# ATLAS OF HUMAN CRANIAL MACROMORPHOSCOPIC TRAITS

# ATLAS OF HUMAN CRANIAL MACROMORPHOSCOPIC TRAITS

JOSEPH T. HEFNER
*Michigan State University, East Lansing, MI, United States*

KANDUS C. LINDE
*Archaeologist, Garcia & Associates, East Lansing, MI, United States*

ELSEVIER

ACADEMIC PRESS
An imprint of Elsevier

Academic Press is an imprint of Elsevier
125 London Wall, London EC2Y 5AS, United Kingdom
525 B Street, Suite 1650, San Diego, CA 92101, United States
50 Hampshire Street, 5th Floor, Cambridge, MA 02139, United States
The Boulevard, Langford Lane, Kidlington, Oxford OX5 1GB, United Kingdom



**Notices**
Knowledge and best practice in this field are constantly changing. As new research and experience broaden our understanding, changes in research methods, professional practices, or medical treatment may become necessary.

Practitioners and researchers must always rely on their own experience and knowledge in evaluating and using any information, methods, compounds, or experiments described herein. In using such information or methods they should be mindful of their own safety and the safety of others, including parties for whom they have a professional responsibility.

To the fullest extent of the law, neither the Publisher nor the authors, contributors, or editors, assume any liability for any injury and/or damage to persons or property as a matter of products liability, negligence or otherwise, or from any use or operation of any methods, products, instructions, or ideas contained in the material herein.

**British Library Cataloguing-in-Publication Data**
A catalogue record for this book is available from the British Library

**Library of Congress Cataloging-in-Publication Data**
A catalog record for this book is available from the Library of Congress

ISBN: 978-0-12-814385-8



*Publisher:* John Fedor
*Acquisition Editor:* Elizabeth Brown
*Editorial Project Manager:* Carlos Rodriguez
*Production Project Manager:* Vijayaraj Purushothaman
*Cover Designer:* Mark Rogers

Typeset by MPS Limited, Chennai, India

# Abstract

Macromorphoscopic traits are quasicontinuous variables of the cranium reflected as soft-tissue differences in living individuals, subdivided into five classes: (1) bone shape; (2) bony feature morphology; (3) suture shape; (4) trait presence/absence; and (5) feature prominence/protrusion. These traits are typically used to estimate ancestry for the purpose of identification, although their use in biodistance studies is becoming more commonplace. In *Linnaean Hierarchical* terms, macromorphoscopic traits would be considered a subtaxon of traditional cranial nonmetric traits, i.e., nonpathological, slight variations of skeletal elements. Tied to E. A. Hooton of Harvard, but with a long and varied history in anatomy, natural philosophy, and anthropology, macromorphoscopic trait data are undergoing a surge in use, in part because of trait standardization and the development of robust statistical methods for classifying an unknown individual into one of a number of reference groups. The *Atlas of Human Cranial Macromorphoscopic Traits* brings together, for the first time, line drawings and photographic exemplars of 17 commonly used macromorphoscopic traits. These photographs illustrate the range in variation each trait can express, while providing the reader a quick reference guide for each trait. Each chapter is supplemented with a treatise on the historical development of these traits, moving well-beyond the Hooton years, back in to the earliest use of these skeletal 'anomalies'. Disambiguation of the trait names is also explored; the nomenclature of each trait is provided in the greatest detail possible. The gross anatomy of each trait and their growth and development is important for understanding how, and potentially why, these traits are expressed differentially between populations, in addition to how they are correlatively expressed in the individual. The adaptive significance and functional morphology for each are similarly important for understanding some of the mechanisms behind their manifestation. To place these traits in a proper context, population-level data on trait manifestation is also provided. These data, drawn from the Macromorphoscopic Databank, are meant to provide the reader a quick guide on trait variability, without falling into the old, typological three-group model of extreme trait values. Of course, implementing these traits into casework is extremely important. Forensic anthropologists are routinely engaged to identify human skeletal remains, usually including some assessment of a decedent's ancestry or geographic origin. To facilitate these analyses, a number of analytical methods are described in detail and include, when appropriate, code for their implementation. All of the individual crania documented herein represent populations encompassing much of human variation. Admittedly, however, we could not capture every nuanced idiosyncrasy nor do we claim to have completely captured the range in trait variation a sample may present. This only confirms the need for additional study and a broadening and deeper understanding of macromorphoscopic traits. Future research efforts will surely focus on additional traits and supplementary character states.

# Contents

# List of Figures

# List of Tables

# Foreword

When I was an undergraduate student in anthropology (with a great interest in forensic anthropology), my osteology course surveyed various methods for estimating components of the biological profile. I remember a particular day in class when my professor handed me several sheets of paper. These seemingly innocuous pages would go on to cause confusion and great frustration in my academic life for over a decade. These three slips of paper each had a line drawing of a skull, labeled as "Caucasoid," "Negroid," and "Mongoloid," and each included a list of nonmetric traits associated with that particular group. Using these traits, our class was tasked to figure out the group membership of the skull resting on the table in front of us. As I started my assignment, I wasn't sure what was meant by "Mongoloid," although I later recognized it as a catch-all term for anyone not considered White or Black but most often referred to as Asian. I read over the trait lists and saw that some of the character states for several traits were listed for more than one group. I became incredibly frustrated because there were no definitions of the traits or their character states and no instruction on how to use them in order to assess group membership. How were we supposed to weigh the traits to ascertain group membership, particularly since many of the traits overlapped between the three 'groups'? At the time, these traits were referred to as cranial nonmetric variables. Although they were linked to a well-received forensic anthropology book, that reference provided little help on the definitions or implementation of these traits in human osteological analysis. And so, on that day, the very foundation for my disdain of cranial nonmetric variables was established, only to become more deep-rooted as I further explored their use.

A few years later, I began graduate school where I met a number of students who would attempt to define the traits for me. Their definitions were generally based on personal experience from studying with an experienced-someone who knew something about these variables and how they were used. The publication of additional forensic anthropology textbooks further focused the discussion of these traits on individual preferences and the author's own understanding of the trait definition. My disdain did not subside, rather it grew as I became more aware of the seeming lack of scientific rigor associated with nonmetric trait analysis. These traits continued to be presented without proper definitions or an analytical method for their application. Furthermore, assumptions regarding the distribution of these traits within a strict three-group model of human variation remained the norm; because they were not used within a statistical framework, they also remained typological and unscientific.

As a graduate student, I was most concerned with human biological variation, the estimation of geographic origin, and the interpretation of population structure using skeletal data, I had already migrated toward well-defined data and variables that were readily applied within deeply ingrained statistical methods. The precisely defined, traditional cranial nonmetric traits were used in bioarchaeological studies and, as such, they were analyzed using relatively robust statistical methods. The nonmetric traits presented in the forensic anthropological literature, however, did not follow that same trajectory. This didn't make sense to me then; however, over the past decade, the traits associated with forensic anthropological research—now coined macromorphoscopic traits—began to make more sense, in large part due to the research and publications of Joe Hefner.

I first saw Joe present a paper on nonmetric traits at the American Academy of Forensic Sciences in 2002, when he detailed the need to better describe the character states of each trait, to better understand their distribution in various population groups, and to implement them within a statistical framework. Joe had the same frustrations others had with nonmetric traits; however, he chose to figure out how to overcome the inherent obstacles. For that paper, he won the J. Lawrence Angel student paper award. In 2009, Joe coined the term *macromorphoscopic traits* and began to publish definitions for the individual traits, their character states, and their frequency distributions among multiple population groups.

*The Visual Atlas of Human Cranial Macromorphoscopic Traits* is the culmination of years of research and analyses and accompanies the debut of a graphical user-interface enabling the estimation of geographic origin using macromorphoscopic variables. Joe has collected data on various world-wide population groups to provide a broader understanding of the biological variation of these traits. This volume fills a huge gap in the literature by providing detailed definitions and line drawings, in addition to R code for the statistical analysis of macromorphoscopic traits. The high-resolution photographs captured by Kandus provide a wonderful addition to the line drawings, more accurately illustrating the range in variation expressed in macromorphoscopic traits.

Today's students and practitioners will not go through the same frustration I once endured. *The Visual Atlas* elaborates on each trait in greater detail, providing a description of the gross anatomy, growth and development, functional morphology, and population variation based on data from the Macromorphoscopic Databank. Researchers will no longer have to choose traits based on preference or their own experience; everyone will be able to collect standardized data appropriate for use within a sound statistical framework.

**Kate Spradley, PhD**
*Professor of Anthropology, Texas State University, San Marcos, TX, United States*

# Quotes

Not only is a skeleton the anchorage for flesh, but also,

at so many points, it is conspicuously present at the surface.

It is the primary factor in proportion, and a means of

great distinction between the sexes.

And what is more, dry bones are objects of masterful design.

Their study should bring profound

respect as well as enlightenment.

***—Stephen R. Peck, Atlas of Human Anatomy for the Artist (1951)***

# Preface

As anthropologists, we have both been fascinated by human variation and the often inconceivable diversity found in the human skeleton. The purpose of this book, *Atlas of Human Cranial Macromorphoscopic Traits*, is to present a thorough and illustrative exposition on cranial macromorphoscopic traits to better understand the diversity found among human groups and to provide a guide for the novice and expert, alike, in the scoring and analysis of macromorphoscopic trait data. In this volume, we present a review of 17 commonly used traits and their associated character states through an examination of their historical development and anatomy, and additional topics covering their growth and development, functional morphology, and between-group population variability. Perhaps most importantly, however, we have tried to provide an exhaustive suite of photographs to illustrate the range in variation possible for each character state.

The idea for this atlas evolved from a need to better understand how macromorphoscopic traits can be most properly implemented in forensic anthropological casework. These traits have a very long history. E. A. Hooton recognized the need for the standardization of cranial nonmetric and metric data, and he began the initial process to systematize their collection. Hooton's efforts serve as a guidepost for this atlas, and he should be acknowledged for the contributions he made nearly 70 years ago.

The unification of art and science should be a careful undertaking, but it can also be a necessary and rewarding one, as we have discovered while preparing this atlas. Photography is an art form; macromorphoscopic trait analysis, as presented herein, is a science; the line drawings associated with these traits fall somewhere in between. By combining these in a single volume, we have attempted to explore the artful science of trait manifestation and analysis. Wanting to contribute more to those who utilize macromorphoscopic traits in forensic anthropological casework and research, photographs seemed like the best way to increase accessibility and better understand the specific traits and their character states. Photographing the human skeleton is a thought-provoking task. You are working with a seemingly inanimate object, while also recognizing its humanness because you know, within your own skin, you too are little more than the bones you will never see.

The skull as "subject" is unmoving and lifeless but also comprises ranging nuances of color, countless depths of field, and fragile and sometimes fragmentary elements, each requiring the subtlest attentions. One must manipulate the environment to create the perfect lighting, while keeping the focus as sharp as possible to capture and accurately represent the feature of interest. The photographs we selected for inclusion were not taken in a studio setting; rather, each one represents the manipulation of a laboratory environment into a photography studio—often using found objects and strong-will. To expedite the photography phase of each data collection trip, the traditional six views of each skull were photographed (i.e., anterior, left lateral, right lateral, inferior, posterior, and superior). Only after data collection did we determine which photographs suitably illustrated a particular trait. Thousands of photographs were taken; we have made every effort to provide those that accurately represent each character state clearly and without ambiguity.

This atlas endeavors to answer questions raised over 200 years ago, when naturalists and early anatomists first identified "anomalies" in the human skeleton and pondered their meaning and presentation. We hope this atlas can serve as a reference text, in research and method development, as well as forensic anthropological case work. The recent surge in interest in macromorphoscopic trait analysis and the ever increasing need for method validation serves as a reminder of the timeliness of this volume and signals a paradigm shift in the analysis of macromorphoscopic traits.

**Joseph T. Hefner and Kandus C. Linde**

# Acknowledgements

The photographs in this atlas and the individual treatises on macromorphoscopic traits sprang from nearly two decades of research, a covenant between skeletal collections, researchers, and a curiosity for the methods associated with forensic anthropology. There have been many individuals associated with the broader project from which this atlas derives and, hopefully, we name all those due their proper acknowledgment.

Quite understandably, this atlas would not have been possible without the skeletal collections from which we drew upon for inspiration and skeletal material. Dr. Nawaporn Techataweewan (Khon Kaen University, Khon Kaen, Thailand), Dr. Todd W. Fenton (Michigan State University, East Lansing, MI) and Drs. David Hunt and Christopher J. Dudar (National Museum of Natural History, Smithsonian Institution, Washington, DC) provided much needed access to their collections. Their eagerness to assist in anyway is remarkable, but their disposition as colleagues and fellow researchers is a true gift and their keen eye for morphology and graciousness as hosts was most welcomed.

Over the years, many skeletal collections have been visited during data collection trips. Although photographs from their collections were not used this time, we are grateful to the following individuals and collections who opened their doors and allowed access to their skeletal collections: Drs. Lee Meadows Jantz, Richard L. Jantz, and Dawnie Steadman (University of Tennessee, Knoxville, TN; William M. Bass Donated Skeletal Collection); Lyman Jellema (Cleveland Museum of Natural History; Hamann-Todd Skeletal Collection); and Dr. M. Kate Spradley (Texas State University, San Marcos, TX; Donated Skeletal Collection).

A number of graduate students contributed directly to this project. Kelly Kamnikar (MSU) and Amber Plemons (MSU) worked very hard to ensure the references were properly formatted and the tables cleanly constructed. Thank you both. Several past and present graduate students from various institutions also worked on early data collection efforts and should be acknowledged for their contributions to this atlas: Felicia Wun, Melody Ratliff, Jane Weigand, and Nicole Jastremski. Thank you.

I (JTH) would like to also pay tribute to the many scholars who paved the way for my academic journey, many of whom I have the pleasure of calling my friend. Ms. Jane Brown, Dr. Dennis Dirkmaat, Dr. Michael Warren, and Dr. Stephen Ousley have provided insight and guidance throughout the years.

There are not many people one can say this about, but Joe Hefner truly wrote the book on macromorphoscopic traits. I (KCL) would like to thank him for the opportunity I was granted in gracing him on this project. Also, thank you Milo Österman, mom, my brothers, and grandpa Jack, for without you, I would not be.

As with any long-term research, many people can have an impact on the final product. This atlas is no different. From our friends who gave us a rain check to the ones actively involved in similar research, we are very grateful to you, each and every one.

We would like to thank Carlos Rodriguez and Elizabeth Brown from Elsevier Publishing. They made this process much easier than expected and provided needed insight into the final product. Finally, some elements of this project were supported by Award No. 2015-DN-BX-K012 through the National Institute of Justice, Office of Justice Programs, United States Department of Justice. The opinions, findings, and conclusions or recommendations expressed in this atlas are those of the authors and do not necessarily reflect the views of the Department of Justice. Of course, we bear all responsibility for the content of this atlas, as well as any errors or omissions.

CHAPTER

# 1

# Introduction

Few books exist that explore cranial nonmetric traits (*sensu stricto*) and there are currently none dedicated exclusively to macromorphoscopic trait manifestations. Consequently, the implementation of these slight variations in the cranial form in research and method building exercises has not yet reached the level of maturity needed to enter general acceptance within the biological anthropological community. The introduction of these traits requires some justification. There are many reasons to undertake the publication of a photographic atlas, but perhaps none are more important than recognizing the gap in current knowledge. In order to fill the gap, a unique set of salutary tools and accessible photographs is essential.

Much of the earlier work and research on macromorphoscopic traits relied on schematic or semischematic line drawings, which only suggested or hinted at a small part of skeletal reality, often failing to capture the range in the expression for any one character state. In contrast, an atlas using photographic exemplars has the advantage of displaying character states *in situ*. Proportions and spatial relationships between singular traits and the cranial complex become more exact and they can be more realistically represented. By including multiple examples of the same character state—some idealized and paradigmatic, others slightly anomalous or irregular—the observer will gain a much broader perspective on interindividual variation and should "walk-away" knowing better how to handle idiosyncratic trait manifestations. Photographs correspond more closely to actual observations made in a laboratory or field setting. While line drawings can display similar information, they lack the texture, lighting, and the level of detail observed on actual specimens. When comparing a specimen to these line drawings or orienting a specimen to effectively score a macromorphoscopic trait, photographs provide the necessary landmarks and contextual clues for correct assessments that are frequently missing from line drawings.

In addition, the existing literature on macromorphoscopic trait analysis—and this is especially true of the early, typological trait lists so popular in forensic anthropological literature—focus almost exclusively on how these traits can be used to predict geographic origin (ancestry or "race") rather than directing the inexperienced to understand the definitions of traits and their individual character states. Consider a similar approach to craniometric analysis. Prior to learning how to successfully implement a discriminant function analysis on a set of measurements, students are first guided through the tedious process of defining the bony landmarks *glabella* and *opisthocranion*, how to properly hold the calipers (or digitizing stylus) to measure between those two points, and are made aware of the many pitfalls associated with data collection and recording errors. Grasping these procedures, the student can now learn to use these new-found abilities to estimate biological distances, posterior probabilities, and likelihood estimates of group membership. Students often find confusion in macromorphoscopic trait analysis, where none should exist; however, they have not been treated the same as their metric counterparts. Before learning how to apply these traits to estimates of geographic origin, their manifestations have to be understood. As a result, several texts and research articles must be consulted, each providing some additional knowledge of trait definitions and character state manifestations. The present atlas, however, will portray macromorphoscopic traits with regard to their expression (i.e., character state) and as objects of human variation rather than matters of extreme expression that may not represent the reality of that variation. Hence, the obstacles to better understanding macromorphoscopic traits are removed, while still providing data on the distribution of these traits within and between populations, benefiting both novice and seasoned human skeletal biologists.

Another goal of this atlas is limiting the text to essential components of macromorphoscopic trait analysis and to offer those components didactically in a simple and self-explanatory manner. Each macromorphoscopic trait is addressed equally: nomenclature—designations used to describe the trait drawn from the literature; gross anatomy—important anatomical structures defining the trait; growth and development—increases in size, changes in proportions, and progression toward maturity through increasing complexity of each trait and the gross

*Atlas of Human Cranial Macromorphoscopic Traits.*
DOI: https://doi.org/10.1016/B978-0-12-814385-8.00001-X

anatomical structures to which they are associated; functional morphology—relationships between a trait and the function of various structures associated with that trait; within population variation—frequency distribution data within worldwide populations; and character states—anatomically based definitions and line drawings, as well as multiple photographs for each character state.

Finally, pedagogical considerations motivate the presentation of these traits. On one hand, observer experience and a detailed understanding of human skeletal variation drive observational data collection, while on the other hand, considerable debate exists regarding the role expertise *should* play in scientific endeavors. Consequently, "I'm an expert" can no longer be used (solely) to explain how and why particular conclusions are reached. Ideally, skeletal biology students sit with an expert to learn appropriate data collection methods of macromorphoscopic traits, distinguishing between various nuanced character states and increasing their understanding of the range and distribution of such features. Photographs will never replace the interaction of mentor and mentee working together with a skull in hand, but they do reinforce and support hands-on learning through more realistic demonstrations of variation than line drawings alone can ever capture.

Most of the traits outlined in this volume existed in the literature well-before the macromorphoscopic method was introduced. Many of these traits have a long history in bioarchaeological and forensic anthropological research. To understand that history and the present state of macromorphoscopic data, a short journey into the past is necessary. But first, what *are* macromorphoscopic traits?

## MACROMORPHOSCOPIC DATA AND DATASETS

Macromorphoscopic traits are quasicontinuous variables of the cranium reflected as soft-tissue differences in living individuals, similar to Brues' second class of characters which "due to the contour of bone in areas where it closely follows the surface..., are apparent in both [the] skeleton and [the] living" (Brues, 1958:559). Macromorphoscopic traits are subdivided into five classes: (1) bone shape (e.g., nasal bone contour); (2) bony feature morphology (e.g., inferior nasal aperture); (3) suture shape (e.g., zygomaticomaxillary suture); (4) trait presence/absence (e.g., postbregmatic depression); and (5) feature prominence/protrusion (e.g., anterior nasal spine). These traits are typically used to estimate ancestry for the purpose of identification, although their use in biodistance studies is becoming more commonplace.

## HISTORICAL TIES

In *Linnaean Hierarchical* terms, macromorphoscopic traits would be considered a subtaxon of traditional cranial nonmetric traits, i.e., nonpathological, slight variations of skeletal elements (Buikstra and Ubelaker, 1994). Macromorphoscopic traits and traditional cranial nonmetric traits are intricately interrelated; not only do they correspond through association by similarity but also through contiguity. Because the terms both belong functionally and structurally to the cranium, the language is occasionally interchangeable. They also share characteristics considered homologs, although any cross-trait functional or structural relationship may be irrelevant. Nevertheless, the historical development of macromorphoscopic traits reflects the development of cranial nonmetric variation.

The five major categories of nonmetric traits in the cranium are: (1) the presence of extra-sutural bone; (2) ossifications and bony bridging; (3) failure of structures to ossify; (4) variation in the expression/manifestation of sutures; and (5) variations in the number and position of foramina. These traits are bilateral and located along the midline. Cranial nonmetric traits include hundreds of traits from the facial skeleton, lateral and posterior vault, and the basilar portion of the cranium, in addition to mandibular and postcranial variations.

The interaction between the genome and the environment in the inheritance and manifestation of cranial nonmetric traits is not well-understood. Regardless, these traits are still used as a measure of relatedness among and between populations due to their correlation to geographic origin and cranial form. Throughout the early 1900s cranial nonmetric traits were thought of as skeletal anomalies worthy of description and naming but of very little analytical value. They only gained a reputation as important contributors to understanding human variation in the 1960s and 1970s. Exploration into the human genome and a deeper understanding of the laws of inheritance led researchers to consciously and more thoroughly explore the use of cranial nonmetric traits in biological distance analysis, kinship studies, and postmarital residence patterns.

E.A. Hooton (1887–1954)—Professor of Physical Anthropology, Harvard—had a keen eye for skeletal variation, and as one of the earliest and certainly one of the most prolific American physical anthropologists, he played an essential role in the reification of cranial nonmetric trait analysis. His work in bioarchaeology, criminal anthropology, and quantitative methods, together with his principal area of research into the nature of "race" and human variation, led to the development of the Harvard Blanks for skeletal analysis. The Harvard Blanks (or occasionally the Harvard List) facilitated data collection on the skeletal variables Hooton assumed useful for differentiating between micro- and pseudoraces of humans. Many of the macromorphoscopic traits used today by forensic anthropologists were included in the Harvard List. Their association with estimations of ancestry is the direct result of Hooton's influence and pedagogic prowess. Hooton's students, like their mentor, included those traits—traits such as anterior nasal spine, palate shape, and postbregmatic depression—as possible indicators of Native American ancestry.

As forensic anthropology matured into a firmly established field, the identification of ancestry from skeletal remains drew heavily from these earlier studies. Until recently, however, there was little effort to standardize how macromorphoscopic data were collected and there were no quantitative methods for analyzing the traits in a manner permitting verification and replication.

## MACROMORPHOSCOPIC DATA IN THE MODERN ERA

The basis of macromorphoscopic trait analysis is the documentation of traits suitable for investigations into relationships among and between populations on the basis of cranial morphology. Whether identifying ancestry for an unknown set of remains, or the identification of biological relatedness in an archeological sample, the traits of interest must be suitable for the construction of classes (groups or individuals). Further generalizations can be made regarding the population from which a sample is drawn. Even though the initial use of these traits was somewhat restricted (i.e., the identification of pseudoraces by Hooton), they pertained to a wider range of meaningful biological generalizations that can be used to estimate ancestry. Hooton recognized their utility. He also recognized the need for refinement, method standardization, and quantitative and qualitative analyses. Even though the collection and interpretation of cranial nonmetric traits were not unusual, the methods were not entirely accepted and very little attention was given to Hooton's warnings regarding the need for standardization and more directed data collection efforts. Researchers of that era agreed with Hooton's call for rigor in trait analysis. Unfortunately, there was no effort to standardize the traits beyond written descriptions of extreme trait values or the occasional line drawing displaying one particular trait or another. When data were collected, samples were often too small for meaningful generalizations. Perhaps more damning, some researchers would present only anecdotal impressions of trait manifestations, with no regard to scientific suitability, implications of confirmation bias, or other issues introduced when authoritative statements were made with no empirical support.

A resurgence in validation studies at the end of the 20th century and now into the 21st—for both craniometric and cranial nonmetric analytical methods—led to refinements in all manners of analysis related to the biological profile, including validation studies focusing on ancestry estimation methods. Personal preferences and individual emphases frequently affect trait importance in a visual, heuristic method. These preferences unduly influence trait selection in future work, even though the often post hoc nature of trait selection is not considered. When no clear protocol is developed for a method, no two authorities are likely to adopt the same traits for their analysis: expertise is the sole determinant. Even when the same traits are used, nomenclature aside, the two could arrive at different decisions on how the trait is manifesting or how much importance a trait should be given. Replication and repeatability between observers is one of the hallmarks of good science and required of any researcher worth her salt.

In order to construct a macromorphoscopic approach to estimate ancestry, many of the traits used since Hooton's day require refinement with standard illustrations, anatomically based definitions (of each trait and each character state), frequency distribution data for large reference samples from around the world, and analytical methods capable of handling categorical data within a classification model.

A fundamental part of method standardization, on any level, is a decrease in overall subjectivity. Standardizing macromorphoscopic trait data collection is essential for data sharing, reference data collection, and, in the end, data analysis on an analytical scale as robust as is currently enjoyed by craniometric analysis. *Macromorphoscopic Traits* (MMS, v1.6) is a data collection computer program for 17 commonly used macromorphoscopic variables. The purpose of MMS is the standardization of trait data for comparison across populations and for use in the analysis of forensically significant remains. Each trait definition is presented with individual character states and line drawings. All data are stored in a two-part relational database for easy data retrieval. MMS is currently available for researchers.

## THE MACROMORPHOSCOPIC DATABANK

Data collected using the MMS program are eventually stored in the Macromorphoscopic Databank (MaMD)—similar in scope and function to the craniometric data stored in the Forensic Databank. The MaMD currently contains macromorphoscopic trait data for 7500 + individuals comprising over 20 populations from around the world and is also available to interested researchers. All of the data in the MaMD were collected using protocols initially developed at the Smithsonian Institution, Repatriation Laboratory in Washington, DC using software designed specifically for data collection of human skeletal remains (https://osteoware.si.edu/).

The MMS program and the MaMD are simply the beginning. The application of macromorphoscopic trait analysis to questions stemming beyond ancestry estimation in forensic anthropology or biological distance analysis in bioarchaeological settings is countless. The inclusion of prehistoric skeletal collections from the United States and international collections from abroad will answer bigger questions about population variability at finer levels of resolution. In turn, the analysis of secular trends within the United States using macromorphoscopic traits will have a far-reaching effect on how we view variation in this country. Tying these data in with genetic, meteorological, and craniometric samples will potentially address some of the long-standing questions on the epigenetic nature of macromorphoscopic traits. Mixed model approaches have great potential for future efforts to understand human variation as it developed *in situ* and these same studies are quite promising for exploring the impact of the genome and the environment on trait manifestation.

## CRANIAL SAMPLES

Many skeletal collections were visited and photographed for this atlas. These are described elsewhere (see Preface) in detail; however, several general points on the selection of individuals to include in this volume should be addressed.

First, any volume attempting to present broad geographic skeletal variation will be biased in some way by the selection of appropriate samples. The clinal nature of trait variation precludes categorizing schemata. So to capture the broadest range in human variability possible, samples from around the world are presented in no particular order and with a blind eye towards categorization by geographic origin.

Second, only adult crania are included in this volume. Even though many of the individuals in the MaMD are of known age, sex, and ancestry, age was not subdivided in this volume beyond the classification, *adult*. When known age was not available, we assessed gross macroscopic age indicators prior to photography or macromorphoscopic data collection. These included dental development, cranial and maxillary suture closure, and fusion of the sphenooccipital synchondrosis.

Finally, certain pathological conditions and many taphonomic variables can impact the expression of a macromorphoscopic trait. Because of the known changes these factors can have, all individuals with known pathological conditions are excluded from this volume whenever possible. For example, individuals with marked antemortem tooth loss will have concomitant bony changes to the vertical portion of the maxilla (e.g., changes in the expression of the anterior nasal spine), the nasal opening (e.g., changes in the expression of the nasal aperture), and facial buttressing [e.g., changes in the expression of the malar tubercle (MT)].

Taphonomic signatures of processed and curated skeletal material vary by collection. For instance, sagittal sectioning was common practice in 19th-century anatomical collections. This practice improves one's ability to photograph inferior nasal aperture morphology; however, that same practice may obfuscate the assessment of postbregmatic depression, anterior nasal spine, nasal bone contour, etc. The more fragile areas of the midface region are often missing or damaged, complicating the data collection for any one particular trait or another. Nasal bones are often broken during the postmortem interval, particularly in collections housing skeletal material in metal drawers or cabinets. This damage can render one trait uncollectable, while other traits in the area are still present and can be collected.

The arrangement of the *Atlas of Human Cranial Macromorphoscopic Traits* is relatively straightforward and is intended to provide interested parties a useful reference. Each macromorphoscopic trait is treated independently, by chapter, outlining various aspects of trait manifestations and other useful considerations for data collection. Photographic atlases generally focus on photographic exemplars, this atlas is no different. The bulk of these pages are dedicated to demonstrating the range of variation a trait may express through visuals of each trait and their respective character states. However, additional information is offered for context and to place the importance of these character states in their appropriate perspective.

To begin, a brief history is provided of each macromorphoscopic trait, including prior use in biological anthropological research, ancestry estimation methods, and, when necessary, disambiguation. Although by no means exhaustive, we have made every effort to provide a thorough background for each trait.

Several of the traits presented herein have undergone name changes throughout their use, so each chapter provides a section documenting many of these names (*Nomenclature*). *Gross Anatomy* identifies the anatomical structures (bones, muscles, ligaments, and tendons) responsible for the presentation or manifestation of each trait. Gross anatomy is complemented by *Growth and Development*, which describes the development of each trait (when known and understood), or the growth and development of the surrounding tissues responsible for trait manifestation. For many traits, there is a functional component. For example, the malar tubercle anchors fibers of the masseter muscle and is usually located close to the zygomaticomaxillary suture. The interaction between musculature and sutural intersections are briefly explored under *Functional Morphology*. In some instances, duplication of these three sections (Gross Anatomy, Growth and Development, and Functional Morphology) was necessary, due in large part to the number of traits a particular bone may express. For example, the nasal bones make up no less than three different traits (Nasal Bone Shape [NBS], Nasal Bone Contour [NBC], and Nasal Overgrowth [NO]).

Each chapter also provides data on the distribution of each character state within multiple populations, identified by geographic origin. Data for the *Within Population Variability* section derive from the MaMD (see above) and are provided to give the reader a sense of the actual trait distribution within and between groups. The bulk of each chapter falls under the *Character States*. In order to demonstrate the range of expression for each character state, multiple photographic exemplars are provided, in addition to line drawings.

The objective of this atlas is to provide emerging human skeletal biologists and other researchers in similar ventures, an inclusive guide to the collection and interpretation of macromorphoscopic trait data. The methods are open-ended enough that, as other traits are documented or new character states identified, they can be added into the macromorphoscopic approach; the valuable criticism already provided by several researchers has contributed exponentially to the method. Of course, continued research on these slight variations in cranial form is necessary for fine-tuning the macromorphoscopic method.

CHAPTER

# 2

# Macromorphoscopic Traits

The following chapter provides rudimentary trait definitions, abbreviations (Table 2.1), and single illustrations for each of the macromorphoscopic traits established by anatomical region, beginning with the anterior view. Descriptive detail for each trait and their designated character states is provided in each respective chapter (Chapters 4–19).

## ANTERIOR VIEW (FIG. 2.1)

### Inferior Nasal Aperture (Chapter 4)

The inferior nasal aperture (INA) is an assessment of the shape of the inferior border of the nasal aperture just lateral to the anterior nasal spine (ANS), which defines the transition from nasal floor to the vertical portion of the maxillae. Character states for INA are scored as: *marked slope* (1), *moderate slope* (2), *abrupt* (3), *weak sill* (4), or *pronounced sill* (5).

### Interorbital Breadth (Chapter 5)

Interorbital breadth (IOB) is the distance between the two orbits in the region of dacryon, relative to the overall breadth of the facial skeleton. IOB is scored using three character states, scored as: *narrow* (1), *medium* (2), or *broad* (3).

### Malar Tubercle (Chapter 6)

Malar tubercle (MT) is a caudally protruding tubercle—varying in size and position—which may occur on the maxillae, the zygomatic bones, or at the intersection between these two bones along the inferior aspect of the zygomaticomaxillary suture (ZS). MT exhibits the following character states and scored as: *no projection* (0), *trace* (1), *medium* (2), and *pronounced* (3).

### Nasal Aperture Shape (Chapter 7)

Nasal aperture shape (NAS) comprises the lateral contours of the nasal opening and the position of greatest projection along the lateral margins, regardless of the overall breadth of the nasal opening. The relative shape of the nasal aperture is mostly defined by the position of greatest lateral projection (i.e., the position of the bony landmark, alare—left and right). NAS comprises three character states, their corresponding scores are: *teardrop* (1), *bell* (2), and *bowed* (3).

### Nasal Aperture Width (Chapter 8)

Nasal aperture width (NAW) includes the width of the nasal aperture relative to the entire facial skeleton using a relative ratio of total facial width to nasal opening. NAW comprises three character states, scored as: *narrow* (1), *intermediate* (2), or *broad* (3).

Atlas of Human Cranial Macromorphoscopic Traits.
DOI: https://doi.org/10.1016/B978-0-12-814385-8.00002-1

**TABLE 2.1** Macromorphoscopic Trait Names and Abbreviations

| Macromorphoscopic trait | Trait abbreviation | Macromorphoscopic trait | Trait abbreviation |
|---|---|---|---|
| Anterior nasal spine | ANS | Nasofrontal suture | NFS |
| Inferior nasal aperture | INA | Orbital shape | OBS |
| Interorbital breadth | IOB | Palate shape | PS |
| Malar tubercle | MT | Postbregmatic depression | PBD |
| Nasal aperture shape | NAS | Posterior zygomatic tubercle | PZT |
| Nasal aperture width | NAW | Supranasal suture | SPS |
| Nasal bone contour | NBC | Transverse palatine suture | TPS |
| Nasal bone shape | NBS | Zygomaticomaxillary suture | ZS |
| Nasal overgrowth | NO | | |

## Nasal Bone Contour (Chapter 9)

Evaluating the nasal bone contour (NBC) is a consideration of the curvature of the midfacial region—specifically, the nasal bones and frontal process of both maxillae—approximately 1 cm below nasion. NBC comprises five character states, scored as: *low and rounded* (0), *oval* (1), *broad plateau* (2), *narrow plateau* (3), and *triangular* (4).

## Nasal Bone Shape (Chapter 10)

Nasal bone shape (NBS) is an assessment of the contour of the nasal bones along the lateral borders. The frontonasal suture, the nasal suture, and the symmetry of the nasal bones should not be considered. NBS comprises four character states, scored as: *straight* (1), *superior pinch* (2), *lateral bulge* (3), and *triangular* (4).

## Nasofrontal Suture (Chapter 12)

Nasofrontal suture is defined as the shape of the suture separating the nasal bones from the frontal bone. To score the trait, hold the cranium in anatomical position with the anterior portion of the cranium facing the observer. There are four character states, scored as: *round* (1), *square* (2), *triangular* (3), and *irregular* (4).

## Orbital Shape (Chapter 13)

Orbital shape (OBS) is defined as the shape of the bony sockets housing the eye. Observers should assess whether the orbital margins are angular (rectangle), curvilinear (circular), or irregular (rhombic). OBS includes the following character states, scored as: *rectangular* (1), *circular* (2), and *rhombic* (3).

## Supranasal Suture (Chapter 17)

Supranasal suture (SPS) is defined as the secondary sutural complex superior to the cranial landmark *nasion* that may persist into adulthood. SPS is not the nasal portion of a persistent metopic suture but is a secondary fusion of the nasal portion of a frontal suture. The SPS appears as a complex suture of interlocking bony spicules at the cranial landmark *glabella*. SPS exhibits three character states, scored as: *obliterated* (0), *unfused* (1), and *closed but visible* (2).

## Zygomaticomaxillary Suture (Chapter 19)

The ZS describes the course of the suture between the maxilla and the zygomatic. The infraorbital suture should be ignored when making a determination. Assessment of ZS is based primarily on the number of major angles present and the approximate location of the greatest lateral projection of the suture. ZS shape has three character states, scored as: *no angles* (0), *one angle* (1), and *two or more angles* (2).

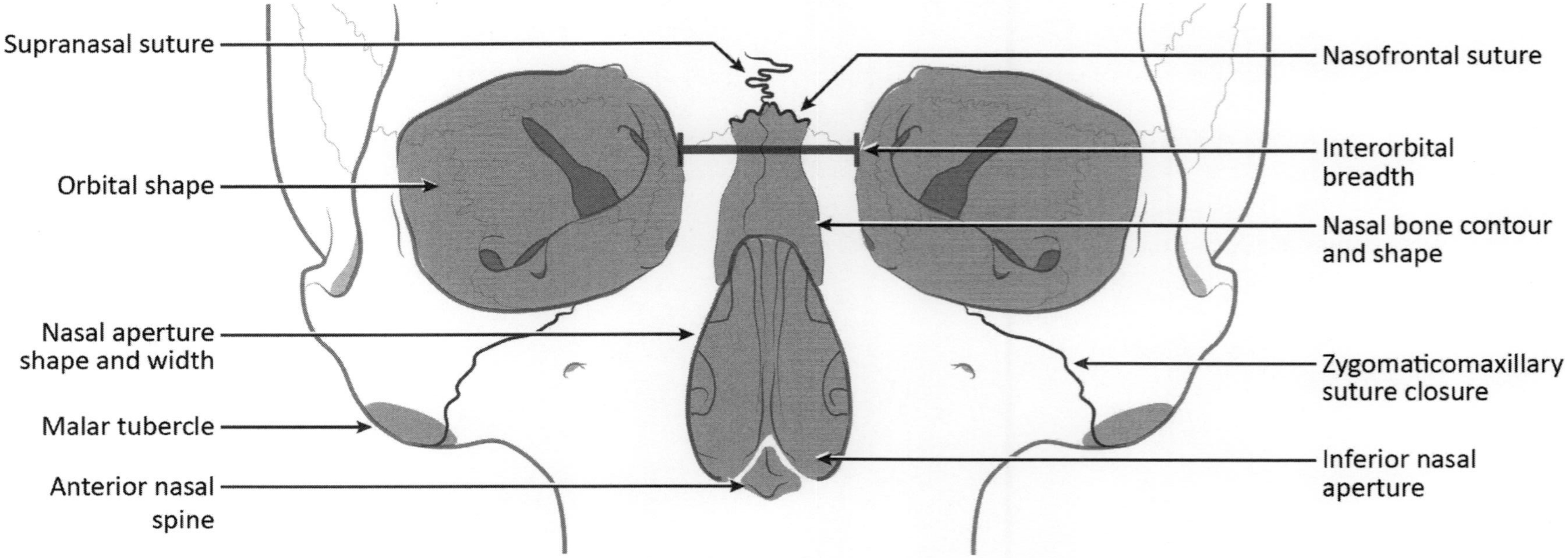


FIGURE 2.1 Anterior view of the cranium providing approximate area of interest of macromorphoscopic traits in the midfacial skeleton. *Image reproduced with permission from Plemons and Hefner (2016).*

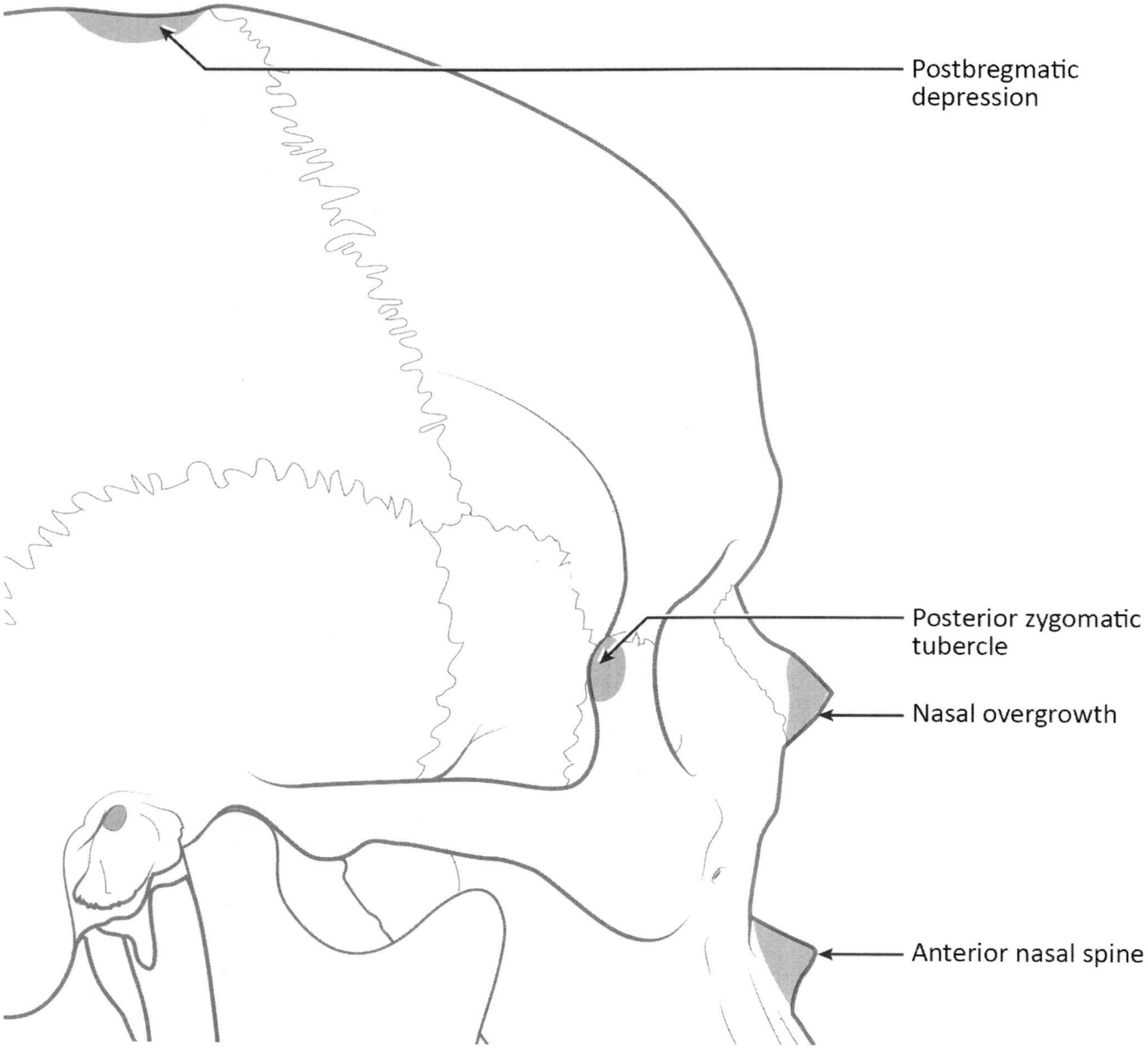


**FIGURE 2.2** Lateral view of the cranium providing approximate area of interest of macromorphoscopic traits. *Image reproduced with permission from Plemons and Hefner (2016).*

## LATERAL VIEW (FIG. 2.2)

### Anterior Nasal Spine (Chapter 3)

The ANS is a uniquely human bony feature located at the inferior border of the nasal aperture, just anterior to the floor of the nasal cavity. This trait exhibits the following character states, scored as: *slight* (1), *intermediate* (2), or *marked* (3).

### Nasal Overgrowth (Chapter 11)

Nasal overgrowth is a projection of the lateral border of the nasal bones at their inferior edge beyond the maxilla at the cranial landmark *nasale inferious*. This trait is visualized by close inspection of the inferior lateral border of the left nasal bone where it meets the maxilla. This trait exhibits two character states, scored as: *absent* (0) or *present* (1).

### Postbregmatic Depression (Chapter 15)

Postbregmatic depression is a slight to broad depression along the sagittal suture, posterior to *bregma*, which is not the result of pathology. Observed in lateral profile, the trait is scored as either absent (no depression) or present. The corresponding scores are: *absent* (0) or *present* (1).

### Posterior Zygomatic Tubercle (Chapter 16)

The posterior zygomatic tubercle (PZT) is a posterior projection of the zygomatic bone at, approximately, mid-orbit. To observe PZT, a small, transparent ruler is placed on the frontal process of the zygomatic from the landmarks *frontomalare posterale* to *jugale*. The extent of bony protrusion beyond the ruler's edge is then assessed with the corresponding scores: *absent* (0), *weak* (1), *moderate* (2), or *marked* (3).

## INFERIOR VIEW (FIG. 2.3)

### Palate Shape (Chapter 14)

Palate shape (PS) considers the contour of the dental arcade, defined by the curvature of the hard palate in the transverse plane viewed from the occlusal/inferior aspect of the maxillae. PS is based on the overall morphology and arch shape of the anterior and posterior dentition, assessed as a midline-projection through the individual teeth along their mesiodistal axis. Assess the overall shape relative to the four character states, scored as: *elliptical* (1), *parabolic A* (2), *parabolic B* (3), or *hyperbolic* (4).

### Transverse Palatine Suture (Chapter 18)

The transverse palatine suture (TPS) is defined as the course of the TPS on the hard bony palate. The entire suture is observed, but each assessment should focus on the medial one-half of the suture. If the suture is asymmetrical, score the general (*gestalt*) shape. TPS has four character states, scored as: *straight* (1), *anterior bulging* (2), *M-shaped (or jagged)* (3), and *posterior bulging* (4).

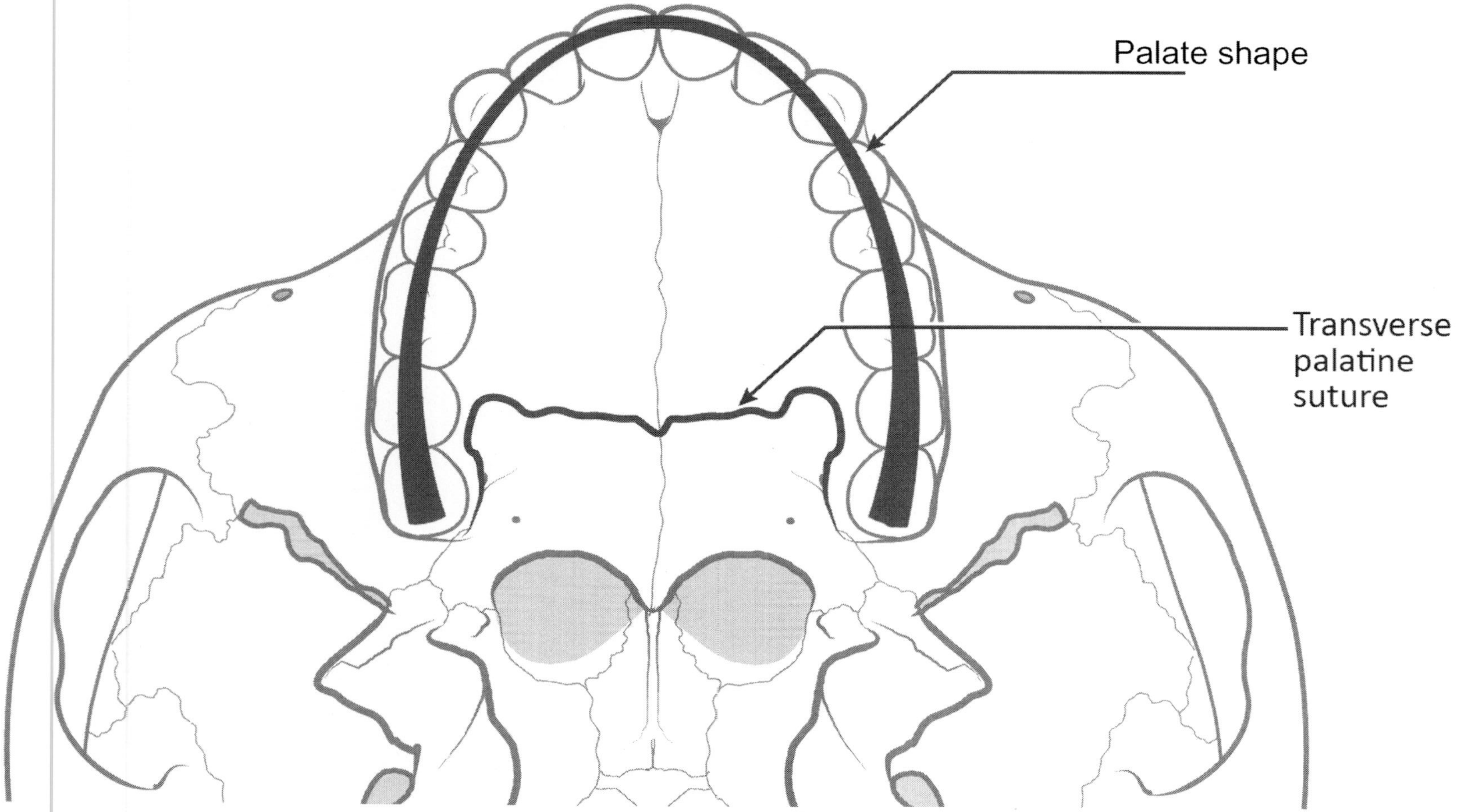


**FIGURE 2.3** Inferior view of the cranium providing approximate area of interest of macromorphoscopic traits in the palate. *Image reproduced and modified with permission from Plemons and Hefner (2016).*

CHAPTER

# 3

# Anterior Nasal Spine

The anterior nasal spine (ANS) is a uniquely human bony feature located at the inferior border of the nasal aperture, just anterior to the floor of the nasal cavity. This trait exhibits the following character states: slight, intermediate, and marked, with corresponding scores: $1 < 2 < 3$. *Slight* (1) indicates minimal to no projection beyond the inferior nasal aperture. *Intermediate* (2) indicates a moderate projection of the ANS beyond the inferior nasal aperture. *Marked* (3) indicates a pronounced projection of the spine beyond the inferior nasal aperture. To score this trait, the cranium should be viewed anteriorly and laterally to assess the degree of projection. Do not score this trait for edentulous individuals.

Hamy (1869) is one of the earlier references to the ANS in ancestry estimation, which is, "in negroes 2.6 mm, in prognathous Europeans 4 mm, and in orthognathous Europeans 5.5 mm." Macalister's (1898) studies of European skulls also touched on the ANS, but only states, "In these crania ... the nasal spine, which remains to support the lower and front part of its cartilaginous portion, projects prominently in the front of the plane of the incisor alveoli." Virchow (1912) used the ANS as an anatomical landmark to calculate his *nasal quadrangle* but only hinted at its use as a nonmetric trait, saying it is the longest in Europeans. Charles (1930) defined the ANS as, "a median remnant of a formerly more prominent intermaxillary bone," which he used again as an anatomical landmark, but did not discuss scoring criteria. A number of other researchers have used various approaches to score or assess ANS (Schultz, 1918; Krogman and Sassouni, 1957; Krogman, 1970, 1978; DeVilliers, 1968; Enlow, 1982; Harris et al., 1977).

Hooton included standard illustrations and a scoring strategy for ANS in the Harvard Blanks (Fig. 3.1: Hooton's Plate 14), which he assessed as: absent, small, medium, and large. He notes that, "Each skull should be fitted into the scale given of plate 14. Note that it is the development of the spine itself, and not the development of the septum that is under consideration" (Hooton, n.d.). A number of researchers since Hooton have assessed the projection of the ANS with regard to ancestry. Brues (1990:5) utilized the Harvard recording system, scoring ANS as absent, small, medium, or large. Burns (1999:154) decreased the number of character states, defining three: medium/tilted, large/long, and little/none. DeVilliers (1968) classified ANS into three classes: absent, slight, and moderate. Gill (1998:299) categorized the ANS as medium, medium-tilted, prominent, straight, and reduced. Rhine (1990:20) scores the feature dichotomously as, "large or small, depending upon the amount of projection." Noback et al. (2011) define the ANS as, "the tip of the median bony process of the maxilla" (2011:602); although they do not indicate categorical variations in the expression of ANS, the results of their geometric morphometric approach to nasal morphology indicate longer and shorter variants dependent on climatic fluctuations. The clinical importance of the ANS has led to a dearth of literature. As an example, Mooney and Siegel (1986) documented ANS development in skeletal specimens ranging in age from 8 weeks prenatal to 8 years, documenting ANS along an ordinal scale following DeVilliers (1968) as: absent, slight, moderate, and prominent. Swenson (2012:31) defined the ANS as the, "anterior tip of the sharp bony process of the maxilla at the lower margin of anterior nasal opening" when studying nasal septum deviation within a longitudinal growth sample.

The ANS is assessed by observing the cranium laterally and assessing the degree of growth from the vertical maxillae/nasal floor juncture. The most reasonable manner is to compare each cranium to the character state illustrations (see the "Character States" section). The fragility of this cranial region, in addition to the projecting nature of an anterior nasal, often leads to peri- or postmortem damage. ANS should not be scored when signs of trauma, pathology (including alveolar resorption or edentulous maxillae), or postmortem damage to the inferior nasal margin are noted.

*Atlas of Human Cranial Macromorphoscopic Traits.*
DOI: https://doi.org/10.1016/B978-0-12-814385-8.00003-3

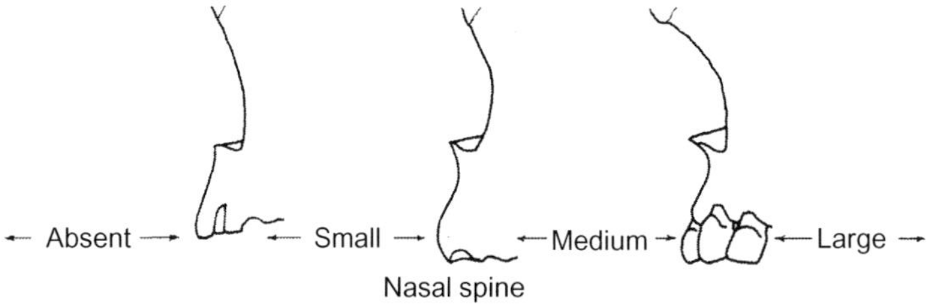


FIGURE 3.1 A detail from E.A. Hooton's unpublished Plate 14 illustrating his scoring strategy for the ANS trait.

## NOMENCLATURE

Anterior nasal spine, anterior inferior nasal spine, anterior nasal spine of maxillae, lower nasal spine, nasal spine, nasospinale, projecting nasal spine, *spina nasalis anterior*, and *spina nasalis anterior maxillae*.

## GROSS ANATOMY

The ANS is a bony projection and cephalometric landmark on the maxilla. Located at the base of the fleshy nose, the ANS serves as the attachment of the *dilator naris posterior mm* and cartilages of the nose. The ANS is formed at the intersection between the two maxillae along the anteroinferior nasal aperture.

## GROWTH AND DEVELOPMENT

Growth and development for the entire midfacial region are relatively predictable and repetitive for most of the macromorphoscopic traits that follow. While redundancy is necessary, the unique pattern of growth and development for each trait is also included.

The ANS develops along the midline of the border of the nasal aperture. Around the fourth week of intrauterine development, five branchial arches form the region of the future head and neck. Each arch gives rise to muscles, connective tissue, vasculature, and neural and skeletal components of the future face, including the maxillae. The first branchial arch is instrumental in the formation of the nasomaxillary region, formed predominantly from the maxillary process of the mandibular arch. Postnatal growth of the nasomaxillary complex is produced through several mechanisms. Primary displacement posteriorly of the posterolateral border of the maxilla (maxillary tuberosity) and passive displacement inferiorly of the entire nasal-maxillary complex leading to a longer, more inferiorly positioned facial complex in adults. Sutural growth (maxillary, frontonasal, frontomaxillary, pterygopalatine, zygomaticotemporal, and the zygomaticomaxillary sutures) leads to downward and forward repositioning of the maxilla. Growth and development continue surface remodeling via bone deposition and resorption leading to an overall increase in size and shape change of the ANS. Enlow and Bang (1965) and Enlow (1982) suggest that ANS formation is the result of resorptive–depository fields of the bony maxilla. As resorption occurs along the labial side of the premaxillary region, depositional (i.e., directional) growth occurs along the lingual surface increasing the overall size of the ANS.

The ANS is present at birth. Analysis of fetal and child crania showed that the ANS projected more in the American White sample than it did in American Black sample (Mooney and Siegel, 1986). The authors suggest this early variance is the result of significant differences between the two samples in the timing and degree of premaxillary–maxillary suture fusion.

## FUNCTIONAL MORPHOLOGY

The ANS is an important skeletal region for determining the soft-tissue morphology of the adult human face. The ANS supports the nasal tip and partially influences the magnitude of projection for the fleshy nose and upper lip. Forming the anteroinferior region of the cartilaginous septum, the ANS anchors the septal cartilages and during early embryonic growth and development communicates to the lower maxilla via the septopremaxillary ligament (Latham, 1970).

# WITHIN POPULATION VARIATION

Data derived from the Macromorphoscopic Databank of the frequency distribution of ANS ($n = 5105$). All data are for adult individuals. When possible, frequency data for males and females are provided separately. When sex could not be estimated reliably, frequency distributions are pooled as "Unknown" (Table 3.1).

**TABLE 3.1** Frequency Distribution of ANS, by Geographic Origin and Sex

| | | 1 | | 2 | | 3 | | |
|---|---|---|---|---|---|---|---|---|
| **Geographic origin** | **Sex** | *n* | % | *n* | % | *n* | % | **Total** |
| **African** | **Female** | 13 | 93 | 1 | 7 | 0 | 0 | 14 |
| | **Male** | 13 | 81 | 3 | 19 | 0 | 0 | 16 |
| | **Unknown** | 0 | 0 | 0 | 0 | 0 | 0 | 0 |
| | **Total** | 26 | 87 | 4 | 13 | 0 | 0 | 30 |
| **American Black** | **Female** | 88 | 65 | 37 | 27 | 10 | 7 | 135 |
| | **Male** | 126 | 53 | 84 | 36 | 26 | 11 | 236 |
| | **Unknown** | 0 | 0 | 0 | 0 | 1 | 100 | 1 |
| | **Total** | 214 | 58 | 121 | 33 | 37 | 10 | 372 |
| **American White** | **Female** | 70 | 27 | 140 | 55 | 45 | 18 | 255 |
| | **Male** | 51 | 19 | 141 | 53 | 75 | 28 | 267 |
| | **Unknown** | 0 | 0 | 0 | 0 | 0 | 0 | 0 |
| | **Total** | 121 | 23 | 281 | 54 | 120 | 23 | 522 |
| **Amerindian** | **Female** | 14 | 32 | 30 | 68 | 0 | 0 | 44 |
| | **Male** | 12 | 31 | 27 | 69 | 0 | 0 | 39 |
| | **Unknown** | 398 | 21 | 1166 | 62 | 313 | 17 | 1877 |
| | **Total** | 424 | 22 | 1223 | 62 | 313 | 16 | 1960 |
| **Chinese** | **Female** | 0 | 0 | 5 | 100 | 0 | 0 | 5 |
| | **Male** | 0 | 0 | 53 | 100 | 0 | 0 | 53 |
| | **Unknown** | 0 | 0 | 0 | 0 | 0 | 0 | 0 |
| | **Total** | 0 | 0 | 58 | 100 | 0 | 0 | 58 |
| **Colombian** | **Female** | 4 | 6 | 31 | 47 | 31 | 47 | 66 |
| | **Male** | 8 | 5 | 68 | 40 | 96 | 56 | 172 |
| | **Unknown** | 0 | 0 | 0 | 0 | 0 | 0 | 0 |
| | **Total** | 12 | 5 | 99 | 42 | 127 | 53 | 238 |
| **El Salvador** | **Female** | 0 | 0 | 0 | 0 | 0 | 0 | 0 |
| | **Male** | 2 | 40 | 3 | 60 | 0 | 0 | 5 |
| | **Unknown** | 0 | 0 | 0 | 0 | 0 | 0 | 0 |
| | **Total** | 2 | 40 | 3 | 60 | 0 | 0 | 5 |
| **Eskimo** | **Female** | 0 | 0 | 0 | 0 | 0 | 0 | 0 |
| | **Male** | 0 | 0 | 0 | 0 | 0 | 0 | 0 |
| | **Unknown** | 237 | 43 | 269 | 49 | 45 | 8 | 551 |
| | **Total** | 237 | 43 | 269 | 49 | 45 | 8 | 551 |

*(Continued)*

TABLE 3.1 (*Continued*)

| | | 1 | | 2 | | 3 | | |
|---|---|---|---|---|---|---|---|---|
| **Geographic origin** | **Sex** | *n* | % | *n* | % | *n* | % | **Total** |
| **European** | **Female** | 2 | 33 | 2 | 33 | 2 | 33 | 6 |
| | **Male** | 1 | 13 | 3 | 38 | 4 | 50 | 8 |
| | **Unknown** | 0 | 0 | 0 | 0 | 0 | 0 | 0 |
| | **Total** | 3 | 21 | 5 | 36 | 6 | 43 | 14 |
| **Guatemalan** | **Female** | 1 | 3 | 27 | 82 | 5 | 15 | 33 |
| | **Male** | 5 | 7 | 41 | 61 | 21 | 31 | 67 |
| | **Unknown** | 0 | 0 | 0 | 0 | 0 | 0 | 0 |
| | **Total** | 6 | 6 | 68 | 68 | 26 | 26 | 100 |
| **Japanese** | **Female** | 0 | 0 | 5 | 100 | 0 | 0 | 5 |
| | **Male** | 0 | 0 | 8 | 100 | 0 | 0 | 8 |
| | **Unknown** | 0 | 0 | 2 | 100 | 0 | 0 | 2 |
| | **Total** | 0 | 0 | 15 | 100 | 0 | 0 | 15 |
| **Mexico** | **Female** | 0 | 0 | 1 | 50 | 1 | 50 | 2 |
| | **Male** | 10 | 42 | 9 | 38 | 5 | 21 | 24 |
| | **Unknown** | 0 | 0 | 0 | 0 | 0 | 0 | 0 |
| | **Total** | 10 | 38 | 10 | 38 | 6 | 23 | 26 |
| **Pacific Island** | **Female** | 30 | 67 | 13 | 29 | 2 | 4 | 45 |
| | **Male** | 47 | 59 | 26 | 33 | 7 | 9 | 80 |
| | **Unknown** | 41 | 55 | 27 | 36 | 7 | 9 | 75 |
| | **Total** | 118 | 59 | 66 | 33 | 16 | 8 | 200 |
| **Peruvian** | **Female** | 0 | 0 | 0 | 0 | 0 | 0 | 0 |
| | **Male** | 0 | 0 | 0 | 0 | 0 | 0 | 0 |
| | **Unknown** | 9 | 56 | 5 | 31 | 2 | 13 | 16 |
| | **Total** | 9 | 56 | 5 | 31 | 2 | 13 | 16 |
| **Southwest (SW) Hispanic** | **Female** | 3 | 50 | 3 | 50 | 0 | 0 | 6 |
| | **Male** | 1 | 14 | 6 | 86 | 0 | 0 | 7 |
| | **Unknown** | 18 | 19 | 56 | 59 | 21 | 22 | 95 |
| | **Total** | 22 | 20 | 65 | 60 | 21 | 19 | 108 |
| **Thai** | **Female** | 175 | 56 | 125 | 40 | 13 | 4 | 313 |
| | **Male** | 219 | 39 | 293 | 52 | 51 | 9 | 563 |
| | **Unknown** | 5 | 36 | 8 | 57 | 1 | 7 | 14 |
| | **Total** | 399 | 45 | 426 | 48 | 65 | 7 | 890 |
| **Total for all groups** | | 1603 | 31 | 2718 | 53 | 784 | 15 | 5105 |

*ANS*, anterior nasal spine.

## CHARACTER STATES

Photographic exemplars of the different character states of ANS are provided below. Each character state is defined following (Hefner; 2009, 2016). When necessary to clarify scoring, more nuanced definitions are provided in the figure captions. ANS should be assessed with the protocol provided in the preceding section. Character states include:

ANS 1 = *Slight*—minimal-to-no projection of the ANS beyond the inferior nasal aperture.

ANS 2 = *Intermediate*—a moderate projection of the ANS beyond the inferior nasal aperture.

ANS 3 = *Marked*—a pronounced projection of the ANS beyond the inferior nasal aperture.

# CHARACTER STATES FOR ANTERIOR NASAL SPINE = 1 (FIGS. 3.2–3.7)

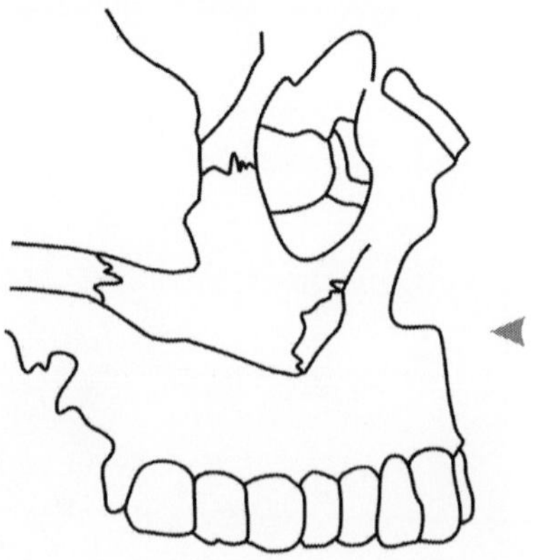


**FIGURE 3.2** Diagrammatic representation of ANS 1. Arrow indicates reference area. *ANS*, anterior nasal spine.

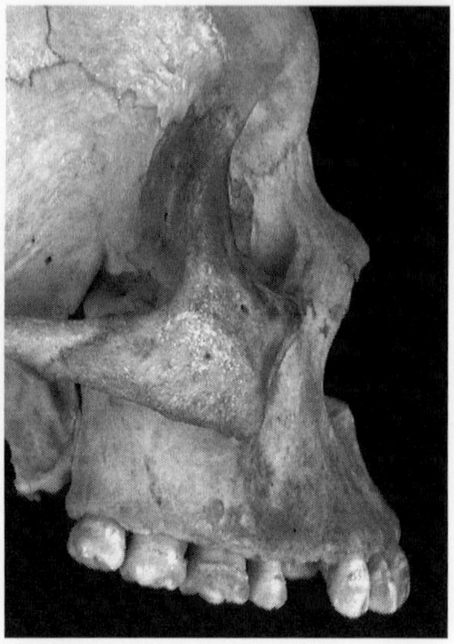

**FIGURE 3.3** Variant of ANS 1. *ANS*, anterior nasal spine.

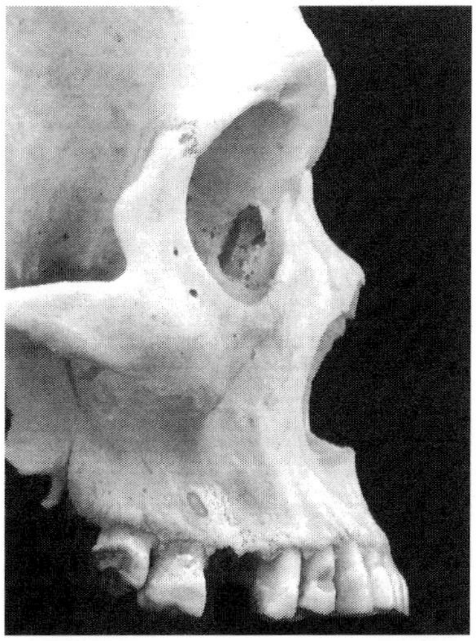

FIGURE 3.4 Variant of ANS 1. *ANS*, anterior nasal spine.

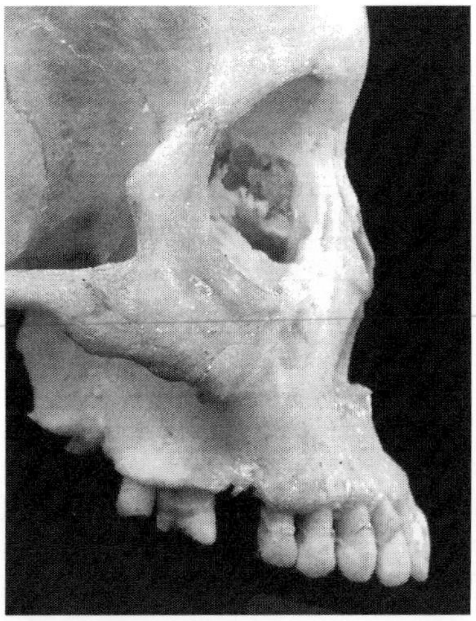

FIGURE 3.5 Variant of ANS 1. *ANS*, anterior nasal spine.

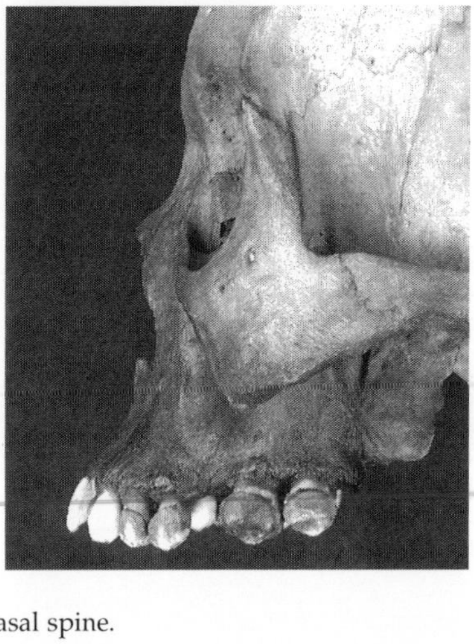

FIGURE 3.6 Variant of ANS 1. *ANS*, anterior nasal spine.

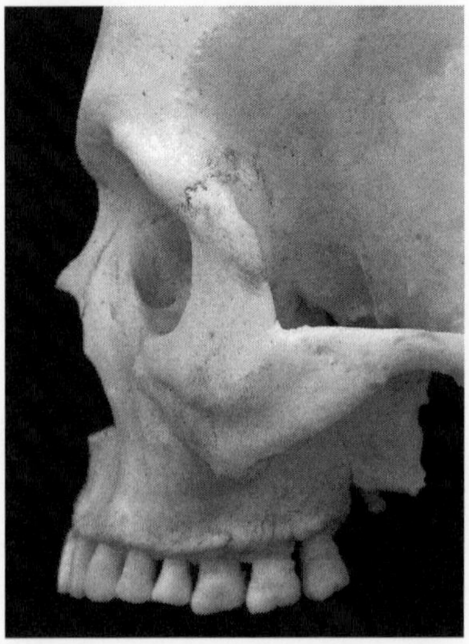

**FIGURE 3.7** Variant of ANS 1. *ANS*, anterior nasal spine.

# CHARACTER STATES FOR ANTERIOR NASAL SPINE = 2 (FIGS. 3.8–3.13)

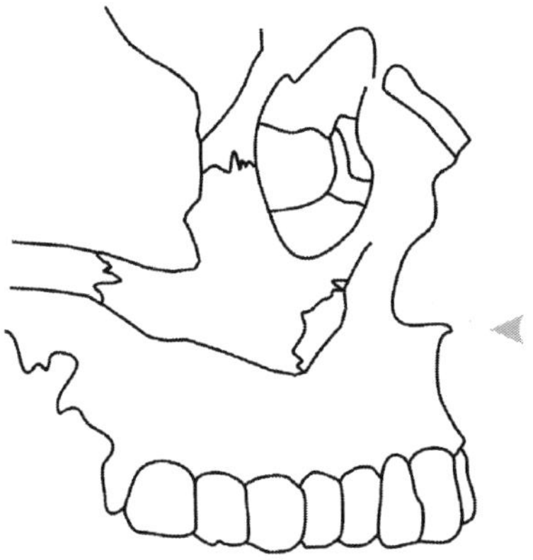

2

FIGURE 3.8 Diagrammatic representation of ANS 2. Arrow indicates reference area. *ANS,* anterior nasal spine.

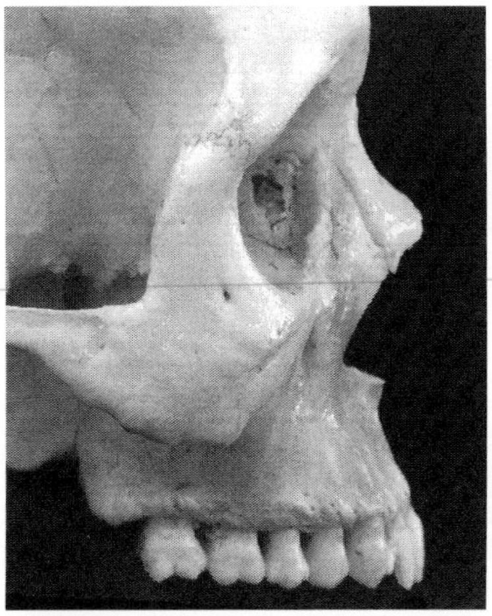

FIGURE 3.9 Variant of ANS 2. *ANS,* anterior nasal spine.

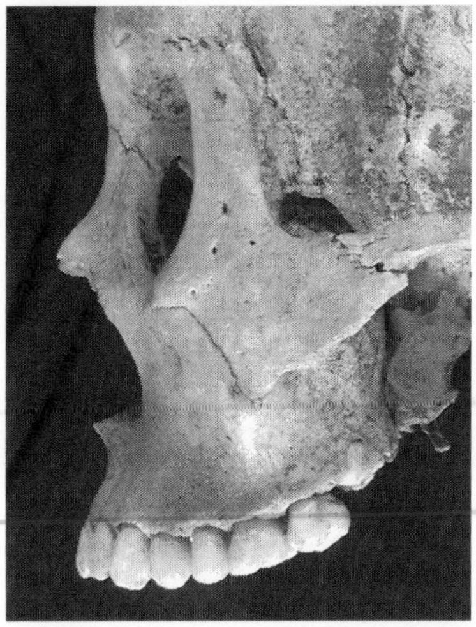

FIGURE 3.10 Variant of ANS 2. *ANS,* anterior nasal spine.

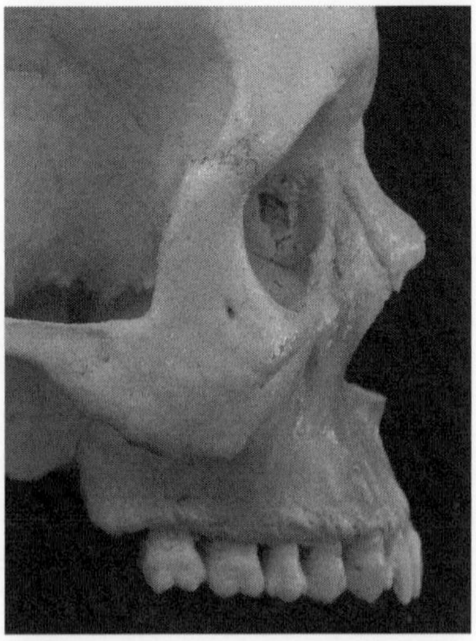

**FIGURE 3.11** Variant of ANS 2. *ANS*, anterior nasal spine.

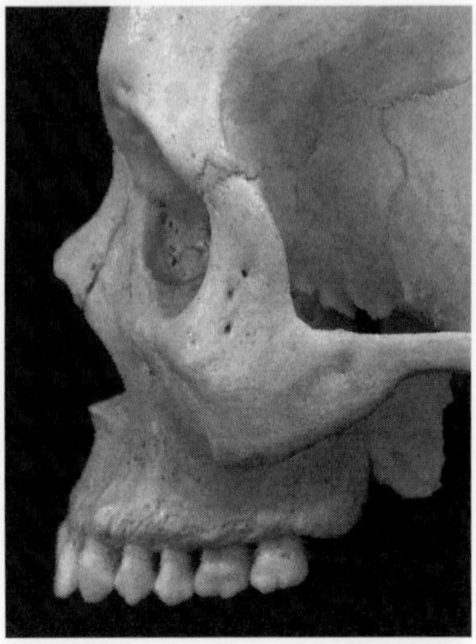

**FIGURE 3.12** Variant of ANS 2. *ANS*, anterior nasal spine.

**FIGURE 3.13** Variant of ANS 2. *ANS*, anterior nasal spine.

## CHARACTER STATES FOR ANTERIOR NASAL SPINE = 3 (FIGS. 3.14–3.19)

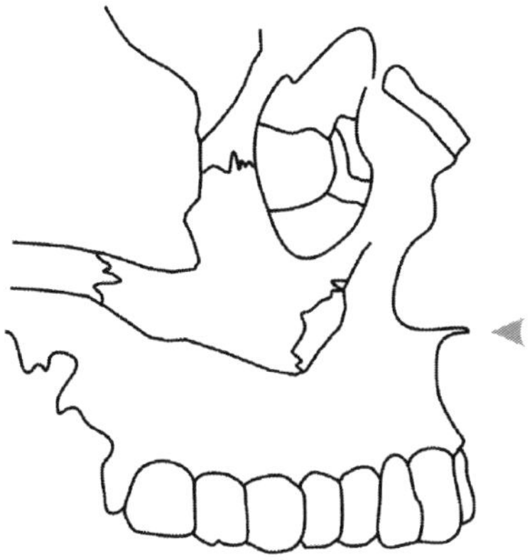

3

FIGURE 3.14 Diagrammatic representation of ANS 3. *ANS*, anterior nasal spine.

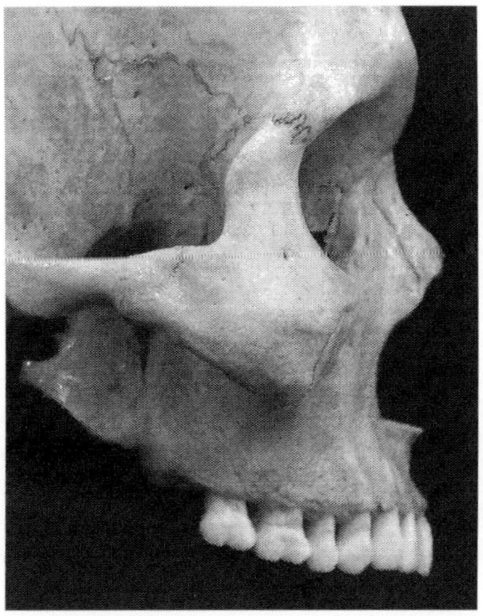

FIGURE 3.15 Variant of ANS 3. *ANS*, anterior nasal spine.

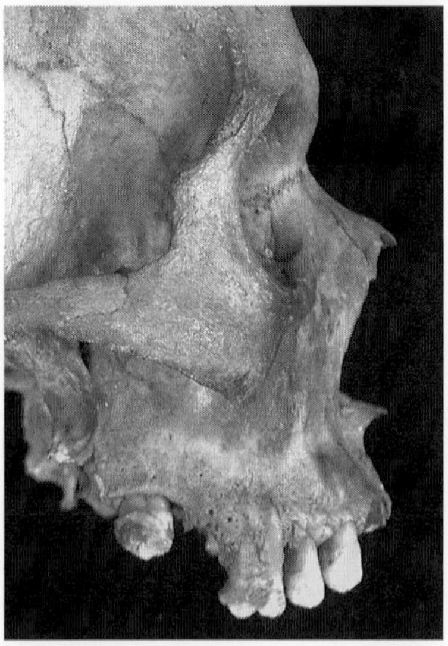

**FIGURE 3.16** Variant of ANS 3. *ANS*, anterior nasal spine.

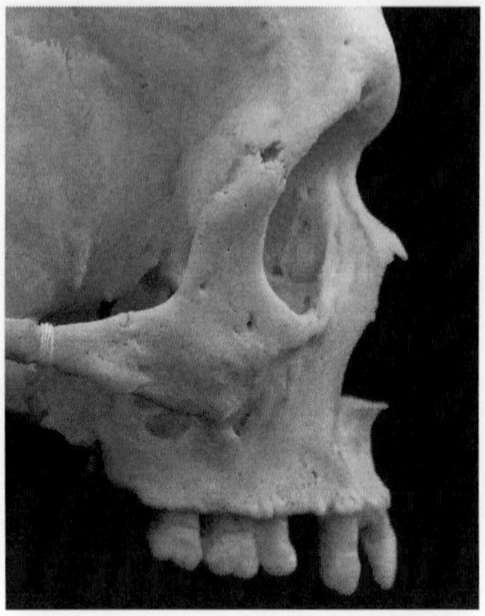

**FIGURE 3.17** Variant of ANS 3. *ANS*, anterior nasal spine.

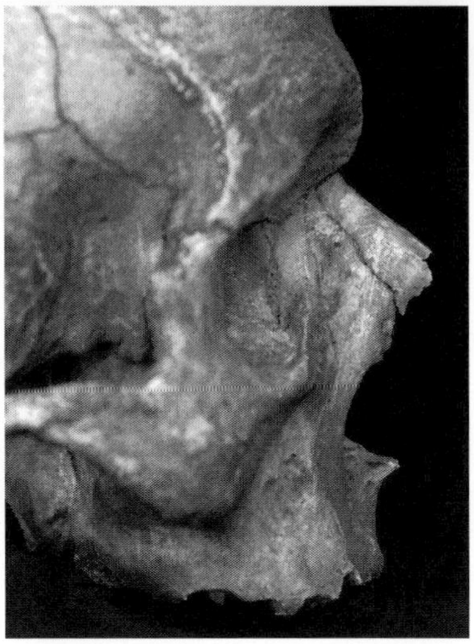

**FIGURE 3.18** Variant of ANS 3. *ANS*, anterior nasal spine.

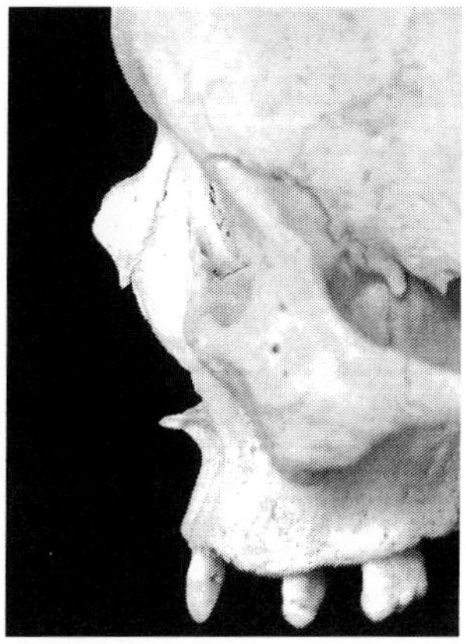

FIGURE 3.19 Variant of ANS 3. *ANS*, anterior nasal spine.

CHAPTER

# 4

# Inferior Nasal Aperture

Assessment of the inferior nasal aperture (INA) considers the shape of the inferior border of the nasal aperture and the transition from the nasal floor to the vertical portion of the maxilla. The entire region is considered when scoring unless bilateral asymmetry is present. In that case, the side with the highest expression is recorded. INA comprises five character states—scored as: $1 < 2 < 3 < 4 < 5$.

The inferior portion of the nasal aperture combined with the lateral alae constitutes the transition from nasal floor to the vertical portion of the maxillae, superior to the anterior dentition. A number of researchers have documented INA. Meil (1850) noted his sample of "Caucasoid" evinced a sharp ridge along the inferior margin of the nasal aperture. Hamy (1869) associated that same ridge with orthognathic crania. Topinard (1881) associated the differences he observed in INA morphology with racial differences, suggesting a rounded morphology was most typical of non-European groups.

The nearly dichotomous nature of these early descriptions was superseded in the late 1880s when Zuckerkandl (1882, 1883, 1895), Mingazzini (1891), and Hovorka (1893) more systematically outlined the various expressions of INA morphology. For example, Hovorka (1893) identified four morphologies of the inferior margin: (1) *Forma anthropina*, (2) *Fossa praenasalis*, (3) *Forma infantilis*, and (4) *Sulcus praenasalis*. Other researchers during this time built upon these morphologies, refining the descriptions and providing more nuanced conditions for expression (Sullivan, 1922; Holl, 1882; Von Bonin, 1912; Gower, 1923). Gower's (1923) contributions had the most lasting effect, and were used exclusively by DeVilliers (1968) who defined the inferior margin of the nasal aperture based on Gower's (1923) crests—lateral crest, spinal crest, and turbinal crest—and the development and fusion of those crests to create six forms, I–VI (DeVilliers, 1968:134).

Hooton (Brues, 1990) included observations for *Nasal Sills* in the Harvard recording form. Unfortunately, if he created illustrations for this feature, they are no longer available. Montague (1951) identified three expressions of the nasal sill: none, dull, and sharp; although this represents Hooton's Harvard recording form, as he borrowed it directly from J.L. Angel, a student of Hooton in the 1940s. Krogman (1955) and Krogman and Işçan (1986) describe three states of the lower nasal margin: (1) sharp, (2) guttered, and (3) troughed. Rhine (1990) describes the morphology of the INA as: deep, shallow, blurred, and guttered (Rhine, 1990:16). Lahr (1996:64–65) identified 10 categories for the *type of narial margins*, which she defined as the distinction between "a sharp line or fossa dividing the nasal floor from the subnasal portion of the maxilla." Byers (2011) identifies three states of the *lower nasal border*: sharp (sill), guttered, and flat/sharp. Mann et al. (2014) identify two manifestations of the inferior nasal margin, guttered and nasal sill.

INA is an assessment of the shape of the inferior border of the nasal aperture just lateral to the anterior nasal spine, which defines the transition from nasal floor to the vertical portion of the maxillae. The morphology of INA ranges from an inferior slope with no delineation of the inferior border (1) to a sharp, vertical ridge of bone, or nasal sill (5).

## NOMENCLATURE

Inferior nasal aperture, *Apertura nasalis, Forma anthropina, Forma infantilis, Fossa praenasalis,* lower nasal margin, inferior margin of the nasal aperture, narial margins, nasal base, nasal guttering, nasal sill, subnasal grooves (*sic*), and *Sulcus praenasalis*.

Atlas of Human Cranial Macromorphoscopic Traits.
DOI: https://doi.org/10.1016/B978-0-12-814385-8.00004-5

## GROSS ANATOMY

The INA is formed by the intersection of the two maxillae, bounded laterally by the thin, sharp margins of the frontal processes of the maxillae and inferiorly by the same as they curve medially, joining at the anterior nasal spine. Comprising the main components of the nasal cavity, this region is usually lined with the *membrane mucosa nasi*, a thick mucus membrane continuous with the external upper lip through the nares.

## GROWTH AND DEVELOPMENT

Near the fourth week of intrauterine development, five branchial arches form the region of the future head and neck. Each arch gives rise to muscles, connective tissue, vasculature, and neural and skeletal components of the future face, including the maxillae. The first branchial arch is instrumental in the formation of the nasomaxillary region, formed predominantly from the maxillary process of the mandibular arch.

Around week 6, the growth of the nasal swellings deepens dorsocaudadly to form the nasal pits and penetrate the underlying mesenchyme. Lying posterior to the primary palate (i.e., the primitive palate), each pit is initially separated from the oral cavity by the oronasal membrane, which eventually breaks down allowing communication between the two structures via the primitive choanae. Following the formation of the secondary palate, the choanae are at the junction between the oral pharynx and the nasal cavities. Posteriorly, the lateral palatine processes fuse with the nasal septum maintaining the separation between the oral and nasal cavities while separating each nasal cavity from the other. The superior, middle, and inferior turbinates develop as elevations on the lateral nasal wall of each nasal cavity. Lined with ectodermal epithelium these structures along the roof of the nasal cavity become specialized for olfaction.

## FUNCTIONAL MORPHOLOGY

The external nose has been the subject of extensive anthropological and clinical study, in part, due to the adaptive significance pertaining to that region of the human face (Bigham et al., 2009; Churchill et al., 2004; Farkas et al., 1986; Ferrario et al., 2007; Franciscus and Long, 1991; Inthavong et al., 2007; Keck and Lindemann, 2010; Noback et al., 2011; Shaffer et al., 2016; Weiner, 1954; Yokley, 2009), but also because of the numerous pathological conditions affecting it (Mooney and Siegel, 2002). The study of the adaptive significance of the external and internal structures of the human nose has generated various conclusions on regional differences in nasal morphology. Nares width has been correlated with temperature and humidity, findings supporting the claim that local climate plays a role in the geographic distribution of nasal form (Zaidi et al., 2017; Farkas et al., 1986; Franciscus and Long, 1991; Churchill et al., 2004; Roseman, 2004; Guo et al., 2014). Others have demonstrated similar correlations between skeletal morphology associated with the human nose and climatic adaptations (Maddux et al., 2016).

Early research looking specifically at functional morphological explanations of INA morphology focused on the dentition and the degree of prognathism. For example, Burkitt and Lightoller (1923) suggested the anterior dentition (incisors and canines) was the primary factor influencing the morphology of the INA. They used the large and curved incisors of nonhuman anthropoids to explain the rounded (guttered or blurred) INA presentation. Reduction in dentition and prognathism likewise reduces guttering and forms a ridge (sill) when the crests of the frontal processes are fused (DeVilliers, 1968). More recent research suggests subnasal morphology is not related entirely to a reduction in the anterior dentition but rather results from ontogenetic resorption of the anterior nasal floor during growth and development (McCollum and Ward, 1997; Nicholas and Franciscus, 2014).

One final note on the functional morphology of the INA is needed. A distinction should be made between subnasal grooves, which represent indentations made by vessels in that area and morphology of the INA (i.e., character states 1 and 2). Subnasal grooves do not reflect the start of the nasal floor and should not be considered when scoring INA.

## WITHIN POPULATION VARIATION

Data derived from the Macromorphoscopic Databank of the frequency distribution of INA ($n = 6215$). All data are for adult individuals. When possible, frequency data for males and females are provided separately. When sex could not be estimated reliably, frequency distributions are pooled as "Unknown" (Table 4.1).

**TABLE 4.1** Frequency Distribution of INA, by Geographic Origin and Sex

| | | 1 | | 2 | | 3 | | 4 | | 5 | | |
|---|---|---|---|---|---|---|---|---|---|---|---|---|
| **Geographic origin** | **Sex** | *n* | % | *n* | % | *n* | % | *n* | % | *n* | % | **Total** |
| **African** | **Female** | 12 | 86 | 2 | 14 | 0 | 0 | 0 | 0 | 0 | 0 | 14 |
| | **Male** | 11 | 69 | 5 | 31 | 0 | 0 | 0 | 0 | 0 | 0 | 16 |
| | **Unknown** | 0 | 0 | 0 | 0 | 0 | 0 | 0 | 0 | 0 | 0 | 0 |
| | **Total** | 23 | 77 | 7 | 23 | 0 | 0 | 0 | 0 | 0 | 0 | 30 |
| **American Black** | **Female** | 49 | 36 | 28 | 20 | 37 | 27 | 22 | 16 | 1 | 1 | 137 |
| | **Male** | 74 | 31 | 42 | 18 | 70 | 29 | 47 | 20 | 7 | 3 | 240 |
| | **Unknown** | 0 | 0 | 0 | 0 | 1 | 100 | 0 | 0 | 0 | 0 | 1 |
| | **Total** | 123 | 33 | 70 | 19 | 108 | 29 | 69 | 18 | 8 | 2 | 378 |
| **American White** | **Female** | 2 | 1 | 28 | 11 | 160 | 61 | 66 | 25 | 5 | 2 | 261 |
| | **Male** | 7 | 3 | 24 | 9 | 183 | 66 | 50 | 18 | 13 | 5 | 277 |
| | **Unknown** | 0 | 0 | 0 | 0 | 0 | 0 | 0 | 0 | 0 | 0 | 0 |
| | **Total** | 9 | 2 | 52 | 10 | 343 | 64 | 116 | 22 | 18 | 3 | 538 |
| **Amerindian** | **Female** | 13 | 29 | 28 | 62 | 4 | 9 | 0 | 0 | 0 | 0 | 45 |
| | **Male** | 17 | 44 | 20 | 51 | 2 | 5 | 0 | 0 | 0 | 0 | 39 |
| | **Unknown** | 222 | 8 | 755 | 29 | 1067 | 40 | 504 | 19 | 92 | 3 | 2640 |
| | **Total** | 252 | 9 | 803 | 29 | 1073 | 39 | 504 | 19 | 92 | 3 | 2724 |
| **Chinese** | **Female** | 2 | 40 | 3 | 60 | 0 | 0 | 0 | 0 | 0 | 0 | 5 |
| | **Male** | 15 | 28 | 36 | 67 | 3 | 6 | 0 | 0 | 0 | 0 | 54 |
| | **Unknown** | 0 | 0 | 0 | 0 | 0 | 0 | 0 | 0 | 0 | 0 | 0 |
| | **Total** | 17 | 29 | 39 | 66 | 3 | 5 | 0 | 0 | 0 | 0 | 59 |
| **Colombian** | **Female** | 5 | 7 | 9 | 13 | 20 | 30 | 15 | 22 | 18 | 27 | 67 |
| | **Male** | 6 | 3 | 20 | 12 | 53 | 31 | 41 | 24 | 53 | 31 | 173 |
| | **Unknown** | 0 | 0 | 0 | 0 | 0 | 0 | 0 | 0 | 0 | 0 | 0 |
| | **Total** | 11 | 5 | 29 | 12 | 73 | 30 | 56 | 23 | 71 | 30 | 240 |
| **El Salvador** | **Female** | 0 | 0 | 0 | 0 | 0 | 0 | 0 | 0 | 0 | 0 | 0 |
| | **Male** | 0 | 0 | 4 | 80 | 1 | 20 | 0 | 0 | 0 | 0 | 5 |
| | **Unknown** | 0 | 0 | 0 | 0 | 0 | 0 | 0 | 0 | 0 | 0 | 0 |
| | **Total** | 0 | 0 | 4 | 80 | 1 | 20 | 0 | 0 | 0 | 0 | 5 |
| **Eskimo** | **Female** | 0 | 0 | 0 | 0 | 0 | 0 | 0 | 0 | 0 | 0 | 0 |
| | **Male** | 0 | 0 | 0 | 0 | 0 | 0 | 0 | 0 | 0 | 0 | 0 |
| | **Unknown** | 173 | 21 | 331 | 41 | 260 | 32 | 49 | 6 | 2 | 0 | 815 |
| | **Total** | 173 | 21 | 331 | 41 | 260 | 32 | 49 | 6 | 2 | 0 | 815 |
| **European** | **Female** | 0 | 0 | 5 | 71 | 2 | 29 | 0 | 0 | 0 | 0 | 7 |
| | **Male** | 2 | 25 | 0 | 0 | 2 | 25 | 4 | 50 | 0 | 0 | 8 |
| | **Unknown** | 0 | 0 | 0 | 0 | 0 | 0 | 0 | 0 | 0 | 0 | 0 |
| | **Total** | 2 | 13 | 5 | 33 | 4 | 27 | 4 | 27 | 0 | 0 | 15 |

*(Continued)*

TABLE 4.1 (*Continued*)

| | | 1 | | 2 | | 3 | | 4 | | 5 | | |
|---|---|---|---|---|---|---|---|---|---|---|---|---|
| **Geographic origin** | **Sex** | *n* | % | *n* | % | *n* | % | *n* | % | *n* | % | **Total** |
| **Guatemalan** | **Female** | 1 | 3 | 4 | 12 | 17 | 52 | 8 | 24 | 3 | 9 | 33 |
| | **Male** | 9 | 13 | 12 | 17 | 21 | 30 | 25 | 36 | 2 | 3 | 69 |
| | **Unknown** | 0 | 0 | 0 | 0 | 0 | 0 | 0 | 0 | 0 | 0 | 0 |
| | **Total** | 10 | 10 | 16 | 16 | 38 | 37 | 33 | 32 | 5 | 5 | 102 |
| **Japanese** | **Female** | 0 | 0 | 5 | 100 | 0 | 0 | 0 | 0 | 0 | 0 | 5 |
| | **Male** | 4 | 50 | 2 | 25 | 0 | 0 | 2 | 25 | 0 | 0 | 8 |
| | **Unknown** | 1 | 50 | 1 | 50 | 0 | 0 | 0 | 0 | 0 | 0 | 2 |
| | **Total** | 5 | 33 | 8 | 53 | 0 | 0 | 2 | 13 | 0 | 0 | 15 |
| **Mexico** | **Female** | 0 | 0 | 0 | 0 | 1 | 50 | 1 | 50 | 0 | 0 | 2 |
| | **Male** | 1 | 4 | 2 | 8 | 13 | 54 | 6 | 25 | 2 | 8 | 24 |
| | **Unknown** | 0 | 0 | 0 | 0 | 0 | 0 | 0 | 0 | 0 | 0 | 0 |
| | **Total** | 1 | 4 | 2 | 8 | 14 | 54 | 7 | 27 | 2 | 8 | 26 |
| **Pacific Island** | **Female** | 7 | 13 | 23 | 42 | 20 | 36 | 4 | 7 | 1 | 2 | 55 |
| | **Male** | 15 | 17 | 36 | 42 | 32 | 37 | 2 | 2 | 1 | 1 | 86 |
| | **Unknown** | 22 | 24 | 47 | 52 | 15 | 17 | 4 | 4 | 2 | 2 | 90 |
| | **Total** | 44 | 19 | 106 | 46 | 67 | 29 | 10 | 4 | 4 | 2 | 231 |
| **Peruvian** | **Female** | 0 | 0 | 0 | 0 | 0 | 0 | 0 | 0 | 0 | 0 | 0 |
| | **Male** | 0 | 0 | 0 | 0 | 0 | 0 | 0 | 0 | 0 | 0 | 0 |
| | **Unknown** | 0 | 0 | 6 | 26 | 12 | 52 | 4 | 17 | 1 | 4 | 23 |
| | **Total** | 0 | 0 | 6 | 26 | 12 | 52 | 4 | 17 | 1 | 4 | 23 |
| **Southwest (SW) Hispanic** | **Female** | 0 | 0 | 0 | 0 | 7 | 88 | 1 | 13 | 0 | 0 | 8 |
| | **Male** | 1 | 10 | 1 | 10 | 5 | 50 | 2 | 20 | 1 | 10 | 10 |
| | **Unknown** | 0 | 0 | 10 | 10 | 63 | 63 | 20 | 20 | 7 | 7 | 100 |
| | **Total** | 1 | 1 | 11 | 9 | 75 | 64 | 23 | 19 | 8 | 7 | 118 |
| **Thai** | **Female** | 27 | 9 | 114 | 36 | 136 | 43 | 37 | 12 | 3 | 1 | 317 |
| | **Male** | 56 | 10 | 227 | 40 | 229 | 40 | 47 | 8 | 7 | 1 | 566 |
| | **Unknown** | 1 | 8 | 5 | 38 | 5 | 38 | 2 | 15 | 0 | 0 | 13 |
| | **Total** | 84 | 9 | 346 | 39 | 370 | 41 | 86 | 10 | 10 | 1 | 896 |
| **Total for all groups** | | 755 | 12 | 1835 | 30 | 2441 | 39 | 963 | 15 | 221 | 4 | 6215 |

*INA*, inferior nasal aperture.

# CHARACTER STATES

Photographic exemplars of the different character states of INA are provided below. Each character state is defined following (Hefner, 2009, 2016). When necessary to clarify scoring, more nuanced definitions are provided in the figure captions. INA morphology should be assessed with the protocol provided in the preceding section. Character states include:

INA 1 = a marked slope of the nasal floor, which starts inside the nasal cavity and terminates on the vertical surface of the maxilla. This gradual slope is a smooth transition between the two anatomical areas.

INA 2 = a moderate slope of the nasal floor to the vertical surface of the maxilla. To differentiate from INA 1, the slope begins more anteriorly in the nasal aperture (more anterior to the insertion of the vomer) and exhibits more angulation at the opening.

INA 3 = an abrupt transition from the nasal floor to the vertical maxilla. There is no slope or intervening projection of bone (sill). This morphology closely resembles a right angle, although a more blunted form may present.

INA 4 = any weak ridge of bone that crosses the anterior nasal floor perpendicularly, resulting in a partial nasal sill.

INA 5 = a pronounced ridge, or nasal sill, obstructing the nasal floor-to-maxilla transition.

## CHARACTER STATES FOR INFERIOR NASAL APERTURE = 1 (FIGS. 4.1–4.7)

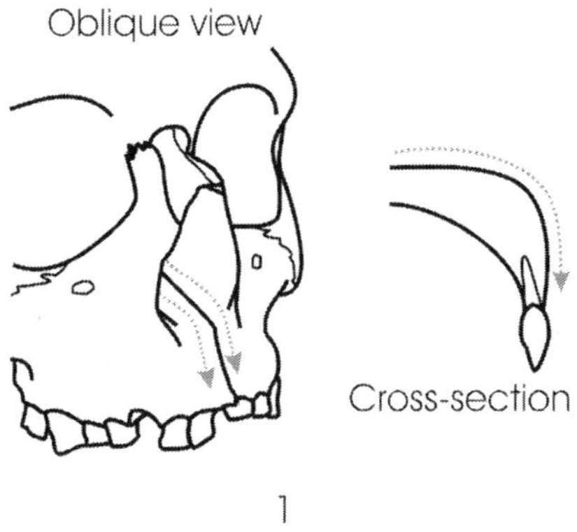


**FIGURE 4.1** Diagrammatic representation of INA 1. *Note:* Arrows indicate transition from nasal cavity floor to vertical maxilla. *INA*, inferior nasal aperture.

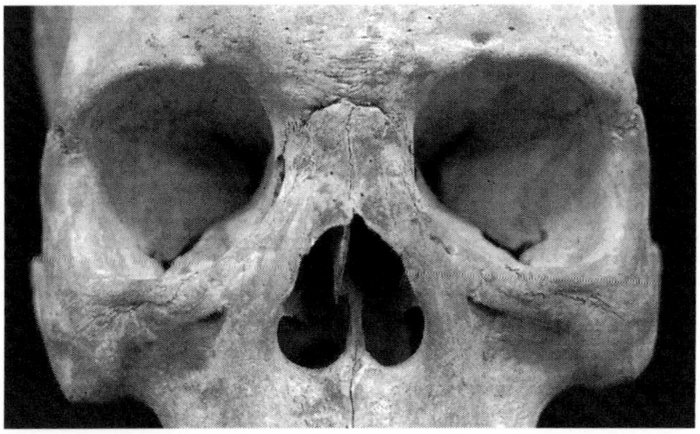

**FIGURE 4.2** Variant of INA 1. *INA*, inferior nasal aperture.

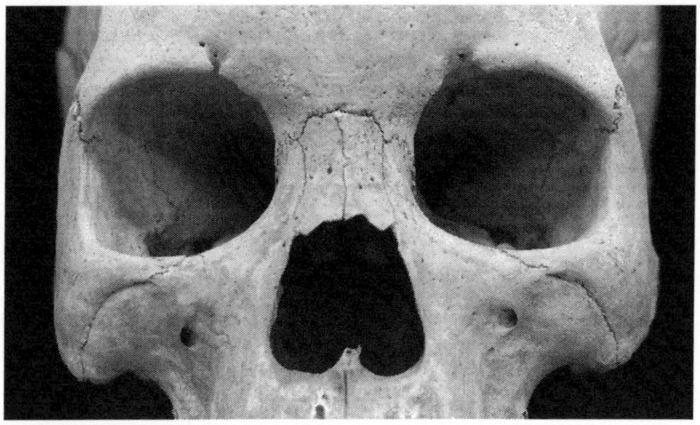

**FIGURE 4.3** Variant of INA 1. *INA*, inferior nasal aperture.

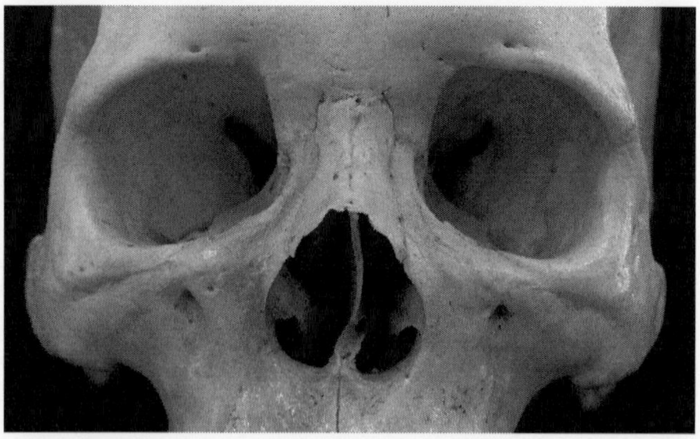

**FIGURE 4.4** Variant of INA 1. *Note:* Lateral grooves along the most inferior aspect of nasal aperture (subnasal grooves) should not be considered when assessing INA. *INA*, inferior nasal aperture.

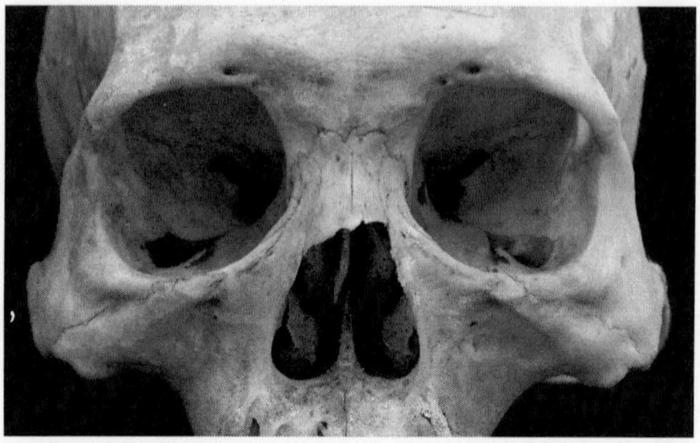

**FIGURE 4.5** Variant of INA 1. *Note:* Lateral grooves along the most inferior aspect of nasal aperture (subnasal grooves) should not be considered when assessing INA. *INA*, inferior nasal aperture.

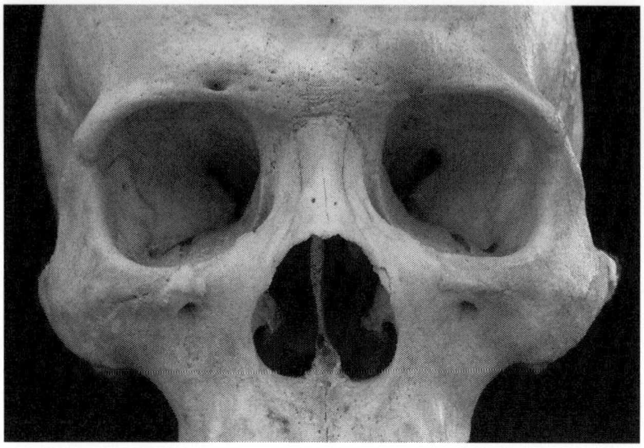

**FIGURE 4.6** Variant of INA 1. *INA*, inferior nasal aperture.

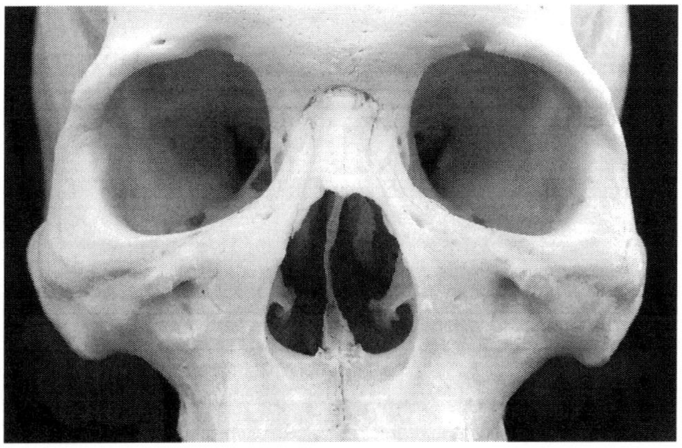

**FIGURE 4.7** Variant of INA 1. *Note:* Relative insertion of vomer is particularly clear in this example. *INA*, inferior nasal aperture.

## CHARACTER STATES FOR INFERIOR NASAL APERTURE = 2 (FIGS. 4.8–4.15)

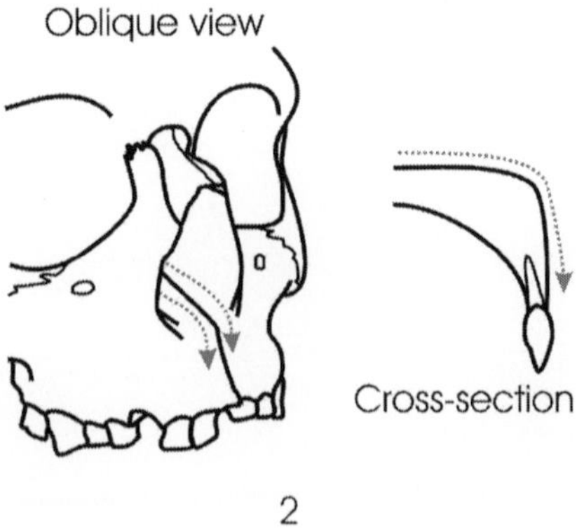


**FIGURE 4.8** Diagrammatic representation of INA 2. *Note:* Arrows indicate transition from nasal cavity floor to vertical maxilla. *INA*, inferior nasal aperture.

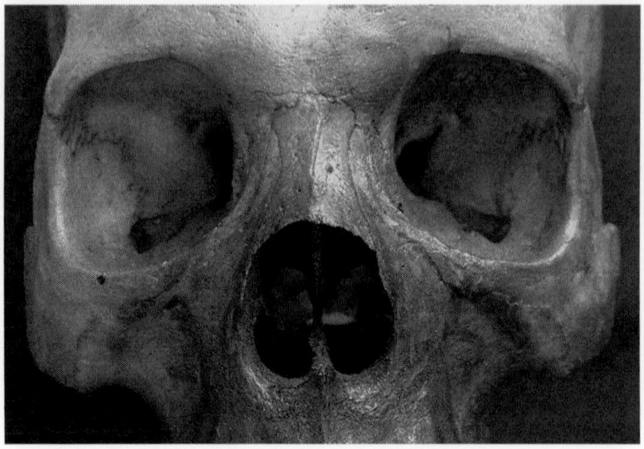

**FIGURE 4.9** Variant of INA 2. *Note:* Position of initial slope (relative to vomer insertion) is more anterior than the position observed in Fig. 4.7. *INA*, inferior nasal aperture.

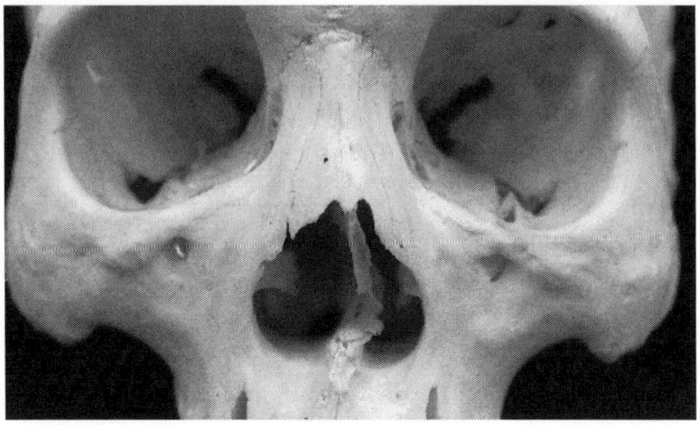

**FIGURE 4.10** Variant of INA 2. *INA*, inferior nasal aperture.

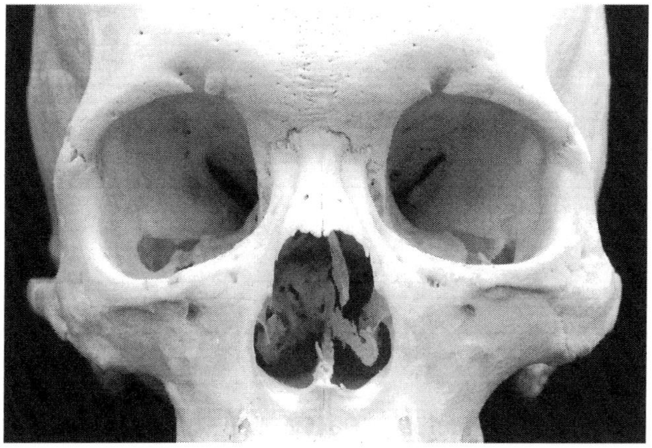

**FIGURE 4.11** Variant of INA 2. *Note:* Lateral grooves along the most inferior aspect of nasal aperture (subnasal grooves) should not be considered when assessing INA. *INA*, inferior nasal aperture.

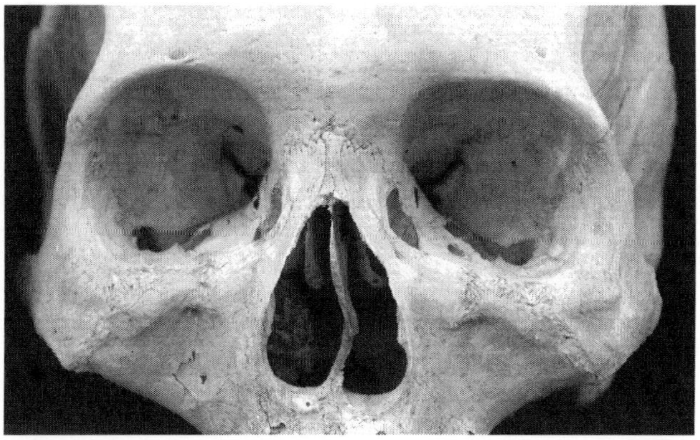

**FIGURE 4.12** Variant of INA 2. *INA*, inferior nasal aperture.

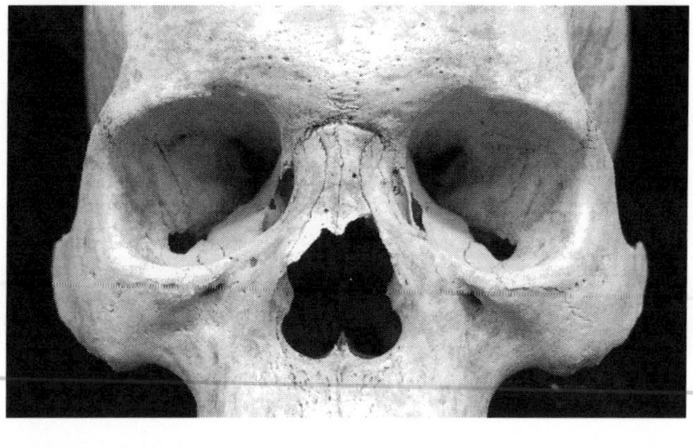

**FIGURE 4.13** Variant of INA 2. *INA*, inferior nasal aperture.

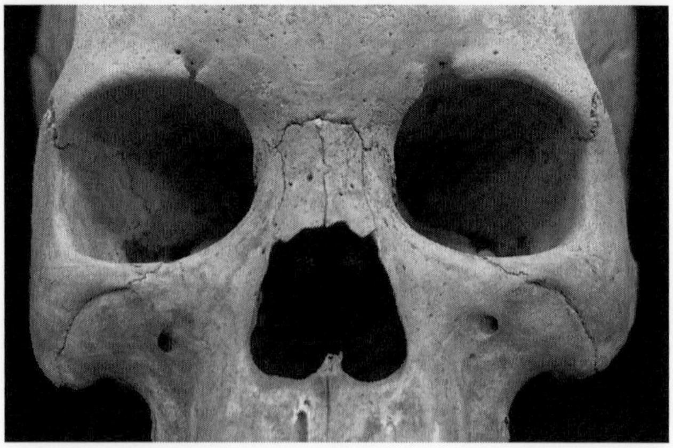

FIGURE 4.14 Variant of INA 2. *INA,* inferior nasal aperture.

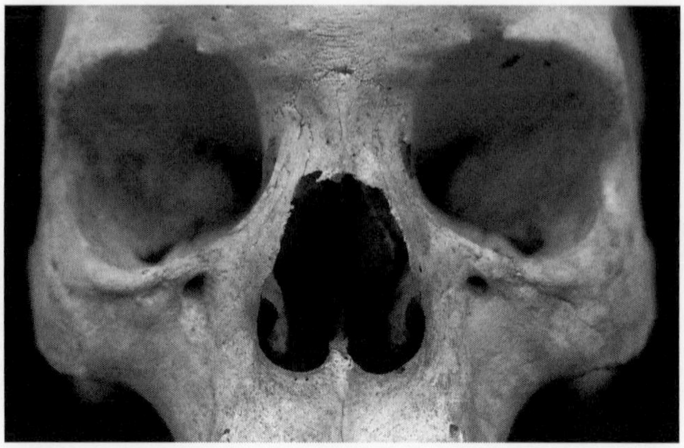

FIGURE 4.15 Variant of INA 2. *INA,* inferior nasal aperture.

## CHARACTER STATES FOR INFERIOR NASAL APERTURE = 3 (FIGS. 4.16–4.22)

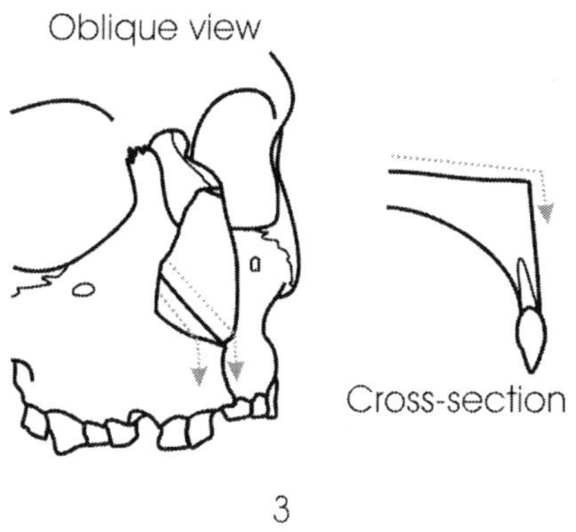


FIGURE 4.16 Diagrammatic representation of INA 3. *Note:* Arrows indicate transition from nasal cavity floor to vertical maxilla. *INA*, inferior nasal aperture.

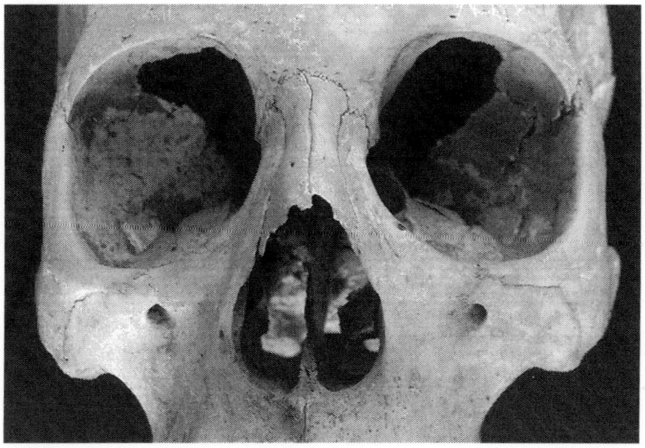

FIGURE 4.17 Variant of INA 3. *Note:* Abrupt transition from nasal floor to vertical maxilla creating an approximately 90° angle. *INA*, inferior nasal aperture.

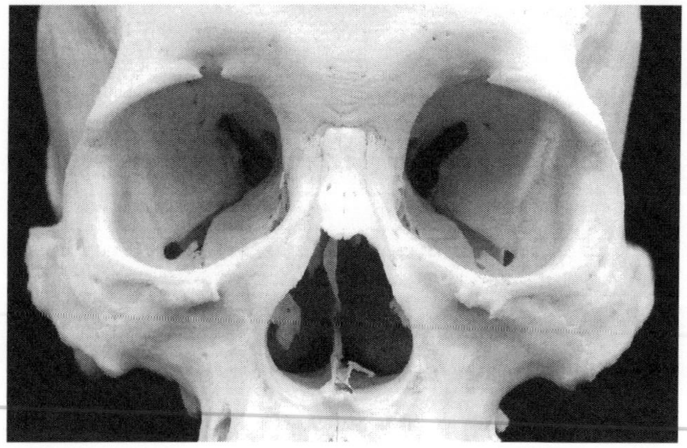

FIGURE 4.18 Variant of INA 3. *INA*, inferior nasal aperture.

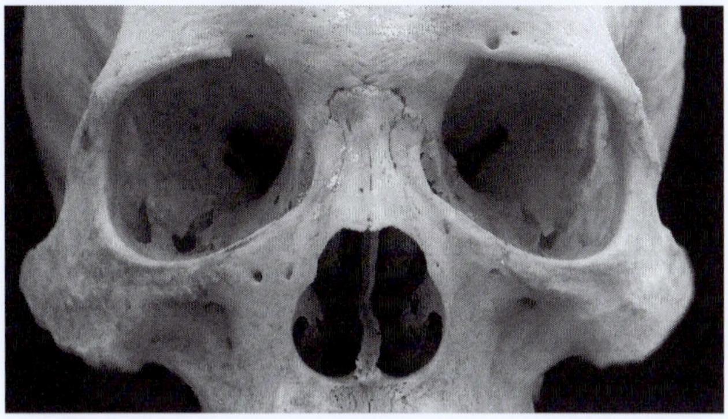

FIGURE 4.19 Variant of INA 3. *INA*, inferior nasal aperture.

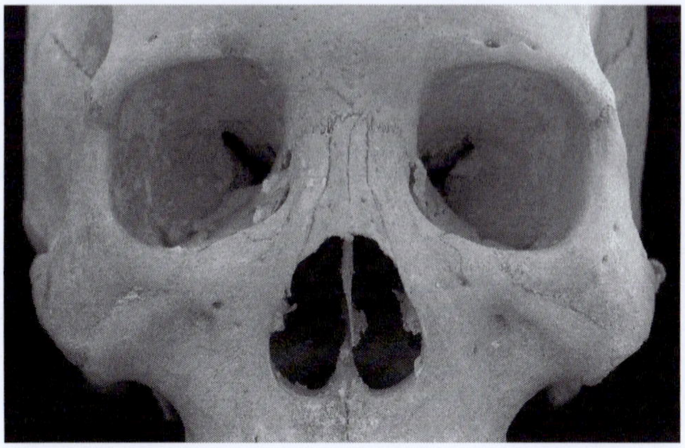

FIGURE 4.20 Variant of INA 3. *INA*, inferior nasal aperture.

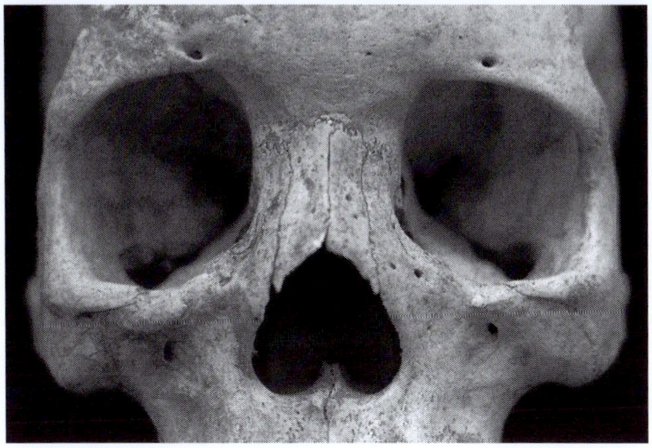

FIGURE 4.21 Variant of INA 3. *INA*, inferior nasal aperture.

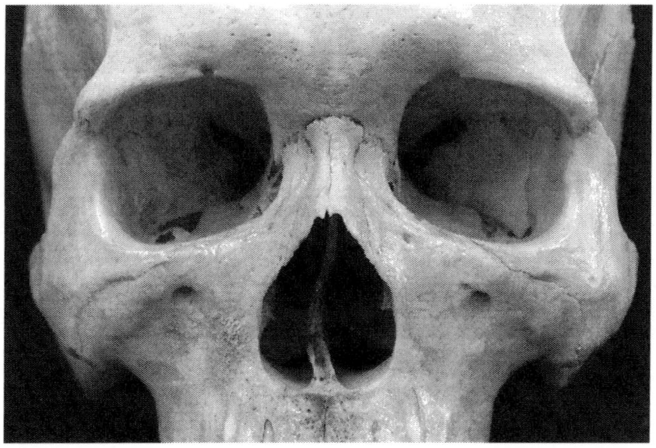

**FIGURE 4.22** Variant of INA 3. *INA*, inferior nasal aperture.

# CHARACTER STATES FOR INFERIOR NASAL APERTURE = 4 (FIGS. 4.23–4.29)

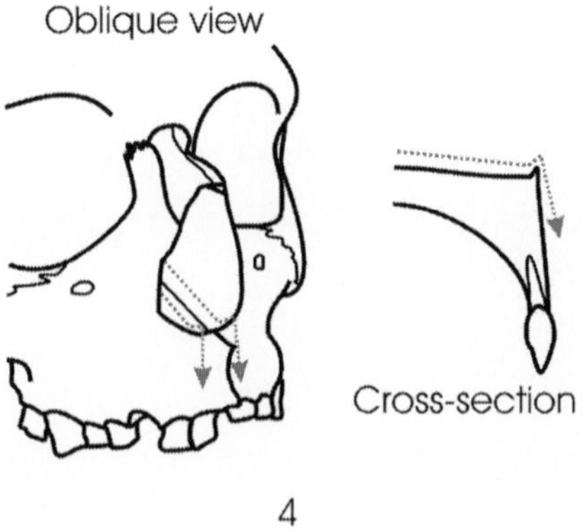


**FIGURE 4.23** Diagrammatic representation of INA 4. *Note:* Arrows indicate transition from nasal cavity floor to vertical maxilla. *INA,* inferior nasal aperture.

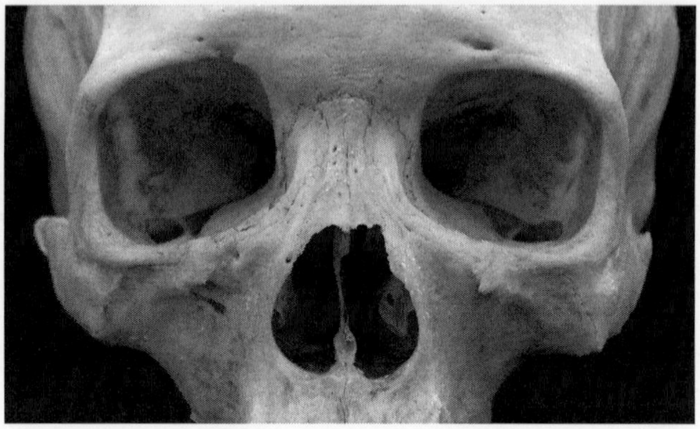

**FIGURE 4.24** Variant of INA 4. *INA,* inferior nasal aperture.

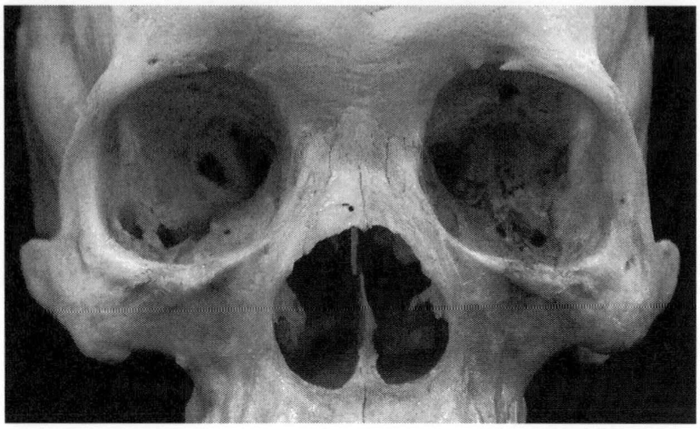

**FIGURE 4.25** Variant of INA 4. *Note:* This is one of the best examples of INA 4. The relative depth of the hard palate is most clear in this image. *INA,* inferior nasal aperture.

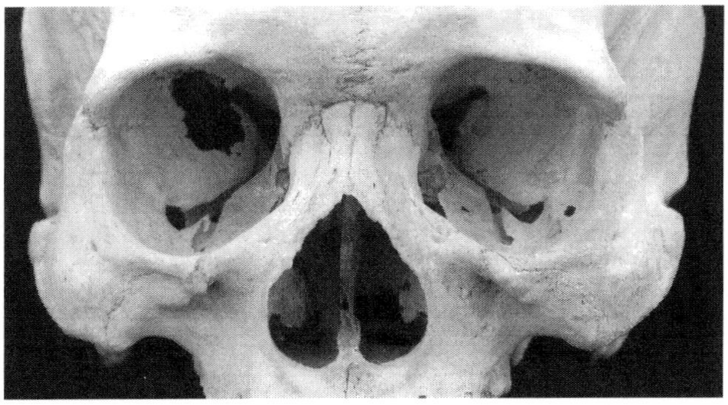

FIGURE 4.26 Variant of INA 4. *INA*, inferior nasal aperture.

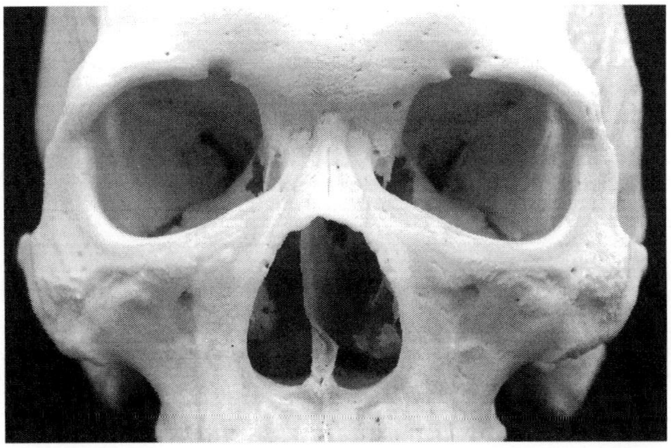

FIGURE 4.27 Variant of INA 4. *INA*, inferior nasal aperture.

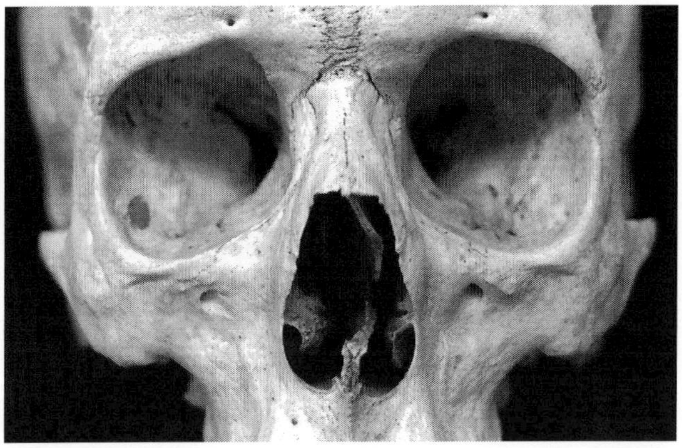

FIGURE 4.28 Variant of INA 4. *INA*, inferior nasal aperture.

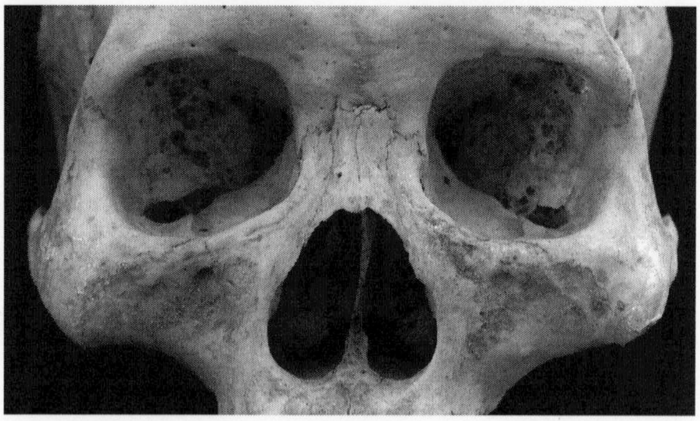

**FIGURE 4.29** Variant of INA 4. *INA*, inferior nasal aperture.

# CHARACTER STATES FOR INFERIOR NASAL APERTURE = 5 (FIGS. 4.30–4.36)

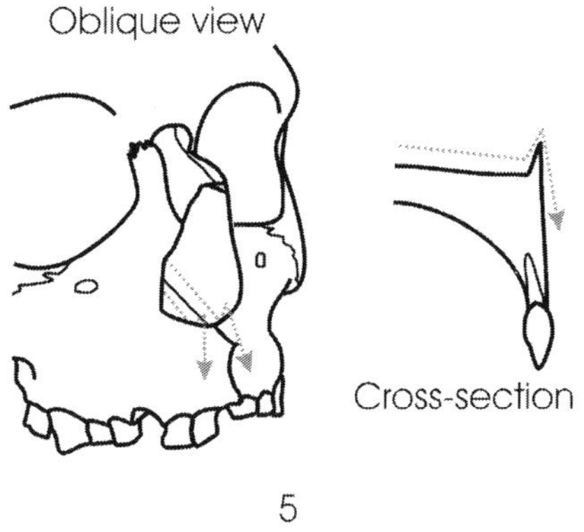


FIGURE 4.30 Diagrammatic representation of INA 5. *Note:* Arrows indicate transition from nasal cavity floor to vertical maxilla. *INA*, inferior nasal aperture.

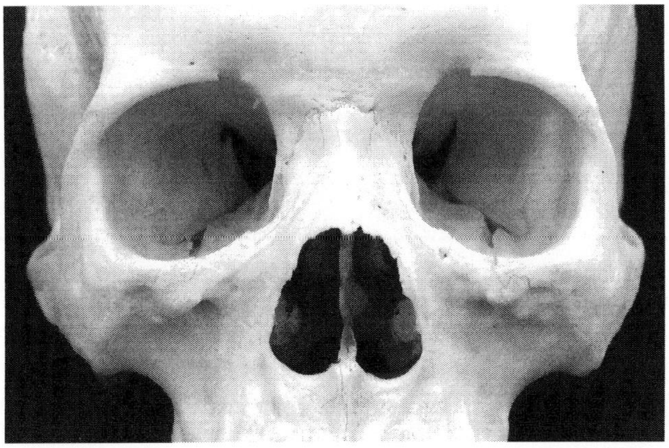

FIGURE 4.31 Variant of INA 5. *Note:* How the nasal floor is not visible in INA 5. *INA*, inferior nasal aperture.

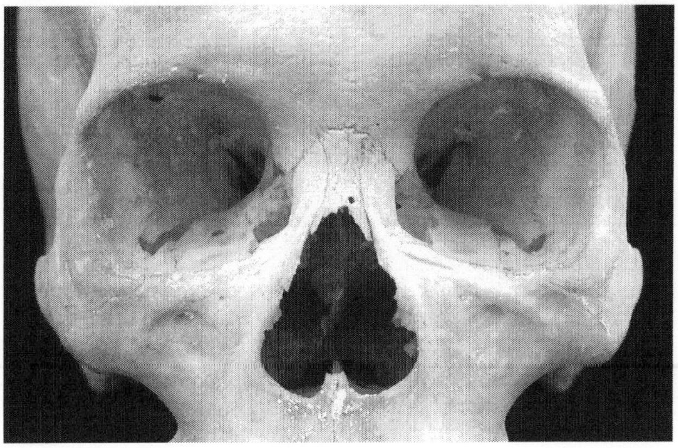

FIGURE 4.32 Variant of INA 5. *INA*, inferior nasal aperture.

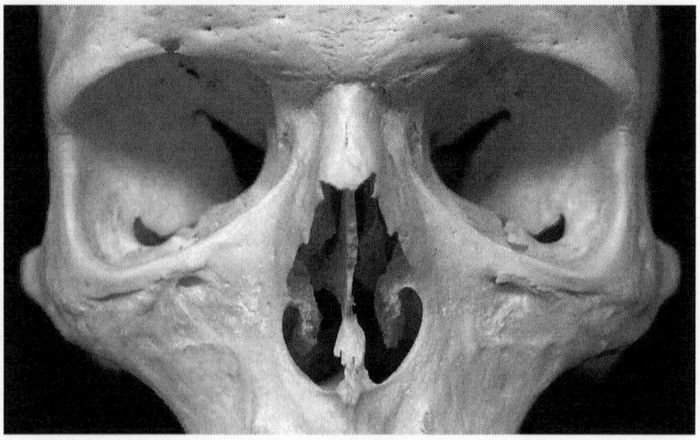

**FIGURE 4.33** Variant of INA 5. *INA*, inferior nasal aperture.

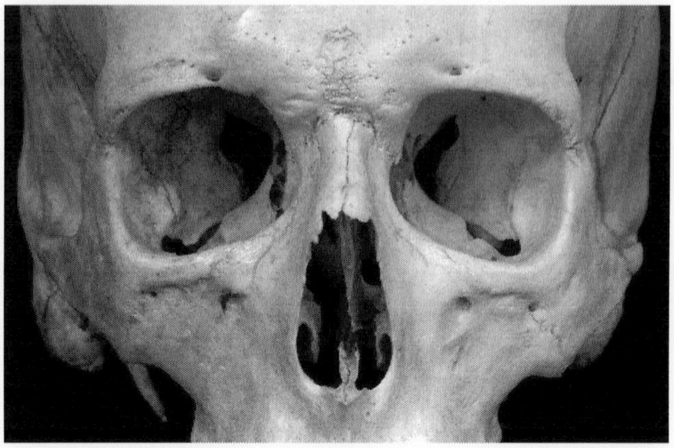

**FIGURE 4.34** Variant of INA 5. *INA*, inferior nasal aperture.

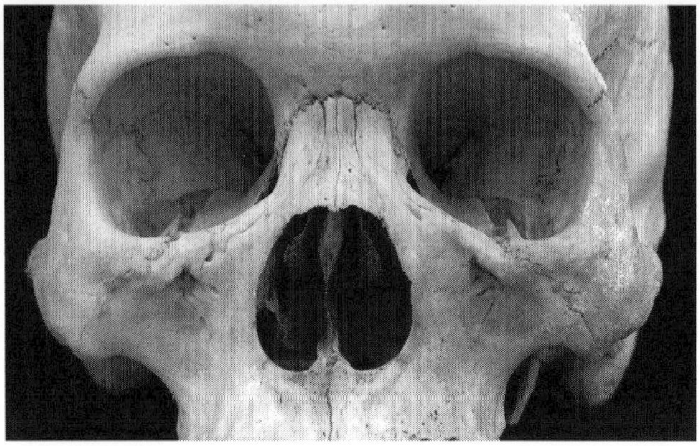

**FIGURE 4.35** Variant of INA 5. *INA*, inferior nasal aperture.

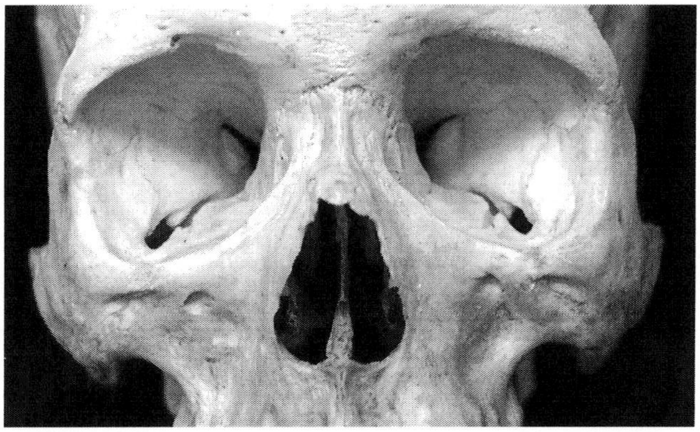

**FIGURE 4.36** Variant of INA 5. *INA*, inferior nasal aperture.

CHAPTER

# 5

# Interorbital Breadth

Assessing the interorbital breadth (IOB) considers the relative distance between the orbits. To score IOB, the entire facial skeleton (from right frontomalare temporale to left frontomalare temporale) is considered (see below).

Knowles (1911) and Martin (1928) studied the correlation between interorbital distance and other craniometric measures. Although they did not provide a cranial nonmetric variant to describe IOB, their work laid the foundation for further study. The first mention we could locate describing IOB in a manner similar to the modern usage is in the introduction to Cameron's (1931:509) treatise on the *Interorbital Width*:

> When a keen observer has his first inspection of the negro (sic) crania in the Hamann Museum, there are at least two very striking features that arrest the attention, namely, their splendid dentitions and the remarkable width between their orbits.

Cameron investigated IOB in a sample of American Black, American White, and Greenlandic Eskimo, using Martin's lacrimal point (*dacryon*), a bony landmark still used today for the metric assessment of this region. He did not, however, include a nonmetric component to his analysis. Likewise, Hooton does not include IOB in the Harvard data collection forms; however, his student J. L. Angel (1944) outlines morphological types, defining a metric *and* a nonmetric component. The latter he simply defined as *narrow* or *wide*. In their study of American Blacks, Anglo-Saxons, and African Blacks, Todd and Tracy (1930) identified two morphological variants of IOB: *narrow* and *wide*. Coon (1962:673), another Hooton student, defined interorbital distance as "[t]he distance between the inner borders of the bony eye-sockets." He does not provide character states per se, but he does use consistent terminology throughout his manuscript to describe the various manifestations. For example, he designates one group having an "interorbital distance [that] is, comparatively speaking, great" (Coon, 1962:27) and another having an "interorbital distance [that] is very narrow ..." (Coon, 1962:Plate 45).

There have not been concerted modern efforts to standardize the character states associated with IOB assessments. Rhine (1990) did not include the assessment of IOB in his list of cranial nonmetric traits. Gill and Gilbert (1990) allude to a visual method, stating: "[w]hites have a high, prominent and narrow interorbital area, while Blacks and American Indians have a low, flat and broad interorbital area" (1990:47). The remainder of that manuscript is devoted to a metric assessment of the interorbital region. Hefner (2003a,b, 2007, 2009) formalized three character states associated with IOB, although the trait was poorly defined: "[IOB] is assessed as: (i) narrow, (ii) intermediate, and (iii) broad. This assessment is made relative to the facial skeleton" (Hefner, 2009:988).

Therefore, IOB is the distance between the two orbits in the region of dacryon, relative to the overall breadth of the facial skeleton scored using three character states: narrow, medium, and broad (i.e., $1 < 2 < 3$). Fig. 5.1 illustrates the relative measures of IOB. When assessing each character state, analysts should consider how much of the interorbital distance comprises the total facial skeleton. If, for example, the interorbital region makes up roughly one-quarter of the upper facial skeleton, the region should be scored "2—medium."

## NOMENCLATURE

Interorbital area, interorbital breadth, interorbital distance, interorbital space, interorbital width, and *latitudinem interorbital*.

*Atlas of Human Cranial Macromorphoscopic Traits.*
DOI: https://doi.org/10.1016/B978-0-12-814385-8.00005-7

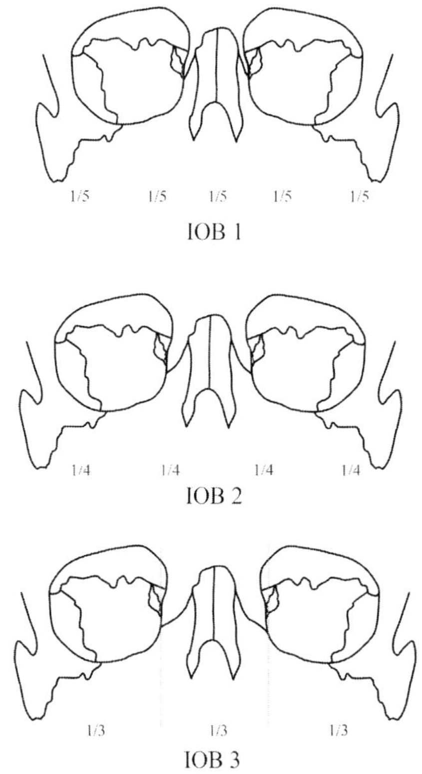


**FIGURE 5.1** Approximations of the relative measures for IOB, from top to bottom: IOB = 1 (narrow); IOB = 2 (medium); and IOB = 3 (broad). *IOB*, interorbital breadth.

## GROSS ANATOMY

Each orbit contains an eye, the orbital and retrobulbar fascia, extraocular muscles, cranial nerves II, III, IV, V, and VI, blood vessels, fat, lacrimal glands and sacs, nasolacrimal ducts, eyelids, the medial and lateral palpebral ligaments, suspensory ligaments, septum, ciliary ganglion, and short ciliary nerves. The medial wall of the orbit anchors the superior, oblique, medial, and inferior rectus muscles. The interorbital region of the midfacial skeleton that should be considered when assessing IOB comprises multiple skeletal elements, including: the medial orbital plate of the frontal bone, the posterior lacrimal crests, both nasal bones, both frontal processes of the maxillae, and, to a lesser degree, the lamina papyracea of the ethmoid.

## GROWTH AND DEVELOPMENT

During the third month in utero, the face of the fetus develops more human-like features, changing in overall appearance from the laterally placed eyes being more anteriorly orientated on the face. Throughout fetal development, orbit height increases as facial development proceeds, and by the 13th week, most principal parts of the eye have developed (cornea, lens, optic nerve, etc.). From this point forward, orbit growth remains linear until birth. Ossification of the bones comprising the majority of the orbit occurs between the 6th (maxilla) and 16th (frontal) week of gestation. There is a general lack of study regarding fetal orbit development in the literature (de Haan et al., 2006; Haas, 1992), which is surprising given the prevalence of developmental defects, such as clefting and midfacial hypoplasias, that affect the region (Barnes, 1994).

## FUNCTIONAL MORPHOLOGY

The interorbital region represents the skeletal connection between the braincase and the nasal region. Comprising the aforementioned skeletal elements (see the "Gross Anatomy" section), the interorbital region houses various soft-tissue structures associated with the eye; it is also an important structure during mastication (Vineyard et al., 2008), serving as a buttress during laterally directed chewing (Ross, 2008:77).

## WITHIN POPULATION VARIATION

Data derived from the Macromorphoscopic Databank of the frequency distribution of IOB ($n = 6098$). All data are for adult individuals. When possible, frequency data for males and females are provided separately. When sex could not be estimated reliably, frequency distributions are pooled as "Unknown" (Table 5.1).

**TABLE 5.1** Frequency Distribution of IOB, by Geographic Origin and Sex

| | | 1 | | 2 | | 3 | | |
|---|---|---|---|---|---|---|---|---|
| **Geographic origin** | **Sex** | *n* | % | *n* | % | *n* | % | **Total** |
| **African** | **Female** | 1 | 7 | 3 | 21 | 10 | 71 | 14 |
| | **Male** | 0 | 0 | 1 | 6 | 15 | 94 | 16 |
| | **Unknown** | 0 | 0 | 0 | 0 | 0 | 0 | 0 |
| | **Total** | 1 | 3 | 4 | 13 | 25 | 83 | 30 |
| **American Black** | **Female** | 23 | 17 | 57 | 42 | 57 | 42 | 137 |
| | **Male** | 39 | 16 | 96 | 40 | 105 | 44 | 240 |
| | **Unknown** | 1 | 100 | 0 | 0 | 0 | 0 | 1 |
| | **Total** | 63 | 17 | 153 | 40 | 162 | 43 | 378 |
| **American White** | **Female** | 140 | 54 | 113 | 43 | 8 | 3 | 261 |
| | **Male** | 130 | 47 | 124 | 45 | 23 | 8 | 277 |
| | **Unknown** | 0 | 0 | 0 | 0 | 0 | 0 | 0 |
| | **Total** | 270 | 50 | 237 | 44 | 31 | 6 | 538 |
| **Amerindian** | **Female** | 28 | 62 | 16 | 36 | 1 | 2 | 45 |
| | **Male** | 21 | 54 | 18 | 46 | 0 | 0 | 39 |
| | **Unknown** | 483 | 19 | 1715 | 69 | 280 | 11 | 2478 |
| | **Total** | 532 | 21 | 1749 | 68 | 281 | 11 | 2562 |
| **Chinese** | **Female** | 3 | 60 | 1 | 20 | 1 | 20 | 5 |
| | **Male** | 23 | 43 | 29 | 54 | 2 | 4 | 54 |
| | **Unknown** | 0 | 0 | 0 | 0 | 0 | 0 | 0 |
| | **Total** | 26 | 44 | 30 | 51 | 3 | 5 | 59 |
| **Colombian** | **Female** | 20 | 30 | 26 | 39 | 21 | 31 | 67 |
| | **Male** | 35 | 20 | 72 | 41 | 70 | 40 | 177 |
| | **Unknown** | 0 | 0 | 0 | 0 | 0 | 0 | 0 |
| | **Total** | 55 | 23 | 98 | 40 | 91 | 37 | 244 |
| **El Salvador** | **Female** | 0 | 0 | 0 | 0 | 0 | 0 | 0 |
| | **Male** | 1 | 20 | 4 | 80 | 0 | 0 | 5 |
| | **Unknown** | 0 | 0 | 0 | 0 | 0 | 0 | 0 |
| | **Total** | 1 | 20 | 4 | 80 | 0 | 0 | 5 |

*(Continued)*

TABLE 5.1 (*Continued*)

| | | 1 | | 2 | | 3 | | |
|---|---|---|---|---|---|---|---|---|
| **Geographic origin** | **Sex** | *n* | % | *n* | % | *n* | % | **Total** |
| **Eskimo** | **Female** | 0 | 0 | 0 | 0 | 0 | 0 | 0 |
| | **Male** | 0 | 0 | 0 | 0 | 0 | 0 | 0 |
| | **Unknown** | 208 | 25 | 543 | 65 | 88 | 10 | 839 |
| | **Total** | 208 | 25 | 543 | 65 | 88 | 10 | 839 |
| **European** | **Female** | 3 | 43 | 4 | 57 | 0 | 0 | 7 |
| | **Male** | 2 | 25 | 6 | 75 | 0 | 0 | 8 |
| | **Unknown** | 0 | 0 | 0 | 0 | 0 | 0 | 0 |
| | **Total** | 5 | 33 | 10 | 67 | 0 | 0 | 15 |
| **Guatemalan** | **Female** | 11 | 32 | 15 | 44 | 8 | 24 | 34 |
| | **Male** | 14 | 20 | 46 | 65 | 11 | 15 | 71 |
| | **Unknown** | 0 | 0 | 0 | 0 | 0 | 0 | 0 |
| | **Total** | 25 | 24 | 61 | 58 | 19 | 18 | 105 |
| **Japanese** | **Female** | 2 | 40 | 3 | 60 | 0 | 0 | 5 |
| | **Male** | 2 | 25 | 5 | 63 | 1 | 13 | 8 |
| | **Unknown** | 1 | 50 | 1 | 50 | 0 | 0 | 2 |
| | **Total** | 5 | 33 | 9 | 60 | 1 | 7 | 15 |
| **Mexico** | **Female** | 1 | 50 | 1 | 50 | 0 | 0 | 2 |
| | **Male** | 12 | 52 | 10 | 43 | 1 | 4 | 23 |
| | **Unknown** | 0 | 0 | 0 | 0 | 0 | 0 | 0 |
| | **Total** | 13 | 52 | 11 | 44 | 1 | 4 | 25 |
| **Pacific Island** | **Female** | 14 | 25 | 30 | 55 | 11 | 20 | 55 |
| | **Male** | 12 | 14 | 58 | 68 | 15 | 18 | 85 |
| | **Unknown** | 18 | 20 | 55 | 61 | 17 | 19 | 90 |
| | **Total** | 44 | 19 | 143 | 62 | 43 | 19 | 230 |
| **Peruvian** | **Female** | 0 | 0 | 0 | 0 | 0 | 0 | 0 |
| | **Male** | 0 | 0 | 0 | 0 | 0 | 0 | 0 |
| | **Unknown** | 11 | 38 | 13 | 45 | 5 | 17 | 29 |
| | **Total** | 11 | 38 | 13 | 45 | 5 | 17 | 29 |
| **Southwest (SW) Hispanic** | **Female** | 4 | 50 | 4 | 50 | 0 | 0 | 8 |
| | **Male** | 4 | 40 | 4 | 40 | 2 | 20 | 10 |
| | **Unknown** | 41 | 41 | 55 | 54 | 5 | 5 | 101 |
| | **Total** | 49 | 41 | 63 | 53 | 7 | 6 | 119 |
| **Thai** | **Female** | 57 | 18 | 206 | 64 | 58 | 18 | 321 |
| | **Male** | 91 | 16 | 403 | 71 | 76 | 13 | 570 |
| | **Unknown** | 3 | 21 | 5 | 36 | 6 | 43 | 14 |
| | **Total** | 151 | 17 | 614 | 68 | 140 | 15 | 905 |
| **Total for all groups** | | 1459 | 24 | 3742 | 61 | 897 | 15 | 6098 |

*IOB*, interorbital breadth.

# CHARACTER STATES

Photographic exemplars of the different character states of IOB are provided below. Each character state is defined following (Hefner, 2009, 2016). When necessary to clarify scoring, more nuanced definitions are provided in the figure captions. IOB should be assessed with the protocol provided in the preceding section. Character states include:

IOB 1 = *Narrow*—approximately 1/5 ratio of the interorbital space relative to the facial skeleton.

IOB 2 = *Medium*—approximately 1/4 ratio of the interorbital space relative to the facial skeleton.

IOB 3 = *Broad*—approximately 1/3 ratio of the interorbital space relative to the facial skeleton.

## CHARACTER STATES FOR INTERORBITAL BREADTH = 1 (FIGS. 5.2–5.8)

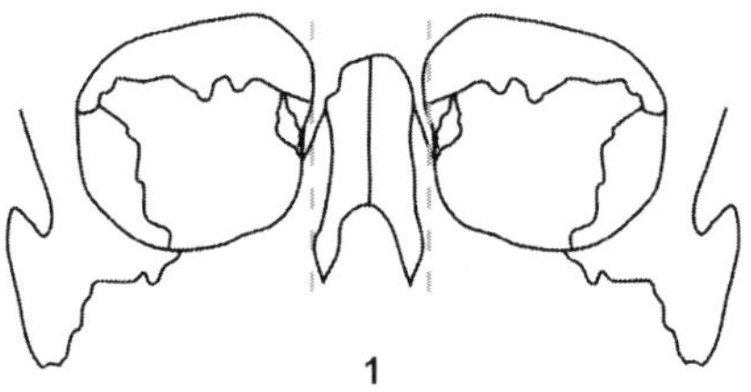


FIGURE 5.2 Diagrammatic representation of IOB 1. Dashed line indicates the plane of reference. *IOB*, interorbital breadth.

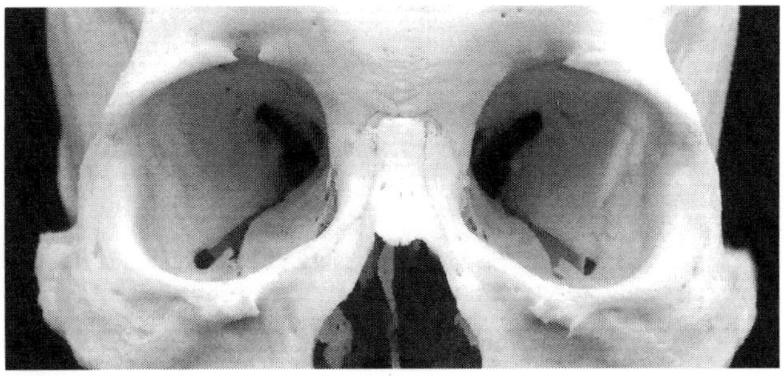

FIGURE 5.3 Variant of IOB 1. *IOB*, interorbital breadth.

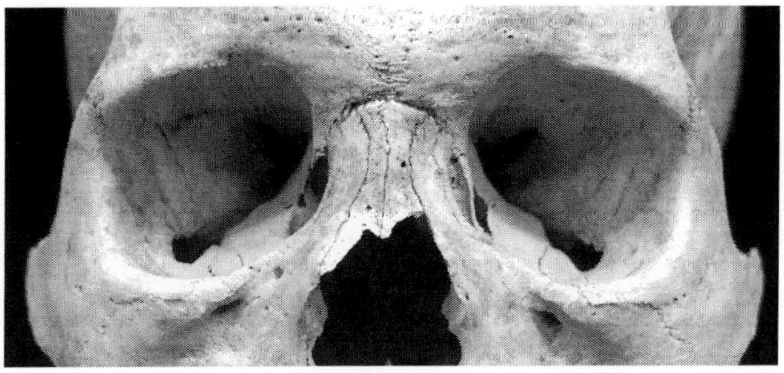

FIGURE 5.4 Variant of IOB 1. *IOB*, interorbital breadth.

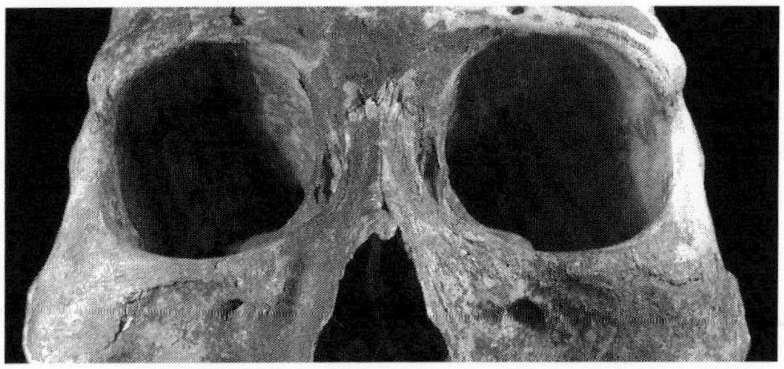

FIGURE 5.5 Variant of IOB 1. *IOB*, interorbital breadth.

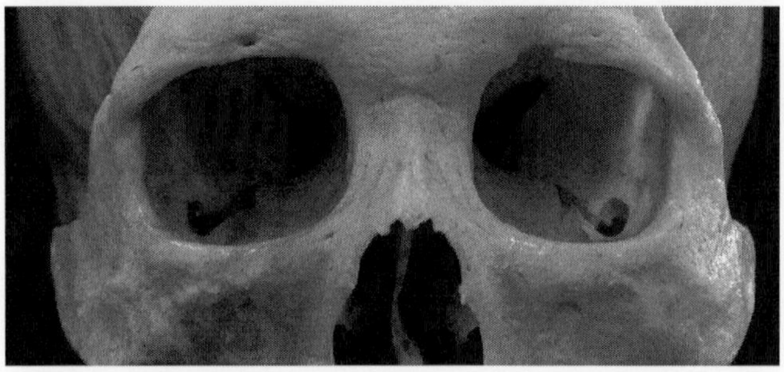

**FIGURE 5.6** Variant of IOB 1. *IOB*, interorbital breadth.

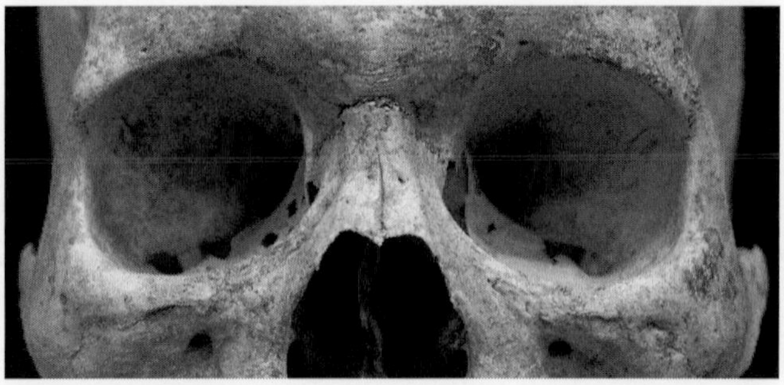

**FIGURE 5.7** Variant of IOB 1. *IOB*, interorbital breadth.

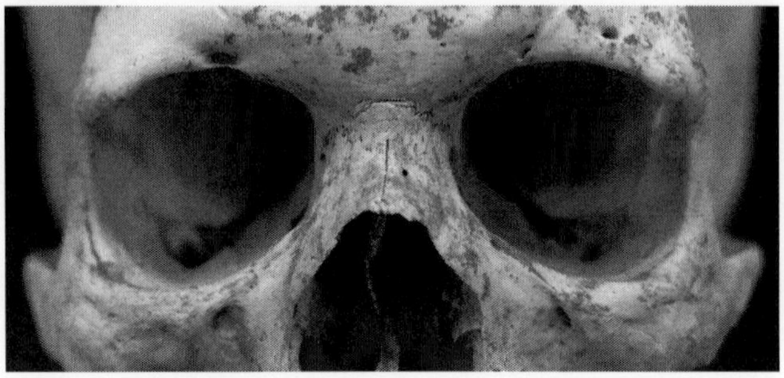

**FIGURE 5.8** Variant of IOB 1. *IOB*, interorbital breadth.

# CHARACTER STATES FOR INTERORBITAL BREADTH = 2 (FIGS. 5.9–5.15)

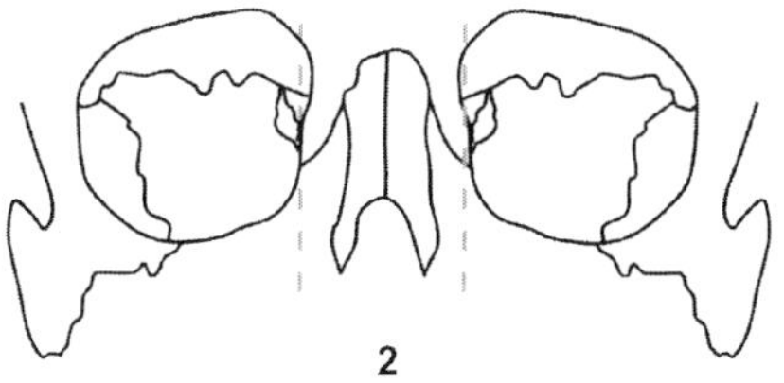


FIGURE 5.9 Diagrammatic representation of IOB 2. Dashed line indicates the plane of reference. *IOB*, interorbital breadth.

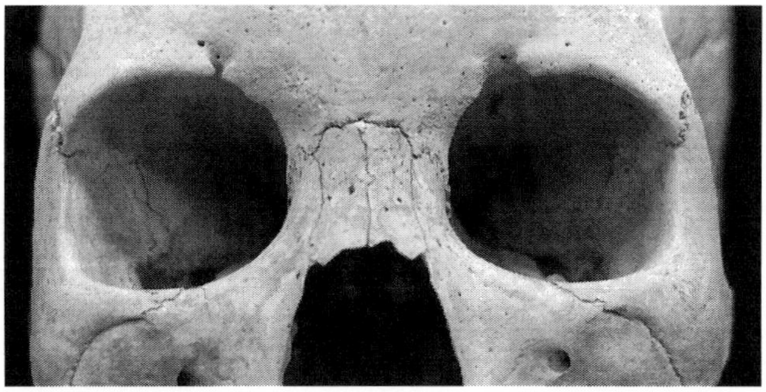

FIGURE 5.10 Variant of IOB 2. *IOB*, interorbital breadth.

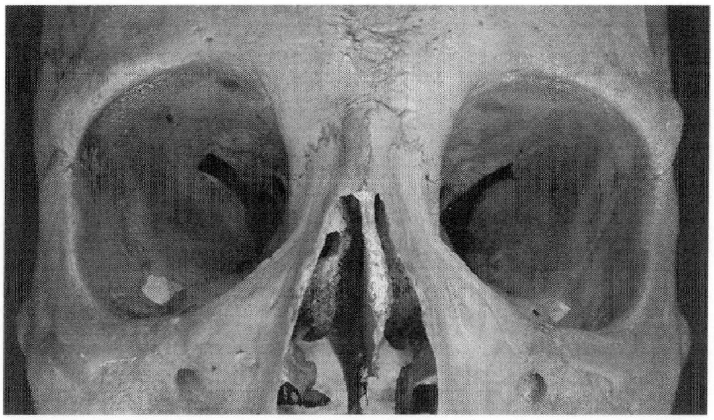

FIGURE 5.11 Variant of IOB 2. *IOB*, interorbital breadth.

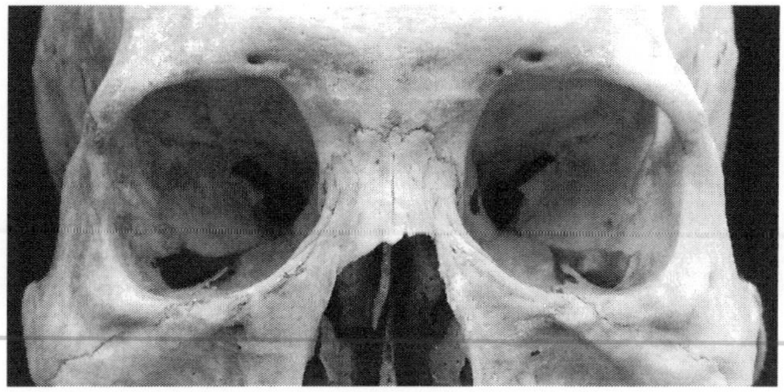

FIGURE 5.12 Variant of IOB 2. *IOB*, interorbital breadth.

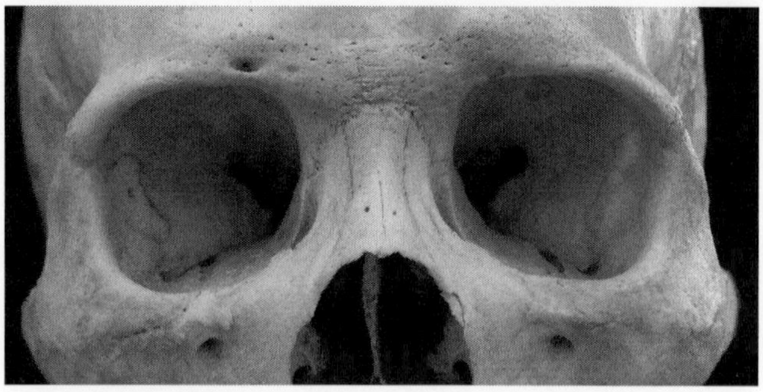

FIGURE 5.13 Variant of IOB 2. *IOB*, interorbital breadth.

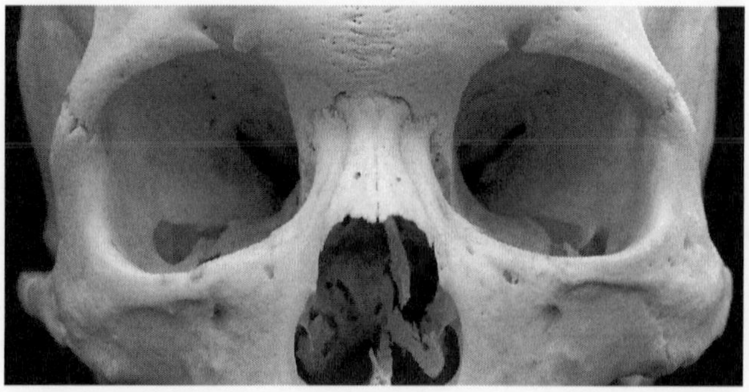

FIGURE 5.14 Variant of IOB 2. *IOB*, interorbital breadth.

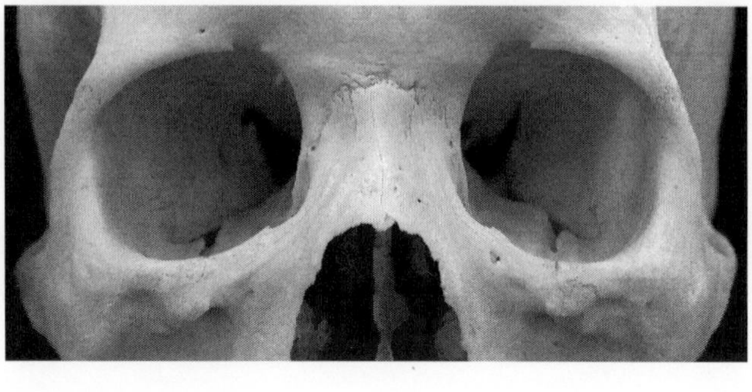

FIGURE 5.15 Variant of IOB 2. *IOB*, interorbital breadth.

## CHARACTER STATES FOR INTERORBITAL BREADTH = 3 (FIGS. 5.16–5.22)

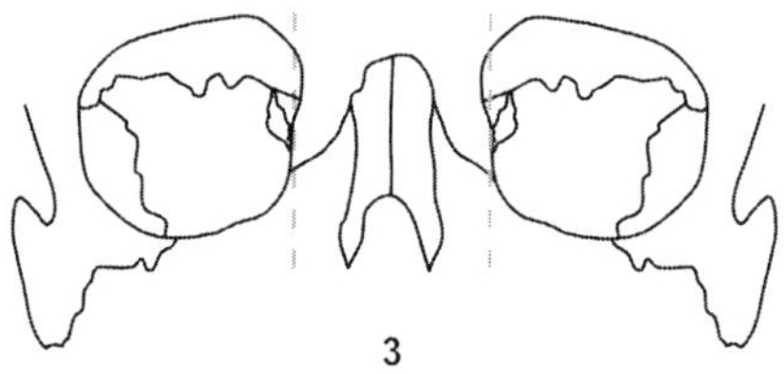


FIGURE 5.16 Diagrammatic representation of IOB 3. Dashed line indicates the plane of reference.

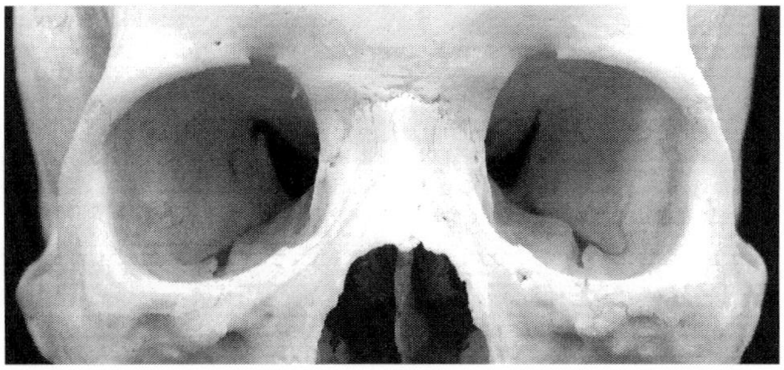

FIGURE 5.17 Variant of IOB 3. *IOB*, interorbital breadth.

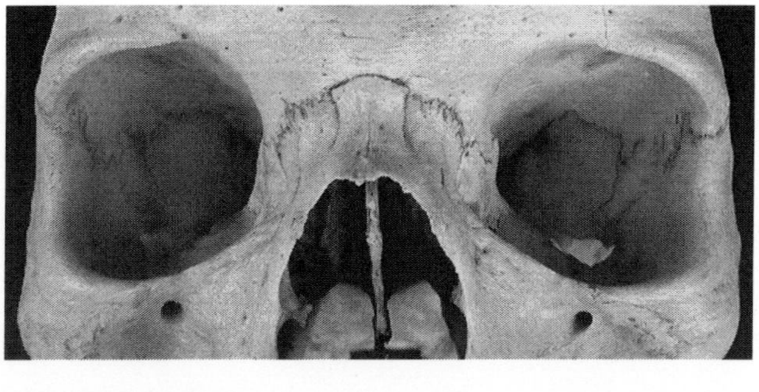

FIGURE 5.18 Variant of IOB 3. *IOB*, interorbital breadth.

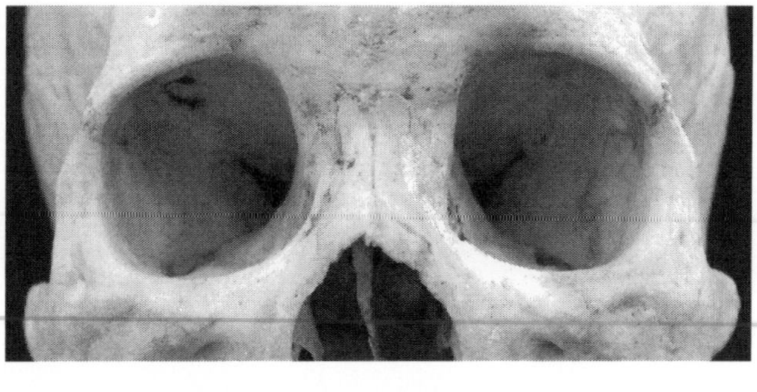

FIGURE 5.19 Variant of IOB 3. *IOB*, interorbital breadth.

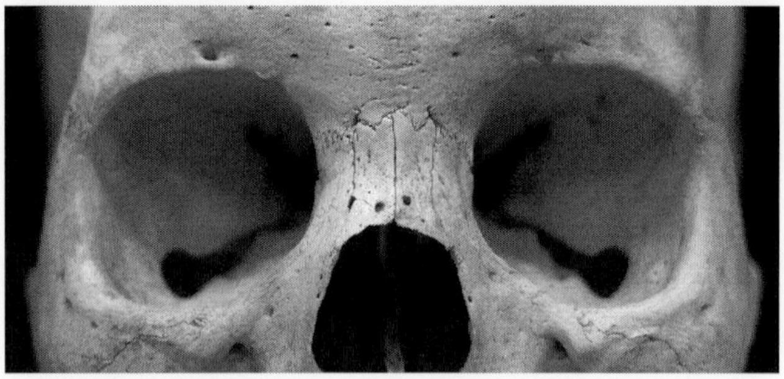

**FIGURE 5.20** Variant of IOB 3. *IOB*, interorbital breadth.

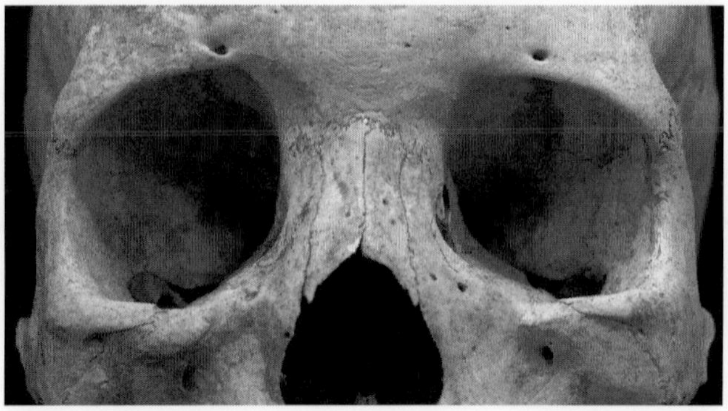

**FIGURE 5.21** Variant of IOB 3. *IOB*, interorbital breadth.

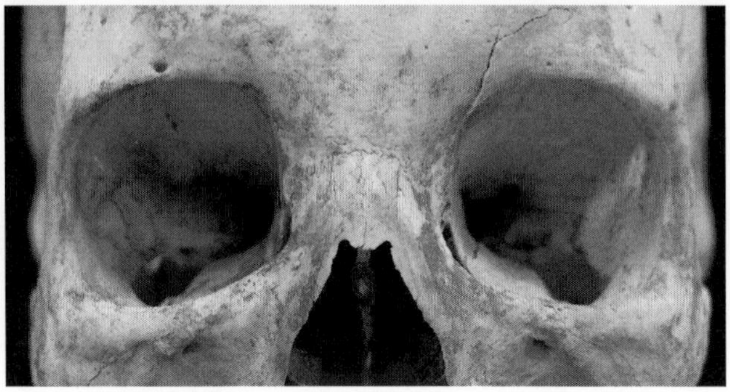

**FIGURE 5.22** Variant of IOB 3. *IOB*, interorbital breadth.

CHAPTER

# 6

# The Malar Tubercle

The malar tubercle (MT) is a caudally protruding tubercle on the inferior margin of the maxilla and zygomatic bones, normally located at the inferior end of the zygomaticomaxillary suture. An MT may be present on the maxilla, zygomatic, or at the inferior aspect of the zygomaticomaxillary suture; a completely absent MT is rare. Observations should not consider any tubercles on the lateral portion of the zygomatic arch. The size of the tubercle is assessed and scored on an ordinal scale ($0 < 1 < 2 < 3$). Observe both sides and record the highest expression.

Numerous researchers have scored MT. Some rely on the visual assessment of the presence of a bony protuberance. Others use an ordinal scale to better capture the range of variation present within a population. Whitnall (1911) is one of the earliest to reference differences in the expression of MT. However, the tubercle he identified and which now bears his name (i.e., Whitnall's tubercle) is "situated on the orbital surface" of the malar (1911:426) and is not synonymous with the contemporary term. His initial description created confusion; "malar tubercle" [sic] is still occasionally used in craniofacial reconstruction literature to refer to Whitnall's tubercle (cf. Wilkinson, 2008).

Rhine (1990:20) recorded the presence of the *zygomatic hook*, a projection on the inferior zygomatic defined as "the tendency for the maxillae and zygomatic to form an inferior projection at the zygomaticomaxillary suture" (Rhine 1990:20). The MT was also outlined by Hauser and De Stefano (1989:76) but under the term *zygomaxillary tubercle*. They provide a detailed ordinal scoring methodology: "a) absent… b) trace… c) medium… d) strong…" (Hauser and De Stefano, 1989:76). Burns (1999) and Gill (1995) attributed this trait to American Indians only and scored the presence of *any* tubercle. Mann et al. (2014) provide photographs of various manifestations of MTs. For a comprehensive review and disambiguation of MT, see Oettlé et al. (2017).

With the purpose of standardizing the definition and identification of MT and the associated character states, the scoring methodology proposed herein follows Hauser and De Stefano (1989:76), Hefner (2009), and Oettlé et al. (2017). MT is assessed by placing a transparent ruler at the intersection of the zygomaticomaxillary suture, across the inferior margin of the malar, extending to the deepest incurvature on the maxilla. A score is assigned with regard to the extent of bone protruding past the ruler's edge. When the tubercle is directly on the zygomaticomaxillary suture, the ruler should extend from the deepest incurvature of the maxilla to the deepest anterior curvature of the zygomatic. By assessing only this portion of the zygomaxillary region, *Whitnall's tubercle* and the *zygomaxillary tuberosity* are excluded from consideration.

## NOMENCLATURE

Malar tubercle, marginal process, *tuber zygomaticum*, *tuberculum zygomaxillare*, zygomaticomaxillary tubercle, zygomaxillary tubercle, and zygomatic hook.

## GROSS ANATOMY

The maxillae articulate with the zygomatic bones bilaterally at the zygomaticomaxillary suture. A caudally protruding tubercle—varying in size and position—may occur on the maxilla, the zygomatic, or at their inferior juncture along the zygomaticomaxillary suture.

*Atlas of Human Cranial Macromorphoscopic Traits.*
DOI: https://doi.org/10.1016/B978-0-12-814385-8.00006-9

## GROWTH AND DEVELOPMENT

Around the fourth week of intrauterine development, five branchial arches form the region of the future head and neck. Each arch gives rise to muscles, connective tissue, vasculature, and neural and skeletal components of the future face, including the maxilla and zygomatic. The first branchial arch is instrumental in the formation of the nasomaxillary region, formed predominantly from the maxillary process of the mandibular arch. Postnatal growth of the nasomaxillary complex is produced through several mechanisms. Primary displacement posteriorly of the posterolateral border of the maxilla (maxillary tuberosity) and passive displacement inferiorly of the entire nasal-maxillary complex leading to a longer, more inferiorly positioned facial complex in adults. Sutural growth (frontonasal, frontomaxillary, pterygopalatine, zygomaticotemporal, and the zygomaticomaxillary sutures) leads to downward and forward repositioning of the maxilla. The nature of sutural growth (i.e., opening of space within sutures resulting from the growth of surrounding soft tissues) leads to bone formation on either side of the suture, resulting in a tension related bone formation at sutural intersections. Growth and development continue surface remodeling via bone deposition and resorption leading to an overall increase in size and shape changes to the facial elements. Gross changes to the functional relationships *between* elements also occur during these stages of growth and development. The zygomatic bone undergoes similar developmental changes. Although the zygomaticomaxillary suture is patent at birth, an MT may be present (Guidotti et al., 1986; Wood, 2012). Baker et al. (2005:47) also identified the presence of an MT: "in older children … [the malar tubercle] is developed and replaces the inferior notch" of the maxilla.

## FUNCTIONAL MORPHOLOGY

Serving as a buttress to direct energy away from the midface and an attachment point for muscles controlling both mastication and facial animation, the zygomaticomaxillary complex plays a significant role in the structure and function of the face. Musculature insertion into or originating from the zygomaticomaxillary complex includes the anterior (superficial) tendinous fibers of the masseter muscle and lesser fibers of the *orbicularis oculi*. The former corresponds closely to the location of the zygomaticomaxillary suture and may play a role in the expression of the MT. The masseter muscle serves as one of the four major muscles of mastication, elevating the mandible and creating forward movement through contraction.

## WITHIN POPULATION VARIATION

Data derived from the Macromorphoscopic Databank of the frequency distribution of MT ($n = 6146$). All data are for adult individuals. When possible, frequency data for males and females are provided separately. When sex could not be estimated reliably, frequency distributions are pooled as "Unknown" (Table 6.1).

**TABLE 6.1** Frequency Distribution of MT, by Geographic Origin and Sex

| | | 0 | | 1 | | 2 | | 3 | | |
|---|---|---|---|---|---|---|---|---|---|---|
| **Geographic origin** | **Sex** | *n* | % | *n* | % | *n* | % | *n* | % | **Total** |
| **African** | **Female** | 0 | 0 | 7 | 50 | 5 | 36 | 2 | 14 | 14 |
| | **Male** | 0 | 0 | 8 | 50 | 4 | 25 | 4 | 25 | 16 |
| | **Unknown** | 0 | 0 | 0 | 0 | 0 | 0 | 0 | 0 | 0 |
| | **Total** | 0 | 0 | 15 | 50 | 9 | 30 | 6 | 20 | 30 |
| **American Black** | **Female** | 8 | 6 | 74 | 54 | 40 | 29 | 15 | 11 | 137 |
| | **Male** | 8 | 3 | 102 | 43 | 92 | 38 | 37 | 15 | 239 |
| | **Unknown** | 0 | 0 | 1 | 100 | 0 | 0 | 0 | 0 | 1 |
| | **Total** | 16 | 4 | 177 | 47 | 132 | 35 | 52 | 14 | 377 |
| **American White** | **Female** | 18 | 7 | 167 | 64 | 60 | 23 | 16 | 6 | 261 |
| | **Male** | 10 | 4 | 172 | 62 | 78 | 28 | 17 | 6 | 277 |
| | **Unknown** | 0 | 0 | 0 | 0 | 0 | 0 | 0 | 0 | 0 |
| | **Total** | 28 | 5 | 339 | 63 | 138 | 26 | 33 | 6 | 538 |
| **Amerindian** | **Female** | 0 | 0 | 21 | 47 | 18 | 40 | 6 | 13 | 45 |
| | **Male** | 0 | 0 | 10 | 26 | 21 | 54 | 8 | 21 | 39 |
| | **Unknown** | 566 | 22 | 1339 | 52 | 575 | 22 | 87 | 3 | 2567 |
| | **Total** | 566 | 21 | 1370 | 52 | 614 | 23 | 101 | 4 | 2651 |
| **Chinese** | **Female** | 0 | 0 | 2 | 40 | 2 | 40 | 1 | 20 | 5 |
| | **Male** | 0 | 0 | 24 | 44 | 19 | 35 | 11 | 20 | 54 |
| | **Unknown** | 0 | 0 | 0 | 0 | 0 | 0 | 0 | 0 | 0 |
| | **Total** | 0 | 0 | 26 | 44 | 21 | 36 | 12 | 20 | 59 |
| **Colombian** | **Female** | 1 | 1 | 31 | 46 | 27 | 40 | 8 | 12 | 67 |
| | **Male** | 6 | 3 | 47 | 27 | 87 | 49 | 37 | 21 | 177 |
| | **Unknown** | 0 | 0 | 0 | 0 | 0 | 0 | 0 | 0 | 0 |
| | **Total** | 7 | 3 | 78 | 32 | 114 | 47 | 45 | 18 | 244 |
| **El Salvador** | **Female** | 0 | 0 | 0 | 0 | 0 | 0 | 0 | 0 | 0 |
| | **Male** | 1 | 20 | 4 | 80 | 0 | 0 | 0 | 0 | 5 |
| | **Unknown** | 0 | 0 | 0 | 0 | 0 | 0 | 0 | 0 | 0 |
| | **Total** | 1 | 20 | 4 | 80 | 0 | 0 | 0 | 0 | 5 |
| **Eskimo** | **Female** | 0 | 0 | 0 | 0 | 0 | 0 | 0 | 0 | 0 |
| | **Male** | 0 | 0 | 0 | 0 | 0 | 0 | 0 | 0 | 0 |
| | **Unknown** | 192 | 24 | 441 | 55 | 147 | 18 | 17 | 2 | 797 |
| | **Total** | 192 | 24 | 441 | 55 | 147 | 18 | 17 | 2 | 797 |
| **European** | **Female** | 0 | 0 | 2 | 29 | 4 | 57 | 1 | 14 | 7 |
| | **Male** | 0 | 0 | 1 | 13 | 5 | 63 | 2 | 25 | 8 |
| | **Unknown** | 0 | 0 | 0 | 0 | 0 | 0 | 0 | 0 | 0 |
| | **Total** | 0 | 0 | 3 | 20 | 9 | 60 | 3 | 20 | 15 |

*(Continued)*

TABLE 6.1 (*Continued*)

| Geographic origin | Sex | 0 *n* | 0 % | 1 *n* | 1 % | 2 *n* | 2 % | 3 *n* | 3 % | Total |
|---|---|---|---|---|---|---|---|---|---|---|
| **Guatemalan** | **Female** | 6 | 18 | 22 | 65 | 5 | 15 | 1 | 3 | 34 |
| | **Male** | 8 | 11 | 30 | 42 | 22 | 31 | 11 | 15 | 71 |
| | **Unknown** | 0 | 0 | 0 | 0 | 0 | 0 | 0 | 0 | 0 |
| | **Total** | 14 | 13 | 52 | 50 | 27 | 26 | 12 | 11 | 105 |
| **Japanese** | **Female** | 0 | 0 | 2 | 40 | 1 | 20 | 2 | 40 | 5 |
| | **Male** | 0 | 0 | 3 | 38 | 3 | 38 | 2 | 25 | 8 |
| | **Unknown** | 0 | 0 | 1 | 50 | 0 | 0 | 1 | 50 | 2 |
| | **Total** | 0 | 0 | 6 | 40 | 4 | 27 | 5 | 33 | 15 |
| **Mexico** | **Female** | 0 | 0 | 2 | 100 | 0 | 0 | 0 | 0 | 2 |
| | **Male** | 4 | 17 | 8 | 33 | 10 | 42 | 2 | 8 | 24 |
| | **Unknown** | 0 | 0 | 0 | 0 | 0 | 0 | 0 | 0 | 0 |
| | **Total** | 4 | 15 | 10 | 38 | 10 | 38 | 2 | 8 | 26 |
| **Pacific Island** | **Female** | 6 | 10 | 30 | 52 | 21 | 36 | 1 | 2 | 58 |
| | **Male** | 7 | 8 | 45 | 52 | 28 | 32 | 7 | 8 | 87 |
| | **Unknown** | 24 | 27 | 37 | 41 | 28 | 31 | 1 | 1 | 90 |
| | **Total** | 37 | 16 | 112 | 48 | 77 | 33 | 9 | 4 | 235 |
| **Peruvian** | **Female** | 0 | 0 | 0 | 0 | 0 | 0 | 0 | 0 | 0 |
| | **Male** | 0 | 0 | 0 | 0 | 0 | 0 | 0 | 0 | 0 |
| | **Unknown** | 7 | 29 | 11 | 46 | 5 | 21 | 1 | 4 | 24 |
| | **Total** | 7 | 29 | 11 | 46 | 5 | 21 | 1 | 4 | 24 |
| **Southwest (SW) Hispanic** | **Female** | 2 | 25 | 5 | 63 | 1 | 13 | 0 | 0 | 8 |
| | **Male** | 0 | 0 | 8 | 80 | 2 | 20 | 0 | 0 | 10 |
| | **Unknown** | 11 | 11 | 64 | 63 | 24 | 24 | 2 | 2 | 101 |
| | **Total** | 13 | 11 | 77 | 65 | 27 | 23 | 2 | 2 | 119 |
| **Thai** | **Female** | 25 | 8 | 181 | 56 | 100 | 31 | 15 | 5 | 321 |
| | **Male** | 40 | 7 | 250 | 44 | 204 | 36 | 77 | 13 | 571 |
| | **Unknown** | 1 | 7 | 7 | 50 | 6 | 43 | 0 | 0 | 14 |
| | **Total** | 66 | 7 | 438 | 48 | 310 | 34 | 92 | 10 | 906 |
| **Total for all groups** | | 951 | 15 | 3159 | 51 | 1644 | 27 | 392 | 6 | 6146 |

*MT*, malar tubercle.

# CHARACTER STATES

Photographic exemplars of the different character states of MT are provided below. Each character state is defined following (Hefner, 2009, 2016). When necessary to clarify scoring, more nuanced definitions are provided in the figure captions. MT should be assessed with the protocol provided in the preceding section. Character states include:

MT 0 = no projection of bone.
MT 1 = a trace tubercle below the ruler's edge, approximately 2 mm or less.
MT 2 = a medium protrusion below the ruler's edge, approximately 2 to 4 mm.
MT 3 = a pronounced tubercle, more than 4 mm below the ruler's edge.

## CHARACTER STATES FOR MALAR TUBERCLE = 0 (FIGS. 6.1–6.3)

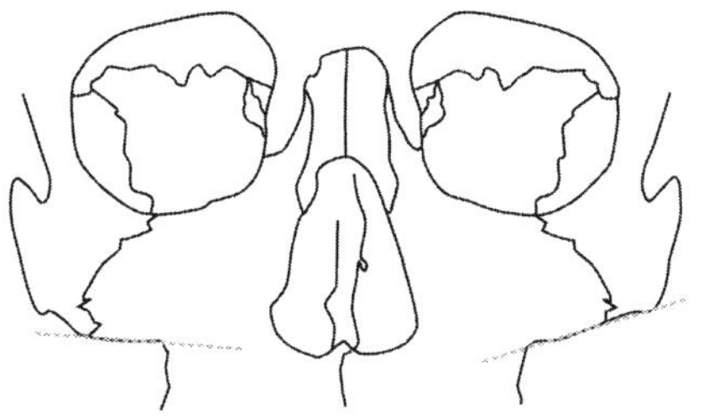


FIGURE 6.1 Diagrammatic representation of MT 0. Dashed line indicates the plane of reference (ruler). *MT*, malar tubercle.

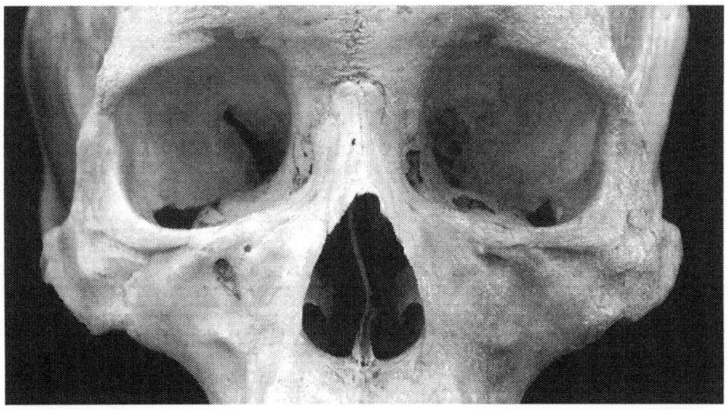

FIGURE 6.2 Variant of MT 0. *Note:* The pronounced tubercle on the inferior aspect of the right zygomatic is not an MT. *MT*, malar tubercle.

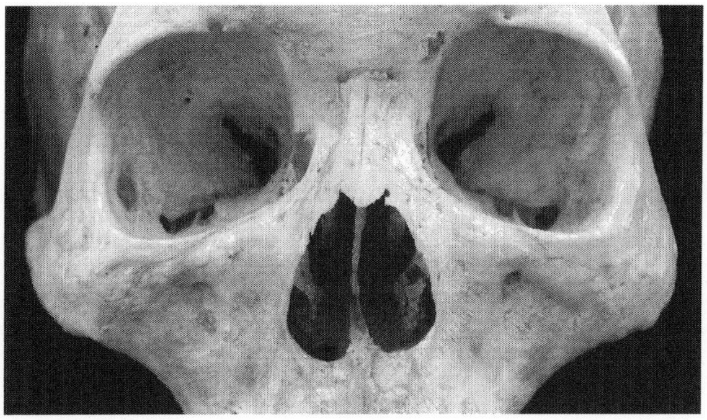

FIGURE 6.3 Variant of MT 0. Slight asymmetry is typical. The side with the greatest expression is recorded. In this example, neither side evinces a tubercle breaking the reference plane. *MT*, malar tubercle.

## CHARACTER STATES FOR MALAR TUBERCLE = 1 (FIGS. 6.4–6.10)

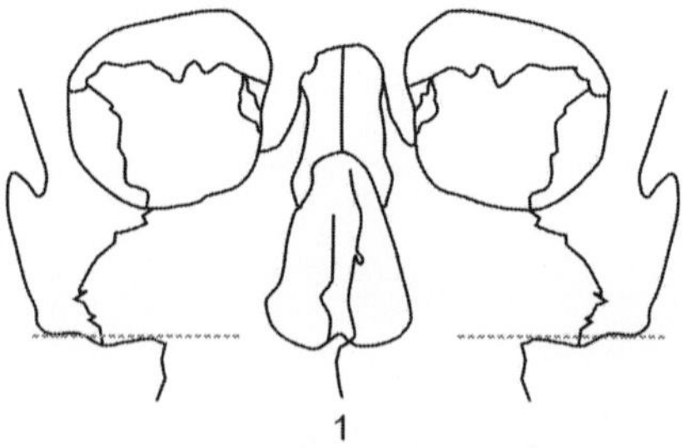


**FIGURE 6.4** Diagrammatic representation of MT 1. Dashed line indicates the plane of reference (ruler). *MT*, malar tubercle.

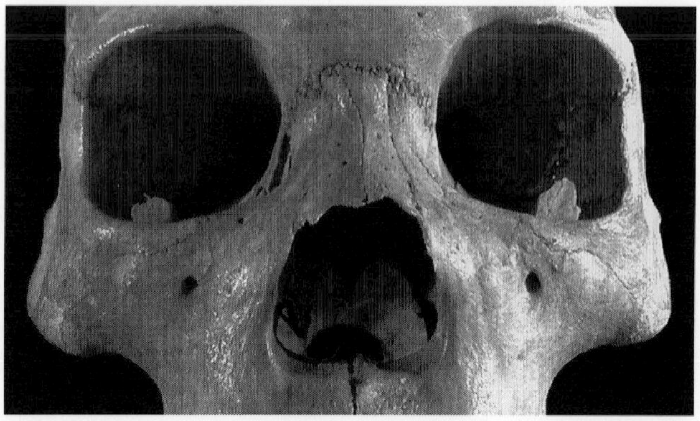

**FIGURE 6.5** Variant of MT 1. Slight asymmetry is typical. The side with the greatest expression is recorded. In this example, the right side is scored 1. *MT*, malar tubercle.

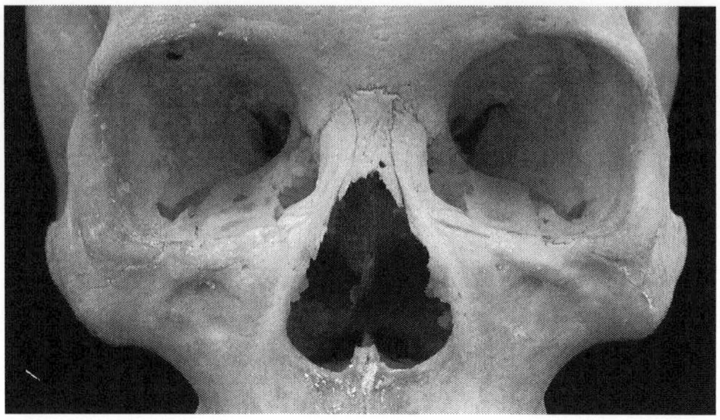

**FIGURE 6.6** Variant of MT 1. *MT*, malar tubercle.

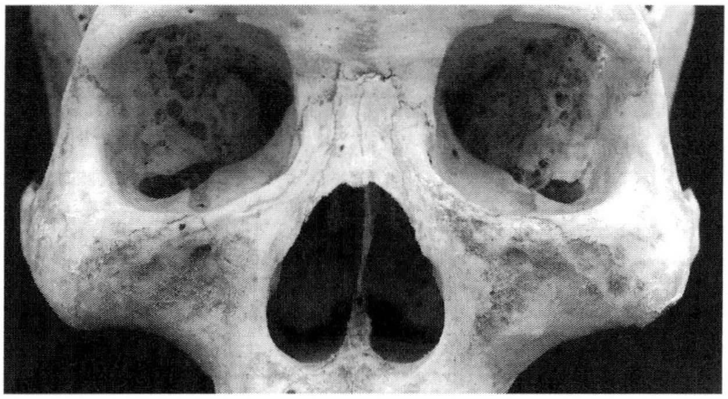

**FIGURE 6.7** Variant of MT 1. Slight asymmetry is typical. The side with the greatest expression is recorded. In this example, the right side is scored 1. *MT*, malar tubercle.

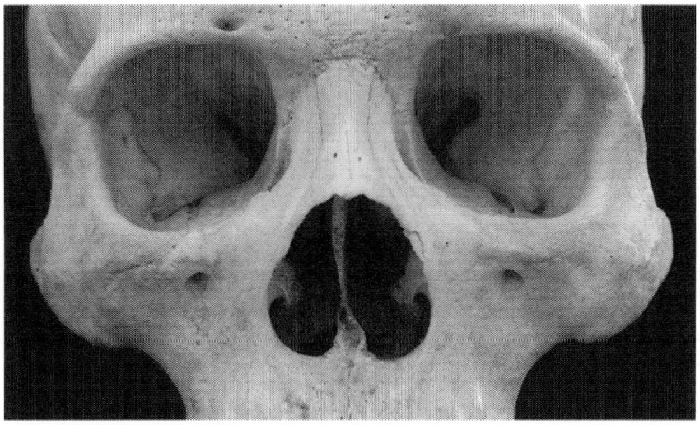

**FIGURE 6.8** Variant of MT 1. *MT*, malar tubercle.

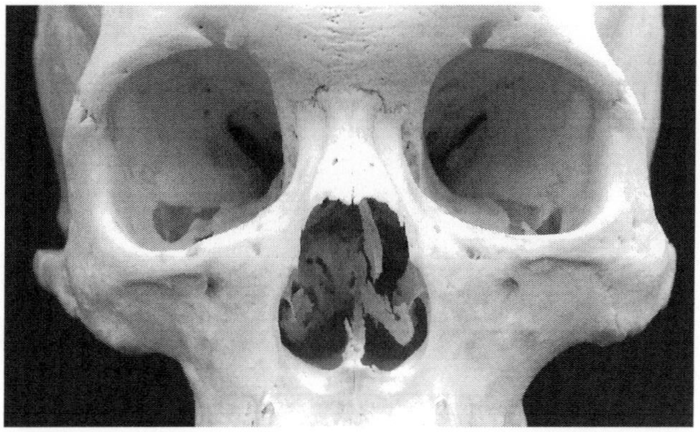

**FIGURE 6.9** Variant of MT 1. Slight asymmetry is typical. The side with the greatest expression is recorded. In this example, both left and right sides are scored 1. *MT*, malar tubercle.

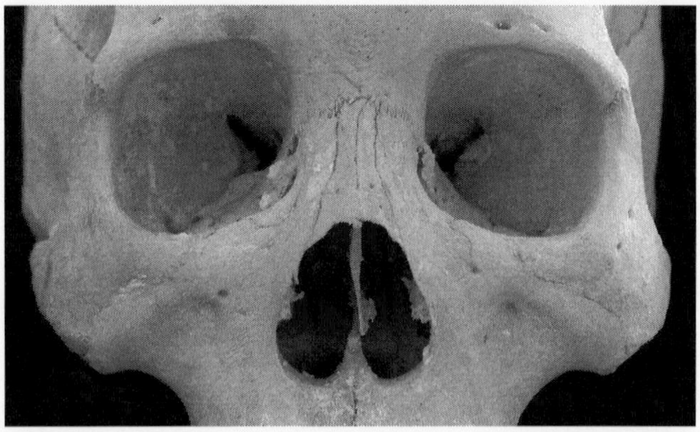

**FIGURE 6.10** Variant of MT 1. Slight asymmetry is typical. The side with the greatest expression is recorded. In this example, both left and right sides are scored 1. *MT*, malar tubercle.

## CHARACTER STATES FOR MALAR TUBERCLE = 2 (FIGS. 6.11–6.17)

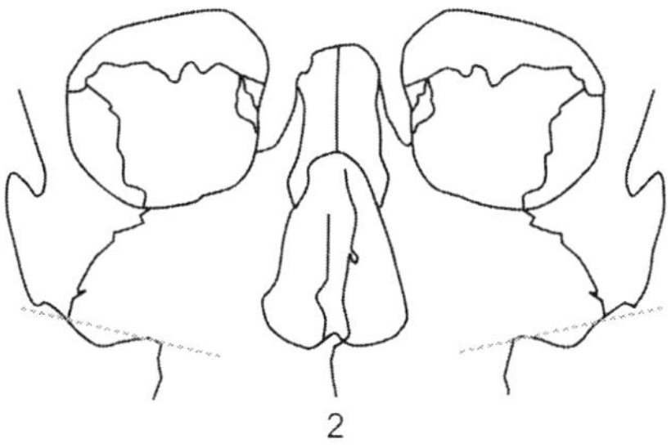


FIGURE 6.11 Diagrammatic representation of MT 2. Dashed line indicates the plane of reference (ruler). *MT*, malar tubercle.

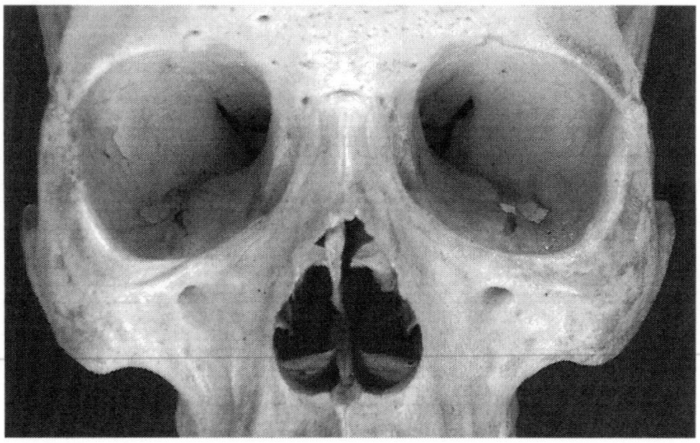

FIGURE 6.12 Variant of MT 2. The deep incurvature of the zygomaticomaxillary complex, in this example, is scored 2 on both sides. *MT*, malar tubercle.

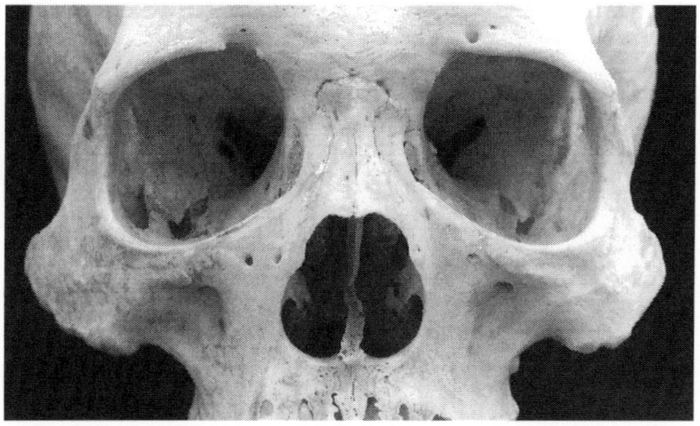

FIGURE 6.13 Variant of MT 2. *Note:* The atypical double MT on the left side. Both sides, in this example, would be scored 2. *MT*, malar tubercle.

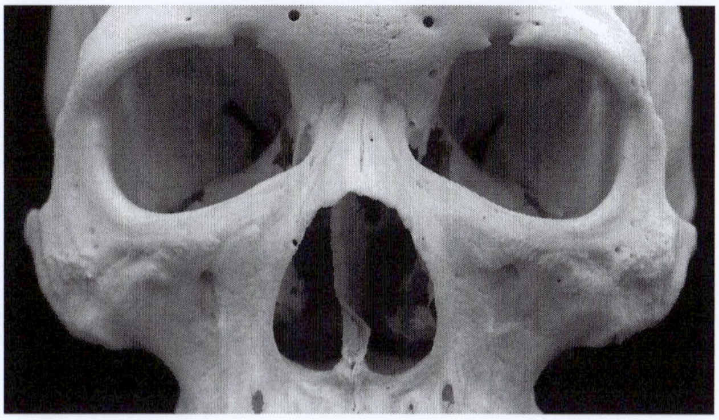

**FIGURE 6.14** Variant of MT 2. *MT*, malar tubercle.

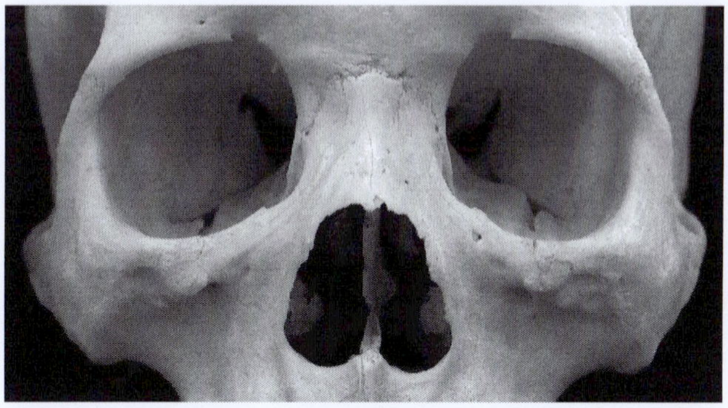

**FIGURE 6.15** Variant of MT 2. Slight asymmetry is typical. The side with the greatest expression is recorded. In this example, the left side is scored 2. *MT*, malar tubercle.

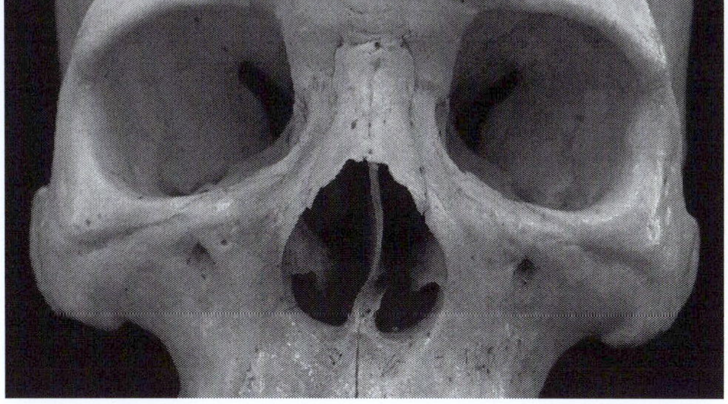

**FIGURE 6.16** Variant of MT 2. *MT*, malar tubercle.

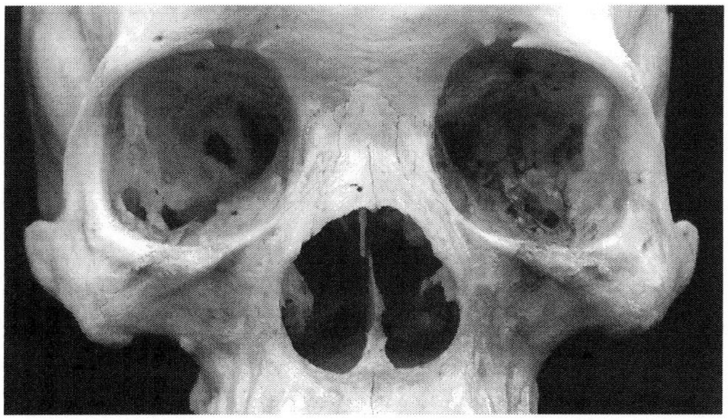

**FIGURE 6.17** Variant of MT 2. *Note:* Bilateral, symmetrical maxillary depression exaggerating the MT. *MT*, malar tubercle.

## CHARACTER STATES FOR MALAR TUBERCLE = 3 (FIGS. 6.18–6.24)

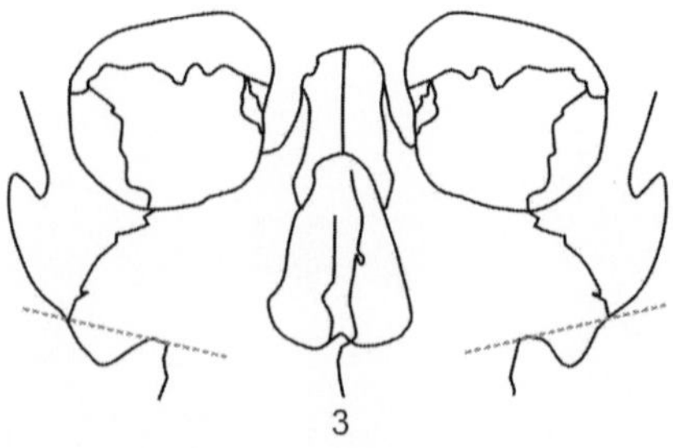


**FIGURE 6.18** Diagrammatic representation of MT 3. Dashed line indicates the plane of reference (ruler). *MT*, malar tubercle.

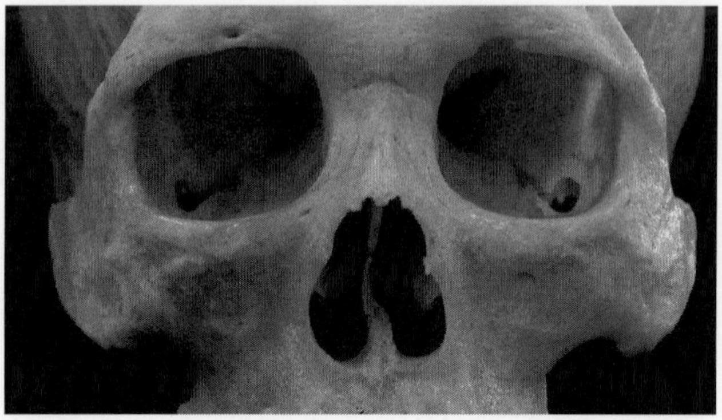

**FIGURE 6.19** Variant of MT 3. Note: The deep incurvature and the pronounced MT are paradigmatic of Rhine's (1990) *zygomatic hook*. *MT*, malar tubercle.

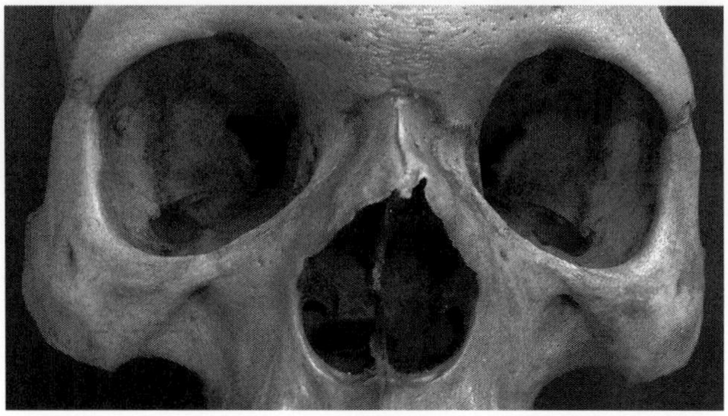

**FIGURE 6.20** Variant of MT 3. Note: Bilateral symmetrical maxillary depression exaggerating the MT. Slight asymmetry is typical. The side with the greatest expression is recorded. In this example, the left side is scored 3. *MT*, malar tubercle.

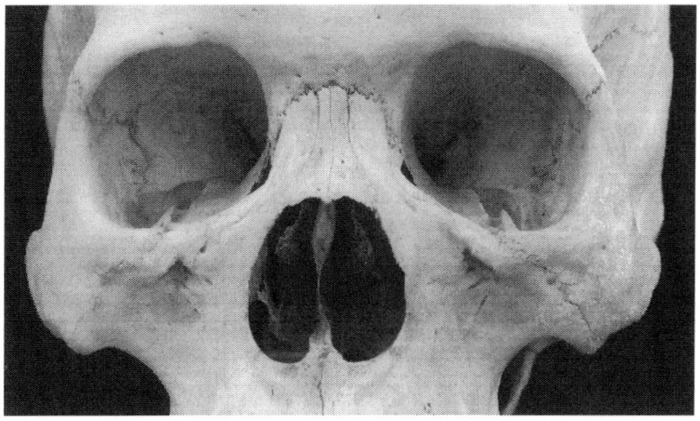

FIGURE 6.21 Variant of MT 3. Slight asymmetry is typical. The side with the greatest expression is recorded. In this example, the left side is scored 3. *MT*, malar tubercle.

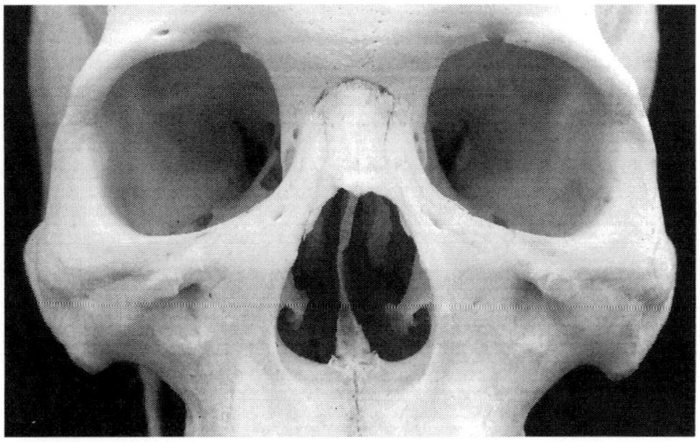

FIGURE 6.22 Variant of MT 3. *MT*, malar tubercle.

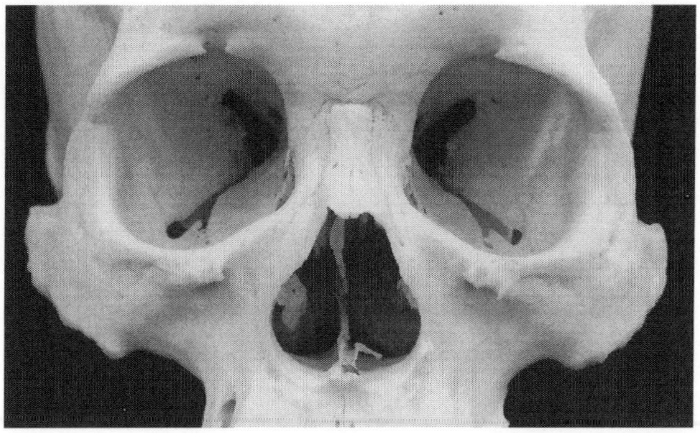

FIGURE 6.23 Variant of MT 3. Note: Rugosity marking an inferior aspect of the zygomaticomaxillary region is not considered when scoring MT. *MT*, malar tubercle.

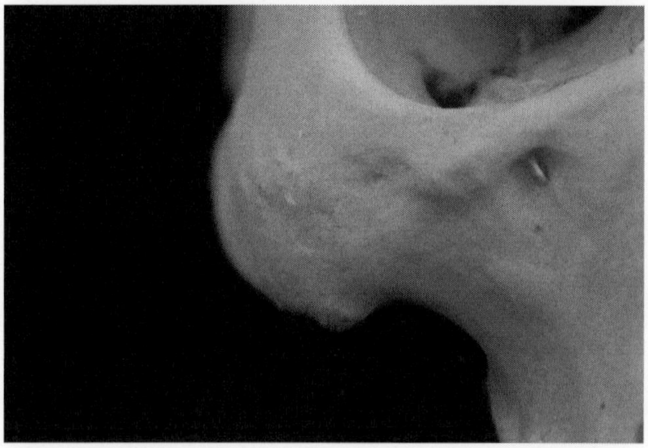

**FIGURE 6.24** Close-up view of MT 3. The deep incurvature and exaggerated superior position of the zygomatic results in an exaggerated MT. *MT*, malar tubercle.

CHAPTER

# 7

# Nasal Aperture Shape

Assessing the nasal aperture shape (NAS) considers the lateral contours of the nasal opening and the position of greatest projection along the lateral margins, regardless of the overall breadth of the nasal opening. The relative shape of the nasal aperture is best defined by the position of greatest lateral projection (i.e., the position of the bony landmark, *alare*—left and right). Bilateral asymmetry is not uncommon but when it does occur the side presenting the highest expression is recorded. Taphonomic damage can obscure or exaggerate NAS expression and should be carefully documented. NAS comprises three character states—scored as: $1 < 2 < 3$.

A number of researchers have documented NAS, albeit in different manners. Gray (1918) defined the nasal aperture as a pear- or heart-shaped opening superiorly circumscribed by the inferior borders of the nasal bones, laterally by the sharp margins separating the anterior and nasal surfaces of the maxilla, and inferiorly by the same structures curving medially to join at the anterior nasal spine.

Wood-Jones (1930, 1931a,b,c) alludes to the shape of the nasal aperture, saying the area is "exceedingly useful in diagnosis of race" (Wood-Jones, 1930:179). Much of the later research focused on the relative width of this area rather than shape (see Chapter 8: Nasal Aperture Width, for complete disambiguation), although the more recent introduction of geometric morphometric (GM) methods of analysis is a return to shape descriptors. Hooton does not consider the shape of the nasal aperture, but he does document several related traits, including nasal bridge breadth and nasal root height (Hooton, 1930). Krogman (1955) and later Krogman and Işçan (1986) identify three character states for nasal opening: *narrow*, *moderately wide*, and *wide*.

Gill (1986) recognizes three types of nasal form: *narrow*, *medium*, and *broad*. Rhine (1990) used the same descriptions as Gill (1986), and Byers (2011) used similar descriptors: *narrow*, *medium*, and *wide*. More recent efforts to quantify the shape of the nasal aperture involved new, complex methods such as elliptical Fourier analysis (EFA) (Nawrocki et al., 2017; McDowell et al., 2012). These methods—part of the larger suite of GM methods—represent great strides in the quantification of cranial nonmetric traits. McDowell et al. (2012:396, 2015) used GM methods to explore shape variation and classification accuracies in a sample originating from South Africa. Using EFA, they identified mean NASs for black and white South Africans (rounded and wide or narrow and constricted). Likewise, Nawrocki et al. (2017:310) utilized EFA methods to explore the shape of the nasal aperture in a sample of 840 American and African specimens, identifying several principal components explaining variation in height: breadth ratios of the aperture.

Hefner (2011:70) formally defined NAS in the Macromorphoscopic Module of *Osteoware* (Smithsonian Institution 2011) as:

> The shape of the nasal aperture (NAS) is assessed by observing both the lateral contours of the nasal aperture and, directly related, the position of greatest lateral projection of the margin. [Character states include:] 1) teardrop, with lateral projection intermediate to 2 and 3; 2) bell shape, with greatest lateral projection at the inferior margin; and, 3) bowed, with greatest lateral projection at midline.

## NOMENCLATURE

*Apertura piriformis*, *cava nasi*, nasal aperture shape, nasal cavities, nasal opening, *nasi foramen figura*, nose form, piriform aperture, and pyriform aperture.

*Atlas of Human Cranial Macromorphoscopic Traits.*
DOI: https://doi.org/10.1016/B978-0-12-814385-8.00007-0

## GROSS ANATOMY

The nasal aperture is the variably-shaped opening of the midface, bounded superiorly by the inferior borders of the nasal bones near *rhinion*, laterally by the maxilla, and inferiorly by the same. Comprising the external components of the nasal cavity, the bony nasal region is divided into two compartments separated internally by the nasal septum. The aperture communicates anteriorly through the fleshy nostrils and posteriorly with the nasopharynx through the choanae. Lined with a mucous membrane and richly vascularized by branches of the maxillary, facial, and ophthalmic arteries, the nasal cavity is innervated via branches of the olfactory, ophthalmic, and maxillary nerves.

## GROWTH AND DEVELOPMENT

Enlow (1990) thoroughly outlines the close relationship between respiratory needs and general growth and development as responses to physiological demands. Respiration is a vital function from birth onward. Significant anatomical changes, predominately in the face, ensure efficient respiration while also permitting growth and development of the facial structures. Other chapters detailing traits from the midface have already outlined the growth and development of structures associated with the nasal aperture (see, for instance, Chapter 4: Inferior Nasal Aperture). However, for continuity, we provide the following details on growth and development of the nasal aperture.

Near the fourth week of intrauterine development, five branchial arches form the region of the future head and neck. Each arch gives rise to muscles, connective tissue, vasculature, and neural and skeletal components of the future face, including the maxillae. The first branchial arch is instrumental in the formation of the nasomaxillary region, formed predominantly from the maxillary process of the mandibular arch.

Around week six, the growth of the nasal swellings deepens dorsocaudally to form the nasal pits and penetrate the underlying mesenchyme. Lying posterior to the primary palate (i.e., the primitive palate), each pit is initially separated from the oral cavity by the oronasal membrane, which eventually breaks down allowing for communication between the two structures via the primitive choanae. Following the formation of the secondary palate, the choanae are at the junction between the oral pharynx and the nasal cavities. Posteriorly, the lateral palatine processes fuse with the nasal septum maintaining the separation between the oral and nasal cavities while separating each nasal cavity from the other. The superior, middle, and inferior turbinates develop as elevations on the lateral nasal wall of each nasal cavity. Lined with ectodermal epithelium, these structures along the roof of the nasal cavity become specialized for olfaction.

## FUNCTIONAL MORPHOLOGY

The nasal cavity is a vital component in olfaction and the respiratory system, heating and humidifying inhaled air. For olfaction, odor is detected and smells are recognized through the nasal aperture. Odor molecules entering into the nasal cavity are distributed (circular movement) through the nasal turbinates. The mucus membrane lining the nasal cavity contains odor binding factors (proteins) that dissolve the odor molecules for transmission to the olfactory receptors through the cribriform plate of the ethmoid. From there, the receptors transmit accumulated signals in glomeruli as neural signals to the brain for interpretation and response. Airflow and associated scalar exchange within the nasal cavity serves to heat and increase the humidity of the inhaled air. Ample research has been dedicated to the role climate plays in the nasal cavity and NAS. Numerous researchers have contributed their investigations to the current body of literature. The following are some the reader should consider for further exploration: Baker (1988), Carey and Steegmann (1981), Churchill et al. (2004), Cole (1982), Davies (1932), Dean (1988), Hall (2005), Havarti (2003), Havarti and Weaver (2006), Hubbi et al. (2009), Lieberman (2011), Mlynski et al. (2001), Shea (1977), Weiner (1954), and Yokley (2009).

## WITHIN POPULATION VARIATION

Data derived from the Macromorphoscopic Databank of the frequency distribution of NAS ($n = 3758$). All data are for adult individuals. When possible, frequency data for males and females are provided separately. When sex could not be estimated reliably, frequency distributions are pooled as "Unknown" (Table 7.1).

**TABLE 7.1** Frequency Distribution of NAS, by Geographic Origin and Sex

| | | 1 | | 2 | | 3 | | |
|---|---|---|---|---|---|---|---|---|
| **Geographic origin** | **Sex** | *n* | % | *n* | % | *n* | % | **Total** |
| **American Black** | **Female** | 0 | 0 | 3 | 60 | 2 | 40 | 5 |
| | **Male** | 0 | 0 | 2 | 100 | 0 | 0 | 2 |
| | **Unknown** | 0 | 0 | 0 | 0 | 0 | 0 | 0 |
| | **Total** | 0 | 0 | 5 | 71 | 2 | 29 | 7 |
| **Amerindian** | **Female** | 0 | 0 | 0 | 0 | 0 | 0 | 0 |
| | **Male** | 0 | 0 | 0 | 0 | 0 | 0 | 0 |
| | **Unknown** | 1488 | 68 | 567 | 26 | 122 | 6 | 2177 |
| | **Total** | 1488 | 68 | 567 | 26 | 122 | 6 | 2177 |
| **El Salvador** | **Female** | 0 | 0 | 0 | 0 | 0 | 0 | 0 |
| | **Male** | 2 | 40 | 2 | 40 | 1 | 20 | 5 |
| | **Unknown** | 0 | 0 | 0 | 0 | 0 | 0 | 0 |
| | **Total** | 2 | 40 | 2 | 40 | 1 | 20 | 5 |
| **Eskimo** | **Female** | 0 | 0 | 0 | 0 | 0 | 0 | 0 |
| | **Male** | 0 | 0 | 0 | 0 | 0 | 0 | 0 |
| | **Unknown** | 509 | 68 | 171 | 23 | 69 | 9 | 749 |
| | **Total** | 509 | 68 | 171 | 23 | 69 | 9 | 749 |
| **Guatemalan** | **Female** | 2 | 100 | 0 | 0 | 0 | 0 | 2 |
| | **Male** | 0 | 0 | 0 | 0 | 0 | 0 | 0 |
| | **Unknown** | 0 | 0 | 0 | 0 | 0 | 0 | 0 |
| | **Total** | 2 | 100 | 0 | 0 | 0 | 0 | 2 |
| **Mexico** | **Female** | 0 | 0 | 0 | 0 | 0 | 0 | 0 |
| | **Male** | 6 | 86 | 0 | 0 | 1 | 14 | 7 |
| | **Unknown** | 0 | 0 | 0 | 0 | 0 | 0 | 0 |
| | **Total** | 6 | 86 | 0 | 0 | 1 | 14 | 7 |
| **Pacific Island** | **Female** | 0 | 0 | 0 | 0 | 0 | 0 | 0 |
| | **Male** | 0 | 0 | 0 | 0 | 0 | 0 | 0 |
| | **Unknown** | 50 | 67 | 24 | 32 | 1 | 1 | 75 |
| | **Total** | 50 | 67 | 24 | 32 | 1 | 1 | 75 |
| **Peruvian** | **Female** | 0 | 0 | 0 | 0 | 0 | 0 | 0 |
| | **Male** | 0 | 0 | 0 | 0 | 0 | 0 | 0 |
| | **Unknown** | 11 | 65 | 3 | 18 | 3 | 18 | 17 |
| | **Total** | 11 | 65 | 3 | 18 | 3 | 18 | 17 |
| **Southwest (SW) Hispanic** | **Female** | 2 | 50 | 0 | 0 | 2 | 50 | 4 |
| | **Male** | 2 | 40 | 0 | 0 | 3 | 60 | 5 |
| | **Unknown** | 0 | 0 | 0 | 0 | 0 | 0 | 0 |
| | **Total** | 4 | 44 | 0 | 0 | 5 | 56 | 9 |
| **Thai** | **Female** | 117 | 53 | 17 | 8 | 87 | 39 | 221 |
| | **Male** | 346 | 73 | 21 | 4 | 108 | 23 | 475 |
| | **Unknown** | 8 | 62 | 0 | 0 | 5 | 38 | 13 |
| | **Total** | 471 | 66 | 38 | 5 | 200 | 28 | 709 |
| **Total for all groups** | | 2544 | 68 | 810 | 22 | 404 | 11 | 3758 |

*NAS*, nasal aperture shape.

## CHARACTER STATES

Photographic exemplars of the different character states of NAS are provided below. Each character state is defined following Hefner (2010). When necessary to clarify scoring, more nuanced definitions are provided in the figure captions. NAS should be assessed with the protocol provided in the preceding section. Character states include:

NAS 1 = *Teardrop*—the greatest projection of the lateral margins is located in the lower 2/3 of the nasal aperture, superior to the location of NAS 2 and inferior to the location of NAS 3.
NAS 2 = *Bell*—the greatest projection of the lateral margins is located at the inferior aspect of the nasal aperture.
NAS 3 = *Bowed*—the greatest projection of the lateral margins is located at the midline of the nasal aperture.

# CHARACTER STATES FOR NASAL APERTURE SHAPE = 1 (FIGS. 7.1–7.7)

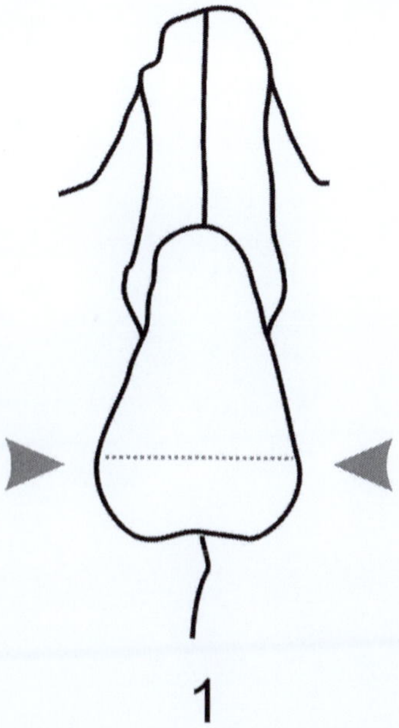


**FIGURE 7.1** Diagrammatic representation of NAS 1. Dashed line indicates the approximate location of greatest breadth (alare). *NAS*, nasal aperture shape.

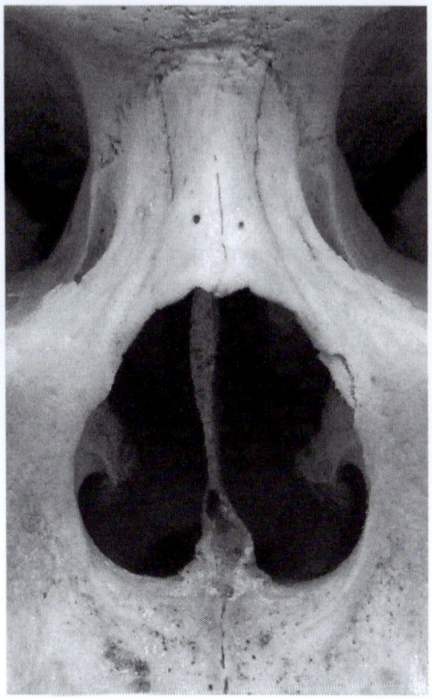

**FIGURE 7.2** Variant of NAS 1. Note: although left lateral aspect is damaged, the approximate location of greatest breadth does not change. *NAS*, nasal aperture shape.

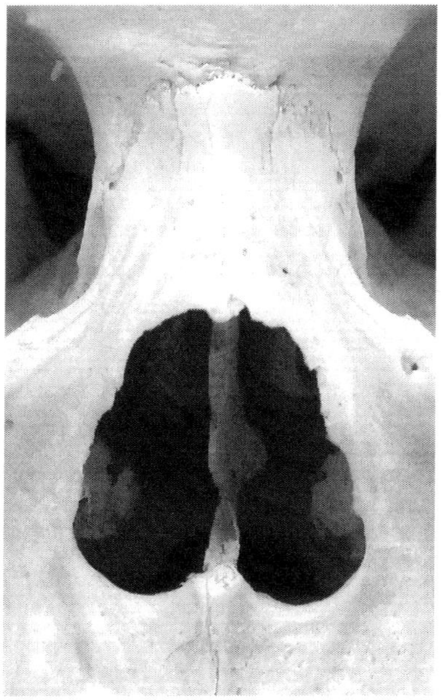

FIGURE 7.3 Variant of NAS 1. *NAS*, nasal aperture shape.

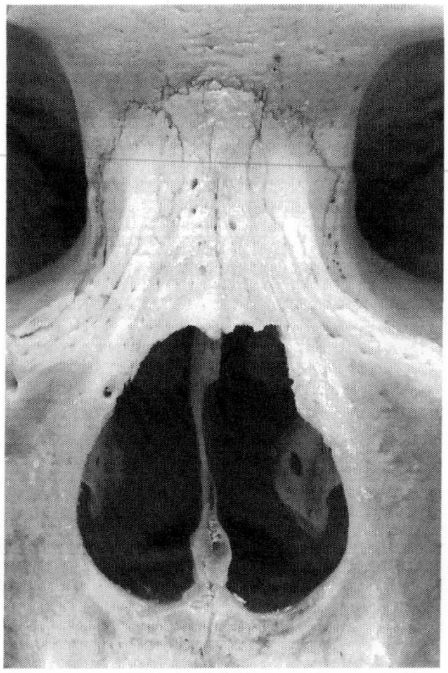

FIGURE 7.4 Variant of NAS 1. Note: slight asymmetry is not uncommon. *NAS*, nasal aperture shape.

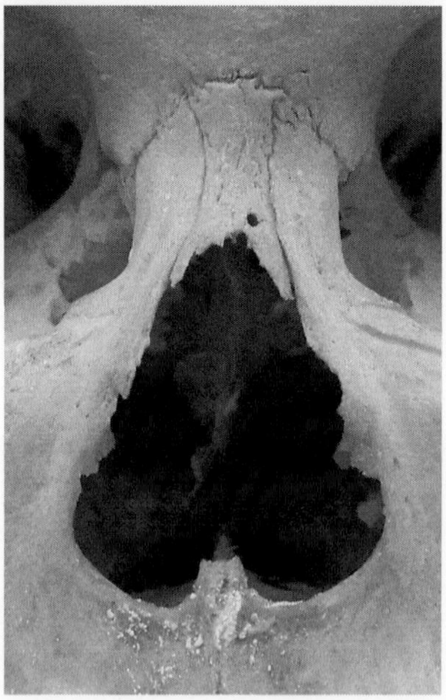

**FIGURE 7.5** Variant of NAS 1. Note: slight taphonomic damage does not affect the score for NAS. *NAS*, nasal aperture shape.

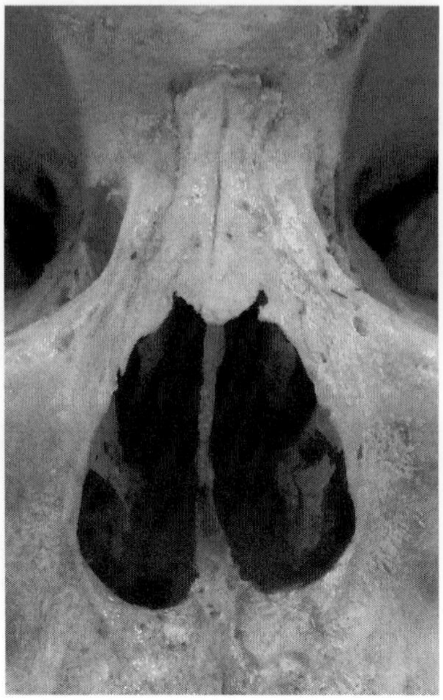

**FIGURE 7.6** Variant of NAS 1. Note: slight asymmetry is not uncommon. *NAS*, nasal aperture shape.

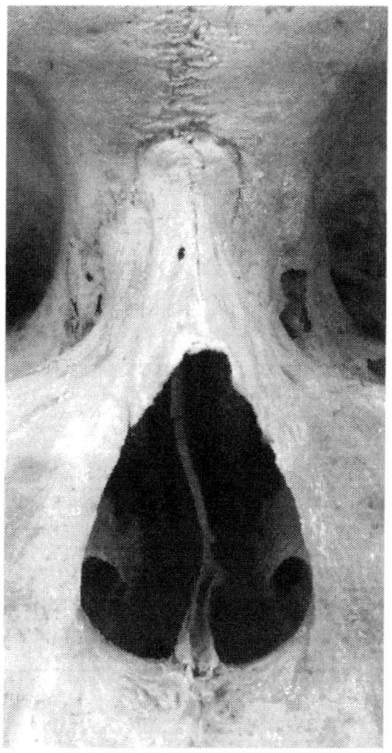

FIGURE 7.7 Variant of NAS 2. Note: one of the best examples of NAS 1. *NAS*, nasal aperture shape.

# CHARACTER STATES FOR NASAL APERTURE SHAPE = 2 (FIGS. 7.8–7.14)

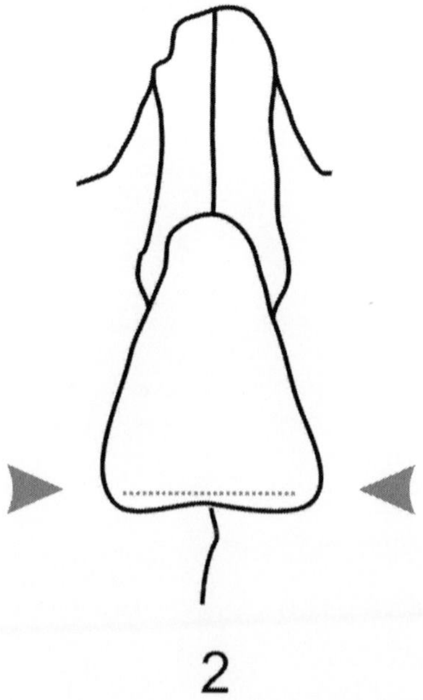


**FIGURE 7.8** Diagrammatic representation of NAS 2. Dashed line indicates the approximate location of greatest breadth (alare). *NAS*, nasal aperture shape.

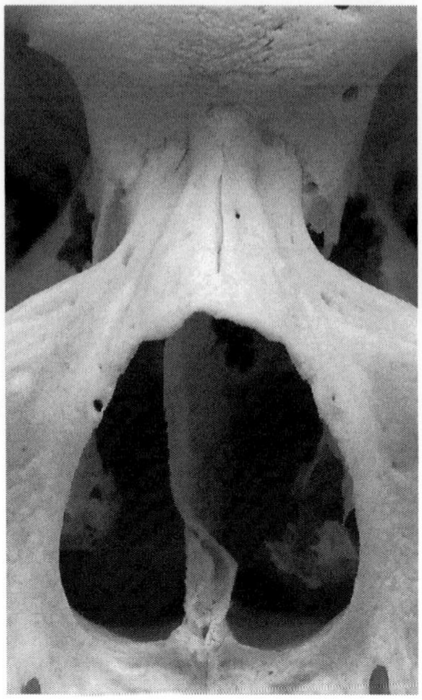

**FIGURE 7.9** Variant of NAS 2. Note: asymmetrical manifestation: higher expression (NAS 2) on the right side is recorded. *NAS*, nasal aperture shape.

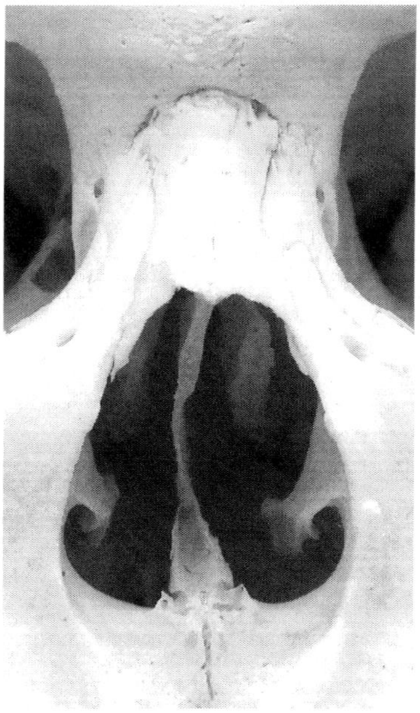

**FIGURE 7.10** Variant of NAS 2. Note: subnasal grooves (see Chapter 4: Inferior Nasal Aperture) exaggerate total height of the nasal cavity. *NAS*, nasal aperture shape.

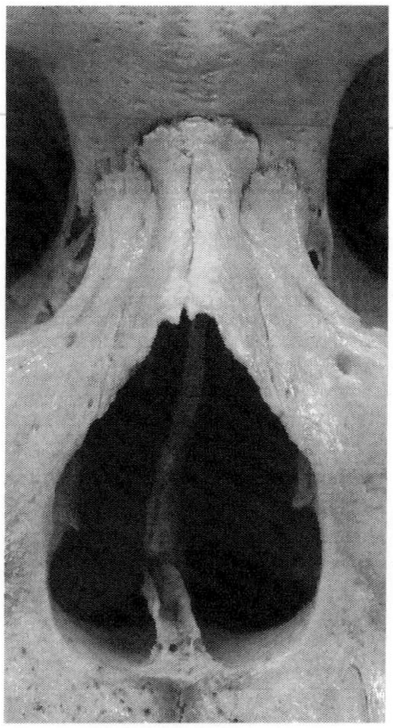

**FIGURE 7.11** Variant of NAS 2. Note: "Squaring-off" of the nasal cavity. *NAS*, nasal aperture shape.

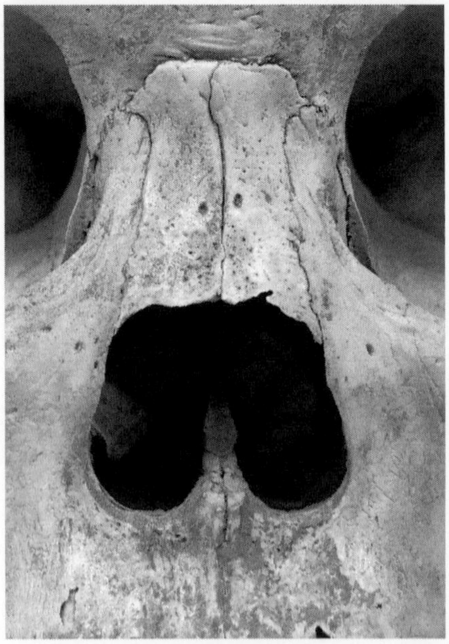

**FIGURE 7.12** Variant of NAS 2. Note: slight asymmetry is not uncommon. *NAS*, nasal aperture shape.

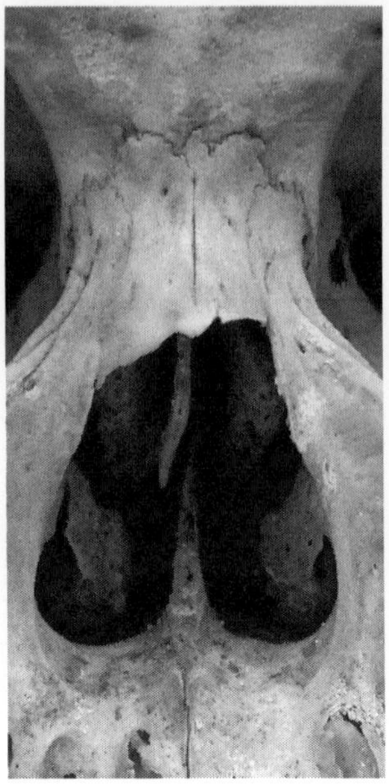

**FIGURE 7.13** Variant of NAS 2. *NAS*, nasal aperture shape.

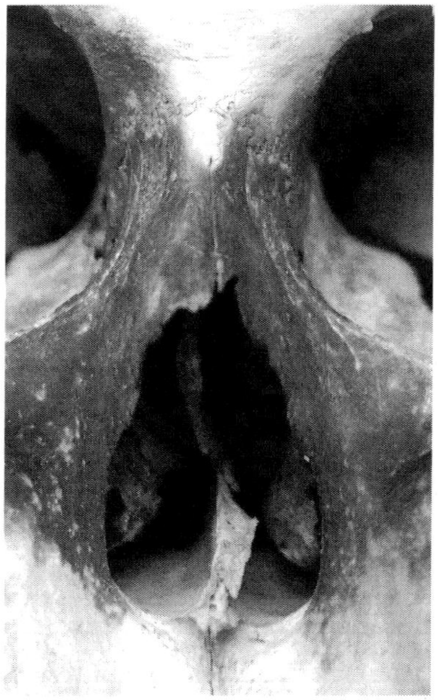

**FIGURE 7.14** Variant of NAS 2. *NAS*, nasal aperture shape.

# CHARACTER STATES FOR NASAL APERTURE SHAPE = 3 (FIGS. 7.15–7.21)

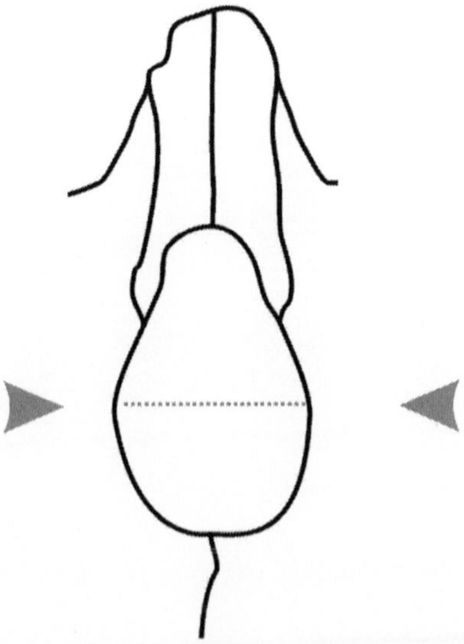


**FIGURE 7.15** Diagrammatic representation of NAS 3. Dashed line indicates the approximate location of greatest breadth (alare). *NAS*, nasal aperture shape.

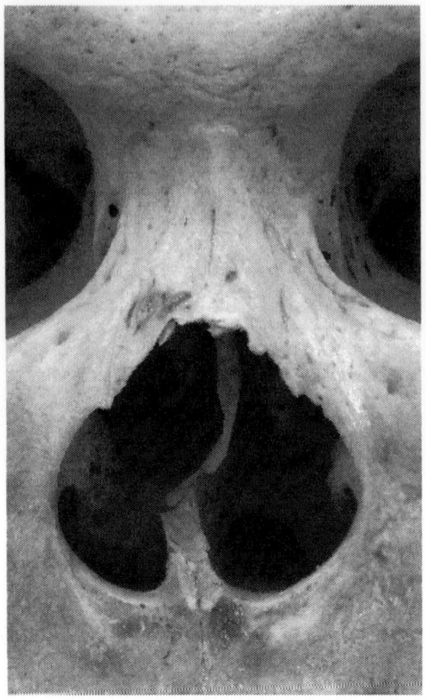

**FIGURE 7.16** Variant of NAS 3. Note: although nasal bones are damaged inferiorly, the greatest lateral breadth can still be observed at the approximate location of the midline. *NAS*, nasal aperture shape.

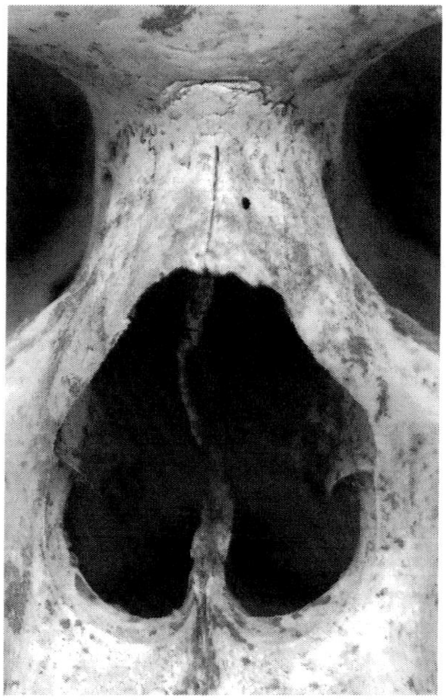

FIGURE 7.17 Variant of NAS 3. Note: subnasal grooves (see Chapter 4: Inferior Nasal Aperture) should not be considered when scoring NAS. *NAS*, nasal aperture shape.

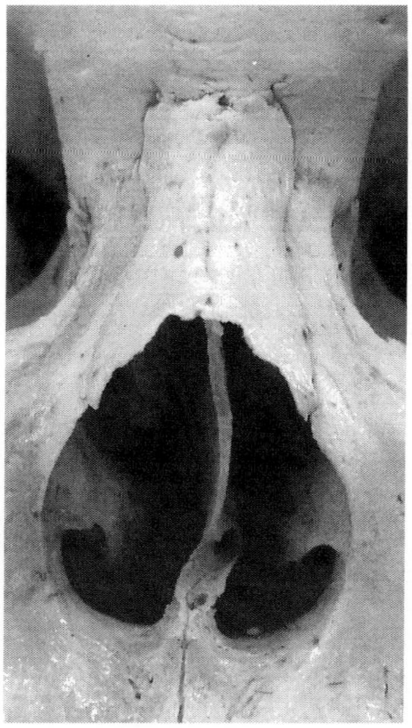

FIGURE 7.18 Variant of NAS 3. Note: slight asymmetry is not uncommon. *NAS*, nasal aperture shape.

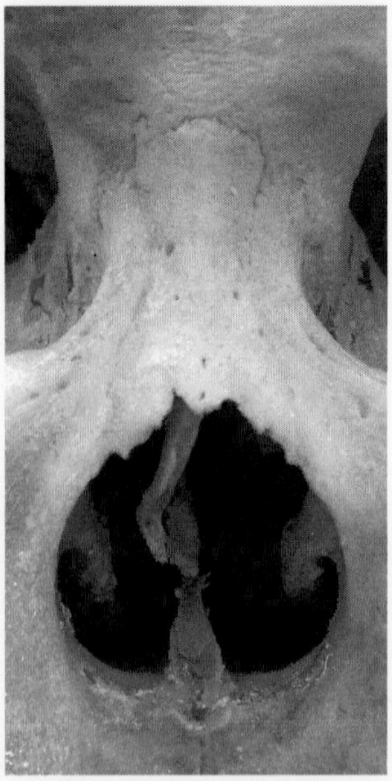

**FIGURE 7.19** Variant of NAS 3. *NAS*, nasal aperture shape.

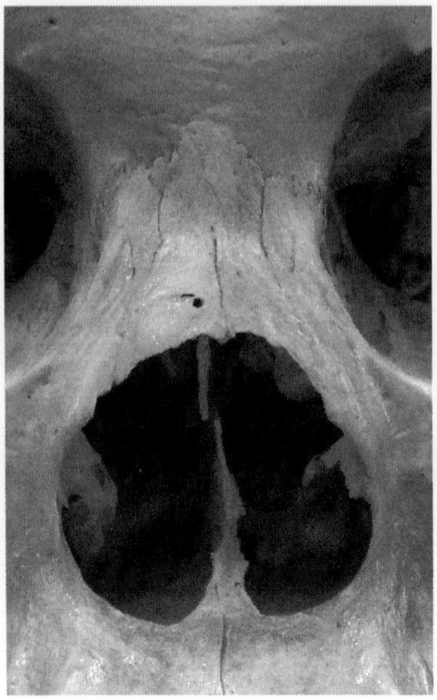

**FIGURE 7.20** Variant of NAS 3. *NAS*, nasal aperture shape.

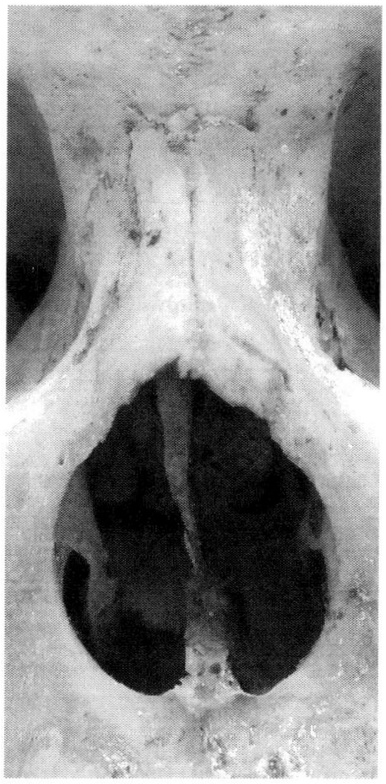

**FIGURE 7.21** Variant of NAS 3. Note: although this nasal cavity is markedly narrower than many of the examples above, the greatest lateral extent of the nasal opening is in the midline (NAS 3). *NAS*, nasal aperture shape.

CHAPTER

# 8

# Nasal Aperture Width

Assessing nasal aperture width (NAW) considers the width of the nasal aperture relative to the entire facial skeleton using a ratio of total facial width to nasal opening. The trait is scored viewing the cranium anteriorly, and dividing the midfacial region into fractions (Fig. 8.1). NAW comprises three character states—scored as: $1 < 2 < 3$.

Most early research into the relationship between the nasal opening and ancestry relied on the metric analysis of NAW (cf. Broca, 1872; Collignon, 1887; Glanville, 1969; Hovorka, 1893; Risley, 1891; Schultz, 1918; Virchow, 1912; Williams, 1956; others). Even more modern work outside of forensic anthropology prefers a metric component. Howells (1973:176), citing Martin (1928), defined nasal breadth (NLB) as the "distance between the anterior edges of the nasal aperture at its widest extent." Jantz and Ousley (2005:104) similarly define NLB as "Nasal Breadth (*al-al*, NLB): The maximum breadth of the nasal aperture" from *alare* (al) to *alare* (al). Liedenberg et al. (2015) used cranial indices, including the nasal index, to evaluate classification accuracies of ancestry in South Africa. Spradley and Jantz (2016) identified NLB as an important variable for the separation of American Black and White males in their craniometric analysis of an American sample. Morphological considerations of NAW followed a similar, though slower, impetus.

Cameron (1930) provides a novel treatment of NAW, identifying *Groups* (1–4) within his sample using average nasal width. Although he does not identify character states, his approach may well represent an early embrace of trait values. For example, Cameron (1930:292—*emphasis added*) suggests Group 4 "contained the representatives of the black races—the American negro, the Australian native, and the Tasmanian native. These three exhibited consistently *wide* nasal apertures." Some of the earliest forensic anthropology texts included more thoughtful definitions of NAW character states.

Krogman (1955) and later Krogman and Isçan (1986) identify three character states for nasal width: narrow, moderately wide, and wide. Similarly, Gill (1998) recognizes three variants: narrow, medium, and broad. Rhine (1990) and Byers (2005) used similar descriptions: narrow, medium, and wide. Bass (2005) identifies two morphologies: narrow and wide. These character states each suffer from lack of objective scoring. Birkby et al. (2008) identified two main character states of NAW useful for the identification of Southwest Hispanics: narrow and moderately wide. Hefner (2003, 2009) defined NAW using three character states. Hurst (2012) used the Hefner (2009) definitions and line drawings to identify Southwest Hispanic trait expressions. Hefner's (2009) definitions of NAW reflect the same lack of an objective measure. That definition identifies three character states:

> NAW—The width of the nasal aperture (NAW) . . . is assessed relative to the facial skeleton. It is scored as 1—narrow; 2—medium; or 3—broad.

To more objectively distinguish character states of NAW, the relative breadth of the nasal aperture should be considered. Fig. 8.1 illustrates the relative measures of NAW. When assessing each character state, analysts should consider how much of the total facial skeleton the nasal cavity comprises. If, for example, the nasal cavity makes up roughly one-quarter of the upper facial skeleton, the region should be scored medium (NAW 2).

## NOMENCLATURE

*Apertura piriformis, Cava nasi*, nasal aperture width, nasal aperture breadth, nasal cavity, nasal opening, and width *foramen nasi*.

*Atlas of Human Cranial Macromorphoscopic Traits.*
DOI: https://doi.org/10.1016/B978-0-12-814385-8.00008-2

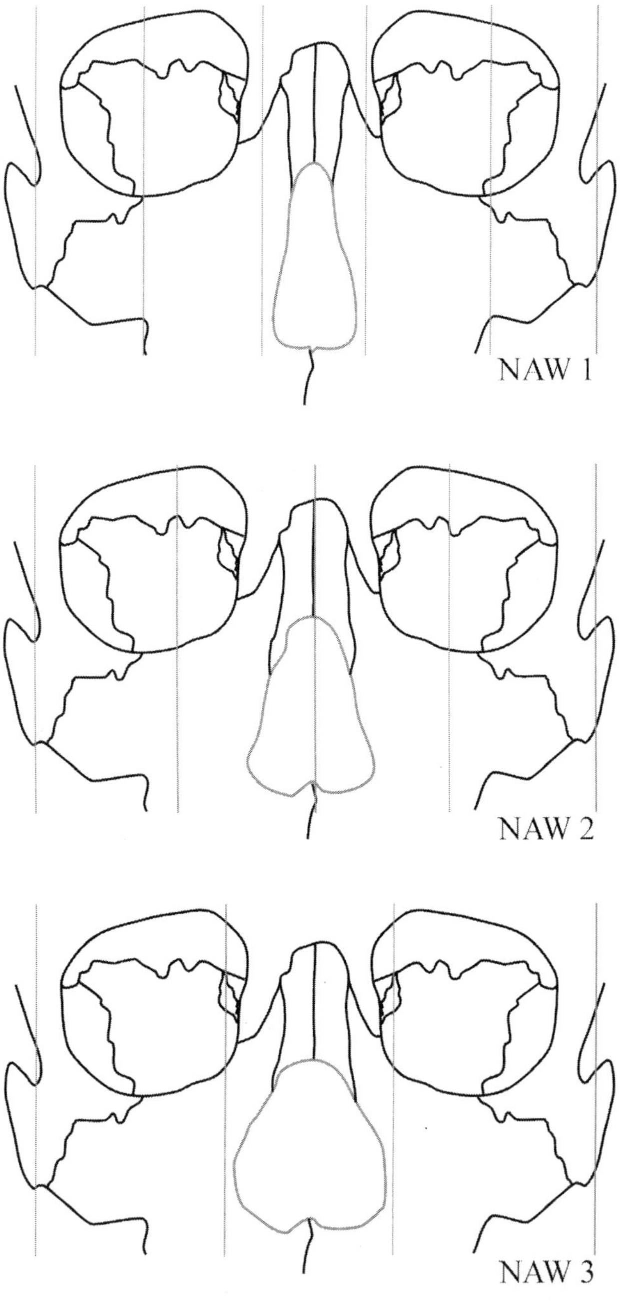


**FIGURE 8.1** Approximation of the 1/5, 1/4, and 1/3 ratios of total facial width to nasal opening.

## GROSS ANATOMY

The nasal aperture is the variably-shaped opening of the midface, bounded superiorly by the inferior borders of the nasal bones near *rhinion*, laterally by the maxilla, and inferiorly by the same. Comprising the external components of the nasal cavity, the bony nasal region is divided into two compartments separated internally by the nasal septum. The aperture communicates anteriorly through the fleshy nostrils and posteriorly with the nasopharynx through the choanae. Lined with a mucous membrane and richly vascularized by branches of the maxillary, facial, and ophthalmic arteries, the nasal cavity is innervated via branches of the olfactory, ophthalmic, and maxillary nerves.

## GROWTH AND DEVELOPMENT

Enlow (1990) thoroughly outlines the close relationship between respiratory needs and general growth and development as responses to physiological demands. Respiration is a vital function from birth onward.

Significant anatomical changes, predominately in the face, ensure efficient respiration while also permitting growth and development of the facial structures. Other chapters detailing traits from the midface have already outlined the growth and development of structures associated with the nasal aperture (see, for instance, Chapter 4: Inferior Nasal Aperture). However, for continuity, we provide the following details on growth and development of the nasal aperture.

Near the fourth week of intrauterine development, five branchial arches form the region of the future head and neck. Each arch gives rise to muscles, connective tissue, vasculature, and neural and skeletal components of the future face, including the maxillae. The first branchial arch is instrumental in the formation of the nasomaxillary region, formed predominantly from the maxillary process of the mandibular arch.

Around week six, the growth of the nasal swellings deepens dorsocaudally to form the nasal pits and penetrate the underlying mesenchyme. Lying posterior to the primary palate (i.e., the primitive palate), each pit is initially separated from the oral cavity by the oronasal membrane, which eventually breaks down allowing for communication between the two structures via the primitive choanae. Following the formation of the secondary palate, the choanae are at the junction between the oral pharynx and the nasal cavities. Posteriorly, the lateral palatine processes fuse with the nasal septum maintaining the separation between the oral and nasal cavities while separating each nasal cavity from the other. The superior, middle, and inferior turbinates develop as elevations on the lateral nasal wall of each nasal cavity. Lined with ectodermal epithelium, these structures along the roof of the nasal cavity become specialized for olfaction.

## FUNCTIONAL MORPHOLOGY

The nasal cavity is a vital component in olfaction and the respiratory system, heating and humidifying inhaled air. For olfaction, odor is detected and smells are recognized through the nasal aperture. Odor molecules entering into the nasal cavity are distributed (circular movement) through the nasal turbinates. The mucus membrane lining the nasal cavity contains odor binding factors (proteins) that dissolve the odor molecules for transmission to the olfactory receptors through the cribriform plate of the ethmoid. From there, the receptors transmit accumulated signals in glomeruli as neural signals to the brain for interpretation and response. Airflow and associated scalar exchange within the nasal cavity serves to heat and increase the humidity of the inhaled air. Ample research has been dedicated to the role climate plays in the nasal cavity and nasal aperture shapes, and numerous researchers have contributed their investigations to the current body of literature. The following are some that the reader should consider for further exploration: Baker (1988), Carey and Steegmann (1981), Churchill et al. (2004), Cole (1982), Davies (1932), Dean (1988), Hall (2005), Havarti (2003), Havarti and Weaver (2006), Hubbi et al. (2009), Lieberman (2011), Mlynski et al. (2001), Shea (1977), Weiner (1954), and Yokley (2009).

## WITHIN POPULATION VARIATION

Data derived from the Macromorphoscopic Databank of the frequency distribution of NAW ($n = 5836$). All data are for adult individuals. When possible, frequency data for males and females are provided separately. When sex could not be estimated reliably, frequency distributions are pooled as "Unknown" (Table 8.1).

**TABLE 8.1** Frequency Distribution of NAW, by Geographic Origin and Sex

| | | 1 | | 2 | | 3 | | |
|---|---|---|---|---|---|---|---|---|
| **Geographic origin** | **Sex** | *n* | % | *n* | % | *n* | % | **Total** |
| **African** | **Female** | 0 | 0 | 5 | 36 | 9 | 64 | 14 |
| | **Male** | 0 | 0 | 2 | 13 | 14 | 88 | 16 |
| | **Unknown** | 0 | 0 | 0 | 0 | 0 | 0 | 0 |
| | **Total** | 0 | 0 | 7 | 23 | 23 | 77 | 30 |
| **American Black** | **Female** | 3 | 2 | 63 | 47 | 69 | 51 | 135 |
| | **Male** | 9 | 4 | 132 | 55 | 98 | 41 | 239 |
| | **Unknown** | 0 | 0 | 1 | 100 | 0 | 0 | 1 |
| | **Total** | 12 | 3 | 196 | 52 | 167 | 45 | 375 |
| **American White** | **Female** | 117 | 45 | 123 | 47 | 19 | 7 | 259 |
| | **Male** | 140 | 51 | 124 | 45 | 13 | 5 | 277 |
| | **Unknown** | 0 | 0 | 0 | 0 | 0 | 0 | 0 |
| | **Total** | 257 | 48 | 247 | 46 | 32 | 6 | 536 |
| **Amerindian** | **Female** | 3 | 7 | 40 | 89 | 2 | 4 | 45 |
| | **Male** | 4 | 10 | 33 | 85 | 2 | 5 | 39 |
| | **Unknown** | 302 | 13 | 1818 | 78 | 205 | 9 | 2325 |
| | **Total** | 309 | 13 | 1891 | 78 | 209 | 9 | 2409 |
| **Chinese** | **Female** | 0 | 0 | 4 | 80 | 1 | 20 | 5 |
| | **Male** | 1 | 2 | 49 | 91 | 4 | 7 | 54 |
| | **Unknown** | 0 | 0 | 0 | 0 | 0 | 0 | 0 |
| | **Total** | 1 | 2 | 53 | 90 | 5 | 8 | 59 |
| **Colombian** | **Female** | 22 | 33 | 21 | 31 | 24 | 36 | 67 |
| | **Male** | 49 | 28 | 87 | 50 | 38 | 22 | 174 |
| | **Unknown** | 0 | 0 | 0 | 0 | 0 | 0 | 0 |
| | **Total** | 71 | 29 | 108 | 45 | 62 | 26 | 241 |
| **El Salvador** | **Female** | 0 | 0 | 0 | 0 | 0 | 0 | 0 |
| | **Male** | 0 | 0 | 4 | 80 | 1 | 20 | 5 |
| | **Unknown** | 0 | 0 | 0 | 0 | 0 | 0 | 0 |
| | **Total** | 0 | 0 | 4 | 80 | 1 | 20 | 5 |
| **Eskimo** | **Female** | 0 | 0 | 0 | 0 | 0 | 0 | 0 |
| | **Male** | 0 | 0 | 0 | 0 | 0 | 0 | 0 |
| | **Unknown** | 140 | 18 | 558 | 73 | 62 | 8 | 760 |
| | **Total** | 140 | 18 | 558 | 73 | 62 | 8 | 760 |
| **European** | **Female** | 3 | 43 | 4 | 57 | 0 | 0 | 7 |
| | **Male** | 7 | 88 | 1 | 13 | 0 | 0 | 8 |
| | **Unknown** | 0 | 0 | 0 | 0 | 0 | 0 | 0 |
| | **Total** | 10 | 67 | 5 | 33 | 0 | 0 | 15 |

*(Continued)*

TABLE 8.1 (*Continued*)

| | | 1 | | 2 | | 3 | | |
|---|---|---|---|---|---|---|---|---|
| **Geographic origin** | **Sex** | *n* | % | *n* | % | *n* | % | **Total** |
| **Guatemalan** | **Female** | 3 | 9 | 18 | 55 | 12 | 36 | 33 |
| | **Male** | 15 | 21 | 43 | 61 | 12 | 17 | 70 |
| | **Unknown** | 0 | 0 | 0 | 0 | 0 | 0 | 0 |
| | **Total** | 18 | 17 | 61 | 59 | 24 | 23 | 103 |
| **Japanese** | **Female** | 0 | 0 | 4 | 80 | 1 | 20 | 5 |
| | **Male** | 0 | 0 | 7 | 88 | 1 | 13 | 8 |
| | **Unknown** | 0 | 0 | 2 | 100 | 0 | 0 | 2 |
| | **Total** | 0 | 0 | 13 | 87 | 2 | 13 | 15 |
| **Mexico** | **Female** | 1 | 50 | 1 | 50 | 0 | 0 | 2 |
| | **Male** | 6 | 25 | 14 | 58 | 4 | 17 | 24 |
| | **Unknown** | 0 | 0 | 0 | 0 | 0 | 0 | 0 |
| | **Total** | 7 | 27 | 15 | 58 | 4 | 15 | 26 |
| **Pacific Island** | **Female** | 5 | 9 | 37 | 70 | 11 | 21 | 53 |
| | **Male** | 10 | 12 | 51 | 59 | 25 | 29 | 86 |
| | **Unknown** | 5 | 6 | 64 | 71 | 21 | 23 | 90 |
| | **Total** | 20 | 9 | 152 | 66 | 57 | 25 | 229 |
| **Peruvian** | **Female** | 0 | 0 | 0 | 0 | 0 | 0 | 0 |
| | **Male** | 0 | 0 | 0 | 0 | 0 | 0 | 0 |
| | **Unknown** | 2 | 15 | 10 | 77 | 1 | 8 | 13 |
| | **Total** | 2 | 15 | 10 | 77 | 1 | 8 | 13 |
| **SW Hispanic** | **Female** | 4 | 50 | 4 | 50 | 0 | 0 | 8 |
| | **Male** | 3 | 30 | 4 | 40 | 3 | 30 | 10 |
| | **Unknown** | 23 | 23 | 75 | 76 | 1 | 1 | 99 |
| | **Total** | 30 | 26 | 83 | 71 | 4 | 3 | 117 |
| **Thai** | **Female** | 17 | 5 | 266 | 84 | 35 | 11 | 318 |
| | **Male** | 27 | 5 | 478 | 84 | 66 | 12 | 571 |
| | **Unknown** | 1 | 7 | 10 | 71 | 3 | 21 | 14 |
| | **Total** | 45 | 5 | 754 | 83 | 104 | 12 | 903 |
| **Total for all groups** | | 922 | 16 | 4157 | 71 | 757 | 13 | 5836 |

*NAW*, nasal aperture width; *SW*, Southwest.

## CHARACTER STATES

Photographic exemplars of the different character states of NAW are provided below. Each character state is defined following Hefner (2009). When necessary to clarify scoring, more nuanced definitions are provided in the figure captions. NAW should be assessed with the protocol provided in the preceding section. Character states include:

NAW 1 = *Narrow*—the nasal aperture takes up 1/5 of the facial skeleton.
NAW 2 = *Intermediate*—the nasal aperture takes up 1/4 of the facial skeleton.
NAW 3 = *Broad*—the nasal aperture takes up 1/3 of the facial skeleton.

# CHARACTER STATES FOR NASAL APERTURE WIDTH = 1 (FIGS. 8.2–8.8)

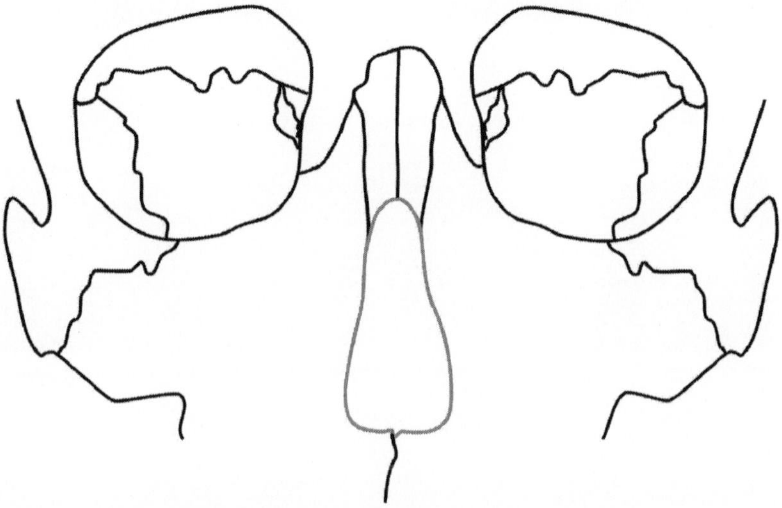


FIGURE 8.2 Diagrammatic representation of NAW 1. *NAW*, nasal aperture width.

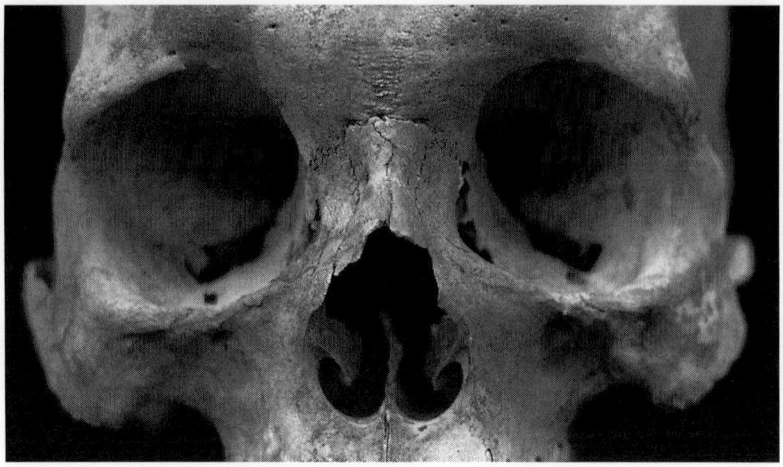

FIGURE 8.3 Variant of NAW 1. *NAW*, nasal aperture width.

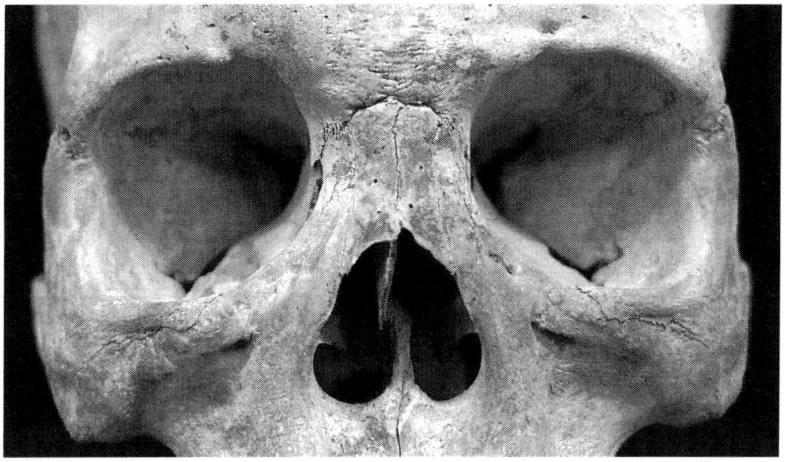

FIGURE 8.4 Variant of NAW 1. *NAW*, nasal aperture width.

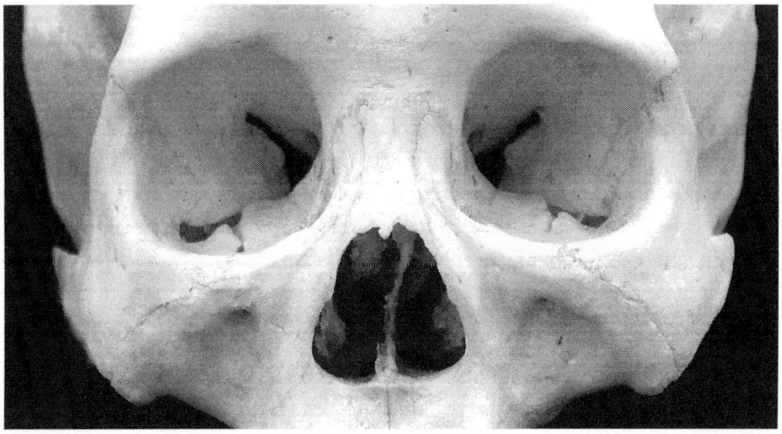

FIGURE 8.5 Variant of NAW 1. *NAW*, nasal aperture width.

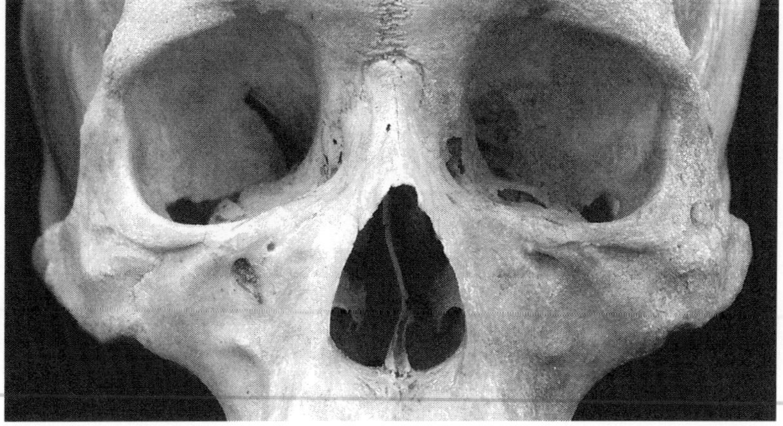

FIGURE 8.6 Variant of NAW 1. *NAW*, nasal aperture width.

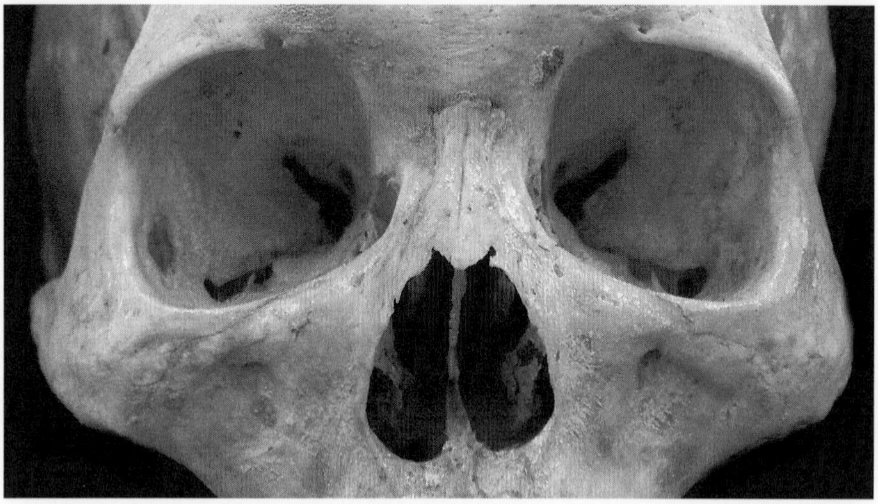

**FIGURE 8.7** Variant of NAW 1. *NAW*, nasal aperture width.

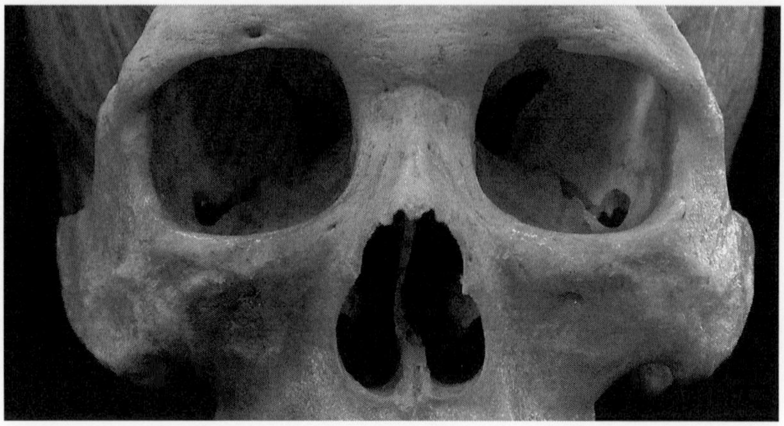

**FIGURE 8.8** Variant of NAW 1. *NAW*, nasal aperture width.

# CHARACTER STATES FOR NASAL APERTURE WIDTH = 2 (FIGS. 8.9–8.15)

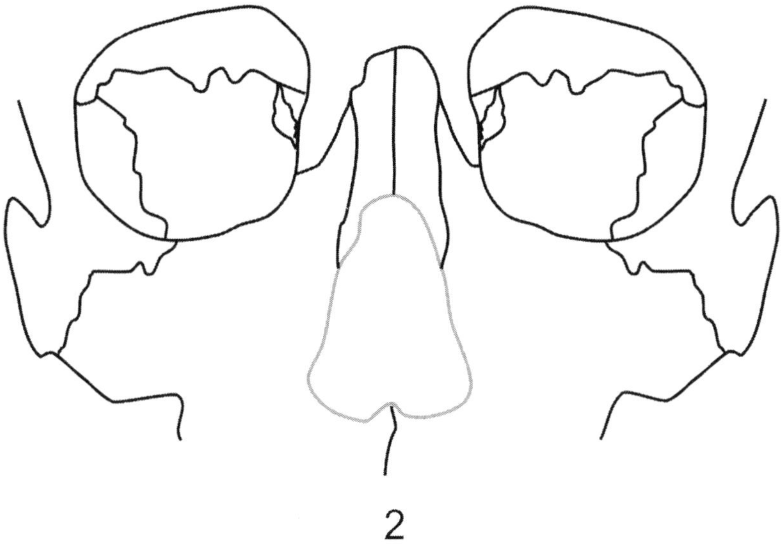


FIGURE 8.9 Diagrammatic representation of NAW 2. *NAW*, nasal aperture width.

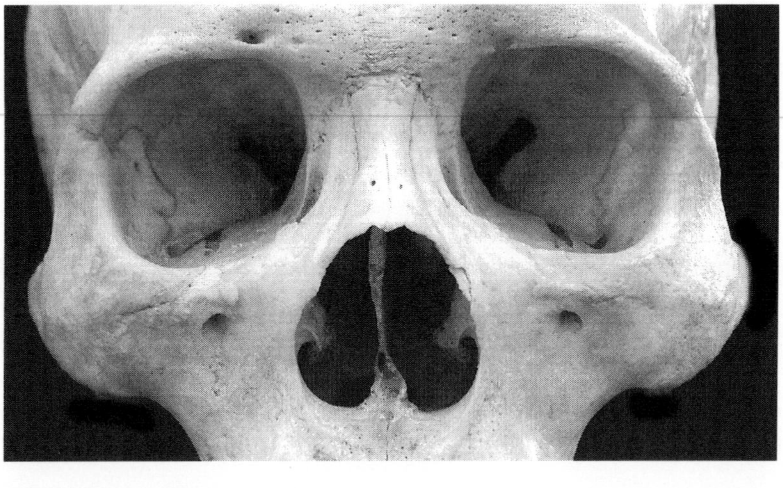

FIGURE 8.10 Variant of NAW 2. *NAW*, nasal aperture width.

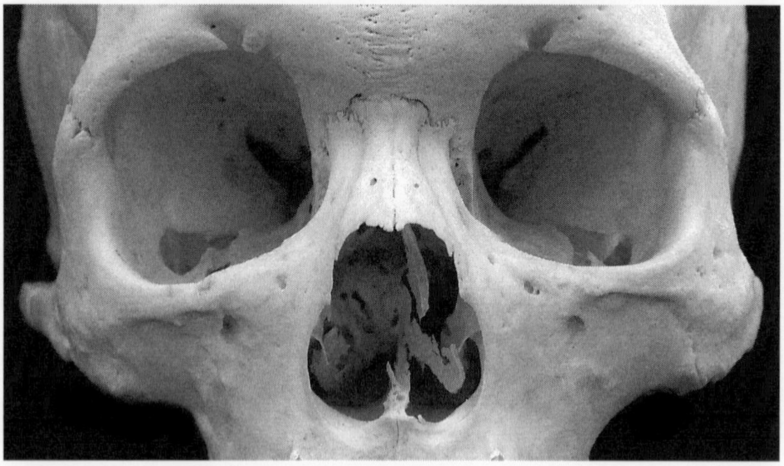

**FIGURE 8.11** Variant of NAW 2. *NAW*, nasal aperture width.

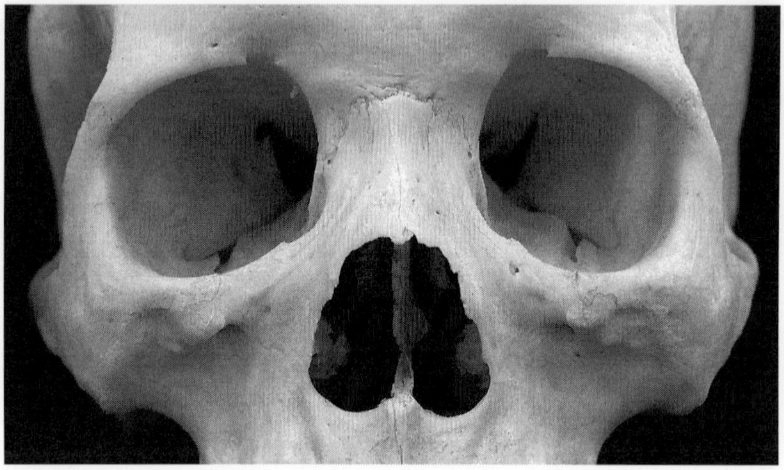

**FIGURE 8.12** Variant of NAW 2. *NAW*, nasal aperture width.

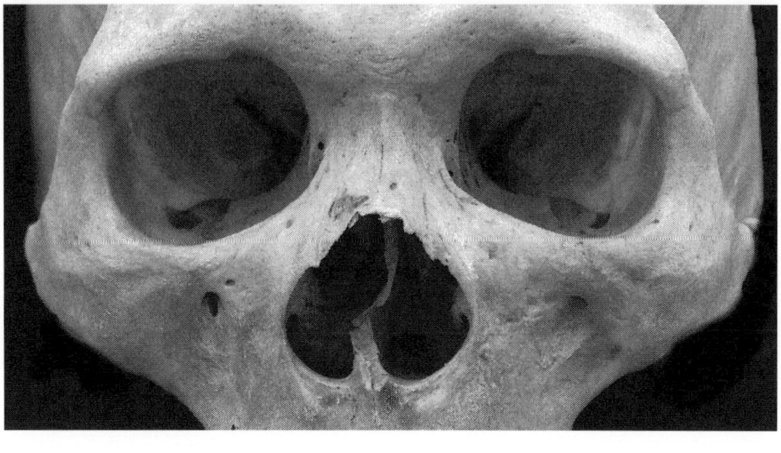

**FIGURE 8.13** Variant of NAW 2. *NAW*, nasal aperture width.

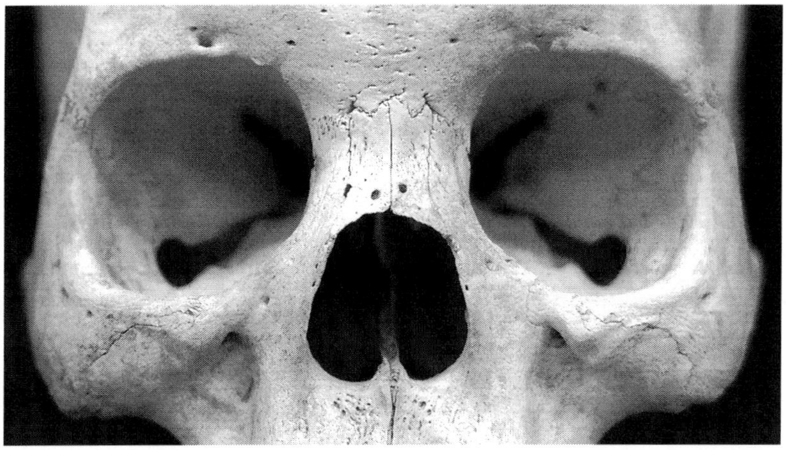

FIGURE 8.14 Variant of NAW 2. *NAW*, nasal aperture width.

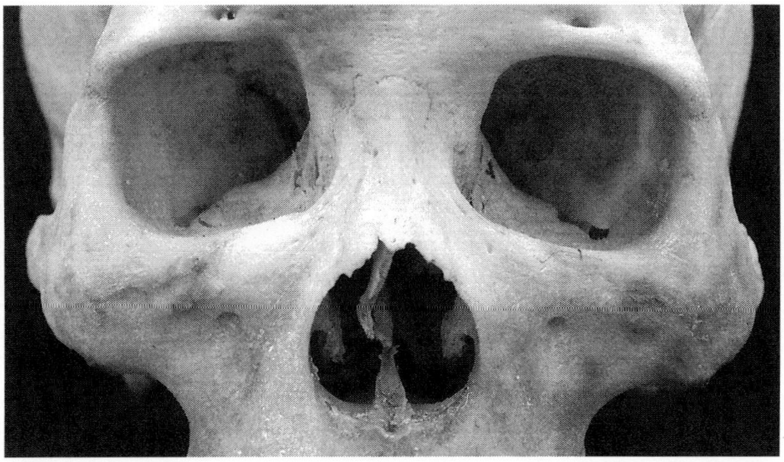

FIGURE 8.15 Variant of NAW 2. *NAW*, nasal aperture width.

## CHARACTER STATES FOR NASAL APERTURE WIDTH = 3 (FIGS. 8.16–8.22)

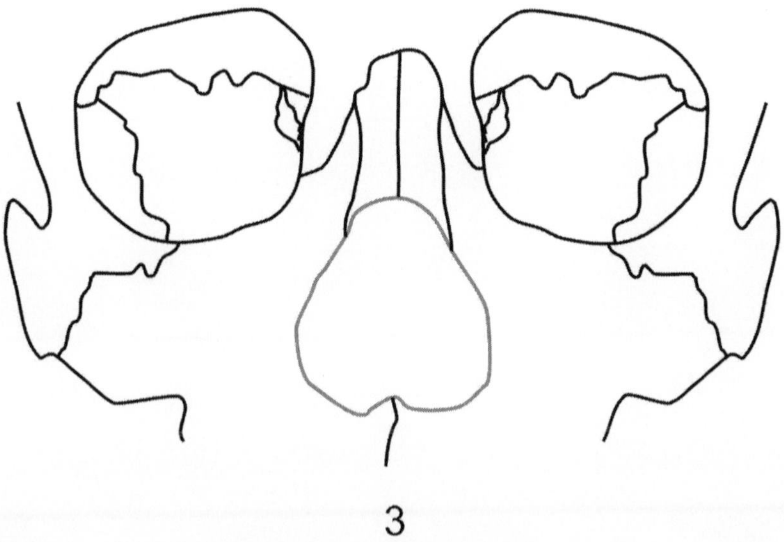


**FIGURE 8.16** Diagrammatic representation of NAW 3. *NAW*, nasal aperture width.

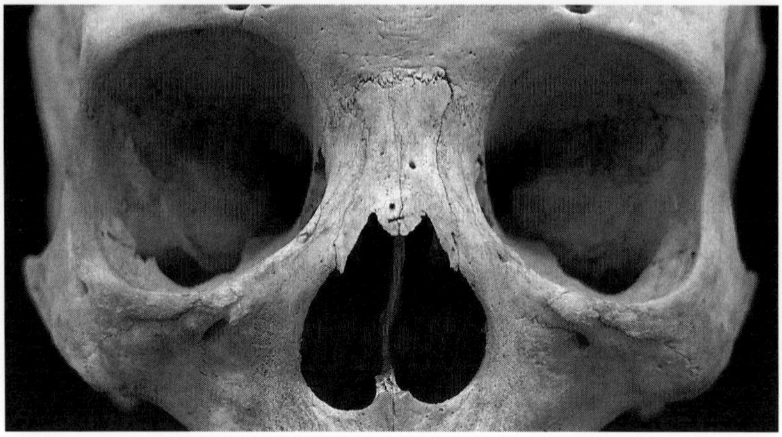

**FIGURE 8.17** Variant of NAW 3. *NAW*, nasal aperture width.

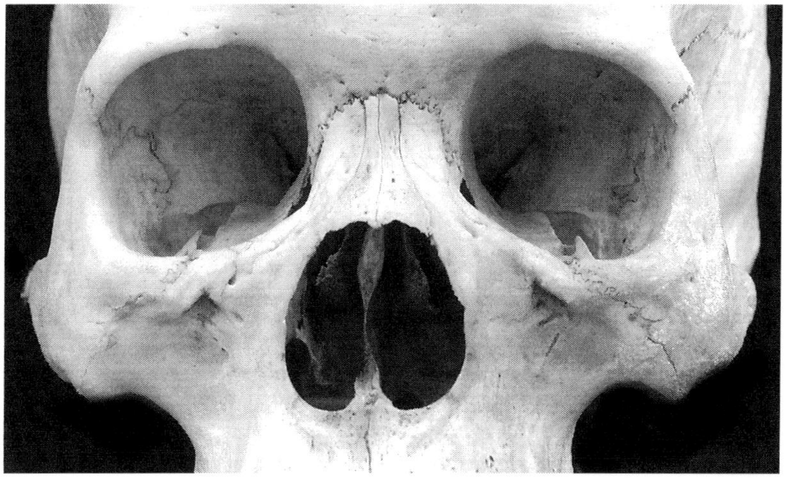

FIGURE 8.18 Variant of NAW 3. *NAW*, nasal aperture width.

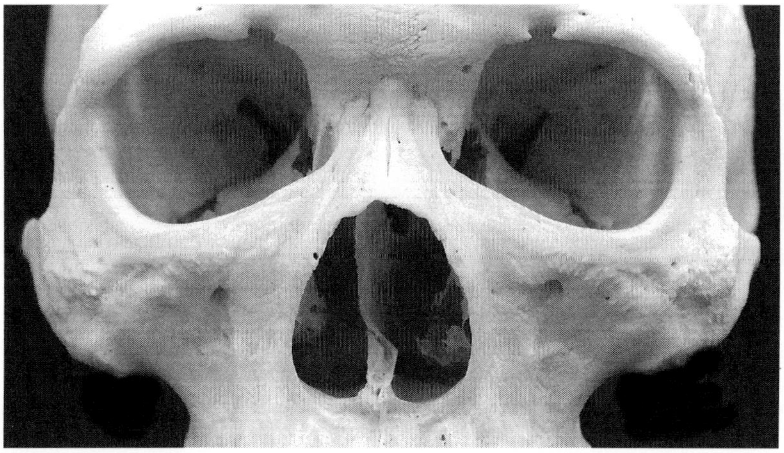

FIGURE 8.19 Variant of NAW 3. *NAW*, nasal aperture width.

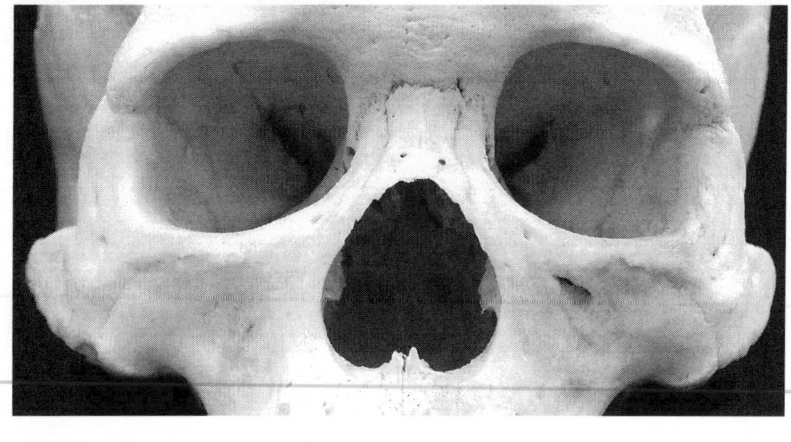

FIGURE 8.20 Variant of NAW 3. *NAW*, nasal aperture width.

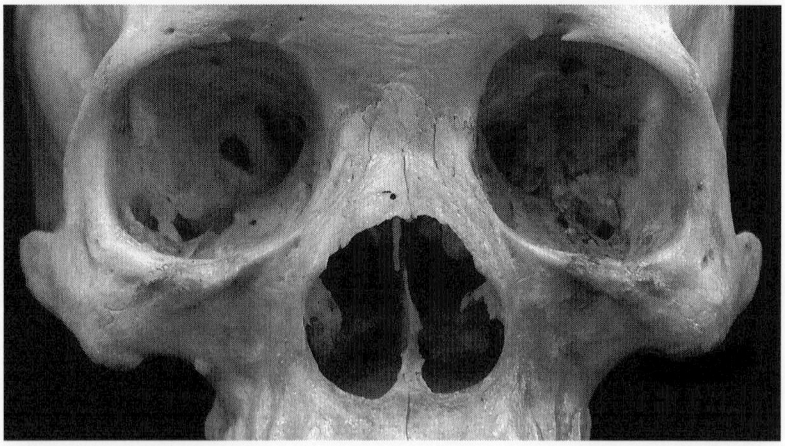

**FIGURE 8.21** Variant of NAW 3. *NAW*, nasal aperture width.

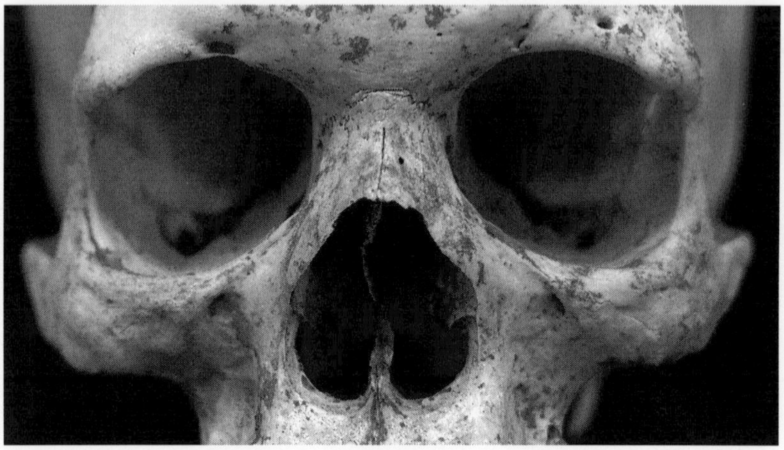

**FIGURE 8.22** Variant of NAW 3. Note: later (sharp) border of maxillae should be considered when assessing NAW. *NAW*, nasal aperture width.

CHAPTER

# 9

# Nasal Bone Contour

Evaluating the nasal bone contour (NBC) is a consideration of the curvature of the midfacial region—specifically the nasal bones and frontal process of both maxillae—approximately 1 cm below the cranial landmark *nasion*. NBC comprises five character states—scored as: $0 < 1 < 2 < 3 < 4$.

Hefner (2003a,b) first introduced nasal bone structure [which he later renamed NBC (Hefner, 2009)] citing Brues (1990) and referring to her nasal root contour as the original description for this trait. However, Brues (1990:5) was describing "three types of horizontal contour[s] across the nasal root … Quonset-hut…, tented…, and… steepled" near *nasion* and not the contour of the nasal bones described by Hefner (2003a,b, 2009). Nevertheless, this trait has proven useful for classifications in forensic anthropological research and casework (Coelho et al., 2016; Klales and Kenyhercz, 2015; Kenyhercz et al., 2016).

A purely visual assessment of NBC is not recommended. A moderate level of inter- and intraobserver error has been noted by several researchers (cf. Hefner, 2009; Klales and Kenyhercz, 2015; L'Abbé et al., 2011). This trait should be recorded using a six inch, stainless steel contour gauge (Fig. 9.1). Contour gauges are ordinarily used for duplicating mechanical parts and transferring prototype contours of ornamental molding, pipes, etc., in various materials, as they readily conform to irregular surfaces.

To assess NBC, the cranium should be placed in a position that allows the observer to gently, but with consistent and balanced pressure, place the contour gauge directly on the nasal bones, approximately 1 cm inferior to *nasion*, while maintaining the gauge roughly perpendicular to the palate and parallel to the orbits (Fig. 9.1). Most observations require approximately 20 mm at the deepest point on the contour gauge for proper

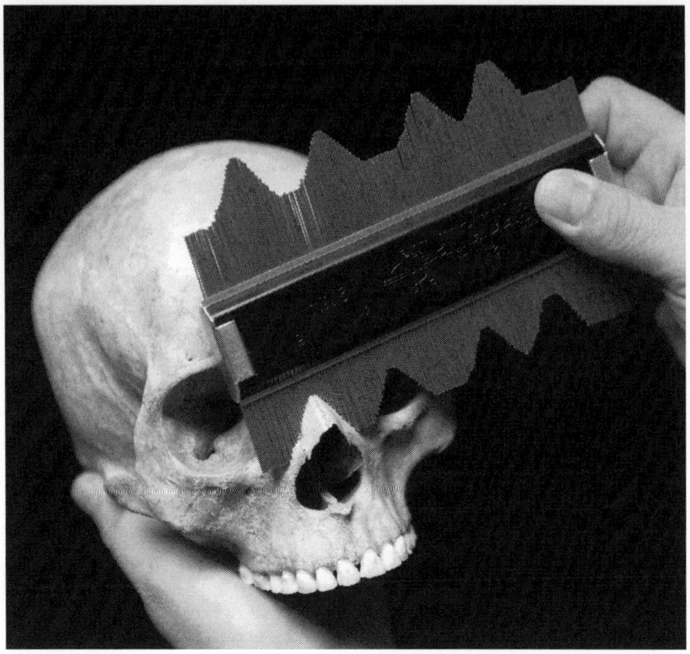

**FIGURE 9.1** Proper use of the contour gauge to assess nasal bone contour (NBC). Note: the gauge is held perpendicular to the orbits, approximately 1 cm below nasion.

*Atlas of Human Cranial Macromorphoscopic Traits*.
DOI: https://doi.org/10.1016/B978-0-12-814385-8.00009-4

assessment, although a lower or higher midface may require adjustments. The contour gauge should be used multiple times to ensure correct assessment. Realign needles after taking each contour, misalignment may result in an incorrect measure.

## NOMENCLATURE

Nasal bone contour, nasal bone structure, and nasal root contour (disambiguation).

## GROSS ANATOMY

The nasal bones are two small, symmetrical oblong bones, each having two surfaces and four borders. Positioned in the midface, at their junction, they form the bridge of the nose superiorly and anchor the upper lateral nasal cartilages inferiorly. The external surface of each nasal bone is covered by the *procerus* and *nasalis muscles*, and each is perforated near the center by a foramen transmitting a small venous complex. The internal surface is transversely concave and contains a groove for the anterior ethmoidal nerve. Each nasal bone articulates with the frontal, ethmoid, opposite nasal, and maxilla. Nasal fractures are common—the most common facial fracture (Wedel and Galloway, 2014)—and usually, a result of blunt force trauma to the nose. Permanent deformity and skeletal manifestation is also common and may preclude an assessment of NBC.

## GROWTH AND DEVELOPMENT

The nasal region undergoes two phases during ontogenesis: the embryonic developmental phase and the growth phase. During embryological development (covered in detail in Chapters 7 and 8), the nose and related skeletal structures are formed. This phase lasts from approximately the third week to three months postconception, during that time the nasal structures (the nasal placode, maxillary and mandibular processes) develop. During the growth phase, which lasts throughout puberty, changes to the various anatomical structures of the nose and an overall increase in size occurs. Around fetal week nine to ten, intramembranous ossification centers appear for each nasal bone (Scheuer and Black, 2000), ossifying from a single center within the cartilaginous nasal capsule. At birth, the nasal bones have a decidedly adult appearance, although the full adult manifestation does not occur until puberty (Scheuer and Black, 2000). Clinical manifestations of nasal bone dysplasia may be assessed as early as the 12th week. Adult manifestations of dysplasia may present with unilateral or bilateral hypoplastic or aplastic nasals (Barnes, 1994).

## FUNCTIONAL MORPHOLOGY

Making up the superior roof of the nasal cavity and anchoring the nasal cartilages, the nasal bones are vital to olfaction and respiration (see Chapters 7 and 8, *Functional Morphology*, for a more detailed exploration of these aspects). Enlow (1990) describes an additional functional component of the nasal bones and associated cartilages in olfaction. The reduced human face resulting from orbital convergence that occurred during hominid evolution required a concomitant reduction of the maxillary complex. The protruding, fleshy human nose and associated skeletal structures direct the nares inferiorly, which then guides inhaled air upward into the nasal cavity to the awaiting sensory nerves of the olfactory bulb.

## WITHIN POPULATION VARIATION

Data derived from the Macromorphoscopic Databank of the frequency distribution of NBC ($n = 5521$). All data are for adult individuals. When possible, frequency data for males and females are provided separately. When sex could not be estimated reliably, frequency distributions are pooled as "Unknown" (Table 9.1).

**TABLE 9.1** Frequency Distribution of NBC, by Geographic Origin and Sex

| | | 0 | | 1 | | 2 | | 3 | | 4 | | |
|---|---|---|---|---|---|---|---|---|---|---|---|---|
| **Geographic origin** | **Sex** | *n* | % | *n* | % | *n* | % | *n* | % | *n* | % | **Total** |
| **African** | Female | 11 | 79 | 2 | 14 | 0 | 0 | 1 | 7 | 0 | 0 | 14 |
| | Male | 12 | 75 | 1 | 6 | 1 | 6 | 1 | 6 | 1 | 6 | 16 |
| | Unknown | 0 | 0 | 0 | 0 | 0 | 0 | 0 | 0 | 0 | 0 | 0 |
| | Total | 23 | 77 | 3 | 10 | 1 | 3 | 2 | 7 | 1 | 3 | 30 |
| **American Black** | Female | 52 | 39 | 39 | 29 | 11 | 8 | 22 | 16 | 10 | 7 | 134 |
| | Male | 71 | 30 | 58 | 25 | 34 | 14 | 48 | 20 | 24 | 10 | 235 |
| | Unknown | 0 | 0 | 0 | 0 | 0 | 0 | 1 | 100 | 0 | 0 | 1 |
| | Total | 123 | 33 | 97 | 26 | 45 | 12 | 71 | 19 | 34 | 9 | 370 |
| **American White** | Female | 16 | 6 | 73 | 29 | 37 | 15 | 64 | 25 | 64 | 25 | 254 |
| | Male | 10 | 4 | 110 | 40 | 52 | 19 | 80 | 29 | 25 | 9 | 277 |
| | Unknown | 0 | 0 | 0 | 0 | 0 | 0 | 0 | 0 | 0 | 0 | 0 |
| | Total | 26 | 5 | 183 | 34 | 89 | 17 | 144 | 27 | 89 | 17 | 531 |
| **Amerindian** | Female | 4 | 9 | 18 | 40 | 16 | 36 | 7 | 16 | 0 | 0 | 45 |
| | Male | 3 | 8 | 6 | 15 | 18 | 46 | 12 | 31 | 0 | 0 | 39 |
| | Unknown | 595 | 28 | 1012 | 48 | 40 | 2 | 255 | 12 | 189 | 9 | 2091 |
| | Total | 602 | 28 | 1036 | 48 | 74 | 3 | 274 | 13 | 189 | 9 | 2175 |
| **Chinese** | Female | 2 | 40 | 2 | 40 | 1 | 20 | 0 | 0 | 0 | 0 | 5 |
| | Male | 11 | 21 | 14 | 26 | 20 | 38 | 7 | 13 | 1 | 2 | 53 |
| | Unknown | 0 | 0 | 0 | 0 | 0 | 0 | 0 | 0 | 0 | 0 | 0 |
| | Total | 13 | 22 | 16 | 28 | 21 | 36 | 7 | 12 | 1 | 2 | 58 |
| **Colombian** | Female | 19 | 28 | 23 | 34 | 1 | 1 | 9 | 13 | 15 | 22 | 67 |
| | Male | 25 | 14 | 101 | 58 | 2 | 1 | 21 | 12 | 26 | 15 | 175 |
| | Unknown | 0 | 0 | 0 | 0 | 0 | 0 | 0 | 0 | 0 | 0 | 0 |
| | Total | 44 | 18 | 124 | 51 | 3 | 1 | 30 | 12 | 41 | 17 | 242 |
| **El Salvador** | Female | 0 | 0 | 0 | 0 | 0 | 0 | 0 | 0 | 0 | 0 | 0 |
| | Male | 0 | 0 | 3 | 60 | 0 | 0 | 1 | 20 | 1 | 20 | 5 |
| | Unknown | 0 | 0 | 0 | 0 | 0 | 0 | 0 | 0 | 0 | 0 | 0 |
| | Total | 0 | 0 | 3 | 60 | 0 | 0 | 1 | 20 | 1 | 20 | 5 |
| **Eskimo** | Female | 0 | 0 | 0 | 0 | 0 | 0 | 0 | 0 | 0 | 0 | 0 |
| | Male | 0 | 0 | 0 | 0 | 0 | 0 | 0 | 0 | 0 | 0 | 0 |
| | Unknown | 284 | 39 | 241 | 33 | 5 | 1 | 73 | 10 | 122 | 17 | 725 |
| | Total | 284 | 39 | 241 | 33 | 5 | 1 | 73 | 10 | 122 | 17 | 725 |
| **European** | Female | 0 | 0 | 1 | 14 | 2 | 29 | 2 | 29 | 2 | 29 | 7 |
| | Male | 0 | 0 | 1 | 13 | 1 | 13 | 3 | 38 | 3 | 38 | 8 |
| | Unknown | 0 | 0 | 0 | 0 | 0 | 0 | 0 | 0 | 0 | 0 | 0 |
| | Total | 0 | 0 | 2 | 13 | 3 | 20 | 5 | 33 | 5 | 33 | 15 |

(*Continued*)

TABLE 9.1 (*Continued*)

| | | 0 | | 1 | | 2 | | 3 | | 4 | | |
|---|---|---|---|---|---|---|---|---|---|---|---|---|
| **Geographic origin** | **Sex** | *n* | % | *n* | % | *n* | % | *n* | % | *n* | % | **Total** |
| **Guatemalan** | Female | 2 | 6 | 8 | 24 | 0 | 0 | 13 | 39 | 10 | 30 | 33 |
| | Male | 4 | 6 | 21 | 30 | 1 | 1 | 30 | 43 | 14 | 20 | 70 |
| | Unknown | 0 | 0 | 0 | 0 | 0 | 0 | 0 | 0 | 0 | 0 | 0 |
| | Total | 6 | 6 | 29 | 28 | 1 | 1 | 43 | 42 | 24 | 23 | 103 |
| **Japanese** | Female | 2 | 40 | 1 | 20 | 2 | 40 | 0 | 0 | 0 | 0 | 5 |
| | Male | 0 | 0 | 0 | 0 | 5 | 71 | 2 | 29 | 0 | 0 | 7 |
| | Unknown | 2 | 100 | 0 | 0 | 0 | 0 | 0 | 0 | 0 | 0 | 2 |
| | Total | 4 | 29 | 1 | 7 | 7 | 50 | 2 | 14 | 0 | 0 | 14 |
| **Mexico** | Female | 0 | 0 | 1 | 50 | 0 | 0 | 1 | 50 | 0 | 0 | 2 |
| | Male | 3 | 13 | 7 | 29 | 1 | 4 | 8 | 33 | 5 | 21 | 24 |
| | Unknown | 0 | 0 | 0 | 0 | 0 | 0 | 0 | 0 | 0 | 0 | 0 |
| | Total | 3 | 12 | 8 | 31 | 1 | 4 | 9 | 35 | 5 | 19 | 26 |
| **Pacific Island** | Female | 7 | 15 | 35 | 76 | 1 | 2 | 1 | 2 | 2 | 4 | 46 |
| | Male | 8 | 10 | 60 | 75 | 1 | 1 | 9 | 11 | 2 | 3 | 80 |
| | Unknown | 25 | 31 | 34 | 42 | 1 | 1 | 9 | 11 | 12 | 15 | 81 |
| | Total | 40 | 19 | 129 | 62 | 3 | 1 | 19 | 9 | 16 | 8 | 207 |
| **Peruvian** | Female | 0 | 0 | 0 | 0 | 0 | 0 | 0 | 0 | 0 | 0 | 0 |
| | Male | 0 | 0 | 0 | 0 | 0 | 0 | 0 | 0 | 0 | 0 | 0 |
| | Unknown | 2 | 8 | 7 | 27 | 2 | 8 | 7 | 27 | 8 | 31 | 26 |
| | Total | 2 | 8 | 7 | 27 | 2 | 8 | 7 | 27 | 8 | 31 | 26 |
| **Southwest (SW) Hispanic** | Female | 1 | 13 | 3 | 38 | 0 | 0 | 3 | 38 | 1 | 13 | 8 |
| | Male | 1 | 10 | 6 | 60 | 0 | 0 | 2 | 20 | 1 | 10 | 10 |
| | Unknown | 4 | 4 | 20 | 22 | 5 | 5 | 55 | 60 | 7 | 8 | 91 |
| | Total | 6 | 6 | 29 | 27 | 5 | 5 | 60 | 55 | 9 | 8 | 109 |
| **Thai** | Female | 188 | 61 | 87 | 28 | 8 | 3 | 23 | 7 | 4 | 1 | 310 |
| | Male | 140 | 25 | 250 | 45 | 36 | 6 | 129 | 23 | 6 | 1 | 561 |
| | Unknown | 5 | 36 | 8 | 57 | 1 | 7 | 0 | 0 | 0 | 0 | 14 |
| | Total | 333 | 38 | 345 | 39 | 45 | 5 | 152 | 17 | 10 | 1 | 885 |
| **Total for all groups** | | 1509 | 27 | 2253 | 41 | 305 | 6 | 899 | 16 | 555 | 10 | 5521 |

*NBC*, nasal bone contour.

## CHARACTER STATES

Photographic exemplars of the different character states of NBC are provided below. Each character state is defined following Hefner (2009, 2016). When necessary to clarify scoring, more nuanced definitions are provided in the figure captions. NBC should be assessed with the protocol provided in the preceding section. Character states include:

NBC 0 = a score of 0 is assigned to NBC exhibiting a low and rounded contour.

NBC 1 = a score of 1 is assigned to NBC exhibiting an oval contour with elongated, high, and rounded lateral walls.

NBC 2 = a score of 2 is assigned to NBC exhibiting steep lateral walls and a broad (approximately 7 mm or more), flat plateau. On the contour gauge, the plateau is identified by a flat cluster of four or more needles.

NBC 3 = a score of 3 is assigned to NBC exhibiting steep-sided lateral walls and a narrow surface plateau.

NBC 4 = a score of 4 is assigned to NBC exhibiting a triangular cross-section and no surface plateau.

## CHARACTER STATES FOR NASAL BONE CONTOUR = 0 (FIGS. 9.2–9.8)

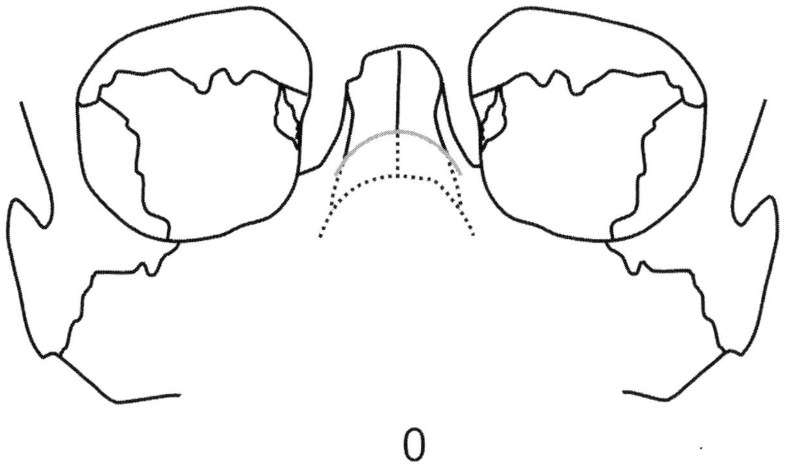


FIGURE 9.2 Diagrammatic representation of NBC 0. Red line indicates the plane of reference. *NBC*, nasal bone contour.

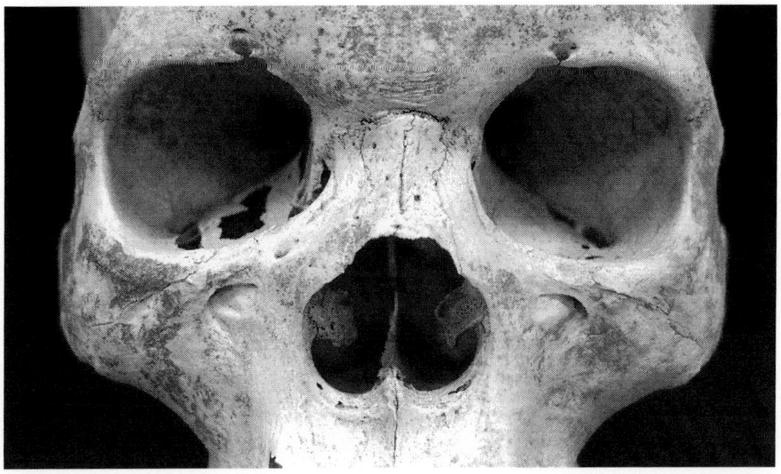

FIGURE 9.3 Variant of NBC 0. *NBC*, nasal bone contour.

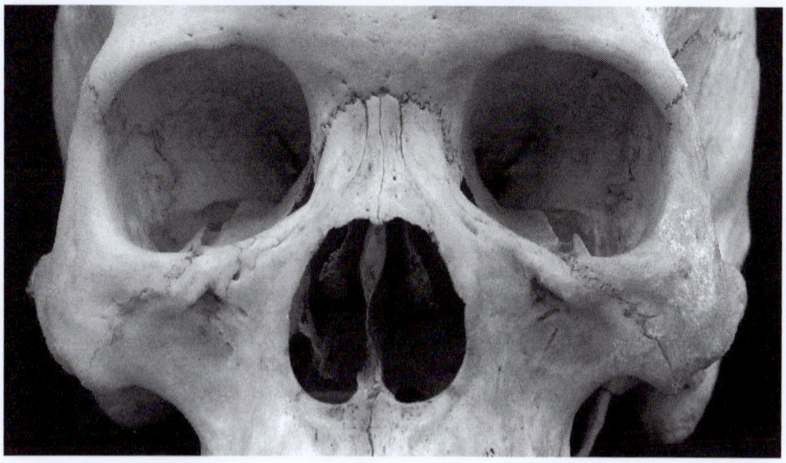

**FIGURE 9.4** Variant of NBC 0. *NBC*, nasal bone contour.

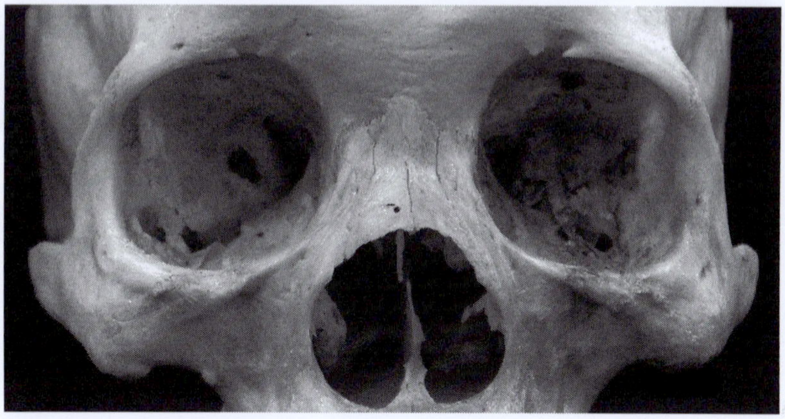

**FIGURE 9.5** Variant of NBC 0. *NBC*, nasal bone contour.

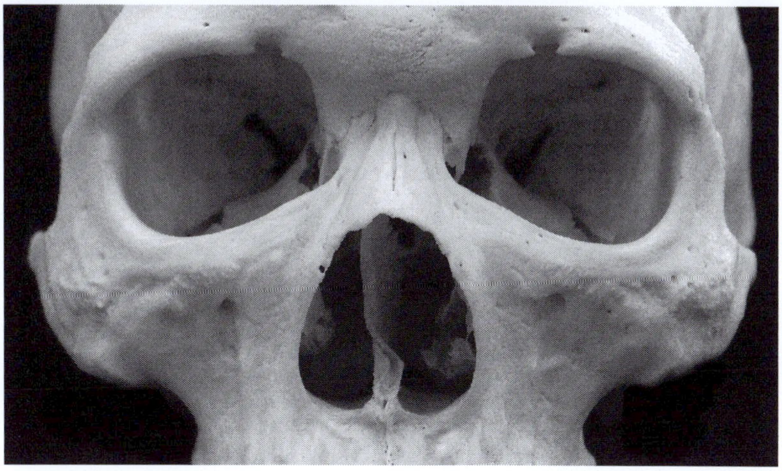

**FIGURE 9.6** Variant of NBC 0. *NBC*, nasal bone contour.

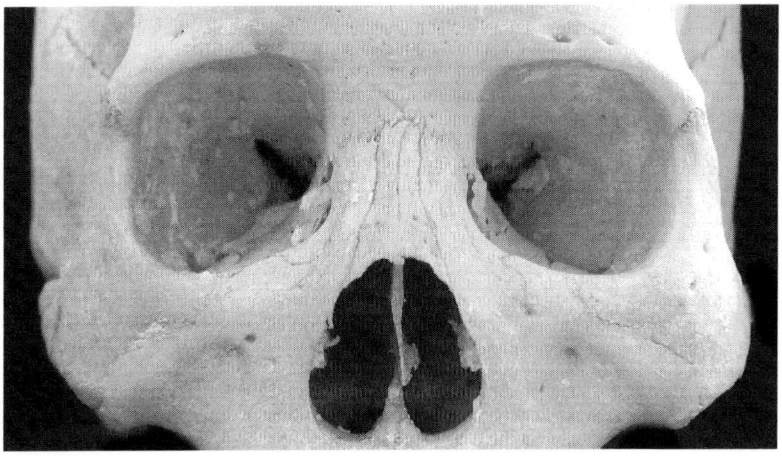

FIGURE 9.7 Variant of NBC 0. *NBC*, nasal bone contour.

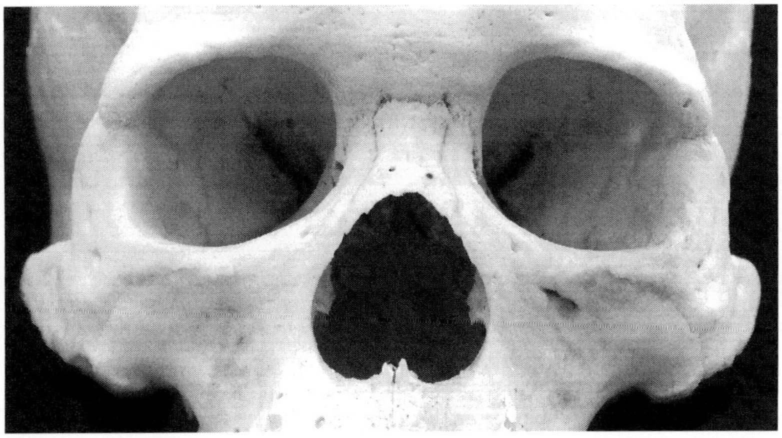

FIGURE 9.8 Variant of NBC 0. *NBC*, nasal bone contour.

# CHARACTER STATES FOR NASAL BONE CONTOUR = 1 (FIGS. 9.9–9.15)

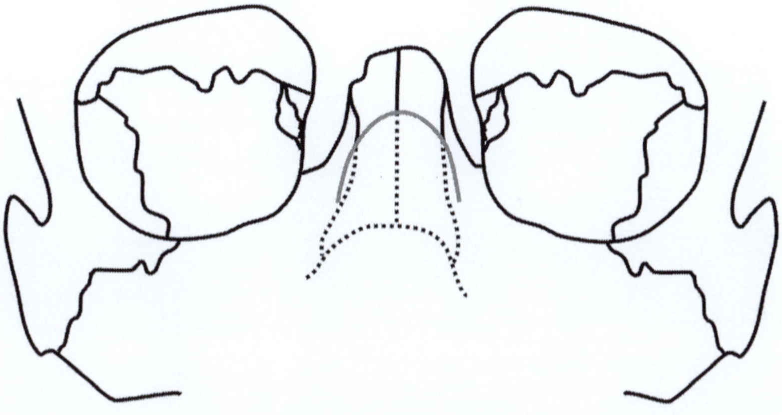


**FIGURE 9.9** Diagrammatic representation of NBC 1. Red line indicates the plane of reference. *NBC*, nasal bone contour.

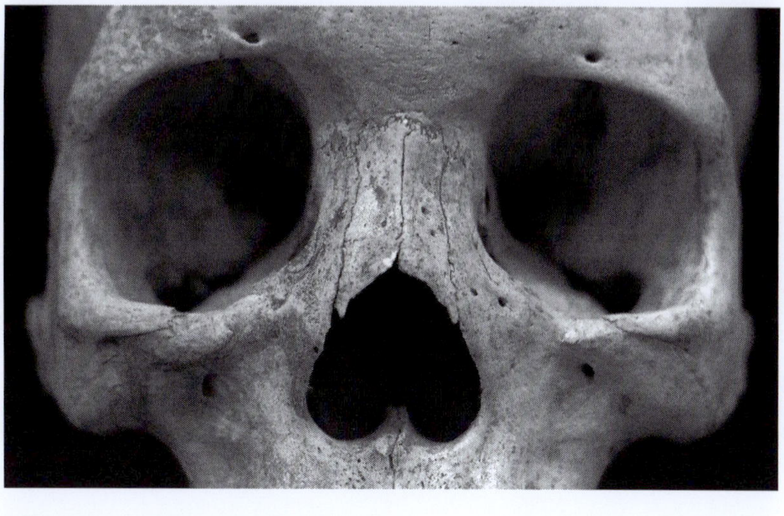

**FIGURE 9.10** Variant of NBC 1. *NBC*, nasal bone contour.

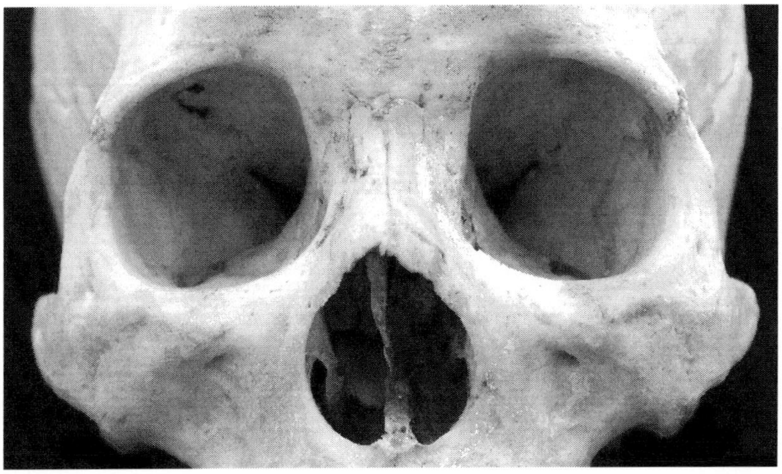

FIGURE 9.11 Variant of NBC 1. *NBC*, nasal bone contour.

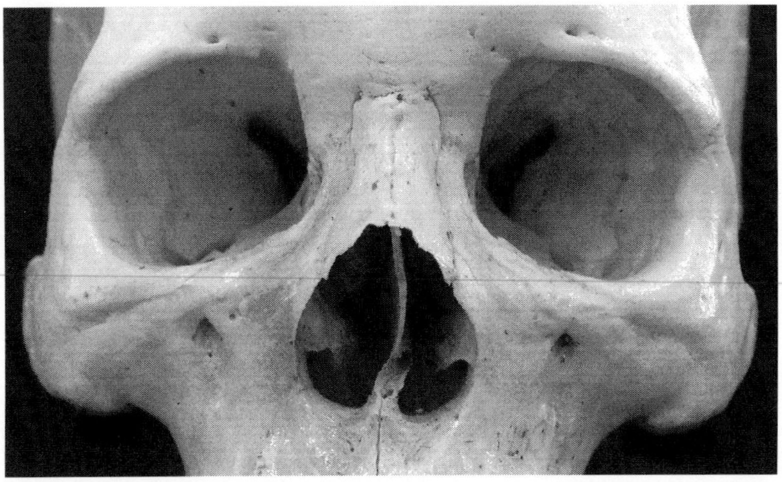

FIGURE 9.12 Variant of NBC 1. *NBC*, nasal bone contour.

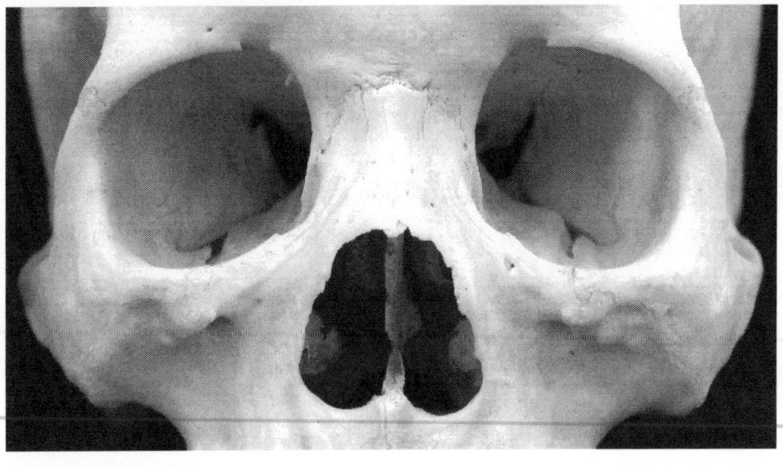

FIGURE 9.13 Variant of NBC 1. *NBC*, nasal bone contour.

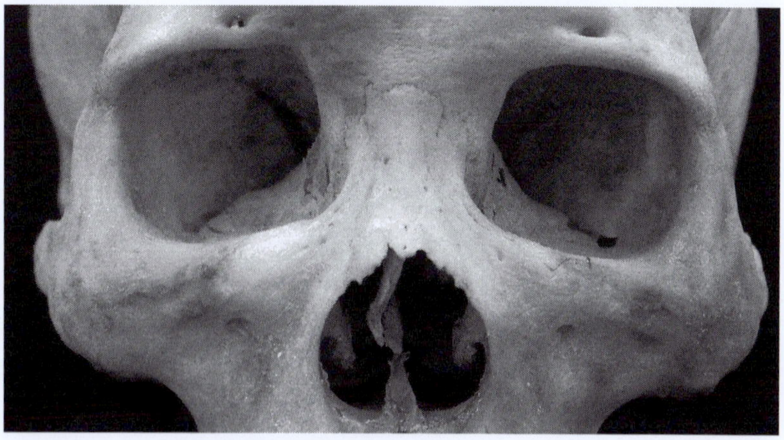

**FIGURE 9.14** Variant of NBC 1. *NBC*, nasal bone contour.

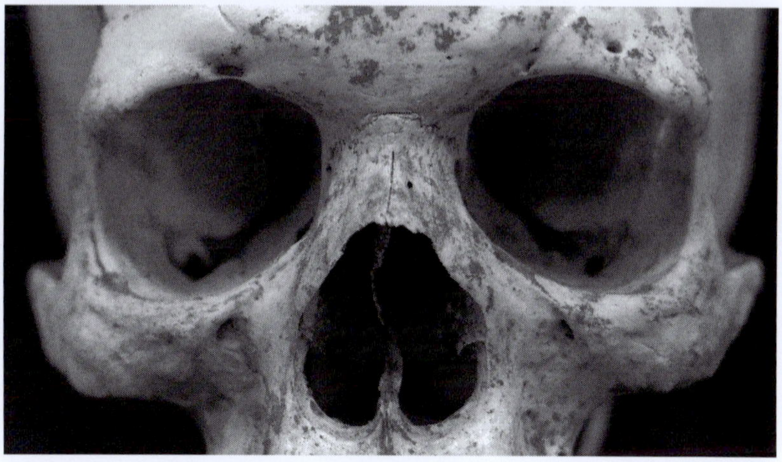

**FIGURE 9.15** Variant of NBC 1. *NBC*, nasal bone contour.

## CHARACTER STATES FOR NASAL BONE CONTOUR = 2 (FIGS. 9.16–9.22)

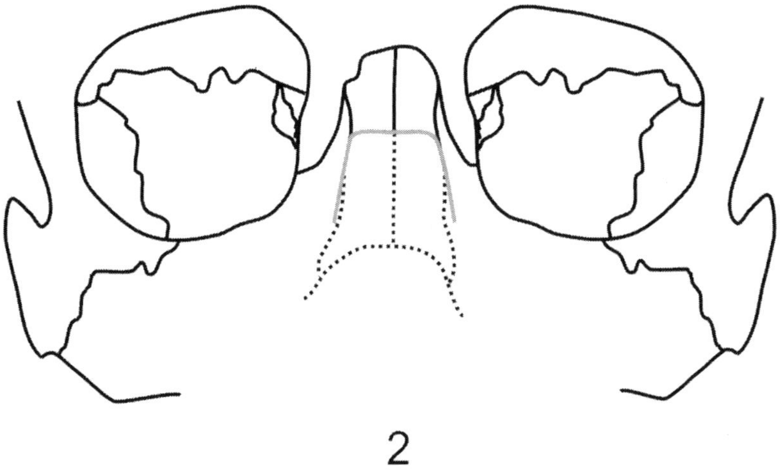


FIGURE 9.16 Diagrammatic representation of NBC 2. Red line indicates the plane of reference. *NBC*, nasal bone contour.

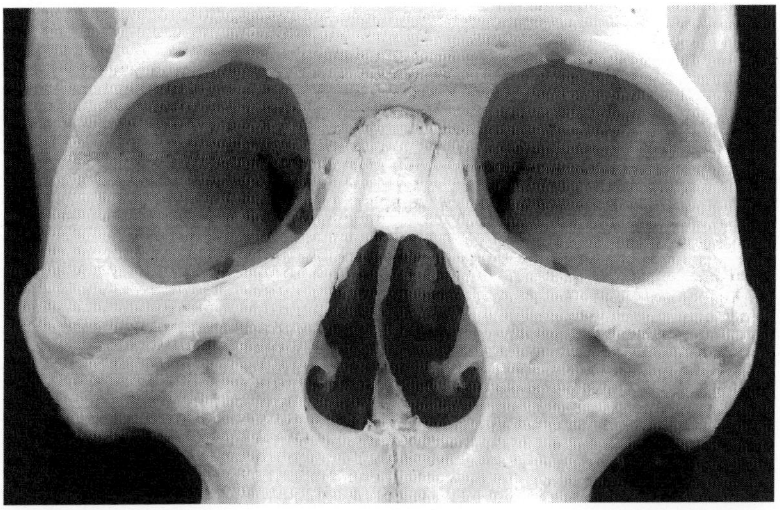

FIGURE 9.17 Variant of NBC 2. *NBC*, nasal bone contour.

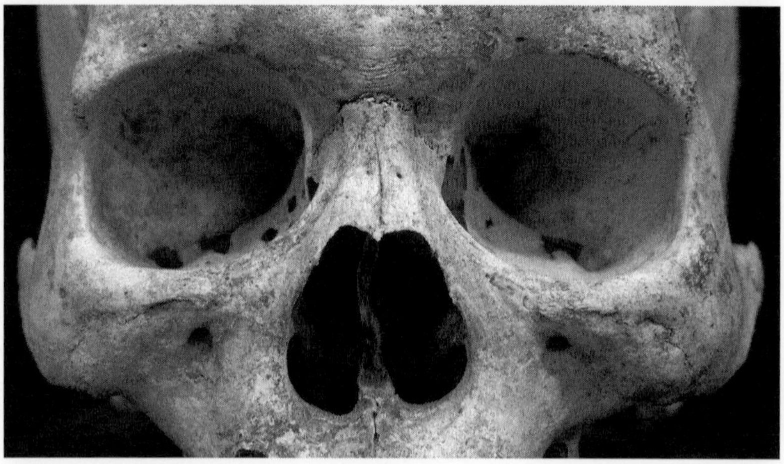

FIGURE 9.18 Variant of NBC 2. *NBC*, nasal bone contour.

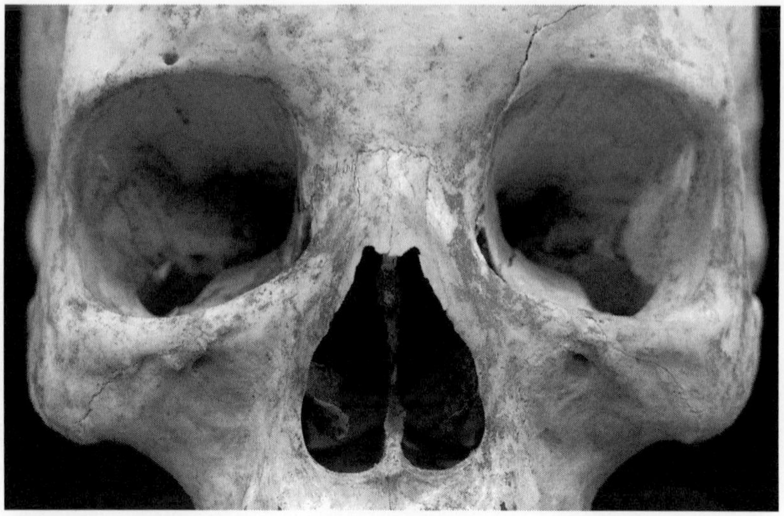

FIGURE 9.19 Variant of NBC 2. *NBC*, nasal bone contour.

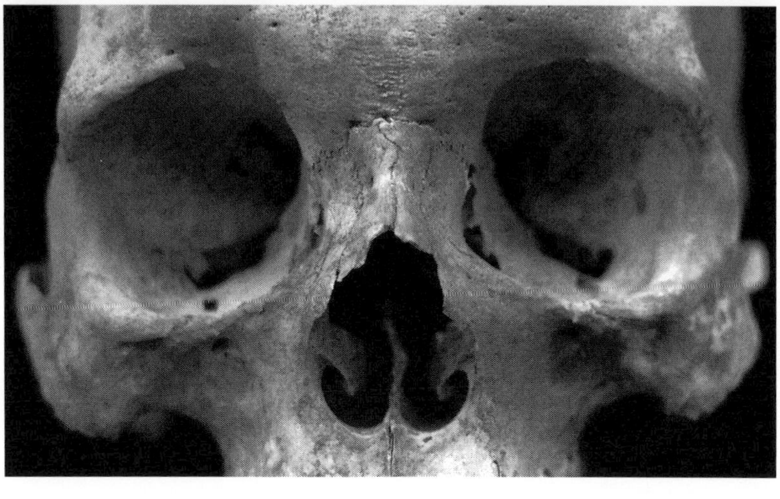

FIGURE 9.20 Variant of NBC 2. *NBC*, nasal bone contour.

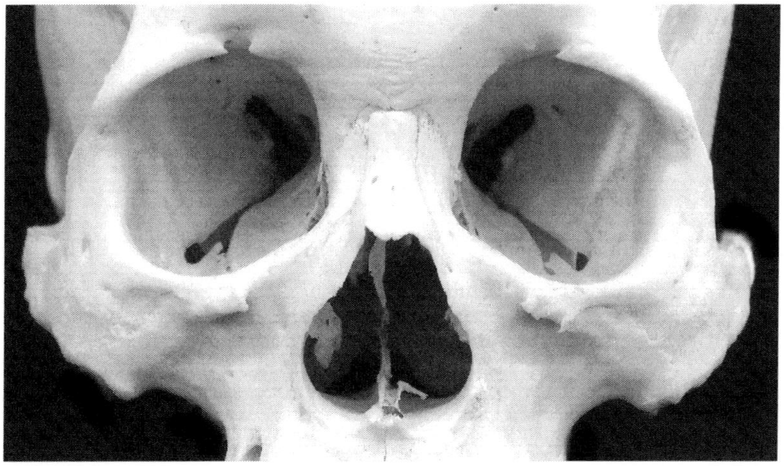

FIGURE 9.21 Variant of NBC 2. *NBC*, nasal bone contour.

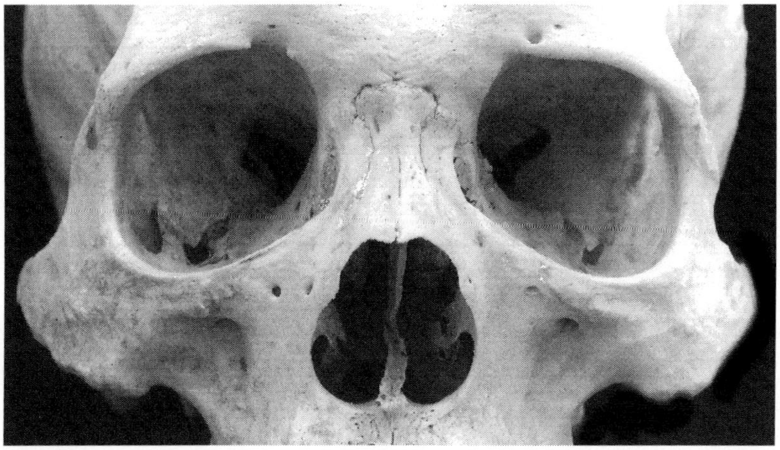

FIGURE 9.22 Variant of NBC 2. *NBC*, nasal bone contour.

## CHARACTER STATES FOR NASAL BONE CONTOUR = 3 (FIGS. 9.23–9.29)

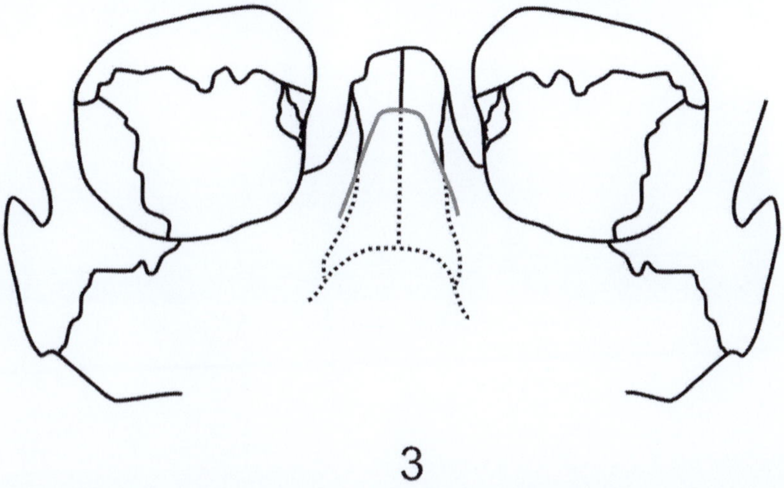


FIGURE 9.23 Diagrammatic representation of NBC 3. Red line indicates the plane of reference. *NBC*, nasal bone contour.

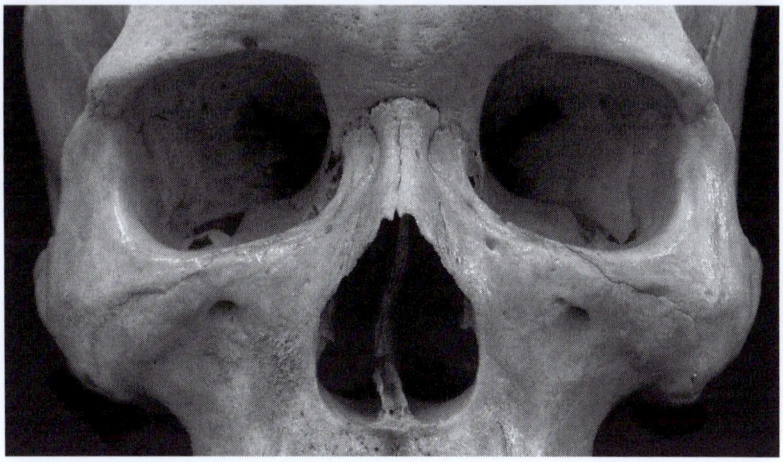

FIGURE 9.24 Variant of NBC 3. *NBC*, nasal bone contour.

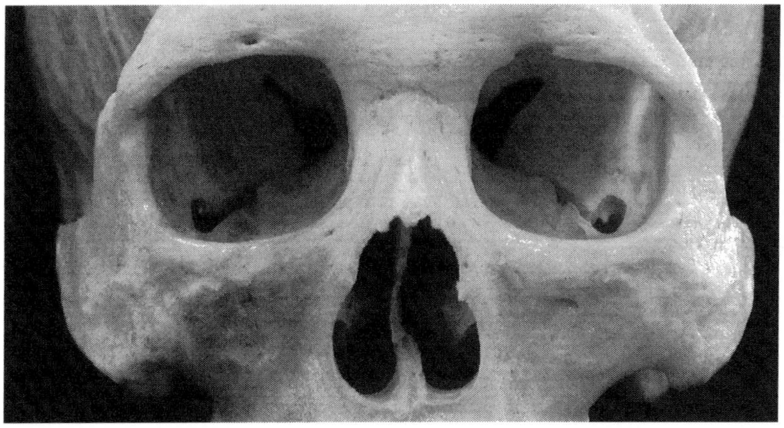

FIGURE 9.25 Variant of NBC 3. *NBC*, nasal bone contour.

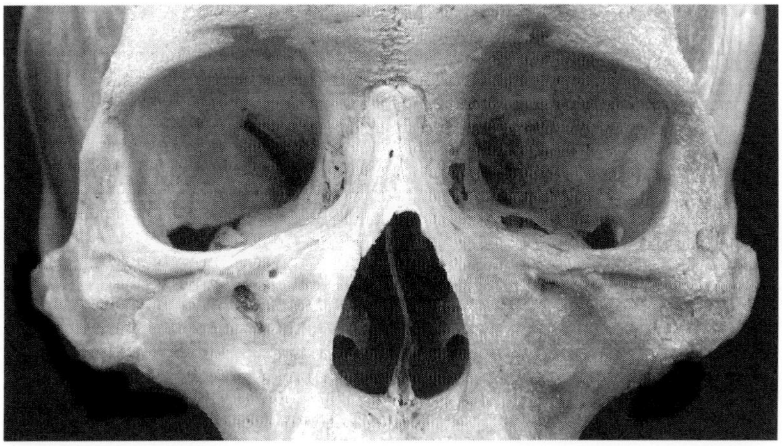

FIGURE 9.26 Variant of NBC 3. *NBC*, nasal bone contour.

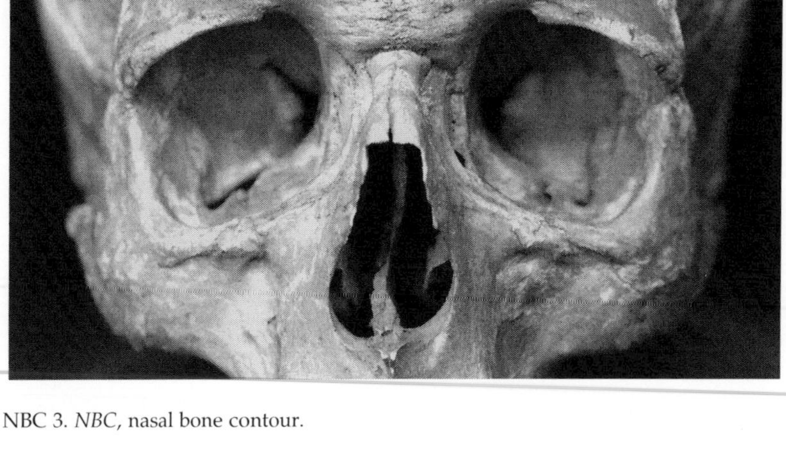

FIGURE 9.27 Variant of NBC 3. *NBC*, nasal bone contour.

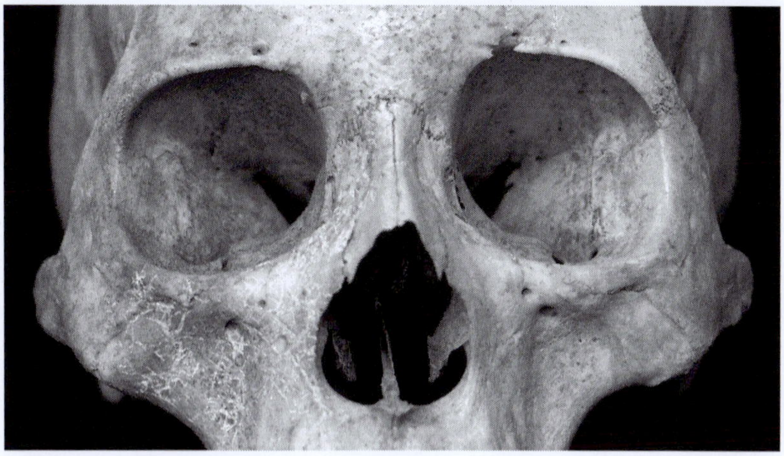

**FIGURE 9.28** Variant of NBC 3. *NBC*, nasal bone contour.

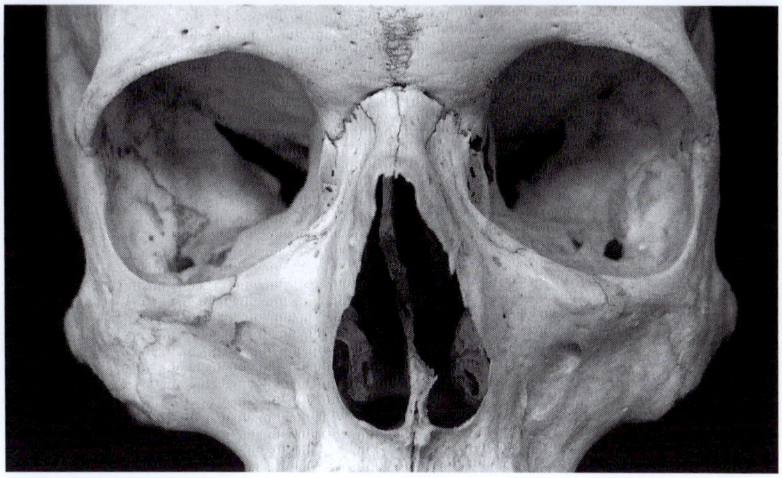

**FIGURE 9.29** Variant of NBC 3. *NBC*, nasal bone contour.

## CHARACTER STATES FOR NASAL BONE CONTOUR = 4 (FIGS. 9.30–9.36)

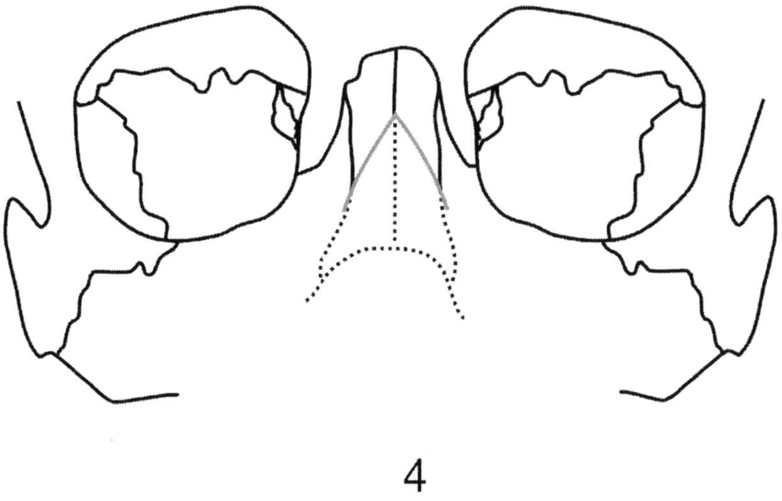


FIGURE 9.30 Diagrammatic representation of NBC 4. Red line indicates the plane of reference. *NBC*, nasal bone contour.

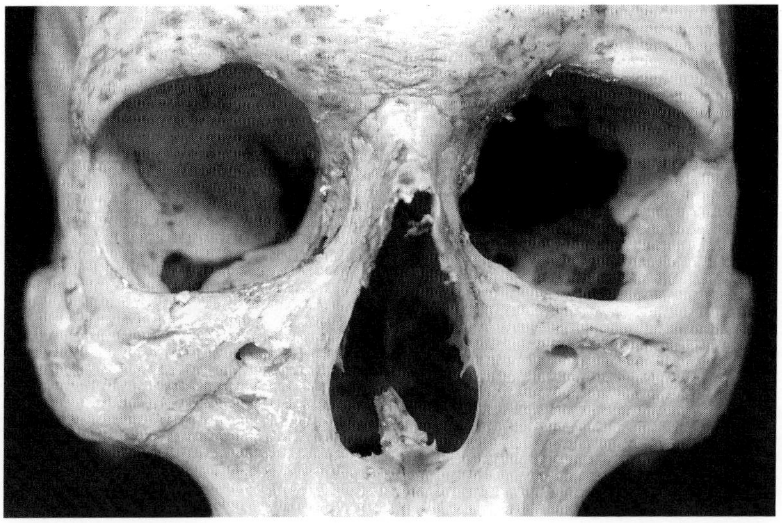

FIGURE 9.31 Variant of NBC 4. *NBC*, nasal bone contour.

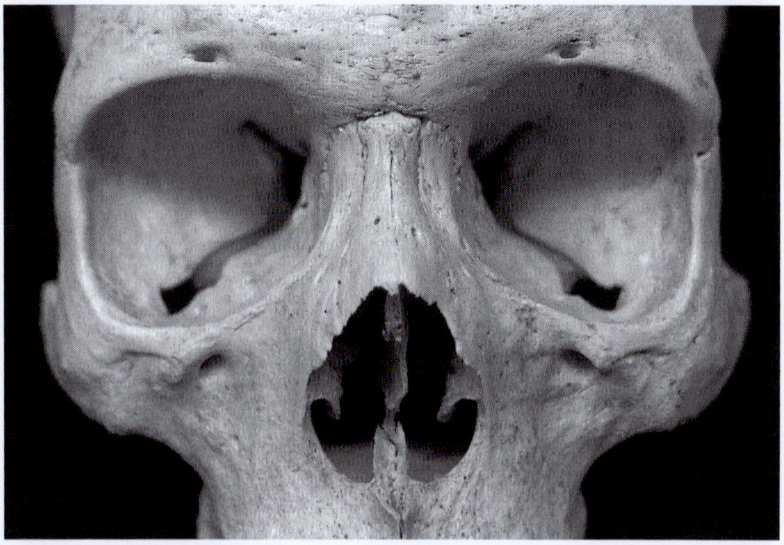

**FIGURE 9.32** Variant of NBC 4. *NBC*, nasal bone contour.

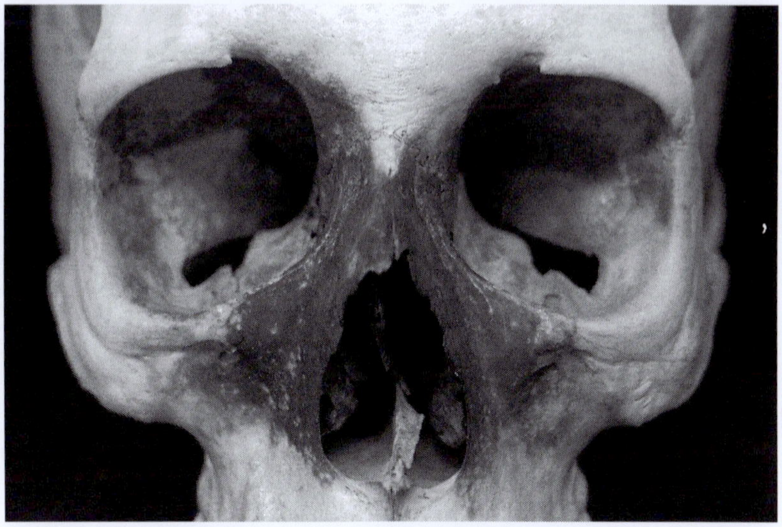

**FIGURE 9.33** Variant of NBC 4. *NBC*, nasal bone contour.

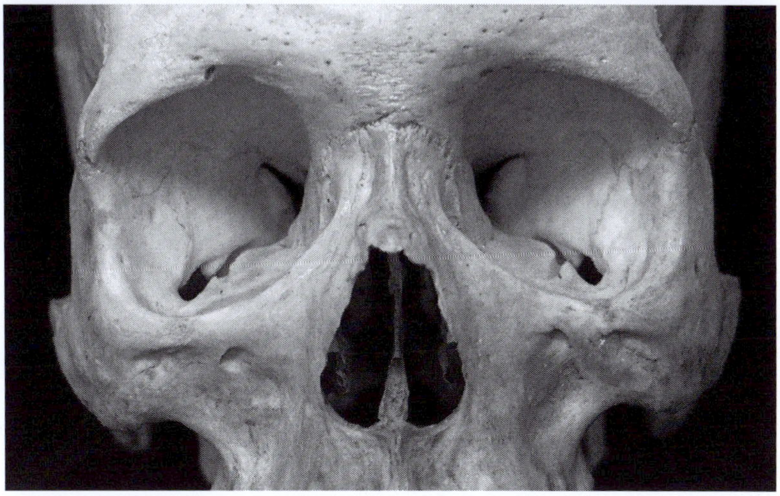

**FIGURE 9.34** Variant of NBC 4. *NBC*, nasal bone contour.

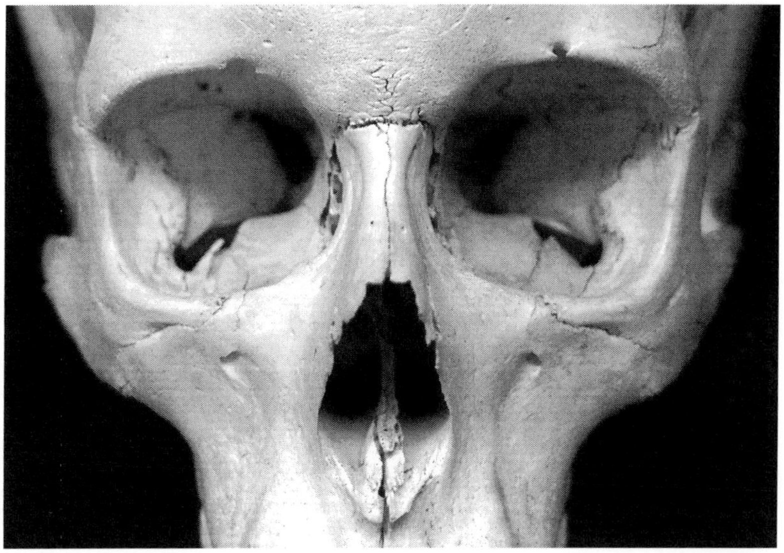

FIGURE 9.35 Variant of NBC 4. *NBC*, nasal bone contour.

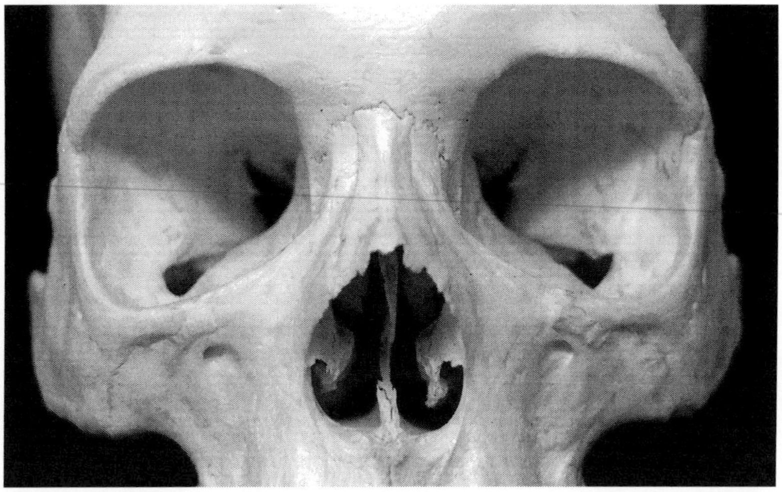

FIGURE 9.36 Variant of NBC 4. *NBC*, nasal bone contour.

CHAPTER

# 10

# Nasal Bone Shape

Nasal bone shape (NBS) is an assessment of the contour of the nasal bones along the lateral borders. This trait is visualized and assessed anteriorly while holding the cranium in approximate anatomical position. In order to make a correct observation, consider the position of the nasal pinch (if present) and the degree of lateral bulging (if present). Observers should not consider the frontonasal suture, the nasal suture, or the symmetry of the nasal bones. NBS comprises four character states—scored as: 1, 2, 3, or 4.

Martin (1928) and Martin and Saller (1957) provide an early description of the NBS. Their illustrations are still used today. In 1928, Martin provided illustrations for the morphologies he felt were most important (Fig. 10.1) and the following description (*translated from the original*—Martin, 1928:943–944):

> [S]ince the widths of the middle and the upper margin of the *ossa nasalia* can combine in many ways, there are very different forms of the nasal bones, of which the most important are provided in Fig. 427. Of these, the broad hourglass shape is large and with lower width ... less common is the ... narrow hourglass shape ...; [the] upturned form Virchow has called *catarrhinia*; Wide nasals with very little difference between the upper and middle projection; [and] ... another one with a lateral extension in the upper corner of the nasal bones called the *processus lateralis* ... The differences in the shape of the nasal bones can also be assessed moderately by a comparison of the smallest and the largest (lower) width expressed.

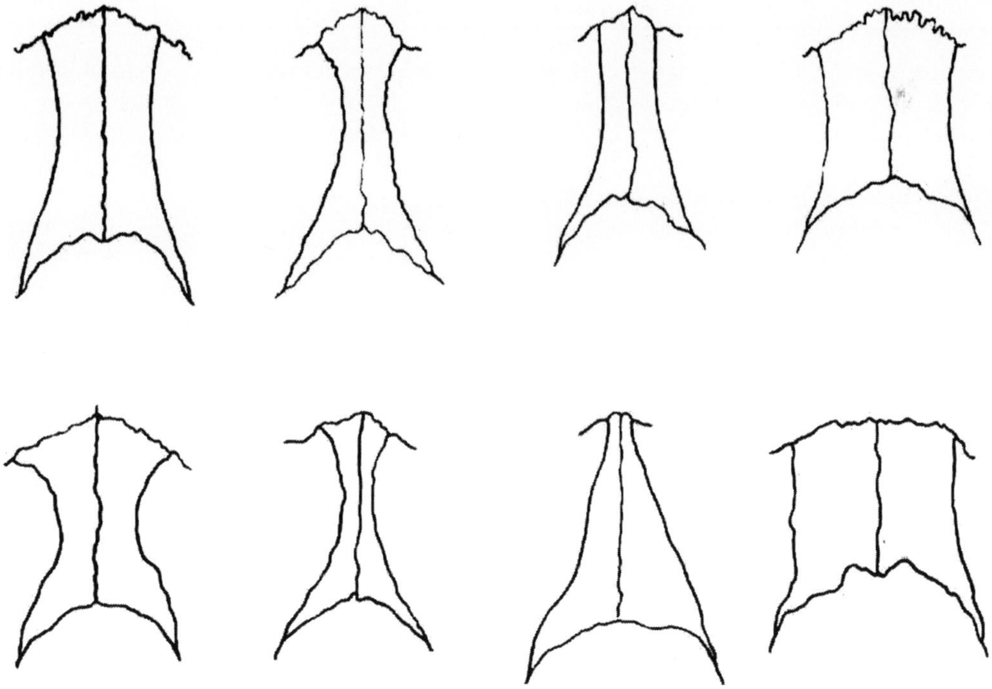

**FIGURE 10.1** Martin and Saller's (1957) illustrations providing the various shapes of the nasal bones.

Atlas of Human Cranial Macromorphoscopic Traits.
DOI: https://doi.org/10.1016/B978-0-12-814385-8.00010-0

DeVilliers (1968) coopted Martin and Saller's (1957) illustrations and definitions to describe the NBS of South Africans. Glanville (1969) observed metric differences in the shape of the nasal region, although his concern was strictly measurement data. Others (some of those mentioned in earlier chapters) deal with the midfacial skeleton and the nasal cavity but do not deal directly with the shape of the nasal bones.

Osteoware (2016:72) includes NBS in the Macromorphoscopic Module, defined as follows: "1 = Nasal bones with no nasal pinch. The nasal bones may be wide or narrow; 2 = Nasal bones with a superior pinch and minimal lateral bulging; 3 = Nasal bones with a superior pinch and pronounced lateral bulging of the inferior region; 4 = Triangular-shaped nasal bones."

## NOMENCLATURE

Nasal bone shape, Nasenbeine beim menschen, *os nasi figura*, and *ossa nasali*.

## GROSS ANATOMY

The nasal bones are two small, symmetrical oblong bones, each having two surfaces and four borders. Positioned in the midface, at their junction they form the bridge of the nose superiorly and anchor the upper lateral nasal cartilages inferiorly. The external surface of each nasal bone is covered by the *procerus* and *nasalis muscles*, and each is perforated near the center by a foramen transmitting a small venous complex. The internal surface is transversely concave and contains a groove for the anterior ethmoidal nerve. Each nasal bone articulates with the frontal, ethmoid, opposite nasal, and maxilla. Nasal fractures are common—the most common facial fracture (Wedel and Galloway, 2014)—and usually, a result of blunt force trauma to the nose.

## GROWTH AND DEVELOPMENT

The nasal region undergoes two phases during ontogenesis: the embryonic developmental phase and the growth phase. During embryological development (covered in detail in Chapters 7 and 8), the nose and related skeletal structures are formed. This phase lasts from approximately the third week to three months postconception, during that time the nasal structures (the nasal placode, maxillary and mandibular processes) develop. During the growth phase, which lasts throughout puberty, changes to the various anatomical structures of the nose and an overall increase in size occurs. Around fetal week nine to ten, intramembranous ossification centers appear for each nasal bone (Scheuer and Black, 2000), ossifying from a single center within the cartilaginous nasal capsule. At birth, the nasal bones have a decidedly adult appearance, although the full adult manifestation does not occur until puberty (Scheuer and Black, 2000). Clinical manifestations of nasal bone dysplasia may be assessed as early as the 12th-week. Adult manifestations of dysplasia may present with unilateral or bilateral hypoplastic or aplastic nasals (Barnes, 1994).

## FUNCTIONAL MORPHOLOGY

Making up the superior roof of the nasal cavity and anchoring the nasal cartilages, the nasal bones are vital to olfaction and respiration (see Chapters 7 and 8, *Functional Morphology*, for a more detailed exploration of these aspects). Enlow (1990) describes an additional functional component of the nasal bones and associated cartilages in olfaction. The reduced human face resulting from orbital convergence that occurred during hominid evolution required a concomitant reduction of the maxillary complex. The protruding, fleshy human nose and associated skeletal structures direct the nares inferiorly, which then guides inhaled air upward into the nasal cavity to the awaiting sensory nerves of the olfactory bulb.

# WITHIN POPULATION VARIATION

Data derived from the Macromorphoscopic Databank of the frequency distribution of NBS ($n = 3844$). All data are for adult individuals. When possible, frequency data for males and females are provided separately. When sex could not be estimated reliably, frequency distributions are pooled as "Unknown" (Table 10.1).

**TABLE 10.1** Frequency Distribution of NBS, by Geographic Origin and Sex

| | | 1 | | 2 | | 3 | | 4 | | |
|---|---|---|---|---|---|---|---|---|---|---|
| **Geographic origin** | **Sex** | *n* | % | *n* | % | *n* | % | *n* | % | **Total** |
| **African** | **Female** | 0 | 0 | 0 | 0 | 0 | 0 | 0 | 0 | 0 |
| | **Male** | 0 | 0 | 0 | 0 | 0 | 0 | 0 | 0 | 0 |
| | **Unknown** | 0 | 0 | 0 | 0 | 0 | 0 | 0 | 0 | 0 |
| | **Total** | 0 | 0 | 0 | 0 | 0 | 0 | 0 | 0 | 0 |
| **American Black** | **Female** | 3 | 20 | 7 | 47 | 5 | 33 | 0 | 0 | 15 |
| | **Male** | 17 | 33 | 17 | 33 | 10 | 20 | 7 | 14 | 51 |
| | **Unknown** | 0 | 0 | 0 | 0 | 1 | 100 | 0 | 0 | 1 |
| | **Total** | 20 | 30 | 24 | 36 | 16 | 24 | 7 | 10 | 67 |
| **American White** | **Female** | 32 | 29 | 62 | 55 | 16 | 14 | 2 | 2 | 112 |
| | **Male** | 51 | 29 | 73 | 41 | 47 | 27 | 5 | 3 | 176 |
| | **Unknown** | 0 | 0 | 0 | 0 | 0 | 0 | 0 | 0 | 0 |
| | **Total** | 83 | 29 | 135 | 47 | 63 | 22 | 7 | 2 | 288 |
| **Amerindian** | **Female** | 0 | 0 | 0 | 0 | 0 | 0 | 0 | 0 | 0 |
| | **Male** | 0 | 0 | 0 | 0 | 0 | 0 | 0 | 0 | 0 |
| | **Unknown** | 169 | 9 | 1332 | 73 | 301 | 16 | 33 | 2 | 1835 |
| | **Total** | 169 | 9 | 1332 | 73 | 301 | 16 | 33 | 2 | 1835 |
| **Chinese** | **Female** | 0 | 0 | 0 | 0 | 0 | 0 | 0 | 0 | 0 |
| | **Male** | 0 | 0 | 0 | 0 | 0 | 0 | 0 | 0 | 0 |
| | **Unknown** | 0 | 0 | 0 | 0 | 0 | 0 | 0 | 0 | 0 |
| | **Total** | 0 | 0 | 0 | 0 | 0 | 0 | 0 | 0 | 0 |
| **Colombian** | **Female** | 0 | 0 | 0 | 0 | 0 | 0 | 0 | 0 | 0 |
| | **Male** | 0 | 0 | 0 | 0 | 0 | 0 | 0 | 0 | 0 |
| | **Unknown** | 0 | 0 | 0 | 0 | 0 | 0 | 0 | 0 | 0 |
| | **Total** | 0 | 0 | 0 | 0 | 0 | 0 | 0 | 0 | 0 |
| **El Salvador** | **Female** | 0 | 0 | 0 | 0 | 0 | 0 | 0 | 0 | 0 |
| | **Male** | 0 | 0 | 3 | 60 | 2 | 40 | 0 | 0 | 5 |
| | **Unknown** | 0 | 0 | 0 | 0 | 0 | 0 | 0 | 0 | 0 |
| | **Total** | 0 | 0 | 3 | 60 | 2 | 40 | 0 | 0 | 5 |
| **Eskimo** | **Female** | 0 | 0 | 0 | 0 | 0 | 0 | 0 | 0 | 0 |
| | **Male** | 0 | 0 | 0 | 0 | 0 | 0 | 0 | 0 | 0 |
| | **Unknown** | 65 | 10 | 465 | 69 | 45 | 7 | 98 | 15 | 673 |
| | **Total** | 65 | 10 | 465 | 69 | 45 | 7 | 98 | 15 | 673 |

*(Continued)*

TABLE 10.1 (*Continued*)

| | | 1 | | 2 | | 3 | | 4 | | |
|---|---|---|---|---|---|---|---|---|---|---|
| **Geographic origin** | **Sex** | *n* | % | *n* | % | *n* | % | *n* | % | **Total** |
| **European** | **Female** | 0 | 0 | 0 | 0 | 0 | 0 | 0 | 0 | 0 |
| | **Male** | 0 | 0 | 0 | 0 | 0 | 0 | 0 | 0 | 0 |
| | **Unknown** | 0 | 0 | 0 | 0 | 0 | 0 | 0 | 0 | 0 |
| | **Total** | 0 | 0 | 0 | 0 | 0 | 0 | 0 | 0 | 0 |
| **Guatemalan** | **Female** | 0 | 0 | 1 | 50 | 0 | 0 | 1 | 50 | 2 |
| | **Male** | 0 | 0 | 1 | 100 | 0 | 0 | 0 | 0 | 1 |
| | **Unknown** | 0 | 0 | 0 | 0 | 0 | 0 | 0 | 0 | 0 |
| | **Total** | 0 | 0 | 2 | 67 | 0 | 0 | 1 | 33 | 3 |
| **Japanese** | **Female** | 0 | 0 | 0 | 0 | 0 | 0 | 0 | 0 | 0 |
| | **Male** | 0 | 0 | 0 | 0 | 0 | 0 | 0 | 0 | 0 |
| | **Unknown** | 0 | 0 | 0 | 0 | 0 | 0 | 0 | 0 | 0 |
| | **Total** | 0 | 0 | 0 | 0 | 0 | 0 | 0 | 0 | 0 |
| **Mexico** | **Female** | 0 | 0 | 0 | 0 | 0 | 0 | 0 | 0 | 0 |
| | **Male** | 4 | 22 | 10 | 56 | 4 | 22 | 0 | 0 | 18 |
| | **Unknown** | 0 | 0 | 0 | 0 | 0 | 0 | 0 | 0 | 0 |
| | **Total** | 4 | 22 | 10 | 56 | 4 | 22 | 0 | 0 | 18 |
| **Pacific Island** | **Female** | 2 | 4 | 36 | 72 | 10 | 20 | 2 | 4 | 50 |
| | **Male** | 1 | 1 | 43 | 52 | 34 | 41 | 4 | 5 | 82 |
| | **Unknown** | 5 | 6 | 52 | 64 | 16 | 20 | 8 | 10 | 81 |
| | **Total** | 8 | 4 | 131 | 62 | 60 | 28 | 14 | 7 | 213 |
| **Peruvian** | **Female** | 0 | 0 | 0 | 0 | 0 | 0 | 0 | 0 | 0 |
| | **Male** | 0 | 0 | 0 | 0 | 0 | 0 | 0 | 0 | 0 |
| | **Unknown** | 2 | 11 | 10 | 53 | 6 | 32 | 1 | 5 | 19 |
| | **Total** | 2 | 11 | 10 | 53 | 6 | 32 | 1 | 5 | 19 |
| **Southwest (SW) Hispanic** | **Female** | 0 | 0 | 7 | 100 | 0 | 0 | 0 | 0 | 7 |
| | **Male** | 2 | 20 | 6 | 60 | 2 | 20 | 0 | 0 | 10 |
| | **Unknown** | 0 | 0 | 0 | 0 | 0 | 0 | 0 | 0 | 0 |
| | **Total** | 2 | 12 | 13 | 76 | 2 | 12 | 0 | 0 | 17 |
| **Thai** | **Female** | 11 | 5 | 143 | 66 | 49 | 22 | 15 | 7 | 218 |
| | **Male** | 31 | 7 | 330 | 70 | 79 | 17 | 34 | 7 | 474 |
| | **Unknown** | 5 | 36 | 5 | 36 | 2 | 14 | 2 | 14 | 14 |
| | **Total** | 47 | 7 | 478 | 68 | 130 | 18 | 51 | 7 | 706 |
| **Total for all groups** | | 400 | 10 | 2603 | 68 | 629 | 16 | 212 | 6 | 3844 |

*NBS*, nasal bone shape.

# CHARACTER STATES

Photographic exemplars of the different character states of NBS are provided below. Each character state is defined following Hefner (2009, 2016). When necessary to clarify scoring, more nuanced definitions are provided in the figure captions. NBS should be assessed with the protocol provided in the preceding section. Character states include:

NBS 1 = the lateral edges of the nasal bones are not pinched and may be wide or narrow.
NBS 2 = the nasal bones exhibit a superior pinch and only minimum bulging along the lateral edges.
NBS 3 = the nasal bones exhibit a superior pinch and pronounced lateral bulging along the inferior margin.
NBS 4 = the lateral edges of the nasal bones form a triangle.

## CHARACTER STATES FOR NASAL BONE SHAPE = 1 (FIGS. 10.2–10.8)

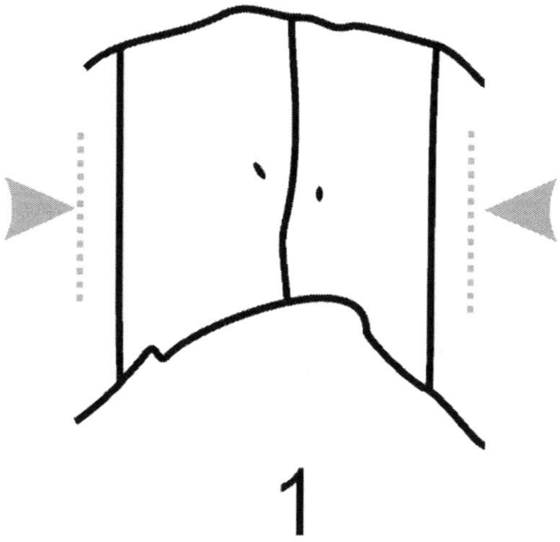


FIGURE 10.2 Diagrammatic representation of NBS 1. *NBS*, nasal bone shape.

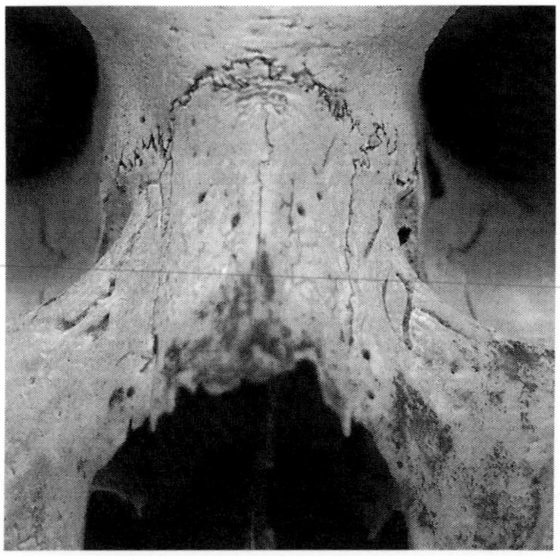

FIGURE 10.3 Variant of NBS 1. *NBS*, nasal bone shape.

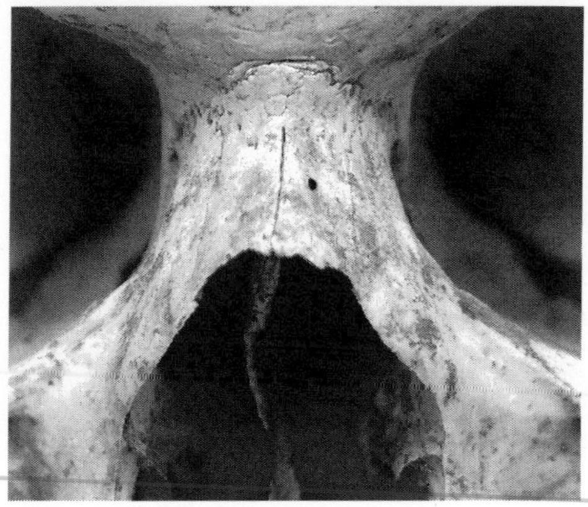

FIGURE 10.4 Variant of NBS 1. *NBS*, nasal bone shape.

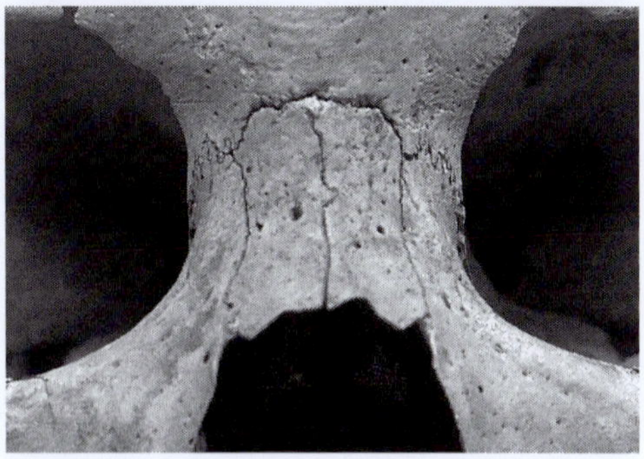

**FIGURE 10.5** Variant of NBS 1. *NBS*, nasal bone shape.

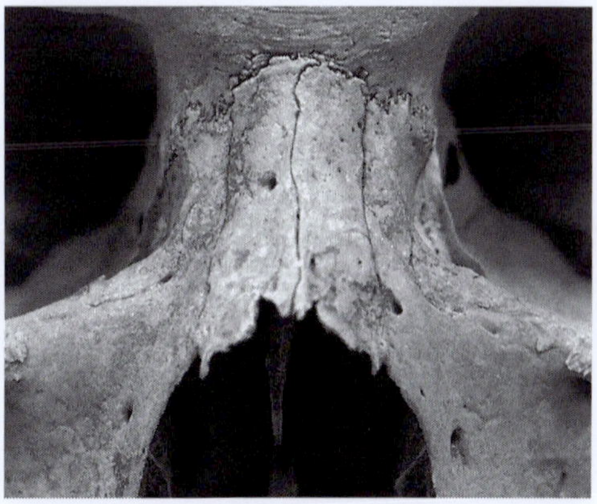

**FIGURE 10.6** Variant of NBS 1. *NBS*, nasal bone shape.

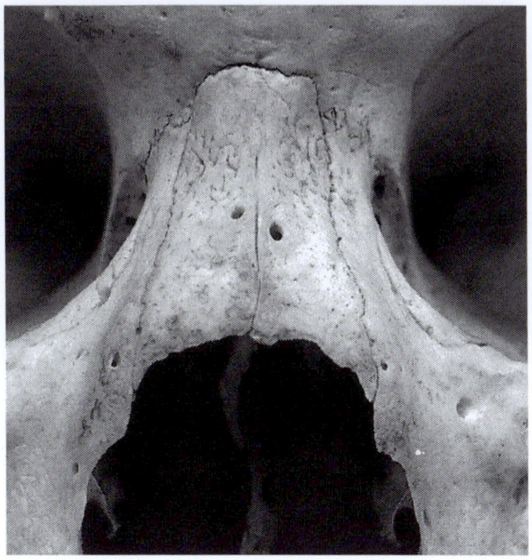

**FIGURE 10.7** Variant of NBS 1. *NBS*, nasal bone shape.

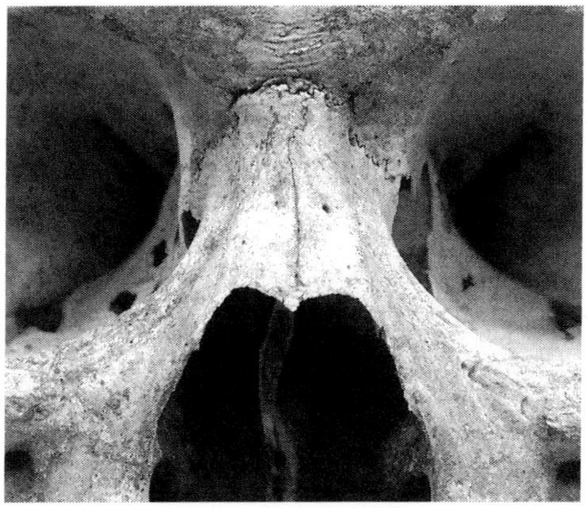

FIGURE 10.8 Variant of NBS 1. *NBS*, nasal bone shape.

# CHARACTER STATES FOR NASAL BONE SHAPE = 2 (FIGS. 10.9–10.15)

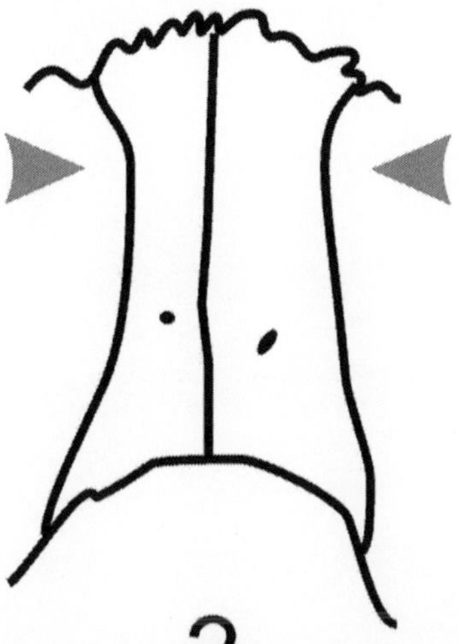


FIGURE 10.9 Diagrammatic representation of NBS 2. *NBS*, nasal bone shape.

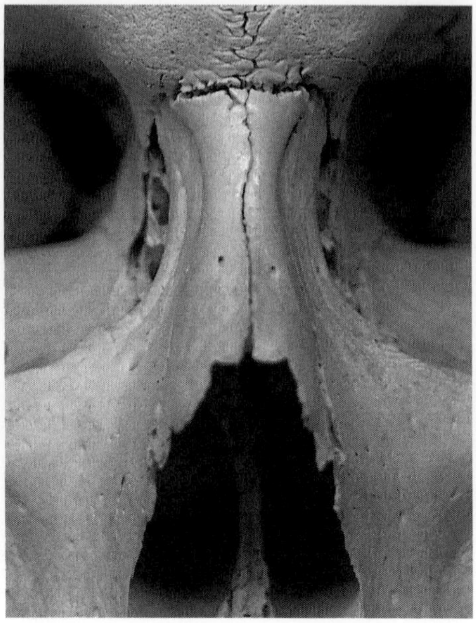

FIGURE 10.10 Variant of NBS 2. *NBS*, nasal bone shape.

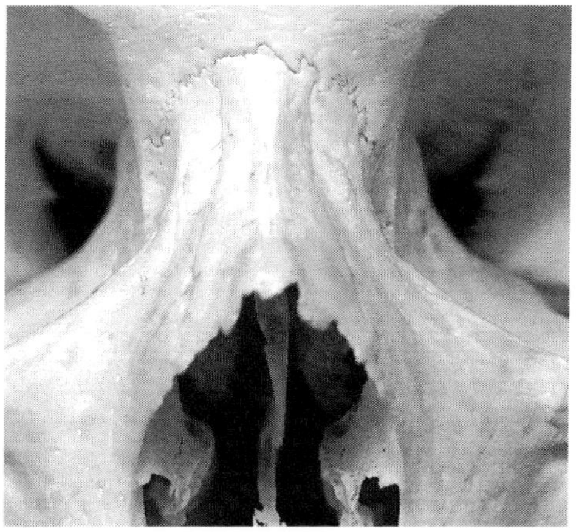

FIGURE 10.11 Variant of NBS 2. *NBS*, nasal bone shape.

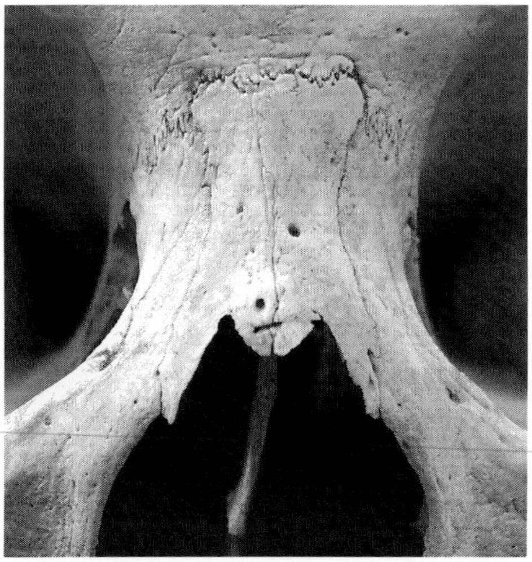

FIGURE 10.12 Variant of NBS 2. *NBS*, nasal bone shape.

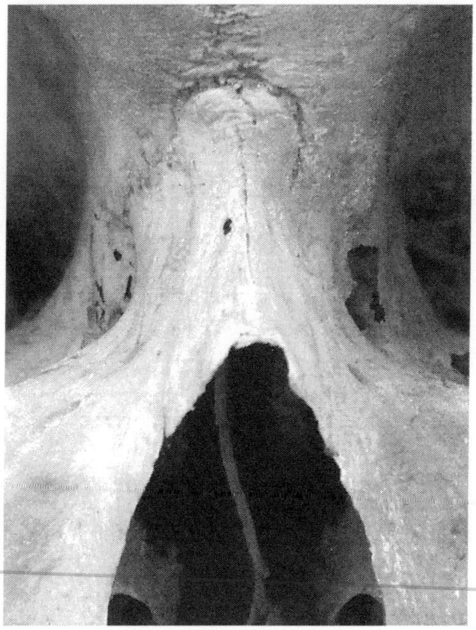

FIGURE 10.13 Variant of NBS 2. *NBS*, nasal bone shape.

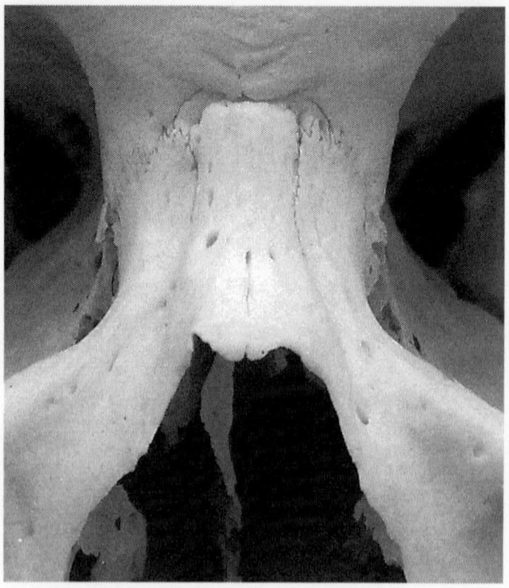

**FIGURE 10.14** Variant of NBS 2. *NBS*, nasal bone shape.

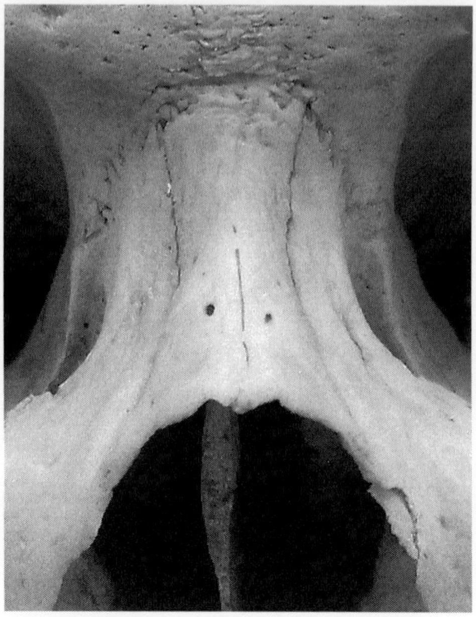

**FIGURE 10.15** Variant of NBS 2. *NBS*, nasal bone shape.

## CHARACTER STATES FOR NASAL BONE SHAPE = 3 (FIGS. 10.16–10.22)

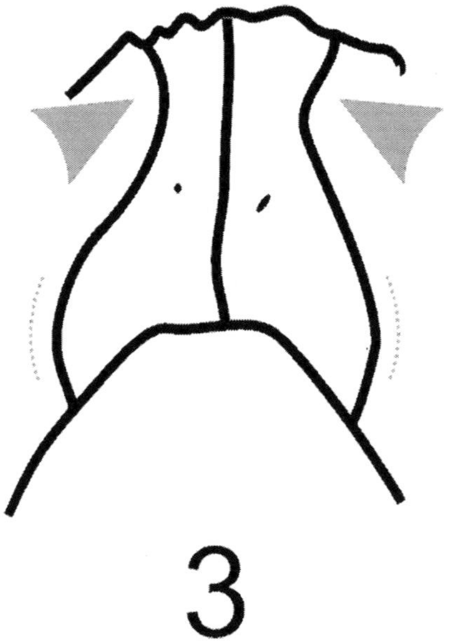


FIGURE 10.16 Diagrammatic representation of NBS 3. *NBS*, nasal bone shape.

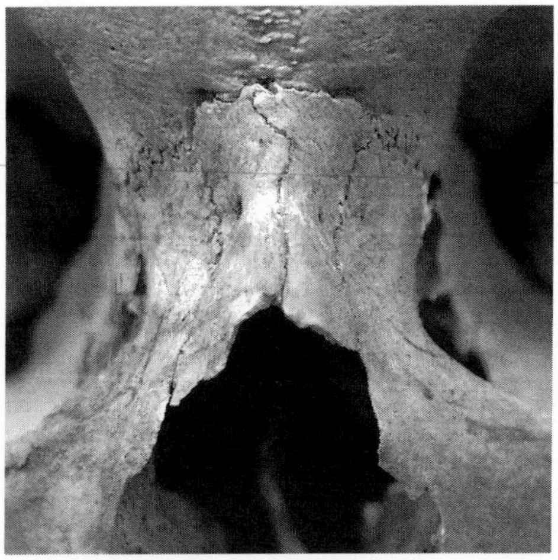

FIGURE 10.17 Variant of NBS 3. *NBS*, nasal bone shape.

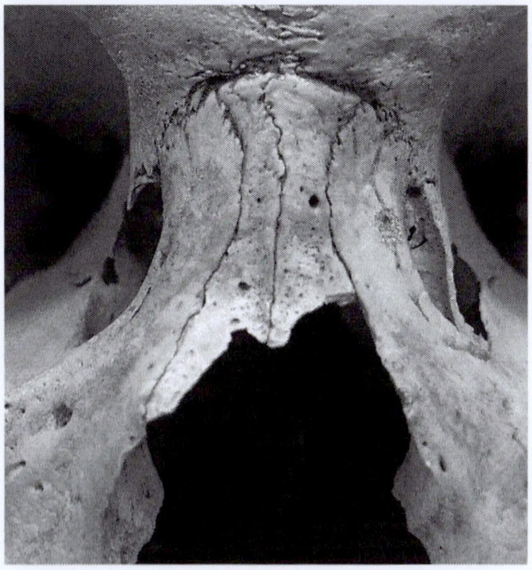

FIGURE 10.18 Variant of NBS 3. *NBS*, nasal bone shape.

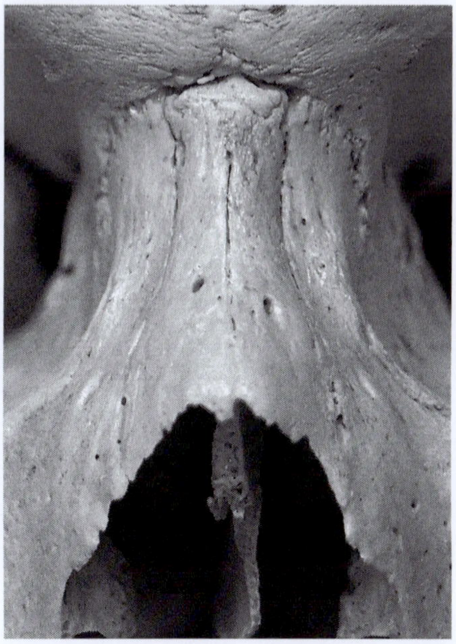

FIGURE 10.19 Variant of NBS 3. *NBS*, nasal bone shape.

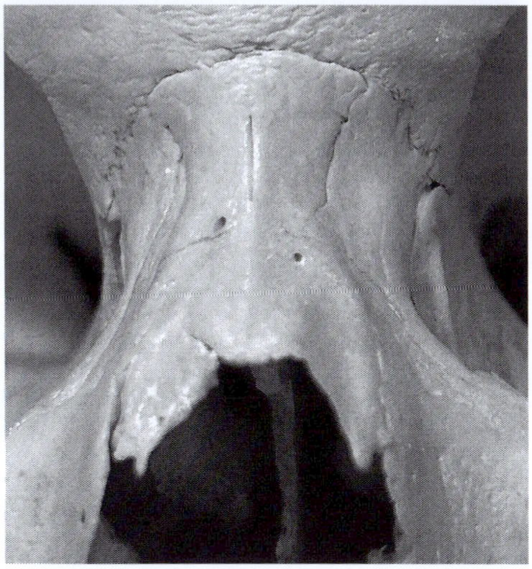

FIGURE 10.20 Variant of NBS 3. *NBS*, nasal bone shape.

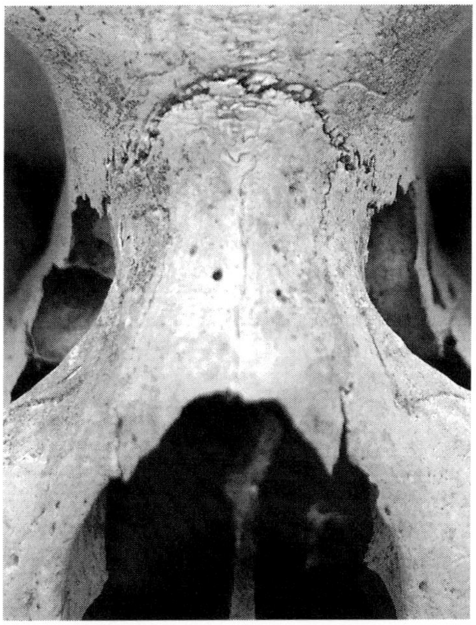

FIGURE 10.21 Variant of NBS 3. *NBS*, nasal bone shape.

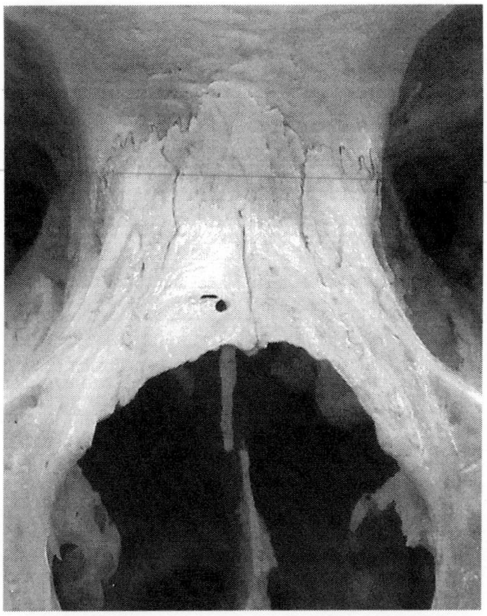

FIGURE 10.22 Variant of NBS 3. *NBS*, nasal bone shape.

## CHARACTER STATES FOR NASAL BONE SHAPE = 4 (FIGS. 10.23–10.29)

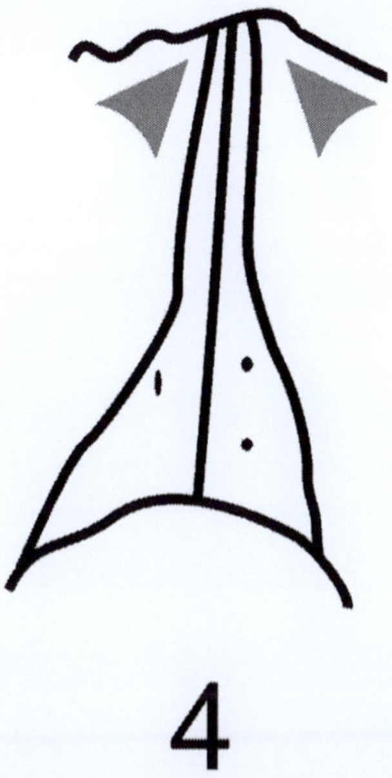


FIGURE 10.23 Diagrammatic representation of NBS 4. *NBS*, nasal bone shape.

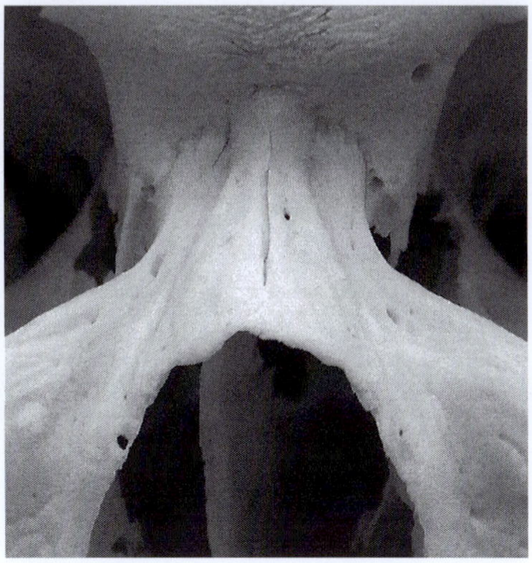

FIGURE 10.24 Variant of NBS 4. *NBS*, nasal bone shape.

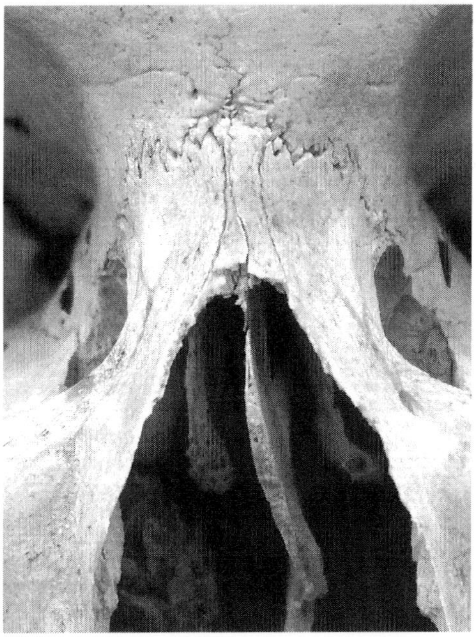

**FIGURE 10.25** Variant of NBS 4. *NBS*, nasal bone shape.

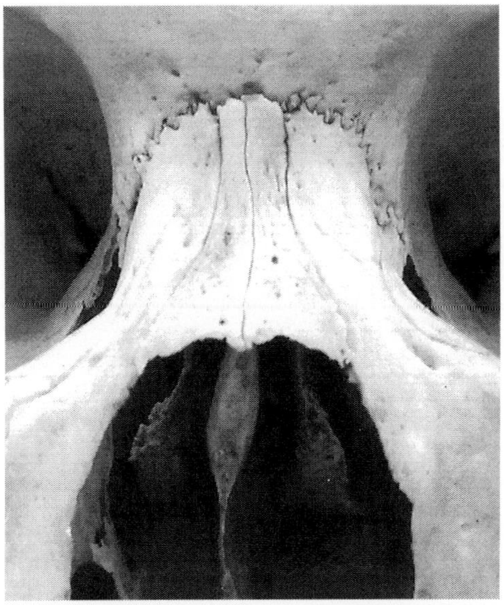

**FIGURE 10.26** Variant of NBS 4. *NBS*, nasal bone shape.

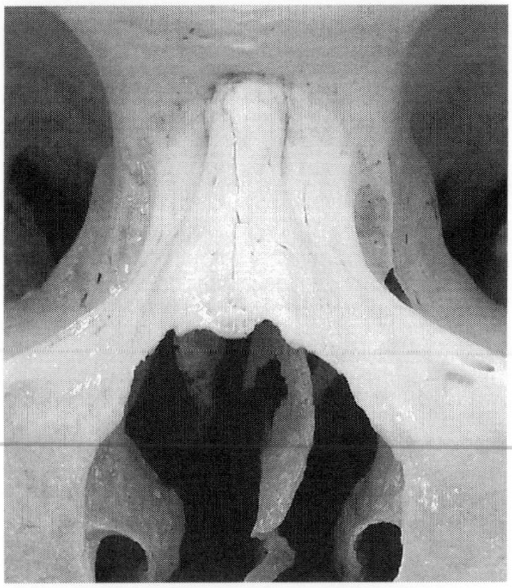

**FIGURE 10.27** Variant of NBS 4. *NBS*, nasal bone shape.

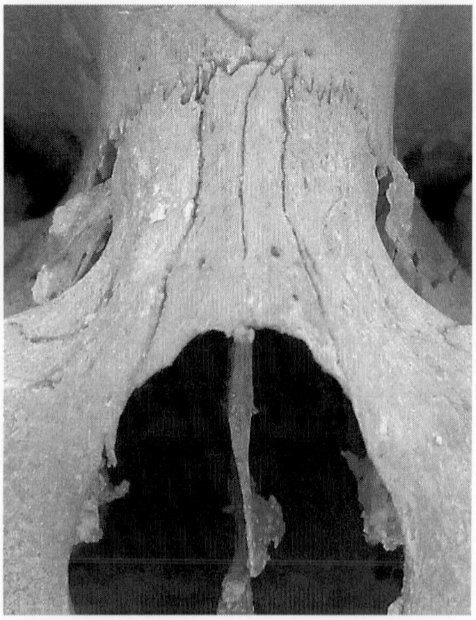

FIGURE 10.28 Variant of NBS 4. *NBS*, nasal bone shape.

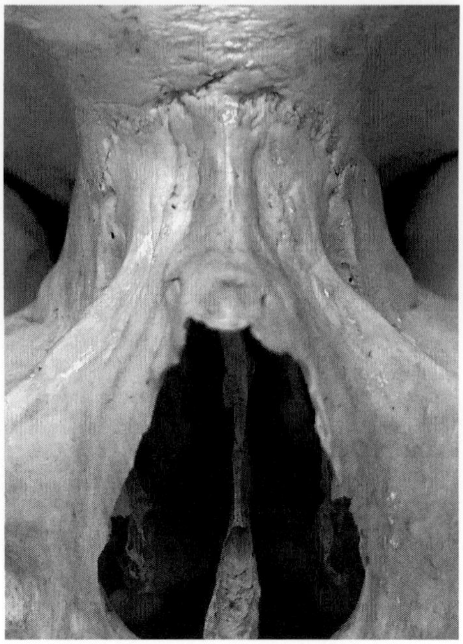

FIGURE 10.29 Variant of NBS 4. *NBS*, nasal bone shape.

# UNIQUE CHARACTER STATES FOR NASAL BONE SHAPE = NA (FIGS. 10.30 AND 10.31)

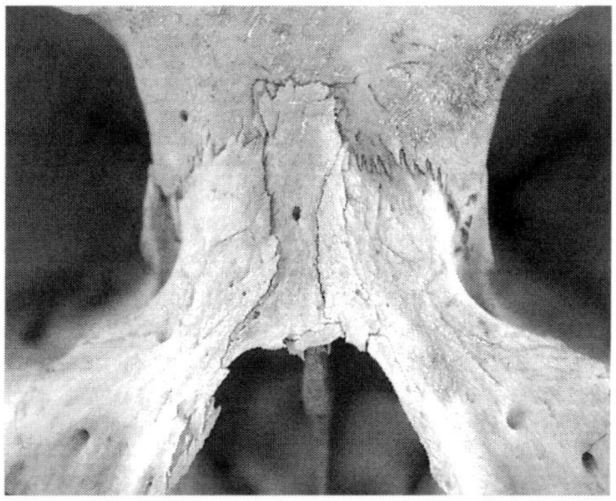

FIGURE 10.30 Unique (idiosyncratic) expression of nasal bone shape.

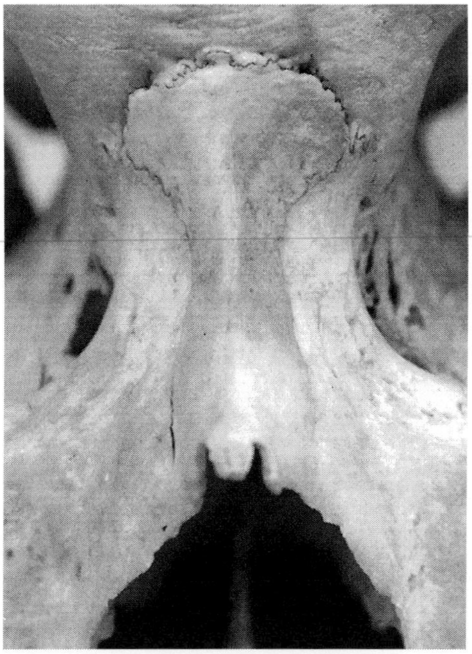

FIGURE 10.31 Unique (idiosyncratic) expression of nasal bone shape. Note the fusion of the nasal suture.

CHAPTER

# 11

# Nasal Overgrowth

Nasal overgrowth (NO) is a projection of the lateral border of the nasal bones at their inferior edge, extending beyond the maxilla at the bony landmark *nasale inferious*. NO is visualized by close inspection of the inferior lateral border where it meets the maxilla. This trait exhibits the following character states: absent or present, with corresponding scores: 0 < 1. If no projection is identified beyond the maxilla, NO is scored *Absent* (0). Any projection of the nasal bones beyond *nasale inferious* should be scored *Present* (1). Gently running your finger along the border of the maxilla and nasal bones at *nasale inferious* may help to determine whether a projection is present. Asymmetry can occur. If asymmetry is present, the side with the highest expression is recorded. If both nasal bones are missing, fractured (ante- or perimortem) or damaged, NO should not be recorded. NO is *only* an assessment of the nasal bones. Any projection or extension of the maxillae should not be considered as an expression of NO (Fig. 11.1).

Duckworth (1901–1902) identified an example (albeit an extreme case) of NO in an Egyptian cranium gifted to the Anatomical Museum at Cambridge, upon which he hypothesized the origin of such an unusual anatomical idiosyncrasy [although DeVilliers (1968) believes Duckworth was describing *lateral overgrowth*, a term he coined]. Birdsell (1949) included three traits related to nasal bone growth: nasal overgrowth, nasal undergrowth, and normal growth. He defined NO as "projection beyond the superior or maxillary border" (Birdsell, 1949:25). This definition seemingly includes any projection (superior or inferior) beyond the maxillary border.

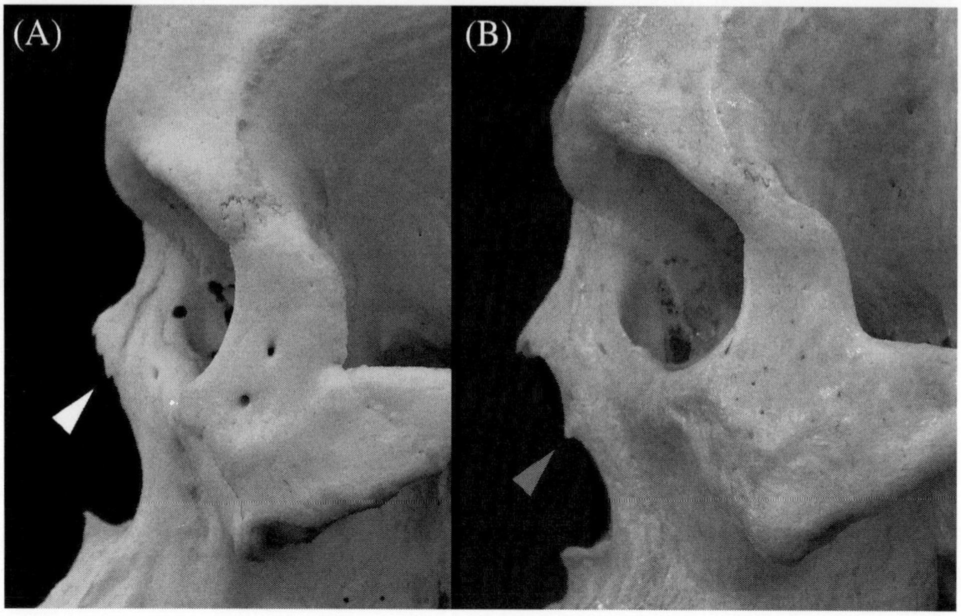


**FIGURE 11.1** Illustrating the distinction between NO [(A) white arrow] and an extension of the maxilla [(B) gray arrow].

*Atlas of Human Cranial Macromorphoscopic Traits.*
DOI: https://doi.org/10.1016/B978-0-12-814385-8.00011-2

Bass (1987:92) identified NO as nasal bones projecting "forward beyond their junction with the frontal portion of the maxilla" (Bass, 1987:92). Rhine (1990:20) defined NO as a "projection of the ends of the nasal bones slightly beyond the maxillae." Birkby et al. (2008) emphasize the importance of NO for the identification of Southwest Hispanics. Finally, Hefner (2009:989) defined NO as "as an inferior projection of the lateral border of the nasal bones beyond the maxillae at *nasale inferious* ... scored dichotomously as 0—absent or 1—present."

## NOMENCLATURE

Nasal overgrowth, *nasi situ vasta*, and projection of the anterior extremity of the nasal bones.

## GROSS ANATOMY

The nasal bones are two small, symmetrical oblong bones, each having two surfaces and four borders. Positioned in the midface, at their junction they form the bridge of the nose superiorly and anchor the upper lateral nasal cartilages inferiorly. The external surface of each nasal bone is covered by the *procerus* and *nasalis muscles*, and each is perforated near the center by a foramen transmitting a small venous complex. The internal surface is transversely concave and contains a groove for the anterior ethmoidal nerve. Each nasal bone articulates with the frontal, ethmoid, opposite nasal, and maxilla. Nasal fractures are common—the most common facial fracture (Wedel and Galloway, 2014)—and usually, a result of blunt force trauma to the nose.

## GROWTH AND DEVELOPMENT

The expression of NO likely results from commencing ossification of the nasal bones extending into the upper portions of the lateral nasal cartilages. The nasal region undergoes two phases during ontogenesis: the embryonic developmental phase and the growth phase. During embryological development (covered in detail in Chapters 7 and 8), the nose and related skeletal structures are formed. This phase lasts from approximately the third week to 3 months postconception, during that time the nasal structures (the nasal placode, maxillary, and mandibular processes) develop. During the growth phase, which lasts through puberty, changes to the various anatomical structures of the nose and an overall increase in size occurs. Around fetal week nine to ten, intramembranous ossification centers appear for each nasal bone (Scheuer and Black, 2000), ossifying from a single center within the cartilaginous nasal capsule. At birth, the nasal bones have a decidedly adult appearance, although the full adult manifestation does not occur until puberty (Scheuer and Black, 2000). Clinical manifestations of nasal bone dysplasia may be assessed as early as the 12th-week. Adult manifestations of dysplasia may present with unilateral or bilateral hypoplastic or aplastic nasals (Barnes, 1994).

## FUNCTIONAL MORPHOLOGY

Making up the superior roof of the nasal cavity and anchoring the nasal cartilages, the nasal bones are vital to olfaction and respiration (see Chapter 7 and 8, *Functional Morphology*, for a more detailed exploration of these aspects). Enlow (1990) describes an additional functional component of the nasal bones and associated cartilages in olfaction. The reduced human face resulting from orbital convergence that occurred during hominid evolution required a concomitant reduction of the maxillary complex. The protruding, fleshy human nose and associated skeletal structures direct the nares inferiorly, which then guides inhaled air upward into the nasal cavity to the awaiting sensory nerves of the olfactory bulb.

## WITHIN POPULATION VARIATION

Data derived from the Macromorphoscopic Databank of the frequency distribution of NO ($n = 4106$). All data are for adult individuals. When possible, frequency data for males and females are provided separately. When sex could not be estimated reliably, frequency distributions are pooled as "Unknown" (Table 11.1).

**TABLE 11.1** Frequency Distribution of NO, by Geographic Origin and Sex

| | | 0 | | 1 | | |
|---|---|---|---|---|---|---|
| **Geographic origin** | **Sex** | *n* | % | *n* | % | **Total** |
| **African** | **Female** | 9 | 82 | 2 | 18 | 11 |
| | **Male** | 11 | 69 | 5 | 31 | 16 |
| | **Unknown** | 0 | 0 | 0 | 0 | 0 |
| | **Total** | 20 | 74 | 7 | 26 | 27 |
| **American Black** | **Female** | 83 | 73 | 30 | 27 | 113 |
| | **Male** | 137 | 62 | 83 | 38 | 220 |
| | **Unknown** | 1 | 100 | 0 | 0 | 1 |
| | **Total** | 221 | 66 | 113 | 34 | 334 |
| **American White** | **Female** | 151 | 63 | 87 | 37 | 238 |
| | **Male** | 148 | 56 | 116 | 44 | 264 |
| | **Unknown** | 0 | 0 | 0 | 0 | 0 |
| | **Total** | 299 | 60 | 203 | 40 | 502 |
| **Amerindian** | **Female** | 18 | 49 | 19 | 51 | 37 |
| | **Male** | 15 | 48 | 16 | 52 | 31 |
| | **Unknown** | 521 | 41 | 754 | 59 | 1275 |
| | **Total** | 554 | 41 | 789 | 59 | 1343 |
| **Chinese** | **Female** | 5 | 100 | 0 | 0 | 5 |
| | **Male** | 39 | 78 | 11 | 22 | 50 |
| | **Unknown** | 0 | 0 | 0 | 0 | 0 |
| | **Total** | 44 | 80 | 11 | 20 | 55 |
| **Colombian** | **Female** | 17 | 27 | 46 | 73 | 63 |
| | **Male** | 15 | 9 | 148 | 91 | 163 |
| | **Unknown** | 0 | 0 | 0 | 0 | 0 |
| | **Total** | 32 | 14 | 194 | 86 | 226 |
| **El Salvador** | **Female** | 0 | 0 | 0 | 0 | 0 |
| | **Male** | 1 | 20 | 4 | 80 | 5 |
| | **Unknown** | 0 | 0 | 0 | 0 | 0 |
| | **Total** | 1 | 20 | 4 | 80 | 5 |
| **Eskimo** | **Female** | 0 | 0 | 0 | 0 | 0 |
| | **Male** | 0 | 0 | 0 | 0 | 0 |
| | **Unknown** | 255 | 80 | 64 | 20 | 319 |
| | **Total** | 255 | 80 | 64 | 20 | 319 |

*(Continued)*

TABLE 11.1 *(Continued)*

| | | 0 | | 1 | | |
|---|---|---|---|---|---|---|
| **Geographic origin** | **Sex** | *n* | % | *n* | % | **Total** |
| **European** | **Female** | 4 | 67 | 2 | 33 | 6 |
| | **Male** | 4 | 57 | 3 | 43 | 7 |
| | **Unknown** | 0 | 0 | 0 | 0 | 0 |
| | **Total** | 8 | 62 | 5 | 38 | 13 |
| **Guatemalan** | **Female** | 20 | 63 | 12 | 38 | 32 |
| | **Male** | 33 | 49 | 35 | 51 | 68 |
| | **Unknown** | 0 | 0 | 0 | 0 | 0 |
| | **Total** | 53 | 53 | 47 | 47 | 100 |
| **Japanese** | **Female** | 4 | 80 | 1 | 20 | 5 |
| | **Male** | 2 | 29 | 5 | 71 | 7 |
| | **Unknown** | 0 | 0 | 2 | 100 | 2 |
| | **Total** | 6 | 43 | 8 | 57 | 14 |
| **Mexico** | **Female** | 0 | 0 | 2 | 100 | 2 |
| | **Male** | 8 | 38 | 13 | 62 | 21 |
| | **Unknown** | 0 | 0 | 0 | 0 | 0 |
| | **Total** | 8 | 35 | 15 | 65 | 23 |
| **Pacific Island** | **Female** | 27 | 77 | 8 | 23 | 35 |
| | **Male** | 52 | 75 | 17 | 25 | 69 |
| | **Unknown** | 55 | 85 | 10 | 15 | 65 |
| | **Total** | 134 | 79 | 35 | 21 | 169 |
| **Peruvian** | **Female** | 0 | 0 | 0 | 0 | 0 |
| | **Male** | 0 | 0 | 0 | 0 | 0 |
| | **Unknown** | 0 | 0 | 12 | 100 | 12 |
| | **Total** | 0 | 0 | 12 | 100 | 12 |
| **Southwest (SW) Hispanic** | **Female** | 4 | 57 | 3 | 43 | 7 |
| | **Male** | 4 | 44 | 5 | 56 | 9 |
| | **Unknown** | 11 | 13 | 73 | 87 | 84 |
| | **Total** | 19 | 19 | 81 | 81 | 100 |
| **Thai** | **Female** | 250 | 83 | 51 | 17 | 301 |
| | **Male** | 444 | 81 | 106 | 19 | 550 |
| | **Unknown** | 10 | 77 | 3 | 23 | 13 |
| | **Total** | 704 | 81 | 160 | 19 | 864 |
| **Total for all groups** | | 2358 | 57 | 1748 | 43 | 4106 |

*NO*, nasal overgrowth; *SW*, Southwest.

# CHARACTER STATES

Photographic exemplars of the different character states of NO are provided below. Each character state is defined following Hefner (2009). When necessary to clarify scoring, more nuanced definitions are provided in the figure captions. NO should be assessed with the protocol provided in the preceding section. Character states include:

NO 0 = Absent—no bony overgrowth at nasale inferious.
NO 1 = Present—any projection of bone from the lateral border of the nasals beyond the maxillary border at nasale inferious.

## CHARACTER STATES FOR NASAL OVERGROWTH = 0 (FIGS. 11.2–11.8)

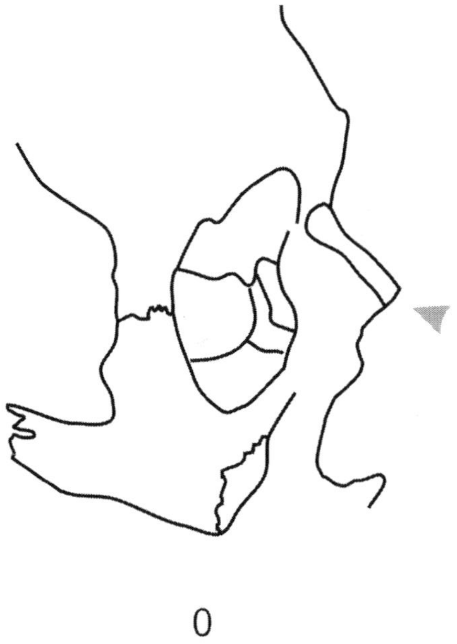


FIGURE 11.2 Diagrammatic representation of NO 0. *NO*, nasal overgrowth.

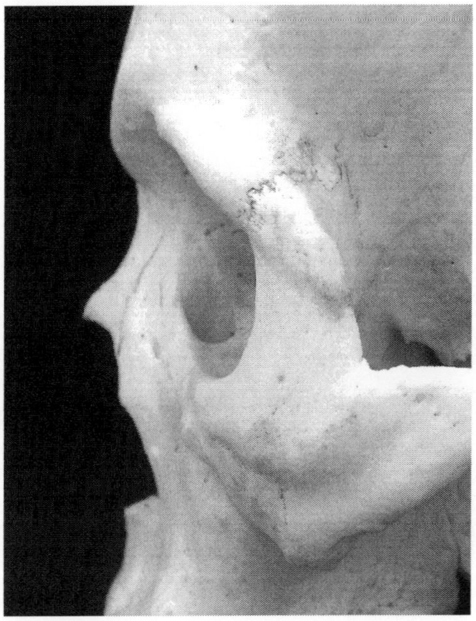

FIGURE 11.3 Variant of NO 0. *NO*, nasal overgrowth.

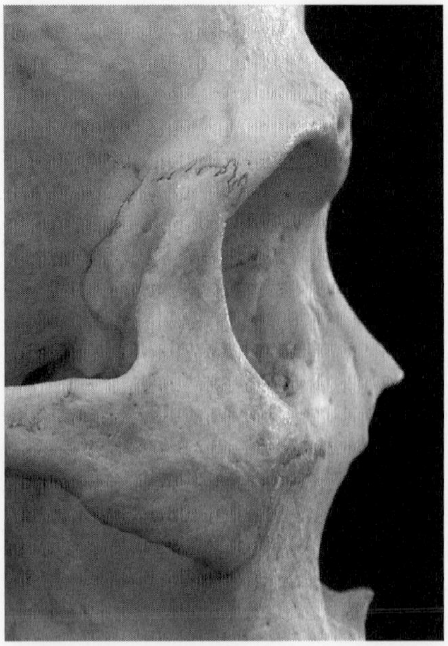

**FIGURE 11.4** Variant of NO 0. *NO*, nasal overgrowth.

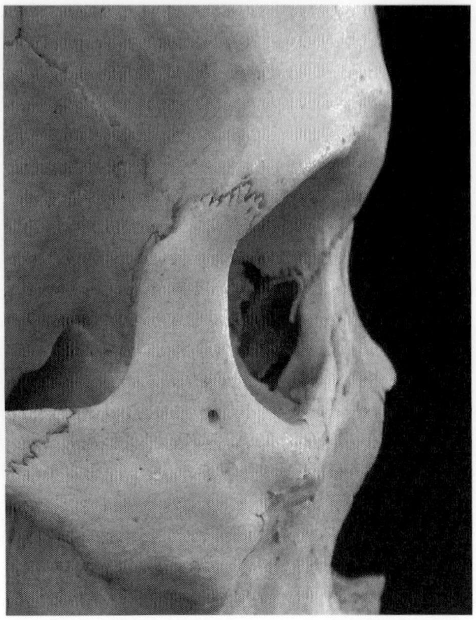

**FIGURE 11.5** Variant of NO 0. Note: although the inferior aspect of the nasal bone is separated from the maxilla, there is no extension beyond. *NO*, nasal overgrowth.

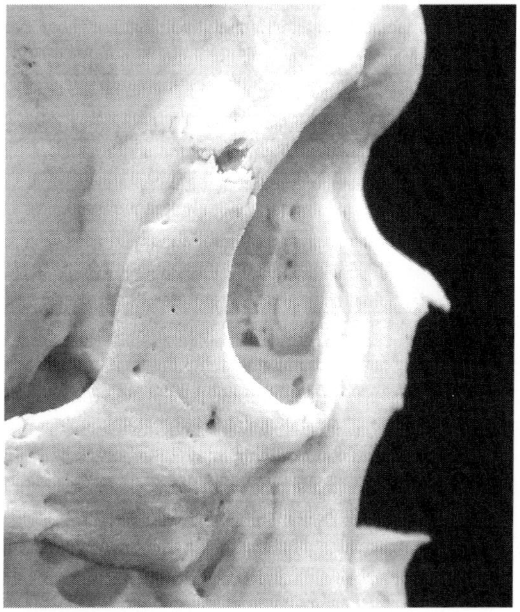

FIGURE 11.6 Variant of NO 0. Note: the extension of the superior aspect of the nasal bones is not considered when scoring NO. *NO*, nasal overgrowth.

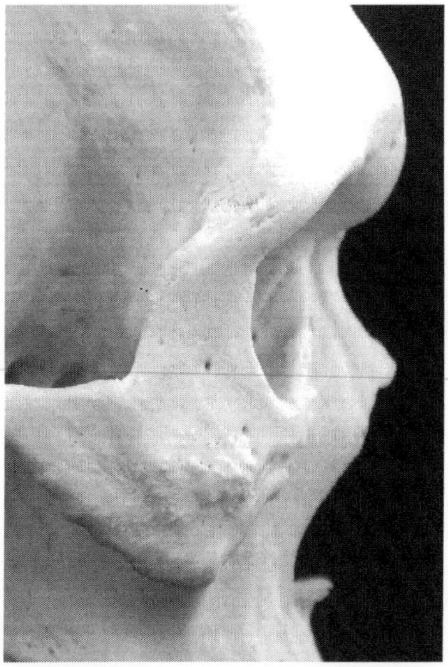

FIGURE 11.7 Variant of NO 0. *NO*, nasal overgrowth.

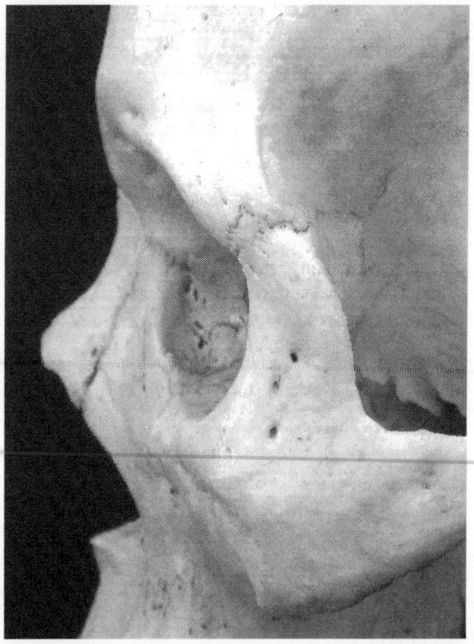

FIGURE 11.8 Variant of NO 0. Note: although the inferior aspect of the nasal bone is separated from the maxilla, there is no extension beyond. *NO*, nasal overgrowth.

# CHARACTER STATES FOR NASAL OVERGROWTH = 1 (FIGS. 11.9–11.15)

**FIGURE 11.9** Diagrammatic representation of NO 1. *NO*, nasal overgrowth.

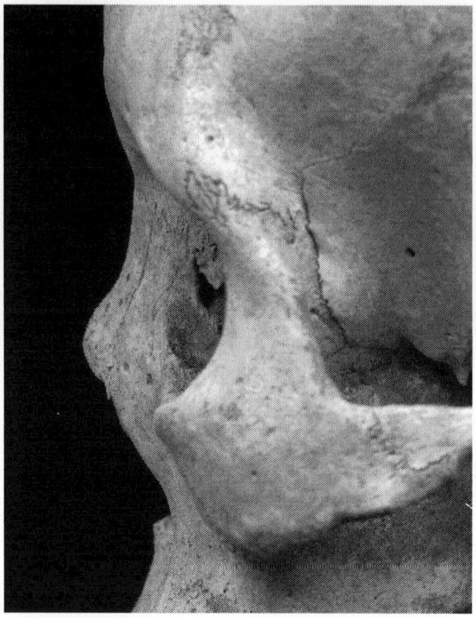

**FIGURE 11.10** Variant of NO 1. *NO*, nasal overgrowth.

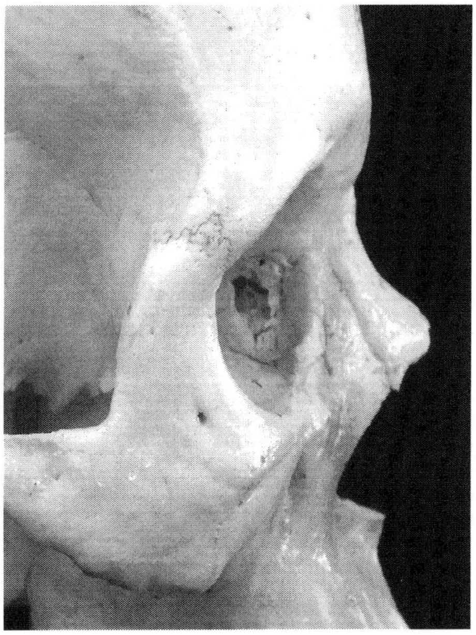

**FIGURE 11.11** Variant of NO 1. *NO*, nasal overgrowth.

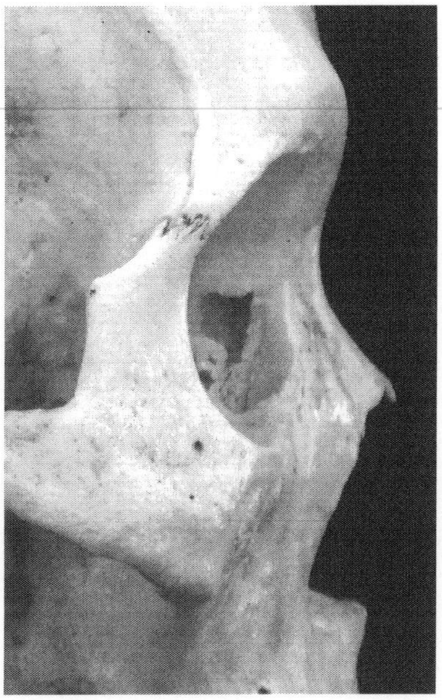

**FIGURE 11.12** Variant of NO 1. *NO*, nasal overgrowth.

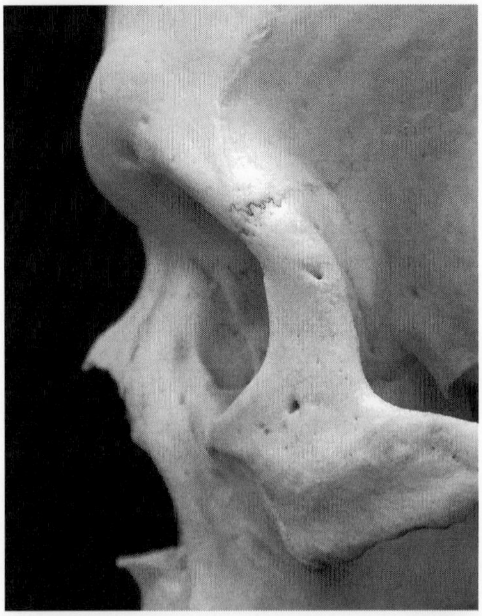

**FIGURE 11.13** Variant of NO 1. *NO*, nasal overgrowth.

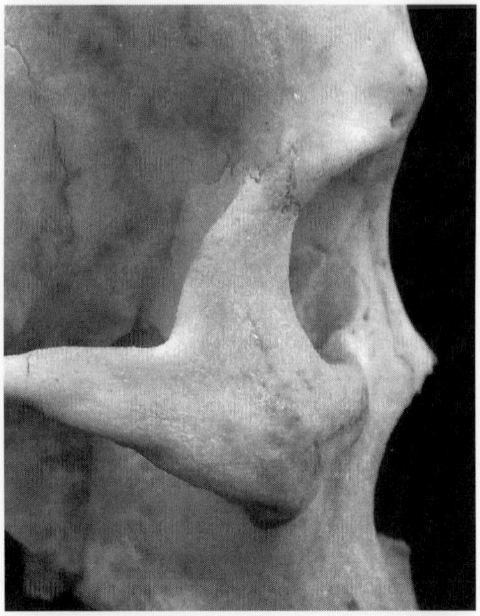

**FIGURE 11.14** Variant of NO 1. Note: although there is only a slight extension, this specimen would still be scored NO 1. *NO*, nasal overgrowth.

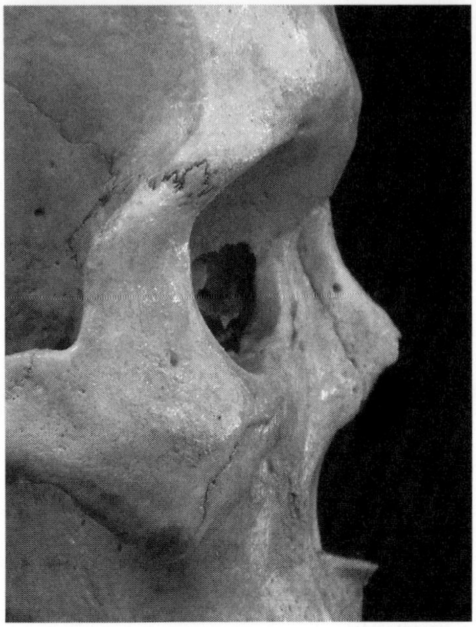

**FIGURE 11.15** Variant of NO 1. *NO*, nasal overgrowth.

CHAPTER

# 12

# Nasofrontal Suture

The nasofrontal suture (NFS) connects the nasal bones to the frontal bone at the ethmoidal notch. There are four variations in the shape of NFS: round, square, triangular, and irregular, with corresponding scores $1 < 2 < 3 < 4$. *Round* (1) indicates the NFS is rounded-over with no angles at the fronto-naso-maxillary junction (i.e., *nasale superious*). *Square* (2) indicates the NFS is quadrangular with approximate right angles at *nasale superious*. A *Triangular* (3) NFS has laterally slanted sides creating a triangular appearance in sutural morphology. Finally, an *Irregular* (4) NFS lacks definitive shape. To score NFS, hold the cranium in anatomical position, with the anterior portion of the cranium facing the observer. Do not assess NFS from a lateral view. When scoring, disregard the symmetry of the nasal bones. If the nasal bones exhibit extreme pinching of the superior border, as it does in nasal bone shape (NBS 4), do not score NFS.

NFS morphology has not received the same level of attention as some of the more common macromorphoscopic traits. However, Oetteking (1920:279) provides a detailed study of the NFS on 88 skulls from San Miguel Island, California. While he noted considerable variability, he was able to identify six forms of the NFS: (1) straight, (2) curved, (3) semicircular, (4) rectangular, (5) trapezoid, and (6) angular (Fig. 12.1). Oetteking's descriptions are very detailed and include a lengthy discussion on the various manifestations of this trait (1920:61):

> The course of the suture is generally described as being of horizontal, or arched, or angular form, both the convexity and the vertex of the angle encroaching on the nasal process of the frontal bone. A closer examination of these conditions admits of further differentiation, giving rise to subdivisions of rather distinct appearance. Progressing from the simplest to the more specialized ones, I succeeded in distinguishing six different varieties, which may be successively educed in the following, by representing each of them by a scheme and an individual case in the series.

Oetteking then provides schematic representations of his six forms, along with a line drawing of the nasal region from a cranium in the San Miguel collection (Fig. 12.2). These illustrations and his definitions provided the basis for Hefner's (2010) illustrations and definitions of NFS. Although Corruccini (1974) calls into question the significance of NFS, it is included as a macromorphoscopic trait for additional study.

## NOMENCLATURE

Nasal root contour, nasofrontal suture, and sutura nasofrontalis.

## GROSS ANATOMY

Viewed in norma frontalis, the facial aspect of the cranium is outlined superiorly by the frontal bone, which articulates to the two nasal bones via the NFS. The NFS is inferior to *glabella* and at its midpoint demarcates the location of *nasion*. The superior border of the nasal bones is generally thick and denticulate (Scheuer and Black, 2000).

*Atlas of Human Cranial Macromorphoscopic Traits.*
DOI: https://doi.org/10.1016/B978-0-12-814385-8.00012-4

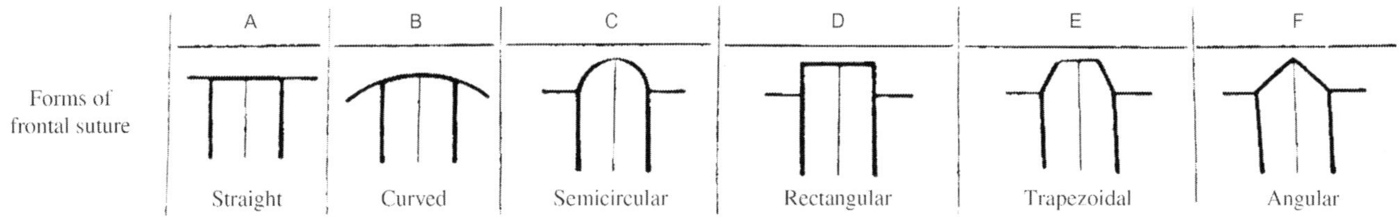


**FIGURE 12.1** Stylized forms of the frontal suture (public domain: Oetteking, 1920).

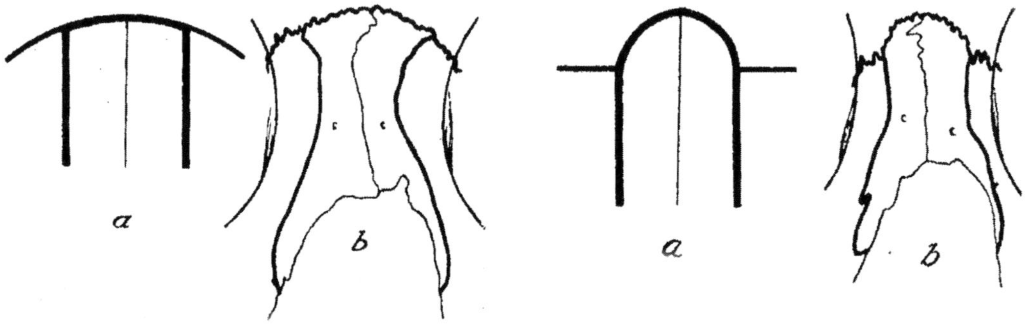


**FIGURE 12.2** Stylized and illustrated examples of the forms of the frontal suture (public domain: Oetteking, 1930).

## GROWTH AND DEVELOPMENT

In embryological development, the NFS manifests early. Like other macromorphoscopic traits of the nasal region, this area undergoes two phases during ontogenesis: the embryonic developmental phase and the growth phase. During embryological development (covered in detail in Chapters 7 and 8), the nose and related skeletal structures are formed. This phase lasts from approximately the third week to three months postconception, during that time the nasal structures (the nasal placode, maxillary and mandibular processes) develop. During the growth phase, which lasts throughout puberty, changes to the various anatomical structures of the nose and an overall increase in size occurs. Around fetal week nine to ten, intramembranous ossification centers appear for each nasal bone (Scheuer and Black, 2000), ossifying from a single center within the cartilaginous nasal capsule. At birth, the nasal bones have a decidedly adult appearance, although the full adult manifestation does not occur until puberty (Scheuer and Black, 2000).

The NFS is also involved in *primary displacement* (Stage 13 of facial growth, Enlow, 1990:118). During this stage, the growth of the ethmomaxillary complex is directed inferiorly, coinciding with overall enlargement of the area through bony resorption and deposition. Bony deposition occurs in the NFS (in addition to other areas of the facial skeleton) through sutural osteogenesis triggered by tension created as the face moves inferiorly and forward during growth.

## FUNCTIONAL MORPHOLOGY

The NFS, like other sutures of the cranium, primarily permits bone growth through sutural osteogenesis. Being the apex of the nasal region and the most robust portion of the nasal bones, the NFS also serves as a bony buttress, supporting and reinforcing the midfacial region. In comparison to other sutures, the NFS contributes less to facial growth (Enlow, 1990; Scott, 1956). Nevertheless, the NFS is likely of morphogenetic importance to the shape of the midfacial region, although the relationship of this suture to other midfacial morphologies and its correlation to other craniometric variables have not been explored.

## WITHIN POPULATION VARIATION

Data derived from the Macromorphoscopic Databank of the frequency distribution of NFS ($n = 3978$). All data are for adult individuals. When possible, frequency data for males and females are provided separately. When sex could not be estimated reliably, frequency distributions are pooled as "Unknown" (Table 12.1).

**TABLE 12.1** Frequency Distribution of NFS, by Geographic Origin and Sex

| | | 1 | | 2 | | 3 | | 4 | | |
|---|---|---|---|---|---|---|---|---|---|---|
| **Geographic origin** | **Sex** | *n* | % | *n* | % | *n* | % | *n* | % | **Total** |
| **American Black** | **Female** | 2 | 33 | 2 | 33 | 1 | 17 | 1 | 17 | 6 |
| | **Male** | 3 | 75 | 1 | 25 | 0 | 0 | 0 | 0 | 4 |
| | **Unknown** | 0 | 0 | 0 | 0 | 0 | 0 | 0 | 0 | 0 |
| | **Total** | 5 | 50 | 3 | 30 | 1 | 10 | 1 | 10 | 10 |
| **American White** | **Female** | 0 | 0 | 0 | 0 | 0 | 0 | 0 | 0 | 0 |
| | **Male** | 1 | 100 | 0 | 0 | 0 | 0 | 0 | 0 | 1 |
| | **Unknown** | 0 | 0 | 0 | 0 | 0 | 0 | 0 | 0 | 0 |
| | **Total** | 1 | 100 | 0 | 0 | 0 | 0 | 0 | 0 | 1 |
| **Amerindian** | **Female** | 0 | 0 | 0 | 0 | 0 | 0 | 0 | 0 | 0 |
| | **Male** | 0 | 0 | 0 | 0 | 0 | 0 | 0 | 0 | 0 |
| | **Unknown** | 1063 | 47 | 584 | 26 | 138 | 6 | 462 | 21 | 2247 |
| | **Total** | 1063 | 47 | 584 | 26 | 138 | 6 | 462 | 21 | 2247 |
| **El Salvador** | **Female** | 0 | 0 | 0 | 0 | 0 | 0 | 0 | 0 | 0 |
| | **Male** | 4 | 80 | 1 | 20 | 0 | 0 | 0 | 0 | 5 |
| | **Unknown** | 0 | 0 | 0 | 0 | 0 | 0 | 0 | 0 | 0 |
| | **Total** | 4 | 80 | 1 | 20 | 0 | 0 | 0 | 0 | 5 |
| **Eskimo** | **Female** | 0 | 0 | 0 | 0 | 0 | 0 | 0 | 0 | 0 |
| | **Male** | 0 | 0 | 0 | 0 | 0 | 0 | 0 | 0 | 0 |
| | **Unknown** | 381 | 51 | 204 | 27 | 51 | 7 | 118 | 16 | 754 |
| | **Total** | 381 | 51 | 204 | 27 | 51 | 7 | 118 | 16 | 754 |
| **Guatemalan** | **Female** | 1 | 50 | 0 | 0 | 0 | 0 | 1 | 50 | 2 |
| | **Male** | 0 | 0 | 0 | 0 | 0 | 0 | 0 | 0 | 0 |
| | **Unknown** | 0 | 0 | 0 | 0 | 0 | 0 | 0 | 0 | 0 |
| | **Total** | 1 | 50 | 0 | 0 | 0 | 0 | 1 | 50 | 2 |
| **Mexico** | **Female** | 0 | 0 | 0 | 0 | 0 | 0 | 0 | 0 | 0 |
| | **Male** | 3 | 43 | 3 | 43 | 1 | 14 | 0 | 0 | 7 |
| | **Unknown** | 0 | 0 | 0 | 0 | 0 | 0 | 0 | 0 | 0 |
| | **Total** | 3 | 43 | 3 | 43 | 1 | 14 | 0 | 0 | 7 |
| **Pacific Island** | **Female** | 19 | 36 | 28 | 53 | 5 | 9 | 1 | 2 | 53 |
| | **Male** | 44 | 56 | 26 | 33 | 4 | 5 | 5 | 6 | 79 |
| | **Unknown** | 56 | 62 | 18 | 20 | 9 | 10 | 7 | 8 | 90 |
| | **Total** | 119 | 54 | 72 | 32 | 18 | 8 | 13 | 6 | 222 |
| **Peruvian** | **Female** | 0 | 0 | 0 | 0 | 0 | 0 | 0 | 0 | 0 |
| | **Male** | 0 | 0 | 0 | 0 | 0 | 0 | 0 | 0 | 0 |
| | **Unknown** | 14 | 50 | 6 | 21 | 1 | 4 | 7 | 25 | 28 |
| | **Total** | 14 | 50 | 6 | 21 | 1 | 4 | 7 | 25 | 28 |

(*Continued*)

TABLE 12.1 (*Continued*)

| Geographic origin | Sex | 1 | | 2 | | 3 | | 4 | | Total |
|---|---|---|---|---|---|---|---|---|---|---|
| | | *n* | % | *n* | % | *n* | % | *n* | % | |
| **Southwest (SW) Hispanic** | **Female** | 0 | 0 | 0 | 0 | 0 | 0 | 4 | 100 | 4 |
| | **Male** | 3 | 60 | 0 | 0 | 0 | 0 | 2 | 40 | 5 |
| | **Unknown** | 0 | 0 | 0 | 0 | 0 | 0 | 0 | 0 | 0 |
| | **Total** | 3 | 33 | 0 | 0 | 0 | 0 | 6 | 67 | 9 |
| **Thai** | **Female** | 45 | 20 | 107 | 49 | 14 | 6 | 54 | 25 | 220 |
| | **Male** | 148 | 32 | 198 | 43 | 33 | 7 | 80 | 17 | 459 |
| | **Unknown** | 5 | 36 | 5 | 36 | 0 | 0 | 4 | 29 | 14 |
| | **Total** | 198 | 29 | 310 | 45 | 47 | 7 | 138 | 20 | 693 |
| **Total for all groups** | | **1792** | **45** | **1183** | **30** | **257** | **6** | **746** | **19** | **3978** |

*NFS*, nasofrontal suture.

## CHARACTER STATES

Photographic exemplars of the different character states of NFS are provided below. Each character state is defined following Hefner (2009, 2016). When necessary to clarify scoring, more nuanced definitions are provided in the figure captions. NFS should be assessed with the protocol provided in the preceding section. Character states include:

NFS 1 = the NFS is round and does not have any angles.

NFS 2 = the NFS is square and contains approximate right angles at *nasale superious*.

NFS 3 = the NFS appears triangular.

NFS 4 = the NFS is irregular and lacks any definitive shape.

## CHARACTER STATES FOR NASOFRONTAL SUTURE = 1 (FIGS. 12.3–12.9)

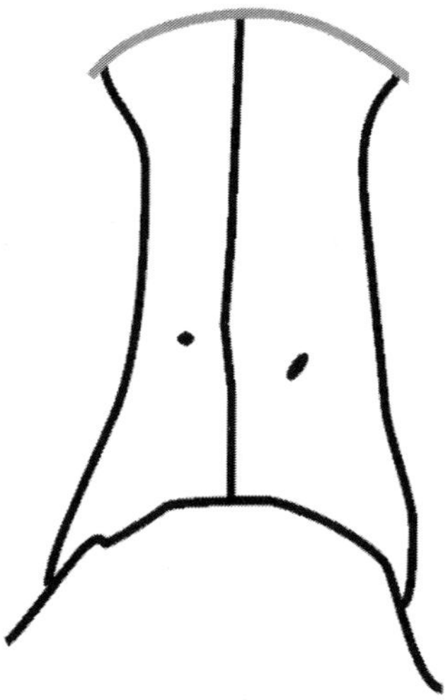


**FIGURE 12.3** Diagrammatic representation of NFS 1. *NFS*, nasofrontal suture.

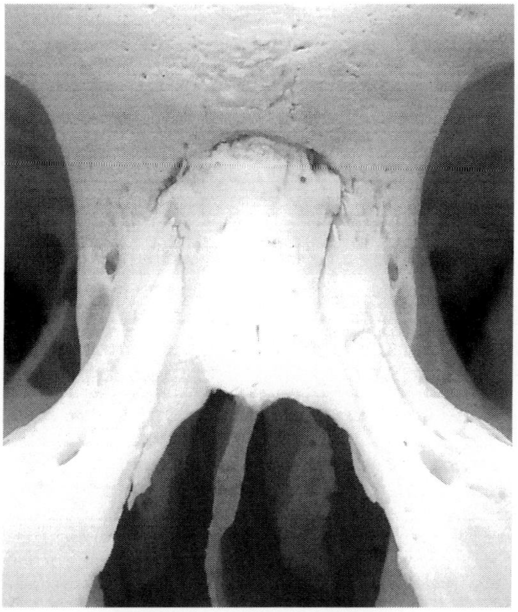

**FIGURE 12.4** Variant of NFS 1. *NFS*, nasofrontal suture.

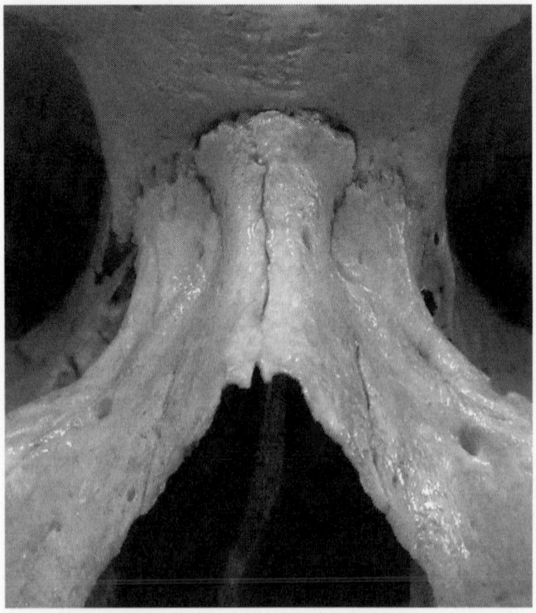

**FIGURE 12.5** Variant of NFS 1. *NFS*, nasofrontal suture.

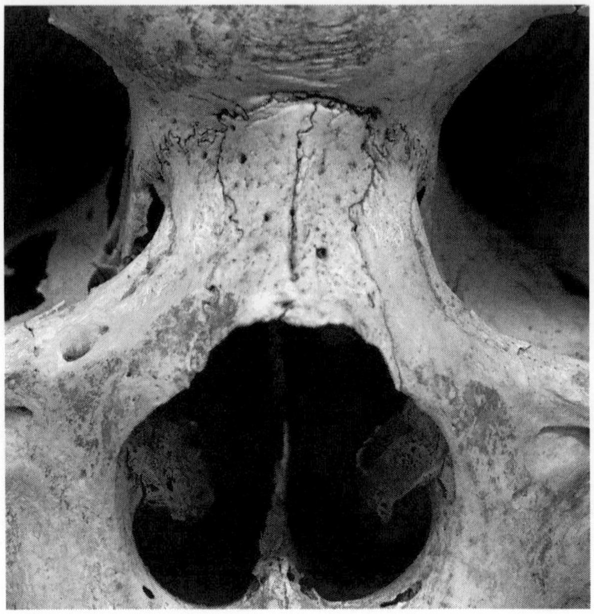

**FIGURE 12.6** Variant of NFS 1. *NFS*, nasofrontal suture.

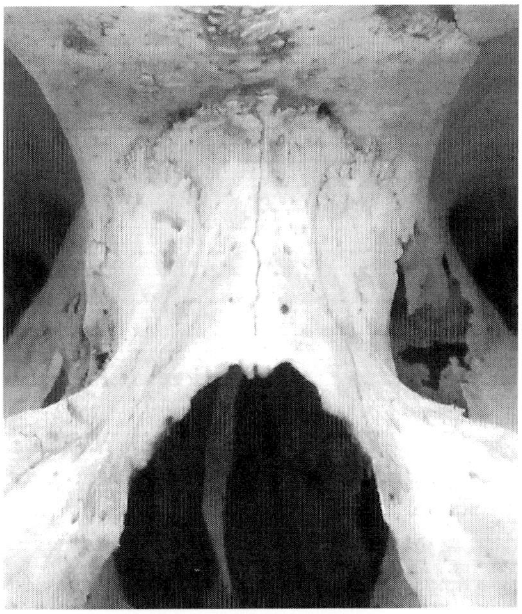

FIGURE 12.7 Variant of NFS 1. *NFS*, nasofrontal suture.

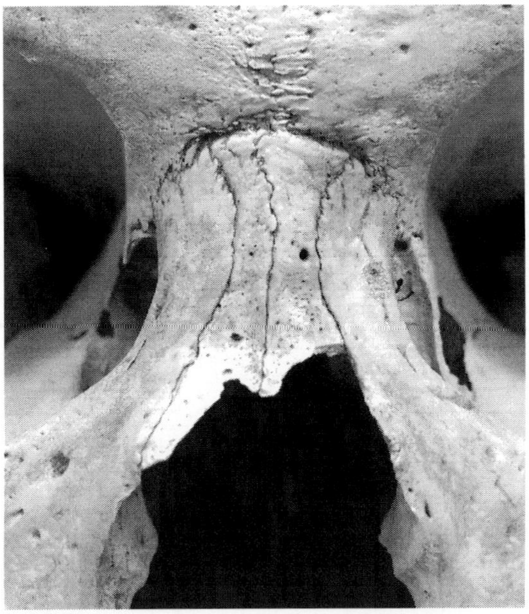

FIGURE 12.8 Variant of NFS 1. *NFS*, nasofrontal suture.

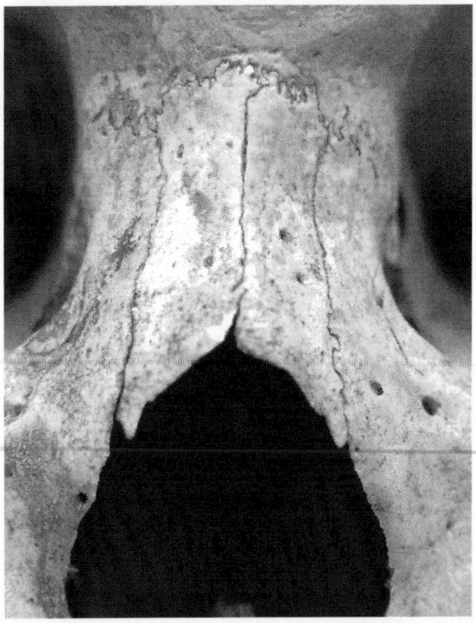

FIGURE 12.9 Variant of NFS 1. *NFS*, nasofrontal suture.

# CHARACTER STATES FOR NASOFRONTAL SUTURE = 2 (FIGS. 12.10–12.16)

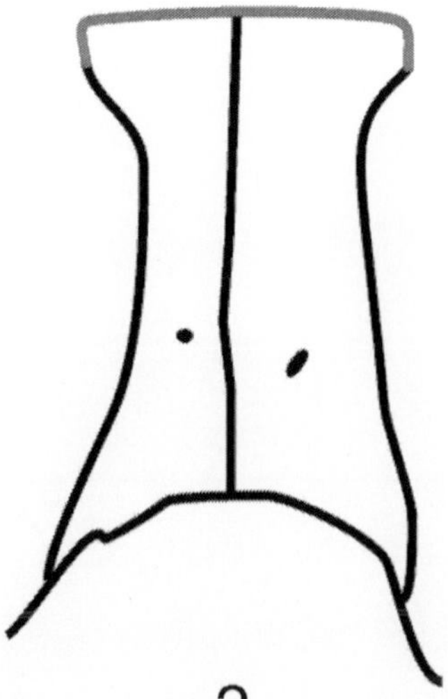


FIGURE 12.10 Diagrammatic representation of NFS 2. *NFS*, nasofrontal suture.

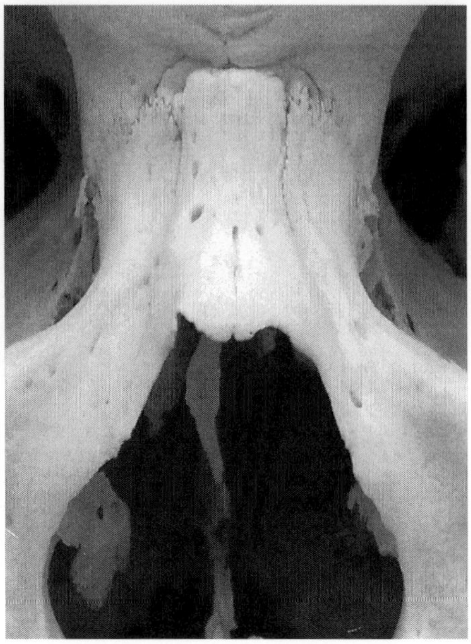

FIGURE 12.11 Variant of NFS 2. *NFS*, nasofrontal suture.

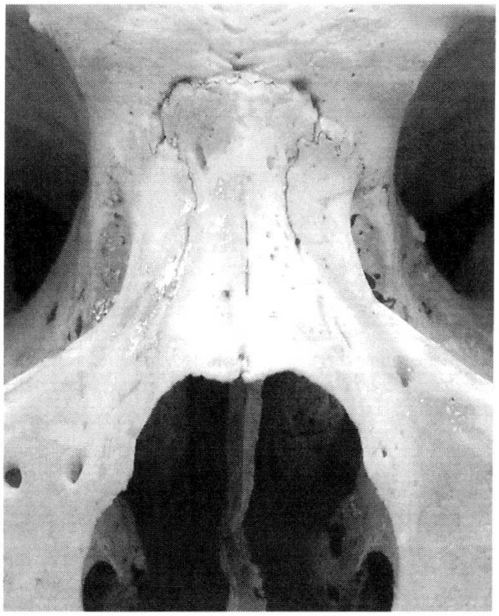

FIGURE 12.12 Variant of NFS 2. *NFS*, nasofrontal suture.

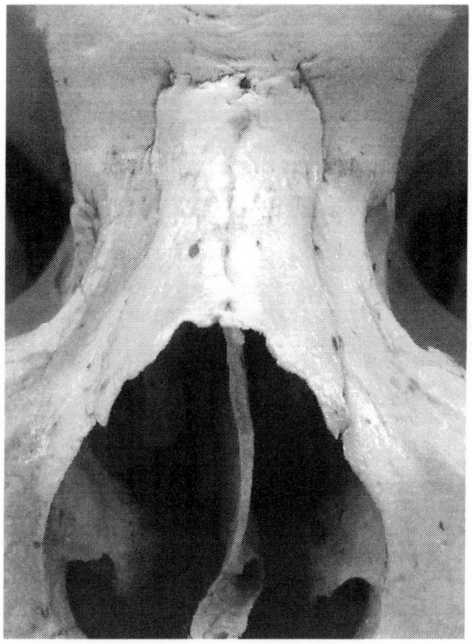

FIGURE 12.13 Variant of NFS 2. *NFS*, nasofrontal suture.

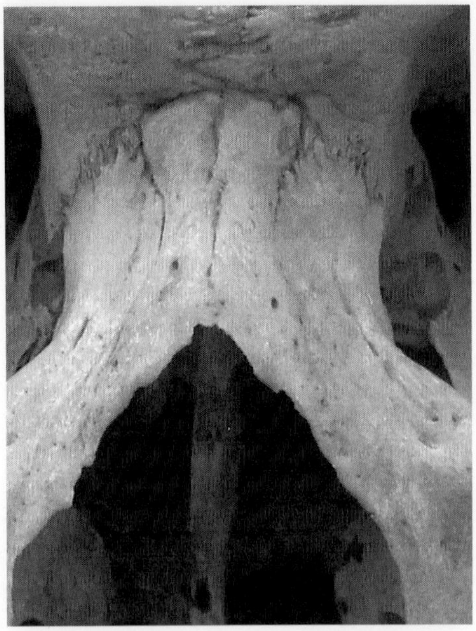

**FIGURE 12.14** Variant of NFS 2. *NFS*, nasofrontal suture.

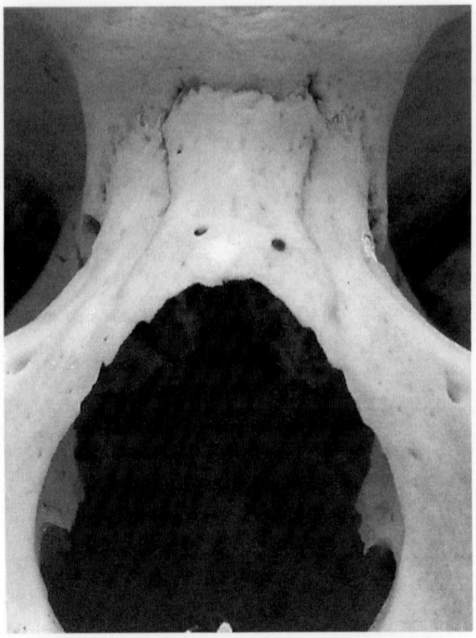

**FIGURE 12.15** Variant of NFS 2. *NFS*, nasofrontal suture.

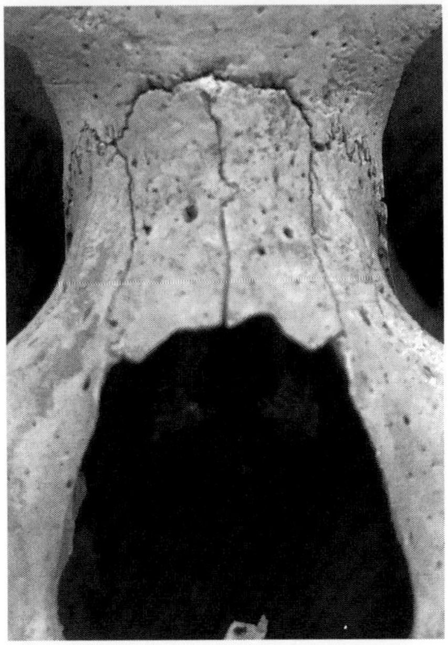

**FIGURE 12.16** Variant of NFS 2. *NFS*, nasofrontal suture.

## CHARACTER STATES FOR NASOFRONTAL SUTURE = 3 (FIGS. 12.17–12.23)

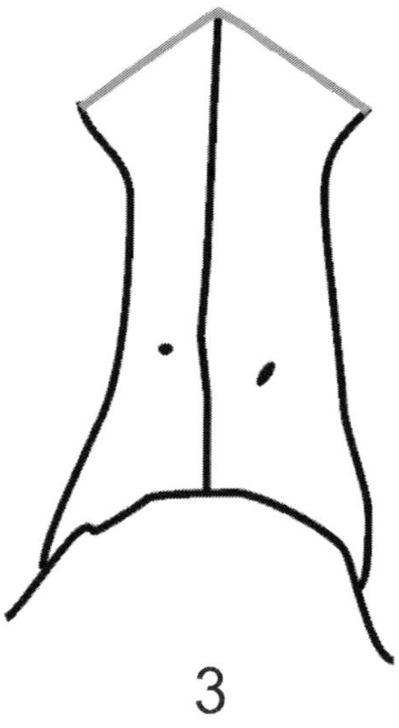


**FIGURE 12.17** Diagrammatic representation of NFS 3. Dashed line indicates the plane of reference (ruler). *NFS*, nasofrontal suture.

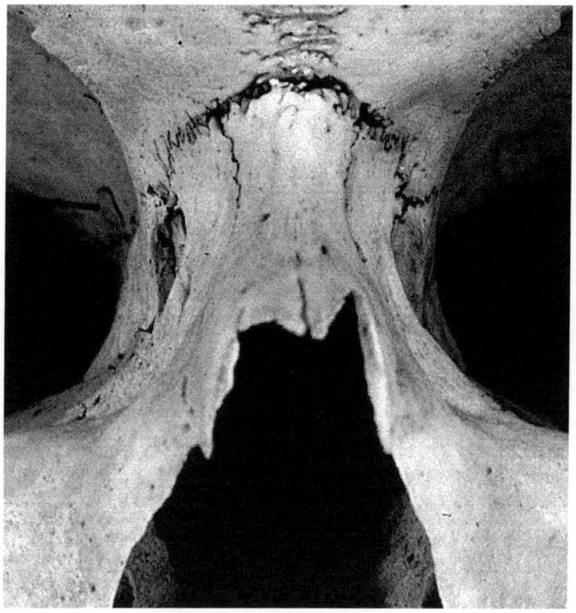

**FIGURE 12.18** Variant of NFS 3. *NFS*, nasofrontal suture.

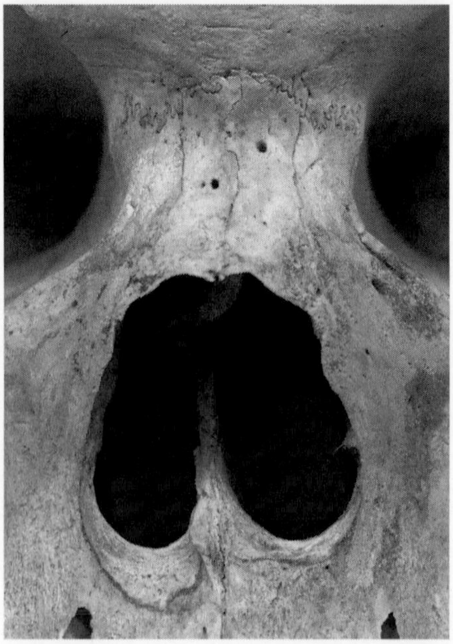

FIGURE 12.19 Variant of NFS 3. *NFS*, nasofrontal suture.

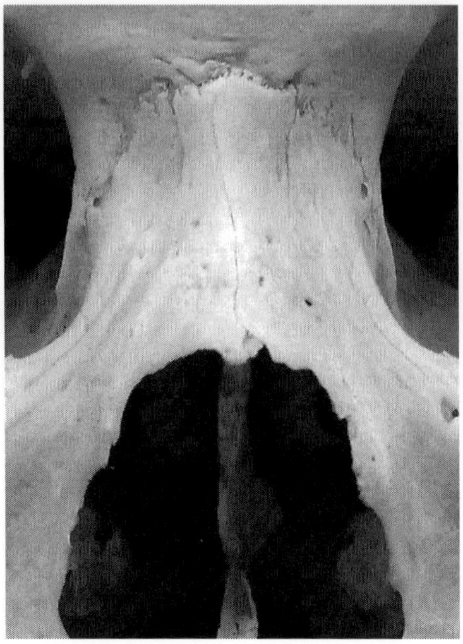

FIGURE 12.20 Variant of NFS 3. *NFS*, nasofrontal suture.

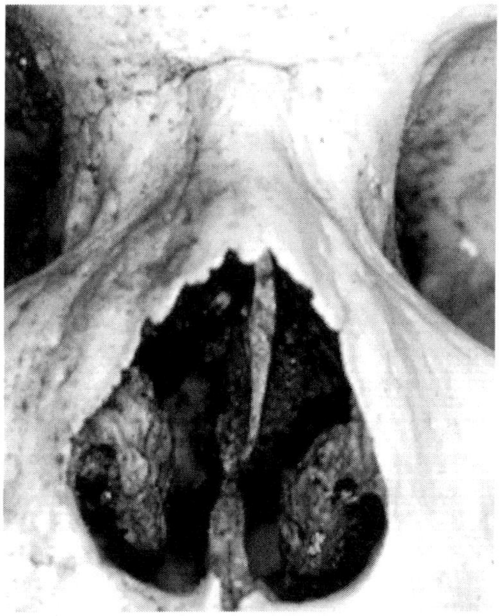

**FIGURE 12.21** Variant of NFS 3. *NFS*, nasofrontal suture.

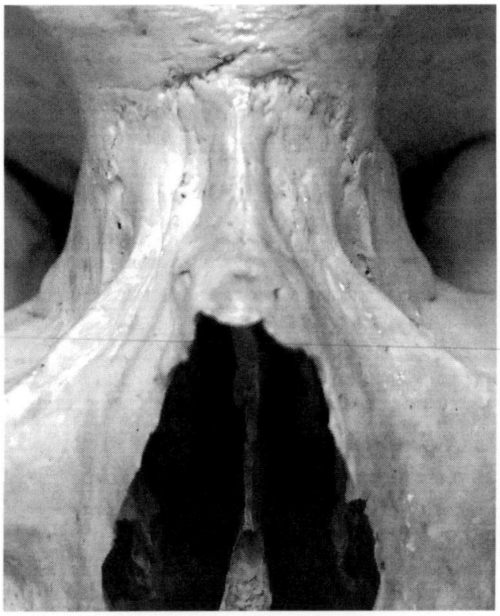

**FIGURE 12.22** Variant of NFS 3. *NFS*, nasofrontal suture.

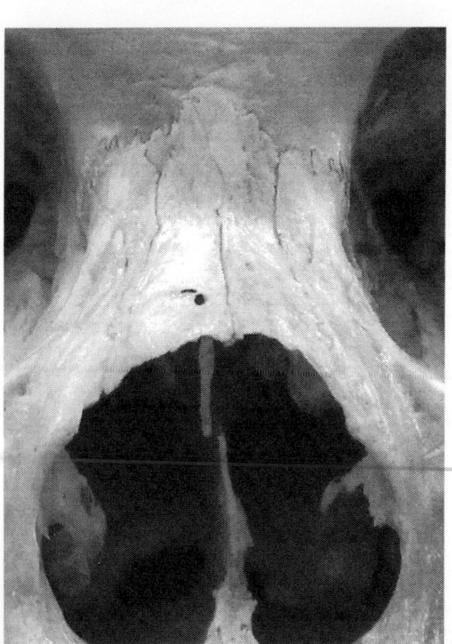

**FIGURE 12.23** Variant of NFS 3. *NFS*, nasofrontal suture.

# CHARACTER STATES FOR NASOFRONTAL SUTURE = 4 (FIGS. 12.24–12.30)

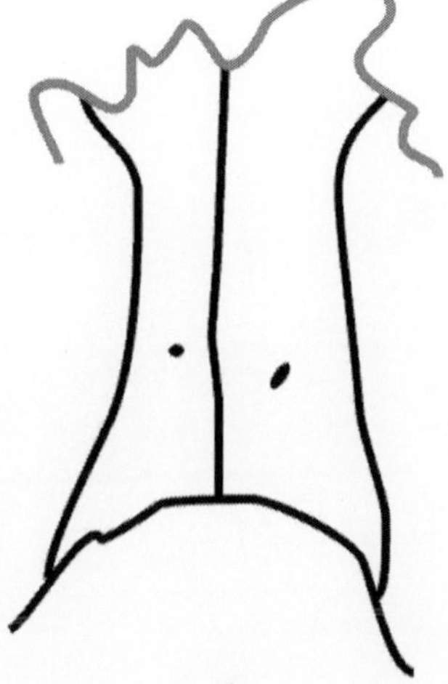


**FIGURE 12.24** Diagrammatic representation of NFS 4. *NFS*, nasofrontal suture.

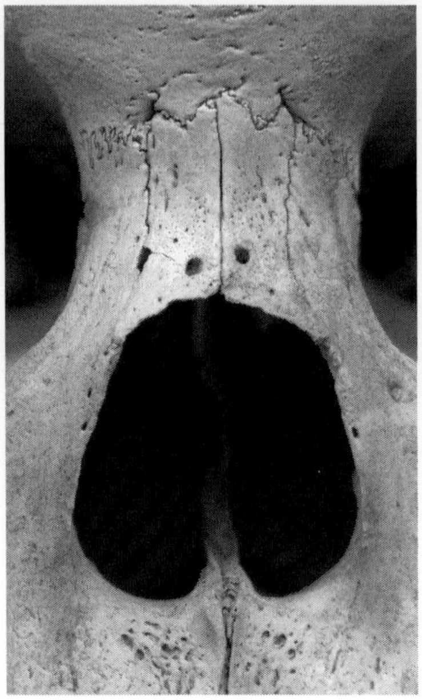

**FIGURE 12.25** Variant of NFS 4. *NFS*, nasofrontal suture.

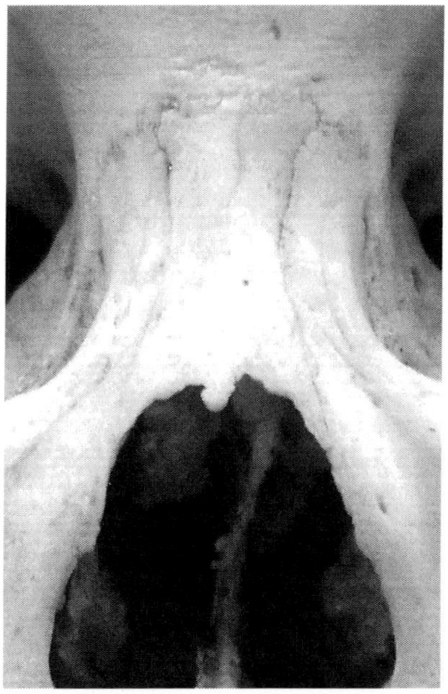

FIGURE 12.26 Variant of NFS 4. *NFS*, nasofrontal suture.

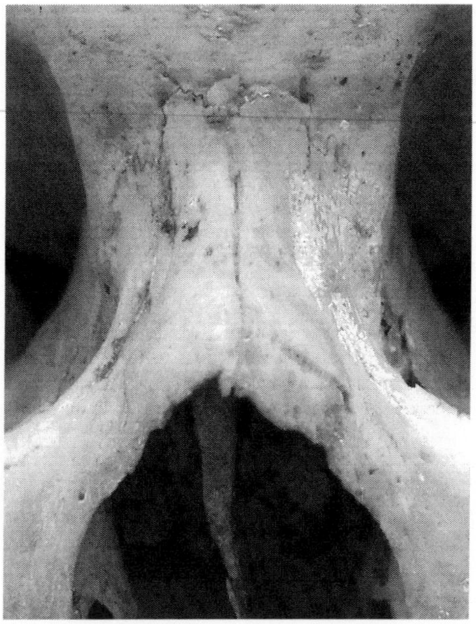

FIGURE 12.27 Variant of NFS 4. *NFS*, nasofrontal suture.

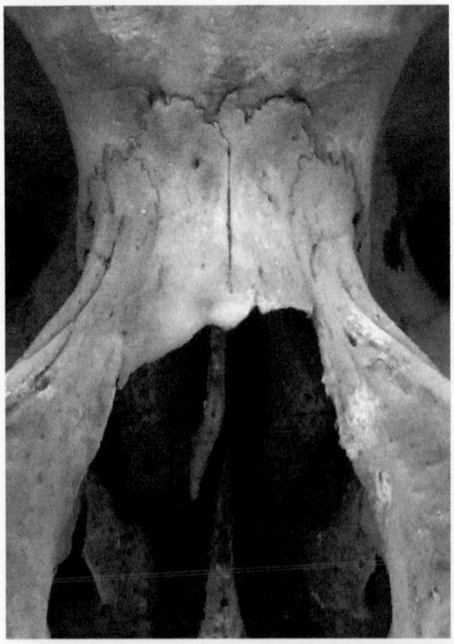

FIGURE 12.28 Variant of NFS 4. *NFS*, nasofrontal suture.

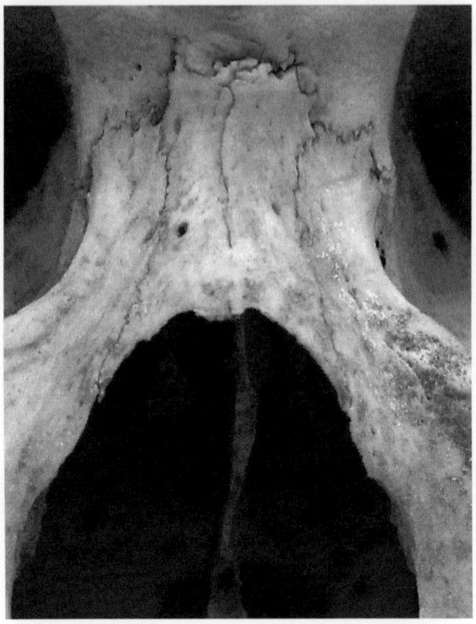

FIGURE 12.29 Variant of NFS 4. *NFS*, nasofrontal suture.

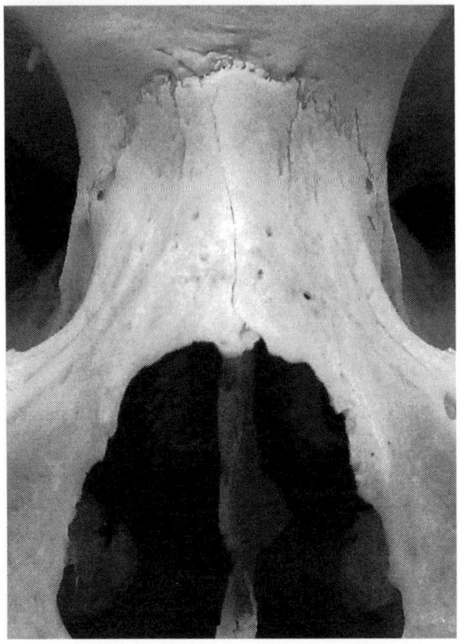

FIGURE 12.30 Variant of NFS 4. *NFS*, nasofrontal suture.

CHAPTER

# 13

# Orbital Shape

Orbital shape (OBS) is defined as the shape of the bony sockets housing the eye. OBS includes the following character states: *rectangular*, *circular*, and *rhombic*—scored as: 1 < 2 < 3. Observation is best from the anterior view. Observers should assess whether the orbital margins are angular (rectangle), curvilinear (circular), or irregular (rhombic). Bilateral asymmetry may occur. All observations should be made from the left orbit.

Hooton (Brues, 1990) included orbit shape in the Harvard Blanks, outlining four morphologies: (1) *ellipsoid*, (2) *square*, (3) *rectangular*, and (4) *rhombic*. Unfortunately, no illustrations have been found (to date) illustrating these morphologies. Krogman (1955) and Krogman and Işcan (1986) include three variants of orbital opening: (1) *angular*, (2) *rectangular*, and (3) *rounded*. An early systematic investigation into orbit shape was Szilvassy (1986), who assessed morphological differences in the orbital opening using frontooccipital radiographs of the skull from a large sample of known genealogy (Fig. 13.1). Szilvassy (1986) identified four distinct shapes: (1) *square*, (2) *trapezoid*, (3) *round*, and (4) *ellipsoid*. Hauser and De Stefano (1986) included the (unmodified) scoring strategy of the Szilvassy (1986) methodology in their text. Others borrowed the Hooton and Szilvassy variations to score orbit shape. Rhine (1990) defined OBS "(obliquity of orbit): [the] tendency towards a *'rounded'*, *'rectangular'*, or *'sloping'* orbit, the latter being a lateral inclination of the orbit." Gill (1998) identifies two variants of the *orbital form*: *round* and *rhomboid*.

Hefner (2010:74) included OBS in the *Macromorphoscopic Module* of Osteoware, defining OBS as:

> Orbital shape includes the following nonmetric variants: Rectangular, Circular, and Rhombic. Observation is best from the anterior view. The shape of the orbit is defined by the orbital margin of the superior, lateral, and inferior borders. The medial border of the orbit is defined by the anterior lacrimal crest and the maxillary process of the frontal bone. Observers should assess whether the margins are angular (rectangle), curvilinear (circular), or irregular (rhombic). Bilateral asymmetry may occur. All observations should be made from the left orbit. 1 = Rectangular – Orbits with horizontal margins longer than the vertical margins, but otherwise parallel (i.e., rectangle); 2 = Circular – Orbital margin is approximately equidistant from center on all sides (i.e., circle); 3 = Rhombic – Medial border height is shorter than lateral border height (aviator sunglasses).

The advent of modern morphometrics changed the way OBS and other macromorphoscopic traits are analyzed. Schleyer et al. (1971) first applied these methods to orbit shape applying elliptical Fourier analysis to radiographs in an effort to define shape differences between males and females (Urbanova, 2011). In the 1980s and 1990s, other researchers followed suit, investigating orbital morphology using advanced three-dimensional techniques to capture and measure orbit morphology (Jacobshagen, 1981, 1982; Lestrel et al., 1997).

More recently, Urbanova (2011) and Gore et al. (2011) explored variation in orbital morphology between populations, sexes, and age-cohorts using similar methods to more objectively treat orbit morphology. These methods are effective for identifying shape differences in orbit morphology; nonetheless, like other complex and labor-intensive methodological approaches, they may not replace the macromorphoscopic trait score approach. Readers interested in a more in-depth look at the promise of geometric morphometric methods of analysis for orbit morphology are encouraged to explore additional literature on the topic (Trask and Moore-Jansen, 2008; Kimmerle et al., 2008; Lestrel, 1988; Pessa and Chen, 2002; Schmittbuhl et al., 1999; Seiffert and Kappelman, 2001; Urbanova, 2009; Williams, 2007).

*Atlas of Human Cranial Macromorphoscopic Traits.*
DOI: https://doi.org/10.1016/B978-0-12-814385-8.00013-6

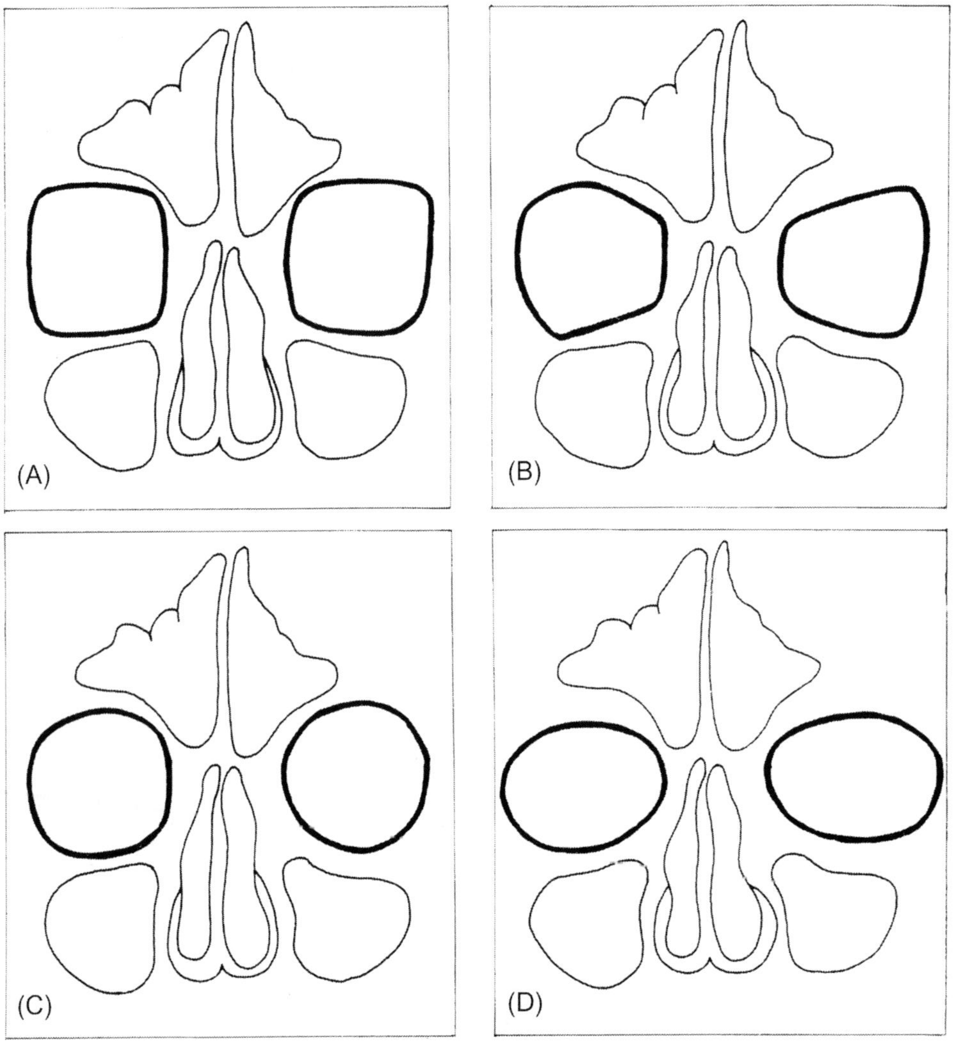


FIGURE 13.1 The categories of orbital shape identified by Szilvassy (1986). *Source: Reproduced from Hauser and De Stefano (1989).*

## NOMENCLATURE

*Aditus orbitae*, orbital cavity, *orbitalis figuras*, orbital opening, orbital shape, and anterior rim of the orbital cavity.

## GROSS ANATOMY

The orbital opening is defined by several bones of the craniofacial skeleton. These include the frontal, lacrimal, maxilla, and zygomatic bones. Four distinct margins define the orbit shape; they include the inferior, lateral, medial, and superior margins, or borders. The inferior margin comprises the orbital surface of the maxilla and horizontal orbital surface of the zygomatic. The lateral margin is made-up entirely of the orbital surface of the zygomatic. The medial border of the orbit is defined by the anterior lacrimal crest and the maxillary process of the frontal bone. Finally, the superior margin comprises the supraorbital margin and the orbital plate of the frontal bone.

## GROWTH AND DEVELOPMENT

The growth of each orbit is proportional to the growth of the human eye. As such, the entire region follows the fascinatingly rapid growth pattern of other neural tissues (Scheuer and Black, 2000). This period of swift development results in proportionately larger eyes (and bony orbits) in infants and young children compared to older adolescents and adults. Morphologically, the fleshy eye first appears as a shallow depression on the medial surface of the neural fold prior to the formalization of the neural tube (Moore and Persaud, 1993). Eventually, the eye expands and, via the optic stalk, establishes a connection to the brain (Franz-Odendaal and Vickaryous, 2006). At this point, the primitive eye undergoes a series of developmental changes (beyond the scope of this work) eventually leading to the more-or-less adult form.

The skeletal tissues associated with (correlated to) the growths of the eye are generally considered the sum total of both osseous and cartilaginous materials. Here, we deal only with the associated osseous remains. The embryo orbit is positioned at the front of the face (directed forward, as in the adult form) and, as already mentioned, is relatively large compared to newborn and adult orbits. At birth, the orbits are roughly circular with sharp supraorbital margins; both the superior and inferior orbital margins are generally vertical and the medial margin is positioned just anterior to the lateral (Enlow, 1990). The medial rim then progresses forward, drawn anteriorly by the nasal wall. Concomitantly, the lateral margin of the orbit is drawn posteriorly as the zygomatic increases in size and is directed laterally and posteriorly. This growth and development draws apart the medial and lateral margins of the orbit in a posteroanterior direction. At the same time, the superior orbital margin is repositioned (overhangs) over the inferior, through the forward growth of the supraorbital ridge and posterior movement (growth) of the zygomatic bone, which creates the obliquely upward and forward slant of the orbit (orbital inclination). Oehmann (1975), as reported in Hauser and De Stefano (1986), outlined four major periods of orbital growth, from a nearly 80% increase in size between birth and age two to a nearly 10% increase in size between ages nine and eleven, when the orbits roughly reach their adult size.

## FUNCTIONAL MORPHOLOGY

The orbital margins function to protect the bony eye and serve as the attachment site for various muscles and the orbital septum. Szilvassy (1986) suggested strong familial associations in the shape of the orbit.

## WITHIN POPULATION VARIATION

Data derived from the Macromorphoscopic Databank of the frequency distribution of OBS ($n = 4403$). All data are for adult individuals. When possible, frequency data for males and females are provided separately. When sex could not be estimated reliably, frequency distributions are pooled as "Unknown" (Table 13.1).

**TABLE 13.1** Frequency Distribution of OBS, by Geographic Origin and Sex

| | | 1 | | 2 | | 3 | | |
|---|---|---|---|---|---|---|---|---|
| **Geographic origin** | **Sex** | *n* | % | *n* | % | *n* | % | **Total** |
| **American Black** | **Female** | 8 | 47 | 8 | 47 | 1 | 6 | 17 |
| | **Male** | 31 | 46 | 33 | 49 | 3 | 4 | 67 |
| | **Unknown** | 0 | 0 | 1 | 100 | 0 | 0 | 1 |
| | **Total** | 39 | 46 | 42 | 49 | 4 | 5 | 85 |
| **American White** | **Female** | 43 | 35 | 72 | 59 | 7 | 6 | 122 |
| | **Male** | 60 | 33 | 98 | 54 | 23 | 13 | 181 |
| | **Unknown** | 0 | 0 | 0 | 0 | 0 | 0 | 0 |
| | **Total** | 103 | 34 | 170 | 56 | 30 | 10 | 303 |

*(Continued)*

TABLE 13.1 (*Continued*)

| Geographic origin | Sex | 1 *n* | 1 % | 2 *n* | 2 % | 3 *n* | 3 % | Total |
|---|---|---|---|---|---|---|---|---|
| **Amerindian** | **Female** | 0 | 0 | 0 | 0 | 0 | 0 | 0 |
| | **Male** | 0 | 0 | 0 | 0 | 0 | 0 | 0 |
| | **Unknown** | 1189 | 53 | 811 | 36 | 245 | 11 | 2245 |
| | **Total** | 1189 | 53 | 811 | 36 | 245 | 11 | 2245 |
| **El Salvador** | **Female** | 0 | 0 | 0 | 0 | 0 | 0 | 0 |
| | **Male** | 1 | 25 | 2 | 50 | 1 | 25 | 4 |
| | **Unknown** | 0 | 0 | 0 | 0 | 0 | 0 | 0 |
| | **Total** | 1 | 25 | 2 | 50 | 1 | 25 | 4 |
| **Eskimo** | **Female** | 0 | 0 | 0 | 0 | 0 | 0 | 0 |
| | **Male** | 0 | 0 | 0 | 0 | 0 | 0 | 0 |
| | **Unknown** | 522 | 68 | 224 | 29 | 26 | 3 | 772 |
| | **Total** | 522 | 68 | 224 | 29 | 26 | 3 | 772 |
| **Guatemalan** | **Female** | 1 | 50 | 1 | 50 | 0 | 0 | 2 |
| | **Male** | 0 | 0 | 1 | 100 | 0 | 0 | 1 |
| | **Unknown** | 0 | 0 | 0 | 0 | 0 | 0 | 0 |
| | **Total** | 1 | 33 | 2 | 67 | 0 | 0 | 3 |
| **Mexico** | **Female** | 0 | 0 | 0 | 0 | 0 | 0 | 0 |
| | **Male** | 7 | 39 | 10 | 56 | 1 | 6 | 18 |
| | **Unknown** | 0 | 0 | 0 | 0 | 0 | 0 | 0 |
| | **Total** | 7 | 39 | 10 | 56 | 1 | 6 | 18 |
| **Pacific Island** | **Female** | 30 | 56 | 11 | 20 | 13 | 24 | 54 |
| | **Male** | 47 | 56 | 24 | 29 | 13 | 15 | 84 |
| | **Unknown** | 71 | 80 | 13 | 15 | 5 | 6 | 89 |
| | **Total** | 148 | 65 | 48 | 21 | 31 | 14 | 227 |
| **Peruvian** | **Female** | 0 | 0 | 0 | 0 | 0 | 0 | 0 |
| | **Male** | 0 | 0 | 0 | 0 | 0 | 0 | 0 |
| | **Unknown** | 7 | 41 | 5 | 29 | 5 | 29 | 17 |
| | **Total** | 7 | 41 | 5 | 29 | 5 | 29 | 17 |
| **Southwest (SW) Hispanic** | **Female** | 3 | 38 | 2 | 25 | 3 | 38 | 8 |
| | **Male** | 7 | 70 | 3 | 30 | 0 | 0 | 10 |
| | **Unknown** | 0 | 0 | 0 | 0 | 0 | 0 | 0 |
| | **Total** | 10 | 56 | 5 | 28 | 3 | 17 | 18 |
| **Thai** | **Female** | 150 | 68 | 60 | 27 | 12 | 5 | 222 |
| | **Male** | 350 | 74 | 94 | 20 | 31 | 7 | 475 |
| | **Unknown** | 11 | 79 | 3 | 21 | 0 | 0 | 14 |
| | **Total** | 511 | 72 | 157 | 22 | 43 | 6 | 711 |
| **Total for all groups** | | 2538 | 58 | 1476 | 34 | 389 | 9 | 4403 |

*OBS*, orbital shape.

## CHARACTER STATES

OBS 1 = the eye orbits are *rectangular* in shape. The horizontal margins are longer than the vertical margins and mainly parallel.

OBS 2 = the eye orbits are *circular* in shape. The orbital margin is approximately equidistant from the center at any point.

OBS 3 = the eye orbits are *rhombic* in shape. The medial border is shorter in height than the lateral border. This shape resembles aviator sunglasses.

## CHARACTER STATES FOR ORBITAL SHAPE = 1 (FIGS. 13.2–13.8)

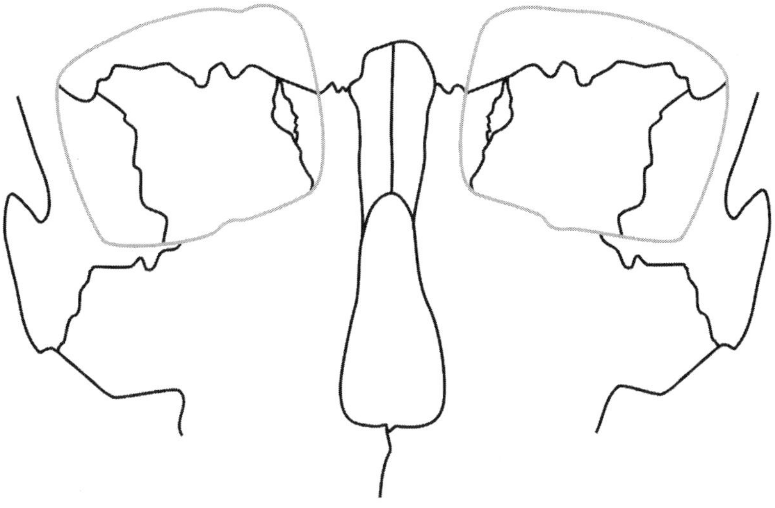


FIGURE 13.2 Diagrammatic representation of OBS 1. *OBS*, orbital shape.

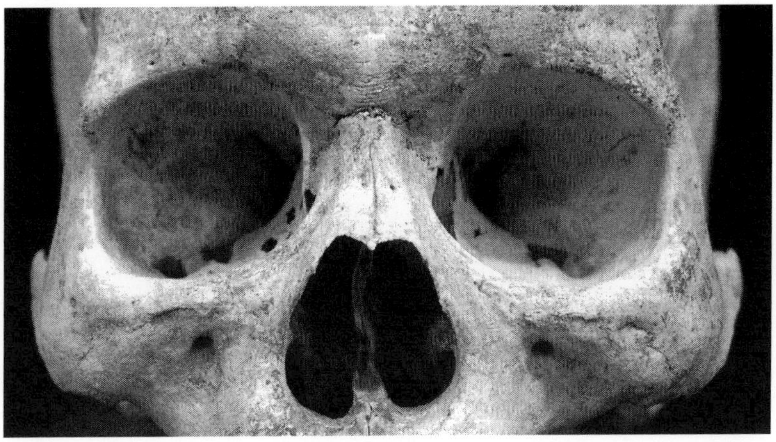

FIGURE 13.3 Variant of OBS 1. *OBS*, orbital shape.

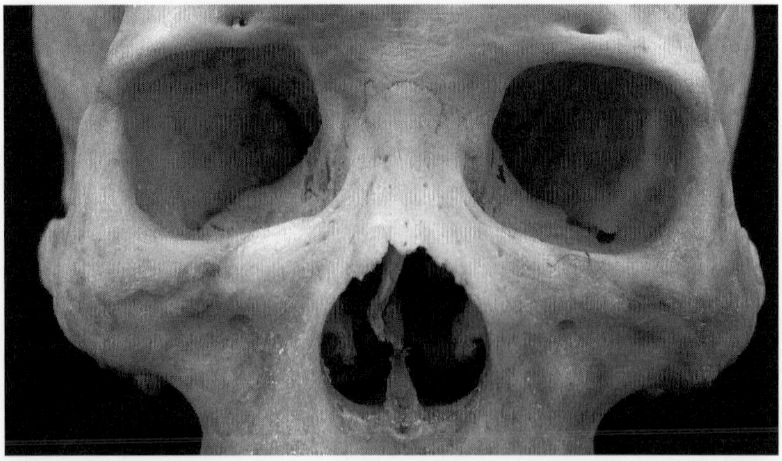

**FIGURE 13.4** Variant of OBS 1. *OBS*, orbital shape.

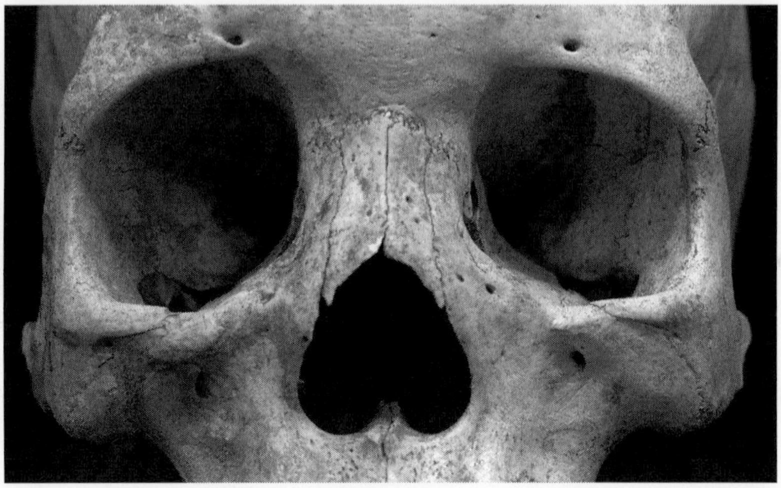

**FIGURE 13.5** Variant of OBS 1. *OBS*, orbital shape.

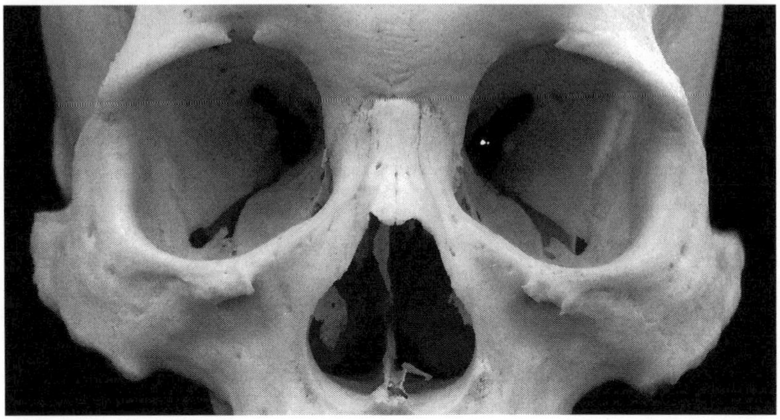

**FIGURE 13.6** Variant of OBS 1. *OBS*, orbital shape.

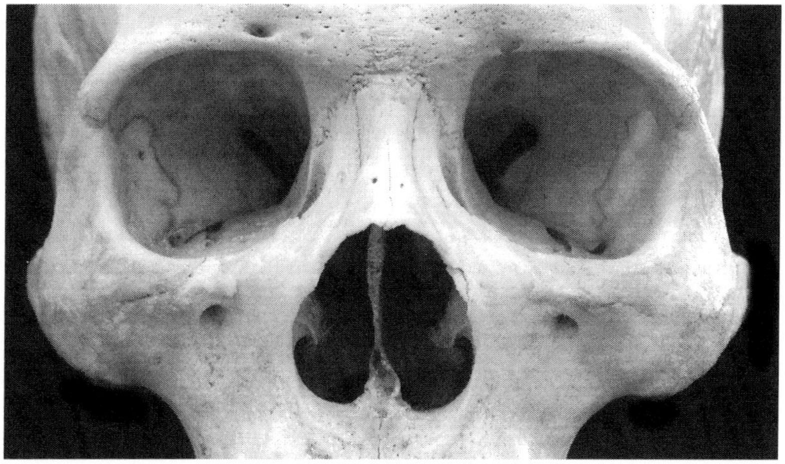

FIGURE 13.7 Variant of OBS 1. *OBS*, orbital shape.

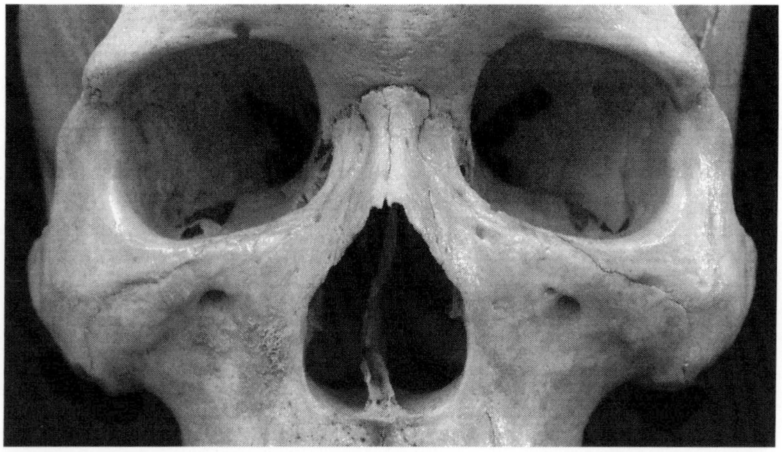

FIGURE 13.8 Variant of OBS 1. *OBS*, orbital shape.

# CHARACTER STATES FOR ORBITAL SHAPE = 2 (FIGS. 13.9–13.15)

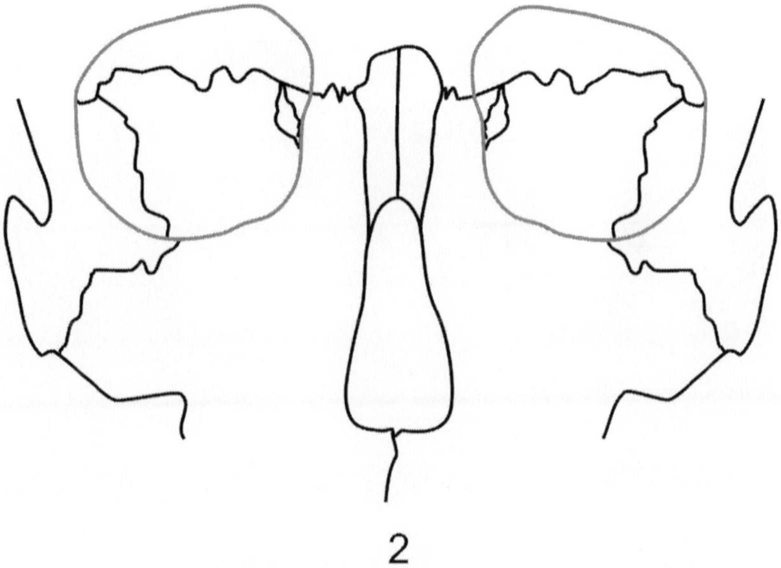


FIGURE 13.9 Diagrammatic representation of OBS 2. *OBS*, orbital shape.

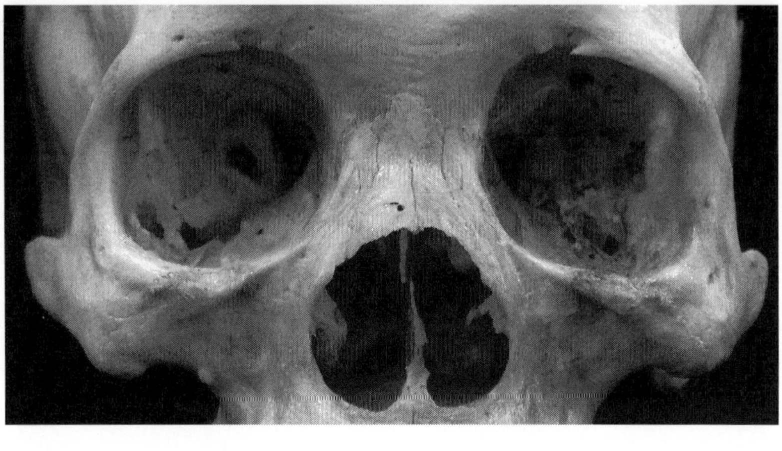

FIGURE 13.10 Variant of OBS 2. *OBS*, orbital shape.

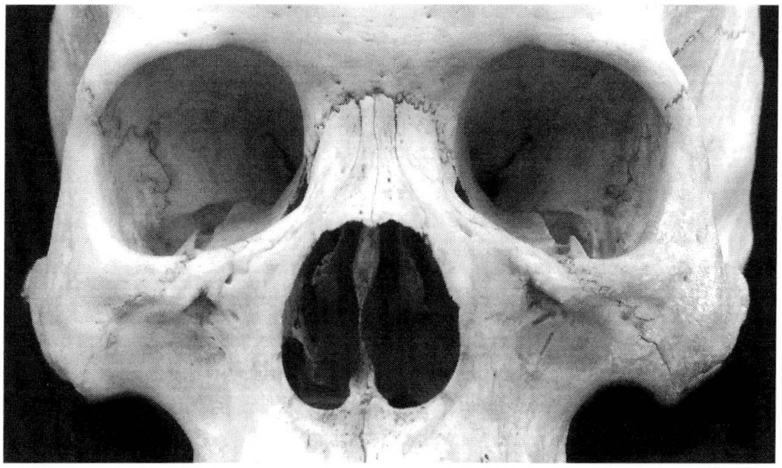

FIGURE 13.11 Variant of OBS 2. *OBS*, orbital shape.

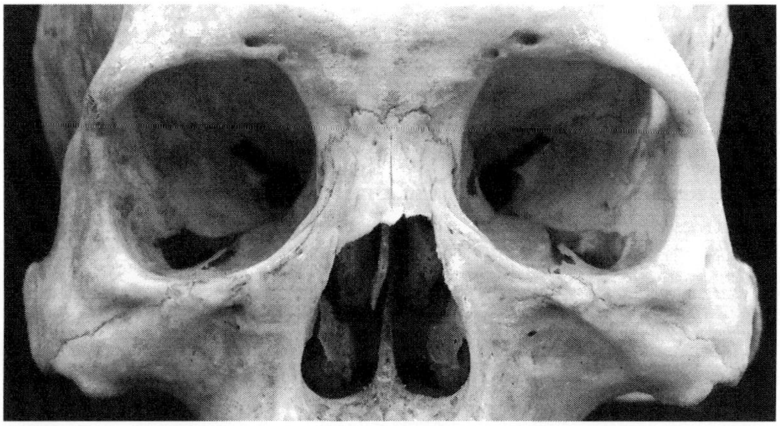

FIGURE 13.12 Variant of OBS 2. *OBS*, orbital shape.

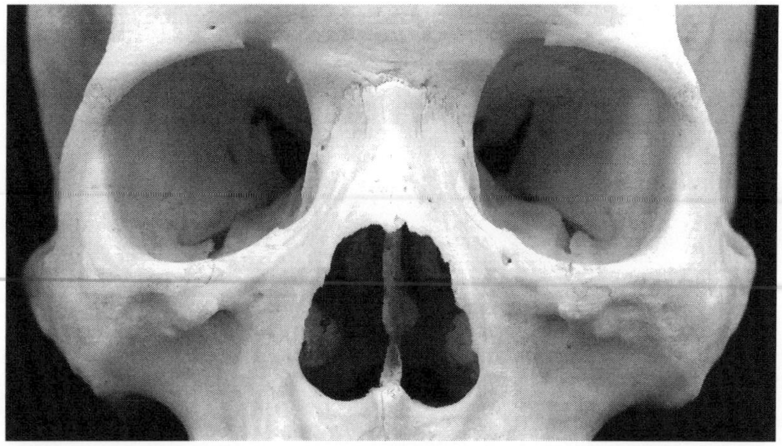

FIGURE 13.13 Variant of OBS 2. *OBS*, orbital shape.

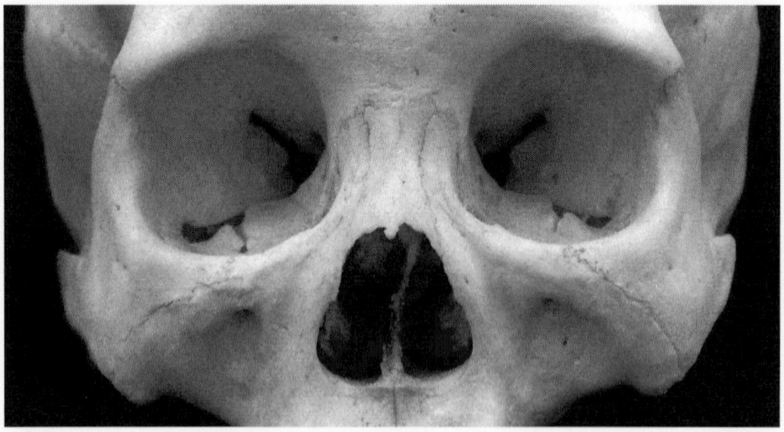

FIGURE 13.14 Variant of OBS 2. *OBS*, orbital shape.

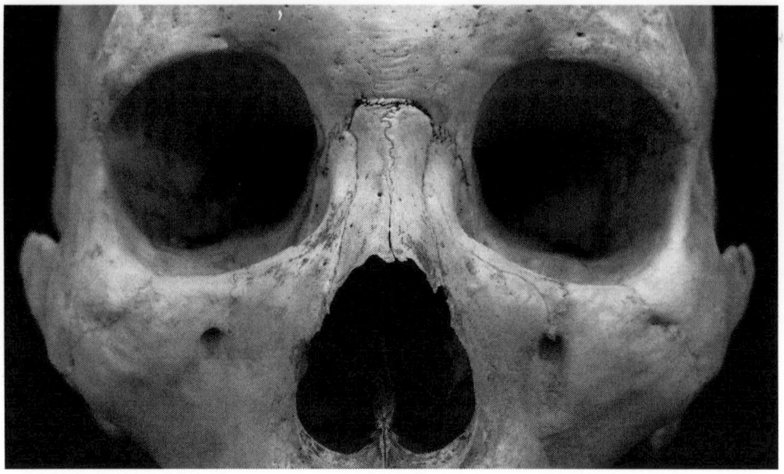

FIGURE 13.15 Variant of OBS 2. *OBS*, orbital shape.

## CHARACTER STATES FOR ORBITAL SHAPE = 3 (FIGS. 13.16–13.22)

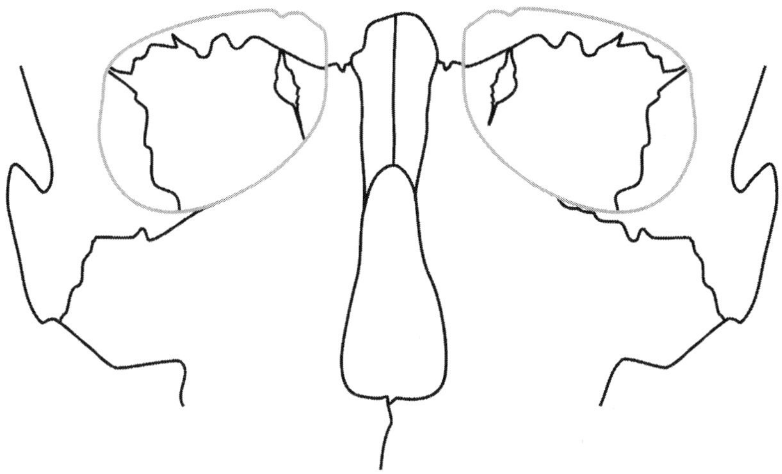


FIGURE 13.16 Diagrammatic representation of OBS 3. *OBS*, orbital shape.

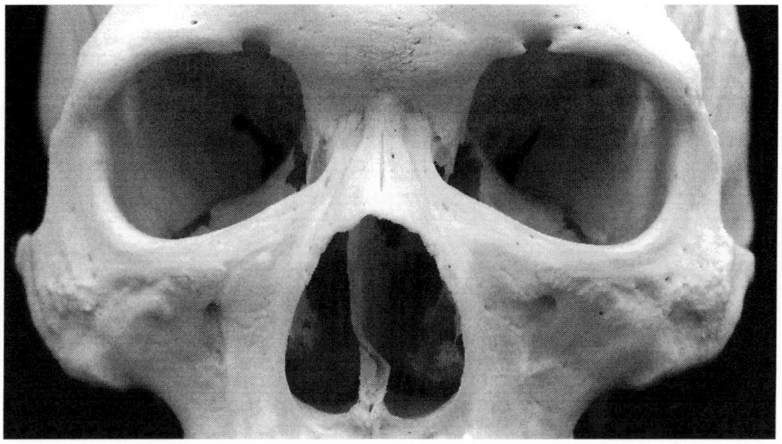

FIGURE 13.17 Variant of OBS 3. *OBS*, orbital shape.

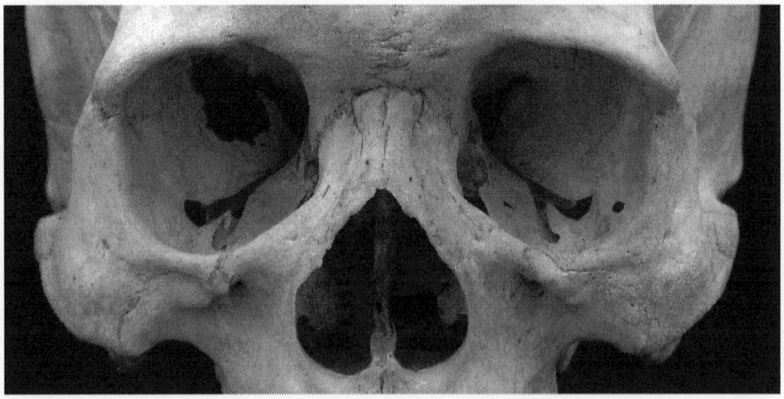

**FIGURE 13.18** Variant of OBS 3. *OBS*, orbital shape.

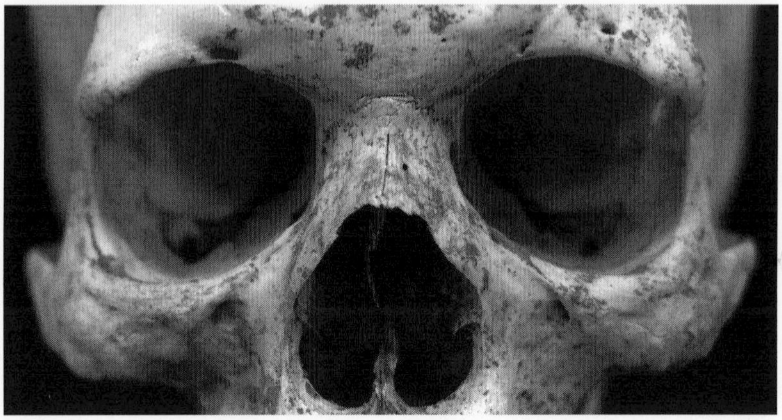

**FIGURE 13.19** Variant of OBS 3. *OBS*, orbital shape.

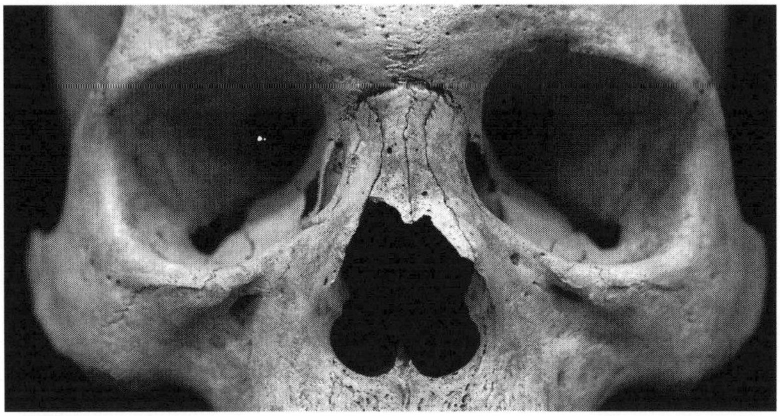

**FIGURE 13.20** Variant of OBS 3. *OBS*, orbital shape.

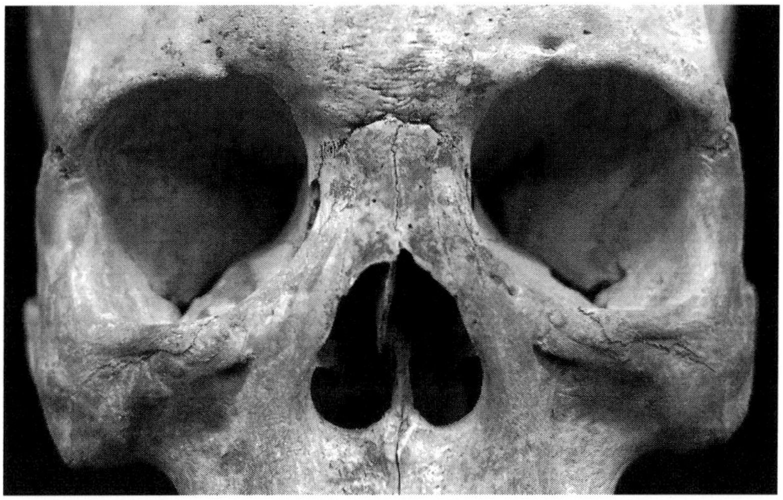

FIGURE 13.21 Variant of OBS 3. *OBS*, orbital shape.

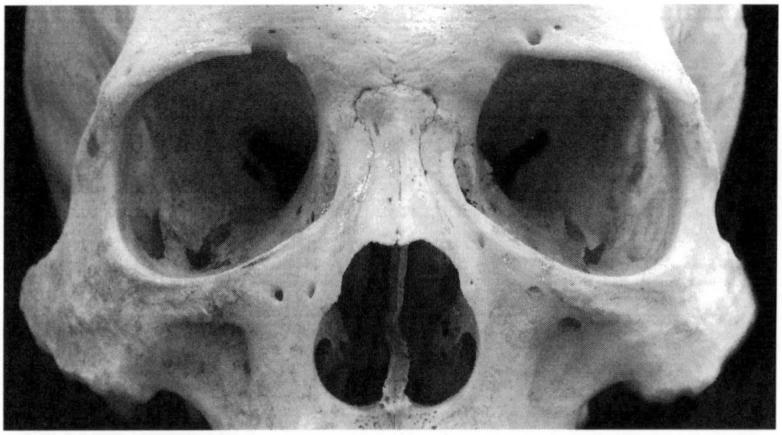

FIGURE 13.22 Variant of OBS 3. *OBS*, orbital shape.

CHAPTER

# 14

# Palate Shape

Palate shape (PS) considers the contour of the dental arcade, defined by the curvature of the hard palate in the transverse plane viewed from the occlusal/inferior aspect of the maxillae. PS is based on the overall morphology and arch shape of the anterior and posterior dentition, assessed as a midline-projection through the individual teeth along their mesiodistal axis. To assess this trait, hold the cranium from the inferior view and focus on the occlusal/inferior aspect of the maxilla. Project a line through the midline-projection of the individual teeth along their mesiodistal axis. Assess the overall shape of this line relative to the four character states: elliptical, parabolic A, parabolic B, hyperbolic; scored as: $1 < 2 < 3 < 4$.

Topinard (1881:260) defined the shape of the palate arch as "the form of the arch [defined] by its inner side, consequently [defining] that of the palate." He identified four classes: (1) *hyperbolic*, (2) *parabolic*, (3) *U-shaped*, and (4) *elliptical*. Duckworth (1904) and Dieufale and Tournier (1908) defined PS similarly; although Duckworth (1904:243) used the terms (1) *hypsiloid*, (2) *parabolic*, and (3) *elliptical*, while Dieufale and Tournier (1908) termed variation in PS as (1) *divergent*, (2) *elliptical*, (3) *hyperbolic*, and (4) *semielliptical*. Shaw (1931) used the same character states as Dieufale and Tournier (1908) to study the palate of South Africans. Galloway (1937) later described three character states: (1) *horseshoe-shaped*, (2) *U-shaped*, and (3) *divergent U-shaped*, which were adopted by DeVilliers (1968) for his study of South African crania.

Hooton (n.d.) included PS in the Harvard Blanks along with standard illustrations and a definition. Hooton's definition of PS is (Fig. 14.1):

> The shape to be considered is arrived at by smoothing the line of the inner edges of the upper teeth surfaces. The ends of the arch so formed may be diverging, parallel, or converging; and it is on this scheme that the scale (plate 15 [Fig. 14.1]) is constructed. It will be noted that no provision is made for a range of "U" shaped palates. To be "U" shaped the ends of the dental arch must be parallel. Size of the palate is described by the standard measurements and need not be repeated as an observation by distinguishing between large and small "Us." Doubtless very few skulls will fit into the new category "simian." The criteria *[sic]* for this category is not a greater degree of convergence, but a greatest width anterior to the second molars. Almost certainly there is no actual human palate like the one pictured at the simian end of the scale, which was concocted to show the direction of change of shape to be sought for.

Clearly, Hooton did not develop PS; rather, like many other macromorphoscopic traits, he standardized how these data were collected and established a systematic approach useful for describing populations like the Pecos Pueblo sample for which he is so well known. Following Hooton's standardization, others followed a similar approach. Krogman (1955) and Krogman and Işcan (1986) included PS in their trait lists, but they moved away from descriptive character states to an approach meant to capture the size of the palate (i.e., *narrow*, *moderately wide*, and *wide*). Rhine (1990) scored *dental arcade shape* as "parabolic (narrower and tapering), elliptic (wider and smoothly curving), or hyperbolic (approaching rectangular)" (Rhine, 1990:20). Similarly, Gill (1986, 1998) identified the same three character states for *palatal form*. Byers et al. (1997) identified archetypes of the various expressions of PS as "(a) *triangular (parabolic)* of Caucasoids, (b) *parallel sided* of Negroids, and (c) *rounded* of Mongoloids" (Byers et al., 1997:4). Maier et al. (2015) mirrored the language of both Rhine and Gill, observing the nonmetric indicators of ancestry for PS as "[t]he parabolic (triangular), the hyperbolic (rectangular), and the elliptical (rounded) palate shapes are linked to white, black, and Asian/Native American ancestry, respectively" (Maier et al., 2015:1129). Wun (2014), working with one of the authors (JTH), developed the scoring strategy for PS used herein. She defined PS as the curvature of the hard palate in the transverse plane based on the overall morphology and arch shape of the anterior and posterior dentition, assessed as a midline-projection through the individual teeth along their mesiodistal axis (Plemons and Hefner, 2016).

*Atlas of Human Cranial Macromorphoscopic Traits.*
DOI: https://doi.org/10.1016/B978-0-12-814385-8.00014-8

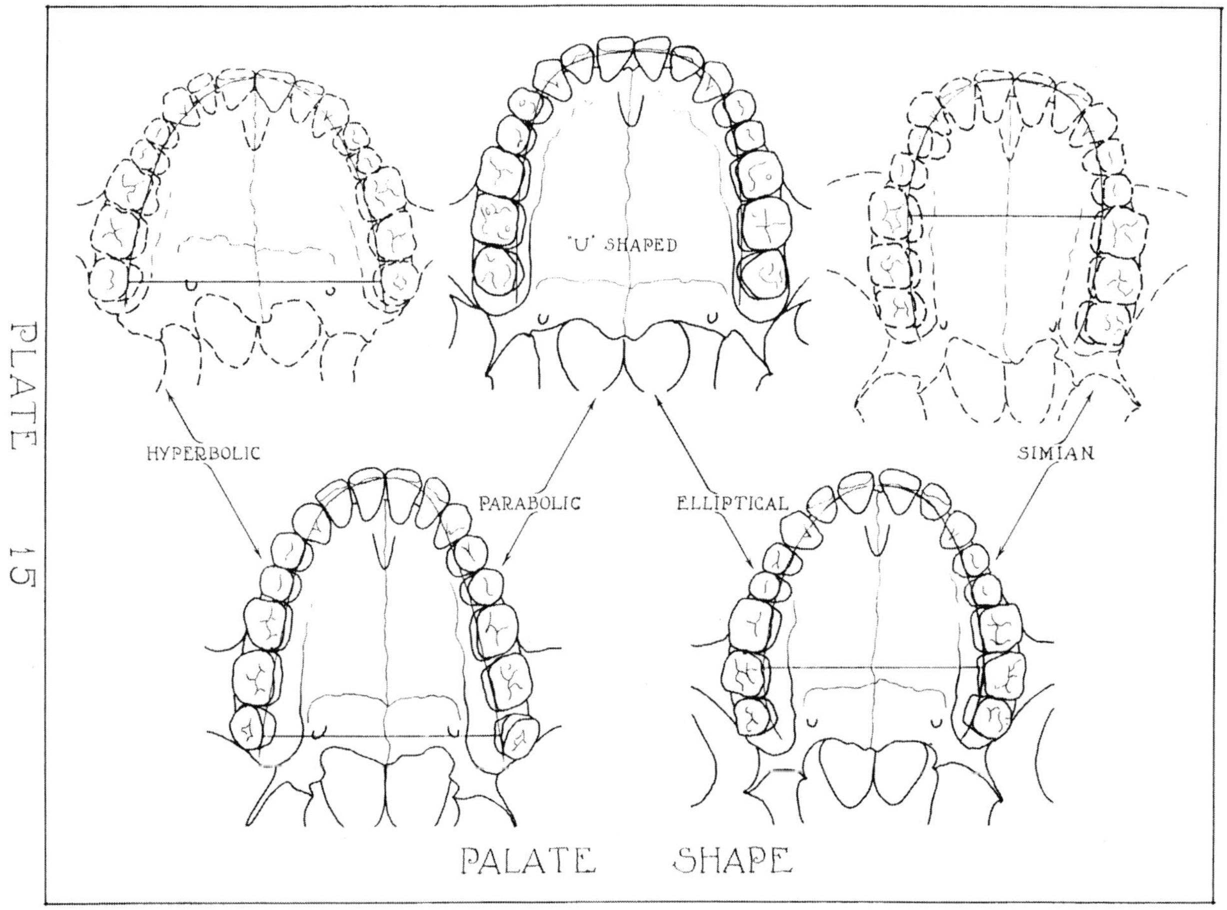


**FIGURE 14.1** Hooton's illustrations of the various character states for palate shape.

## NOMENCLATURE

Dental arcade shape, *figura palatum*, palate form, palatal form, palate shape, superior maxillary arch, palate arch, and shape of palate.

## GROSS ANATOMY

The human palate is defined by several skeletal elements. The anterior two-thirds of the hard palate is formed by the palatine processes of the maxillae (White, 2000), while the posterior one-third comprises the horizontal portions of the palatine bones. The maxilla and palatine are connected via the transverse palatine suture (see Chapter 18: Transverse Palatine Suture); the left and right maxillae articulate via the median palatine suture. The alveoli and associated dentition also contribute to PS as they are used to define the mesiodistal axis for the assessment of PS.

## GROWTH AND DEVELOPMENT

The maxillae each ossify from two main centers of ossification—the maxillary and the premaxillary (White and Folkens, 1991). By the ninth week in utero, these are fully fused in humans. The left and right halves of the maxillae may never fully fuse at the anterior median palatine suture. The palatine bones ossify from a single center. The two halves may never fully fuse along the posterior median palatine suture. PS is demonstrable early in growth and development. Wood (2012, 2015) notes several authors describing PS differences within and between populations as early as fetal development (Feik and Glover, 1998; Limson, 1932; Weinberg et al., 2005).

## FUNCTIONAL MORPHOLOGY

Much of the functional morphology of the palate is under strong selective pressures related to mastication. The morphology of the palate is associated with the dental alveolus housing, the dentition and the variation inherent in palate morphology resulting from differential loading in this skeletal region (masticatory loading) (Menegaz et al., 2009). Palate morphology—including its dimensions and underlying cortical and trabecular bone concentration—is determined, at least in part, by the variation introduced through differential masticatory loadings (Pilloud et al., 2014). The palatine sutures (incisive, median palatine, and transverse) provide anterior and lateral growth up to their obliteration and are directly linked to the development of the soft palate.

## WITHIN POPULATION VARIATION

Data derived from the Macromorphoscopic Databank of the frequency distribution of PS ($n = 988$). All data are for adult individuals. When possible, frequency data for males and females are provided separately. When sex could not be estimated reliably, frequency distributions are pooled as "Unknown" (Table 14.1).

**TABLE 14.1** Frequency Distribution of PS, by Geographic Origin and Sex

| | | 1 | | 2 | | 3 | | 4 | | |
|---|---|---|---|---|---|---|---|---|---|---|
| **Geographic origin** | **Sex** | *n* | % | *n* | % | *n* | % | *n* | % | **Total** |
| **American Black** | **Female** | 7 | 58 | 2 | 17 | 2 | 17 | 1 | 8 | 12 |
| | **Male** | 14 | 22 | 14 | 22 | 15 | 23 | 22 | 34 | 65 |
| | **Unknown** | 1 | 100 | 0 | 0 | 0 | 0 | 0 | 0 | 1 |
| | **Total** | 22 | 28 | 16 | 21 | 17 | 22 | 23 | 29 | 78 |
| **American White** | **Female** | 53 | 45 | 34 | 29 | 16 | 14 | 14 | 12 | 117 |
| | **Male** | 61 | 35 | 59 | 34 | 34 | 20 | 20 | 11 | 174 |
| | **Unknown** | 0 | 0 | 0 | 0 | 0 | 0 | 0 | 0 | 0 |
| | **Total** | 114 | 39 | 93 | 32 | 50 | 17 | 34 | 12 | 291 |
| **El Salvador** | **Female** | 0 | 0 | 0 | 0 | 0 | 0 | 0 | 0 | 0 |
| | **Male** | 0 | 0 | 1 | 20 | 1 | 20 | 3 | 60 | 5 |
| | **Unknown** | 0 | 0 | 0 | 0 | 0 | 0 | 0 | 0 | 0 |
| | **Total** | 0 | 0 | 1 | 20 | 1 | 20 | 3 | 60 | 5 |
| **Guatemalan** | **Female** | 0 | 0 | 0 | 0 | 1 | 100 | 0 | 0 | 1 |
| | **Male** | 0 | 0 | 1 | 100 | 0 | 0 | 0 | 0 | 1 |
| | **Unknown** | 0 | 0 | 0 | 0 | 0 | 0 | 0 | 0 | 0 |
| | **Total** | 0 | 0 | 1 | 50 | 1 | 50 | 0 | 0 | 2 |

*(Continued)*

TABLE 14.1 (*Continued*)

| Geographic origin | Sex | 1 | | 2 | | 3 | | 4 | | Total |
|---|---|---|---|---|---|---|---|---|---|---|
| | | *n* | % | *n* | % | *n* | % | *n* | % | |
| **Mexico** | **Female** | 0 | 0 | 0 | 0 | 0 | 0 | 0 | 0 | 0 |
| | **Male** | 6 | 33 | 5 | 28 | 6 | 33 | 1 | 6 | 18 |
| | **Unknown** | 0 | 0 | 0 | 0 | 0 | 0 | 0 | 0 | 0 |
| | **Total** | 6 | 33 | 5 | 28 | 6 | 33 | 1 | 6 | 18 |
| **Pacific Island** | **Female** | 12 | 24 | 35 | 70 | 3 | 6 | 0 | 0 | 50 |
| | **Male** | 16 | 20 | 61 | 76 | 3 | 4 | 0 | 0 | 80 |
| | **Unknown** | 1 | 7 | 12 | 86 | 1 | 7 | 0 | 0 | 14 |
| | **Total** | 29 | 20 | 108 | 75 | 7 | 5 | 0 | 0 | 144 |
| **Southwest (SW) Hispanic** | **Female** | 0 | 0 | 4 | 57 | 3 | 43 | 0 | 0 | 7 |
| | **Male** | 1 | 11 | 3 | 33 | 4 | 44 | 1 | 11 | 9 |
| | **Unknown** | 0 | 0 | 0 | 0 | 0 | 0 | 0 | 0 | 0 |
| | **Total** | 1 | 6 | 7 | 44 | 7 | 44 | 1 | 6 | 16 |
| **Thai** | **Female** | 14 | 11 | 48 | 38 | 61 | 48 | 3 | 2 | 126 |
| | **Male** | 30 | 10 | 139 | 47 | 122 | 41 | 7 | 2 | 298 |
| | **Unknown** | 1 | 10 | 7 | 70 | 1 | 10 | 1 | 10 | 10 |
| | **Total** | 45 | 10 | 194 | 45 | 184 | 42 | 11 | 3 | 434 |
| **Total for all groups** | | 217 | 22 | 425 | 43 | 273 | 28 | 73 | 7 | 988 |

*PS*, palate shape.

## CHARACTER STATES

Photographic exemplars of the different character states of PS are provided below. Each character state is defined following Hefner (2009, 2016). When necessary to clarify scoring, more nuanced definitions are provided in the figure captions. PS should be assessed with the protocol provided in the preceding section. Character states include:

PS 1 = *elliptical*; smooth, round curvature of the anterior portion of the palate combined with a midarch (ca. M1 and M2) widening relative to M3, contributing to the appearance of constricted (medially positioned) third molars.

PS 2 = *parabolic A*; smooth rounded curvature of the anterior portion of the palate, combined with an even, gradual flaring of the posterior dentition.

PS 3 = *parabolic B*; smooth, rounded curvature of the anterior portion of the palate, but combined with an even, gradual flaring of the posterior dentition. The only distinction is the longer relative length to breadth ratio in Form B.

PS 4 = *hyperbolic*; smooth, slightly flattened curvature of the anterior portion of the palate, combined with a straight, more-or-less parallel configuration of the posterior portions of the arch.

## CHARACTER STATES FOR PALATE SHAPE = 1 (FIGS. 14.2–14.8)

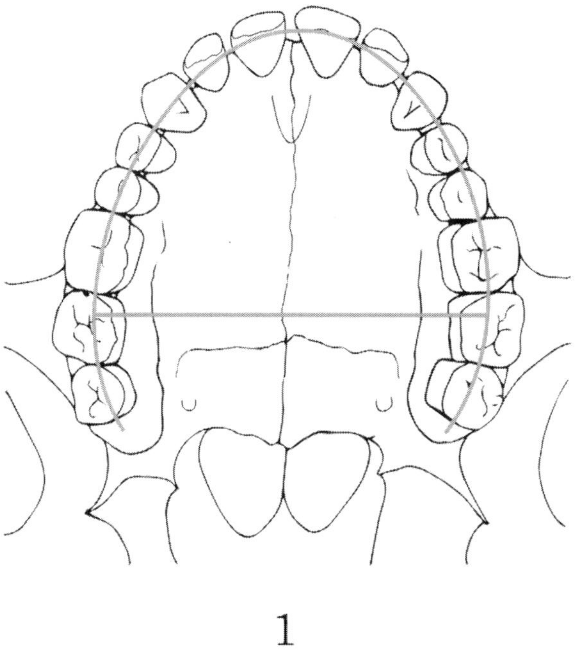


FIGURE 14.2 Diagrammatic representation of PS 1. Arch indicates the plane of reference. *PS*, palate shape.

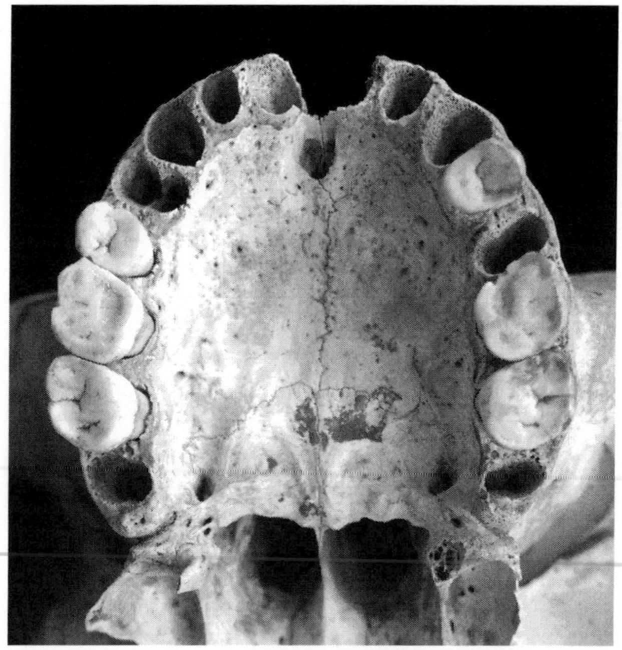

FIGURE 14.3 Variant of PS 1. Note: even when the teeth are missing, assessing PS is possible. *PS*, palate shape.

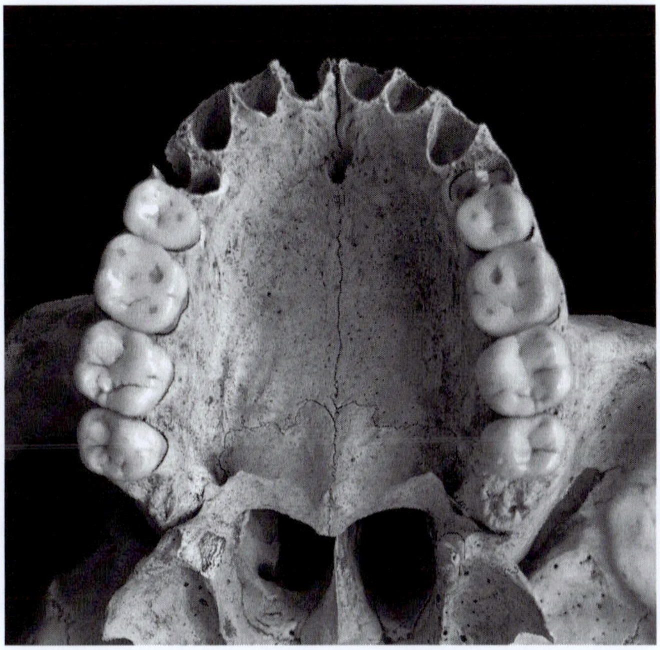

**FIGURE 14.4** Variant of PS 1. *PS*, palate shape.

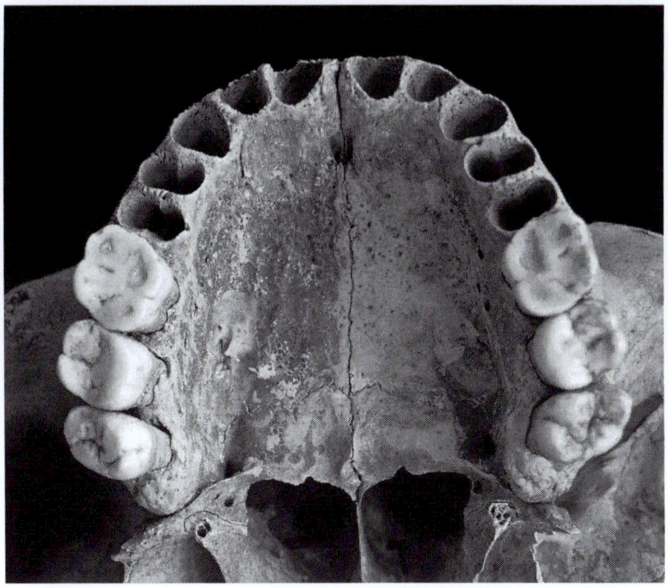

**FIGURE 14.5** Variant of PS 1. *PS*, palate shape.

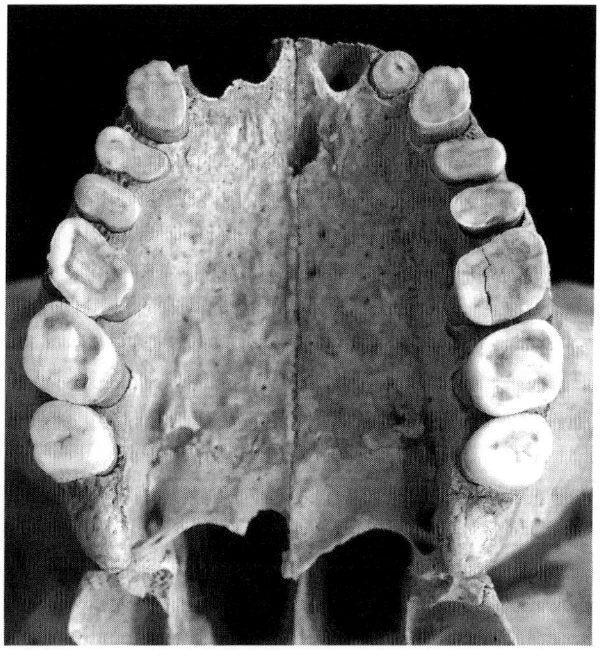

FIGURE 14.6 Variant of PS 1. *PS*, palate shape.

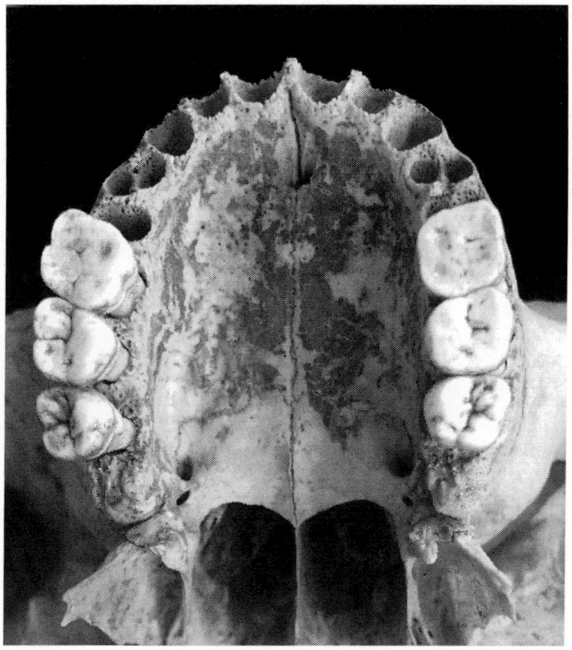

FIGURE 14.7 Variant of PS 1. *PS*, palate shape.

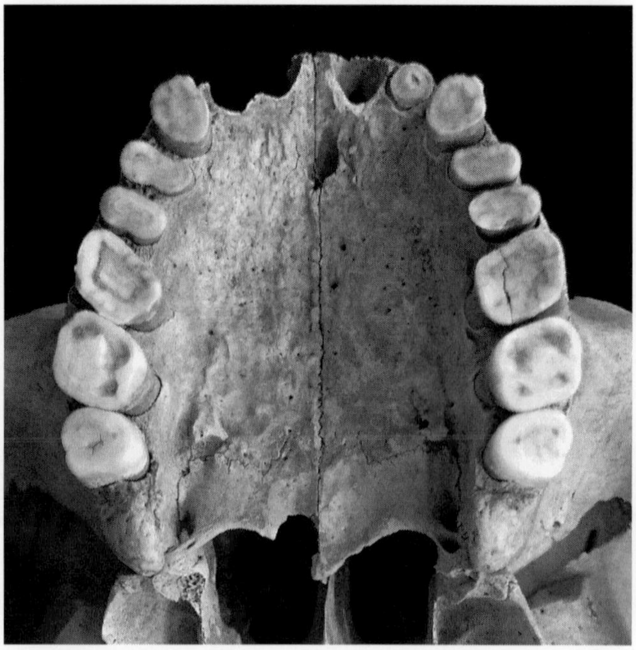

**FIGURE 14.8** Variant of PS 1. *PS*, palate shape.

## CHARACTER STATES FOR PALATE SHAPE = 2 (FIGS. 14.9–14.15)

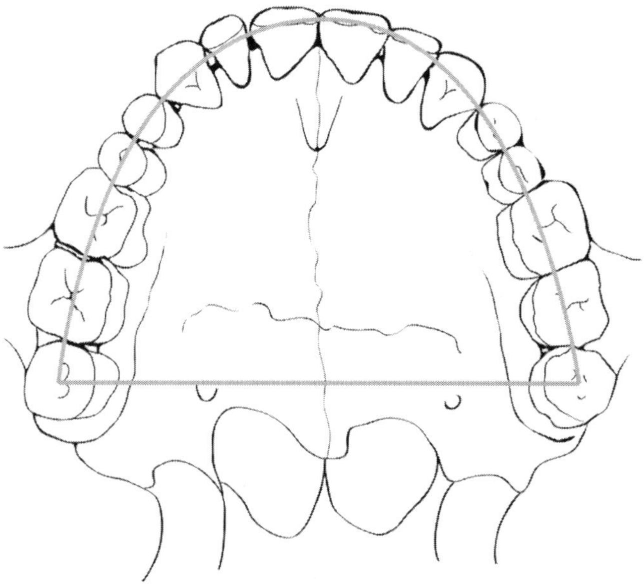

2

FIGURE 14.9 Diagrammatic representation of PS 2. Arch indicates the plane of reference. *PS*, palate shape.

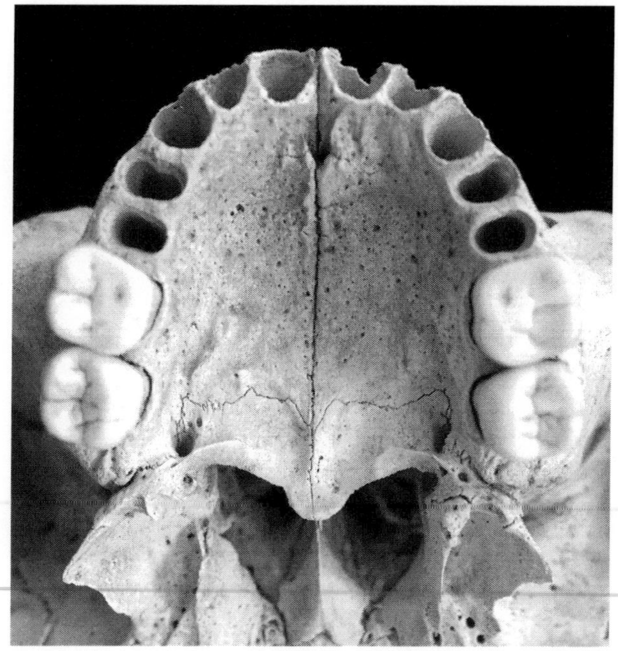

FIGURE 14.10 Variant of PS 2. Note: even when the teeth are missing, assessing PS is possible. *PS*, palate shape.

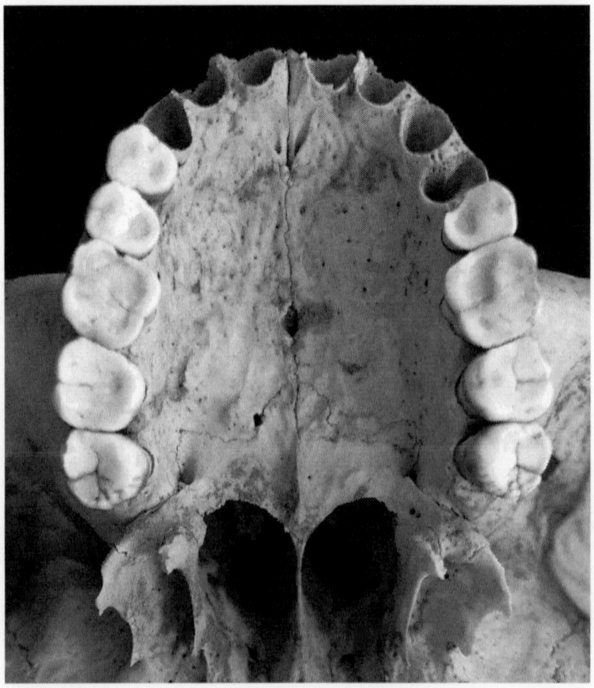

**FIGURE 14.11** Variant of PS 2. *PS*, palate shape.

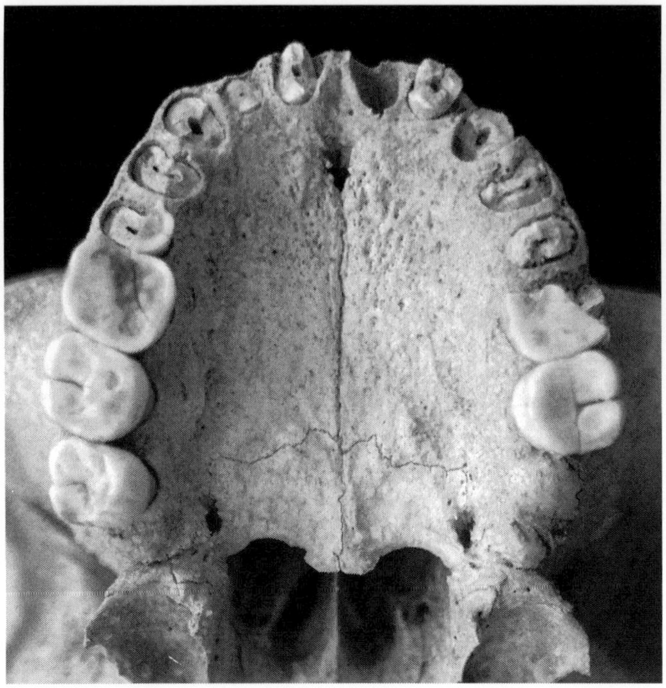

**FIGURE 14.12** Variant of PS 2. *PS*, palate shape.

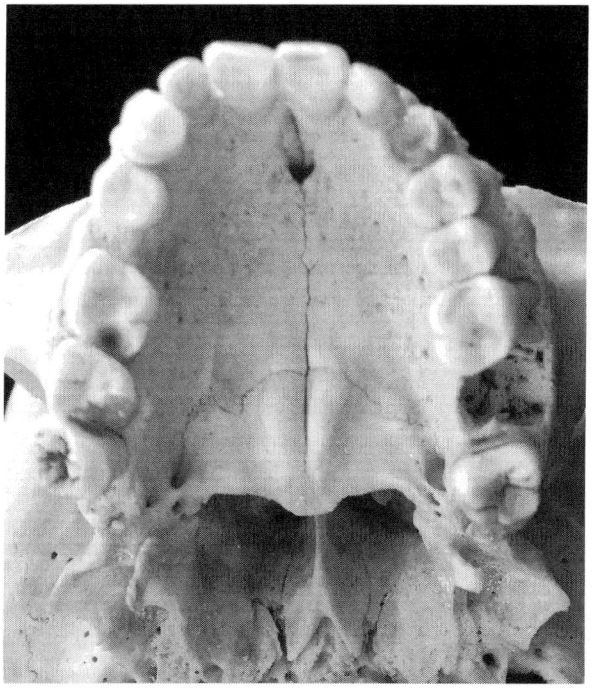

FIGURE 14.13 Variant of PS 2. *PS*, palate shape.

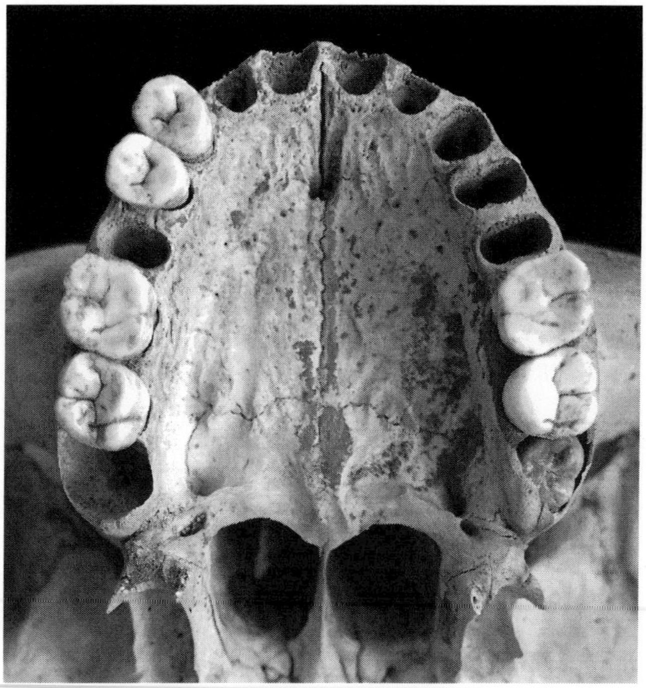

FIGURE 14.14 Variant of PS 2. *PS*, palate shape.

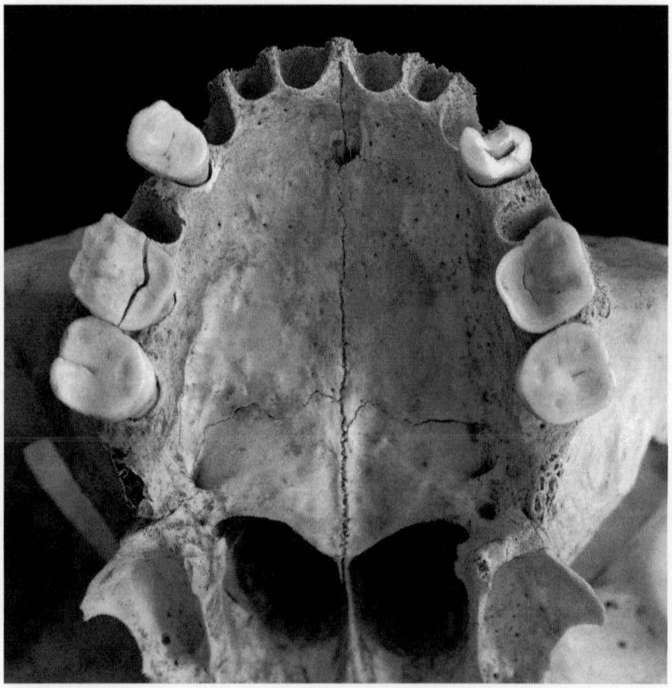

**FIGURE 14.15** Variant of PS 2. *PS*, palate shape.

## CHARACTER STATES FOR PALATE SHAPE = 3 (FIGS. 14.16–14.22)

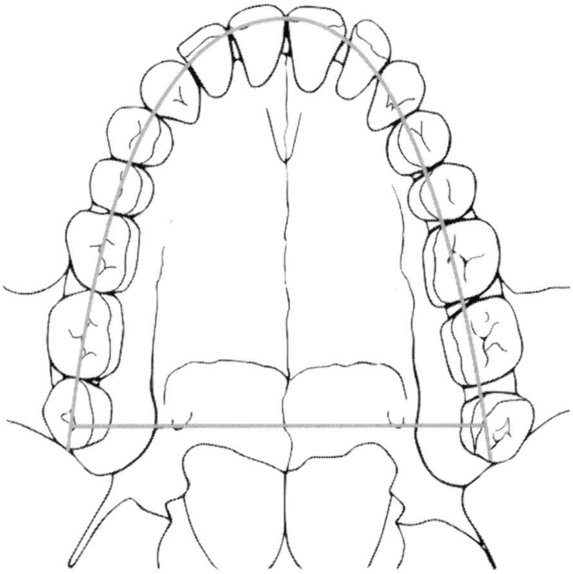

3

**FIGURE 14.16** Diagrammatic representation of PS 3. Arch indicates the plane of reference. *PS*, palate shape.

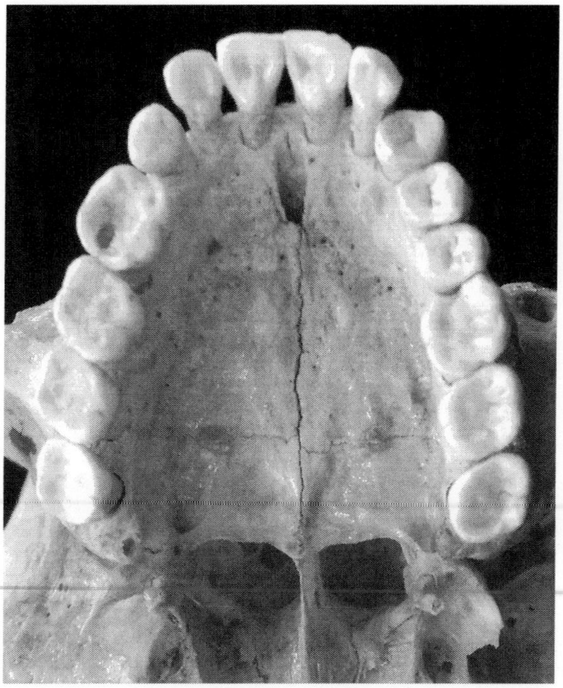

**FIGURE 14.17** Variant of PS 3. *PS*, palate shape.

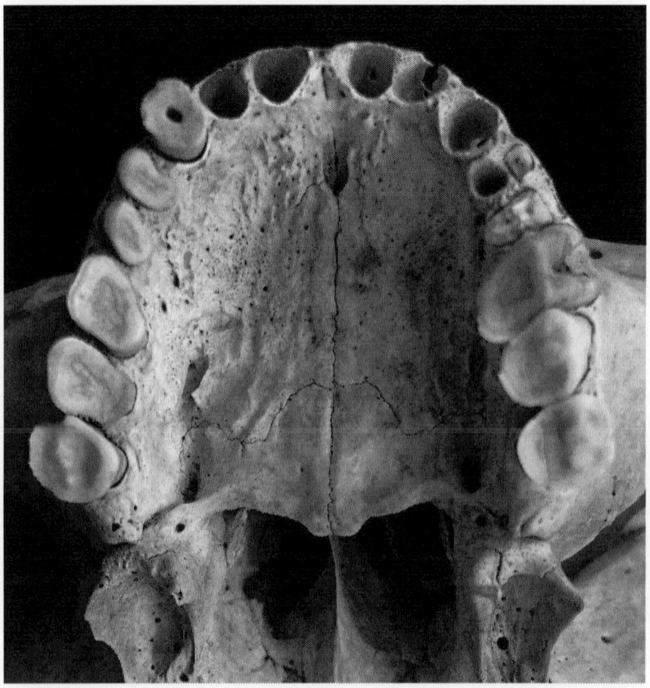

**FIGURE 14.18** Variant of PS 3. *PS*, palate shape.

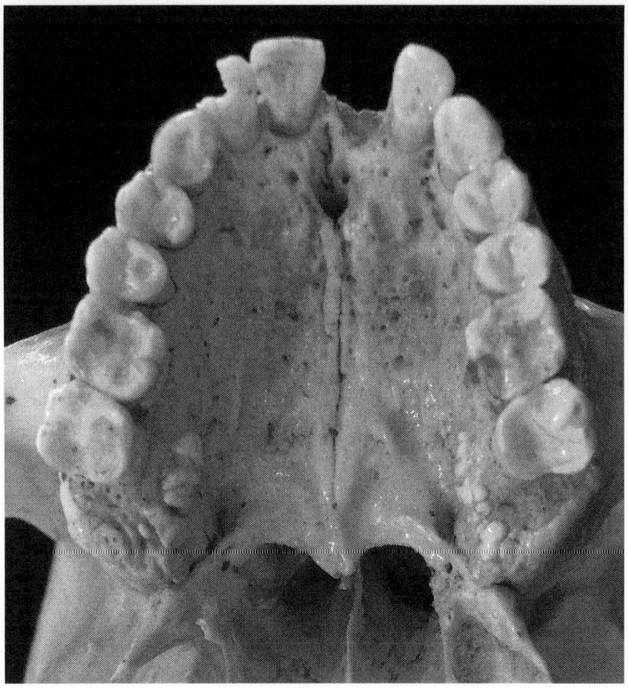

**FIGURE 14.19** Variant of PS 3. *PS*, palate shape.

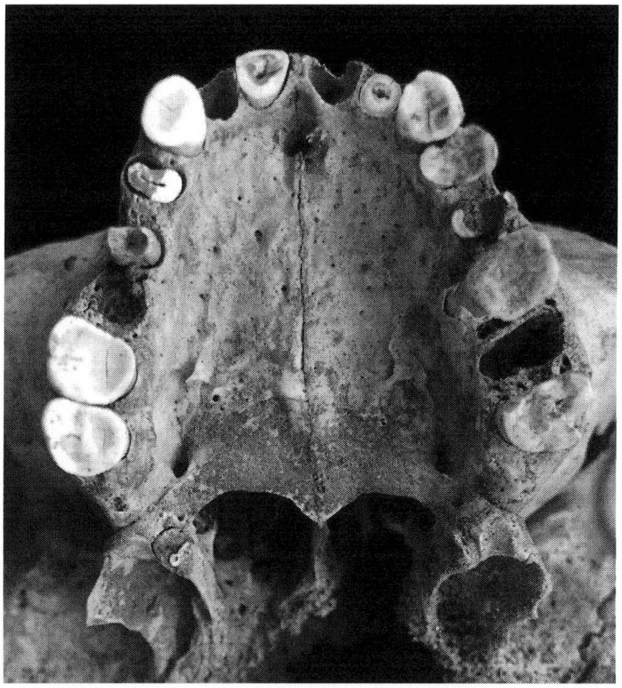

FIGURE 14.20 Variant of PS 3. *PS*, palate shape.

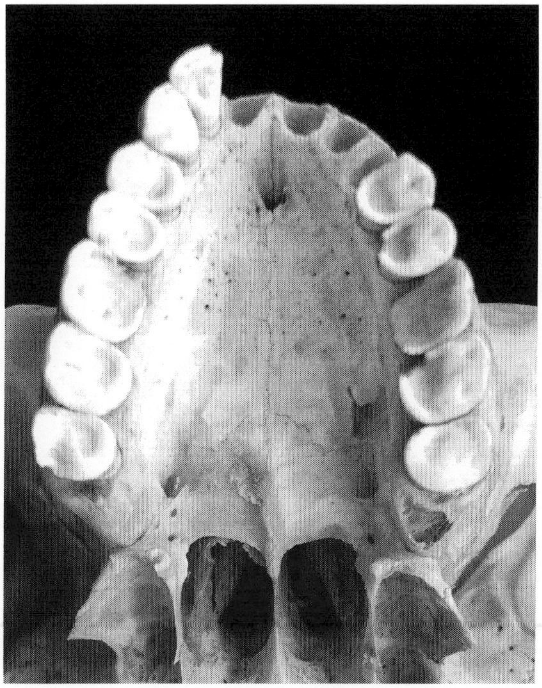

FIGURE 14.21 Variant of PS 3. *PS*, palate shape.

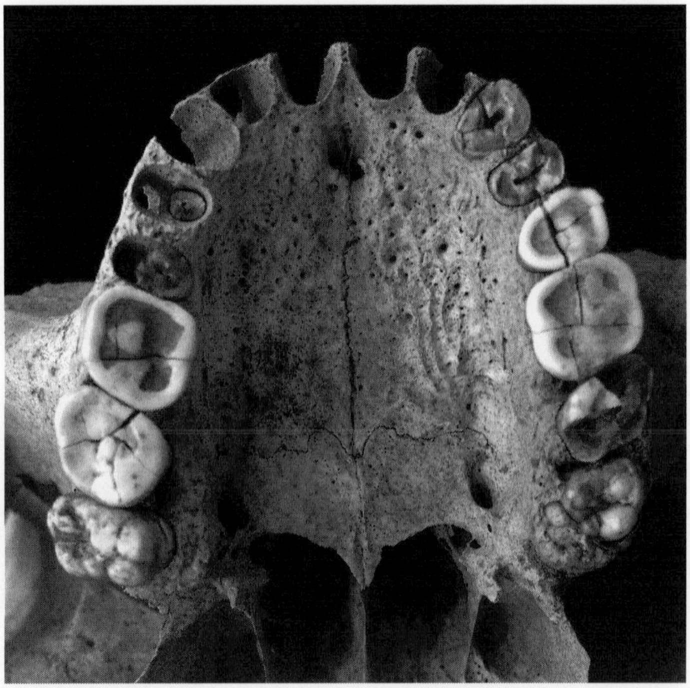

**FIGURE 14.22** Variant of PS 3. *PS*, palate shape.

## CHARACTER STATES FOR PALATE SHAPE = 4 (FIGS. 14.23–14.29)

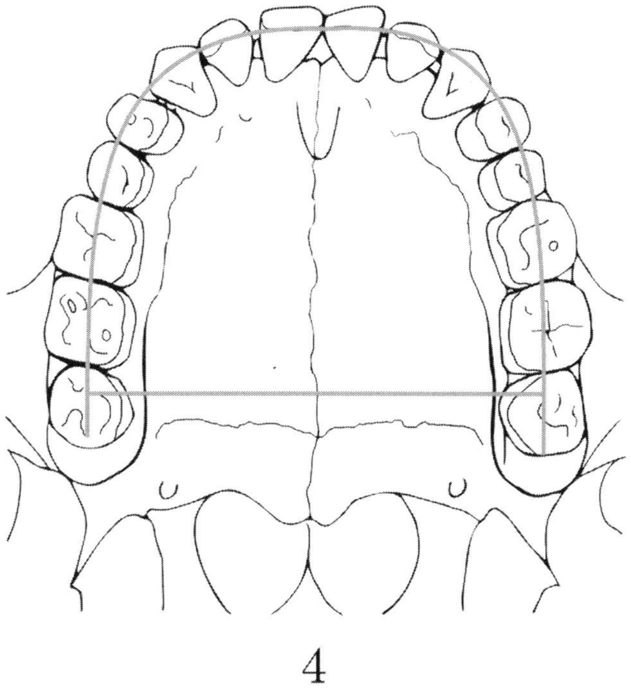


**FIGURE 14.23** Diagrammatic representation of PS 4. Arch indicates the plane of reference. *PS*, palate shape.

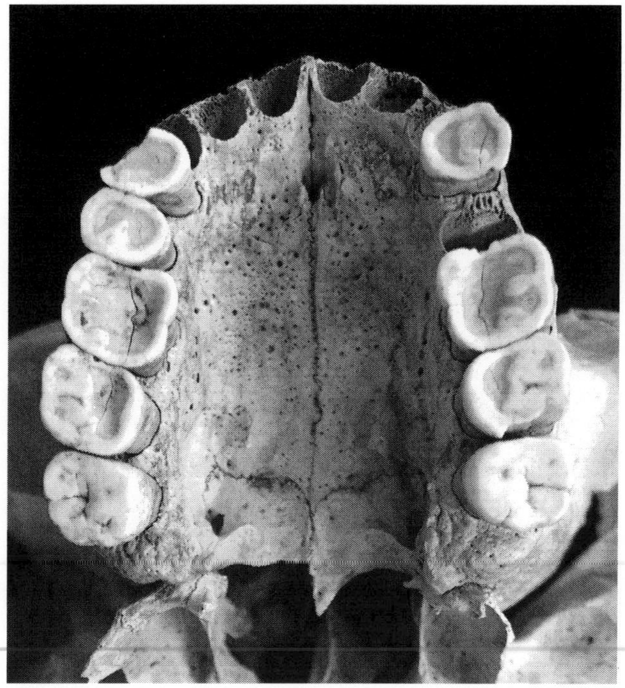

**FIGURE 14.24** Variant of PS 4. *PS*, palate shape.

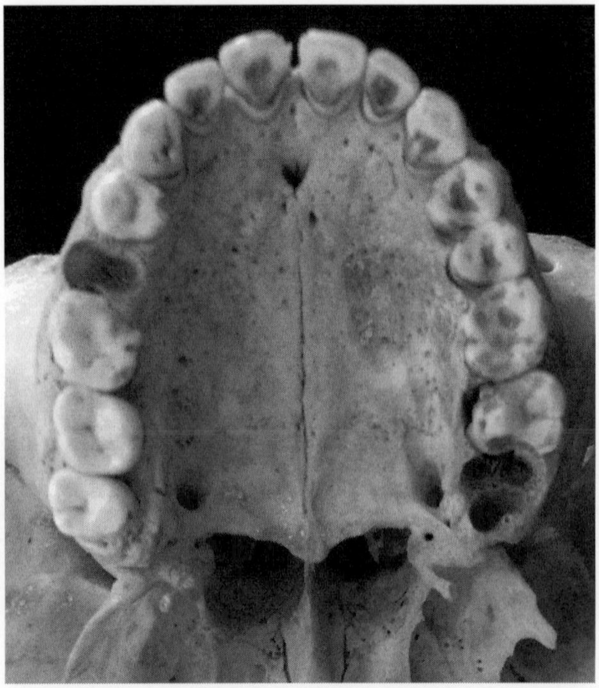

**FIGURE 14.25** Variant of PS 4. *PS*, palate shape.

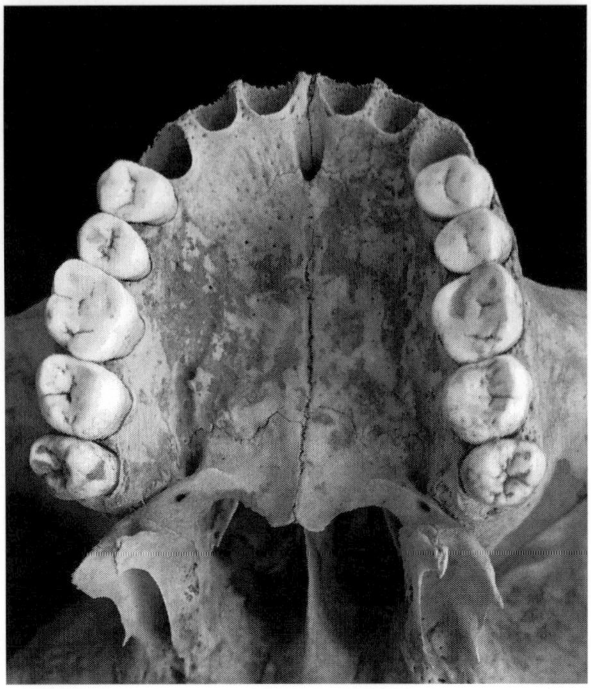

**FIGURE 14.26** Variant of PS 4. *PS*, palate shape.

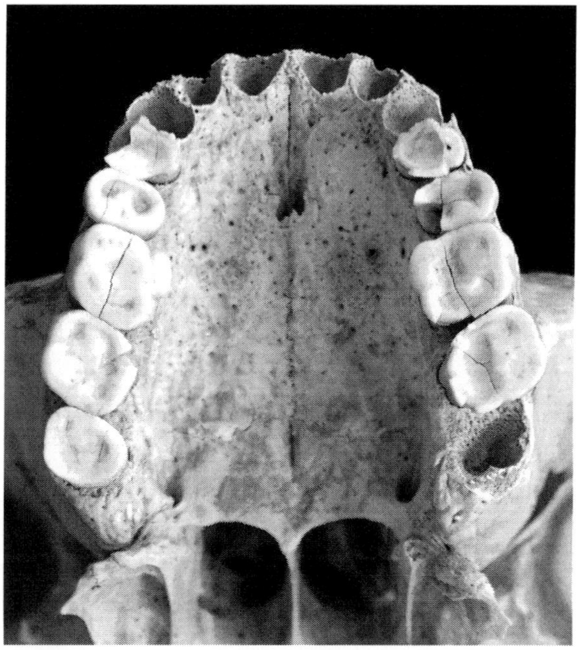

FIGURE 14.27 Variant of PS 4. *PS*, palate shape.

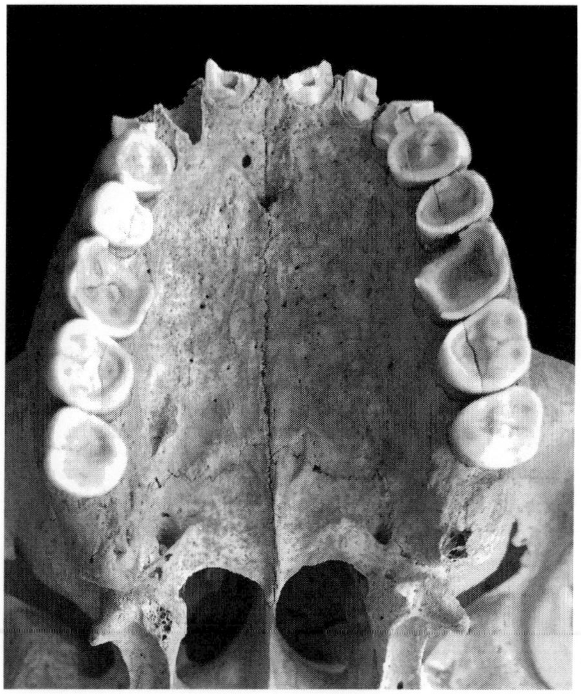

FIGURE 14.28 Variant of PS 4. *PS*, palate shape.

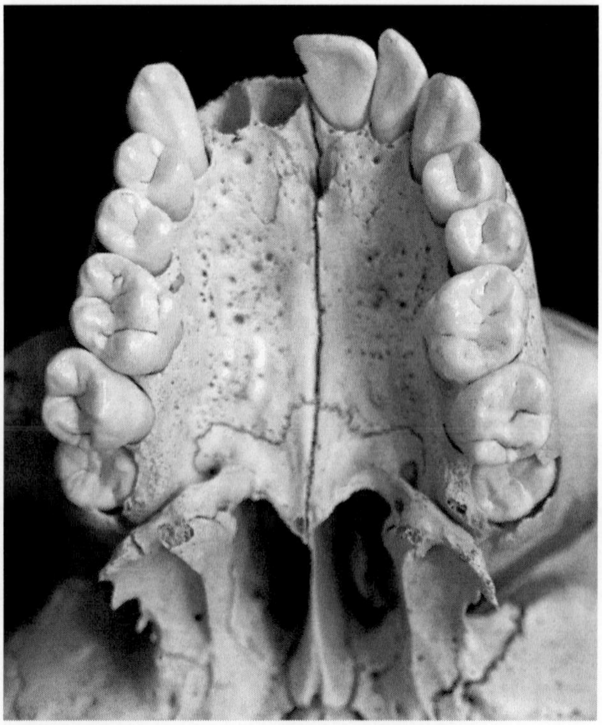

**FIGURE 14.29** Variant of PS 4. *PS*, palate shape.

C H A P T E R

# 15

# Postbregmatic Depression

Postbregmatic depression (PBD) is a slight to broad depression along the sagittal suture, posterior to bregma, which is not the result of pathology. Observed in lateral profile, the trait is scored as either absent (no depression) or present, with corresponding scores: $0 < 1$. This depression can range in expression from slight to marked. To score PBD, hold the cranium in a lateral profile view and look for a depression posterior to *bregma*. It may be helpful to palpate the area.

In 1889, Allen (1889:52) described a depression posterior to the coronal suture common "in Negroes [sic] ... [which] when well marked may receive the name of the post-bregmal portion." He continues throughout his discussion describing various depressions along the sagittal suture, termed variously as a postcoronal depression, coronal depression, and postbregmal depression. Several authors are noted by Allen, including a coronal depression described by Cleland (1870) and the postcoronal depression attributed to Rolleston (1885). Unfortunately, efforts to further identify these two sources were not successful.

MacDonnell (1904:190)—a Karl Pearson student—studied levels of variation and correlations using craniometric data and several still-utilized morphological traits. His sample represents crania from England; in it, MacDonnell describes a depression just behind *bregma*, which he calls the postcoronal depression. In 1981, Cunningham described a "slight hollowing of the surface of the parietals behind the coronal suture" as a common finding in the anatomy of the skull. This description appears to be a distinctly different trait; however, when Cunningham describes the location and appearance of postcoronal depression "just anterior to the cranial vertex" he may be referring to PBD. Hrdlička (1941) describes a slight depression in Koniag crania, but this expression is most likely the result of artificial cranial deformation.

Hrdlička (1930) noted the presence of a PBD in the Krapina 1 cranium. Hooton (n.d.) included recordings for postcoronal depression in the Harvard Blanks, scoring it *small*, *medium*, or *large*. If they exist, Hooton's illustrations or definitions of postcoronal depression have never been recovered. Goldstein (1943) observed *pre-* and *postbregmatic depression* among a sample of crania from Mexico. Finnegan (1976) mentions *postbregmatic flattening* but does not define the trait. Likewise, Bass (1985) includes *bregmatic depression* in his laboratory field manual, but he does not define the trait or provide a scoring strategy; in fact, his illustration of a Negroid (*sic*) (Bass, 1985:85) places the depressed region anterior to *bregma*. Rhine (1990:19) defines PBD as "a thumb-sized depression immediately posterior to *bregma* centered on the sagittal suture," he does not provide a scoring strategy and his data table seems to indicate presence/absence. Pope (1992:265) noted one *Homo erectus* specimen that was "noticeably depressed in the postbregmatic area."

Hefner (2003a,b:34) defined PBD as "a slight to broad depression along the sagittal suture located posterior to bregma ... scored as either *absent* (no depression) or *present*." In 2010, Hefner (2010:74) slightly modified his original definition (which is more or less the definition used herein), as follows:

> [A] slight to broad depression along the sagittal suture, posterior to bregma, which is not the result of pathology. Observed in lateral profile, the trait is scored as either absent (no depression) or present. 0 = No depression present; 1 = A marked depressed area posterior to bregma along the mid-sagittal plane.

## NOMENCLATURE

Postbregmatic depression, bregmal depression, bregmatic depression, postbregmatic flattening, postbregmatic furrow, and postcoronal depression.

*Atlas of Human Cranial Macromorphoscopic Traits.*
DOI: https://doi.org/10.1016/B978-0-12-814385-8.00015-X

## GROSS ANATOMY

The frontal bone and the two parietal bones articulate via the coronal suture; the two parietal bones articulate in the midline of the head via the sagittal suture. These two sutures intersect perpendicularly at the bony landmark *bregma* (Greek: top of the head) in the superior middle portion of the head. Known as the anterior fontanelle during infancy ["Now mind his little fontanelle"], this region begins as a membranous cover just deep to the skin, which is completely closed in most individuals by the second year of life (Scheuer and Black, 2000).

## GROWTH AND DEVELOPMENT

Each of the three bones contributing to the bregmatic region undergoes intramembranous ossification, forming from one (frontal) or two (parietals) primary centers of ossification. The primary center of ossification associated with the frontal bone forms around week six or seven of gestation, it is fully formed and the two halves are fused by the second year of life. Similarly, by week eight, the two primary centers of ossification are formed for both parietals. At birth, each parietal is fully formed and gradually attains the adult morphology throughout adolescence. Growth and developmental function of the PBD is poorly understood. Wood (2012) identified a present PBD in two individuals aged birth to 3 years and multiple individuals between 3 and 20 years. This suggests a PBD may be present early in life and remain well into adulthood. Wood (2012:238) attributes this early manifestation and age stability to "redirection of sutural growth vectors once the fontanelles are obliterated."

## FUNCTIONAL MORPHOLOGY

Like other fontanelles, the anterior fontanelle enables flexion between the frontal and parietals; thus, allowing the head to pass more easily through the birth canal. Wood (2012) provides the clearest functional explanation of the presence of a PBD. She suggests a PBD may stem from intrinsic (cranial stenosis, neural development, and musculature) or extrinsic (ontogenetic stressors, such as developmental disruptions or cranial deformation) factors during development. Moreover, she suggests the presence of a PBD may be due to dissipative forces reacting to either one or both of these intrinsic and extrinsic factors.

## WITHIN POPULATION VARIATION

Data derived from the Macromorphoscopic Databank of the frequency distribution of PBD ($n = 5906$). All data are for adult individuals. When possible, frequency data for males and females are provided separately. When sex could not be estimated reliably, frequency distributions are pooled as "Unknown" (Table 15.1).

**TABLE 15.1** Frequency Distribution of PBD, by Geographic Origin and Sex

| | | 0 | | 1 | | |
|---|---|---|---|---|---|---|
| **Geographic origin** | **Sex** | *n* | % | *n* | % | **Total** |
| **African** | **Female** | 9 | 64 | 5 | 36 | 14 |
| | **Male** | 5 | 33 | 10 | 67 | 15 |
| | **Unknown** | 0 | 0 | 0 | 0 | 0 |
| | **Total** | 14 | 48 | 15 | 52 | 29 |
| **American Black** | **Female** | 48 | 41 | 69 | 59 | 117 |
| | **Male** | 110 | 65 | 58 | 35 | 168 |
| | **Unknown** | 0 | 0 | 0 | 0 | 0 |
| | **Total** | 158 | 55 | 127 | 45 | 285 |
| **American White** | **Female** | 92 | 72 | 36 | 28 | 128 |
| | **Male** | 65 | 73 | 24 | 27 | 89 |
| | **Unknown** | 0 | 0 | 0 | 0 | 0 |
| | **Total** | 157 | 72 | 60 | 28 | 217 |
| **Amerindian** | **Female** | 35 | 95 | 2 | 5 | 37 |
| | **Male** | 36 | 97 | 1 | 3 | 37 |
| | **Unknown** | 2570 | 93 | 203 | 7 | 2773 |
| | **Total** | 2641 | 93 | 206 | 7 | 2847 |
| **Chinese** | **Female** | 5 | 100 | 0 | 0 | 5 |
| | **Male** | 44 | 88 | 6 | 12 | 50 |
| | **Unknown** | 0 | 0 | 0 | 0 | 0 |
| | **Total** | 49 | 89 | 6 | 11 | 55 |
| **Colombian** | **Female** | 38 | 57 | 29 | 43 | 67 |
| | **Male** | 108 | 61 | 68 | 39 | 176 |
| | **Unknown** | 0 | 0 | 0 | 0 | 0 |
| | **Total** | 146 | 60 | 97 | 40 | 243 |
| **El Salvador** | **Female** | 0 | 0 | 0 | 0 | 0 |
| | **Male** | 4 | 80 | 1 | 20 | 5 |
| | **Unknown** | 0 | 0 | 0 | 0 | 0 |
| | **Total** | 4 | 80 | 1 | 20 | 5 |
| **Eskimo** | **Female** | 0 | 0 | 0 | 0 | 0 |
| | **Male** | 0 | 0 | 0 | 0 | 0 |
| | **Unknown** | 699 | 87 | 104 | 13 | 803 |
| | **Total** | 699 | 87 | 104 | 13 | 803 |
| **European** | **Female** | 3 | 60 | 2 | 40 | 5 |
| | **Male** | 8 | 100 | 0 | 0 | 8 |
| | **Unknown** | 0 | 0 | 0 | 0 | 0 |
| | **Total** | 11 | 85 | 2 | 15 | 13 |

(*Continued*)

TABLE 15.1 (*Continued*)

| | | 0 | | 1 | | |
|---|---|---|---|---|---|---|
| **Geographic origin** | **Sex** | *n* | % | *n* | % | **Total** |
| **Guatemalan** | **Female** | 26 | 79 | 7 | 21 | 33 |
| | **Male** | 62 | 87 | 9 | 13 | 71 |
| | **Unknown** | 0 | 0 | 0 | 0 | 0 |
| | **Total** | 88 | 85 | 16 | 15 | 104 |
| **Japanese** | **Female** | 5 | 100 | 0 | 0 | 5 |
| | **Male** | 7 | 88 | 1 | 13 | 8 |
| | **Unknown** | 1 | 50 | 1 | 50 | 2 |
| | **Total** | 13 | 87 | 2 | 13 | 15 |
| **Mexico** | **Female** | 2 | 100 | 0 | 0 | 2 |
| | **Male** | 11 | 85 | 2 | 15 | 13 |
| | **Unknown** | 0 | 0 | 0 | 0 | 0 |
| | **Total** | 13 | 87 | 2 | 13 | 15 |
| **Pacific Island** | **Female** | 49 | 82 | 11 | 18 | 60 |
| | **Male** | 76 | 83 | 16 | 17 | 92 |
| | **Unknown** | 69 | 73 | 26 | 27 | 95 |
| | **Total** | 194 | 79 | 53 | 21 | 247 |
| **Peruvian** | **Female** | 0 | 0 | 0 | 0 | 0 |
| | **Male** | 0 | 0 | 0 | 0 | 0 |
| | **Unknown** | 22 | 76 | 7 | 24 | 29 |
| | **Total** | 22 | 76 | 7 | 24 | 29 |
| **Southwest (SW) Hispanic** | **Female** | 2 | 50 | 2 | 50 | 4 |
| | **Male** | 2 | 40 | 3 | 60 | 5 |
| | **Unknown** | 67 | 74 | 23 | 26 | 90 |
| | **Total** | 71 | 72 | 28 | 28 | 99 |
| **Thai** | **Female** | 236 | 74 | 82 | 26 | 318 |
| | **Male** | 446 | 79 | 122 | 21 | 568 |
| | **Unknown** | 9 | 64 | 5 | 36 | 14 |
| | **Total** | 691 | 77 | 209 | 23 | 900 |
| **Total for all groups** | | 4971 | 84 | 935 | 16 | 5906 |

*PBD*, postbregmatic depression.

## CHARACTER STATES

Photographic exemplars of the different character states of PBD are provided below. Each character state is defined following Hefner (2010). When necessary to clarify scoring, more nuanced definitions are provided in the figure captions. PBD should be assessed with the protocol provided in the preceding section.

Character states include:

PBD 0 = *absent*; no depression posterior to *bregma*.
PBD 1 = *present*; any depression posterior to *bregma* along the midsagittal plane.

## CHARACTER STATES FOR POSTBREGMATIC DEPRESSION = 0 (FIGS. 15.1–15.7)

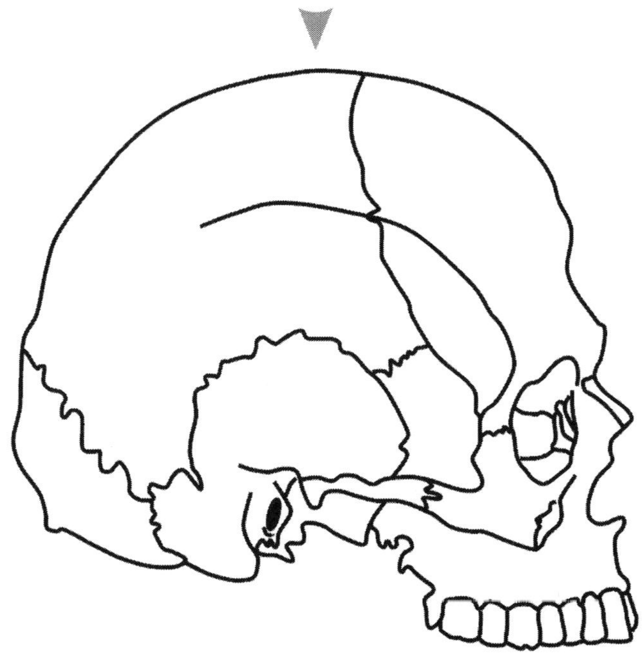

0

FIGURE 15.1 Diagrammatic representation of PBD 0. *PBD*, postbregmatic depression.

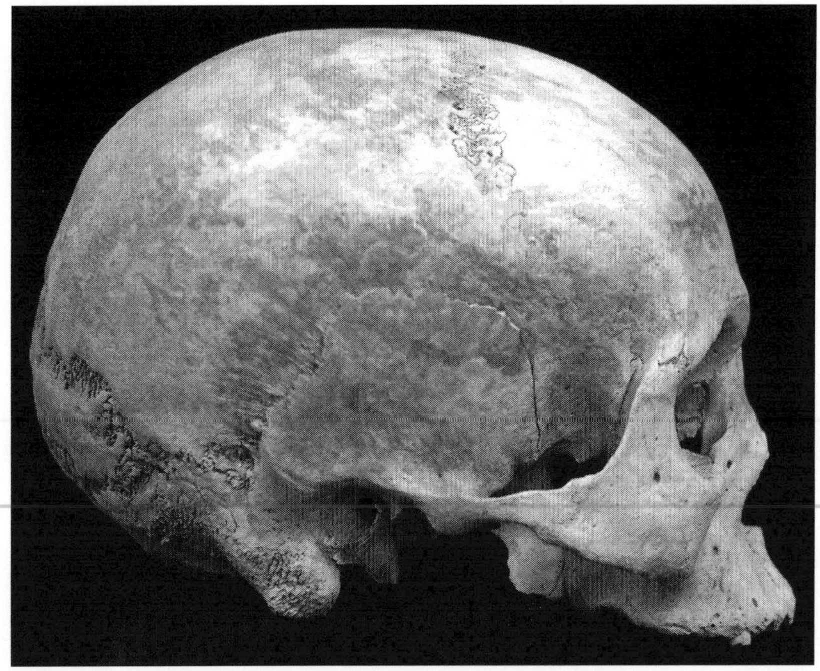

FIGURE 15.2 Variant of PBD 0. *PBD*, postbregmatic depression.

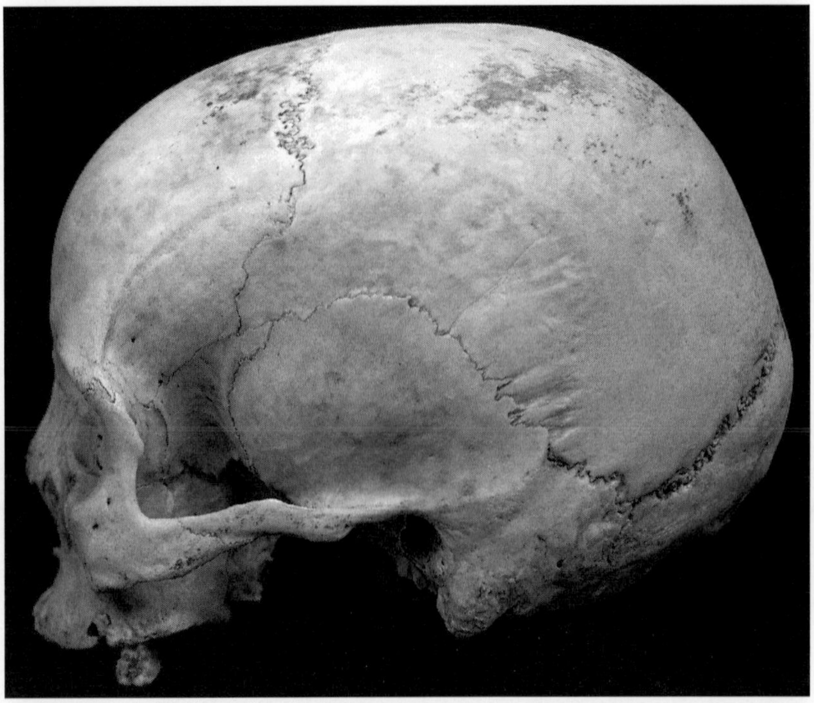

**FIGURE 15.3** Variant of PBD 0. *PBD*, postbregmatic depression.

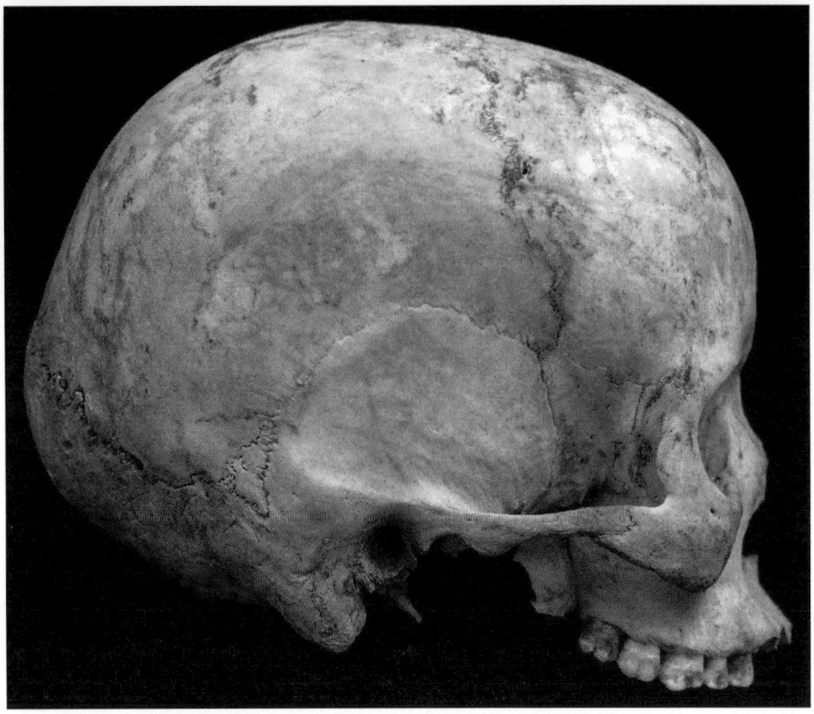

**FIGURE 15.4** Variant of PBD 0. *PBD*, postbregmatic depression.

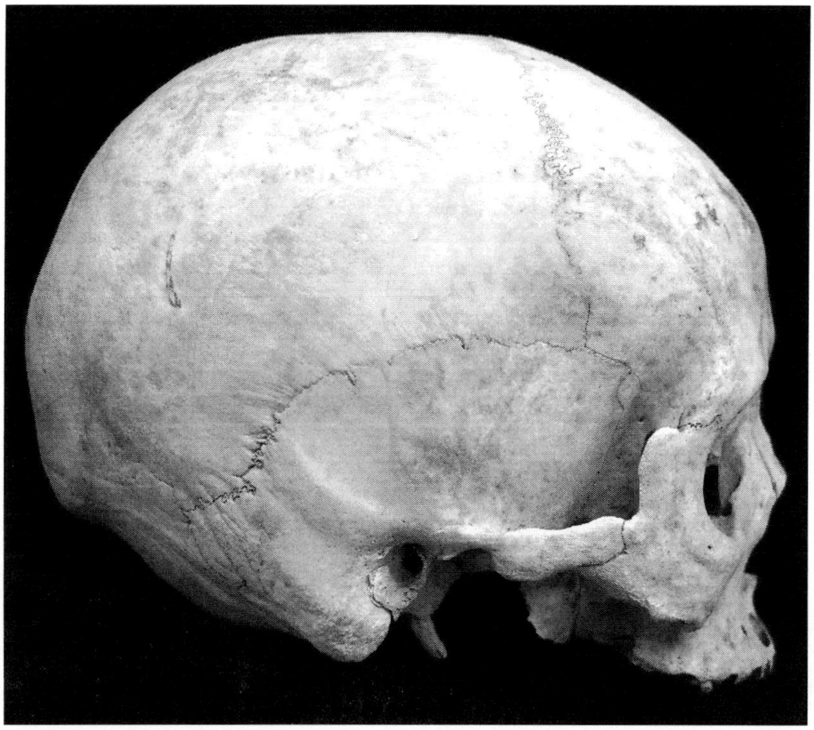

FIGURE 15.5 Variant of PBD 0. *PBD*, postbregmatic depression.

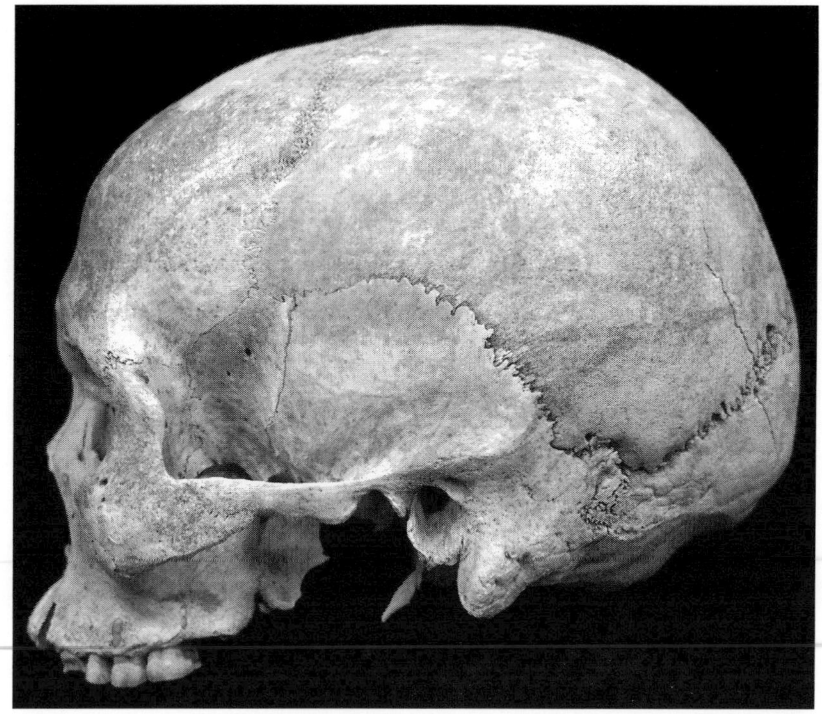

FIGURE 15.6 Variant of PBD 0. *PBD*, postbregmatic depression.

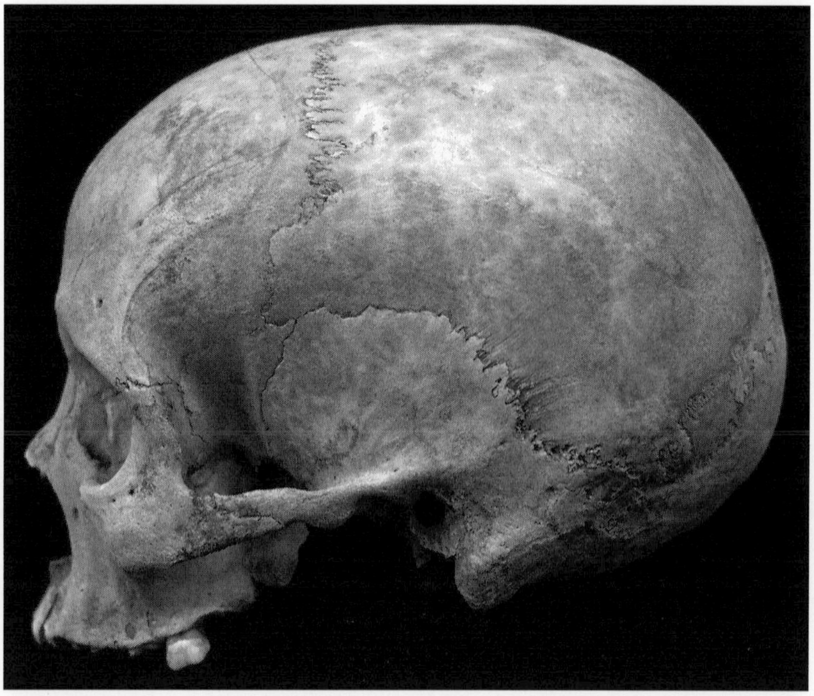

**FIGURE 15.7** Variant of PBD 0. *PBD*, postbregmatic depression.

## CHARACTER STATES FOR POSTBREGMATIC DEPRESSION = 1 (FIGS. 15.8–15.14)

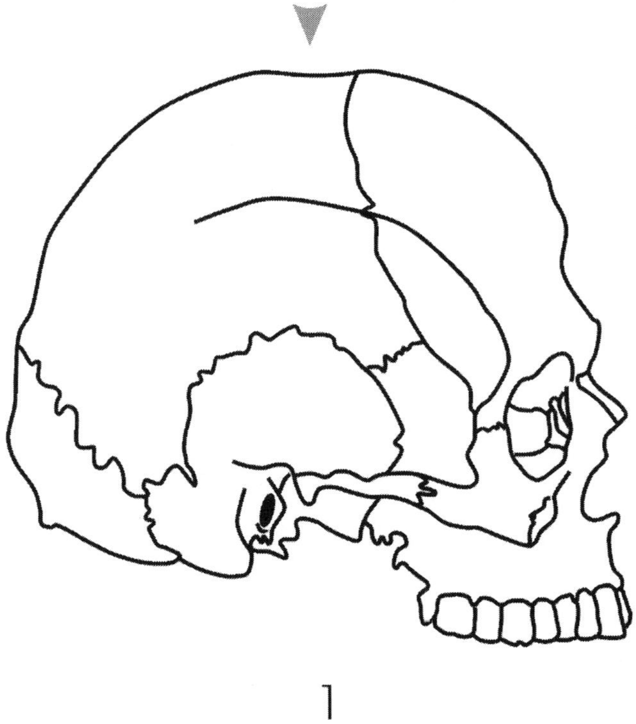


**FIGURE 15.8** Diagrammatic representation of PBD 1. *PBD*, postbregmatic depression.

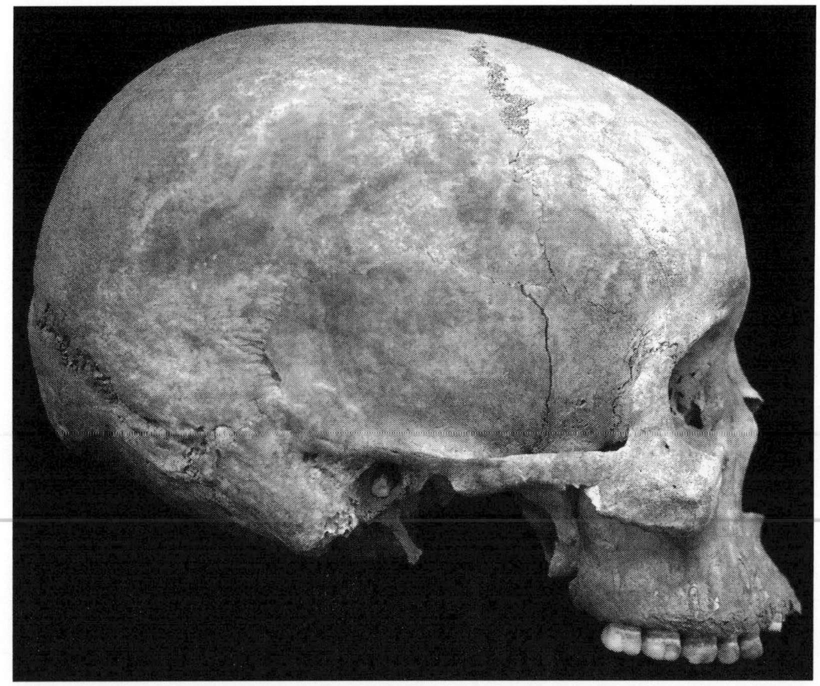

**FIGURE 15.9** Variant of PBD 1. *PBD*, postbregmatic depression.

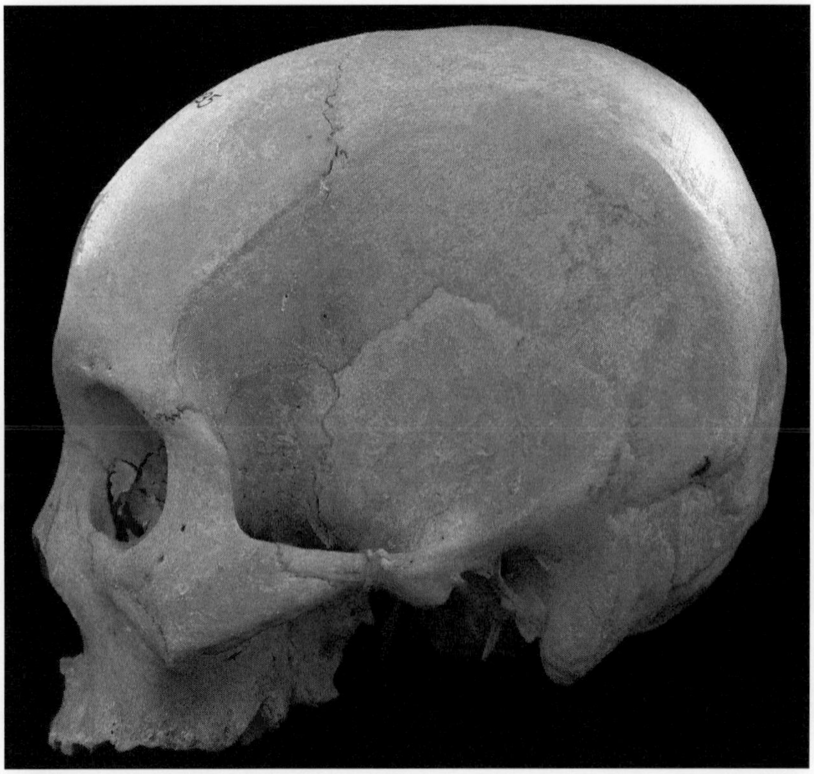

**FIGURE 15.10** Variant of PBD 1. *PBD*, postbregmatic depression.

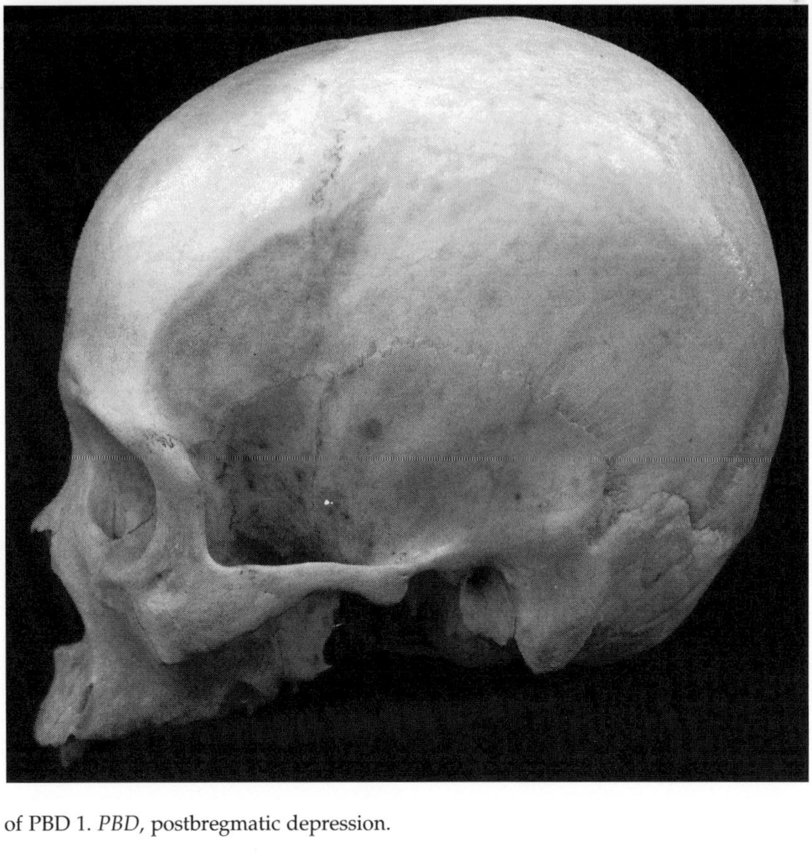

**FIGURE 15.11** Variant of PBD 1. *PBD*, postbregmatic depression.

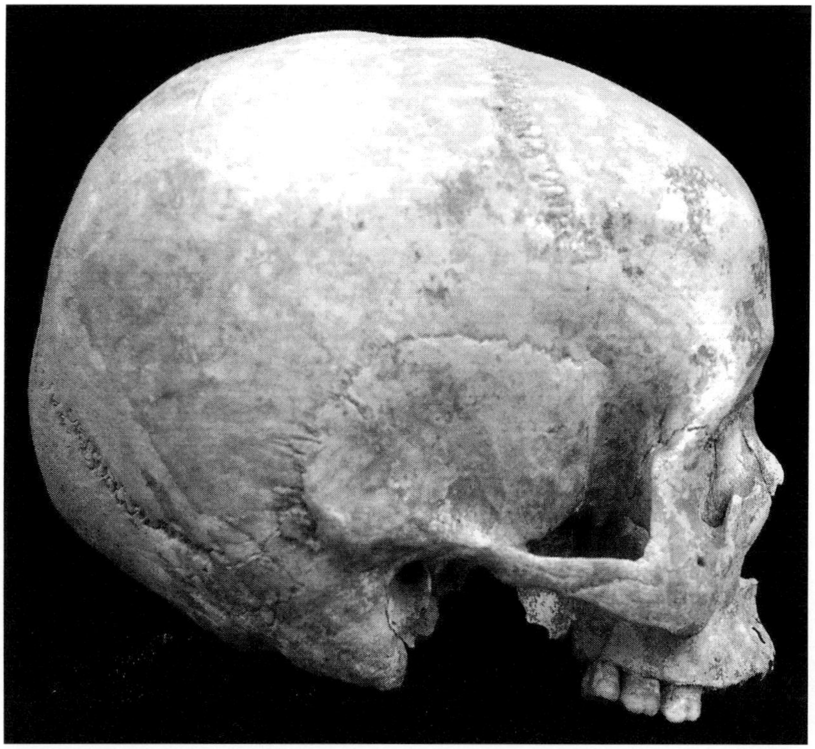

FIGURE 15.12 Variant of PBD 1. *PBD*, postbregmatic depression.

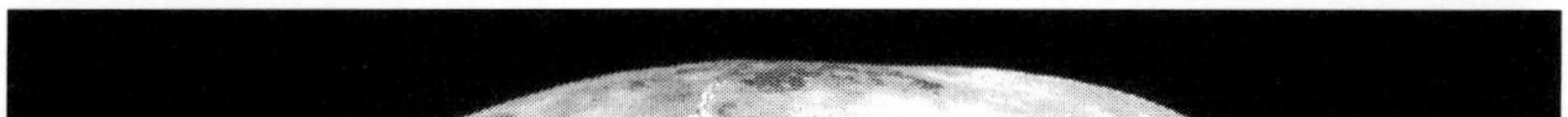

FIGURE 15.13 Variant of PBD 1. *PBD*, postbregmatic depression.

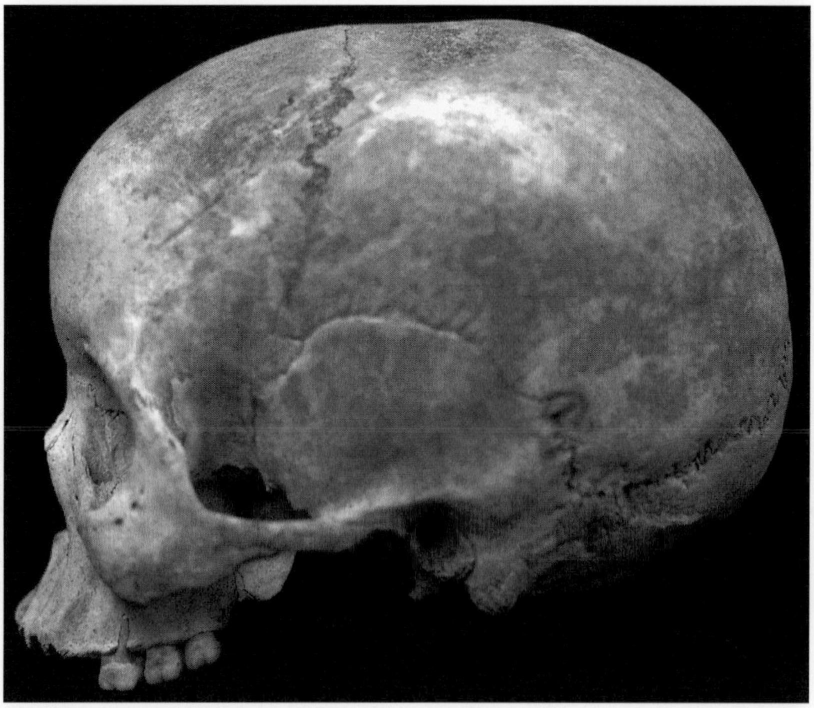

**FIGURE 15.14** Variant of PBD 1. *PBD*, postbregmatic depression.

CHAPTER

# 16

# Posterior Zygomatic Tubercle

The posterior zygomatic tubercle (PZT), or the marginal process, is a posterior projection of the zygomatic bone at approximately midorbit as viewed in lateral plane. To observe the various degrees of expression, a small, transparent ruler is placed on the frontal process of the zygomatic between the landmarks *frontomalare posterale* and *jugale*. The extent of bony protrusion beyond the ruler's edge is then assessed as: *absent*, *weak*, *moderate*, or *marked*, with corresponding scores: $0 < 1 < 2 < 3$.

Luschan (1914) studied the morphological development of the PZT, believing large versions resulted from a secondary center of ossification, although Luschka (1869) believed the expression of a *marginal tubercle* was related to the strong fibers of the temporal fascia inserting along this region of the zygomatic. Neither of these studies dealt directly with the range of variation of the posterior zygomatic process. Martin (1928:695) included the *processus marginalis* among his recommended cranioscopic traits, defining it as "[t]he protrusion or recession of the zygoma above or behind the cranial contour, as viewed in *norma verticalis* and assessed by holding the skull eye level and determining the amount of protrusion. A ruler may be used for assessment" (translated from the original). Oetteking (1930) included the *processus marginalis* in his study on the craniology of the populations found on the Pacific North Coast, but he did not provide or outline a definition for that trait. He did, however, score processus marginalis as small or large.

Hooton (n.d.) included the *marginal process* in the Harvard Blanks, scoring that trait as: absent-to-submedium or medium-to-large. Hooton's illustrations (if he created them) have not been discovered in his archives. Czarnetzi (1972) and Perizonius (1979) scored the presence and absence of *marginal tubercles* and *processus marginalis*, respectively. Hauser and DeStefano (1987, 1989) scored four character states for the *marginal tubercle*: absent, weak, medium, and strong, defined into three grades: "weak = projecting up to 4 mm, medium = projection between 4 and 7 mm, and strong = projections of more than 7 mm" (Hauser and De Stefano, 1989:228). Their methodology was refined by Hefner (2003a,b, 2010). Rhine (1990:20) defined the *zygomatic posterior tubercle* as a "projection posteriorly of the zygomatic at approximately mid orbit as viewed in normal [sic] lateralis," which he scored as present or absent. Hefner (2010:75) defined the PZT as

> a posterior projection of the zygomatic bone at approximately midorbit viewed in the lateral plane, assessed using a small, transparent ruler placed on the frontal process of the zygomatic from the landmarks *frontomalare posterale* to *jugale*. The extent of bony protrusion beyond the ruler's edge is then assessed as: absent, weak, moderate, or marked, with corresponding scores: $0 < 1 < 2 < 3$.

## NOMENCLATURE

*Apophysis pyramidalis*, marginal tubercle, posterior zygomatic tubercle, *processus marginalis*, processus Sömmeringi, *tuberculum posterius zygomaticus*, and zygomatic posterior tubercle.

## GROSS ANATOMY

The zygomatic bone, upon which the PZT is situated, forms the lateral aspect of the cheek, part of the lateral orbit, and the temporal and infratemporal fossae (Gray, 1966). The superoposterior border of the frontal process may show a tubercle or projection of bone varying in size and shape, which is known by various names including the PZT.

*Atlas of Human Cranial Macromorphoscopic Traits.*
DOI: https://doi.org/10.1016/B978-0-12-814385-8.00016-1

## GROWTH AND DEVELOPMENT

The primary ossification center of the zygomatic bone appears in utero around the 8th week of fetal development. By the 6th month, the zygomatic has essentially developed its adult morphology. Around the 2nd or 3rd year of life, the PZT has developed. According to Wood (2012) PZT becomes age-stable between 15 and 20 years old. Note that Wood (2012) did observe a PZT (*marginal tubercle*) in all of her age groups (fetal to 20 years), although their incidence in the younger ages was rare.

## FUNCTIONAL MORPHOLOGY

The PZT serves as the origin for a strong slip (strong fibers) of the temporal fascia, which eventually gives rise to the most anterior superficial layers of the temporalis muscle. These muscles function during mastication and are important for to the crushing and grinding activity of the molars. Tamura et al. (1998) investigated a suite of muscles—including the temporalis—important during suckling activity in a sample of infants. They identified the temporalis as an early muscle dictating suckling behavior, a finding supporting Wood's (2012) conclusions and Hauser and DeStefano's (1989) hypothesis on the manifestation of a marginal tubercle in newborns.

## WITHIN POPULATION VARIATION

Data derived from the Macromorphoscopic Databank of the frequency distribution of PZT ($n = 5752$). All data are for adult individuals. When possible, frequency data for males and females are provided separately. When sex could not be estimated reliably, frequency distributions are pooled as "Unknown" (Table 16.1).

**TABLE 16.1** Frequency Distribution of PZT, by Geographic Origin and Sex

| | | 0 | | 1 | | 2 | | 3 | | |
|---|---|---|---|---|---|---|---|---|---|---|
| **Geographic origin** | **Sex** | *n* | % | *n* | % | *n* | % | *n* | % | **Total** |
| **African** | **Female** | 0 | 0 | 1 | 9 | 7 | 64 | 3 | 27 | 11 |
| | **Male** | 0 | 0 | 1 | 8 | 6 | 50 | 5 | 42 | 12 |
| | **Unknown** | 0 | 0 | 0 | 0 | 0 | 0 | 0 | 0 | 0 |
| | **Total** | 0 | 0 | 2 | 9 | 13 | 57 | 8 | 35 | 23 |
| **American Black** | **Female** | 4 | 3 | 59 | 50 | 36 | 31 | 19 | 16 | 118 |
| | **Male** | 4 | 2 | 64 | 40 | 64 | 40 | 30 | 19 | 162 |
| | **Unknown** | 0 | 0 | 0 | 0 | 0 | 0 | 0 | 0 | 0 |
| | **Total** | 8 | 3 | 123 | 44 | 100 | 36 | 49 | 18 | 280 |
| **American White** | **Female** | 1 | 1 | 81 | 59 | 46 | 34 | 9 | 7 | 137 |
| | **Male** | 1 | 1 | 54 | 56 | 34 | 35 | 7 | 7 | 96 |
| | **Unknown** | 0 | 0 | 0 | 0 | 0 | 0 | 0 | 0 | 0 |
| | **Total** | 2 | 1 | 135 | 58 | 80 | 34 | 16 | 7 | 233 |
| **Amerindian** | **Female** | 0 | 0 | 24 | 53 | 19 | 42 | 2 | 4 | 45 |
| | **Male** | 0 | 0 | 17 | 45 | 17 | 45 | 4 | 11 | 38 |
| | **Unknown** | 186 | 7 | 1345 | 52 | 763 | 29 | 312 | 12 | 2606 |
| | **Total** | 186 | 7 | 1386 | 52 | 799 | 30 | 318 | 12 | 2689 |

*(Continued)*

TABLE 16.1 (*Continued*)

| | | 0 | | 1 | | 2 | | 3 | | |
|---|---|---|---|---|---|---|---|---|---|---|
| **Geographic origin** | **Sex** | *n* | % | *n* | % | *n* | % | *n* | % | **Total** |
| **Chinese** | **Female** | 0 | 0 | 1 | 25 | 1 | 25 | 2 | 50 | 4 |
| | **Male** | 0 | 0 | 13 | 28 | 21 | 46 | 12 | 26 | 46 |
| | **Unknown** | 0 | 0 | 0 | 0 | 0 | 0 | 0 | 0 | 0 |
| | **Total** | 0 | 0 | 14 | 28 | 22 | 44 | 14 | 28 | 50 |
| **Colombian** | **Female** | 0 | 0 | 38 | 57 | 25 | 37 | 4 | 6 | 67 |
| | **Male** | 1 | 1 | 76 | 43 | 79 | 45 | 21 | 12 | 177 |
| | **Unknown** | 0 | 0 | 0 | 0 | 0 | 0 | 0 | 0 | 0 |
| | **Total** | 1 | 0 | 114 | 47 | 104 | 43 | 25 | 10 | 244 |
| **El Salvador** | **Female** | 0 | 0 | 0 | 0 | 0 | 0 | 0 | 0 | 0 |
| | **Male** | 0 | 0 | 2 | 40 | 2 | 40 | 1 | 20 | 5 |
| | **Unknown** | 0 | 0 | 0 | 0 | 0 | 0 | 0 | 0 | 0 |
| | **Total** | 0 | 0 | 2 | 40 | 2 | 40 | 1 | 20 | 5 |
| **Eskimo** | **Female** | 0 | 0 | 0 | 0 | 0 | 0 | 0 | 0 | 0 |
| | **Male** | 0 | 0 | 0 | 0 | 0 | 0 | 0 | 0 | 0 |
| | **Unknown** | 96 | 12 | 467 | 58 | 195 | 24 | 47 | 6 | 805 |
| | **Total** | 96 | 12 | 467 | 58 | 195 | 24 | 47 | 6 | 805 |
| **European** | **Female** | 0 | 0 | 2 | 40 | 2 | 40 | 1 | 20 | 5 |
| | **Male** | 0 | 0 | 1 | 14 | 4 | 57 | 2 | 29 | 7 |
| | **Unknown** | 0 | 0 | 0 | 0 | 0 | 0 | 0 | 0 | 0 |
| | **Total** | 0 | 0 | 3 | 25 | 6 | 50 | 3 | 25 | 12 |
| **Guatemalan** | **Female** | 2 | 6 | 16 | 47 | 11 | 32 | 5 | 15 | 34 |
| | **Male** | 2 | 3 | 19 | 27 | 32 | 46 | 17 | 24 | 70 |
| | **Unknown** | 0 | 0 | 0 | 0 | 0 | 0 | 0 | 0 | 0 |
| | **Total** | 4 | 4 | 35 | 34 | 43 | 41 | 22 | 21 | 104 |
| **Japanese** | **Female** | 0 | 0 | 2 | 50 | 2 | 50 | 0 | 0 | 4 |
| | **Male** | 0 | 0 | 2 | 25 | 3 | 38 | 3 | 38 | 8 |
| | **Unknown** | 0 | 0 | 0 | 0 | 2 | 100 | 0 | 0 | 2 |
| | **Total** | 0 | 0 | 4 | 29 | 7 | 50 | 3 | 21 | 14 |
| **Mexico** | **Female** | 0 | 0 | 0 | 0 | 1 | 50 | 1 | 50 | 2 |
| | **Male** | 0 | 0 | 5 | 38 | 4 | 31 | 4 | 31 | 13 |
| | **Unknown** | 0 | 0 | 0 | 0 | 0 | 0 | 0 | 0 | 0 |
| | **Total** | 0 | 0 | 5 | 33 | 5 | 33 | 5 | 33 | 15 |
| **Pacific Island** | **Female** | 6 | 10 | 25 | 43 | 20 | 34 | 7 | 12 | 58 |
| | **Male** | 2 | 2 | 33 | 37 | 37 | 42 | 17 | 19 | 89 |
| | **Unknown** | 9 | 10 | 56 | 62 | 25 | 27 | 1 | 1 | 91 |
| | **Total** | 17 | 7 | 114 | 48 | 82 | 34 | 25 | 11 | 238 |

(*Continued*)

TABLE 16.1 (*Continued*)

| | | 0 | | 1 | | 2 | | 3 | | |
|---|---|---|---|---|---|---|---|---|---|---|
| **Geographic origin** | **Sex** | *n* | % | *n* | % | *n* | % | *n* | % | **Total** |
| **Peruvian** | **Female** | 0 | 0 | 0 | 0 | 0 | 0 | 0 | 0 | 0 |
| | **Male** | 0 | 0 | 0 | 0 | 0 | 0 | 0 | 0 | 0 |
| | **Unknown** | 4 | 16 | 13 | 52 | 7 | 28 | 1 | 4 | 25 |
| | **Total** | 4 | 16 | 13 | 52 | 7 | 28 | 1 | 4 | 25 |
| **Southwest (SW) Hispanic** | **Female** | 0 | 0 | 2 | 50 | 1 | 25 | 1 | 25 | 4 |
| | **Male** | 0 | 0 | 2 | 40 | 2 | 40 | 1 | 20 | 5 |
| | **Unknown** | 2 | 2 | 52 | 52 | 31 | 31 | 15 | 15 | 100 |
| | **Total** | 2 | 2 | 56 | 51 | 34 | 31 | 17 | 16 | 109 |
| **Thai** | **Female** | 15 | 5 | 182 | 57 | 99 | 31 | 25 | 8 | 321 |
| | **Male** | 13 | 2 | 264 | 46 | 203 | 36 | 91 | 16 | 571 |
| | **Unknown** | 0 | 0 | 7 | 50 | 2 | 14 | 5 | 36 | 14 |
| | **Total** | 28 | 3 | 453 | 50 | 304 | 34 | 121 | 13 | 906 |
| **Total for all groups** | | 348 | 6 | 2926 | 51 | 1803 | 31 | 675 | 12 | 5752 |

*PZT*, posterior zygomatic tubercle.

## CHARACTER STATES

Photographic exemplars of the different character states of PZT are provided below. Each character state is defined following Hefner (2009, 2010). When necessary to clarify scoring, more nuanced definitions are provided in the figure captions. PZT should be assessed with the protocol provided in the preceding section. Character states include:

PZT 0 = *absent;* no projection of bone past the ruler's edge.
PZT 1 = *weak;* a modest projection of bone that extends less than 4 mm past the ruler's edge.
PZT 2 = *moderate;* a moderate projection of bone that extends approximately 4–6 mm past the ruler's edge.
PZT 3 = *marked;* a significant projection of bone extending more than 6 mm past the ruler's edge.

## CHARACTER STATES FOR POSTERIOR ZYGOMATIC TUBERCLE = 0 (FIGS. 16.1–16.7)

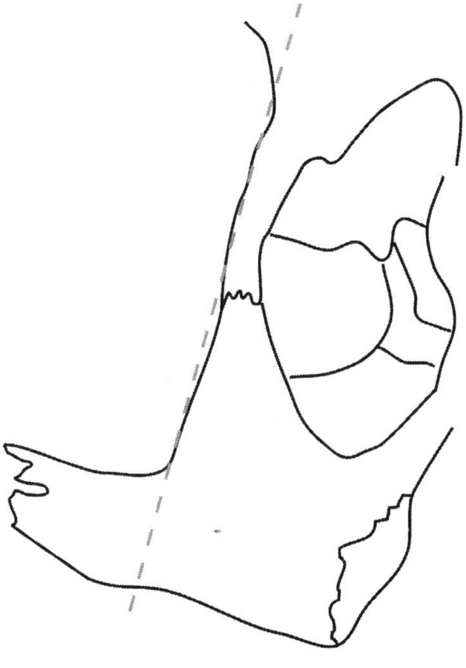

0

**FIGURE 16.1** Diagrammatic representation of PZT 0. Dashed line indicates the plane of reference (ruler). *PZT*, posterior zygomatic tubercle.

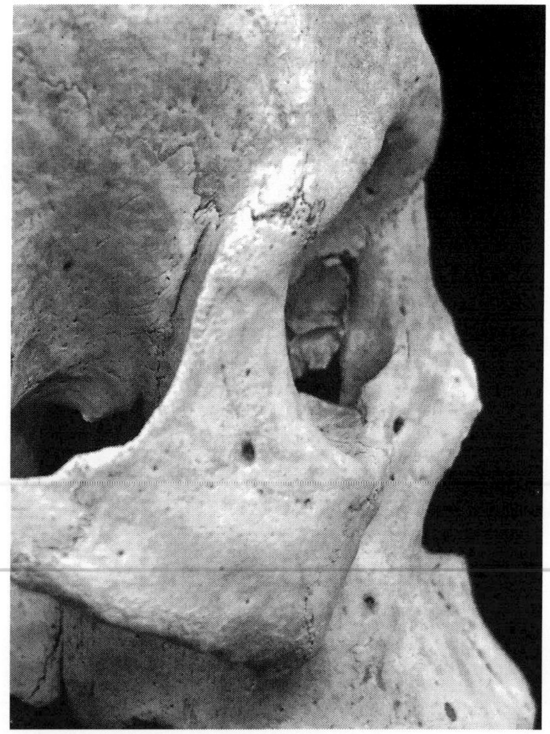

**FIGURE 16.2** Variant of PZT 0. *PZT*, posterior zygomatic tubercle.

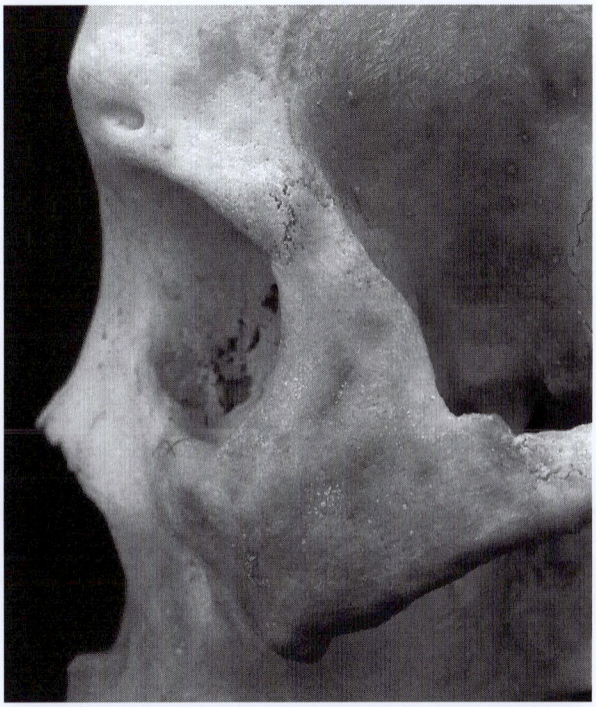

**FIGURE 16.3** Variant of PZT 0. *PZT*, posterior zygomatic tubercle.

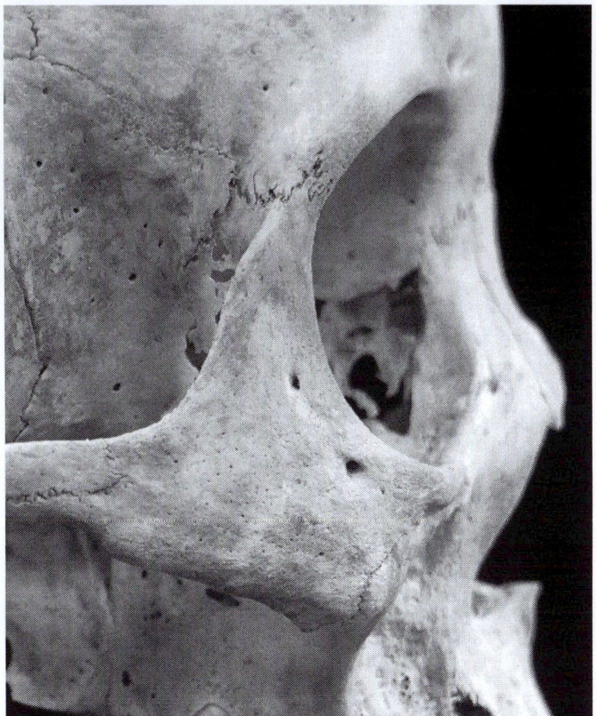

**FIGURE 16.4** Variant of PZT 0. *PZT*, posterior zygomatic tubercle.

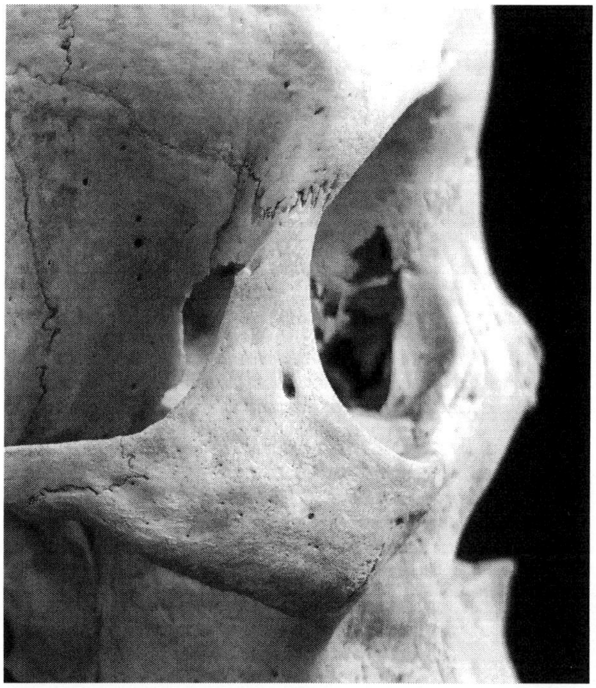

**FIGURE 16.5** Variant of PZT 0. *PZT*, posterior zygomatic tubercle.

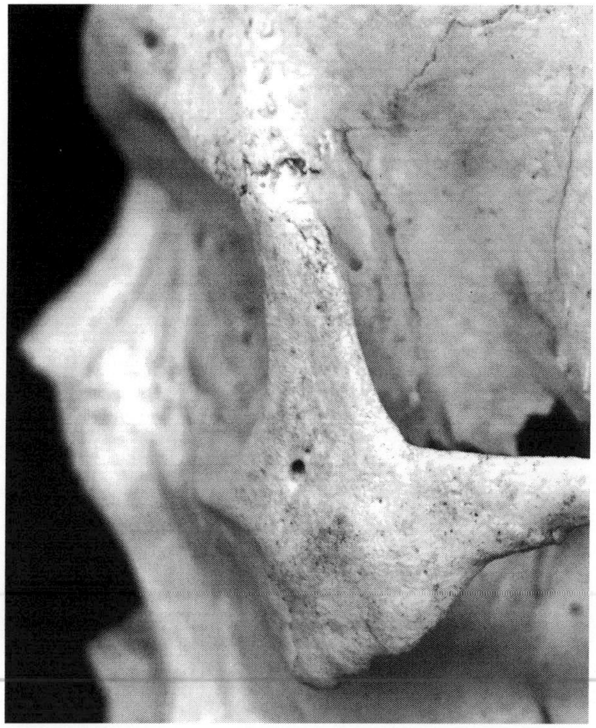

**FIGURE 16.6** Variant of PZT 0. *PZT*, posterior zygomatic tubercle.

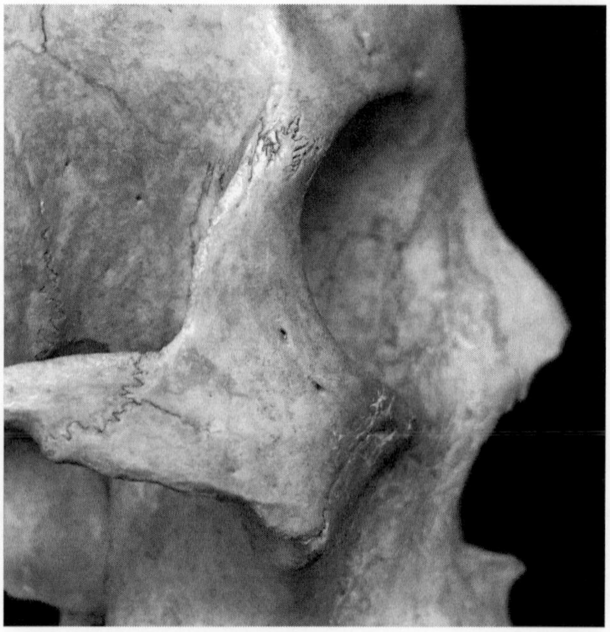

**FIGURE 16.7** Variant of PZT 0. *PZT*, posterior zygomatic tubercle.

# CHARACTER STATES FOR POSTERIOR ZYGOMATIC TUBERCLE = 1 (FIGS. 16.8–16.14)

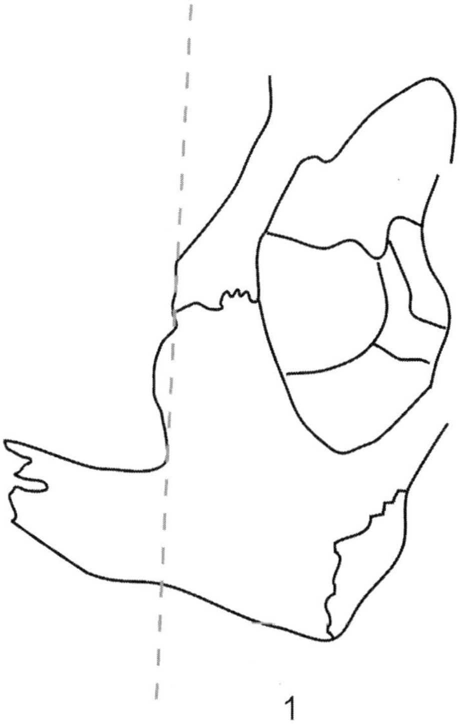


FIGURE 16.8 Diagrammatic representation of PZT 1. Dashed line indicates the plane of reference (ruler). *PZT*, posterior zygomatic tubercle.

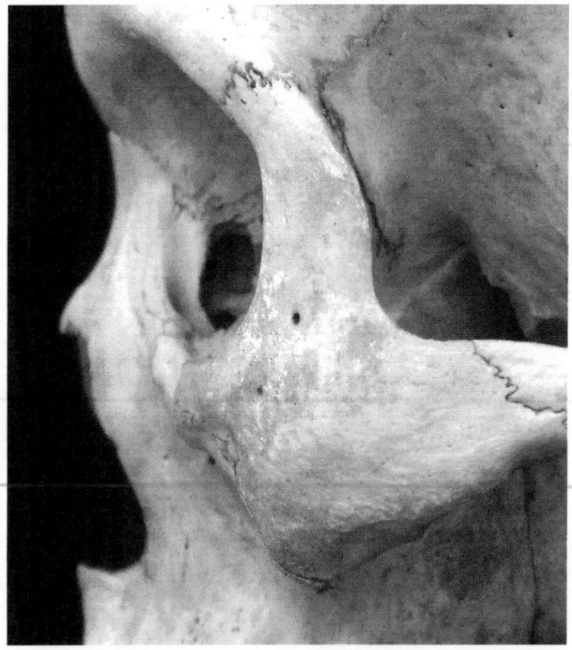

FIGURE 16.9 Variant of PZT 1. *PZT*, posterior zygomatic tubercle.

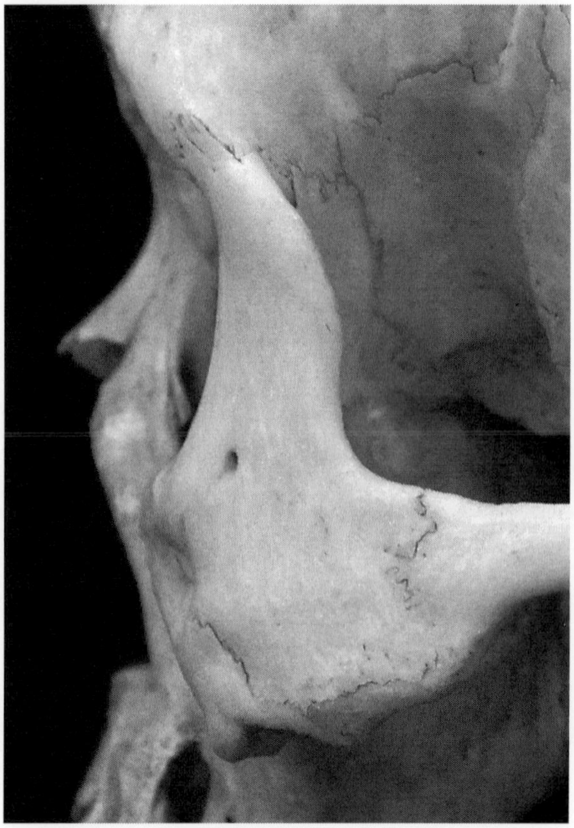

**FIGURE 16.10** Variant of PZT 1. *PZT*, posterior zygomatic tubercle.

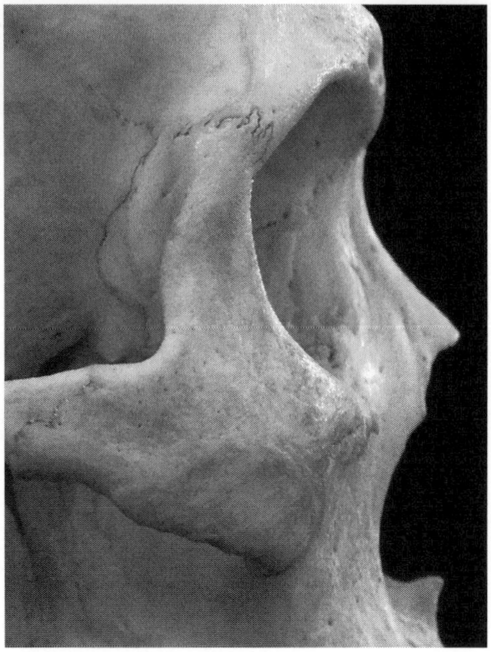

**FIGURE 16.11** Variant of PZT 1. *PZT*, posterior zygomatic tubercle.

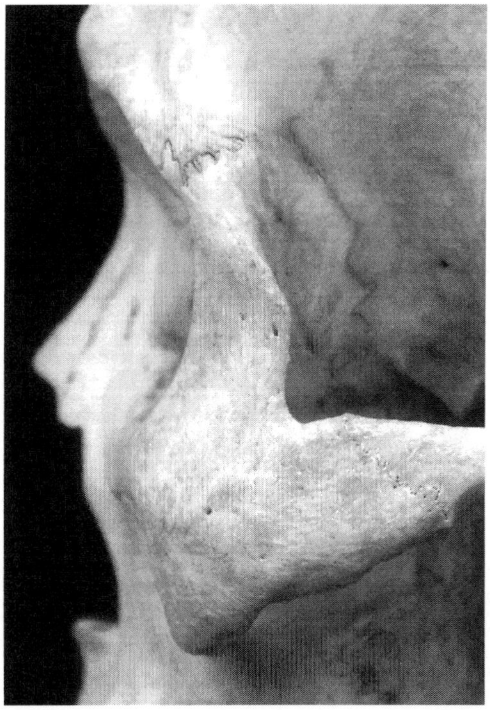

FIGURE 16.12 Variant of PZT 1. *PZT*, posterior zygomatic tubercle.

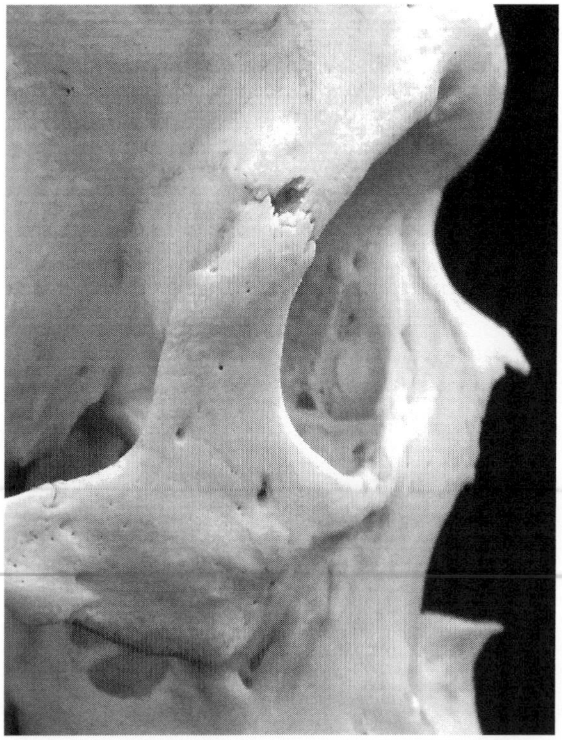

FIGURE 16.13 Variant of PZT 1. *PZT*, posterior zygomatic tubercle.

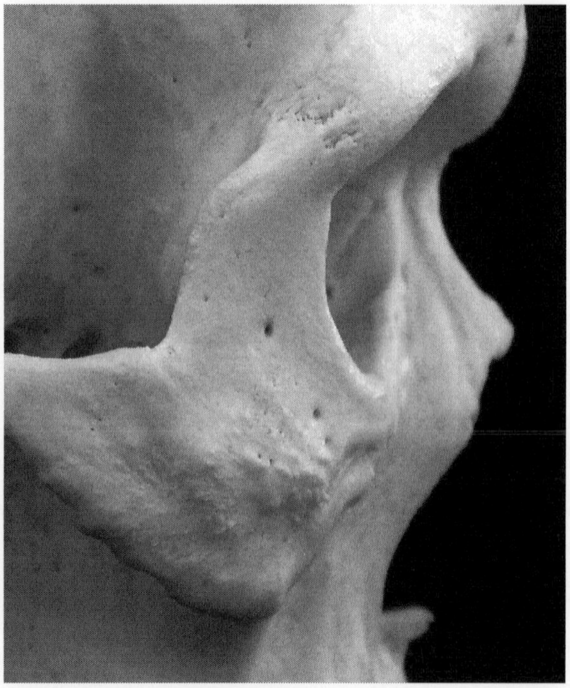

**FIGURE 16.14** Variant of PZT 1. *PZT*, posterior zygomatic tubercle.

# CHARACTER STATES FOR POSTERIOR ZYGOMATIC TUBERCLE = 2 (FIGS. 16.15–16.21)

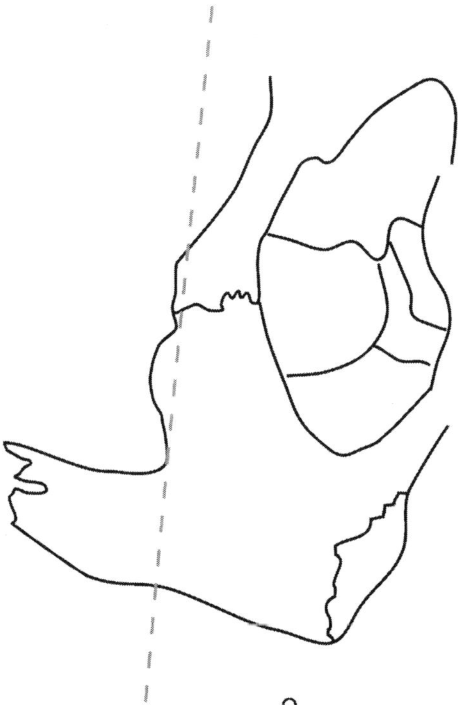


**FIGURE 16.15** Diagrammatic representation of PZT 2. Dashed line indicates the plane of reference (ruler). *PZT*, posterior zygomatic tubercle.

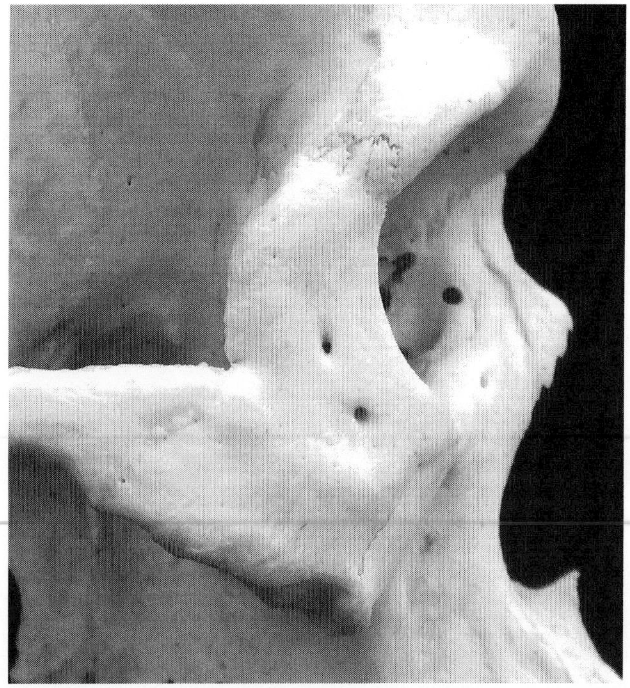

**FIGURE 16.16** Variant of PZT 2. *PZT*, posterior zygomatic tubercle.

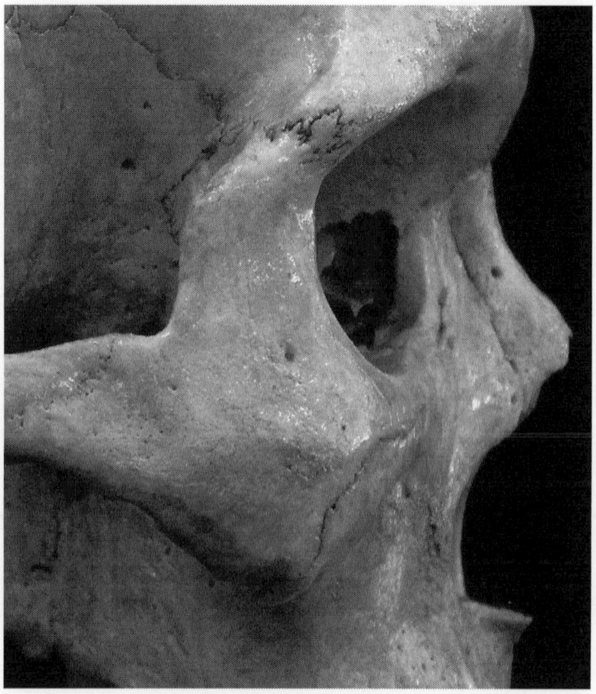

**FIGURE 16.17** Variant of PZT 2. *PZT*, posterior zygomatic tubercle.

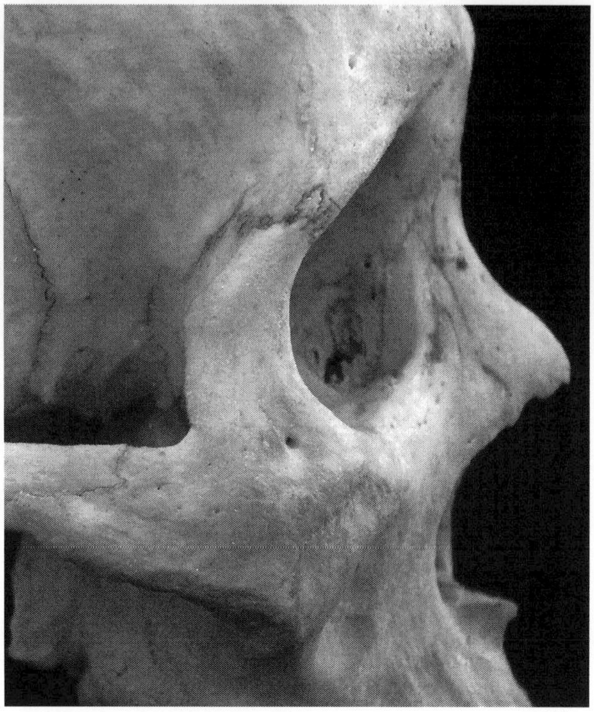

**FIGURE 16.18** Variant of PZT 2. *PZT*, posterior zygomatic tubercle.

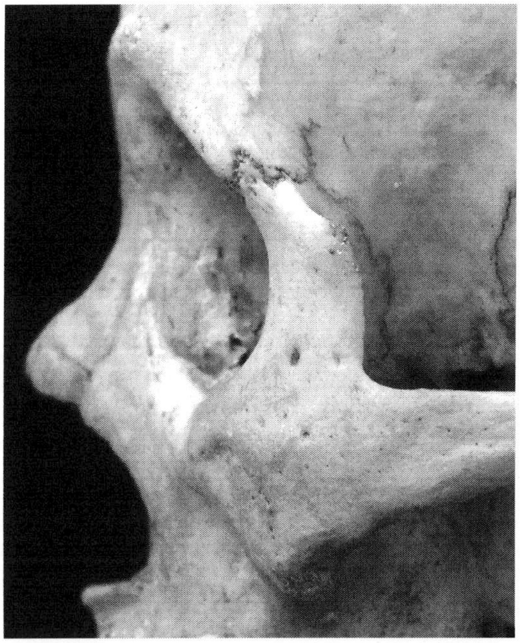

FIGURE 16.19 Variant of PZT 2. *PZT*, posterior zygomatic tubercle.

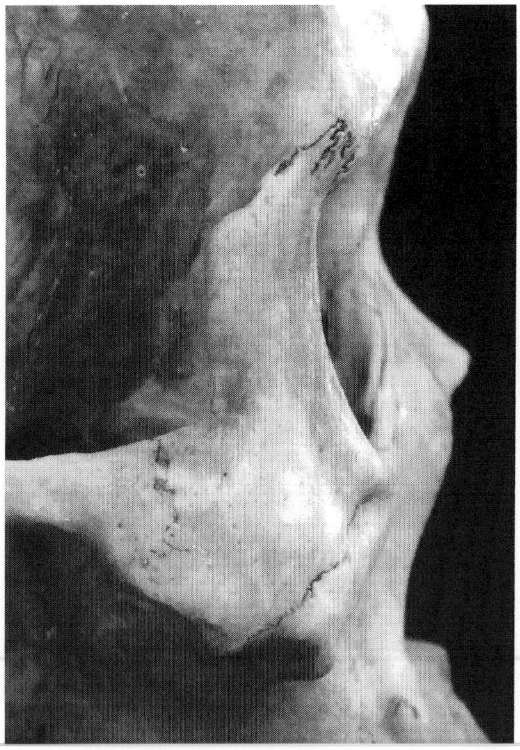

FIGURE 16.20 Variant of PZT 2. *PZT*, posterior zygomatic tubercle.

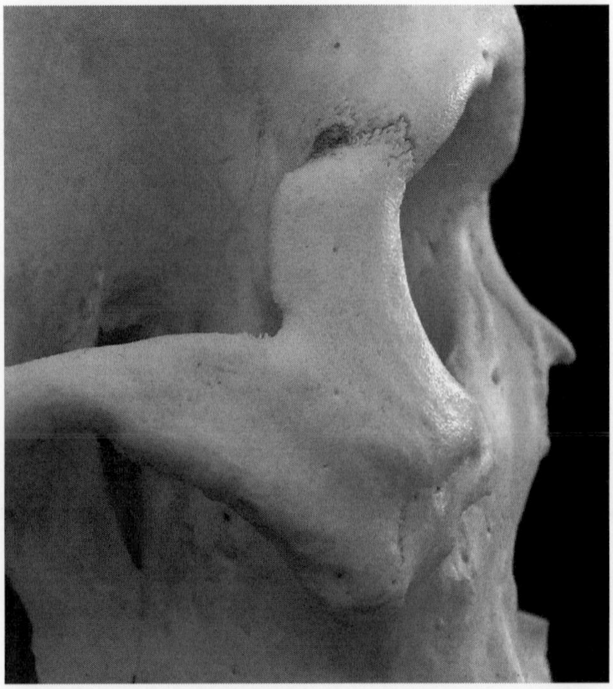

**FIGURE 16.21** Variant of PZT 2. *PZT*, posterior zygomatic tubercle.

# CHARACTER STATES FOR POSTERIOR ZYGOMATIC TUBERCLE = 3 (FIGS. 16.22–16.28)

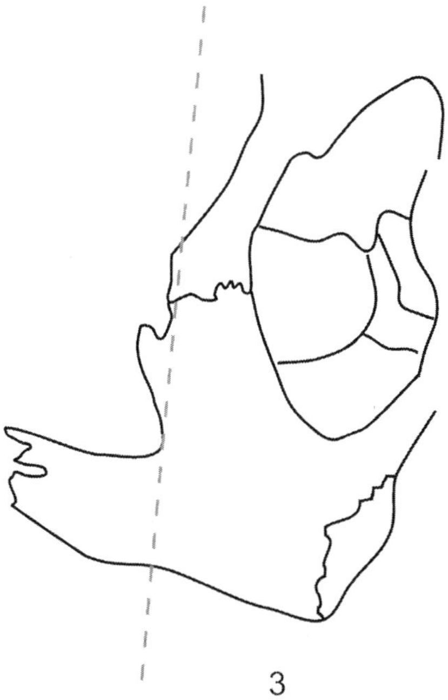


**FIGURE 16.22** Diagrammatic representation of PZT 3. Dashed line indicates the plane of reference (ruler). *PZT*, posterior zygomatic tubercle.

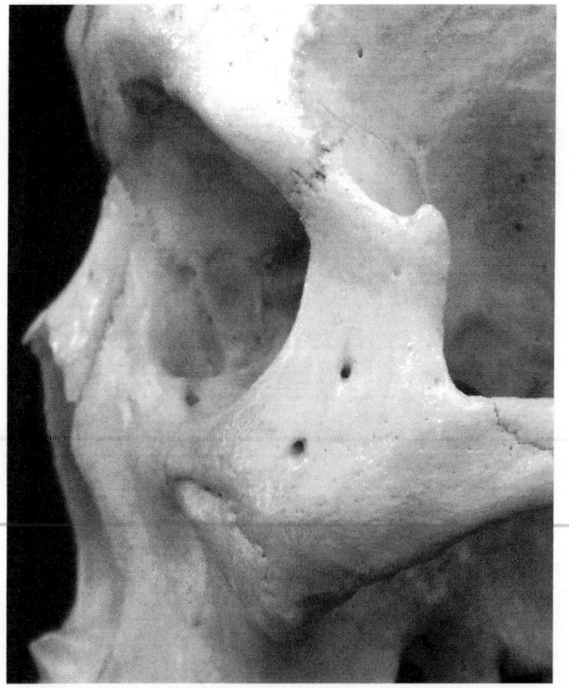

**FIGURE 16.23** Variant of PZT 3. *PZT*, posterior zygomatic tubercle.

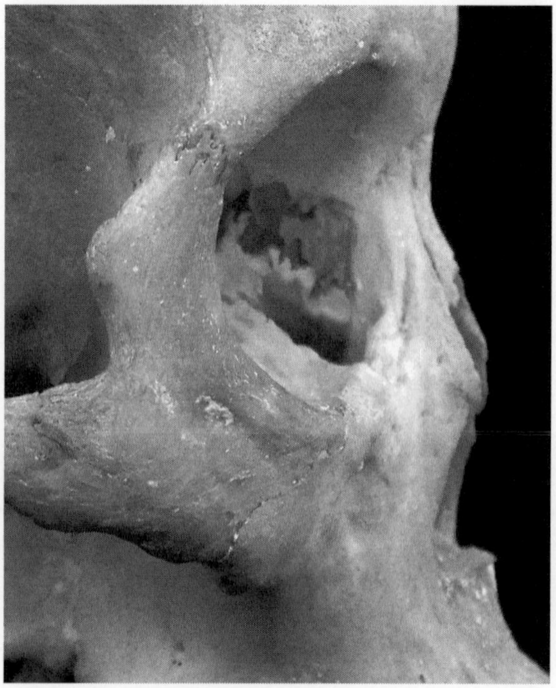

**FIGURE 16.24** Variant of PZT 3. *PZT*, posterior zygomatic tubercle.

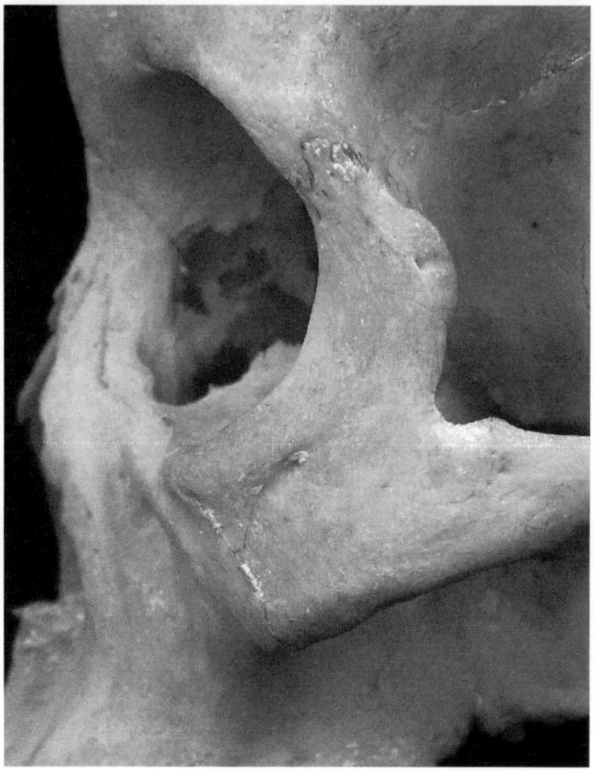

**FIGURE 16.25** Variant of PZT 3. *PZT*, posterior zygomatic tubercle.

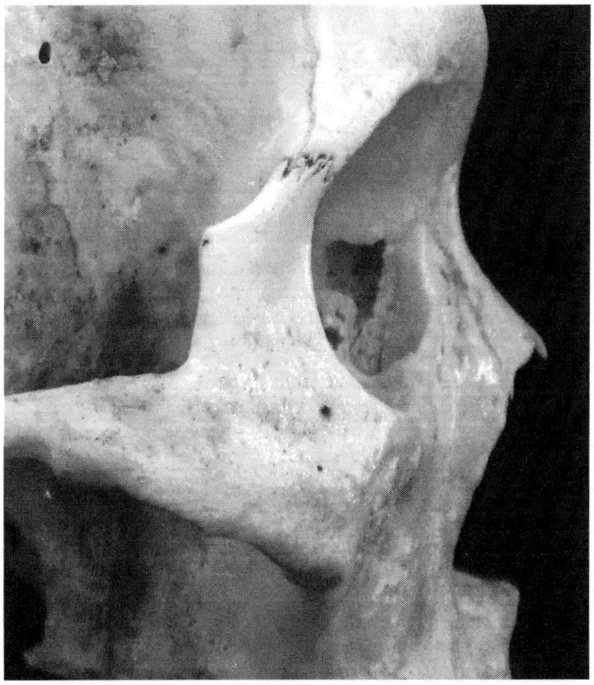

FIGURE 16.26 Variant of PZT 3. *PZT*, posterior zygomatic tubercle.

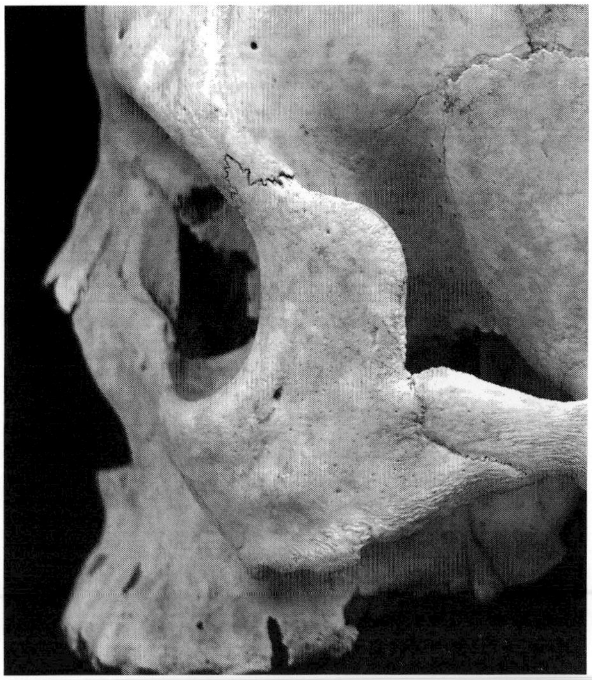

FIGURE 16.27 Variant of PZT 3. *PZT*, posterior zygomatic tubercle.

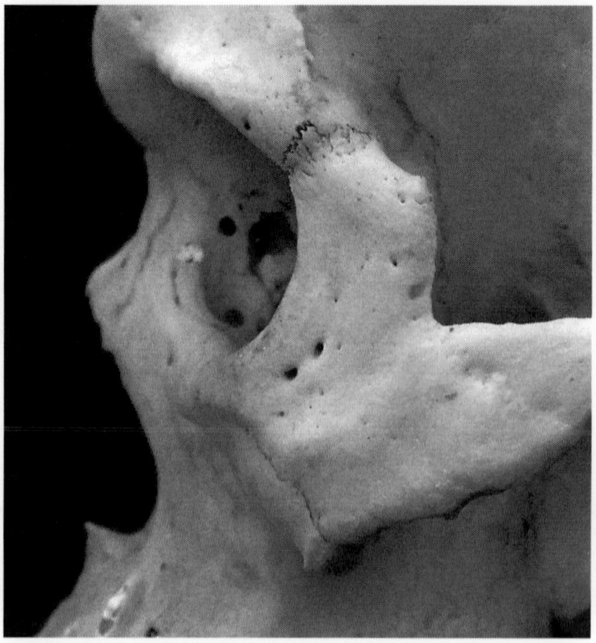

**FIGURE 16.28** Variant of PZT 3. *PZT*, posterior zygomatic tubercle.

CHAPTER

# 17

# Supranasal Suture

Supranasal suture (SPS) is defined as the secondary sutural complex superior to the cranial landmark *nasion* that may persist into adulthood. SPS exhibits three character states: *obliterated, unfused,* and *closed but visible,* scored as: $0 < 1 < 2$. Scored by viewing the cranium anteriorly, SPS is not the nasal portion of a persistent metopic suture, but is the secondary fusion of the nasal portion of a frontal suture. The SPS appears as a complex suture of interlocking bony spicules at the cranial landmark *glabella.*

Velepeau (1837) first described the *sutura supernasalis* as an *os fontanellæ supranasalis.* However, Schwalbe (1901) considers the SPS a result of irregular frontal (metopic) suture formation. Later, Rauber (1906) agreed with Schwalbe's etiology of the SPS, while Mair (1923) argue that the two sutures were unrelated by establishing a connection between the SPS and the superciliary arches. Toldt (1914) confirmed the latter, establishing a relationship between SPS formation/persistence to frontal bone contour and the sex of the individual.

Hooton did not collect data on the SPS. Hauser and De Stephano (1986:46) score SPS according to the degree of persistence—*open; closed, but visible; closed, barely visible;* and *obliterated not visible*—and shape—*uniform; oscillation larger towards nose; oscillation smaller towards nose;* and *supranasal triangle.* The scoring strategy of Hauser and De Stefano (1986) was adopted by Hefner (2003a,b) and later modified only slightly by Hefner (2009). See below for a more thorough description of the Hefner's (2009) definition. Schiwy-Bochat (2001) identified sex-related variation in SPS morphology using fractal analysis but did not provide a nonmetric equivalent. Mann et al. (2014) identify multiple expressions of the SPS using the Hauser and De Stefano (1986) methodology. They, like other authors, point out the difficulties inherent in establishing the exact etiology of the SPS, misidentifying the SPS with trace metopic sutures, and the role of a secondary center of ossification in the formation of SPS.

Hefner (2009, 2010) formalized a scoring methodology, borrowing the methodology outlined by Hauser and De Stefano (1986). He (2010:75) defined SPS as:

> A secondary complex suture may persist, which is generally referred to as the supranasal suture, or *sutura supranasalis.* This suture does not represent the nasal portion of a persistent metopic suture, which is generally a single, non-oscillating line, but rather is the fusion of the nasal portion of a frontal suture. SPS appears as a complex of interlocking bony spicules at glabella. 0 = completely obliterated; 1 = open (unfused); 2 = closed, but visible.

## NOMENCLATURE

Supranasal sutura, supranasal suture, and *sutura supernasalis.*

## GROSS ANATOMY

In adults and older adolescents, a small sutural complex may form between the two frontal bones in the approximate region of the bony landmark *glabella.* This secondary suture, when present, does not represent a trace metopic suture (Mann et al., 2014; Pietrusewsky and Douglas, 2002; Tavassoli, 2001), but rather is a secondary center of ossification manifesting during late adolescence, a state corresponding to Wood's (2012) endpoint of growth in the adult.

*Atlas of Human Cranial Macromorphoscopic Traits.*
DOI: https://doi.org/10.1016/B978-0-12-814385-8.00017-3

## GROWTH AND DEVELOPMENT

Frontal bone growth and development begins as two halves with the initial formation of primary ossification centers in utero between the sixth and seventh week (Scheuer and Black, 2000) and continues until complete fusion of the metopic suture takes place, generally by the fourth year of life. In some individuals, a complete or trace metopic suture may persist into adulthood. A number of researchers suggest that the SPS is associated with sexual maturation (Hauser and De Stefano, 1989; Mair, 1923; Wood, 2012). Wood (2012) noted a persistent SPS more frequently in association with robust male crania (Wood, 2012:251) suggesting SPS is a more reliable indication of sex than it would be for geographic origin.

## FUNCTIONAL MORPHOLOGY

Hauser and De Stefano (1986) and Wood (2012) have suggested the SPS may be associated with increased superciliary arches from increased robusticity among males and mechanical stressors enhanced by increased masticatory strains. No other functional morphological explanations for the SPS were identified.

## WITHIN POPULATION VARIATION

Data derived from the Macromorphoscopic Databank of the frequency distribution of SPS ($n = 5131$). All data are for adult individuals. When possible, frequency data for males and females are provided separately. When sex could not be estimated reliably, frequency distributions are pooled as "Unknown" (Table 17.1).

**TABLE 17.1** Frequency Distribution of SPS, by Geographic Origin and Sex

| | | 0 | | 1 | | 2 | | |
|---|---|---|---|---|---|---|---|---|
| **Geographic origin** | **Sex** | *n* | % | *n* | % | *n* | % | **Total** |
| **African** | **Female** | 0 | 0 | 0 | 0 | 0 | 0 | 0 |
| | **Male** | 0 | 0 | 2 | 29 | 5 | 71 | 7 |
| | **Unknown** | 0 | 0 | 0 | 0 | 0 | 0 | 0 |
| | **Total** | 0 | 0 | 2 | 29 | 5 | 71 | 7 |
| **American Black** | **Female** | 43 | 62 | 3 | 4 | 23 | 33 | 69 |
| | **Male** | 12 | 13 | 9 | 10 | 71 | 77 | 92 |
| | **Unknown** | 0 | 0 | 0 | 0 | 0 | 0 | 0 |
| | **Total** | 55 | 34 | 12 | 7 | 94 | 58 | 161 |
| **American White** | **Female** | 19 | 24 | 4 | 5 | 55 | 71 | 78 |
| | **Male** | 6 | 8 | 11 | 14 | 60 | 78 | 77 |
| | **Unknown** | 0 | 0 | 0 | 0 | 0 | 0 | 0 |
| | **Total** | 25 | 16 | 15 | 10 | 115 | 74 | 155 |
| **Amerindian** | **Female** | 0 | 0 | 1 | 14 | 6 | 86 | 7 |
| | **Male** | 0 | 0 | 0 | 0 | 15 | 100 | 15 |
| | **Unknown** | 1099 | 41 | 234 | 9 | 1338 | 50 | 2671 |
| | **Total** | 1099 | 41 | 235 | 9 | 1359 | 50 | 2693 |

*(Continued)*

TABLE 17.1 (*Continued*)

| Geographic origin | Sex | 0 n | 0 % | 1 n | 1 % | 2 n | 2 % | Total |
|---|---|---|---|---|---|---|---|---|
| **Chinese** | **Female** | 0 | 0 | 0 | 0 | 1 | 100 | 1 |
| | **Male** | 0 | 0 | 1 | 25 | 3 | 75 | 4 |
| | **Unknown** | 0 | 0 | 0 | 0 | 0 | 0 | 0 |
| | **Total** | 0 | 0 | 1 | 20 | 4 | 80 | 5 |
| **El Salvador** | **Female** | 0 | 0 | 0 | 0 | 0 | 0 | 0 |
| | **Male** | 0 | 0 | 0 | 0 | 5 | 100 | 5 |
| | **Unknown** | 0 | 0 | 0 | 0 | 0 | 0 | 0 |
| | **Total** | 0 | 0 | 0 | 0 | 5 | 100 | 5 |
| **Eskimo** | **Female** | 0 | 0 | 0 | 0 | 0 | 0 | 0 |
| | **Male** | 0 | 0 | 0 | 0 | 0 | 0 | 0 |
| | **Unknown** | 274 | 34 | 241 | 30 | 283 | 35 | 798 |
| | **Total** | 274 | 34 | 241 | 30 | 283 | 35 | 798 |
| **European** | **Female** | 0 | 0 | 1 | 100 | 0 | 0 | 1 |
| | **Male** | 0 | 0 | 1 | 25 | 3 | 75 | 4 |
| | **Unknown** | 0 | 0 | 0 | 0 | 0 | 0 | 0 |
| | **Total** | 0 | 0 | 2 | 40 | 3 | 60 | 5 |
| **Guatemalan** | **Female** | 1 | 33 | 0 | 0 | 2 | 67 | 3 |
| | **Male** | 0 | 0 | 0 | 0 | 0 | 0 | 0 |
| | **Unknown** | 0 | 0 | 0 | 0 | 0 | 0 | 0 |
| | **Total** | 1 | 33 | 0 | 0 | 2 | 67 | 3 |
| **Japanese** | **Female** | 0 | 0 | 0 | 0 | 0 | 0 | 0 |
| | **Male** | 0 | 0 | 0 | 0 | 1 | 100 | 1 |
| | **Unknown** | 0 | 0 | 0 | 0 | 0 | 0 | 0 |
| | **Total** | 0 | 0 | 0 | 0 | 1 | 100 | 1 |
| **Mexico** | **Female** | 0 | 0 | 1 | 50 | 1 | 50 | 2 |
| | **Male** | 0 | 0 | 5 | 38 | 8 | 62 | 13 |
| | **Unknown** | 0 | 0 | 0 | 0 | 0 | 0 | 0 |
| | **Total** | 0 | 0 | 6 | 40 | 9 | 60 | 15 |
| **Pacific Island** | **Female** | 43 | 75 | 0 | 0 | 14 | 25 | 57 |
| | **Male** | 24 | 27 | 7 | 8 | 59 | 66 | 90 |
| | **Unknown** | 46 | 48 | 12 | 13 | 37 | 39 | 95 |
| | **Total** | 113 | 47 | 19 | 8 | 110 | 45 | 242 |
| **Peruvian** | **Female** | 0 | 0 | 0 | 0 | 0 | 0 | 0 |
| | **Male** | 0 | 0 | 0 | 0 | 0 | 0 | 0 |
| | **Unknown** | 6 | 19 | 8 | 26 | 17 | 55 | 31 |
| | **Total** | 6 | 19 | 8 | 26 | 17 | 55 | 31 |

(*Continued*)

TABLE 17.1 (*Continued*)

| Geographic origin | Sex | 0 | | 1 | | 2 | | Total |
|---|---|---|---|---|---|---|---|---|
| | | *n* | % | *n* | % | *n* | % | |
| **Southwest (SW) Hispanic** | **Female** | 0 | 0 | 1 | 25 | 3 | 75 | 4 |
| | **Male** | 0 | 0 | 1 | 20 | 4 | 80 | 5 |
| | **Unknown** | 27 | 27 | 13 | 13 | 61 | 60 | 101 |
| | **Total** | 27 | 25 | 15 | 14 | 68 | 62 | 110 |
| **Thai** | **Female** | 170 | 53 | 16 | 5 | 133 | 42 | 319 |
| | **Male** | 55 | 10 | 152 | 27 | 360 | 63 | 567 |
| | **Unknown** | 3 | 21 | 1 | 7 | 10 | 71 | 14 |
| | **Total** | 228 | 25 | 169 | 19 | 503 | 56 | 900 |
| **Total for all groups** | | 1828 | 36 | 725 | 14 | 2578 | 50 | 5131 |

*SPS*, supranasal suture.

## CHARACTER STATES

Photographic exemplars of the different character states of SPS are provided below. Each character state is defined following Hefner (2010). When necessary to clarify scoring, more nuanced definitions are provided in the figure captions. SPS should be assessed with the protocol provided in the preceding section. Character states include:

SPS 0 = *obliterated*; complete obliteration of the SPS.
SPS 1 = *open (unfused)*; an open, visible, and unfused SPS.
SPS 2 = *closed, but visible*; although the SPS is closed it remains distinctly visible.

## CHARACTER STATES FOR SUPRANASAL SUTURE = 0 (FIGS. 17.1–17.7)

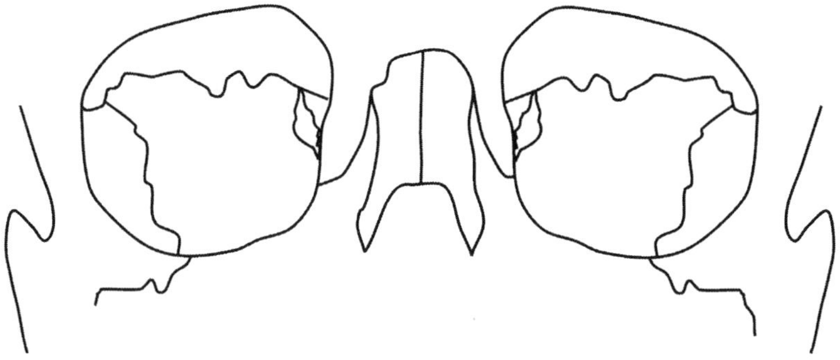


FIGURE 17.1 Diagrammatic representation of SPS 0. *SPS*, supranasal suture.

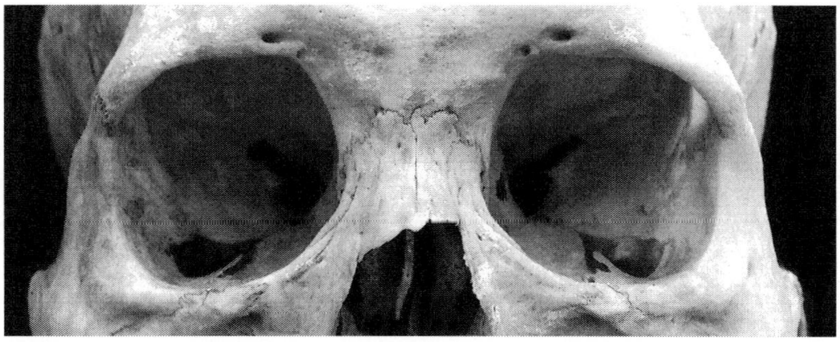

FIGURE 17.2 Variant of SPS 0. *SPS*, supranasal suture.

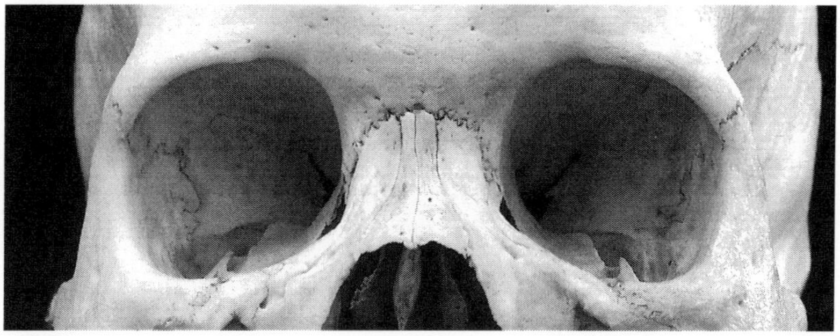

FIGURE 17.3 Variant of SPS 0. *SPS*, supranasal suture.

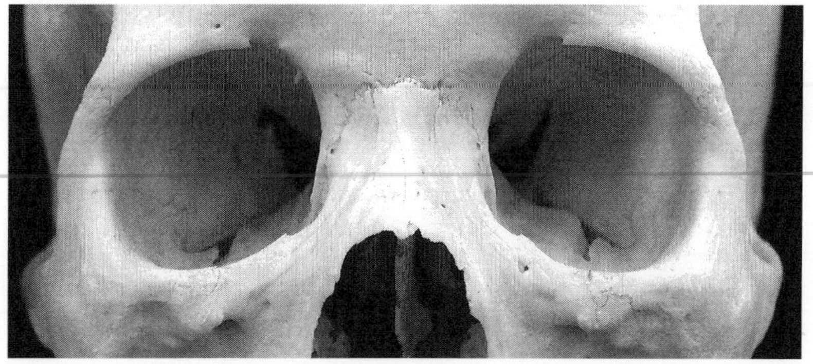

FIGURE 17.4 Variant of SPS 0. *SPS*, supranasal suture.

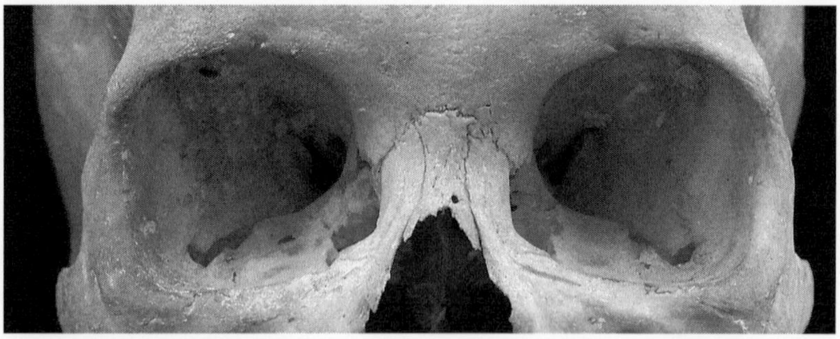

**FIGURE 17.5** Variant of SPS 0. *SPS*, supranasal suture.

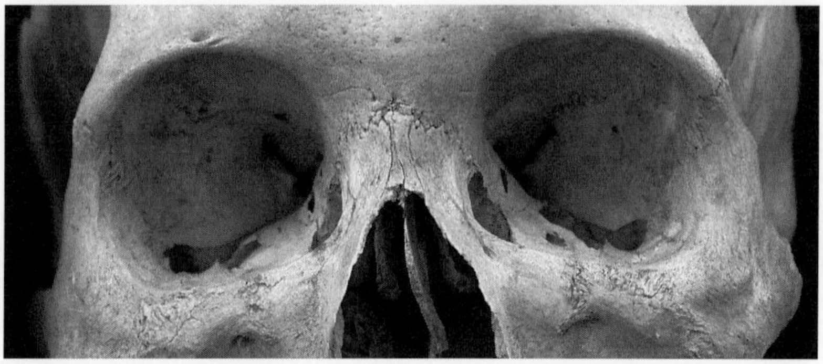

**FIGURE 17.6** Variant of SPS 0. *SPS*, supranasal suture.

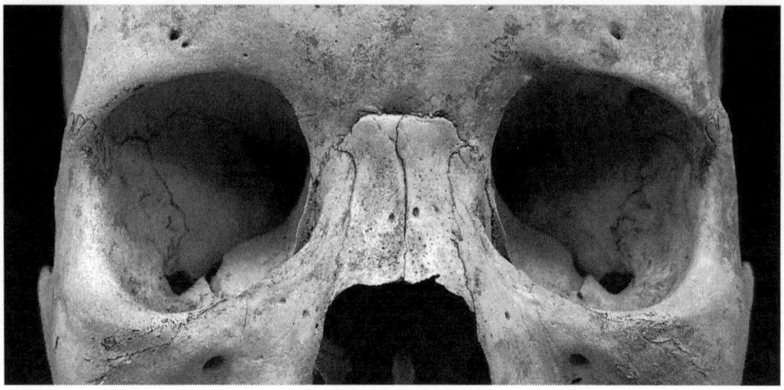

**FIGURE 17.7** Variant of SPS 0. *SPS*, supranasal suture.

## CHARACTER STATES FOR SUPRANASAL SUTURE = 1 (FIGS. 17.8–17.14)

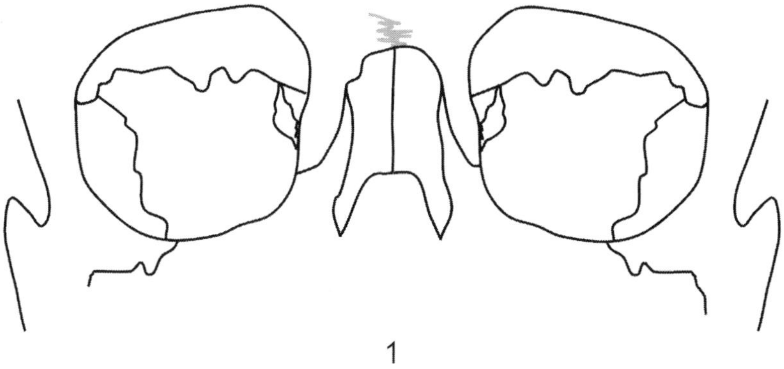


FIGURE 17.8 Diagrammatic representation of SPS 1. *SPS*, supranasal suture.

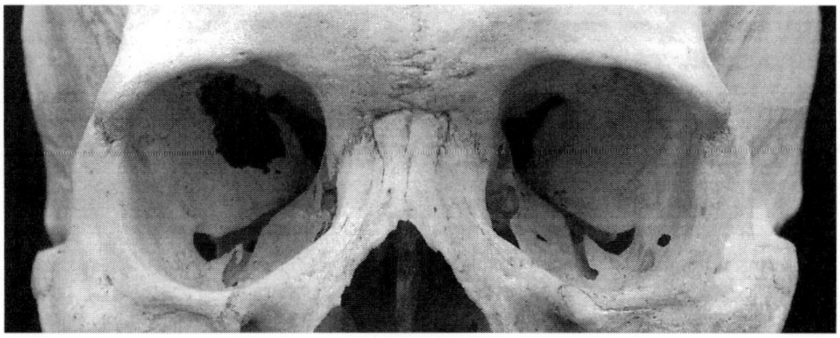

FIGURE 17.9 Variant of SPS 1. *SPS*, supranasal suture.

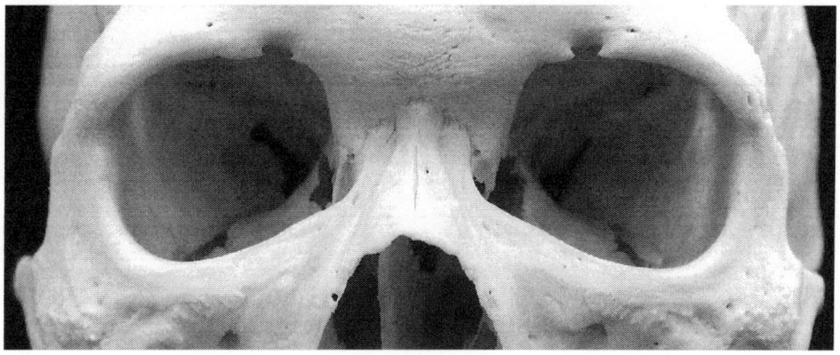

FIGURE 17.10 Variant of SPS 1. *SPS*, supranasal suture.

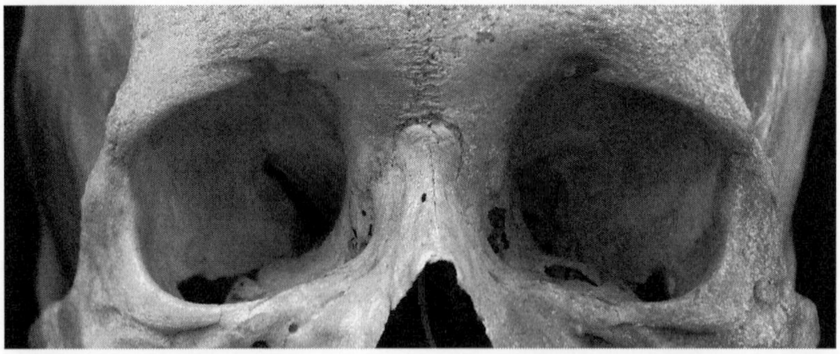

**FIGURE 17.11** Variant of SPS 1. *SPS*, supranasal suture.

**FIGURE 17.12** Variant of SPS 1. *SPS*, supranasal suture.

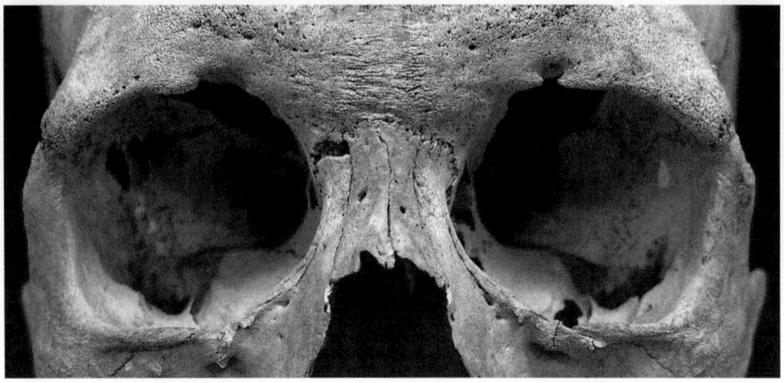

**FIGURE 17.13** Variant of SPS 1. *SPS*, supranasal suture.

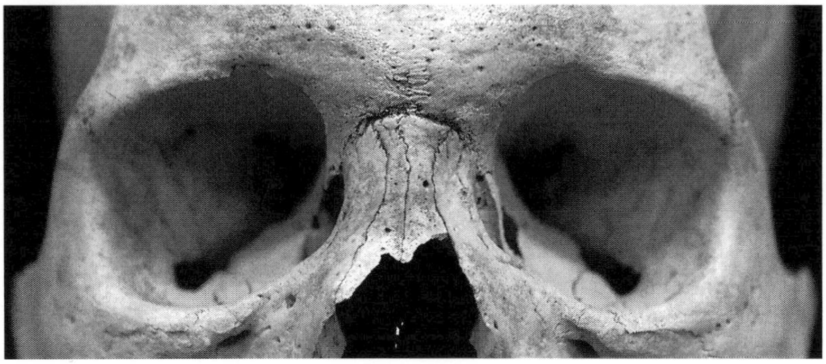

**FIGURE 17.14** Variant of SPS 1. *SPS*, supranasal suture.

## CHARACTER STATES FOR SUPRANASAL SUTURE = 2 (FIGS. 17.15–17.21)

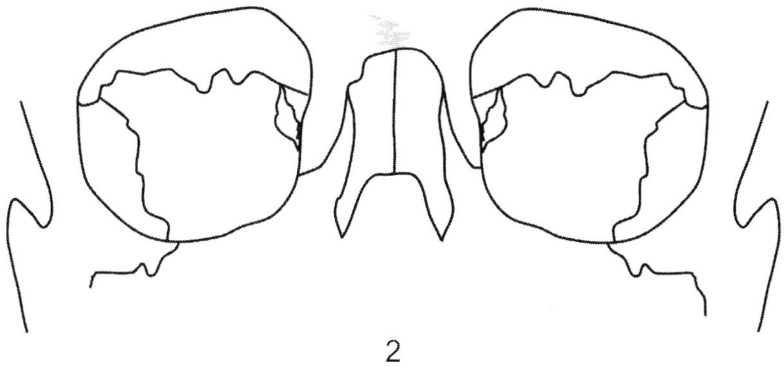


FIGURE 17.15 Diagrammatic representation of SPS 2. *SPS*, supranasal suture.

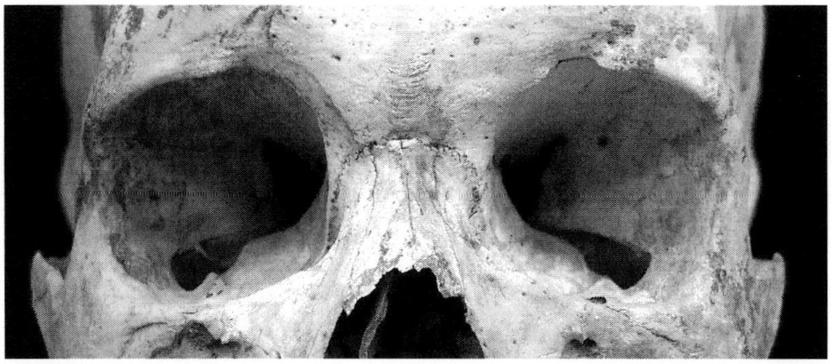

FIGURE 17.16 Variant of SPS 2. *SPS*, supranasal suture.

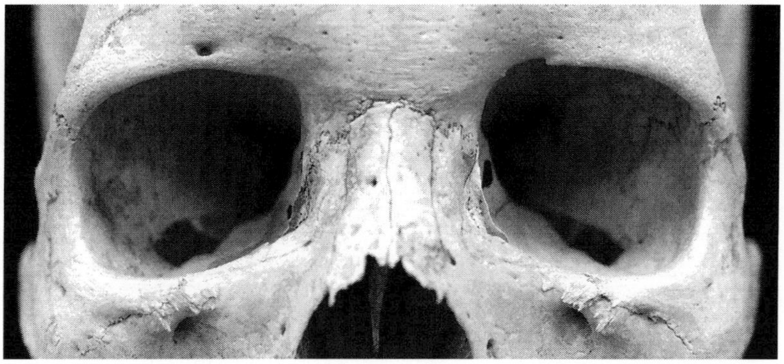

FIGURE 17.17 Variant of SPS 2. *SPS*, supranasal suture.

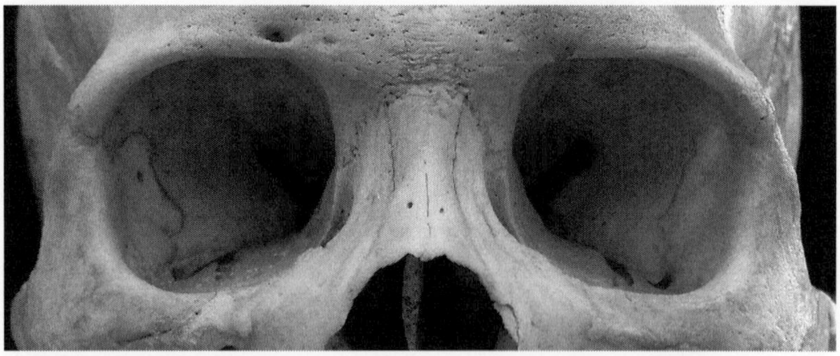

FIGURE 17.18 Variant of SPS 2. *SPS*, supranasal suture.

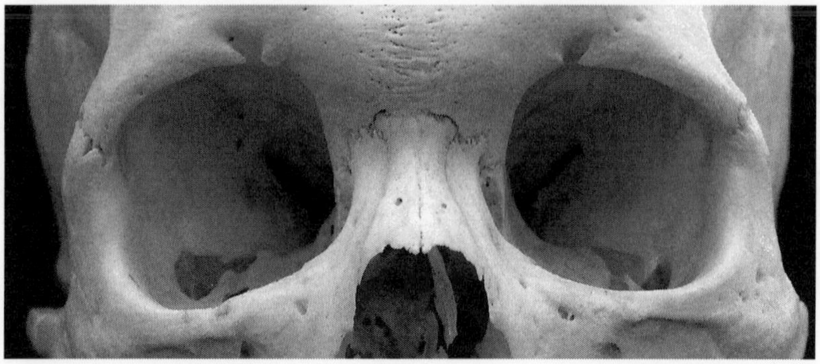

FIGURE 17.19 Variant of SPS 2. *SPS*, supranasal suture.

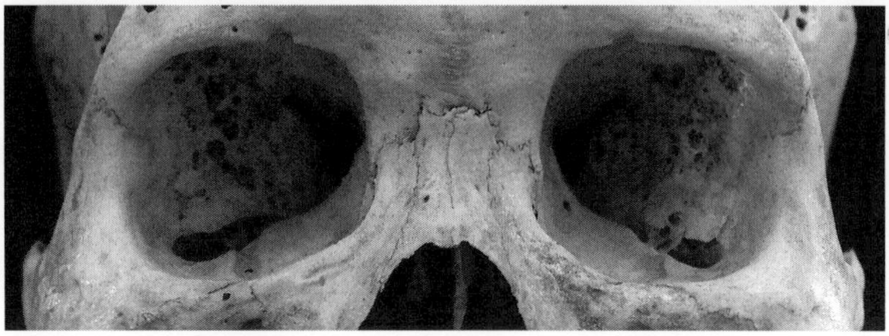

FIGURE 17.20 Variant of SPS 2. *SPS*, supranasal suture.

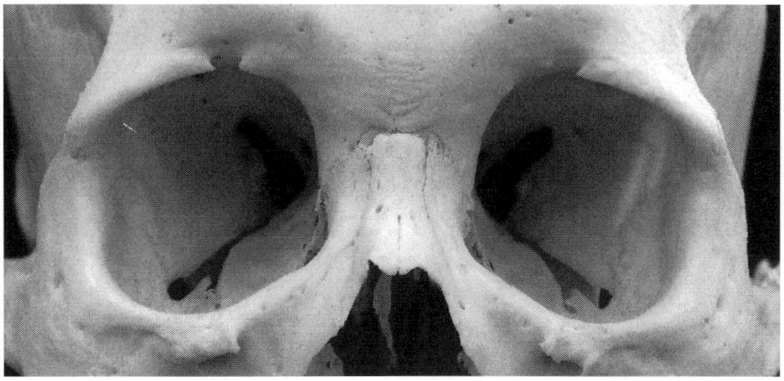

FIGURE 17.21 Variant of SPS 2. *SPS*, supranasal suture.

CHAPTER

# 18

# Transverse Palatine Suture

The transverse palatine suture (TPS) is defined as the course of the TPS on the hard bony palate. The entire suture is observed, but each assessment should focus on the medial one-half of the suture. If the suture is asymmetrical, score the general (*gestalt*) shape. TPS has four character states: *straight*, *anterior bulging*, *M-shaped (or jagged)*, and *posterior bulging*, scored as: $1<2<3<4$. If the suture is obliterated, do not score TPS; and, do not consider slight undulations in sutural morphology when scoring TPS. To assess this trait, view the cranium inferiorly, at the hard palate. Follow the transverse suture and note if, and how, the deviation occurs near the intersection with the median palatine suture.

TPS morphology has been scrutinized for over 200 years. Meckel (1815) first identified a *backward curving* (posterior bulging) TPS, whereas Topinard (1881) and Gegenbaur (1898) identified the anterior bulging and straight morphologies, respectively. Stieda (1894) formalized a scoring methodology for TPS, identifying four character states: *transverse*, *forward*, *backward*, and *irregular* forms. His *irregular* form was any combination of the other three (now identified as asymmetrical). In 1906, Le Double (cited in Woo, 1949a,b,c) further modified this scoring strategy, identifying seven character states.

Throughout the late 1800s, anatomists and skeletal biologists continued to work with the various manifestations of the TPS. Some of them, such as Stieda (1894) and Killerman (1894) attempted to use those manifestations as an indication of geographic origin (i.e., *racial differences*). Others attempted to explain the various presentations of TPS as a mechanism of growth and development (Calori, 1868; Stieda, 1894) or directional growth and hyperdevelopment (Augier, 1931; Woo, 1949a,b,c).

Woo (1948) and later Woo (1949a,b,c) used Le Double's (1906a,b) character states to deliver one of the more robust early investigations into the TPS morphology. He documented the manifestation of TPS in five groups ($n=1531$), outlining the following four character states: *anterior*, *posterior*, *transverse*, and *irregular*. As a side note, Woo (1949a,b,c) used the sagittally sectioned crania from the Terry Collection (Smithsonian Institution, National Museum of Natural History, Washington, DC) to argue that TPS does not represent a serrate suture as many anatomists before him argued, but rather it belongs to a type of *squamosal suture* since the palatal border overlaps the maxillary border.

Hooton (1920) assessed the *palatine transverse suture direction* in the Harvard Blanks, permitting three character states: *transverse*, *anterior*, and *posterior*. Hauser and De Stefano (1989) provide nine character states: (1) *straight transverse, symmetric*, (2) *straight transverse, posterior protrusions*, (3) *straight transverse, scalaris*, (4) *straight transverse, posterior protrusion at midline*, (5) *convex, posterior protrusion*, (6) *irregular, posterior protrusion at midline*, (7) *transverse symmetric, anterior protrusion*, (8) *convex, anterior protrusion*, and (9) *median rectangular, anterior protrusion* (Hauser and De Stefano, 1989:173). Rhine (1990:20) identified two character states: *straight* and *bulging*, while Burns (1999:38) reported three: *straight*, *Z-shaped*, and *arched*. Gill (1998:151) identified three morphologies: *straight*, *curved*, and *jagged*.

Initially, Hefner (2003a,b) did not formally define TPS, but later (Hefner, 2009:990) provided additional insight and guidance on a scoring methodology: "The course of the TPS ... is highly variable, although certain themes persist." Therefore, TPS is defined as *the shape of the course of the TPS on the hard bony palate* expressed as *straight*, *anterior bulging*, *M-shaped (or jagged)*, or *posterior bulging*.

## NOMENCLATURE

*Sutura palatina transversa*, *sutura palatina transversa scalaris*, transverse palatine suture, palatine suture, palatine transverse suture direction, and transverse palatomaxillary suture.

*Atlas of Human Cranial Macromorphoscopic Traits*.
DOI: https://doi.org/10.1016/B978-0-12-814385-8.00018-5

## GROSS ANATOMY

The hard palate is made up of four cranial bones: the paired maxillae and the paired palatine bones. The maxillae are situated anteriorly and cover the majority of the area between the two sides of the dental arch. Medially, the maxillae articulate to one another via the anterior median palatine suture. Posteriorly, the maxillae articulate with the two horizontal palatine processes at the *TPS*. The palatine bones articulate along the midline of the palate by means of the posterior median palatine suture. The anterior portion of the palate (sensu stricto) is bordered anteriorly and laterally by the maxillary teeth. In life, the posterior aspect of the hard palate connects directly to the soft palate, a muscular structure bound by a thick, tendinous aponeurosis of the *tensor veli palatini* muscles (aponeurotic plate).

## GROWTH AND DEVELOPMENT

The maxillae each ossify from two main centers of ossification—the maxillary and the premaxillary (White and Folkens, 1991); by the 9th week in utero, these are fully fused in humans. The left and right halves of the maxillae may never fully fuse at the anterior median palatine suture. The palatine bones ossify from a single center. The two halves may never fully fuse along the posterior median palatine suture. Wood (2012) noted age-stability in TPS shape by 7–10 years and predictable regional variability in TPS morphology in fetal remains for some populations.

## FUNCTIONAL MORPHOLOGY

The hard palate functions both in feeding and speech. At birth, the hard and soft palates create a vacuum that forces liquid into the mouth. Birth defects (e.g., cleft palate) can interfere with this process, requiring extensive and often invasive surgeries. The palate is also essential to the creation of certain phonetic sounds during speech. The TPS serves as a zone of growth during development. As mentioned earlier, much of the functional morphology of the palate is under strong selective pressures related to mastication. The morphology of the palate is associated with the dental alveolus housing the dentition and the variation inherent in palate morphology resulting from differential loading in this skeletal region (masticatory loading) (Menegaz et al., 2009). Palate morphology—including its dimensions and underlying cortical and trabecular bone concentration—is determined, at least in part, by the variation introduced through differential masticatory loadings (Pilloud et al., 2014). The palatine sutures, including the TPS, provide anterior and lateral growth up to obliteration.

## WITHIN POPULATION VARIATION

Data derived from the Macromorphoscopic Databank of the frequency distribution of TPS ($n = 3981$). All data are for adult individuals. When possible, frequency data for males and females are provided separately. When sex could not be estimated reliably, frequency distributions are pooled as "Unknown" (Table 18.1).

**TABLE 18.1** Frequency Distribution of TPS, by Geographic Origin and Sex

| Geographic origin | Sex | 1 | | 2 | | 3 | | 4 | | Total |
|---|---|---|---|---|---|---|---|---|---|---|
| | | *n* | % | *n* | % | *n* | % | *n* | % | |
| **American Black** | **Female** | 2 | 17 | 8 | 67 | 2 | 17 | 0 | 0 | 12 |
| | **Male** | 0 | 0 | 39 | 68 | 18 | 32 | 0 | 0 | 57 |
| | **Unknown** | 1 | 0 | 0 | 0 | 0 | 0 | 0 | 0 | 1 |
| | **Total** | 3 | 4 | 47 | 67 | 20 | 29 | 0 | 0 | 70 |
| **American White** | **Female** | 22 | 23 | 50 | 53 | 21 | 22 | 2 | 2 | 95 |
| | **Male** | 31 | 22 | 80 | 58 | 28 | 20 | 0 | 0 | 139 |
| | **Unknown** | 0 | 0 | 0 | 0 | 0 | 0 | 0 | 0 | 0 |
| | **Total** | 53 | 23 | 130 | 56 | 49 | 21 | 2 | 1 | 234 |
| **Amerindian** | **Female** | 0 | 0 | 0 | 0 | 0 | 0 | 0 | 0 | 0 |
| | **Male** | 0 | 0 | 0 | 0 | 0 | 0 | 0 | 0 | 0 |
| | **Unknown** | 1120 | 56 | 654 | 33 | 85 | 4 | 132 | 7 | 1991 |
| | **Total** | 1120 | 56 | 654 | 33 | 85 | 4 | 132 | 7 | 1991 |
| **El Salvador** | **Female** | 0 | 0 | 0 | 0 | 0 | 0 | 0 | 0 | 0 |
| | **Male** | 2 | 40 | 3 | 60 | 0 | 0 | 0 | 0 | 5 |
| | **Unknown** | 0 | 0 | 0 | 0 | 0 | 0 | 0 | 0 | 0 |
| | **Total** | 2 | 40 | 3 | 60 | 0 | 0 | 0 | 0 | 5 |
| **Eskimo** | **Female** | 0 | 0 | 0 | 0 | 0 | 0 | 0 | 0 | 0 |
| | **Male** | 0 | 0 | 0 | 0 | 0 | 0 | 0 | 0 | 0 |
| | **Unknown** | 310 | 48 | 209 | 32 | 72 | 11 | 59 | 9 | 650 |
| | **Total** | 310 | 48 | 209 | 32 | 72 | 11 | 59 | 9 | 650 |
| **Guatemalan** | **Female** | 0 | 0 | 2 | 100 | 0 | 0 | 0 | 0 | 2 |
| | **Male** | 0 | 0 | 0 | 0 | 0 | 0 | 0 | 0 | 0 |
| | **Unknown** | 0 | 0 | 0 | 0 | 0 | 0 | 0 | 0 | 0 |
| | **Total** | 0 | 0 | 2 | 100 | 0 | 0 | 0 | 0 | 2 |
| **Mexico** | **Female** | 0 | 0 | 0 | 0 | 0 | 0 | 0 | 0 | 0 |
| | **Male** | 4 | 29 | 7 | 50 | 3 | 21 | 0 | 0 | 14 |
| | **Unknown** | 0 | 0 | 0 | 0 | 0 | 0 | 0 | 0 | 0 |
| | **Total** | 4 | 29 | 7 | 50 | 3 | 21 | 0 | 0 | 14 |
| **Pacific Island** | **Female** | 12 | 24 | 16 | 32 | 14 | 28 | 8 | 16 | 50 |
| | **Male** | 21 | 28 | 40 | 53 | 12 | 16 | 3 | 4 | 76 |
| | **Unknown** | 37 | 47 | 26 | 33 | 11 | 14 | 5 | 6 | 79 |
| | **Total** | 70 | 34 | 82 | 40 | 37 | 18 | 16 | 8 | 205 |
| **Peruvian** | **Female** | 0 | 0 | 0 | 0 | 0 | 0 | 0 | 0 | 0 |
| | **Male** | 0 | 0 | 0 | 0 | 0 | 0 | 0 | 0 | 0 |
| | **Unknown** | 4 | 31 | 1 | 8 | 2 | 15 | 6 | 46 | 13 |
| | **Total** | 4 | 31 | 1 | 8 | 2 | 15 | 6 | 46 | 13 |
| **Southwest (SW) Hispanic** | **Female** | 3 | 50 | 3 | 50 | 0 | 0 | 0 | 0 | 6 |
| | **Male** | 4 | 44 | 5 | 56 | 0 | 0 | 0 | 0 | 9 |
| | **Unknown** | 0 | 0 | 0 | 0 | 0 | 0 | 0 | 0 | 0 |
| | **Total** | 7 | 47 | 8 | 53 | 0 | 0 | 0 | 0 | 15 |
| **Thai** | **Female** | 181 | 60 | 90 | 30 | 16 | 5 | 15 | 5 | 302 |
| | **Male** | 323 | 69 | 103 | 22 | 32 | 7 | 13 | 3 | 471 |
| | **Unknown** | 8 | 89 | 0 | 0 | 1 | 11 | 0 | 0 | 9 |
| | **Total** | 512 | 65 | 193 | 25 | 49 | 6 | 28 | 4 | 782 |
| **Total for all groups** | | 2085 | 52 | 1336 | 34 | 317 | 8 | 243 | 6 | 3981 |

*TPS*, transverse palatine suture.

## CHARACTER STATES

Photographic exemplars of the different character states of TPS are provided below. Each character state is defined following Hefner (2009, 2016). When necessary to clarify scoring, more nuanced definitions are provided in the figure captions. TPS should be assessed with the protocol provided in the preceding section. Character states include:

TPS 1 = *straight*; suture crosses the palate perpendicular to the median palatine suture. There is no significant deviation, anteriorly or posteriorly.
TPS 2 = *anterior bulging*; suture crosses the palate perpendicular to the median palatine suture; however, there is an anterior deviation, or bulge, near the intersection of the two.
TPS 3 = *M-shaped (or jagged)*; as the suture crosses the palate, there are deviations both anteriorly and posteriorly, resulting in a jagged intersection with the median palatine suture.
TPS 4 = *posterior bulging*; suture crosses the palate perpendicular to the median palatine suture; however, there is a posterior deviation, or bulge, near the intersection of the two.

## CHARACTER STATES FOR TRANSVERSE PALATINE SUTURE = 1 (FIGS. 18.1–18.7)

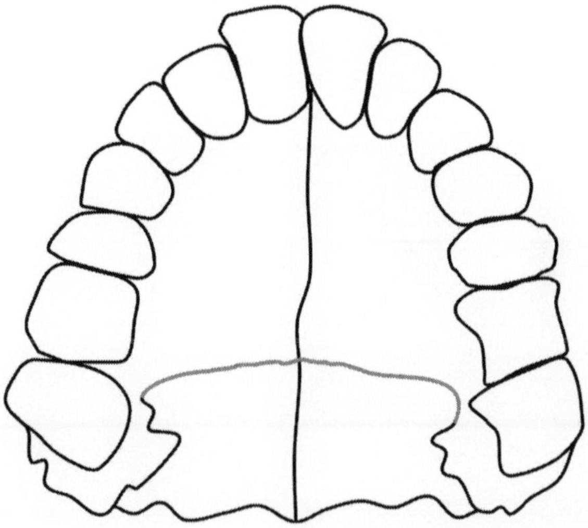


FIGURE 18.1 Diagrammatic representation of TPS 1. *TPS*, transverse palatine suture.

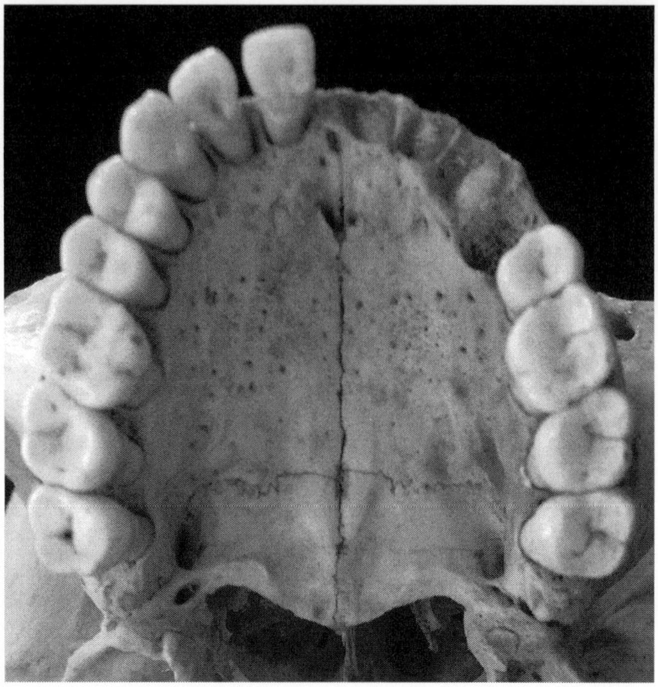

FIGURE 18.2 Variant of TPS 1. Note: slight asymmetry may occur. Although the two branches of the suture do not connect at midline, the general theme (i.e., "straight") is considered. *TPS*, transverse palatine suture.

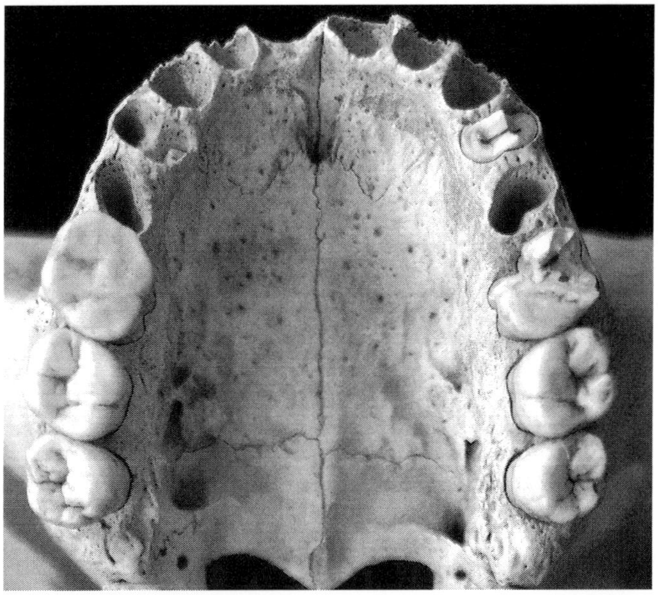

**FIGURE 18.3** Variant of TPS 1. Note: slight asymmetry may occur. Although the two branches of the suture do not connect at midline, the general theme (i.e., "straight") is considered. *TPS*, transverse palatine suture.

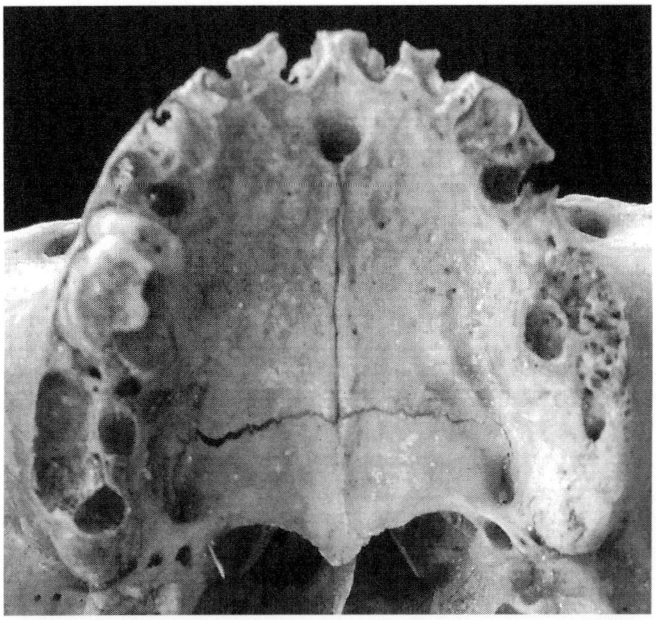

**FIGURE 18.4** Variant of TPS 1. *TPS*, transverse palatine suture.

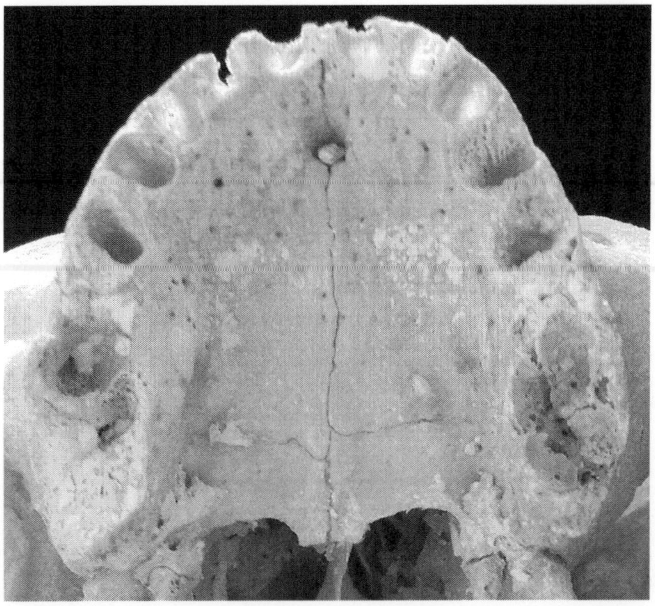

**FIGURE 18.5** Diagrammatic representation of TPS 1. Note: slight asymmetry may occur. Although the two branches of the suture do not connect at midline, the general theme (i.e., "straight") is considered. *TPS*, transverse palatine suture.

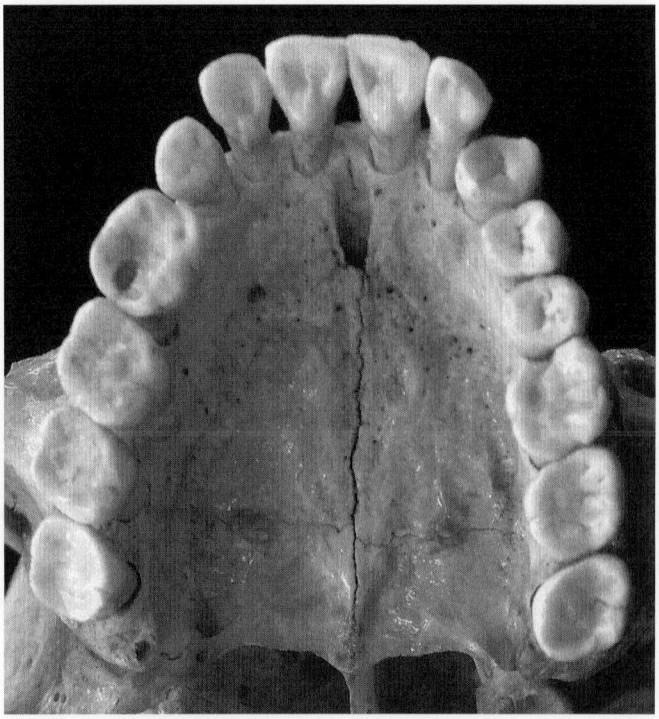

**FIGURE 18.6** Variant of TPS 1. Note: slight asymmetry may occur. Although the two branches of the suture do not connect at midline, the general theme (i.e., "straight") is considered. *TPS*, transverse palatine suture.

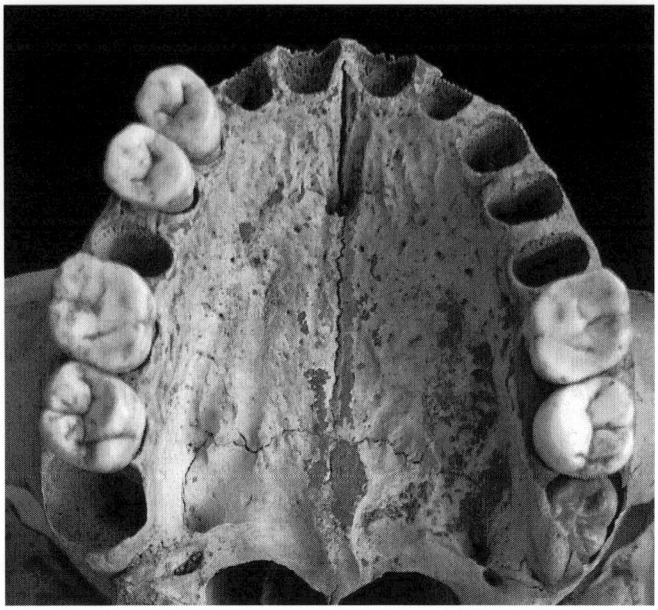

**FIGURE 18.7** Variant of TPS 1. Note: slight undulations at midline are not considered true deviations. *TPS*, transverse palatine suture.

## CHARACTER STATES FOR TRANSVERSE PALATINE SUTURE = 2 (FIGS. 18.8–18.14)

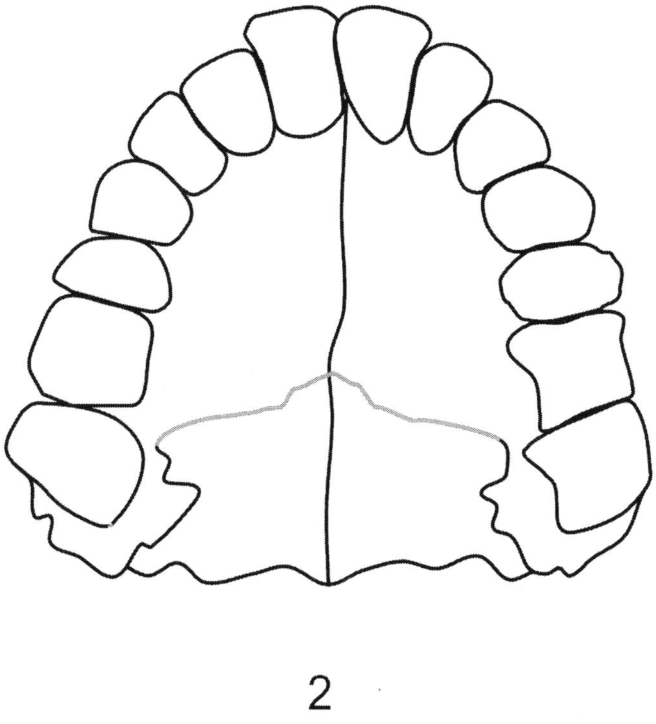


FIGURE 18.8 Diagrammatic representation of TPS 2. *TPS*, transverse palatine suture.

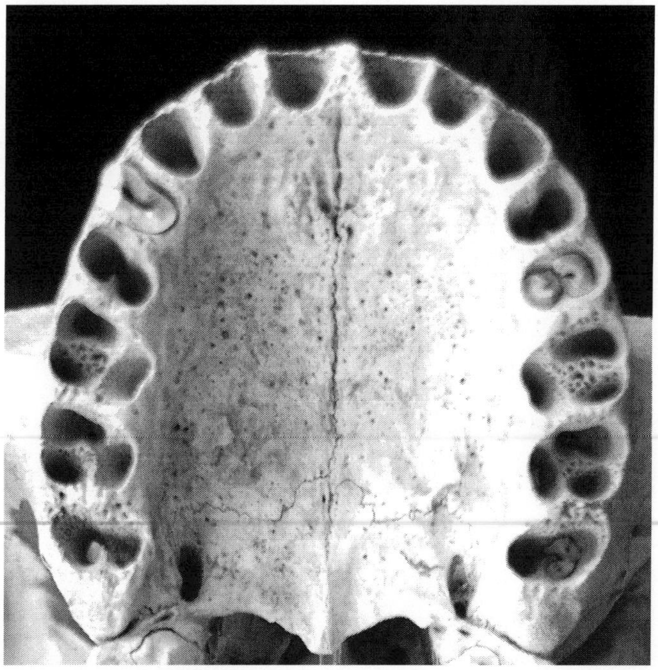

FIGURE 18.9 Variant of TPS 2. *TPS*, transverse palatine suture.

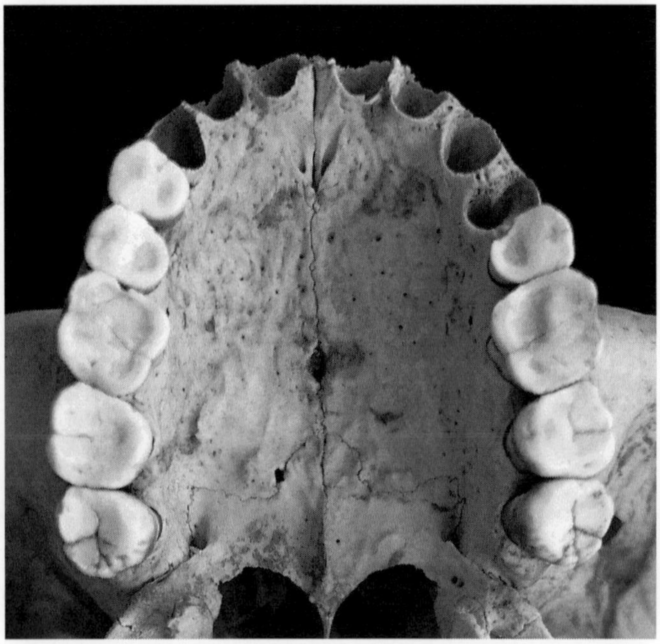

**FIGURE 18.10** Variant of TPS 2. *TPS*, transverse palatine suture.

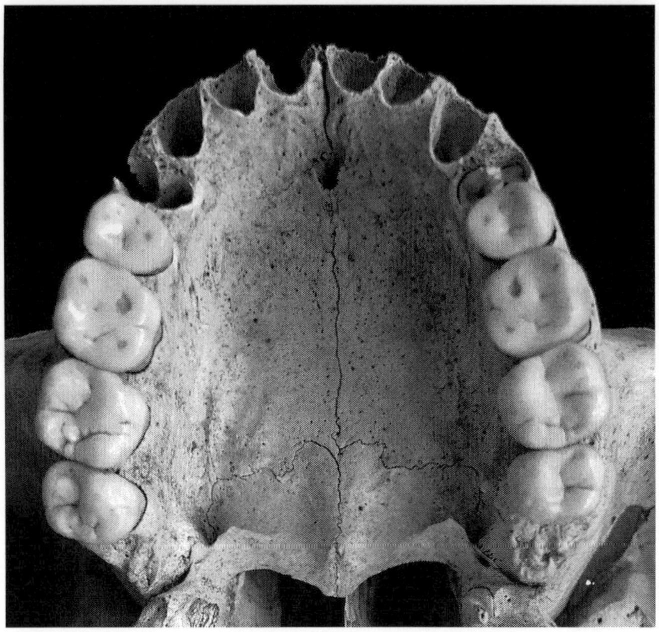

**FIGURE 18.11** Variant of TPS 2. Note: slight undulations at midline are not considered true deviations.

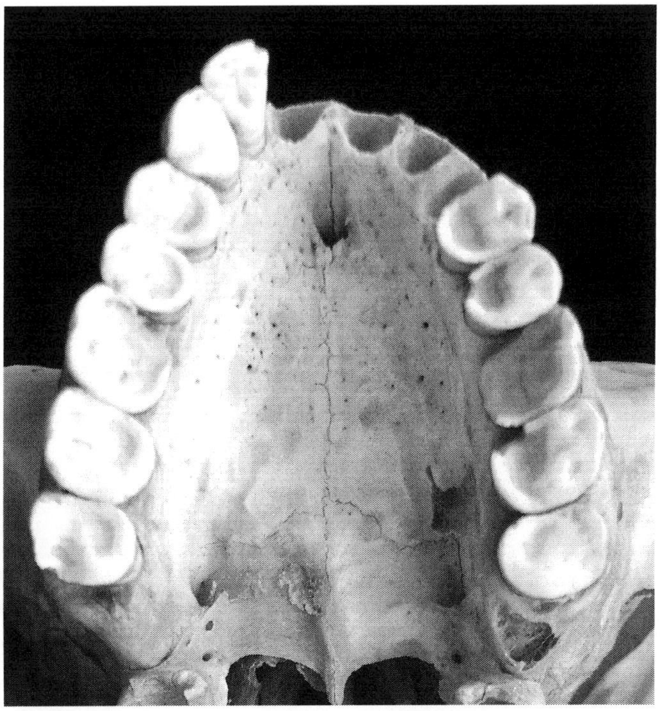

FIGURE 18.12 Variant of TPS 2. Note: slight asymmetry may occur. Although the two branches of the suture do not connect at midline, the general theme (i.e., "anterior bulging") is considered.

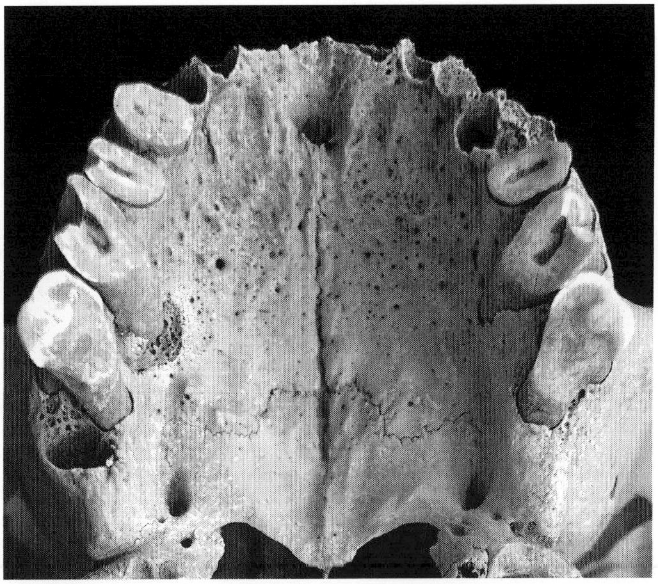

FIGURE 18.13 Variant of TPS 2. *TPS*, transverse palatine suture.

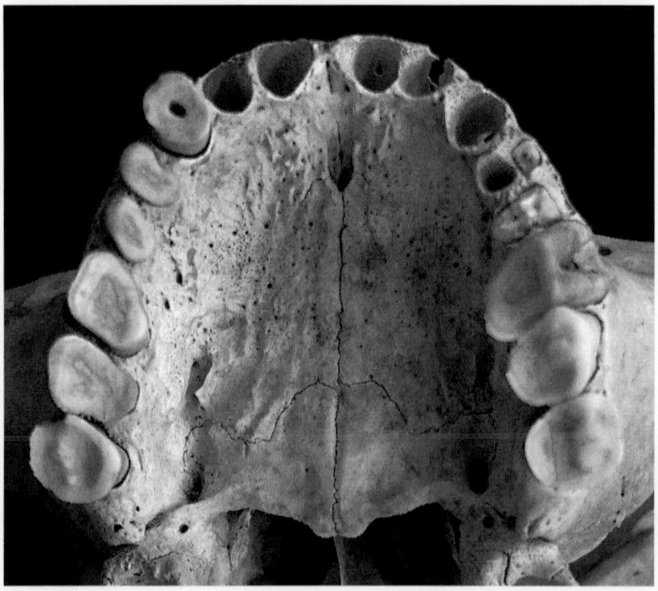

**FIGURE 18.14** Variant of TPS 2. *TPS*, transverse palatine suture.

# CHARACTER STATES FOR TRANSVERSE PALATINE SUTURE = 3 (FIGS. 18.15–18.21)

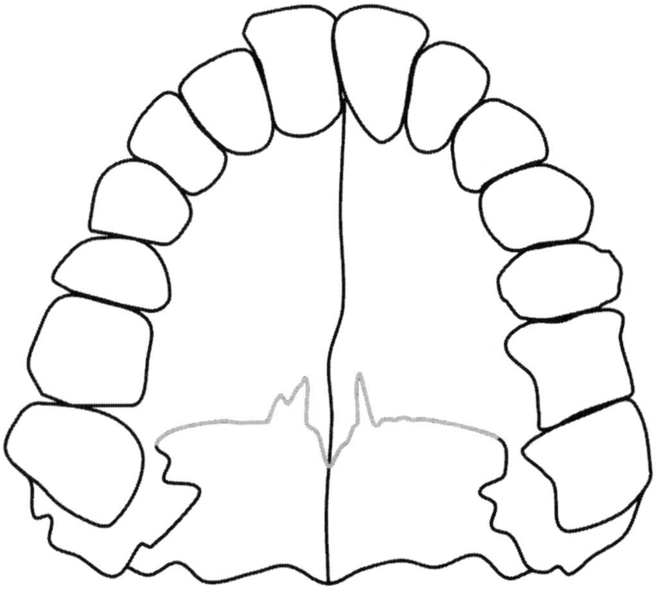

3

FIGURE 18.15 Diagrammatic representation of TPS 3. *TPS*, transverse palatine suture.

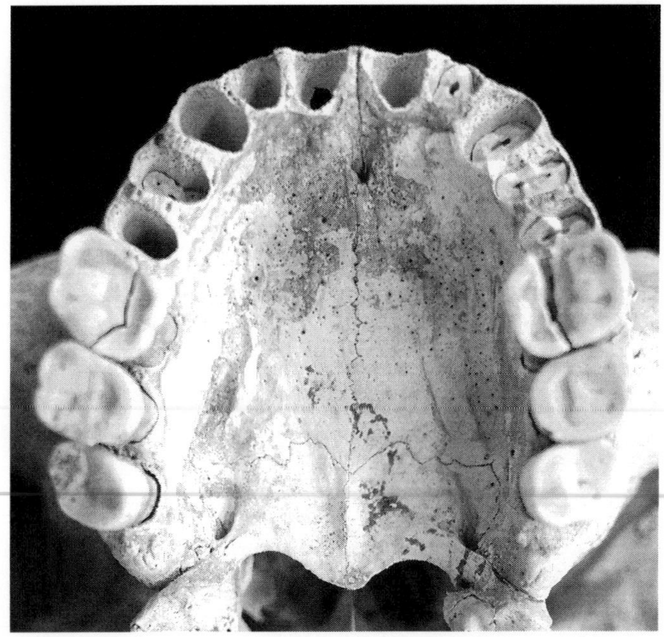

FIGURE 18.16 Variant of TPS 3. *TPS*, transverse palatine suture.

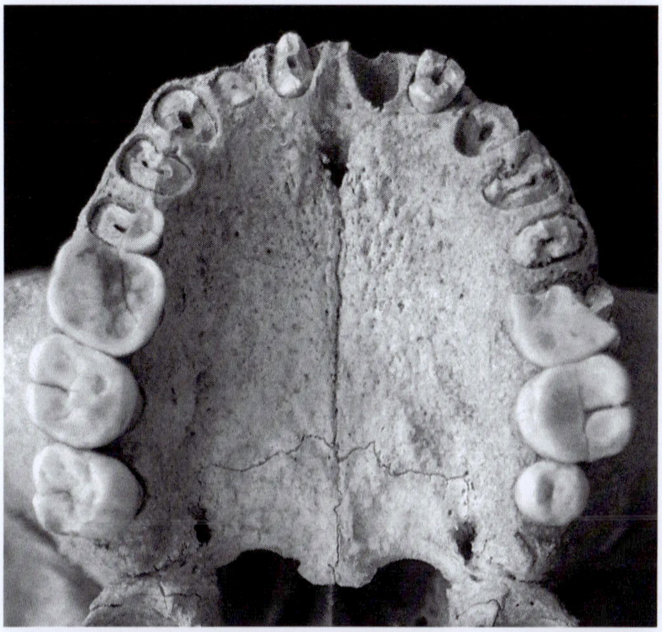

**FIGURE 18.17** Variant of TPS 3. *TPS*, transverse palatine suture.

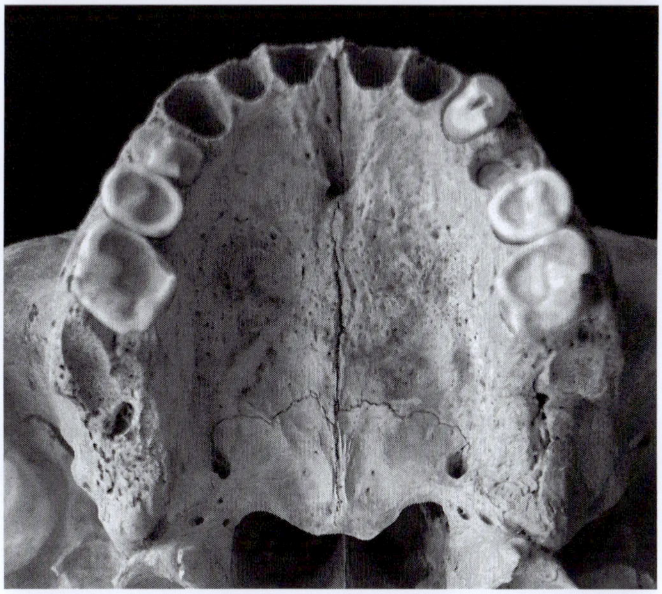

**FIGURE 18.18** Variant of TPS 3. *TPS*, transverse palatine suture.

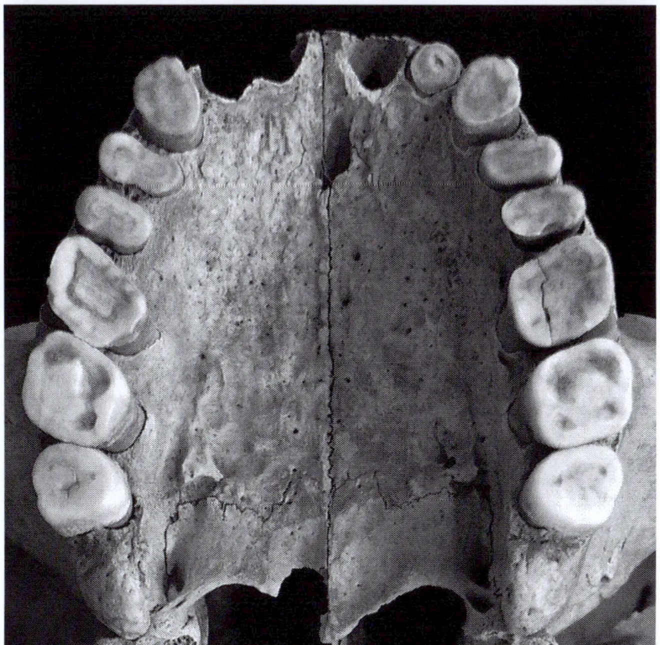

**FIGURE 18.19** Variant of TPS 3. *TPS*, transverse palatine suture.

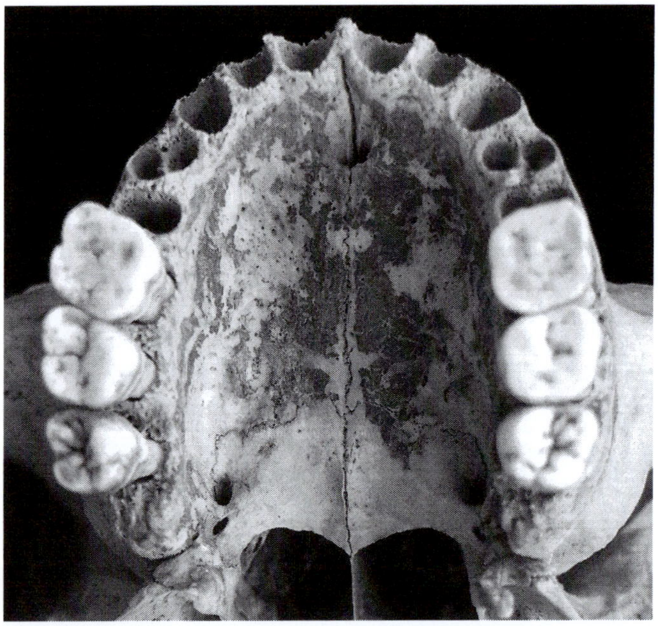

**FIGURE 18.20** Variant of TPS 3. *TPS*, transverse palatine suture.

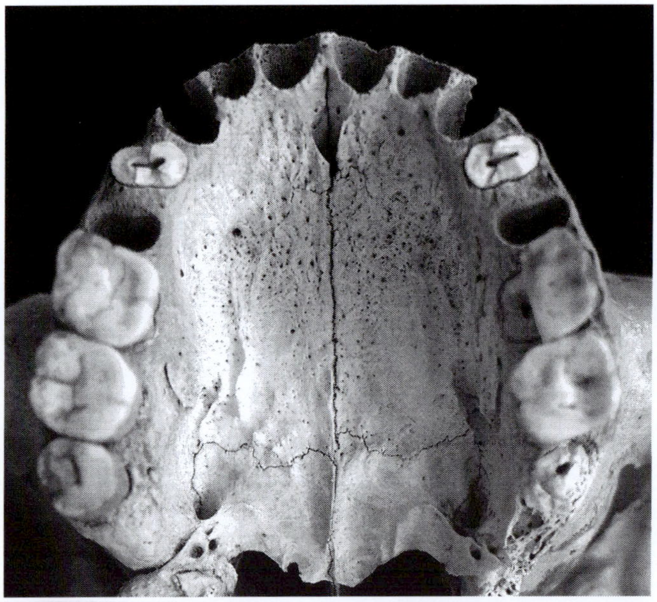

**FIGURE 18.21** Variant of TPS 3. Note: slight asymmetry may occur. Although the two branches of the suture do not connect at midline, the general theme (i.e., "M-shaped") is considered. *TPS*, transverse palatine suture.

# CHARACTER STATES FOR TRANSVERSE PALATINE SUTURE = 4 (FIGS. 18.22–18.28)

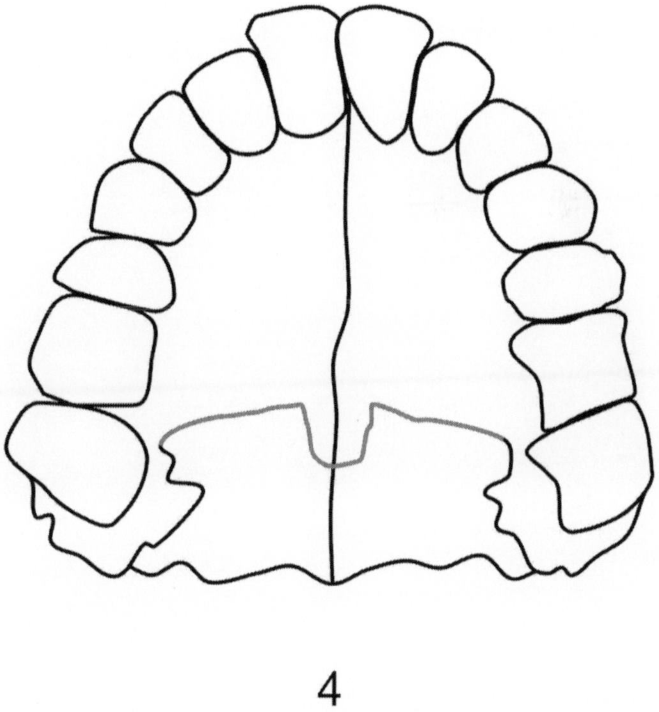


FIGURE 18.22 Diagrammatic representation of TPS 4. *TPS*, transverse palatine suture.

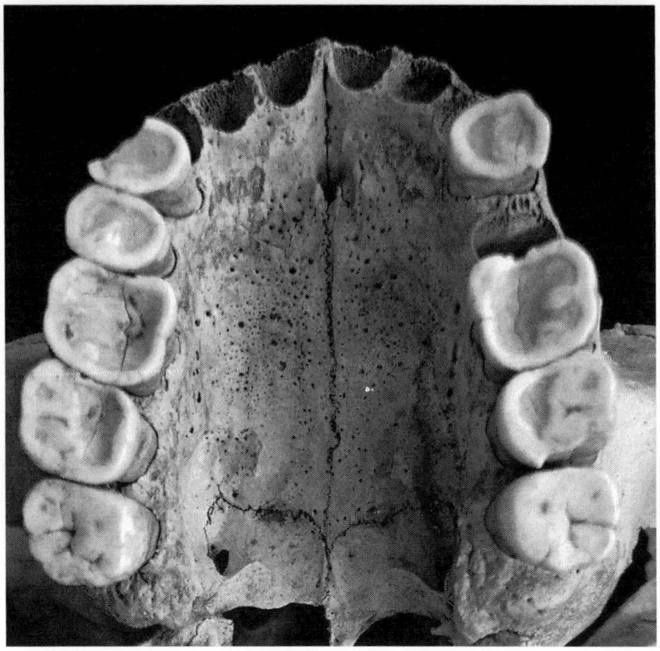

FIGURE 18.23 Variant of TPS 4. *TPS*, transverse palatine suture.

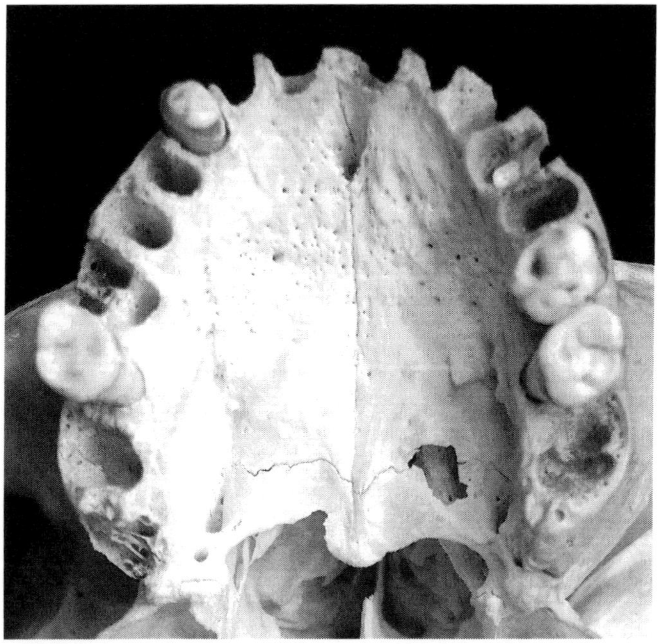

FIGURE 18.24 Variant of TPS 4. *TPS*, transverse palatine suture.

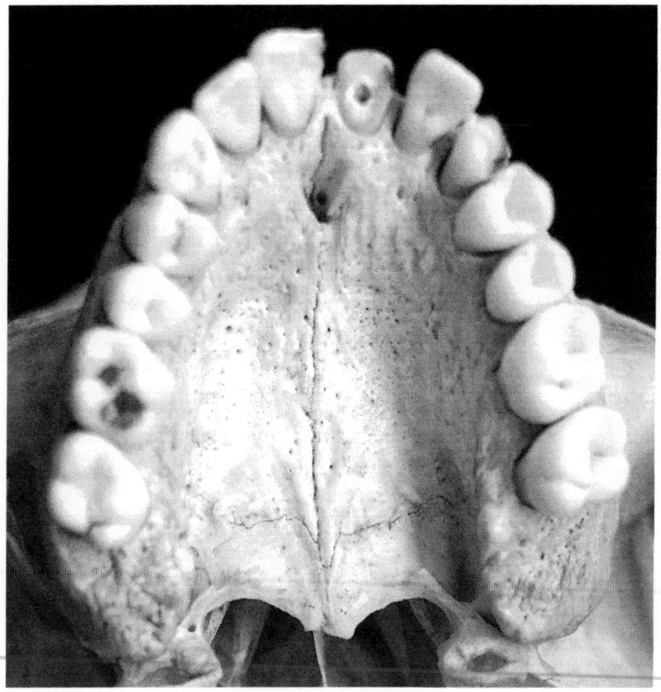

FIGURE 18.25 Variant of TPS 4. *TPS*, transverse palatine suture.

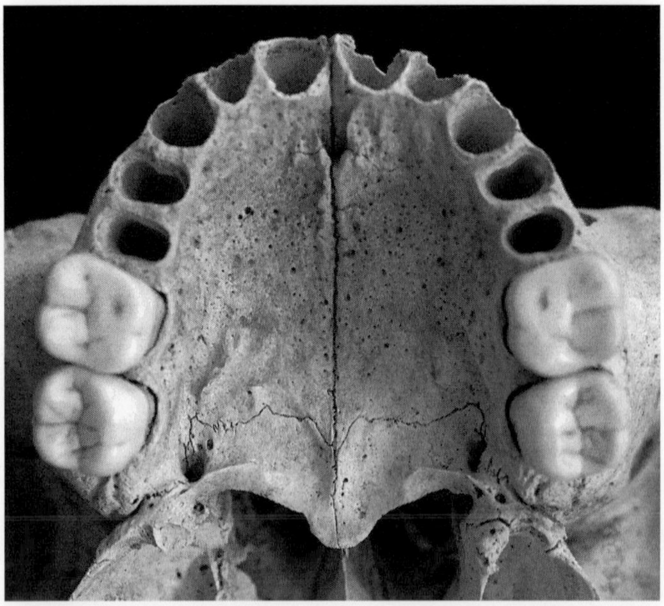

FIGURE 18.26 Variant of TPS 4. *TPS*, transverse palatine suture.

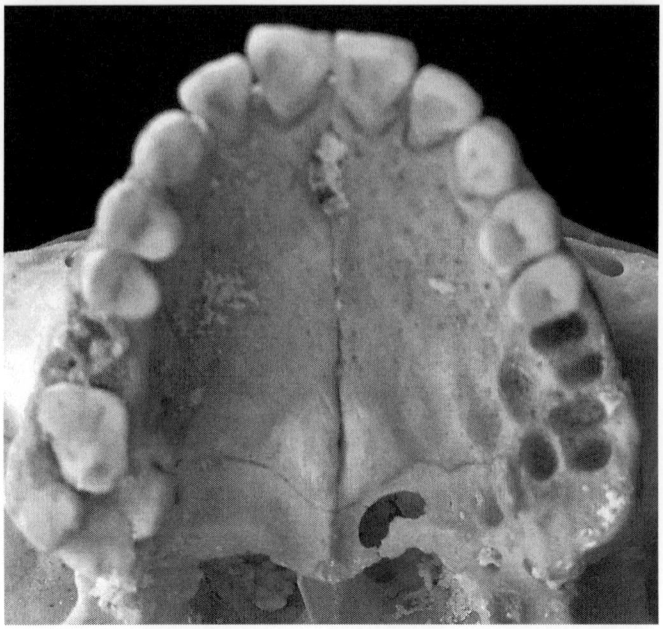

FIGURE 18.27 Variant of TPS 4. *TPS*, transverse palatine suture.

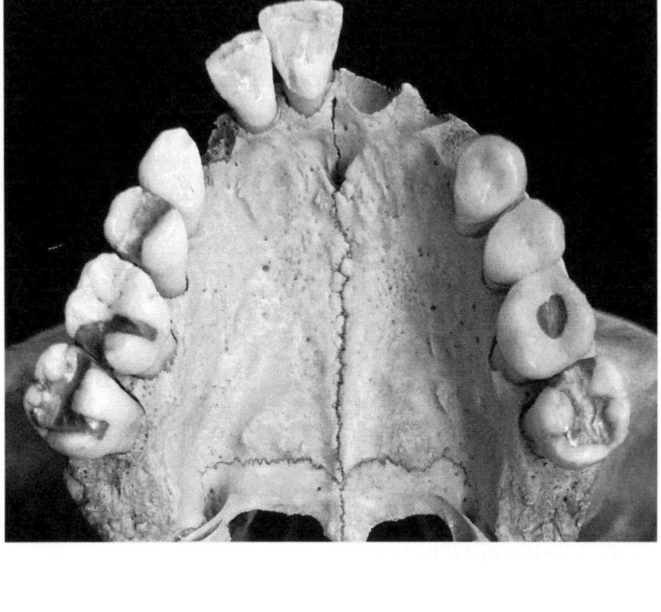

FIGURE 18.28 Variant of TPS 4. *TPS*, transverse palatine suture.

CHAPTER

# 19

# Zygomaticomaxillary Suture

The zygomaticomaxillary suture (ZS) describes the course of the suture between the maxilla and the zygomatic. When asymmetry occurs, the side presenting the highest expression is recorded. The infraorbital suture should be ignored when making a determination. Assessment of ZS is based primarily on the number of major angles present and the approximate location of the greatest lateral projection of the suture. Sutures having greatest lateral projection at the inferior margin, but a slight angle near the midpoint of the suture should be scored as 0. The course of the suture is best observed in the anterior view. ZS shape has three character states: *no angles, one angle*, and *two or more angles*, scored as: $0 > 1 > 2$.

Martindale and Gilbert (1984) introduced a scoring system for *zygomaxillary suture* shape, attributing two patterns (*angled* and *curved*) to their Amerindian and American White sample. Gill (1995, 1998) used the same expressions to describe zygomaxillary sutures among a slightly larger sample. Rhine (1990) retitled this trait ZS. He used the Martindale and Gilbert (1984) character states but further described the two variants as: "either '*curved*' (a general 'S' shape), or '*angled*' from orbit to cheek" (Rhine, 1990:20; italics added). Burns (1999:38) recorded similar definitions for the *zygomaxillary suture*, describing three character states: *angled, jagged, or S-shaped*, and *curved, or S-shaped* (Burns, 1999:38).

Holborow (2002) used larger samples and incorporated a metric component (three linear measures) to quantify suture shape. Similarly, Sholts and Wärmländer (2012) used more robust geometric morphometrics to explore shape variability between populations.

Hefner (2003a,b, 2009), and subsequently Hefner (2010) who defined ZS for the *Osteoware* program (Smithsonian Institution, 2015), provides the scoring methodology proposed herein (with slight modifications). ZS is defined as (Hefner, 2010:75):

> ...the suture between the maxilla and the zygomatic. The course of the suture is best observed in the anterior view ... The infraorbital suture should be ignored when making a determination. Assessment of ZS is based primarily on the approximate location of greatest lateral projection of the suture, and also on the number of major angles present. Sutures having greatest lateral projection at the inferior margin, but a slight angle near the midpoint of the suture should be scored as 0. 0 = A suture with no angles and greatest lateral projection at the inferior margin of the malar (note: Sutures having greatest lateral projection at the inferior margin, but a slight angle near the midpoint of the suture should be scored as 0); 1 = A suture with one angle and greatest lateral projection near the midline; 2 = A suture with two or more angles (presenting a jagged and/or S-shaped appearance) with variable greatest lateral projection.

## NOMENCLATURE

*Os zygomaticum bipartitum, sutura mediojugalis, sutura zygomatica*, zygomaxillary suture, zygomaticomaxillary sutura, zygomaticomaxillary suture, *sutura infraorbitalis, sutura zygomaticomaxillaris*, and suture zygomaticomaxillaire.

## GROSS ANATOMY

The zygomaticomaxillary region comprises the maxillae and the zygomatic bones. These bones articulate at the ZS, a weakly serrated suture connecting the maxillary process of the zygomatic bone to the zygomatic process of the maxilla.

*Atlas of Human Cranial Macromorphoscopic Traits.*
DOI: https://doi.org/10.1016/B978-0-12-814385-8.00019-7

## GROWTH AND DEVELOPMENT

The maxillae each ossify from two main centers of ossification—the maxillary and the premaxillary (White and Folkens, 1991). By the ninth week in utero, these are fully fused in humans. The maxillae reach their adult morphology by the 14th year of life (following complete development of the second permanent molars). The zygomatic bones each ossify from a single center of ossification, which appears during the eighth week, in utero. The zygomatic reaches adult-like proportions by the second or third year of life (Scheur and Black, 2000). The ZS provides lateral and forward growth of the face. The nature of sutural growth (i.e., opening of space within sutures resulting from the growth of surrounding soft tissues) leads to bone formation on either side of the suture, resulting in a tension-related bone formation at sutural intersections. Growth and development continues surface remodeling via bone deposition and resorption leading to an overall increase in size and shape changes to the facial elements.

## FUNCTIONAL MORPHOLOGY

Serving as a buttress to direct energy away from the midface and an attachment point for muscles controlling both mastication and facial animation, the zygomaticomaxillary complex plays a significant role in the structure and function of the face. Musculature insertion into or originating from the zygomaticomaxillary complex includes the anterior (superficial) tendinous fibers of the masseter muscle and lesser fibers of the *orbicularis oculi*. The former corresponds closely to the location of the ZS and may play a role in the expression of the malar tubercle. The masseter muscle serves as one of the four major muscles of mastication, elevating the mandible and creating forward movement through contraction.

## WITHIN POPULATION VARIATION

Data derived from the Macromorphoscopic Databank of the frequency distribution of ZS ($n = 5512$). All data are for adult individuals. When possible, frequency data for males and females are provided separately. When sex could not be estimated reliably, frequency distributions are pooled as "Unknown" (Table 19.1).

**TABLE 19.1** Frequency Distribution of ZS, by Geographic Origin and Sex

| | | 0 | | 1 | | 2 | | |
|---|---|---|---|---|---|---|---|---|
| **Geographic origin** | **Sex** | *n* | % | *n* | % | *n* | % | **Total** |
| **African** | **Female** | 0 | 0 | 5 | 42 | 7 | 58 | 12 |
| | **Male** | 0 | 0 | 5 | 33 | 10 | 67 | 15 |
| | **Total** | 0 | 0 | 10 | 37 | 17 | 63 | 27 |
| **American Black** | **Female** | 10 | 9 | 50 | 44 | 54 | 47 | 114 |
| | **Male** | 40 | 25 | 60 | 38 | 57 | 36 | 157 |
| | **Unknown** | 0 | 0 | 0 | 0 | 0 | 0 | 0 |
| | **Total** | 50 | 18 | 110 | 41 | 111 | 41 | 271 |
| **American White** | **Female** | 16 | 14 | 48 | 41 | 53 | 45 | 117 |
| | **Male** | 17 | 19 | 36 | 40 | 37 | 41 | 90 |
| | **Unknown** | 0 | 0 | 0 | 0 | 0 | 0 | 0 |
| | **Total** | 33 | 16 | 84 | 41 | 90 | 43 | 207 |

*(Continued)*

TABLE 19.1 (*Continued*)

| Geographic origin | Sex | 0 | | 1 | | 2 | | Total |
|---|---|---|---|---|---|---|---|---|
| | | *n* | % | *n* | % | *n* | % | |
| **Amerindian** | **Female** | 0 | 0 | 14 | 32 | 30 | 68 | 44 |
| | **Male** | 0 | 0 | 10 | 26 | 28 | 74 | 38 |
| | **Unknown** | 1651 | 66 | 647 | 26 | 218 | 9 | 2516 |
| | **Total** | 1651 | 64 | 671 | 26 | 276 | 11 | 2598 |
| **Chinese** | **Female** | 0 | 0 | 1 | 25 | 3 | 75 | 4 |
| | **Male** | 3 | 6 | 14 | 30 | 30 | 64 | 47 |
| | **Unknown** | 0 | 0 | 0 | 0 | 0 | 0 | 0 |
| | **Total** | 3 | 6 | 15 | 29 | 33 | 65 | 51 |
| **Colombian** | **Female** | 10 | 15 | 42 | 64 | 14 | 21 | 66 |
| | **Male** | 22 | 13 | 126 | 72 | 28 | 16 | 176 |
| | **Unknown** | 0 | 0 | 0 | 0 | 0 | 0 | 0 |
| | **Total** | 32 | 13 | 168 | 69 | 42 | 17 | 242 |
| **El Salvador** | **Female** | 0 | 0 | 0 | 0 | 0 | 0 | 0 |
| | **Male** | 1 | 20 | 2 | 40 | 2 | 40 | 5 |
| | **Unknown** | 0 | 0 | 0 | 0 | 0 | 0 | 0 |
| | **Total** | 1 | 20 | 2 | 40 | 2 | 40 | 5 |
| **Eskimo** | **Female** | 0 | 0 | 0 | 0 | 0 | 0 | 0 |
| | **Male** | 0 | 0 | 0 | 0 | 0 | 0 | 0 |
| | **Unknown** | 544 | 71 | 171 | 22 | 46 | 6 | 761 |
| | **Total** | 544 | 71 | 171 | 22 | 46 | 6 | 761 |
| **European** | **Female** | 0 | 0 | 2 | 29 | 5 | 71 | 7 |
| | **Male** | 0 | 0 | 3 | 50 | 3 | 50 | 6 |
| | **Unknown** | 0 | 0 | 0 | 0 | 0 | 0 | 0 |
| | **Total** | 0 | 0 | 5 | 38 | 8 | 62 | 13 |
| **Guatemalan** | **Female** | 13 | 59 | 8 | 36 | 1 | 5 | 22 |
| | **Male** | 27 | 57 | 19 | 40 | 1 | 2 | 47 |
| | **Unknown** | 0 | 0 | 0 | 0 | 0 | 0 | 0 |
| | **Total** | 40 | 58 | 27 | 39 | 2 | 3 | 69 |
| **Japanese** | **Female** | 0 | 0 | 1 | 33 | 2 | 67 | 3 |
| | **Male** | 0 | 0 | 4 | 57 | 3 | 43 | 7 |
| | **Unknown** | 0 | 0 | 1 | 100 | 0 | 0 | 1 |
| | **Total** | 0 | 0 | 6 | 55 | 5 | 45 | 11 |
| **Mexico** | **Female** | 2 | 100 | 0 | 0 | 0 | 0 | 2 |
| | **Male** | 5 | 38 | 4 | 31 | 4 | 31 | 13 |
| | **Unknown** | 0 | 0 | 0 | 0 | 0 | 0 | 0 |
| | **Total** | 7 | 47 | 4 | 27 | 4 | 27 | 15 |

(*Continued*)

TABLE 19.1 (*Continued*)

| Geographic origin | Sex | 0 *n* | 0 % | 1 *n* | 1 % | 2 *n* | 2 % | Total |
|---|---|---|---|---|---|---|---|---|
| **Pacific Island** | **Female** | 37 | 70 | 7 | 13 | 9 | 17 | 53 |
| | **Male** | 48 | 55 | 25 | 28 | 15 | 17 | 88 |
| | **Unknown** | 43 | 48 | 40 | 44 | 7 | 8 | 90 |
| | **Total** | 128 | 55 | 72 | 31 | 31 | 13 | 231 |
| **Peruvian** | **Unknown** | 12 | 57 | 7 | 33 | 2 | 10 | 21 |
| | **Total** | 12 | 57 | 7 | 33 | 2 | 10 | 21 |
| **Southwest (SW) Hispanic** | **Female** | 3 | 75 | 1 | 25 | 0 | 0 | 4 |
| | **Male** | 4 | 80 | 0 | 0 | 1 | 20 | 5 |
| | **Unknown** | 47 | 47 | 36 | 36 | 16 | 16 | 99 |
| | **Total** | 54 | 50 | 37 | 34 | 17 | 16 | 108 |
| **Thai** | **Female** | 139 | 44 | 80 | 25 | 100 | 31 | 319 |
| | **Male** | 190 | 35 | 208 | 38 | 151 | 28 | 549 |
| | **Unknown** | 8 | 57 | 4 | 29 | 2 | 14 | 14 |
| | **Total** | 337 | 38 | 292 | 33 | 253 | 29 | 882 |
| **Total for all groups** | | 2892 | 52 | 1681 | 30 | 939 | 17 | 5512 |

*ZS*, zygomaticomaxillary suture.

## CHARACTER STATES

Photographic exemplars of the different character states of ZS are provided below. Each character state is defined following Hefner (2009, 2016). When necessary to clarify scoring, more nuanced definitions are provided in the figure captions. ZS should be assessed with the protocol provided in the preceding section. Character states include:

ZS 0 = *no angles*; greatest lateral projection of the suture is at the inferior margin of the malar.
ZS 1 = *one angle*; greatest lateral projection is near the midline.
ZS 2 = *two or more angles*; a jagged or S-shaped appearance. The greatest lateral projection is variable.

# CHARACTER STATES FOR ZYGOMATICOMAXILLARY SUTURE = 0 (FIGS. 19.1–19.7)

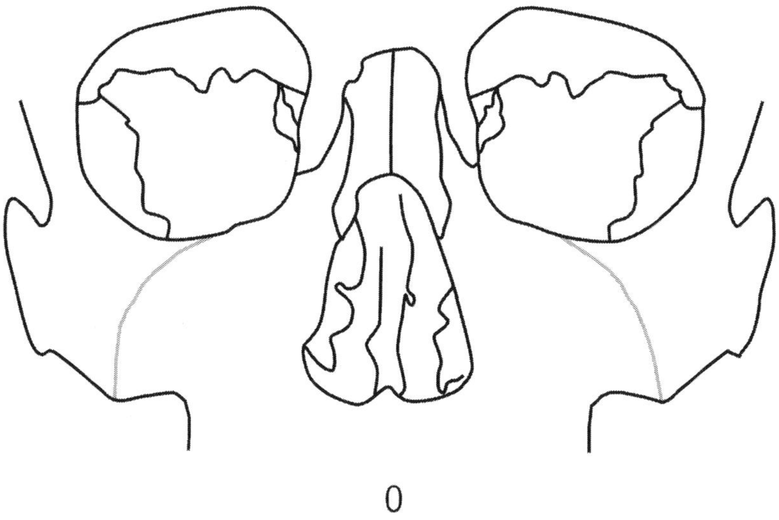


**FIGURE 19.1** Diagrammatic representation of ZS 0. *ZS*, zygomaticomaxillary suture.

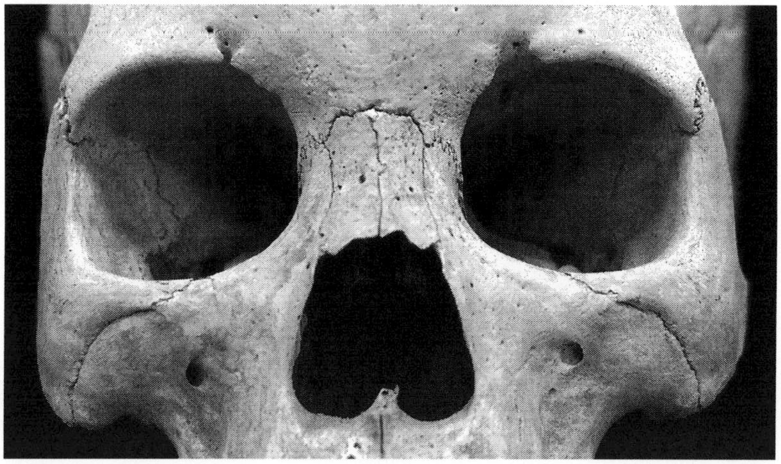

**FIGURE 19.2** Variant of ZS 0. Note: slight undulations of the infraorbital suture should not be considered when scoring ZS. *ZS*, zygomaticomaxillary suture.

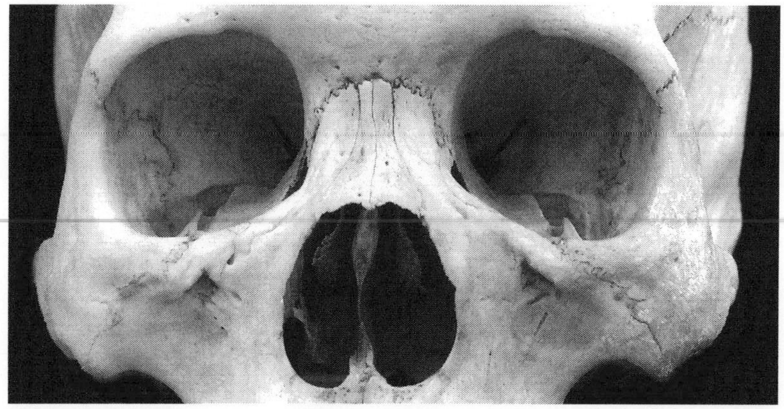

**FIGURE 19.3** Variant of ZS 0. *ZS*, zygomaticomaxillary suture.

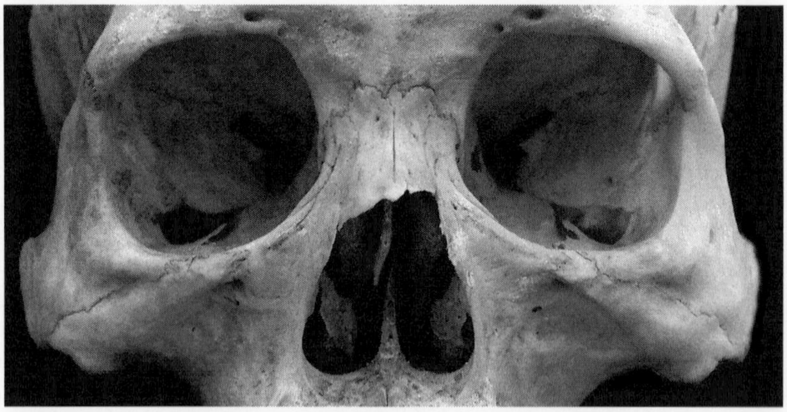

**FIGURE 19.4** Variant of ZS 0. *ZS*, zygomaticomaxillary suture.

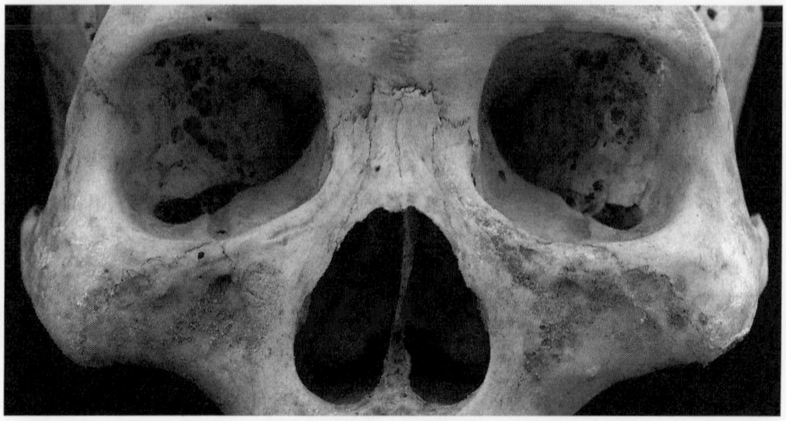

**FIGURE 19.5** Variant of ZS 0. *ZS*, zygomaticomaxillary suture.

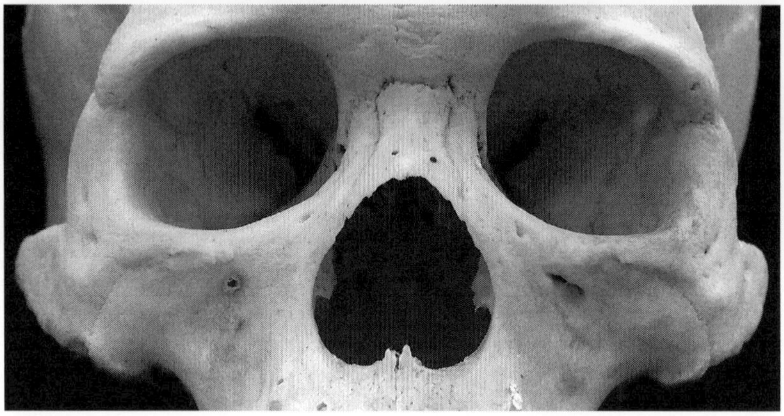

**FIGURE 19.6** Variant of ZS 0. Note: slight undulations of the infraorbital suture should not be considered when scoring ZS. In this example, the right infraorbital suture is projecting somewhat medially. *ZS*, zygomaticomaxillary suture.

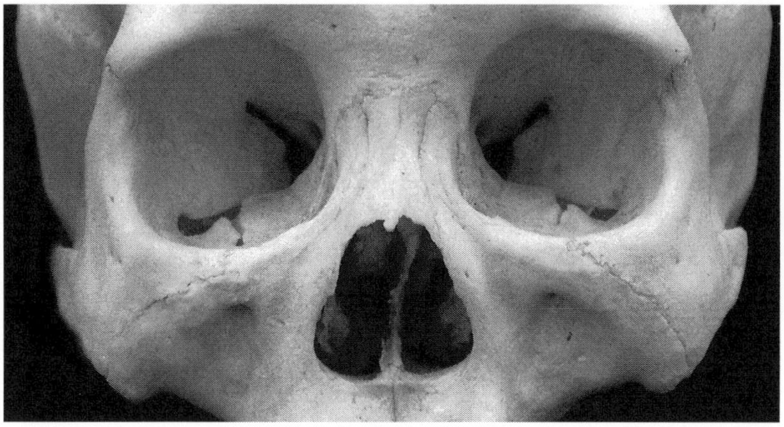

**FIGURE 19.7** Variant of ZS 0. Note: slight undulations of the infraorbital suture should not be considered when scoring ZS. In this example, the right infraorbital suture is projecting somewhat inferiorly before commencing to the right lateral aspect of the zygoma. *ZS*, zygomaticomaxillary suture.

# CHARACTER STATES FOR ZYGOMATICOMAXILLARY SUTURE = 1 (FIGS. 19.8–19.14)

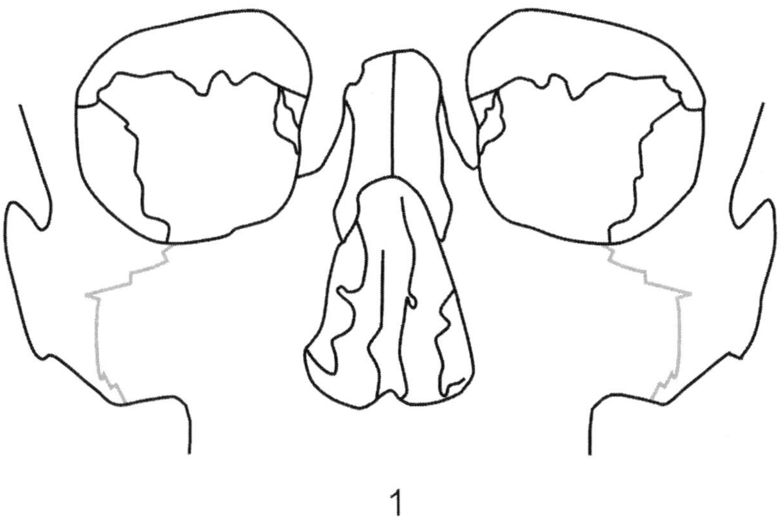


**FIGURE 19.8** Diagrammatic representation of ZS 1. *ZS*, zygomaticomaxillary suture.

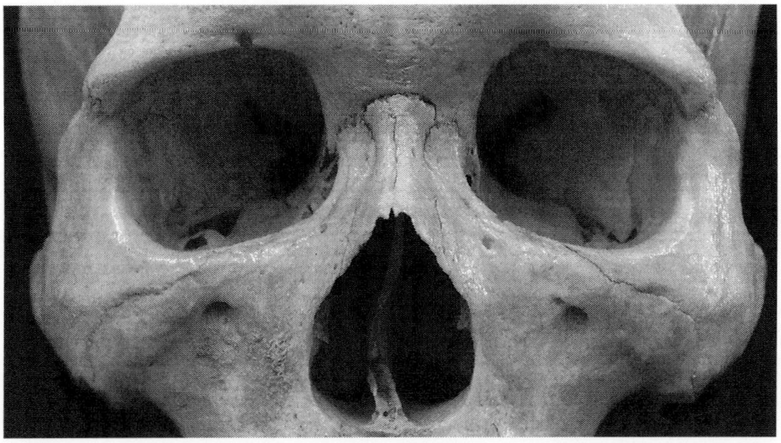

**FIGURE 19.9** Variant of ZS 1. *ZS*, zygomaticomaxillary suture.

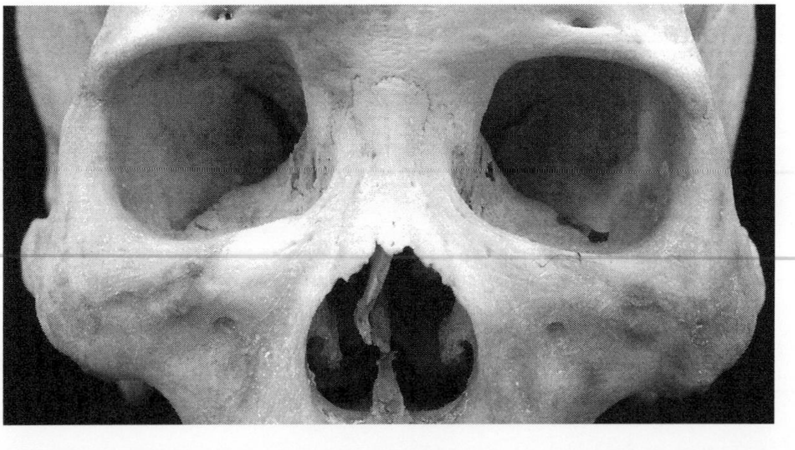

**FIGURE 19.10** Variant of ZS 1. Note: right side is expressing ZS 1 and left side is expressing ZS 0. *ZS*, zygomaticomaxillary suture.

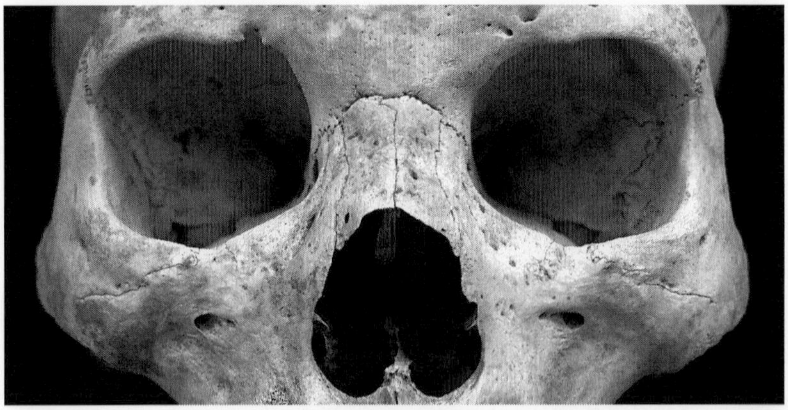

FIGURE 19.11 Variant of ZS 1. *ZS*, zygomaticomaxillary suture.

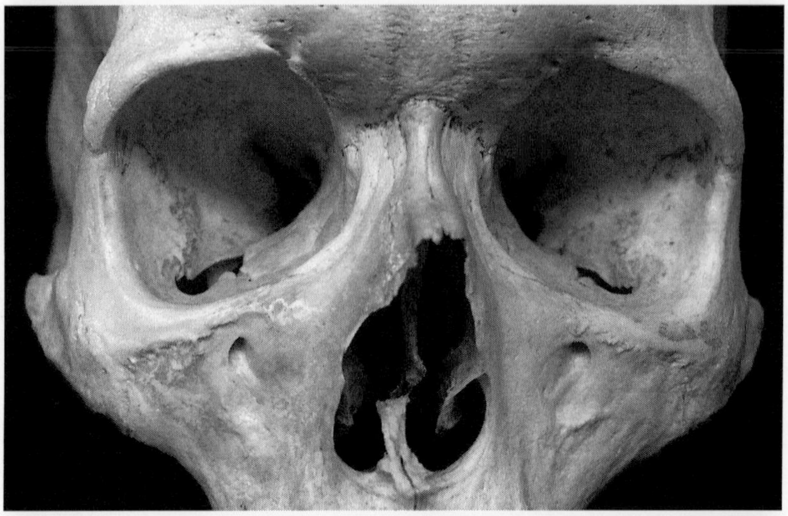

FIGURE 19.12 Variant of ZS 1. *ZS*, zygomaticomaxillary suture.

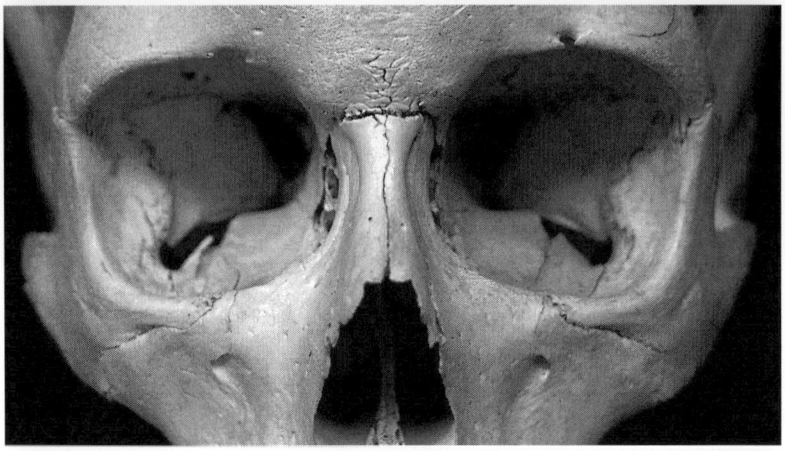

FIGURE 19.13 Variant of ZS 1. *ZS*, zygomaticomaxillary suture.

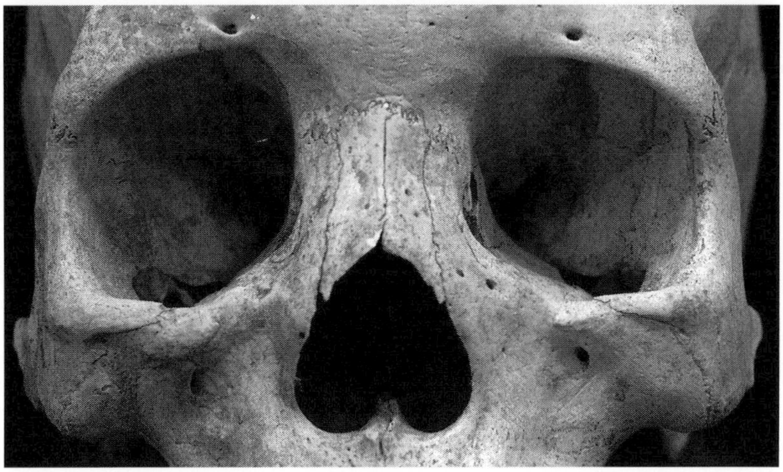

FIGURE 19.14 Variant of ZS 1. *ZS*, zygomaticomaxillary suture.

## CHARACTER STATES FOR ZYGOMATICOMAXILLARY SUTURE = 2 (FIGS. 19.15–19.21)

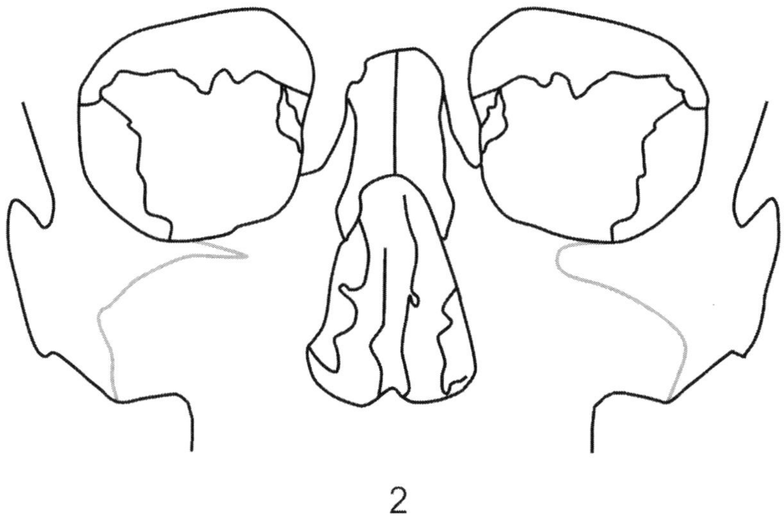


**FIGURE 19.15** Diagrammatic representation of ZS 2. *ZS*, zygomaticomaxillary suture.

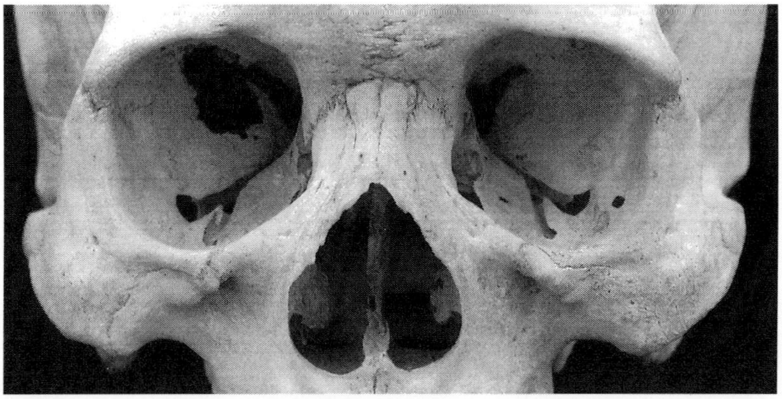

**FIGURE 19.16** Variant of ZS 2. *ZS*, zygomaticomaxillary suture.

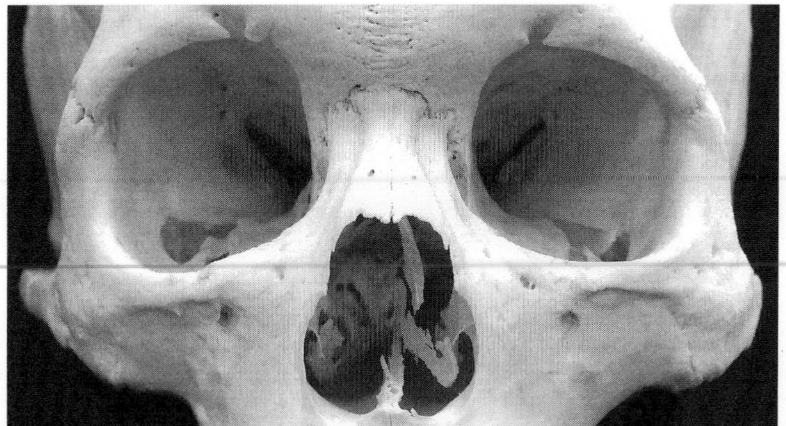

**FIGURE 19.17** Variant of ZS 2. *ZS*, zygomaticomaxillary suture.

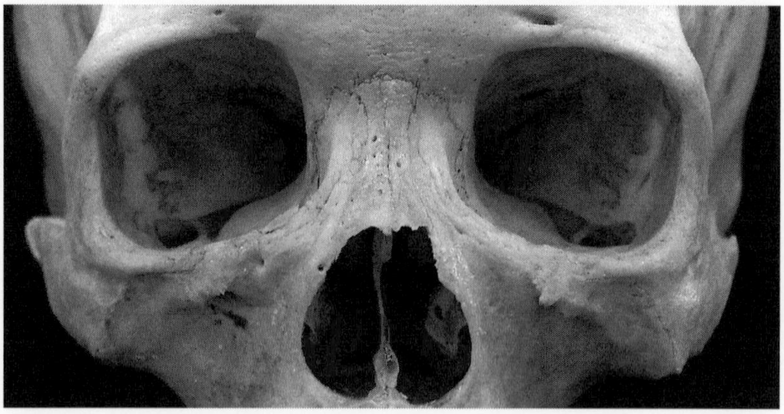

**FIGURE 19.18** Variant of ZS 2. *ZS*, zygomaticomaxillary suture.

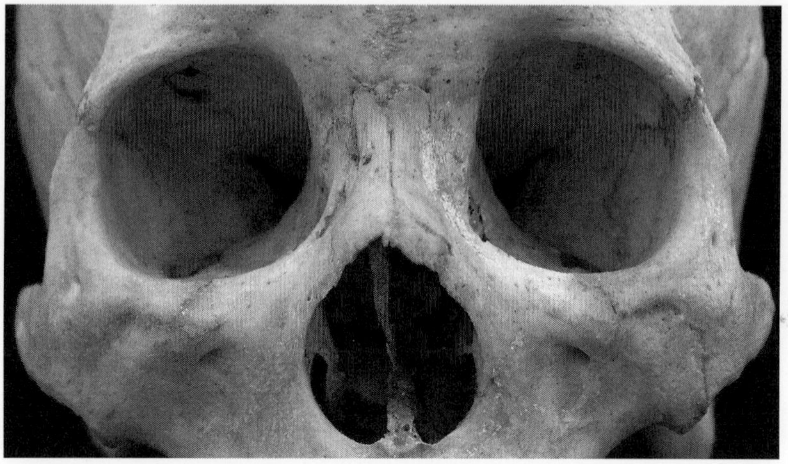

**FIGURE 19.19** Variant of ZS 2. *ZS*, zygomaticomaxillary suture.

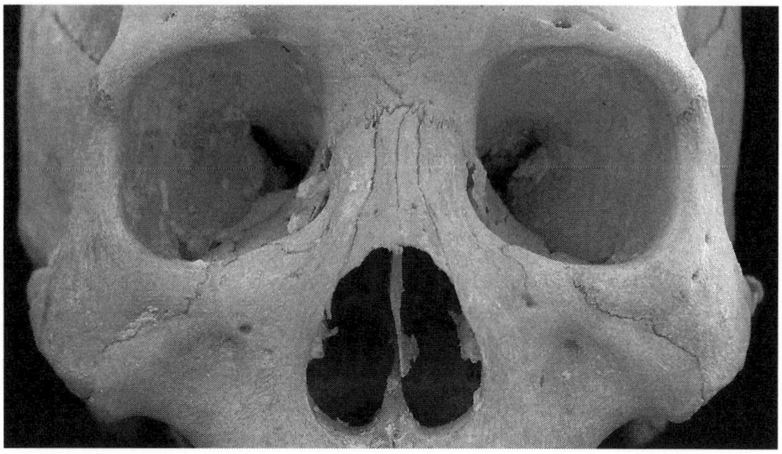

**FIGURE 19.20** Variant of ZS 2. *ZS*, zygomaticomaxillary suture.

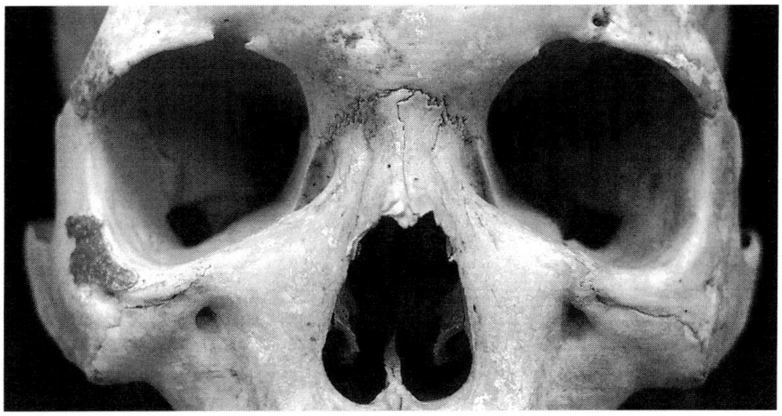

**FIGURE 19.21** Variant of ZS 2. *ZS*, zygomaticomaxillary suture.

CHAPTER

# 20

# Analytical Methods

The decision-making process is an integral part of everyday life, one that usually leads to some conclusion, prediction, or solution based on past experience and observation of similar events. Even when past experiences seem too encompass the available data for a particular observation or outcome, there remains a great deal of unaccounted for and seemingly uncontrollable information. Having countless past experiences upon which one can draw from years of training and practice would seem to make these efforts easier. However, only by establishing models from observations that (hopefully) sufficiently capture consistencies in responses can we successfully predict future observations. And, while an expert may try to build an accurate model using nothing more than the knowledge she has gained through years of practice, the information (*the data*) are far too complex and the underlying structures (*variation and covariation*) contained within a large dataset are not well enough understood—even by an expert!—to generate a flawless and accurate model based *only* on past experiences. Statistical models using a sample from the population can accurately summarize the question, while also accounting for noise and variability.

For macromorphoscopic trait scores, the question may be whether some combination of those traits can be used to characterize a population. That decision, and associated particulars of classification, intimately depends on the distribution of a traits character states within and between that population and others. There are a great number of factors influencing cranial morphology. They do so to varying degrees and often in multidimensional, complex ways. Even when the interaction between all of these factors is known, the data for each factor needs to be processed and accounted for in some fashion if an accurate predictive model is to be built. Trying to predict, or classify, an individual to a geographic origin based on a suite of macromorphoscopic traits is even more difficult, because many of these interactions are not known or they are poorly understood.

Constructing flexible models which best explain, or "fit," the data is only possible when variability in observations is accounted for in a statistical framework. The benefit of that statistical model is obvious: if we can explain our observations, two things follow: (1) we can also be confident in successful future predictions (correct classifications), and (2) we can quantify how often those future predictions will be wrong (error rate). Likewise, if we cannot explain how a particular decision was reached ("I'm an expert, so I must be right"), then our confidence in the prediction of future occurrences is critically diminished.

Even within a statistical framework, problems can materialize that greatly influence and impact model confidence. For example, a particular set of best-fit parameters in a probabilistic model should provide some level of understanding into the underlying processes of macromorphoscopic trait formation, but that will not always be the case. The model is a simplification of reality, so there will always be aspects of the data not accounted for by any model, no matter how complex it may be. Similarly, identifying which aspects are relevant for prediction, or classification, and which are merely noise in the dataset, is not always easy to understand or know with any degree of certainty. This is even truer when the observer's experience, *alone*, is used to draw a conclusion or judge a complex set of interacting variables. Any subsequent predictions would be clouded by the inevitability of noise in the dataset and an incomplete understanding of the underlying processes leading to these complex distributions.

The solution to the aforementioned issues in modeling our predictions using macromorphoscopic traits is to find objective scoring strategies and to analyze those data in as objective a manner as possible. The preceding chapters have provided the necessary standardization of the traits, leaving only an exploration into the analytical methods appropriate for that type of data. As mentioned in the introduction, categorical data like macromorphoscopic traits do not follow the same distribution as their craniometric counterparts that are distributed in a normal, continuous fashion.

*Atlas of Human Cranial Macromorphoscopic Traits.*
DOI: https://doi.org/10.1016/B978-0-12-814385-8.00020-3

Many of the earliest methods of analysis using cranial nonmetric data focused predominately on asymmetric expressions in trait manifestation; they failed to account for intertrait correlations, which have been demonstrated in the human cranial macromorphoscopic literature. Moreover, these methods were not useful for classification purposes, as they could not place a single unknown individual into any one reference population based on the manifestations of the various cranial nonmetric traits. Appropriate methods for categorical data analysis have only recently been established. Like their metric counterparts, macromorphoscopic data require large samples and a probabilistic calculation (or likelihood) for the classification, the heart of all good science is knowing how often a prediction will be right or wrong (i.e., an estimated error rate).

This chapter examines several appropriate and novel statistical methods for classifying an unknown cranium into one of several reference groups. The minutiae and mathematical rational of each method is not always presented; rather, this chapter is meant to guide the reader to suitable methods of analysis. A forthcoming analytical program by Hefner et al. will incorporate these methods in a single, user-friendly analytical program. An exact release date is not yet available, but the expectation is December 2018.

## ANALYTICAL METHODS

The following methods, previously outlined in Hefner and Ousley (2014), are by no means the only classification methods useful for human cranial macromorphoscopic traits. They represent some types of analytical approach suitable for macromorphoscopic (MMS) trait data and are presented, in no particular order to guide the reader through the process of method selection. R code (R Development Core Team 2018) is provided in Appendix A for methods using that program which are discussed in detail.

### Correspondence Analysis

Frequency table data, or contingency tables, are quite common in research dealing with categorical data. Many studies on cranial macromorphoscopic traits begin with them and generally a Pearson's $\chi^2$ test of association to assess significant differences between groups. To graphically represent these data, and to shed light on the mechanisms behind documented differences, many researchers now use a correspondence analysis. Correspondence analysis is an ordination procedure that transforms contingency table information into a two-dimensional graphical representation to visualize patterns, relative dispersions, and total variance in a dataset. To do so, correspondence analysis incorporates three interrelated concepts drawn from a contingency table: profile, mass, and chi-square distances.

The profile of a correspondence analysis is the computed percentages of the response variables for each category, making each row profile a unique point in multidimensional space. Reducing dimensionality in this way facilitates visualization of these relationships into a format we can understand—two or three-dimensional graphs. Each cell frequency divided by the grand total is the mass and is used to assign a weight to each cell proportional to the number of respondents for that category. Finally, the chi-square distance is used to measure distances between profile points in space to properly plot the profiles on to a correspondence map.

Correspondence analysis cannot be used to test hypotheses; however, these analyses are used to map the relationships of variables to one another in multivariate space. Perhaps more practically, the method can be used to make complicated analytical methods, like discriminant function analysis, more easily understood. For instance, a frequency table may show the distribution of a given trait's character states for three groups, but the correspondence map demonstrates the relationship of each character state to each group.

R code for a simple correspondence analysis is provided in Appendix A.

### Optimized Summed Scored Attributes

The optimized summed scored attributes (OSSA) method was developed by Hefner and Ousley (2014) to serve the needs of forensic anthropologists working predominately in the United States where the majority of the casework revolves around establishing an individual as American Black or White.

OSSA is a heuristic method (not a statistic) that uses six macromorphoscopic traits: anterior nasal spine, inferior nasal aperture (INA), interorbital breadth, nasal aperture width, nasal bone contour, and postbregmatic depression. The OSSA method creates a bimodal distribution of each trait between the two groups. To optimize that distribution, each trait score is dichotomized (e.g., 1, 2, 3, 4 transformed to 0, 1) in a manner to maximize between-group differences through heuristic optimization (i.e., ordering the newly derived variables in a manner that maximizes differences). Hefner and Ousley (2014) scored character states more common in American Blacks a "0" and those more common in American Whites as "1." For example, to maximize the INA, a threshold is determined based on the frequency distribution of each character state (Table 20.1). If the threshold is set between character states 3 and 4 for INA, we can expect to be correct almost 80% of the time for American Blacks and 72% for American Whites. Once all six traits were converted into the new binary OSSA variables, the sum of all six traits was calculated to produce the OSSA distribution presented in Fig. 20.1. Macromorphoscopic data for an unknown individual is collected using the original character states and compressed to their respective OSSA value. After compression, the scores are summed and the resulting value is compared to the sectioning point of 4 and below for American Blacks, and 4 and above for American Whites. The value "4" is a revised threshold value identified by Kenyhercz et al. (2017) to increase correct classifications.

A data collection sheet for OSSA is provided in Appendix A. For a worksheet incorporating OSSA, please visit http://macromorphoscopic.com/.

# NAÏVE BAYESIAN

Naïve Bayesian analysis is a probabilistic classifier based on Bayes' theorem. The method removes a training sample from the dataset to calculate prior and conditional probabilities. Using these parameters, Naïve Bayesian estimates posterior probabilities for the entire dataset. Naïve Bayesian is considered naïve because all variables are equally weighted in the model. Naïve Bayesian is calculated as a conditional model, following

$$p(C|F_1, F_2, \ldots, F_n)$$

**TABLE 20.1** Frequency Table Showing Original Scores and Compressed OSAA Scores for the Inferior Nasal Aperture

| | American White ($N = 184$) | | American Black ($N = 180$) | | |
|---|---|---|---|---|---|
| **Original Score** | **Cumul. %** | **%** | **%** | **Cumul. %** | **OSSA Score** |
| 1 | 100 | 0.5 | **35.6** | 23.9 | 0 |
| 2 | 99.5 | 3.3 | **32.8** | 68.4 | 0 |
| 3 | 96.2 | 22.3 | **18.3** | **86.7** | 0 |
| 4 | **73.9** | **41.3** | 10 | 96.7 | 1 |
| 5 | 32.6 | **32.6** | 3.3 | 100 | 1 |

*OSSA*, optimized summed scored attributes. Note: Bold text signifies threshold values used to determine OSSA cut-off values for optimizing trait scores.

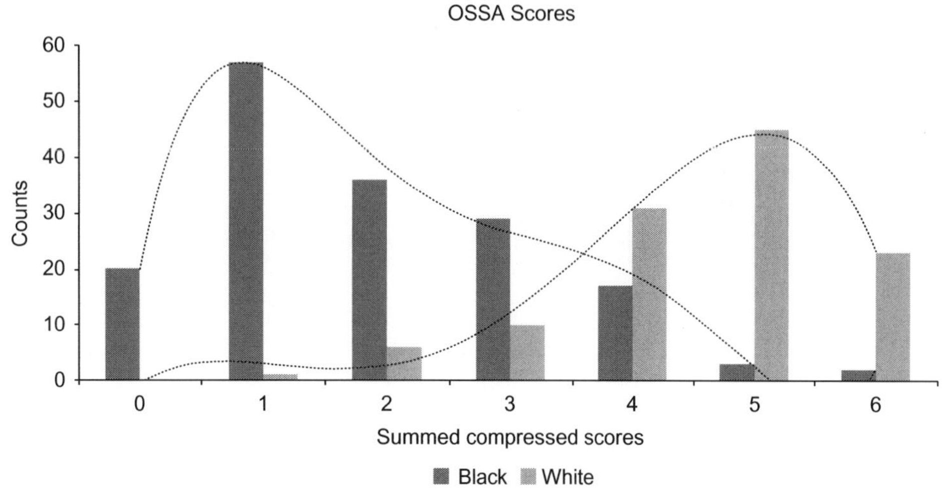


**FIGURE 20.1** Distribution of optimized summed scored attributes, OSSA, for six traits.

where the probability, $p$, of a given class variable, $C$, is conditional on several features, $F$. Using the Bayesian model, we can express the model as

$$p(C|F_1, F_2, \ldots, F_n) = \frac{p(C)p(F_1, F_2, \ldots, F_n|C)}{p(F_1, F_2, \ldots, F_n)}$$

Naïve Bayesian assumes independence among all features of interest. However, because the model is probabilistic, Naïve Bayesian, like discriminant function, correctly allocates crania as long as the correct population is more probable than any other. Put in another way, if the overall cross-validated classification accuracy is high enough, serious violations in underlying model assumptions can be ignored with little consequence to the overall model.

R code for a Naïve Bayesian analysis is provided in Appendix A.

## K-NEAREST NEIGHBOR

Nearest neighbor classification is one of the easiest classification statistics to use and understand, in part because it works similarly to the way we reason through organization of the physical world. In short, objects that are close to each other are more similar. If you know the prediction value of one object, you can predict the same values for its nearest neighbors. Nearest neighbor is generally used for prediction in a supervised learning environment. The *k*-nearest neighbor (*k*-NN) algorithm classifies objects on the basis of a subset of individuals in multivariate space used as a training set (thus, a supervised learning model). The training set is initially plotted into multidimensional space and is separated into regions by a priori class labels. When an unknown individual is placed in this space, they are assigned to the class of their *k*-NNs in the training sample. Choosing the optimal number of neighbors for a classification depends principally on the dataset; generally, larger values of *k* not only blur boundaries between the classes but also reduce any noise inherent in a dataset that may seriously weaken the classificatory power of *k*-NN.

R code for a *k*-NN is provided in Appendix A.

## MULTINOMIAL LOGISTIC REGRESSION

Multinomial logistic regression (MLR) is a semiparametric classification statistic that generalizes logistic regression to multiclass problems (e.g., more than two possible outcomes). MLR predicts the probabilities of the various outcomes of a categorically distributed dependent variable using a combination of independent variables of any class (e.g., binary, ordinal, continuous). To predict group membership, MLR uses the log odds ratio rather than probabilities and an iterative maximum likelihood method rather than a least squares method to fit the final model. Assumptions of MLR include (1) each independent variable should have a single value for each case; (2) collinearity is assumed to be relatively low, though not necessarily completely independent; and (3) there should be independence of irrelevant alternatives (IIA). IIA defines the odds of preferring one class over another, regardless of the presence of other unrelated and irrelevant alternatives.

MLR does not, unfortunately, produce typicality probabilities that are useful for assessing how well the model is classifying, but Hefner and Ousley (2014) suggest substituting these measures with nonparametric methods such as ranked probabilities and ranked interindividual similarity measures (Hefner and Ousley 2014). Cross-validation methods can be used to test the performance of logistic regression and to obtain a reliability estimate of the model.

## CANONICAL ANALYSIS OF THE PRINCIPAL COORDINATES

One of the more robust methods of analysis for macromorphoscopic trait data is a canonical analysis of the principal coordinates (CAP) method. The CAP method very effectively deals with macromorphoscopic data, enabling classification and visualization of the groups in a manner approximating craniometric analyses. Legendre and Legendre (1998) proposed a robust statistical approach for numerical ecology data that incorporated a canonical discriminant analysis performed on the transformed values of the principal coordinates (PCOs). In short, CAP calculates the PCOs (interindividual measures) using any one of several distance measures (Anderson and Willis, 2003). Using these transformed values essentially converts the categorical responses of macromorphoscopic traits into continuous, normally distributed variables appropriate for a canonical analysis. The following mathematical description of the CAP method is a summarization of Anderson and Willis's (2003) treatment of the same and is drawn predominately from Hefner (2016).

Consider an $N \times p$ matrix (*Y*) comprising macromorphoscopic trait data for a population, where $N =$ number of individuals and $p =$ the number of macromorphoscopic traits. An $N \times q$ matrix (*X*) represents the populations. CAP performs a nonparametric canonical analysis testing the effect of $Y$, if any, on $X$ using an a priori distance measure. Since **Y** contains predictor (explanatory) variables, the result is a generalized discriminant analysis for classification purposes.

The first step in a CAP analysis is to generate an interindividual distance matrix. Let $\mathbf{D} = (d_{ij})$ be an $(N \times N)$ distance matrix calculated from trait values from **Y**, using distance measure, ***J***. Allowing $\mathbf{A} = (a_{ij}) = \left(-1/2d_{ij}^2\right)$, calculate Gower's (1966) centered matrix (***G***) of **A**:

$$G = \left(I - \left(\frac{1}{N}\right)1 \cdot 1'\right) A \left(I - \left(\frac{1}{N}\right)1 \cdot 1'\right)$$

where 1 is a column of 1's the length of $N$ and ***I*** is an identity matrix. Decomposing matrix **G** into component eigenvalues and corresponding orthonormal eigenvectors, we get ***Q***. A subset of these eigenvectors ($m$) is then selected to form a matrix ($\boldsymbol{Q_m}$) for the canonical analysis. To avoid overfitting the model, ***m*** is kept small relative to $N$. To avoid overfitting and subjective selection of ***m***, the derived diagnostic information for appropriate dimensionality recommended by Anderson (2002) should be used for the canonical analyses. Next, we calculate the influence, or hat, matrix which is idempotent; thus by definition, $\mathbf{H}^2 = \mathbf{HH} = \mathbf{H}$. So, the hat matrix is

$$H = X\left[X'X\right]^{-1}X'$$

[which Anderson (2002) attributes to Johnson and Wichern (1992)]. The canonical test statistic (the trace) is calculated as

$$tr(Q_m' H Q_m)$$

Two issues to consider during a CAP analysis include (1) choosing the number of appropriate axes $m$ and (2) selecting the most appropriate distance/dissimilarity measure. Anderson and Willis (2003) consider the selection of the number of PCO axes retained a fundamental issue in a CAP analysis. If the number of axes is too small, then pertinent information contained in the data may be lost, and if the number is too large, overfitting the data may occur. They suggest increasing the value of $m$ until the residual error or the misclassification rate (for generalized discriminant function) is minimized. In addition, Anderson and Willis (2003) suggest that the selected $m$ axes should explain at least 60% of the variation in the dataset but should never reach 100% (i.e., overfitting).

Anderson and Willis (2003) briefly discuss the second issue and suggest using a methodological approach. They analyze their datasets using multiple distance measures and then plot the proportion of correct allocations against the number of axes (1-misclassification) to identify which distance measure provides the highest proportion of correct allocations using the lowest value $m$. Hefner (2007) performed a similar analysis using multiple distance measures on a sample of macromorphoscopic data. He identified the chi-square distance measure as the most likely appropriate measure for use with categorical, nonmetric cranial traits (Table 20.2).

**TABLE 20.2** Classification Accuracy in a Two-Way CAP Analysis. Eight Best Distance Measures Included

| Distance measure | Variables | $m$ | Black | White | %Correct |
|---|---|---|---|---|---|
| **Chi-square** | 5 | 3 | 81 | 93 | 87 |
| **Chi-square (metric)** | 13 | 10 | 88 | 80 | 84 |
| **Euclidean** | 5 | 3 | 83 | 84 | 84 |
| **Bray–Curtis** | 5 | 3 | 83 | 84 | 84 |
| **Manhattan** | 5 | 3 | 82 | 84 | 83 |
| **Orloci's** | 5 | 3 | 80 | 84 | 82 |
| **Canberra** | 5 | 3 | 73 | 88 | 81 |
| **Jaccard** | 5 | 3 | 63 | 85 | 74 |

The CAP method accounts for variable correlations, unlike other statistics (e.g., Naïve Bayesian). This is particularly important in light of earlier research by Hefner (2003a,b) who demonstrated intertrait correlations between macromorphoscopic variables. By accounting for the correlative structure in the response matrix, significant patterns in the dataset may be elucidated, particularly with regard to a priori labels.

R code for a CAP analysis is provided in Appendix A.

CHAPTER

# 21

# Concluding Remarks

This chapter's title may be a misnomer, since this effort is really only the beginning of macromorphoscopic trait standardization, development, and implementation. The macromorphoscopic approach to the investigation of human skeletal variation has an extensive history and, over those years, has proven successful in the estimation of ancestry when applied in a systematic manner *and* within a statistical framework. Herein, we have attempted to provide an atlas useful to the uninitiated budding scholar and to the seasoned expert. We have not relied on extreme trait values supposedly linked to one ancestry or another. Rather, we offer a manual explicitly dedicated to macromorphoscopic trait variation that thoroughly illustrates the wide-ranging variation one may encounter when collecting these data.

All of the individual crania documented in these pages represent the populations that encompass much of our human variation. Admittedly, however, we have not captured every nuanced idiosyncrasy; nor do we claim to have completely captured the range in trait variation a sample may present. This only confirms the need for additional study and a broadening and deeper understanding of macromorphoscopic traits. Future research efforts will surely focus on additional traits and supplementary character states that we did not explore here.

Defining the significant traits for ancestry estimation and biological distance analysis—and properly describing the individual character states for that trait—hearkens back to the age of Hooton and his efforts to create a comprehensive list of standardized observations. The *Harvard Blanks*, nearly 90 years in use and counting, represent Hooton's concerted effort to formalize data collection efforts. And while Hooton may not have been the first to implement many of these traits, he was the first "forensic" anthropologist to propose a set of standard observations, each meticulously coded for data analysis, documenting the skeletal variation within a sample. Hooton used his analysis of those data to draw larger conclusions about a population. Just as Hooton called for further refinement and standardization in his observational data, so too should the macromorphoscopic approach be tested, refined, and validated. Additional analysis of the many skeletal collections around the world is necessary, but those data must be collected using standard illustrations and definitions in order to generate comparable datasets truly useful for explorations into modern (and past) human variation.

Forthcoming research efforts will also certainly focus on determining the precise role the genome and the environment play in macromorphoscopic trait expression. We currently know very little about the genetic contributions to macromorphoscopic trait development. But that needn't be the case. Each macromorphoscopic trait has an underlying genetic template, a threshold concretely defining character state expression. Measuring the influence of the genome and the environment on their expression and disentangling these from individual idiosyncrasy (sporadic appearances of unique morphological manifestations) and developmental defects require sufficient reference data, preferably paired to genetic, environmental, and epigenetic information.

Current research exploring face shape shows great promise. Quantifying the shape of a face with regard to genetic data has been systematically tested and the foundations for predictive modeling of faces are just around the corner. These methods will use DNA from a crime scene to predict a perpetrator's face, ancient DNA from archeological sites to model our ancestors' appearance, and so much more. Since macromorphoscopic traits so closely follow the contour of the soft tissue, correlating structures identified in these studies to skeletal morphology (and macromorphoscopic traits) is a logical next step to broaden our understanding of their genetics.

Measuring the effects climate imparts on cranial form is also receiving new found attention. Researchers using craniometric data have thoroughly documented the correlation between those data and genetic distance; when genetic data is managed (controlled), the underlying associations between biological (craniometric) distances and geographical (climactic) distances indicate a significant relationship between human cranial form and the climate. Such research is easily transferable to macromorphoscopic data.

*Atlas of Human Cranial Macromorphoscopic Traits*.
DOI: https://doi.org/10.1016/B978-0-12-814385-8.00021-5

## OTHER CONSIDERATIONS

Some of the macromorphoscopic traits presented herein—such as nasal bone shape, nasofrontal suture, postbregmatic depression, and supranasal suture—may not prove effective in ancestry estimation or biological distance analysis. The distribution of these traits in the Macromorphoscopic Databank (MaMD) and the weight these traits are provided in classification algorithms and predictive models are not ideal. And, perhaps more importantly, error rates associated with the collection of these traits are underwhelming, suggesting uncertainty and bias in both data collection and interpretation. Inter- and intraobserver error associated with macromorphoscopic traits suggest several sources of error, including (1) unclear descriptions; (2) a significant role for observer experience; (3) difficulty in identifying between character states; (4) atypical trait manifestations (character states outside the standard definitions and expressions); and, most importantly, (5) error in the underlying methodology.

Nasal bone shape (NBS) is an excellent example of a trait with very little variation within and between populations. This lack of variation does not preclude the use of NBS, but it does suggest classifications will not weigh this trait as heavily as a trait having much more variation between groups.

With the introduction of the Macromorphoscopic Traits (MMS) program, much of the subjectivity and observer error inherent in the cranial nonmetric approach is removed. However, measuring the impact of the MMS program on observer bias and the continued role of observer experience on macromorphoscopic trait analysis requires large, geographically diverse reference samples (to assess variation), with repeated measures. To function wholly as a data collection repository and as an analytical tool for future work, the MaMD requires cooperation and data sharing among researchers in both forensic anthropology and more generally among biological anthropologists. Future efforts have great potential to refine estimates of geographic origin, including among juveniles.

Presently, the bulk of the modern MaMD data has been collected by the Macromorphoscopic Laboratory at Michigan State University. Other data sources include individual researchers, medical examiner's offices, government-based forensic anthropology laboratories, museums (curators and repatriation laboratory staff), and university-based forensic anthropologists. As of September 2017, the MaMD contained cranial macromorphoscopic trait data for 7397 cases. Of those, 2363 are maintained in the modern dataset; 84.7% of those have known (confirmed) geographic origin, 86% have known sex, and 71% have known age, future identifications will lead to higher numbers for each of these categories.

# References


Baker, P.T., 1988. Human adaptability. In: Harrison, G.A., Tanner, J.M., Tanner, J.M., Pilbeam, D.R., Baker, P.T. (Eds.), Human Biology: An Introduction to Human Evolution, Variation, Growth and Adaptability. Oxford University Press, Oxford, pp. 437–547.

Bass, W.M., 1987. Human Osteology: A Laboratory and Field Manual, third ed., Missouri Archaeological Society, Columbia, MO.

Bigham, A.W., Mao, X., Mei, R., Brutsaert, T., Wilson, M.J., Julian, C.G., et al., 2009. Identifying positive selection candidate loci for high-altitude adaptation in Andean populations. Hum. Genomics 4, 79–90.

Birkby, W.H., Fenton, T.W., Anderson, B.E., 2008. Identifying southwest Hispanics using nonmetric traits and the cultural profile. J. Forensic Sci. 53, 29–33.

Broca, P., 1872. Recherches sup I'indice nasale. Revue de I'anthrop. I.

Brues, A.M., 1958. Identification of skeletal remains. J. Crim. Law Criminol. Police Sci. 48, 551–563.

Brues, A.M., 1990. The once and future diagnosis of race. In: Gill, Rhine S. (Ed.), Skeletal Attribution of Race: Methods for Forensic Anthropology. MaxwellMuseum of Anthropology, Albuquerque, NM, pp. 1–9.

Buikstra, J.E., Ubelaker, D., 1994. Standards for data collection from human skeletal remains. In: Proceedings of a Seminar at the Field Museum of Natural History. Arkansas Archeological Survey Research Series #44, Arkansas.

Burns, K., 1999. Forensic Anthropology Training Manual. Prentice Hall, New Jersey.

Byers, S.N., 2011. Introduction to Forensic Anthropology: A Textbook, fourth ed Allyn & Bacon, Toronto, ON.

Cameron, J., 1931. The interorbital width. A new cranial dimension. Its significance in modern and fossil man and in lower mammals. Am. J. Phys. Anthropol. 15, 509–519.

Carey, J.W., Steegmann, A.T., 1981. Human nasal protrusion, latitude, and climate. Am. J. Phys. Anthropol. 56, 313–319.

Charles, C.M., 1930. The cavum nasi of the American Negro. Am. J. Phys. Anthropol. 14, 177-153.

Churchill, S.E., Shackelford, L.L., Georgi, J.N., Black, M.T., 2004. Morphological variation and airflow dynamics in the human nose. Am. J. Hum. Biol. 16, 625–638.

Cole, P., 1982. Upper respiratory airflow. In: Proctor, D.F., Andersen, I.B. (Eds.), The Nose: Upper Airway Physiology and The Atmospheric Environment. Elsevier Biomedical Press, Amsterdam, pp. 163–189.

Collignon, R., 1887. La nomenclature quinaire de i'indice nasal du vivant. Revue de l'anthropologie 11, 8.

Coon, C.S., 1962. The Origin of Races. Alfred A. Knopf, New York, NY.

Corruccini, R.S., 1974. An examination of the meaning of cranial discrete traits for human skeletal biological studies. Am. J. Phys. Anthropol. 40, 425–446.

Davies, A., 1932. A re-survey of the morphology of the nose in relation to climate. J. R. Anthropol. Inst. 62, 337–359.

Dean, M.C., 1988. Another look at the nose and the functional significance of the face and nasal mucous membrane for cooling the brain in fossil hominids. J. Hum. Evol. 17, 715–718.

de Haan, A.B., Willekens, B., Klooster, J., Los, A.A., van Zwieten, J., Botha, C.P., et al., 2006. The prenatal development of the human orbit. Strabismus 14, 51–56.

DeVilliers, H., 1968. The skull of the South African Negro: a biometrical and morphological study. Witwatersrand University Press, Johannesburg.

Farkas, L.G., Kolar, J.C., Munro, I.R., 1986. Geography of the nose: a morphometric study. Aesthetic. Plast. Surg. 10, 191–223.

Feik, S.A., Glover, J.E., 1998. Growth of children's faces. In: Clement, J.G., Ranson, D.L. (Eds.), Craniofacial Identification in Forensic Medicine. Oxford University Press, New York, NY.

Ferrario, V.F., Mian, F., Peretta, R., Rosati, R., Sforza, C., 2007. Three-dimensional computerized anthropometry of the nose: landmark representation compared to surface analysis. Cleft Palate Craniofac. J. 44, 278–285.

Finnegan, M., 1976. Walnut Creek massacre: identification and analysis. Am. J. Phys. Anthropol. 45, 737–742.

Franciscus, R.G., Long, J.C., 1991. Variation in human nasal height and breadth. Am. J. Phys. Anthropol. 85, 419–427.

Gill, G.W., 1986. Craniofacial criteria in forensic race identification. In: Reichs, K.J. (Ed.), Forensic Osteology: Advances in the Identification of Human Remains. Charles C Thomas, Springfield, IL, pp. 143–159.

Gill, G.W., 1995. Challenge on the frontier: discerning American Indians from whites osteologically. J. Forensic Sci. 40, 783–788.

Gill, G.W., 1998. Craniofacial criteria in the skeletal attribution of race. In: Reichs, K.J. (Ed.), Forensic Osteology, second ed., Charles C Thomas, Springfield, IL, pp. 293–317.

Gill, G.W., Gilbert, R., 1990. Race identification from the midfacial skeleton: American blacks and whites. In: Gill, G.W., Rhine, S. (Eds.), Skeletal Attribution of Race: Methods for Forensic Anthropology. Maxwell Museum of Anthropology, Albuquerque, NM, pp. 47–54.

Glanville, E.V., 1969. Nasal shape, prognathism and adaptation in man. Am. J. Phys. Anthropol. 30, 29–37.

Goldstein, M., 1943. Observations on Mexican Crania. Am. J. Phys. Anthropol. 1 (1), 83–93.

Gray, H., 1980. In: Williams, P.L., Warwick, R. (Eds.), Gray's Anatomy, 36th ed., Churchill, London.

Guidotti, A., Bastianini, A., De Stefano, G.F., Hauser, G., 1986. Variations of supraorbital bony structures in Sienese skull. Acta Anat. 127, 1–6.

Guo, J., Tan, J., Yang, Y., Zhou, H., Hu, S., Hashan, A., 2014. Variation and signatures of selection on the human face. J. Hum. Evol. 75, 143–152.

Hall, R.L., 2005. Energetics of nose and mouth breathing, body size, body composition, and nose volume in young adult males and females. Am. J. Hum. Biol. 17, 321–330.

Hamy, E.T., 1869. De l'épine nasale antérieure dans l'ordre des primates. Bull. Soc. Anthropol. 2, 13.

Harris, J.E., Kowalski, C.J., LeVasseur, F.A., Nasjleti, C.E., 1977. Age and race as factors in craniofacial growth and development. J. Dent. Res. 56, 266.
Harvati, K., 2003. The Neanderthal taxonomic position: models of intra- and inter-specific craniofacial variation. J. Hum. Evol. 44, 107–132.
Harvati, K., Weaver, T.D., 2006. Human cranial anatomy and the differential preservation of population history and climate signatures. Anat. Rec. 288, 1225–1233.
Hauser, G., De Stefano, G.F., 1989. Epigenetic Variants of the Human Skull. E. Schweizerbart, Stuttgart.
Hefner, J.T., 2003a. Assessing Nonmetric Cranial Traits Currently used in the Forensic Determination of Ancestry. Department of Anthropology. University of Florida, Gainesville, FL.
Hefner, J.T., 2003b. The utility of nonmetric cranial traits in ancestry determination—Part II. In: Proc AAFS. Chicago, IL. Colorado Springs, CO: American Academy of Forensic Sciences.
Hefner, J.T., 2007. The Statistical Determination of Ancestry Using Cranial Nonmetric Traits. Department of Anthropology, University of Florida, Gainesville, FL.
Hefner, J.T., 2009. Cranial nonmetric variation and estimating ancestry. J. Forensic Sci. 54, 985–995.
Hefner, J.T., 2016. Biological distance analysis, cranial morphoscopic traits, and ancestry assessment in forensic anthropology. In: Pilloud, M. A., Hefner, J.T. (Eds.), Biological Distance Analysis: Forensic and Bioarchaeological Perspectives. Elsevier, New York, NY, pp. 310–314.
Hefner, J.T., Ousley, S.D., 2014. Statistical classification methods for estimating ancestry using morphoscopic traits. J. Forensic Sci. 59, 883–890.
Holborow, A.A., 2002. The Zygomaticomaxillary Suture: A Study of the Frequencies of Suture Shapes within Various Major Populations of Homo Sapiens. Department of Anthropology, University of Wyoming, Laramie, WY.
Hooton, E.A., no date. The Test. Unpublished manuscript by EA Hooton. Peabody Museum Archives, Cambridge.
Hooton, E.A., 1930. The Indians of Pecos Pueblo. Yale University Press, New Haven, CT.
Hovorka, O., 1893. Die aufiere Nase. Alfred Holder, Vienna.
Howells, W.W., 1973. Cranial variation in man: a study by multivariate analysis of patterns of difference among recent human populations, Papers of the Peabody Museum of Archaeology and Ethnology, Vol. 67. Harvard University, Cambridge, The Museum,.
Hrdlička, A., 1930. The skeletal remains of early man, Smithsonian Miscellaneous Collections, Vol. 83. Smithsonian Institution, Washington, DC.
Hrdlička A. 1941. Diseases and artifacts on the skulls and bones from Kodial Island. Smithsonian Miscellaneous Collections, 101(4): 1–25, Washington, DC: Smithsonian Institute Press.
Hubbe, M., Hanihara, T., Harvati, K., 2009. Climate signatures in the morphological differentiation of worldwide modern human populations. Anat. Rec. 292, 1720–1733.
Hurst, C.V., 2012. Morphoscopic trait expressions used to identify southwest Hispanics. J. Forensic Sci. 57, 859–865.
Inthavong, K., Tian, Z.F., Tu, J.Y., 2007. CFD simulations on the heating capability in a human nasal cavity. In: 16th Australasian Fluid Mechanics Conference (AFMC). School of Engineering, The University of Queensland.
Jacobshagen, B., 1981. Comparison of morphological factors in the cranial variation of the great apes and man. In: Chiarelli, A.B., Corruccini, R.S. (Eds.), Primate Evolutionary Biology. Springer, Berlin, pp. 98–108.
Jacobshagen, B., 1982. Variations in size and shape of the orbital contour. A comparison between man and the greater apes using Fourier analysis. Man and his origin. Anthropos (Brno) 21, 113–130.
Jantz, R., Ousley, S., 2005. FORDISC 3: Computerized Forensic Discriminant Functions. The University of Tennessee, Knoxville, TN.
Keck, T., Lindemann, J., 2010. Numerical simulation and nasal air-conditioning. GMS Curr. Opin. Otolaryngol. 9, 1–18.
Klales, A.R., Kenyhercz, M.W., 2015. Morphological assessment of ancestry using cranial macromorphoscopics. J. Forensic Sci. 60, 13–20.
Krogman, W.M., 1955. A guide to the identification of human skeletal remains. FBI Law Enforcement Bull. 3, 3–31.
Krogman, W.M., 1970. Growth of the head, face, trunk, and limbs in Philadelphia White and Negro children of elementary and high school age. Monogr. Soc. Res. Child 35, 1–80.
Krogman, W.M., Işcan, M.Y., 1986. The Human Skeleton in Forensic Anthropology, second ed Charles C Thomas Press, Springfield, IL.
Krogman, W.M., Sassouni, V., 1957. A Syllabus of Roentgenographic Cephalometry. University of Pennsylvania School of Medicine, Philadelphia, PA, p. 233.
L'Abbé, E.N., van Rooyen, C., Nawrocki, S.P., Becker, P.J., 2011. An evaluation of non-metric cranial traits used to estimate ancestry in a South African sample. Forensic Sci. Int. 209, 1–3.
Lahr, M.M., 1996. The Evolution of Modern Human Diversity: A Study of Cranial Variation. Cambridge University Press, Cambridge.
Latham, R.A., 1970. Maxillary development and growth: the septo-premxillary ligament. J. Anat. 107, 471–478.
Le Double, A.F., 1906a. Traite des variations des os de la face de l'homme. Vigot Freres, Paris.
Le Double, A.F., 1906b. Traité des variations des os de la face de l'homme et leur signification au point de vue de l'anthropologie zoologique. Vigot Frères, Paris.
Lestrel, P.E., Read, D.W., Wolfe, C., 1997. Size and shape of the rabbit orbit: 3-D Fourier descriptors. In: Lestrel, P.E. (Ed.), Fourier Descriptors and Their Applications in Biology. Cambridge University Press, Cambridge, pp. 359–378.
Liebenberg, L., Stull, K.E., L'Abbé, E.N., Botha, D., 2015. Evaluating the accuracy of cranial indices in ancestry estimation among South African groups. J. Forensic Sci. 60, 1277–1282.
Lieberman, D.E., 2011. The Evolution of the Human Head. Belknap Press, Cambridge.
Limson, M., 1932. Observations on the bones of the skull in white and Negro fetuses and infants. Contrib. Embryol. 23, 205–222.
Long, J.C., 1991. The genetic structure of admixed populations. Genetics 127, 417–428.
Luschan, F., 1914. Uber das Vorkommen eines os postmalare beim Menschen. Zoo Ethno 46, 37–45.
Luschka, H.V., 1869. Der processus marginalis des menschlichen Jochbeins. Arch. Anat. Physiol. Wiss. Med. 8, 326–330.
Macalister, A., 1898. The aperture pyriformis. J. Anat. Physiol. 32, 223.
Maddux, S.D., Yokley, T.R., Svoma, B.M., Franciscus, R.G., 2016. Absolute humidity and the human nose: a reanalysis of climate zones and their influence on nasal form and function. Am. J. Phys. Anthropol. 161, 309–320.

Maier, C.A., Zhang, K., Manhein, M.H., Li, X., 2015. Palate shape and depth: a shape-matching and machine learning method for estimating ancestry from human skeletal remains. J. Forensic Sci. 60, 1129–1134.

Mair, R., 1923. Zur Kenntnis der Fontanella metopica und der Stirnnaht. Anat. Anz. 57, 149–157.

Mann, R.W., Hunt, D.R., Lozanoff, S., 2014. Photographic Regional Atlas of Non-Metric Traits and Anatomical Variants of the Human Skeleton. Charles C Thomas Publishers, Springfield, IL.

Martin, R., Saller, K., 1957. Lehrbuch der Anthropologie. Systematischer Darstellung. Fischer, Stuttgart.

Martin, R., 1928. Lehrbuch der anthropologie, second ed Fischer, Jena.

Martindale SW, Gilbert BM. 1984. Race determination from craniofacial variation in American Indians and Whites. In: Paper Presented at the Symposium on Racial Identification, 36th Annual Meeting of the American Academy of Forensic Sciences, Anaheim, CA.

McDowell, J.L., L'Abbé, E.N., Kenyhercz, M.W., 2012. Nasal aperture shape evaluation between black and white South Africans. Forensic Sci. Int. 222, 1–3.

Mingazzini, G., 1891. Uber die onto- und philogenetische Bedeutung der verschiedenen Formen der Apertura pyriformis. Arch. Anthropol. 20, 171–180.

Mlynski, G., Grutzenmacher, S., Plontke, S., Mlynski, B., Lang, C., 2001. Correlation of nasal morphology and respiratory function. Rhinology 39, 197–201.

Mooney, M., Siegel, M., 2002. Understanding Craniofacial Anomalies: The Etiopathogenesis of Craniosynostoses and Facial Clefting. Wiley and Sons, Canada.

Mooney, M.P., Siegel, M.I., 1986. Developmental relationship between premaxillary-maxillary suture patency and anterior nasal spine morphology. Cleft Palate J. 23, 101–107.

Noback, M.L., Harvati, K., Spoor, F., 2011. Climate-related variation of the human nasal cavity. Am. J. Phys. Antropol. 145, 599–614.

Oetteking, B., 1930. Craniology of the North Pacific Coast. The Jesup North Pacific Expedition 11. Forgotten Books, London.

Oettlé, A.C., Demeter, F.P., L'Abbé, E.N., 2017. Ancestral variations in the shape and size of the zygoma. Anat. Rec. 300, 196–208.

Perizonius, W.R.K., 1979. Non–metric cranial traits: sex difference and age dependence. J. Hum. Evol. 8, 679–684.

Plemons, A.M., Hefner, J.T., 2016. Ancestry estimation using macromorphoscopic traits. Acad. Forensic Pathol 6, 400–412.

Pessa, J.E., Chen, Y., 2002. Curve analysis of the aging orbital aperture. Plast. Reconstr. Surg. 109, 756–757.

Pope, G., 1992. Craniofacial evidence for the origin of modern humans in China. Yearb. Phys. Anthropol. 35, 243–298.

Rauber, A., 1906. Suturae supranasales, Gegenbaurs Morph. Jb. Leipzig 35, 362–376.

Rhine, S., 1990. Nonmetric skull racing. In: Gill, G.W., Rhine, S. (Eds.), Skeletal Attribution of Race: Methods for Forensic Anthropology. Maxwell Museum of Anthropology, Albuquerque, NM, pp. 9–20.

Risley, H., 1891. The study of ethnology in India. J. Anthropol. Inst. 20, 235–263.

Roseman, C.C., 2004. Detecting interregionally diversifying natural selection on modern human cranial form by using matched molecular and morphometric data. Proc. Natl. Acad. Sci. USA 101, 12824–12829.

Ross, C.F., 2008. Does the primate face torque. In: Vineyard, C., Ravosa, M.J., Wall, C. (Eds.), Primate Craniofacial Function and Biology. Springer Science, New York, NY, pp. 63–80.

Scheuer, L., Black, S., 2000. Developmental Human Osteology. Academic Press, London.

Schiwy-Bochat, K.H., 2001. The roughness of the supranasal region e a morphological sex trait. Forensic Sci. Int. 117 (1–2), 7–13.

Schleyer, F., Ihm, P., Bensch, W., 1971. Über die geschlechts verschiedenheit des umrisses der knöchernen orbita. Zierschrift für Rechtsmedizin 69, 168–172.

Schmittbuhl, M., Le Minor, J.M., Allenbach, B., Schaaf, A., 1999. Shape of the orbital opening: individual characterization and analysis of variability in modern humans, Gorilla gorilla, and Pan troglodytes. Ann. Anat. 181, 299–307.

Schultz, A.H., 1918. The fontanella metopica and its remnants in an adult skull. Am. J. Anat. 23, 259–271.

Schwalbe, G., 1901. Ueber den supranasalen Theil der Stirnnaht. Z. Morph. Anthrop 3, 208–220.

Scott, J.H., 1956. Growth at facial sutures. Am. J. Orthodont. 42, 381–387.

Seiffert, E.R., Kappelman, J., 2001. Morphometric variation in the hominoid orbital aperture: a case study with implications for the use of variable characters in Miocene cararrhine systematics. J. Hum. Evol. 40, 301–318.

Shaffer, J.R., Orlova, E., Lee, M.K., Leslie, E.J., Raffensperger, Z.D., Heike, C.L., et al., 2016. Genome-wide association study reveals multiple loci influencing normal human facial morphology. PLoS Genet. 12, e1006149.

Shaw, J.C.M., 1931. The Teeth, The Bony Palate, and The Mandible in The Bantu Races of South Africa. Bale and Danielsson, London.

Shea, B.T., 1977. Eskimo craniofacial morphology, cold stress and maxillary sinus. Am. J. Phys. Anthropol. 47, 289–300.

Spradley, M.K., Jantz, R.L., 2016. Ancestry estimation in forensic anthropology: geometric morphometric versus standard and nonstandard interlandmark distances. J. Forensic Sci. 61, 892–897.

Sullivan, L.R., 1922. The frequency and distribution of some anatomical variations in American crania. Am. Museum Nat. Hist. Anthropol. Pap. 23, 203–358.

Swenson, K.E., 2012. Nasal Septal Deviation in a Longitudinal Growth Sample. The University of Iowa, Iowa City.

Szilvassy, J., 1986. Eine neue methode zur intraserialen analyse von gräberfeldern. Mitteilungen der Berliner Gesellschaft für Anthropologie, Ethnologie, und Urgeschichte 7, 49–62.

Todd, T.W., Tracy, B., 1930. Racial features in the American Negro cranium. Am. J. Phys. Anthropol. 15, 53–110.

Toldt, C., 1914. Brauenwuelste, Tori supraorbitales, und BrauenboÈgen, Arcus superciliares, und ihre mechanische Bedeutung, Mitt. Anthrop. Ges. Wien 44, 235–315.

Topinard, P., 1881. Du bord inferieur des narines sur les cranes des caracteres de superiorte ou d'inferiorite qu'il fournit. Chapmna & Hall, London.

Trask, W.R., Moore-Jansen, P.H., 2008. Group variation and sexual dimorphism in orbital aperture shape. Am. J. Phys. Anthropol. 135, 209.

Velepeau, A.L.M., 1837. A Complete Treatise on the Surgical Anatomy of the Human Body, Both General and Regional. Velepeau and Co, Paris.

Vineyard, C., Ravosa, M.J., Wall, C., 2008. Primate Craniofacial Function and Biology. Springer Science, New York, NY.

Virchow, H., 1912. Die anthropologische Untersuchung der Nase. Zeitschrift für Ethnologie 44, 289–337.
Weinberg, S.M., Putz, D.A., Mooney, M.P., Siegel, M.I., 2005. Evaluation of non-metric variation in the crania of black and white perinates. Forensic Sci. Int. 151, 177–185.
Weiner, J.S., 1954. Nose shape and climate. Am. J. Phys. Anthropol. 12, 615–618.
White, T.D., 2000. Human Osteology. Academic Press, London.
Whitnall, S.E., 1911. On a tubercle on the malar bone, and the lateral attachments of the tarsal plates. Anat. Physiol. 54, 426–432.
Wilkinson, C., 2008. Forensic Facial Reconstruction. Cambridge University Press, Cambridge.
Williams, R.I., 1956. The nasal index: anthropological and clinical. Ann. Otol. 65, 171–190.
Williams, S.E., 2007. A new method for evaluating orbit shape. Proc. AAFS 13, 352–354.
Woo, J.K., 1949a. Ossification and growth of the human maxilla, premaxilla and palate bone. Anat. Rec. 105, 737–753.
Woo, J.K., 1949b. Racial and sexual differences in the frontal curvature and its relation to metopism. Am. J. Phys. Anthropol. 7, 215–226.
Woo, J.K., 1949c. Direction and type of the transverse Palatine suture and its relation to the form of the hard Palate. Am. J. Phys. Anthropol. 7, 385–396.
Wood-Jones, F., 1931a. The non-metrical morphological characters of the skull as criteria for racial diagnosis: Part I: General discussion of the morphological characters employed in racial diagnosis. J. Anat. 65, 179–195.
Wood-Jones, F., 1931b. The non-metrical morphological characters of the skull as criteria for racial diagnosis: Part II: The non-metrical morphological characters of the Hawaiian skull. J. Anat. 65, 368–378.
Wood-Jones, F., 1931c. The non-metrical morphological characters of the skull as criteria for racial diagnosis: Part III: The non-metrical morphological characters of the skulls of prehistoric inhabitants of Guam. J. Anat. 65, 438–445.
Zimmerman, L.J., 2005. Public heritage, a desire for a "White" history for America, and some impacts of the Kennewick man/Ancient One decision. Int. J. Cult. Property 12, 265–274.
Zuckerkandl, E., 1882. Normale und pathologische Anatomie der Nasenhole und ihre pneumatischen Anhange. 2 Bde. W. Braumtiller, Wein.
Zuckerkandl, E., 1895. Fossae pranasalis. Mitth. Anthrop. Ges. 24, 57–59.

## *Further Reading*

Adachi, B., 1904. Die Orbita und die Hauptmaße des Schädels der Japaner und die Methode der Orbitamessung. Z. Morphol. Anthropol. 7, 379–480.
Adachi, N., Suzuki, T., Sakaue, K., Takigawa, W., Ohshima, N., Dodo, Y., 2006. Kinship analysis of the Jomon skeletons unearthed from a double burial at the Usu-Moshiri site, Hokkaido, Japan. Anthropol. Sci. 114, 29–34.
Adams, J., Ward, R.H., 1973. Admixture studies and the detection of selection. Science 180, 1137–1143.
Adis-Castro, E., Neumann, G.K., 1948. The incidence of ear exostoses in the Hopewell people of Illinois Valley. Indiana Acad. Sci. Proc. 57, 33–36.
Agur, A.M.R., 1991. Grant's Atlas of Anatomy, ninth ed William & Wilkins Press, Cambridge.
Akabori, E., 1933. Crania nipponica recentia I. Analytical inquiries into the non-metric variations in the Japanese Skull. Jpn. J. Med. Sci. 1: Anat. 4, 61–315.
Alciati, G., 1974. Morfologia del foro e del canale infraorbitali, con particolare riguardo al primo anno di età. Quaderni Anatomia. Pratica 30, 75–96.
Almond, D.V., 2006. Is the 1918 influenza pandemic over? Long-term effects of in utero influenza exposure in the post-1940 U.S. population. J. Pol. Econ. 114, 672–712.
AlQahtani, S.J., 2009. Atlas of tooth development and eruption. ⟨http://www.smd.qmul.ac.uk/atlas⟩ (last accessed Dec 8, 2011).
Alt, K.W., Brace, C.L., Turp, J.C., 1998. The history of dental anthropology. In: Alt, K.W., Rösing, F.W., Teschler-Nicola, M. (Eds.), Dental Anthropology: Fundamentals, Limits, and Prospects. Springer, New York, NY, pp. 15–39.
Alvesalo, L., 1997. Sex chromosomes and human growth. Hum. Genet. 101, 1–5.
Anderson, J.E., 1960. The development of the tympanic plate. Nat. Mus. Can. Bull. 180, 143–153.
Anderson, J.E., 1962. The development of the tympanic plate. Nat. Mus. Can. Bull. 180. Anthropol. Ser., 57:143-153.
Anderson, J.E., 1968a. Skeletal "anomalies" as genetic indicators. In: Brothwell, D.R. (Ed.), The Skeletal Biology of Earlier Human Populations. Pergamon Press, Oxford, pp. 135–147.
Anderson, J.E., 1968b. The Serpent Mounds site physical anthropology. In: Royal Ontario Museum. Art and Archaeology Division. Occasional paper 11. Royal Ontario Museum, University of Toronto, Toronto.
Angel, J.L., Kelley, J.O., 1990. Inversion of the posterior edge of the jaw ramus: new race trait. In: Gill, G.W., Rhine, S. (Eds.), Skeletal Attribution of Race: Methods for Forensic Anthropology. Maxwell Museum Anthropological Papers No. 4, Albuquerque, NM, pp. 33–39.
Anscombe, F.J., 1948. The transformation of Poisson, binomial and negative-binomial data. Biometrika 35, 246–254.
Anson, B.J., Bast, T.H., Richany, S.F., 1955. The fetal and early postnatal development of the tympanic ring and related structures in man. Ann. Otol. Rhinol. Laryngol. 64, 802–823.
Armelagos, G.J., Goodman, A.H., 1998. Race, racism, and anthropology. In: Goodman, A.F., Leatherman, T.L. (Eds.), Building a New Biocultural Synthesis: Political-Economic Perspectives on Human Biology. University of Michigan Press, Ann Arbor, MI, pp. 359–378.
Armelagos, G.J., Carlson, D.S., Van Gerven, D.P., 1982. The theoretical foundations and development of skeletal biology. In: Spencer, F. (Ed.), A History of American Physical Anthropology, 1930–1980. Academic Press, New York, NY, pp. 305–328.
Azouley, O., Regnault, O., 1893. Variation in the form of the teeth. Bull. Mem. Soc. Anthropol. Paris 4, 266.
Balakrishan, V., Sanghvi, L.D., 1968. Distance between populations on the basis of attribute data. Biometrics 24, 859–865.
Bamshad, M.J., Wooding, S., Watkins, W.S., Ostler, C.T., Batzer, M.A., Jorde, L.B., 2003. Human population genetic structure and inference of group membership. Am. J. Hum. Genet. 72, 578–589.
Bandioli, F., Corruccini, R.S., Macchiarelli, R., 1986. Familial segregation in the iron age community of Alfedena, Abruzzo, Italy, based on osteodental trait analysis. Am. J. Phys. Anthropol. 71, 393–400.
Bartels, P., 1904. Über Rassenunterschiede am Schädel. Monatschrift für Anatomy und Physio 21, 137–194.

Bastir, M., Rosas, A., 2004. Facial heights: evolutionary relevance of postnatal ontogeny for facial orientation and skull morphology in humans and chimpanzees. J. Hum. Evol. 47, 359–381.

Beals, K.L., 1972. Head form and climatic stress. Am. J. Phys. Anthropol. 37, 85–92.

Beals, K.L., Smith, C.L., Dodd, S.M., 1983. Climate and the evolution of brachycephalization. Am. J. Phys. Anthropol. 62, 425–437.

Beals, K.L., Smith, C.L., Dodd, S.M., 1984. Brain size, cranial morphology, climate and time machines. Curr. Anthropol. 25, 301–330.

Bedrick, E.J., Lapidus, J., Powell, J.F., 2000. Estimating the Mahalanobis distance from mixed continuous and discrete data. Biometrics 56, 394–401.

Belcher, R.L., Armelagos, G.J., 2005. Forensic misclassification of Ancient Nubian crania: implications for assumptions about human variation. Curr. Anthropol. 46, 340–346.

Bendyshe, T., 1969. The Anthropological treatises of Johann Blumenbach. Publications for the Anthropological Society. Longman Green Press, London.

Benfer, R.A., 1970. Associations among cranial traits: brief communication. Am. J. Phys. Anthropol. 32, 463.

Bennett, K.A., 1965. The etiology and genetics of wormian bones. Am. J. Phys. Anthropol. 23, 255–260.

Bentley, G.R., 1986. Dental morphology and social reconstruction at Early Bronze age Bab edh-Dhra', Jordan. Am. J. Phys. Anthropol. 69, 175.

Bergman, M., Wendler, D., Bertolini, R., 1984. Accessory mandibular canals in the human. Anat. Anz. Jena 156, 293–302.

Berry, A.C., 1974. The use of non-metrical variation of the cranium in the study of Scandinavian population movements. Am. J. Phys. Anthropol. 40, 345–358.

Berry, A.C., 1975. Factors affecting the incidence of non–metrical skeletal variants. J. Anat. 101, 361–379.

Berry, A.C., Berry, R.J., 1967. Epigenetic variation in the human cranium. J. Anat. 101, 361–379.

Berry, A.C., Berry, R.J., 1971. In: Chiarelli, A.B. (Ed.), Epigenetic Polymorphism in the Primate Skeleton. Academic Press, London, pp. 12–42.

Berry, A.C., Berry, R.J., 1972. Origins and relationships of the ancient Egyptians. Based on a study of non-metrical variations in the skull. J. Hum. Evol. 1, 199–208.

Berry, A.C., Berry, R., Ucko, P.J., 1967. Genetical change in ancient Egypt. Man 2, 551–568.

Berry, R.J., 1963. Epigenetic polymorphism in wild populations of *Mus musculus*. Genet. Res. 4, 193–220.

Berry, R.J., 1968. Biology and non-metrical variation in mice and men. In: Brothwell, D.R. (Ed.), The Skeletal Biology of Earlier Human Populations. Pergamon Press, Oxford, pp. 101–133.

Berry, R.J., Searle, A.G., 1963. Epigenetic polymorphism of the rodent skeleton. Proc. Zool. Soc. Lond. 140, 577–615.

Betti, L., Balloux, F., Hanihara, T., Manica, A., 2010. The relative role of drift and selection in shaping the human skull. Am. J. Phys. Anthropol. 141, 76–82.

Billy, G., 1955. Recherche sur les trous parietaux. Bull. Mem. Soc. Anthropol. Paris 6, 147–158.

Binford, L.R., 1962. Archaeology as anthropology. Am. Antiq. 28, 217–225.

Binford, L.R., 1964. A consideration of archaeological research design. Am. Antiq. 29, 425–441.

Black, G.V., 1902. Descriptive anatomy of the teeth, fourth ed S.S. White, Philadelphia, PA.

Black-MacLaughlin, S., Scheuer, L., 1996. Occipitalization of the atlas with reference to its embryological development. Int. J. Osteoarch. 6, 189–194.

Blumenbach, J.F., 1775. De generis humani varietate nativa liber [On the Natural Variety of Mankind]. Vandenhoek et Ruprecht, Goettingae.

Blumenbach, J.F., 1795. De Generis Humani Varietate Nativa Liber, third ed., Bergman Publishers, Gottingae, Germany.

Bogin, B., 1999. Patterns of Human Growth, second ed Cambridge University Press, Cambridge.

Bogin, B., Smith, B.H., 2000. Evolution of the human life cycle. In: Stinson, S., Bogin, B., Huss-Ashmore, R., O'Rourke, D. (Eds.), Human Biology: An Evolutionary and Biocultural perspective. Wiley-Liss, New York, NY, pp. 377–424.

Bondioli, L., Corruccini, R., Macchiarelli, R., 1986. Familial segregation in the Iron Age community of Alfedena, Abruzzo, Italy, based on osteodental trait analysis. Am. J. Phys. Anthropol. 71, 393–400.

Bookstein, F.L., 1991. Morphometric Tools for Landmark Data. Cambridge University Press, New York, NY.

Bookstein, F.L., Gunz, P., Mitterœcker, P., Prossinger, H., Schæfer, K., Seidler, H., 2003. Cranial integration in Homo: singular warps analysis of the midsagittal plane in ontogeny and evolution. J. Hum. Evol. 44, 167–187.

Bos, K.I., Harkins, K.M., Herbig, A., Coscolla, M., Weber, N., Comas, I., et al., 2014. Pre-Columbian mycobacterial genomes reveal seals as a source of New World human tuberculosis. Nature 514, 494–497.

Boudreaux, M.C., Lord, W.D., Dutra, R.L., 1999. Child abduction: aged-based analysis of offender, victim and offense characteristics in 550 cases of alleged child disappearance. J. Forensic Sci. 44, 539–553.

Boyd, G.I., 1930. The emissary foramina of the cranium in man and the anthropoids. J. Anat. 65, 108–121.

Brace, C.L., 1992. A four-letter word called "race.". In: Reynolds, L.J., Lieberman, L. (Eds.), Race and Other Miscalculations and Mismeasures: Papers in Honor of Ashley Montague. General Hall Publishers, New York, NY, pp. 106–141.

Brace, C.L., 1995. Region does not mean "race"—reality versus convention in Forensic Anthropology. J. Forensic Sci. 40, 171–175.

Brace, C.L., 2005a. "Race" is a Four-Letter Word: The Genesis of the Concept. Oxford University Press, New York, NY.

Brace, C.L., 2005b. Does race exist? An antagonist's perspective. ⟨http://www.pbs.org/wgbh/nova/first/brace.html⟩ (accessed March 6, 2005).

Brace, C.L., Hunt, K.D., 1990. A nonracial craniofacial perspective on human variation: A(ustralia) to Z(uni). Am. J. Phys. Anthropol. 82, 341–360.

Brace, C.L., Tracer, D.P., Hunt, K.D., 1990. Human craniofacial form and the evidence for the peopling of the Pacific. Bull. Indo-Pac. Pre. Hi. 11, 247–269.

Bräuer, G., 1988. Osteometrie. In: Knußmann, R. (Ed.), Anthropologie—Handbuch der vergleichenden Biologie des Menschen. Gustav Fischer Verlag, Stuttgart, pp. 160–232.

Breathnach, A.S., 1958. Frazer's Anatomy of the Human Skeleton, fifth ed Churchill, London.

Broca, M.P., 1863. Review of the Proceedings of the Anthropological Society of Paris. Anthropol. Rev. 1, 274–310.

Brooks, S., Brooks, R.H., France, D., 1990. Alveolar prognathism contour, an aspect of Racial Identification. In: Gill, G.W., Rhine, S. (Eds.), Skeletal Attribution of Race. Maxwell Museum of Anthropology: Anthropological Papers No. 4. Maxwell Museum of Anthropology, Albuquerque, NM, pp. 41–46.

Brotherton, P., Endicott, P., Sanchez, J.J., Beaumont, M., Barnett, R., Austin, J., et al., 2007. Novel high-resolution characterization of ancient DNA reveals C > U-type base modification events as the sole cause of post mortem miscoding lesions. Nucleic Acids Res. 35, 5717–5728.

Brothwell, D.R., 1959. The use of non-metrical characters of the skull in differentiating populations. Homo (supplement). Bericht über die 6. Tagung der Deutschen Gesellschaft für Anthropologie in Kiel, 1958.

Brothwell, D.R., 1963a. Digging Up Bones. British Museum, London.

Brothwell, D.R., 1963b. Dental Anthropology. Pergamon, New York, NY.

Brothwell, D.R., 1981. Digging Up Bones, third ed Cornell University Press, Ithaca, NY.

Brown, T., 1992. Developmental, morphological and functional aspects of occlusion in Australian Aboriginals. J. Hum. Ecol. (Special Issue) 2, 73–85.

Brown, J.A., 1977. Current directions in midwestern archaeology. Ann. Rev. Anthropol. 6, 161–179.

Brown, K.M., Keppel, R.D., 2007. Child abduction murder: an analysis of the effect of time and distance separation between murder incident sites on solvability. J. Forensic Sci. 52, 137–145.

Brues, A.M., 1977. People and Races. Macmillan, New York, NY.

Bryce, F., Young, M., 1916. Observations on metopism. J. Anat. 11, 153–163.

Buck, T.J., Strand Vidarsdottir, U., 2004. A proposed method for the identification of race in sub-adult skeletons: a geometric morphometric analysis of mandibular morphology. J. Forensic Sci. 49, 1159–1164.

Buettner-Janusch, J., 1969. Division of anthropology: the nature and future of physical anthropology. Trans. N.Y. Acad. Sci. 31 (2 Series II), 128–138.

Buikstra, J.E., 1972. Techniques for coping with the age–regressive nature of non–metric traits. Paper presented before the American Association of Physical Anthropologists.

Buikstra, J.E., 1974. Non-metric traits—control of environmental noise. Am. J. Phys. Anthropol. 41, 471.

Buikstra, J.E., 1976. Hopewell in the Lower Illinois Valley: A Regional Approach to the Study of Human Biological Variability and Prehistoric Behavior. Northwestern University, Evanston, IL.

Buikstra, J.E., 1980. Epigenetic distance: a study of biological variability in the lower Illinois River region. In: Browman, D.L. (Ed.), Early Native Americans: Prehistoric Demography, Economy, and Technology. Mouton, New York, NY, pp. 271–300.

Buikstra, J.E., 2006. An historical introduction. In: Buikstra, J.E., Beck, L.A. (Eds.), Bioarchaeology: The Contextual Analysis of Human Remains. Academic Press, San Diego, CA, pp. 7–25.

Buikstra, J.E., Frankenberg, S.R., Konigsberg, L.W., 1990. Skeletal biological distance studies in American Physical Anthropology: recent trends. Am. J. Phys. Anthropol. 82, 1–7.

Bulygina, E., Mitteroecker, P., Aiello, L., 2006. Ontogeny of facial dimorphism and patterns of individual development within one human population. Am. J. Phys. Anthropol. 131, 432–443.

Buschang, P.H., Tanguay, R., LaPalme, L., Demirjian, A., 1990. Mandibular growth prediction: mean growth increments versus mathematical models. Eur. J. Orthod. 12, 290–296.

Cabana, G.S., Lewis Jr., Cecil M., Tito, R.Y., Covey, R.A., Cáceres, A.M., Cruz, A.F., et al., 2014. Population genetic structure of traditional populations in the Peruvian Central Andes and implications for South American population history. Hum. Biol. 86, 147–165.

Cadien, J., Harris, E.F., Jones, W.P., Mandarino, L.J., 1976. Biological lineages, skeletal populations and microevolution. Yearb. Phys. Anthropol. 18, 194–201.

Campbell, N.A., 1978. Multivariate analysis in biological anthropology: some further considerations. J. Hum. Evol. 7, 197–203.

Campbell, T.D., 1925. The dentition and palate of the Australian Aboriginal. Hassell Press, Adelaide, SA.

Camper, P., 1791. Over het natuurlijk verschil der wezenstrekken in menschen van onderscheiden landaart en ouderdom; over het schoon in antyke beelden en gesneedene stenen. Utrecht.

Cann, R.L., Stoneking, M., Wilson, A.C., 1987. Mitochondrial DNA and human evolution. Nature 325, 31–36.

Cardoso, H.F.V., 2007. Environmental effects on skeletal versus dental development: using a documented subadult skeletal sample to test a basic assumption in human osteological research. Am. J. Phys. Anthropol. 132, 223–233.

Carlson, D.S., Van Gerven, D.P., 1977. Masticatory function and post-Pleistocene evolution in Nubia. Am. J. Phys. Anthropol. 81, 561–580.

Carson, E.A., 2006. Maximum-likelihood variance components analysis of heritabilities of cranial nonmetric traits. Hum. Biol. 78, 383–402.

Cattaneo, C., 2007. The skeletal remains of a child, victim of organized crime: the study of postmortem interval, personal identification and cause and manner of death. In: Brickley, M.B., Ferllini, R. (Eds.), Forensic Anthropology: case studies from Europe. Charles C Thomas, Springfield, IL, pp. 137–150.

Cavalli-Sforza, L.L., Piazza, A., Menozzi, P., Mountain, J., 1988. Reconstruction of human evolution: bringing together genetic, archaeological, and linguistic data. Proc. Natl. Acad. Sci. U.S.A. 85, 6002–6006.

Cesnys, G., 1982. Relation of non-metric cranial traits to sex and age in the $1^{st}$–$2^{nd}$ millennia A. D. Lithuanian craniological materials. Hum. Biol. Budapest 10, 19–24.

Cesnys, G., 1985. Variability of discrete cranial traits in the skulls of Lithuanian children. Anat. Anz. 159, 45–54.

Chakraborty, R., Kamboh, M.I., Nwankwo, M., Ferrell, R.E., 1992. Caucasian genes in American Negroes: New data. Am. J. Hum. Genet. 50, 145–155.

Chambellan, V., 1883. Etude anatomique et anthropologique sur les os wormiens. A. Delahaye et E. Lecrosnier.

Cheatle, A.H., 1900. The petro-squamosal sinus: its anatomy and pathological importance. J. Rhinol. Laryngol. Otol. 15, 13–23. N.S.N.

Cheverud, J., 1981. Phenotypic, genetic, and environmental morphological integration in the cranium. Evolution 36, 499–516.

Cheverud, J.M., 1988. A comparison of genetic and phenotypic correlations. Evolution 42, 958–968.

Cheverud, J.M., Buikstra, J.E., 1981. Quantitative genetics of skeletal nonmetric traits in the rhesus macaques on Cayo Santiago. I. Single trait heritabilities. Am. J. Phys. Anthropol. 54, 43–49.

Cheverud, J.M., Buikstra, J.E., 1982. Quantitative genetics of skeletal nonmetric traits in the rhesus macaques on Cayo Santiago. III. Phenotypic, genetic, and environmental correlations between traits. Am. J. Phys. Anthropol. 59, 151–155.

Chima, S.C., Ryschlewitsch, C.F., Fan, K.J., Stoner, G.L., 2000. Polyomavirus JC genotypes in an urban United States population reflect the history of African origin and genetic admixture in modern African Americans. Hum. Biol. 72, 837–850.

Chouke, K.S., 1946. On the incidence of the foramen of Civinini and the porus crotaphitico-buccinatorius in American Whites and Negroes. I. Observations on 1544 skulls. Am. J. Phys. Anthropol. 4, 203–225.

Chouke, K.S., 1947. On the incidence of the foramen of Civinini and the porus crotaphitico-buccinatorius in American Whites and Negroes. II. Observations on 2745 additional skulls. Am. J. Phys. Anthropol. 5, 79–86.

Christensen, A., 2004. The impact of Daubert: implications for testimony and research in Forensic Anthropology (and the use of frontal sinuses in personal identification). J. Forensic Sci. 49, 1–4.

Church, M.S., 1995. Determination of race from the skeleton through forensic anthropological methods. Forensic Sci. Rev. 7, 1–39.

Clemente, C.D., 1975. Anatomy: A Regional Atlas of the Human Body. Lea & Feibeger, Philadelphia, PA.

Cobb, S., O'Higgins, P., 2002. The ontogeny of form variation in the African ape facial skeleton: a hierarchical approach to the interspecific comparison of ontogenetic trajectories. Am. J. Phys. Anthropol. 34 (Suppl), 55.

Cohen, J., 1988. Statistical Power Analysis for the Behavioral Sciences, second ed Lawrence Erlbaum & Associates, Hillsdale, MI.

Collins, H.B., 1926. The temporo-frontal articulation in man. Am. J. Phys. Anthropol. 9, 343–348.

Collins, H.B., 1951. The origin and antiquity of the Eskimo. Annual Report of the Smithsonian Institute for 1950. Smithsonian Institute Press, Washington, DC, pp. 423–467.

Comas, J., 1942. Contribution a l'étude du metopisme. Archives Suisses d'Anthropolgie. Gen 10, 273–412.

Constandse-Westermann, T.S., 1972. Coefficients of Biological Distance; An Introduction to The Various Methods of Assessment of Biological Distances between Populations, with Special Reference to Human Biological Problems. Anthropological Publications, Oosterhout.

Cook, R.D., 1982. Residuals and Influence in Regression. Chapman & Hall, New York, NY.

Coon, C.S., Garn, S.M., Birdsell, J.B., 1950. Races. Charles C Thomas, Springfield, IL.

Cooper, A., Poinar, H., 2000. Ancient DNA: do it right or not at all. Science 289, 1139.

Coqueugniot, H., Weaver, T.D., 2007. Brief communication: infracranial maturation in the skeletal collection from Coimbra, Portugal: new aging standards for epiphyseal union. Am. J. Phys. Anthropol. 134, 424–437.

Corruccini, R.S., 1975. Multivariate analysis in biological anthropology: some considerations. J. Hum. Evol. 4, 1–19.

Corruccini, R.S., 1984. An epidemiologic transition in dental occlusion in world populations. Am. J. Orthod. 82, 371–376.

Corruccini, R.S., 1991. Anthropological aspects of orofacial and occlusal variations and anomalies. In: Kelley, M.A., Larsen, C.S. (Eds.), Advances in Dental Anthropology. Wiley-Liss, New York, NY, pp. 295–323.

Corruccini, R.S., Choudhury, A.F.H., 1985. Dental occlusion variation among rural and urban Bengali youths. Hum. Biol. 5, 61–66.

Corruccini, R.S., Potter, R.H.Y., Dahlberg, A.A., 1981. Changing occlusal variation in Pima Amerinds. Am. J. Phys. Anthropol. 62, 317–324.

Corruccini, R.S., Kaul, S.S., Chopra, S.R.K., Karosas, J., Larsen, M.D., Morrow, C., 1983. Epidemiological survey of occlusion in north India. Br. J. Orthod. 10, 44–47.

Corruccini, R.S., Townsend, G.C., Brown, T., 1990. Occlusal variation in Australian Aboriginals. Am. J. Phys. Anthropol. 82, 257–265.

Corruccini, R.S., Nesbitt, R., Ciochon, R., 1992. Occlusofacial morphological changes in relation to masticatory function. Am. J. Phys. Anthropol. (Suppl.) 14, 63–64.

Corruccini, R.S., Shimada, I., Shinoda, K., 2002. Dental and mtDNA relatedness among thousand-year-old remains from Huaca Loro, Peru. Dent. Anthropol. 16, 9–14.

Cowgill, L.W., 2010. The ontogeny of Holocene and Late Pleistocene human postcranial strength. Am. J. Phys. Anthropol. 141, 16–37.

Cox, K., Tayles, N.G., Buckley, H.R., 2006. Forensic Identification of "Race": the issues in New Zealand. Forensic Identification of "Race": the issues in New Zealand. Curr. Anthropol. 47, 869–874.

Crognier, E., 1981. Climate and anthropometric variation in Europe and the Mediterranean area. Ann. Hum. Biol. 8, 99–107.

Cunha, E., 1995. Testing identification records: evidence from the Coimbra identified skeletal collections ($19^{th}$ and $20^{th}$ centuries). In: Saunders, S.R., Herring, A. (Eds.), Grave Reflections: Portraying the Past through Cemetery studies. Canadian Scholars Press, Toronto, ON, pp. 179–198.

Czarnetzki, A., 1971. Epigenetische Skelettmerkmaie im Populationsvergleich, II. Frequenzunterschiede zwischen den Geschlechtern. Zeitschriftfur Morphologie und Anthropologic 63, 341–350.

Czarnetzki, A., 1975. On the question of correlation between the size of the epigenetic distance and the degree of allopatry in different populations. J. Hum. Evol. 4, 483–489.

Dahinten, S.L., Pucciarelli, H.M., 1981. Effect of sex, age and nutrition on discontinuous traits from a rat skull. Acta Anat. 110, 159–163.

Dahinten, S.L., Pucciarelli, H.M., 1983. Effects of protein-calorie malnutrition during suckling and post weaning periods on discontinuous cranial traits in rats. Am. J. Phys. Anthropol. 60, 425–430.

Dahlberg, A.A., 1971. Penetrance and expressivity of dental traits. In: Dahlberg, A.A. (Ed.), Dental Morphology and Evolution. University of Chicago Press, Chicago, IL, pp. 257–262.

Dahlberg, A.A., Cederquist, R., Mayhall, J., Owen, D., 1978. Eskimo craniofacial studies. In: Jamieson, P.L., Zegura, S.L., Milan, F.A. (Eds.), Eskimos of Northwestern Alaska: A Biological Perspective. Hutchinson & Ross, Stroudsburg, PA, pp. 94–115.

Dahm, M.C., Shepherd, R.K., Clark, G.M., 1993. The postnatal growth of the temporal bone and its implications for cochlear implants in children. Acta Oto-Laryngol. 505 (Suppl), 1–27.

Dalley, M., 2009. 2008 Missing Children Reference Report. National Missing Children Services, National Police Services, Royal Canadian Mounted Police. Minister of Public Works and Government Services, Canada.

Daniel, W.W., 1991. Biostatistics: A Foundation for Analysis in the Health Sciences, fifth ed Wiley, New York, NY, pp. 586–592.

Darwin, C., 1871. The Descent of Man. John Murray, London.

Daubert v. Merrell Dow Pharmaceuticals, Inc., 509 U.S. 579 (1993).

Davida, E., 1914. Über die Varientäten des Verlaufes der sutura infraorbitalis sagittalis. Anat. Anz. 44, 203–210.

Del Papa, M.C., Perez, S.I., 2007. The influence of artificial cranial vault deformation on the expression of cranial nonmetric traits: its importance in study of evolutionary relationships. Am. J. Phys. Anthropol. 134, 251–262.

Deol, M.S., Truslove, G.M., 1957. Genetical studies on the skeleton of the mouse. XX. Maternal physiology and variations in the skeleton of C57BL mice. J. Genet. 55, 288–312.

DiBennardo, R., Taylor, J.V., 1983. Multiple discriminant function analysis of sex and race in the postcranial skeleton. Am. J. Phys. Anthropol. 61, 305–314.

Dirkmaat, D.C., Cabo, L.L., Ousley, S.D., Symes, S.A., 2008. New perspectives in forensic anthropology. Yearb. Phys. Anthropol. 51, 33–52.

Dixon, A.F., 1904. On certain markings due to nerves and blood vessels upon the cranial vault; their significance, and the relative frequency of their occurrence in the different races of mankind. J. Anat. 38, 337–398.

Dodo, Y., 1974. Non-metrical cranial traits in the Hokkaido Ainu and the northern Japanese of recent times. J. Anthropol. Soc. Nippon 82, 31–51.

Dodo, Y., 1980. Appearance of bony bridging of the hypoglossal canal during the fetal period. J. Anthropol. Soc. Nippon 88, 229–238.

Dodo, Y., 1986. Observations on the bony bridging of the jugular foramen in man. J. Anat. 144, 153–165.

Dodo, Y., 1987. Supraorbital foramen and hypoglossal canal bridging: the two most suggestive non-metric cranial traits in discriminating major racial groupings of man. J. Anthropol. Soc. Nippon 95, 19–35.

Dodo, Y., Ishida, H., 1987. Incidences of nonmetric cranial variants in several population samples from East Asia and North America. J. Anthropol. Soc. Nippon 95, 161–177.

Dodo, Y., Ishida, H., 1990. Population history of Japan as viewed from cranial nonmetric variation. J. Anthropol. Soc. Nippon 98, 269–287.

Dodo, Y., Ishida, H., 1992. Consistency of nonmetric cranial trait expression during the last 2,000 years in the habitants of the central islands of Japan. J. Anthropol. Soc. Nippon 100, 417–423.

Dodo, Y., Doi, N., Kondo, O., 1998. Ainu and Ryukyuan cranial nonmetric variation: evidence which disputes the Ainu–Ryukyu common origin theory. Anthropol. Sci. 106, 99–120.

Donlon, D.A., 2000. The value of infracranial nonmetric variation in studies of modern *Homo sapiens*: an Australian focus. Am. J. Phys. Anthropol. 113, 349–368.

Dorsey, G.A., 1897. Wormian bones in artificially deformed Kwakiutl crania. Am. Anthropol. 10, 169–173.

Droessler, J., 1981. Craniometry and Biological Distance: Biocultural Continuity and Change at the Late-Woodland-Mississippian Interface. Center for American Archaeology, Evanston, IL.

Dror, I.E., Charlton, D., Peron, A.E., 2005. Contextual information renders experts vulnerable to making erroneous identifications. Forensic Sci. Int. 156, 74–78.

Duke-Elder, S., 1963. System of Ophthalmology, Vol 3, Normal and Abnormal Development, Part 1. Kimpton, London, pp. 211–219.

Dutilleul, P., Stockwell, J.D., Frigon, D., Legendre, P., 2000. The Mantel test versus Pearson's correlation analysis: assessment of the differences for biological and environmental studies. J. Agric. Biol. Environ. Stat. 5, 131–150.

Eby, T.L., Nadol, J.B., 1986. Postnatal growth of the human temporal bone. Implications for cochlear implants in children. Ann. Otol. Rhinol. Laryngol. 95, 356–364.

Edgar, H.J.H., 2007. Microevolution of African American dental morphology. Am. J. Phys. Anthropol. 132, 535–544.

Edgar, H.J.H., 2013. Estimation of ancestry using dental morphological characteristics. J. Forensic Sci. 58, S3–S8.

Edgar, H.J.H., Lease, L.R., 2007. Correlations between deciduous and permanent tooth morphology in a European American sample. Am. J. Phys. Anthropol. 133, 726–734.

Edgar, H.J.H., Jolie, E.A., Powell, J.F., Watkins, J.E., 2007. Contextual issues in Paleoindian repatriation: Spirit Cave Man as a case study. J. Soc. Archaeol. 7, 101–122.

England, M., 1996. Facial growth and the ontogeny of morphological variation. J. Zool. 264, 37–47.

Enlow, D.H., 1968. The Human Face: An Account of the Postnatal Growth and Development of the Craniofacial Skeleton. Harper and Row, New York, NY.

Enlow, D.H., 1975. Handbook of Facial Growth. Saunders, Philadelphia, PA.

Enlow, D.H., Hans, M.G., 1996. Essentials of Facial Growth. W.B. Saunders Co., Toronto, ON.

Enoki, K., Dahlberg, A.A., 1958. Rotated maxillary central incisors. Orthod. J. Jpn. 17, 157–169.

Falconer, D.S., 1965. The inheritance of liability to certain diseases, estimated from distances among relatives. Ann. Hum. Genet. 29, 51–76.

Falconer, D.S., 1967. The inheritance of liability to diseases with variable age of onset, with particular reference to diabetes mellitus. Ann. Hum. Genet. 31, 1–20.

Falconer, D.S., 1989. Introduction to Quantitative Genetics, third ed Longman, London.

Farkas, L.G., Posnick, J.C., Hreczko, T.M., Pron, G.E., 1992a. Growth patterns in the orbital region: a morphometric study. Cleft Palate Craniofac. J. 29, 315–318.

Farkas, L.G., Posnick, J.C., Hreczko, T.M., 1992b. Growth patterns of the face: a morphometric study. Cleft Palate Craniofac. J. 29, 308–314.

Farkas, L.G., Posnick, J.C., Hreczko, T.M., Pron, G.E., 1992c. Growth patterns of the nasiolabial region: a morphometric study. Cleft Palate Craniofac. J. 29, 318–324.

Farkas, L.G., Hreczko, T.M., Katic, M., 1992d. Anthropometric growth patterns in the nasal root and intercanthal widths of a North American Caucasian population. Anthropologie 30, 227–231.

Farkas, L.G., Katic, M.J., Forrest, C.R., 2005. International anthropometric study of facial morphology in various ethnic groups/races. J. Craniofac. Surg. 16, 615–646.

Feldesman, M.R., 2002. Classification trees as an alternative to linear discriminant analysis. Am. J. Phys. Anthropol. 119, 257–275.

Finkelhor, D., 1997. The homicides of children and youth: a developmental perspective. In: Kantor, G.K., Jasinski, J.L. (Eds.), Out of the Darkness: Contemporary Perspectives on Family Violence. Sage Publications, Thousand Oaks, CA, pp. 17–34.

Finnegan, M., McGuire, S.A., 1979. Classification systems for discrete variables used in forensic anthropology. Am. J. Phys. Anthropol. 51, 547–553.

Fish, A., 2006. Indigenous bodies in colonial courts: anthropological science and the (physical) laws of the remaining human. Wicazo Sa Rev. Spring, 77–95.

Fisher, R.A., 1936a. "The coefficient of racial likeness" and the future of craniometry. J. R. Anthropol. Inst. 66, 57–63.

Fisher, R.A., 1936b. The use of multiple measurements in taxonomic problems. Ann. Eugen. 7, 179–188.

FitzGerald, C.M., Rose, J.C., 2000. Reading between the lines: dental development and subadult age assessment using the microstructural growth markers of teeth. In: Katzenberg, M.A., Saunders, S.R. (Eds.), Skeletal Biology of Past Peoples: Research Methods. John Wiley & Sons, Inc, New York, NY, pp. 163–186.

Franklin, D., Freedman, L., Milne, N., 2005. Three-dimensional technology for linear morphological studies: a re-examination of cranial variation in four Southern African indigenous populations. Homo 56, 17–34.

Franklin, D., Freedman, L., Milne, N., Oxnard, L.E., 2007. Geometric morphometric study of population variation in indigenous South African crania. Am. J. Hum. Biol. 19, 20–33.

Freeman, M.F., Tukey, J.W., 1950. The use of inverse sine transformations in the analysis of non-metric cranial data. Am. J. Physical. Anthropol. 45, 61–68.

Frelich, L., Hunt, D.R., 2007. Morphological characteristics of ancestry in the fetal/newborn human skeleton. Proc AAFS. American Academy of Forensic Sciences, San Antonio, TX; Colorado Springs, CO.

Fukumine, T., Hanihara, T., Nishime, A., Ishida, H., 2006. Nonmetric variation of early modern human skeletal remains from Kumejima, Okinawa and the peopling of the Ryukyu Islands. Anthropol. Sci. 14, 141–151.

Garn, S.M., 1965. Human Races, second ed Charles C Thomas, Springfield, IL.

Garn, S.M., Lewis, A.B., Kerewsky, R.S., 1964. Sex difference in tooth size. J. Dent. Res. 43, 306.

Garn, S.M., Lewis, A.B., Dahlberg, A.A., Kerewsky, R.S., 1966. Interaction between relative molar size and relative number of cusps. J. Dent. Res. 45, 1240.

Garn, S.M., Osborne, R., McCabe, K., 1979. The effects of prenatal factors on crown dimesions. Am. J. Phys. Anthropol. 51, 665–678.

Giles, E., Elliot, O., 1962. Race identification from cranial measurements. J. Forensic Sci. 7, 147–157.

Gill, G.W., 1971. The Prehistoric Inhabitants of Northern Coastal Nayarit: Skeletal Analysis and Description of Burials. Department of Anthropology. University of Kansas, Lawrence, KS.

Gill, G.W., 1984. A forensic test case for a new method of geographical race determination. In: Rathburn, T.A., Buikstra, J.E. (Eds.), Human Identification: Case Studies in Forensic Anthropology. Charles C Thomas, Springfield, IL, pp. 329–339.

Gill, G.W., 2005. Does race exist? A proponent's perspective. ⟨http://www.pbs.org/wgbh/nova/first/gill.html⟩ (accessed March 6, 2005).

Gill, G.W., Rhine, S., 1990. Skeletal Attribution of Race: Methods for Forensic Anthropology. Maxwell Museum of Anthropology, Albuquerque, NM.

Gill, G.W., Hughes, S.S., Bennett, S.M., Gilbert, B.M., 1988. Racial identification from the midfacial skeleton with special reference to North American Indians & Whites. J. Forensic Sci. 13, 92–99.

Gindhart, P.S., 1989. An early twentieth-century skeletal collection. J. Forensic Sci. 34, 887–893.

Glass, B., Li, C.C., 1953. The dynamics of racial intermixture—an analysis based on the American Negro. Am. J. Hum. Genet. 5, 1–20.

Godde, K., 2010. An examination of proposed causes of auditory exostoses. Int. J. Osteoarch. 20, 486–490.

Gonzalez, P.N., Perez, S.I., Bernal, V., 2010. Ontogeny of robusticity of craniofacial traits in modern humans: a study of South American Populations. Am. J. Phys. Anthropol. 142, 367–379.

González-José, R., Ramíez-Rozzi, F., Sardi, M., Martínez-Abadí, N., Hernández, M., Pucciarelli, H.M., 2005. Functional–cranial approach to the influence of economic strategy on skull morphology. Am. J. Phys. Anthropol. 128, 757–771.

Goodman, A.H., 1997. Bred in the bone? Sciences 37 (2), 20–25.

Goodman, A.H., Armelagos, G.J., 1985. Factors affecting the distribution of enamel hypoplasias within the permanent human dentition. Am. J. Phys. Anthropol. 68, 479–493.

Goodman, A.H., Armelagos, G.J., 1996. The resurrection of race: the concept of race in physical anthropology in the 1990s. In: Reynolds, L., Lieberman, L. (Eds.), Race and Other Misadventures: Essays in Honor of Ashley Montagu in His Ninetieth Year. General Hall, Dix Hills, NY, pp. 174–186.

Goodman, A.H., Rose, J.C., 1991. Dental enamel hypoplasia as indicators of nutritional status. In: Kelley, M.A., Larsen, C.S. (Eds.), Advances in Dental Anthropology. Wiley-Liss, New York, NY, pp. 279–293.

Goodman, A.H., Armelagos, G.J., Rose, J.C., 1980. Enamel hypoplasia as indicators of stress in three prehistoric populations from Illinois. Hum. Biol. 52, 515–528.

Goodman, A.H., Heath, D., Lindee, M.S., 2003. Genetic Nature/Culture: Anthropology and Science Beyond the Two-Culture Divide. University of California Press, Berkeley, CA.

Goose, D.H., 1956. Variability in the form of maxillary permanent incisors. J. Dent. Res. 35, 902–908.

Goose, D.H., 1963. Dental measurement: an assessment of its value in anthropological studies. In: Brothwell, D.R. (Ed.), Dental Anthropology. Pergamon, New York, NY, pp. 125–148.

Goose, D.H., Appleton, J., 1982. Human Dentofacial Growth. Pergamon Press, London.

Goss, C.M., 1973. Gray's Anatomy, 29th ed Lea & Febiger Press, Philadelphia, PA.

Gould, S.J., 1996. The Mismeasure of Man. WI Norton, New York, NY.

Gravetter, F.J., Wallnau, L.B., 2004. Statistics for the Behavioral Sciences, sixth ed Bellmont, Wadsworth.

Gravlee, C.C., Bernard, H.R., Leonard, W.R., 2003. Heredity, environment, and cranial form: a re-analysis of Boas's immigrant data. Am. Anthropol. 105, 125–138.

Gray, H., 1918. Anatomy of the Human Body. Retrieved from ⟨www.bartleby.com⟩ (on 27 September 2012).

Green, R.F., Suchey, J.M., Gokhale, D.V., 1979. The statistical treatment of correlated bilateral traits in the analysis of cranial material. Am. J. Phys. Anthropol. 50 (4), 629–634.

Greene, D.L., 1982. Discrete dental variations and biological distances of Nubian populations. Am. J. Physical. Anthropol. 58, 75–79.

Greene, R.F., Suchey, J., 1976. The use of inverse sine transformation in the analysis of non-metrical data. Am. J. Phys. Anthropol. 45, 61–68.

Gregoricka, L.A., 2013. Geographic origins and dietary transitions during the bronze age in the oman peninsula. Am. J. Phys. Anthropol. 152, 353–369.

Grewal, M., 1962. The rate of divergence in the C57BL strain of mice. Genet. Res. 3, 226–237.

Grüneberg, H., 1952. Genetical studies on the skeleton of the mouse. IV. Quasi-continuous variations. J. Genet. 51, 95–114.

Grüneberg, H., 1955. Genetical studies on the skeleton of the mouse XV. Relations between major and minor variants. J. Genet. 53, 515–533.

Grüneberg, H., 1963. The Pathology of Development: A Study of Inherited Skeletal Disorders in Animals. Blackwell Scientific Publications, Oxford.

Gualdi-Russo, E., Tasca, M.A., Brasili, P., 1999. Scoring of nonmetric cranial traits: a methodological approach. J. Anat. 195, 543–550.

Guglielmino-Matessi, C.R., Gluckman, P., Cavalli-Sforza, L.L., 1979. Climate and the evolution of skull metrics in man. Am. J. Phys. Anthropol. 50, 549–564.

Gupta, N., Ray, B., Ghosh, S., 2005. Anatomic characteristics of foramen Vesalius. Kathmandu Univ. Med. J. 3, 155–158.

Haas, A., Weiglein, C., Faschinger, K., Müllner, K., 1993. Fetal development of the human orbit. Graefes Arch. Clin. Exp. Ophthalmol. 231, 217–220.

Haeussler, A.M., Irish, J.D., Morris, D.H., Turner II, C.G., 1989. Morphological and metrical comparison of San and Central Sotho dentitions from Southern African. Am. J. Phys. Anthropol. 78, 115–122.

Halder, I., Yang, B.Z., Kranzler, H.R., Stein, M.B., Shriver, M.D., Gelernter, J., 2009. Measurement of admixture proportions and description of admixture structure in different U.S. populations. Hum. Mutat. 30, 1299–1309.

Halffman, C.M., Scott, G.R., Pedersen, P.O., 1992. Palatine torus in the Greenlandic Norse. Am. J. Phys. Anthropol. 88, 145–161.

Hallgrimsson, B., Donnabháin, B.O., Walters, G.B., Cooper, D.M., Gudbjartsson, D., Stefansson, K., 2004. Composition of the founding population of Iceland: biological distance and morphological variation in early historic Atlantic Europe. Am. J. Phys. Anthropol. 124, 257–274.

Hallgrimsson, B., Donnabháin, B.O., Blom, D.E., Lozada, M.C., Willmore, K.T., 2005. Why are rare traits unilaterally expressed?: Trait frequency and unilateral expression for cranial nonmetric traits in humans. Am. J. Phys. Anthropol. 128, 14–25.

Handt, O., Richards, M., Trommsdorff, M., Kilger, C., Simanainen, J., Georgiev, O., et al., 1994. Molecular genetic analyses of the Tyrolean Ice Man. Science 264, 1775–1778.

Hanihara, K., 1954. Studies on the deciduous dentition of the Japanese and the Japanese-American hybrids: I. Deciduous incisors. J. Anthropol. Soc. Nippon 63, 168–185.

Hanihara, K., 1955. Studies on the deciduous dentition of the Japanese and the Japanese-American hybrids: II. Deciduous canines. J. Anthropol. Soc. Nippon 64, 63–82.

Hanihara, K., 1976. Mongoloid dental complex in the deciduous dentition. J. Anthropol. Soc. Nippon 74, 61–70.

Hanihara, K., 1978. Differences in sexual dimorphism in dental morphology among several human populations. In: Bulter, P.M., Joysey, K.A. (Eds.), Development, Function and Evolution of Teeth. Academic Press, London, pp. 127–134.

Hanihara, T., 1992. Population prehistory of East Asia and the Pacific as viewed from craniofacial morphology: the basic populations in East Asia, IV. Am. J. Phys. Anthropol. 88, 163–182.

Hanihara, T., 1996. Comparison of craniofacial features of major human groups. Am. J. Phys. Anthropol. 99, 389–412.

Hanihara, T., 1997. Craniofacial affinities of Mariana Islanders and circum-Pacific peoples. Am. J. Phys. Anthropol. 104, 411–425.

Hanihara, T., 2000. Frontal and facial flatness of major human populations. Am. J. Phys. Anthropol. 111, 105–134.

Hanihara, T., 2008. Morphological variation of major human populations based on nonmetric dental traits. Am. J. Phys. Anthropol. 136, 169–182.

Hanihara, T., Ishida, H., 2001a. Os incae: variation in frequency in major human population groups. J. Anat. 198, 137–152.

Hanihara, T., Ishida, H., 2001b. Frequency variations of discrete traits in major human populations. I. Supernumerary ossicle variations. J. Anat. 198, 689–706.

Hanihara, T., Ishida, H., 2001c. Frequency variations of discrete traits in major human populations. II. Hypostotic variations. J. Anat. 198, 707–725.

Hanihara, T., Ishida, H., 2001d. Frequency variations of discrete traits in major human populations. III. Hyperstotic variations. J. Anat. 199, 251–272.

Hanihara, T., Ishida, H., 2001e. Frequency variations of discrete traits in major human populations. IV. Vessel and nerve related variations. J. Anat. 199, 273–287.

Hanihara, T., Ishida, H., 2009. Regional differences in craniofacial diversity and the population history of Jomon Japan. Am. J. Phys. Anthropol. 139, 311–322.

Hanihara, T., Ishida, H., Dodo, Y., 1998a. Os zygomaticum bipartitum: frequency distribution in major human populations. J. Anat. 192, 539–555.

Hanihara, T., Ishida, H., Dodo, Y., 1998b. Place of the Hokkaido Ainu (Northern Japan) among circumpolar and other peoples of the world: a comparison of the frequency variations of discrete cranial traits. Int. J. Circumpolar Health 57, 257–275.

Hanihara, T., Ishida, H., Dodo, Y., 2003. Characterization of biological diversity through analysis of discrete cranial traits. Am. J. Phys. Anthropol. 121, 241–251.

Harkins, K.M., Buikstra, J.E., Campbell, T., Bos, K.I., Johnson, E.D., Krause, J., et al., 2015. Screening ancient tuberculosis with qPCR: challenges and opportunities. Philos. Trans. R. Soc. London, Ser. B 370, 20130622.

Harpending, H.C., Jenkins, T., 1973. Genetic distance among southern African populations. In: Crawford, M.H., Workman, P. (Eds.), Methods and Theories of Anthropological Genetics. University of New Mexico Press, Albuquerque, NM, pp. 177–199.

Harris, M., 1968. Rise of Anthropological Theory. Thomas Y. Crowell Company, New York, NY.

Harris, E.F., 2007. Carabelli's trait and tooth size of human maxillary first molars. Am. J. Phys. Anthropol. 132, 238–246.

Harris, E.F., McKee, J.H., 1990. Tooth mineralization standards for blacks and whites from the middle southern United States. J. Forensic Sci. 35, 859–872.

Harris, E.F., Sjøvold, T., 2004. Calculation of Smith's mean measure of divergence for intergroup comparisons using nonmetric data. Dent. Anthropol. 17, 83–93.
Hastie, R., Dawes, R.M., 2001. Rational Choice in an Uncertain World: The Psychology of Judgment and Decision Making, second ed., Sage Publications, California.
Hauser, G., De Stefano, G.F., Bastianini, A., Guidotti, A., 1984. Supraorbital minor skeletal variants in fetuses and newborns. Anthropol. Kozl.—Anthropol. Commun. 28, 63–70.
Hefner, J.T., 2002. An assessment of craniofacial nonmetric traits currently used in forensic determination of ancestry. Proc. AAFS. American Academy of Forensic Sciences, Atlanta. Colorado Springs, CO.
Hefner, J.T., 2015. Cranial morphoscopic traits and the assessment of American Black, American White, and Hispanic ancestry. In: Berg, G.E., Ta'ala, S.C. (Eds.), Biological Affinity in Forensic Identification of Human Skeletal Remains. CRC Press, Boca Raton, FL, pp. 27–42.
Hefner, J.T., Emanovsky, P.D., Byrd, J., Ousley, S.D., 2007. The value of experience, education, and methods in ancestry prediction. Proc. AAFS. American Academy of Forensic Sciences, Seattle. Colorado Springs, CO.
Hefner, J.T., Ousley, S.D., Dirkmaat, D.C., 2012. Morphoscopic traits and the assessment of ancestry. In: Dirkmaat, D.C. (Ed.), A Companion to Forensic Anthropology. Wiley-Blackwell, Malden, MA, pp. 287–310.
Hefner, J.T., Spradley, M.K., Anderson, B., 2014. Ancestry assessment using random forest modeling. J. Forensic Sci. 59, 583–589.
Hefner, J.T., Pilloud, M.A., Black, C.J., Anderson, B.E., 2015. Morphoscopic trait expression in "Hispanic" populations. J. Forensic Sci. 60, 1135–1139.
Hennessy, R.J., Stringer, C.G., 2002. Geometric morphometrics study of the regional variation of modern human craniofacial form. Am. J. Phys. Anthropol. 117, 37–48.
Hernández, M., Fox, C.L., Garcia-Moro, C., 1997. Fueguian cranial morphology: the adaptation to a cold, harsh environment. Am. J. Phys. Anthropol. 103, 103–117.
Hertzog, K.P., 1968. Associations between discontinuous cranial traits. Am. J. Phys. Anthropol. 29, 397–404.
Hess, L., 1946. Ossicula wormiana. Hum. Biol. 18, 61–80.
Higa, T., Hanihara, T., Sunakawa, H., Ishida, H., 2003. Dental variation of Ryukyu Islanders: a comparative study among Ryukyu, Ainu and other Asian populations. Am. J. Hum. Biol. 15, 127–143.
Higuchi, R.G., Bowman, B., Freiberger, M., Ryder, A.O., Wilson, A.C., 1984. DNA sequence from the quagga, an extinct member of the horse family. Nature 312, 282–284.
Hillson, S., 1996. Dental Anthropology. Cambridge University Press, Cambridge.
Hillson, S., FitzGerald, C., Flinn, H., 2005. Alternative dental measurements: proposals and relationships with other measurements. Am. J. Phys. Anthropol. 126, 413–426.
Holliday, R., 1990. DNA methylation and epigenetic inheritance. Philos. Trans. R. Soc. London, Ser. B 326, 329–338.
Hooton, E.A., 1918. On certain Eskimoid characters in Icelandic skulls. Am. J. Phys. Anthropol. 1, 53–76.
Hooton, E.A., 1926a. Significance of the term race. Science 63, 75–81.
Hooton, E.A., 1926b. Lecture Notes of EA Hooton. Peabody Museum Archives, Cambridge.
Hooton, E.A., 1931. Lecture Notes of EA Hooton. Unpublished manuscripts of the Peabody Museum Archives of E. A. Hooton. Cambridge.
Hooton, E.A., 1946a. Up from the Apes. Macmillan, New York, NY.
Hooton, E.A., 1946b. Lecture Notes of EA Hooton. Unpublished manuscripts of the Peabody Museum Archives of E. A. Hooton. Cambridge.
Howe, W.L., Parsons, P.A., 1967. Genotype and environment in the determination of minor skeletal variants and body weight in mice. J. Embryol. Exp. Morphol. 17, 283–292.
Howells, W.W., 1970. Multivariate analysis for the identification of race from the crania. In: Stewart, T.D. (Ed.), Personal Identification in Mass Disasters. Smithsonian Institution Press, Washington, DC, pp. 111–112.
Howells, W.W., 1989. Skull shapes and the map: craniometric analyses in the dispersion of modern homo, Papers of the Peabody Museum of Archaeology and Ethnology, Vol. 79. Harvard University, Cambridge, The Museum,.
Howells, W.W., 1995. Who's who in skulls: ethnic identification of crania from measurements, Papers of the Peabody Museum of Archaeology and Ethnology, Vol. 82. Harvard University, Cambridge, The Museum,.
Hrdlička, A., 1911. Human dentition and teeth from the evolutionary and racial standpoint. Dom. Dent. J. 23, 403–421.
Hrdlička, A., 1920a. Anthropometry. Wistar Institute of Anatomy and Biology, Philadelphia, PA.
Hrdlička, A., 1920b. Shovel shaped teeth. Am. J. Phys. Anthropol. 3, 429–465.
Hrdlička, A., 1921. Further studies of tooth morphology. Am. J. Phys. Anthropol. 4, 141–176.
Hrdlička, A., 1924. New data on the teeth of early man and certain fossil European apes. Am. J. Phys. Anthropol. 7, 109–132.
Hrdlička, A., 1927a. Anthropology of the American negro. Historical notes. Am. J. Phys. Anthropol. 10, 205–233.
Hrdlička, A., 1927b. Catalogue of human crania in the United States National Museum Collection. Proceedings of the United States Museum. Washington Smithsonian Institution Press, pp. 1–127.
Hrdlička, A., 1935a. Ear exostoses. Am. J. Phys. Anthropol. 20, 489–490.
Hrdlička, A., 1935b. Ear exostoses, Smithsonian Miscellaneous Collections, 93. Smithsonian Institute Press, Washington, DC, pp. 1–100.
Hrdlička, A., 1952. Practical Anthropometry, fourth ed Wistar Institute of Anatomy and Biology, Philadelphia, PA.
Hughes, T., Dempsey, P., Richards, L., Townsend, G.C., 2000. Genetic analysis of deciduous tooth size in Australian twins. Arch. Oral Biol. 45, 997–1004.
Hughes, S.S., 1980. Differences in nasal projections between American Indian and Caucasoid crania. Wyo. Contrib. Anthropol. 2, 96–113.
Humphrey, T., 1969. The relation between human fetal mouth opening reflexes and closure of the palate. Am. J. Anat. 125, 317–344.
Humphrey, L.T., 1998. Growth patterns in the modern skeleton. Am. J. Phys. Anthropol. 105, 57–72.
Humphrey, L.T., Scheuer, L., 2006. Age of closure of the foramen of Huschke: an osteological study. Int J Osteoarch 16, 47–60.
Hunt, N., 1998. Muscle function and the control of facial form. In: Harris, M., Edgar, M., Meghji, S. (Eds.), Clinical Oral Science. Wright, Oxford, pp. 120–133.

Hunt, D.R., 1990. Sex determination in the subadult ilia: an indirect test of Weaver's nonmetric sexing method. J. Forensic Sci. 35, 881–885.
Hunt, D.R., Albanese, J., 2005. History and demographic composition of the Robert J. Terry Anatomical Collection. Am. J. Phys. Anthropol. 127, 406–417.
Hunter, J.P., Guatelli-Steinberg, D., Weston, T.C., Durner, R., Betsinger, T.K., 2010. Model of tooth morphogenesis predicts Carabelli cusp expression, size, and symmetry in humans. PLoS One 5, e11844.
Huss-Ashmore, R., Goodman, A.H., Armelagos, G.J., 1982. Nutritional inference from paleopathology. Adv. Archaeol. Method Theory 5, 395–474.
Huxley, A.K., 2005. Gestational age discrepancies due to acquisition artifact in the forensic fetal osteology collection at the National Museum of Natural History, Smithsonian Institute Press, USA. Am. J. Forensic Med. Pathol. 26, 216–220.
Hylander, W., 1977. The adaptive significance of Eskimo craniofacial morphology. In: Dahlberg, A., Graber, T.M. (Eds.), Orofacial Growth and Development. Mouton, The Hague, pp. 129–169.
Hylander, W., Picq, P., Johnson, K., 1992. Bone strain and the supraorbital region in primates. In: Carlson, D., Goldstein, S. (Eds.), Bone Biodynamics in Orthodontic and Orthopaedic Treatment. Center for Human Growth and Development, Ann Arbor, MI, pp. 315–349.
Ingelmark, B.E., 1947. Uber das craniovertebrale Grenzgebiet beim Menschen. Acta Anat. S6, 5–113.
Ingervall, B., Thilander, B., 1974. Relations between facial morphology and activity of the masticatory muscles: an electromyographic and radiographic cephalometric investigation. J. Oral. Rehabil. 1, 131–147.
Inke, G., 1962. Quantitative anatomie der innenfläche des unterkiefers beim menschen und bei den simiae I,II. Gegenbaurs Morphol. Jahrb. 103, 303–331. 332–360.
Irish, J., 2010. The mean measure of divergence: its utility in model-free and model-bound analyses relative to the Mahalanobis D2 distance for nonmetric traits. Am. J. Hum. Biol. 22, 378–395.
Irish, J.D., 1997. Characteristic high- and low-frequency dental traits in sub-Saharan African populations. Am. J. Phys. Anthropol. 102, 455–467.
Irish, J.D., 1998a. Ancestral dental traits in recent Sub-Saharan Africans and the origins of modern humans. J. Hum. Evol. 34, 81–98.
Irish, J.D., 1998b. Dental morhpological indications of population discontinuity and Egyptian gene flow in post-Paleolithic Nubia. In: Lukas, J. R. (Ed.), Human Dental Development, Morphology, and Pathology: A Tribute to Albert A. Dahlberg. Department of Anthropology, University of Oregon, Eugene, OR, pp. 155–172.
Irish, J.D., Turner, C.G., 1990. West African dental affinity of late Pleistocene Nubian peopling of the Eurafrican-South Asian triangle. Homo 41, 42–53.
Irmak, M.K., Korkmaz, A., Erogul, O., 2004. Selective brain cooling seems to be a mechanism leading to human craniofacial diversity observed in different geographical regions. Med. Hypotheses 63, 974–979.
Irwin, J.A., Leney, M.D., Loreille, O., Barritt, S.M., Christensen, A.F., Holland, T.D., et al., 2007. Application of low copy number STR typing to the identification of aged, degraded skeletal remains. J. Forensic Sci. 52, 1322–1327.
Iscan, M.Y., 1983. Assessment of race from the pelvis. Am. J. Phys. Anthropol. 62, 205–208.
Işçan, M.Y., 1990. A comparison of techniques on the determination of race, sex, and stature from the Terry and Hamann–Todd Collections. In: Gill, G.W., Rhine, S. (Eds.), Skeletal Attribution of Race: Methods for Forensic Anthropology. Maxwell Museum of Anthropology, Albuquerque, NM, pp. 73–81.
Ishida, H., Dodo, Y., 1993. Nonmetric cranial variation and the population affinities of the Pacific peoples. Am. J. Phys. Anthropol. 90, 49–57.
Ishida, H., Dodo, Y., 1997. Cranial variation in prehistoric human skeletal remains from the Marianas. Am. J. Phys. Anthropol. 104, 399–410.
Ishida, H., Hanihara, T., Kondo, O., Fukumine, T., 2009. Craniometric divergence history of the Japanese populations. Anthropol. Sci. 117, 147–156.
Israel, H., 1978. The fundamentals of cranial and facial growth. In: Falkner, F., Tanner, J.M. (Eds.), Human GROWTH: POSTNATAL GROWTH. Plenum Press, New York, NY, pp. 357–380.
Jacobshagen, B., 1986. Size and shape of the orbital outline: a multivariate comparison and analysis of intraspecific variation in four hominid species. In: Else, J., Lee, P.C. (Eds.), Primate Evolution, Volume 1. Cambridge University Press, Cambridge, pp. 281–288.
Jacobson, A., 1990. Craniofacial growth studies and prediction in Orthodontics. Apes to Angels: Essays in Anthropology in Honor of Phillip V. Tobias. Wiley-Liss, New York, NY, pp. 261–268.
Jamison, P.L., Meier, R.J., Thompson-Jacob, D., 1989. Meaning of biodistances statistics: a test case using adult monozygotic twins. Am. J. Phys. Anthropol. 80, 485–492.
Jantz, R.L., 2001. Cranial change in Americans:1850–1975. J. Forensic Sci. 46, 784–787.
Jantz, R.L., Owsley, D.W., 1994. Growth and development in Arikara children. In: Jantz, R.L., Owsley, D.W. (Eds.), Skeletal Biology in the Great Plains: Migration, Warfare, Health, and Subsistence. Smithsonian Institute Press, Washington, DC, pp. 247–258.
Jantz, R.L., Hunt, D.R., Falsetti, A.B., Key, P.J., 1992. Variation among North Amerindians: analysis of Boas's anthropometric data. Hum. Biol. 64, 435–461.
Jernvall, J., Jung, H.-S., 2000. Genotype, phenotype, and developmental biology of molar tooth characters. Yearb. Phys. Anthropol. 43, 171–190.
Johnson, K., Paul, K., 2015. Bioarchaeology and kinship: integrating theory, social relatedness, and biology in ancient family research. J. Arch. Res. 24, 1–49.
Jorde, L.B., 1980. The genetic structure of subdivided human populations: a review. In: Mielke, J.H., Crawford, M.H. (Eds.), Current Developments in Anthropological Genetics, Volume 1: Theory and Methods. Plenum Press, New York, NY, pp. 135–208.
Jørgensen, K.D., 1956. The deciduous dentition: a descriptive and comparative anatomical study. Acta Odontol. Scand. 14 (suppl. 20), 1–120.
Kamnikar, K.R., Plemons, A.M., Hefner, J.T., 2017. Intraobserver error in macromorphoscopic trait data. J. Forensic Sci. 63 (2), 361–370.
Kellock, W.L., Parsons, P.A., 1970. Variation of minor non-metrical cranial variants in Australian aborigines. Am. J. Phys. Anthropol. 32, 409–421.
Kennedy, G.E., 1986. The relationship between exostoses and cold water: a latitudinal analysis. Am. J. Phys. Anthropol. 71, 401–415.
Kerckring, T., 1670. Spicilegium anatomicum continens osteogeniam foetuum. Amstelodami.

Keyes, J.E.L., 1935. Observations on four thousand optic foramina in human skulls of known origin. Arch. Ophthalmol. 13, 538–568.
Kieser, J.A., 1990. Human Adult Odontometrics: The Study of Variation in Adult Tooth Size. Cambridge University Press, Cambridge.
Klaus, H.D., Wilbur, A.K., Temple, D.H., Buikstra, J.E., Stone, A.C., Fernandez, M., et al., 2010. Tuberculosis on the north coast of Peru: skeletal and molecular paleopathology of late pre-Hispanic and postcontact mycobacterial disease. J. Arch. Sci. 37, 2587–2597.
Klepinger, L.L., 2006. Fundamentals of Forensic Anthropology. John Wiley & Sons Inc, Hoboken, NJ.
Knip, A.S., 1970. Metrical and non-metrical measurements on the skeletal remains of Christian populations from two sites in Sudanese Nubia. Proc. K. Ned. Akad. Wet. Hum. Biol. C 73, 433–468.
Knip, A.S., 1971. The frequencies of non-metrical variants in Tellem and Nokara skulls from the Mali Republic, I, II. Proc. K. Ned. Akad. Wet. Hum. Biol. C 74, 422–443.
Knudson, K.J., Stojanoski, C.M., 2008. New directions in bioarchaeology: recent contributions to the study of human social identities. J. Arch. Res. 16, 397–432.
Kodama, K., Inoue, K., Nagashima, M., Matsumura, G., Watanabe, S., Kodama, G., 1997. Studies on the foramen vesalius in the Japanese juvenile and adult skulls. Hokkaido Igaku Zasshi 72 (6), 667–674 [Article in Japanese].
Komar, D., 1996. Identifying racial affinities in skeletal remains: utilizing infracranial non-metric traits and the Rubison procedure to determine racial identity. Can. Soc. Forensic Sci. J. 29, 155–164.
Komar, D., 2005. A potential new morphological indicator of biological affinity in human skeletal remains. In: Poster Presented at the 2005 Meetings of the American Academy of Forensic Sciences, New Orleans.
Komar, D.A., Buikstra, J.E., 2008. Forensic Anthropology: Contemporary Theory and Practice. Oxford University Press, New York, NY.
Komar, D.A., Grivas, C., 2008. Manufactured populations: what do contemporary reference skeletal populations represent? A comparative study using the Maxwell Museum Documented Collection. Am. J. Phys. Anthropol. 137, 224–233.
Konigsberg, L., Blangero, J., 1993. Multivariate quantitative genetic simulations in anthropology with an example from the South Pacific. Hum. Biol. 65, 897–915.
Konigsberg, L., Kohn, L.A., Cheverud, J.M., 1993. Cranial deformation and nonmetric trait variation. Am. J. Phys. Anthropol. 90, 35–48.
Konigsberg, L.W., 2006. A post-Neumann history of biological and genetic distance studies in bioarchaeology. In: Buikstra, J.E., Beck, L.A. (Eds.), Bioarchaeology: The Contextual Analysis of Human Remains. Academic Press, Amsterdam, pp. 263–280.
Konigsberg, L.W., 1990a. Analysis of prehistoric biological variation under a model of isolation by geographic and temporal distance. Hum. Biol. 62, 49–70.
Konigsberg, L., 1990b. Temporal aspects of biological distance: serial correlation and trend in a prehistoric skeletal lineage. Am. J. Phys. Anthropol. 82, 45–52.
Konigsberg, L.W., Ousley, S.D., 1995. Multivariate quantitative genetics of anthropometric traits from the Boas data. Hum. Biol. 67, 481–498.
Königstein, L., 1896. Notizen zur Anatomie und Physiologie der Orbita. Deutschmanns Beitr Augenheilkd 25, 399–447.
Korey, K.A., 1980. The incidence of bilateral nonmetric skeletal traits: a reanalysis of sampling procedures. Am. J. Phys. Anthropol. 53, 19–23.
Kraus, B.S., 1951. Carabelli's anomaly of the maxillary molar teeth. Am. J. Hum. Genet. 3, 348–355.
Kraus, B.S., 1959. Occurrence of the Carabelli trait in Southwest ethnic groups. Am. J. Phys. Anthropol. 17, 117–123.
Krogman, W.M., 1927. Anthropological aspects of the human teeth and dentition. J. Dent. Res. 7, 1–108.
Krogman, W.M., 1962. The Human Skeleton in Forensic Medicine. Charles C Thomas, Springfield, IL.
Krovitz, G.E., Thompson, J.L., Nelson, A.J., 2003. Hominid growth and development from Australopithecines to Middle Pleistocene Homo. In: Thompson, J.L., Krovitz, G.E., Nelson, A.J. (Eds.), Growth and Development in the Genus Homo. Cambridge University Press, Cambridge, pp. 271–292.
Krzanowski, W., 2003. Non-parametric estimation of distance between groups. J. Appl. Stat. 30, 743–750.
Kuba, C.L., 2006. Nonmetric Traits and the Detection of Family Groups in Archaeological Remains. Department of Anthropology: Arizona State University, Phoenix, AZ, Unpublished dissertation.
Lahr, M.M., 1994. The multiregional model of modern human origins: a reassessment of its morphological basis. J. Hum. Evol. 26, 23–56.
Lahr, M.M., 1995. Patterns of modern human diversification: implications for Amerindian origins. Yearb. Phys. Anthropol. 38, 163–198.
Lane, R., 1977. The Allegany Seneca: A Test of the Genetic Reliability of Nonmetric Osteological Traits for Intrapopulation Analysis. Department of Anthropology. University of Texas, Austin, TX.
Lane, R.A., Sublett, A.J., 1972. Osteology of social organization: residence pattern. Am. Antiq. 37, 186–201.
Lanfear, R., Calcott, B., Ho, S.Y., Guindon, S., 2012. PartitionFinder: combined selection of partitioning schemes and substitution models for phylogenetic analyses. Mol. Biol. Evol. 29, 1695–1701.
Lang, J., 1985. VII. Orbita. In: Lang, J., Lanz, T., von Wachsmuth, W. (Eds.), Praktische Anatomie, Vol 1. Springer, Berlin, pp. 205–212.
Lang, J., Brückner, B., 1981. Über dicke und dünne Zonen des Neurocranium, Impressiones gyrorum und Foramina parietalia bei Kindern und Erwachsenen. Anat. Anz. 149, 11–50.
Lang, J., Hetterich, A., 1983. Beitrag zur postnatalen Entwicklung des Processus pterygoideus. Anat. Anz. 154, 1–31.
Láng-Bottyán, O., 1972. Changes in the palate owing to age. Advances in the Biology of Human Populations. Akadémiai Kiadó, Budapest, pp. 473–477.
Larsen, C.S., 1997. Bioarchaeology: Interpreting Behavior from the Human Skeleton. Cambridge University Press, Cambridge.
Larson, J.L., 1994. Interpreting Nature: The Science of Living Form from Linnaeus to Kant. Johns Hopkins University Press, Baltimore, MD.
Lasker, G.W., 1945. Observations on the teeth of Chinese born and reared in China and America. Am. J. Phys. Anthropol. 3, 129–150.
Lasker, G.W., 1950. Genetic analysis of racial traits of the teeth. Cold Spring Harbor Symposia on Quantitative Biology. Cold Spring Harbor Laboratory Press, Cold Spring Harbor, NY, pp. 191–203.
Lasker, G.W., Lee, M.M., 1957. Racial traits in the human teeth. J. Forensic Sci. 2, 401–419.
Lauc, T., 2003. Influence of inbreeding on the Carabelli Trait in a human isolate. Dent. Anthropol. 16, 65–72.
Laughlin, W.S., 1960. Aspects of current physical anthropology: method and theory. Southwest J. Anthropol. 16, 75–92.
Laughlin, W.S., 1963. Eskimos and Aleuts: their origins and evolution. Science 142, 633–645.
Laughlin, W.S., Jorgenson, J.B., 1956. Isolate variation in Greenlandic Eskimo crania. Acta Genet. Stat. Med. 6, 3–12.

Le Double, A.F., 1903a. Traite des variations des os du crane de l'homme. Vigot Freres, Paris.

Le Double, A.F., 1903b. Traité des variations des os du crane de l'homme et leur signification au point de vue de l'anthropologie zoologique. Vigot Frères, Paris.

Le Double, A.F., 1903c. Le canal cranio-pharyngien, hypophysaire ou pituitaire de l'homme. Bull. Mem. Soc. Anthropol. Paris 4, 82–99.

Le Double, A.F., 1912. Variations de la colonne vertebrate de l'homme. Vigot Freres, Paris.

Lenth, R.V., 2001. Some practical guidelines for effective sample size determination. Am. Stat. 55, 187–193.

Lestrel, P.E., Huggare, J.A., 1997. Cranial base changes in shunt-treated hydrocephalics: Fourier descriptor. In: Lestrel, P.E. (Ed.), Fourier Descriptors and their Applications in Biology. Cambridge University Press, Cambridge, MA, pp. 322–339.

Levine, P., 1945. Anti-Hr Sera. Nature 156, 418.

Lewis, M.E., 2007. The Bioarchaeology of Children: Perspectives from Biological and Forensic Anthropology. Cambridge University Press, Cambridge.

Lewis, M.E., Rutty, G.N., 2003. The endangered child: the personal identification of children in forensic anthropology. Sci. Justice 43, 201–209.

Lewis, W.H., 1920. The cartilaginous skull of a human embryo twenty-one millimeters in length. Contrib. Embryol. Carnegie Inst. 9, 299–324.

Lewontin, R.C., 1972. The apportionment of human diversity. Evol. Biol. 6, 381–398.

Libby, W.F., 1952. Radiocarbon Dating. University of Chicago Press, Chicago, IL.

Lieberman, D.E., 1996. How and why humans grow thin skulls: experimental evidence for systematic cortical robusticity. Am. J. Phys. Anthropol. 101, 217–236.

Lieberman, D.E., 2000. Ontogeny, homology and phylogeny in the hominid cranio- facial skeleton: the problem of the browridge. In: O'Higgins, Cohn M. (Ed.), Development, Growth and Evolution: Implications for the Study of Hominid Skeletal Evolution. Academic Press, London, pp. 85–112.

Lieberman, D.E., McBratney, B.M., Krovitz, G., 1999. The evolution and development of cranial form in Homo sapiens. Proc. Natl. Acad. Sci. U.S.A. 99, 1134–1139.

Lieberman, D.E., Krovitz, G.E., Yates, F.W., Devlin, M., St Clair, M., 2004. Effects of food processing on masticatory strain and craniofacial growth in a retrognathic face. J. Hum. Evol. 46, 655–677.

Lillie, R.D., 1917. Variations of the canalis hypoglossi. Anat. Rec. 13, 131–144.

Lovejoy, C.O., Meindl, R.S., Mensforth, R.P., Barton, T.J., 1985. Multifactorial determination of skeletal age at death: a method and blind tests of its accuracy. Am. J. Phys. Anthropol. 68, 1–14.

Madrigal, L., 2000. Statistics for Anthropology. Cambridge University Press, Cambridge.

Mahalanobis, P., 1948. Appendix 1. Historical note on the D2-statistic. Sankhya 9, 237–239.

Mahalanobis, P.C., 1936. On the generalized distance in statistics. Proc. Natl. Inst. Sci. India 2, 49–55.

Manzi, G., Vienna, A., 1997. Cranial non-metric traits as indicators of hypostosis or hyperostosis. Riv. Antropol. 75, 41–61.

Manzi, G., Vienna, A., Hauser, G., 1996. Developmental stress and cranial hypostosis by epigenetic trait occurrence and distribution: an exploratory study on the Italian Neandertals. J. Hum. Evol. 30, 511–527.

Manzi, G., Gracia, A., Arsuaga, J.L., 2000. Cranial discrete traits in the middle Pleistocene humans from Sima de los Huesos (Sierra de Atapuerca, Spain). Does hypostosis represent any increase in 'ontogenetic stress' along the Neandertal lineage? J. Hum. Evol. 38, 425–446.

Marks, J., 1995. Human Biodiversity: Genes, Race and History. Aldine De Gruyter, New York, NY.

Martin, R., 1914. Lehrbuch der Anthropologie in systematischer Darstellung mit besonderer Berücksichtigung der anthropologischen Methoden. Gustav Fischer, Jena.

Martinez-Abadias, N., Esparza, M., Sjøvold, T., González-José, R., Santos, M., Hernández, M., 2009. Heritability of human cranial dimensions: comparing the evolvability of different cranial traits and biological affinities of North African late Holocene populations. J. Anat. 214, 19–35.

Matthews, W., Wortman, J.L., Billings, J.S., 1893. Human bones of the Hemenway collection in the United States Army Medical Museium. Mem. Natl. Acad. Sci. 6, 141–186.

Mayhall, J.T., Saunders, S.R., Belier, P.L., 1982. The dental morphology of North American whites: a reappraisal. In: Kurten, B. (Ed.), Teeth: Form, Function and Evolution. Columbia University Press, New York, NY, pp. 245–258.

McBratney-Owens, B., Lieberman, D.E., 2003. Postnatal ontogeny of facial position in Homo sapiens and Pan troglodytes. In: Thompson, J.L., Krovitz, G.E., Nelson, A.J. (Eds.), Patterns of Growth and Development in the Genus Homo. Cambridge University Press, Cambridge, pp. 45–72.

McGee, R., Warms, R.L., 2012. Anthropological Theory: An Introductory History, fifth ed., McGraw-Hill, New York, NY.

McGrath, J.W., Cheverud, J.M., Buikstra, J.E., 1984. Genetic correlations between sides and heritability of asymmetry for nonmetric traits in Rhesus Macaques on Cayo Santiago. Am. J. Phys. Anthropol. 64, 401–411.

McLaurin, J.W., 1973. Trauma and infections of the external ear. In: Paparella, M.M., Shumrick, D.A. (Eds.), Otolaryngology, Vol 2: Ear. WB Saunders, Philadelphia, PA, pp. 24–32.

McNeill, R.W., Newton, G.N., 1965. Cranial base morphology in association with intentional cranial vault deformation. Am. J. Phys. Anthropol. 23, 241–254.

Meehl, P., 1986. Clinical Versus Statistical Prediction: A Theoretical Analysis and Review of the Literature. University of Minnesota Press, Minneapolis, MN.

Meier, A., 1949. A study of the racial ancestry of the Mississippi College Negro. Am. J. Phys. Anthropol. 7, 227–239.

Meindl, R.S., Russell, K.F., Lovejoy, C.O., 1990. Reliability of age at death in the Hamann–Todd Collection: validity of subselection procedures used in blind tests of the summary age technique. Am. J. Phys. Anthropol. 83, 349–357.

Mensforth, R.P., Latimer, B.M., 1989. Hamann–Todd Collection aging studies: osteoporosis fracture-syndrome. Am. J. Phys. Anthropol. 80, 461–479.

Merkel, F., 1871. Die Linea Nuchae Suprema. Engelman, Leipzig.

Meyerhoff, W.L., Caruso, V.G., 1991. Trauma and infections of the external ear. In: Paparella, M.M., Shumrick, D.A., Gluckman, J.L., Meyerhoff, W.L. (Eds.), Otolaryngology, thirrd ed WB Saunders, Philadelphia, PA, pp. 1227–1235.

Mizoguchi, Y., 1985. Shovelling: a statistical analysis of its morphology. University Museum, University of Tokyo, Bulletin 26.
Mizoguchi, Y., 1997. Human bones from Ikenohata-shichikencho relics. In: Ikenohata- shichikencho Iseki (Keianji-Ato). Taito-ku Ikenohata-shichikencho Chosakai, Tokyo, pp. 289–303. [In Japanese].
Mo, D., 2005. A Study of Juvenile Nasal Morphology Oriented Toward Ancestry Differentiation and Elucidation of Ontogenetic Patterns. Unpublished MSC Thesis. University of Toronto.
Molloy, H.P.L., Newfields, T., 2004. Some preliminary thoughts on statistics and background information on SPSS (Part 1). Shiken: JALT Test. Eval. SIG Newsl. 8, 2–5.
Molnar, S., 2002. Human Variation: Races, Types and Ethnic Groups, fifth ed., Prentice Hall, New Jersey.
Molto, J.E., 1983. Biological relationships of Southern Woodland Peoples: The Evidence of Discontinuous Cranial Morphology. National Museums of Canada, Archaeological Survey of Canada, Ottawa, ON, Paper No. 117.
Monsalve, M.V., Stone, A.C., Lewis, C.M., Rempel, A., Richards, M., Straathof, D., et al., 2002. Brief communication: molecular analysis of the Kwaday Dan Ts'finchi ancient remains found in a glacier in Canada. Am. J. Phys. Anthropol. 119, 288–291.
Montagu, A., 1966. A Handbook of Anthropometry. Charles C Thomas, Springfield, IL.
Montagu, A., 1974. Man's Most Dangerous Myth: The Fallacy of Race, fifth ed Oxford University Press, London.
Montagu, M.F.A., 1937. The medio-frontal suture and the problem of metopism in the primates. J. R. Anthropol. Inst. 67, 157–201.
Moore, K.L., 1992. Clinically Oriented Anatomy, third ed., Williams & Wilkins, Baltimore, MD.
Moore-Jansen, P.H., Ousley, S.D., Jantz, R.L., 1994. Data Collection Procedures for Forensic Skeletal Material. The University of Tennessee Forensic Anthropology Series, Knoxville, TN.
Moorrees, C.F.A., 1957. The Aleut Dentition. Harvard University Press, Cambridge.
Moorrees, C.F.A., Reed, R.B., 1954. Correlations among crown diameters of human teeth. Arch. Oral Biol. 9, 685–697.
Morant, G.M., 1923. A first study of the Tibetan Skull. Biometrika 14, 193–260.
Morant, G.M., 1924. A study of certain oriental series of crania including the Nepalese and Tibetan series in the British Museum (Natural History). Biometrika 16, 1–105.
Morant, G.M., 1925. A study of Egyptian craniology from Prehistoric to Roman times. Biometrika 17, 1–52.
Morild, I., Hamre, S.S., Huel, R., Parsons, T.J., 2015. Identification of missing norwegian World War II soldiers, in Karelia Russia. J. Forensic Sci. 60, 1104–1110.
Morimoto, N., Ogihara, N., Katayama, K., Shiota, K., 2008. Three-dimensional ontogenetic shape changes in the human cranium during the fetal period. J. Anat. 212, 627–635.
Morton, N., 1975. Kinship, information and biological distance. Theor. Popul. Biol. 7, 246–255.
Morton, R.J., Lord, W.D., 2002. Detection and recovery of abducted and murdered children: behavioral and taphonomic influences. In: Haglund, W.D., Sorg, M.H. (Eds.), Advances in Forensic Taphonomy: Method, Theory and Archaeological Perspectives. CRC Press, New York, NY, pp. 151–171.
Morton, R.J., Lord, W.D., 2006. Taphonomy of child-sized remains: a study of scattering and scavenging in Virginia, USA. J. Forensic Sci. 51, 475–479.
Morton, R.J., Lord, W.D., Goff, M., 1999. Taphonomic effects on child sized remains located in surface and shallow burial disposal sites. Proc AAFS. American Academy of Forensic Sciences, Colorado Springs, CO.
Morton, S.G., 1839. Crania Americana; or, a comparative view of the skulls of various aboriginal nations of North and South America: to which is prefixed an essay of the variaties of the human species. Philadelphia, PA.
Morton, S.G., 1844. Crania Aegyptica. John Penington, Philadelphia, PA.
Moss, M., 1956. The functional matrix concept and its relationship to temporomandibular joint dysfunction and treatment. Dent. Clin. N. Am. 27, 445–455.
Moss, M., 1964. Vertical growth of the human face. Am. J. Orthod. 50, 359–376.
Moss, M., 1968. The primacy of functional matrices on orofacial growth. Dent. Pract. 19, 65–73.
Moss, M., Salentijn, L., 1971. The logarithmic growth of the human mandible. Acta Anat. 77, 341–360.
Moss, M.L., 1958. The pathogenesis of artificial cranial deformation. Am. J. Phys. Anthropol. 16, 269–286.
Moss, M.L., 1973. A functional cranial analysis of primate craniofacial growth. In: Zingeser, M. (Ed.), Fourth International Congress of Primatologists, vol. 3. Karger, Basel, pp. 191–208.
Moss, M.L., 1978. Analysis of developmental processes possible related to human dental sexual dimorphism. In: Bulter, P.M., Joysey, K.A. (Eds.), Development, Function and Evolution of Teeth. Academic Press, London, pp. 135–144.
Mouri, T., 1976. A study of non-metrical cranial variants of the modern Japanese in the Kinki district. J. Anthropol. Soc. Nippon 84, 191–203.
Mouri, T., 1996. Nonmetric cranial variants in a medieval Japanese sample from the Ichikishima-jinja site. Anthropol. Sci. 104, 89–98.
Mullis, K.B., Faloona, F.A., 1987. Specific synthesis of DNA in vitro via a polymerase catalyzed chain reaction. Methods Enzymol. 155, 335–350.
Mundorff, A.Z., Bartelink, E.J., Mar-Cash, E., 2009. DNA preservation in skeletal elements from the World Trade Center disaster: recommendations for mass fatality management. J. Forensic Sci. 54, 739–745.
Nakajima, M., 2000. Morphological study on the Japanese skeletons of the Edo era (17–19th c.): a case study of skeletal anthropology for the Ikenohata-shichikencho site. Anthropol. Sci.: J. Anthropol. Soc. Nippon 108, 77.
Napoli, M.L., Birkby, W.H., 1990. Racial differences in the visibility of the oval window in the middle ear. In: Gill, G.W., Rhine, S. (Eds.), Skeletal Attribution of Race. Maxwell Museum of Anthropology: Anthropological Papers No. 4. Maxwell Museum of Anthropology, New Mexico, pp. 27–32.
Nei, M., Roychoudhury, A.K., 1993. Evolution in relationships of human populations on a global scale. Mol. Biol. Evol. 10, 927–943.
Nelson, C.T., 1938. The teeth of the Indians of Pecos Pueblo. Am. J. Phys. Anthropol. 23, 261–293.
Nethery, K., 2004. Non-Familial Abductions that End in Homicide: An Analysis of the Distance Patterns and Disposal Sites. Unpublished Masters of Arts Thesis for the School of Criminology, Simon Fraser University.
Neumann, G.K., 1942. Types of artificial cranial deformation in the eastern United States. Am. Antiq. 7, 306–310.

Neumann, G.K., 1951. The Hopewellian culture in the lower Wabash valley. Ill. State Archaeol. Soc. J. 1, 113–118.

Neumann, G.K., 1952. Archaeology and race in the American Indian. In: Griffen, J.B. (Ed.), Archeology of the Eastern United States. University of Chicago Press, Chicago, IL, pp. 13–34.

Newman, M.T., 1953. The application of ecological rules to the racial anthropology of the aboriginal New World. Am. Anthropol. 55, 311–327.

Nicholson, E., Havarti, K., 2006. Quantitative analysis of human mandibular shape using three-dimensional geometric morphometrics. Am. J. Phys. Anthropol. 131, 368–383.

Nikita, E., Mattingly, D., Lahr, M.M., 2012. Sahara: barrier or corridor? Nonmetric cranial traits and biological affinities of North African late Holocene populations. Am. J. Phys. Anthropol. 147, 280–292.

Oetteking, B., 1919. The processus frontosphenoidalis of the zygoma and its bearing on the configuration of the orbit. Anat. Rec. 17, 24–41.

Oetteking, B., 1924a. The Santa Barbara Crania. Museum of the American Indian, Heye Foundation, New York, NY.

Oetteking, B., 1924b. Declination of the Pars Basilaris in Normal and in Artificially Deformed Skulls. No. 25-27. Museum of the American Indian. Heye Foundation, New York, NY.

Oetteking, B., Hantzsch, B., 1908. Ein Beitrag zur Kraniologie der Eskimo. Teubner.

Oetteking, B., Davis, E.H., Heye, G.G., Teggart, F.J., 1921. Morphological and Metrical Variation in Skulls from San Miguel Island, California: I. The Sutura Nasofrontalis. Museum of the American Indian, Heye Foundation, New York, NY.

O'Higgins, P., Jones, N., 1998. Facial growth in *Cercocebus torquatus*: an application of three dimensional geometric morphometric techniques to the study of morphological variation. J. Anat. 193, 251–272.

O'Higgins, P., Strand Vidarsdottir, U., 1999. New approaches to the quantitative analysis of craniofacial growth and variation. In: Hoppa, R. D., Fitzgerald, C.M. (Eds.), Human Growth in the Past: Studies from Bones and Teeth. Cambridge University Press, Cambridge, pp. 128–160.

O'Higgins, P., Chadfield, P., Jones, N., 2001. Facial growth and the ontogeny of morphological variation within and between *Cebus paella* and *Cercocebus torquatus*. J. Zool. 254, 337–357.

Okumura, M.M.M., Boyadjian, C.H.C., Eggers, S., 2007. Auditory exostoses as an aquatic activity marker: a comparison of coastal and inland skeletal remains from tropical and subtropical regions of Brazil. Am. J. Phys. Anthropol. 132, 558–567.

Ortner, D.J., 2003. Identification of Pathological Conditions in Human Skeletal Remains, second ed., Academic Press, London.

Ossenberg, N.S., 1969. Discontinuous morphological variation in the human cranium. Department of Anthropology: University of Toronto, Toronto, Canada.

Ossenberg, N.S., 1970. The influence of artificial cranial deformation on discontinuous morphological traits. Am. J. Phys. Anthropol. 33, 357–371.

Ossenberg, N.S., 1976. Within and between race distances in population studies based on discrete traits of the human skull. Am. J. Phys. Anthropol. 45, 701–709.

Ossenberg, N.S., 1981. An argument for the use of total side frequencies of bilateral nonmetric skeletal traits in population distance analysis: the regression of symmetry on incidence. Am. J. Phys. Anthropol. 54, 471–479.

Ossenberg, N.S., 1986. Isolate conservatism and hybridization in the population history of Japan: the evidence of nonmetric cranial traits. In: Akazawa, T., Aikens, C.M. (Eds.), Prehistoric Hunter-Gatherers in Japan. Tokyo University Press, Tokyo, pp. 199–215.

Ossenberg, N.S., 1987. Retromolar foramen of the human mandible. Am. J. Phys. Anthropol. 73, 119–128.

Ossenberg, N.S., 2013. Cranial Nonmetric Trait Database. Nancy S. Ossenberg (producer). Queen's University Library, Data and Government Information Centre (distributor), Kingston, Ontario.

Ossenberg, N.S., Dodo, Y., Maeda, T., Kawakubo, Y., 2006. Ethnogenesis and craniofacial change in Japan from the perspective of nonmetric traits. Anthropol. Sci. 114, 99–115.

Oudhof, H.A.J., 1982. Sutural growth. Cells Tissues Organs 112, 58–68.

Ousley, S., Jantz, R.L., Fried, D., 2009. Understanding race and human variation: why forensic anthropologists are good at identifying race. Am. J. Phys. Anthropol. 139, 68–76.

Ousley, S.D., Hefner, J.T., 2005. The statistical determination of ancestry. In: Proc AAFS. Seattle, WA.

Ousley, S.D., Jantz, R.L., 1998. The forensic data bank: documenting skeletal trends in the United States. In: Reichs, K.J. (Ed.), Forensic osteology: Advances in the Identification of Human Remains. Charles C Thomas, Springfield, IL, pp. 441–458.

Overholser, M.D., Alexander, W.F., Trotter, M., 1956. Can Missouri continue the teaching of human anatomy effectively? Mod. Med. 53, 474–476.

Owen, R., 1845. Odontography, Or, a Treatise on the Comparative Anatomy of the Teeth, Their Physiological Relations, Mode of Developement, and Microscipic Structure, in the Vertebrate Animals: Text. Bailliere.

Owsley, D.W., Bennett, S.M., Jantz, R.L., 1982. Intercemetery morphological variation in Arikara crania from the mobridge site. Am. J. Phys. Anthropol. 58, 179–185.

Pääbo, S., 1985a. Molecular cloning of ancient Egyptian mummy DNA. Nature 314, 644–645.

Pääbo, S., 1985b. Preservation of DNA in ancient Egyptian mummies. J. Arch. Sci. 12, 411–417.

Pääbo, S., 1986. Molecular genetic investigations of ancient human remains. Cold Spring Harbor Symposia on Quantitative Biology. Cold Spring Harbor Laboratory Press, Cold Spring Harbor, NY, pp. 441–446.

Pallant, J., 2007. SPSS Survival Manual, third ed., McGraw-Hill, New York, NY.

Parra, E., Marcini, A., Akey, J., Martinson, J., Batzer, M.A., Cooper, R., et al., 1998. Estimating African-American admixture proportions by use of population-specific alleles. Am. J. Hum. Genet. 63, 1839–1851.

Parra, E., Kittles, R., Argyropoulos, G., Pfaff, C., Heister, K., Bonilla, C., et al., 2001. Ancestral proportions and admixture dynamics in geographically defined African Americans living in South Carolina. Am. J. Phys. Anthropol. 114, 18–29.

Paschetta, C., de Azevedo, S., Castillo, L., Martínez-Abadías, N., Hernandez, M., Lieberman, D., et al., 2010. The influence of masticatory loading on craniofacial morphology: a test case across technological transitions in the Ohio Valley. Am. J. Phys. Anthropol. 141, 297–314.

Paul, K.S., Stojanowski, C.M., Butler, M.M., 2013. Biological and spatial structure of an Early Classic Period cemetery at Charco Redondo, Oaxaca. Am. J. Phys. Anthropol. 152, 217–229.

Pearson, K., 1926. On the coefficient of racial likeness. Biometrika 18, 105–117.
Peat, J., 2001. Health Science Research: A Handbook of Quantitative Methods. Allen & Unwin, Sydney, NSW.
Penrose, L.S., 1952. Distance, size, and shape. Ann. Eugen. 18, 337–343.
Pensa, A., 1907. Osservazioni sulla "spina supra meatum". Bollettino della Societa' Medico-Chirurgica di Pavia.
Perino, G., 1962. Excavation of the Klunk and Koster mounds. Plains Anthropol. 7, 86–88.
Persson, M., 1995. The role of sutures in normal and abnormal craniofacial growth. Acta Odontol. Scand. 53, 152–161.
Petersen, H., 2000. On statistical methods for comparison of intrasample morphometric variability: Zalavar revisited. Am. J. Phys. Anthropol. 113, 79–84.
Petersen, H., 2007. Mahalanobis distance, missing values, and the end of the Mesolithic. Am. J. Phys. Anthropol. S44, 188.
Pietrusewsky, M., Chang, C., 2003. Taiwan aboriginals and peoples of the Pacific-Asia region: multivariate craniometric comparisons. Anthropol. Sci. 111, 293–332.
Pilloud, M.A., Hillson, S., 2012. Brief communication: the use of alternative dental measurements on deciduous teeth. Am. J. Phys. Anthropol. 149, 299–306.
Pilloud, M.A., Larsen, C.S., 2011. "Official" and "Practical" kin: inferring social community structure from dental phenotype at Neolithic Çatalhöyük, Turkey. Am. J. Phys. Anthropol. 145, 519–530.
Pink, C.M., 2013. Striking Out and Digging. A Bioarchaeological Perspective on the Impacts of the Wari Expansion on Populations in the Peruvian Central Highlands. Department of Anthropology. University of Tennessee, Knoxville, TN.
Prahl-Andersen, B., Ligthelm-Bakker, A.S.W.M.R., Wattel, E., Nanda, R., 1995. Adolescent growth changes in soft tissue profile. Am. J. Orthod. Dentofacial Orthop. 107, 476–483.
Raab, D.M., Smith, E.L., Crenshaw, T.D., Thomas, D.P., 1990. Bone mechanical properties after exercise training in young and old rats. J. Appl. Physiol. 68, 130–134.
Raff, J., Tackney, J., O'Rourke, D.H., 2010. South from Alaska: a pilot aDNA study of genetic history on the Alaska Peninsula and the Eastern Aleutians. Hum. Biol. 82, 677–693.
Raghavan, M., DeGiorgio, M., Albrechtsen, A., Moltke, I., Skoglund, P., Korneliussen, T.S., et al., 2014. The genetic prehistory of the New World Arctic. Science 345, 1255832.
Ranly, D., 1980. A Synopsis of Facial Growth. Appleton & Lange, Norwalk, CT.
Rao, C.R., 1948. The utilization of multiple measurements in problems of biological classification. J. R. Stat. Soc. Ser. B (Methodol.) 10, 159–203.
Rao, C.R., 1989. Statistics and Truth: Putting Chance to Work, second ed., World Scientific, London.
Reid, C., Van Reenan, J.F., Groeneveld, H.T., 1991. Tooth size and the Carabelli trait. Am. J. Phys. Anthropol. 84, 427–432.
Relethford, J.H., 1994. Craniometric variation among modern human populations. Am. J. Phys. Anthropol. 95, 53–62.
Relethford, J.H., 2001. Global analysis of regional differences in craniometric diversity and population substructure. Hum. Biol. 73 (5), 629–636.
Relethford, J.H., 2002. Apportionment of global human genetic diversity based on craniometrics and skin color. Am. J. Phys. Anthropol. 118, 393–398.
Relethford, J.H., 2008. Geostatistics and spatial analysis in Biological Anthropology. Am. J. Phys. Anthropol. 136, 1–10.
Relethford, J.H., 2009. Race and global patterns of phenotypic variation. Am. J. Phys. Anthropol. 139, 16–22.
Relethford, J.H., 2010. Population-specific deviations of global human craniometric variation from a neutral model. Am. J. Phys. Anthropol. 142, 105–111.
Relethford, J.H., Blangero, J., 1990. Detection of differential gene flow from patterns of quantitative variation. Hum. Biol. 62, 5–25.
Relethford, J.H., Harpending, H.C., 1994. Craniometric variation, genetic theory, and modern human origins. Am. J. Phys. Anthropol. 95, 249–270.
Relethford, J.H., Lees, F., 1982. The use of quantitative traits in the study of human population structure. Yearb. Phys. Anthropol. 25, 113–132.
Relethford, J.H., Crawford, M., Blangero, J., 1997. Genetic drift and gene flow in post-famine Ireland. Hum. Biol. 69, 443–465.
Ricci, F., Fornai, C., Tiesler Blos, V., Rickards, O., Di Lernis, S., Manzi, G., 2010. Evidence of artificial cranial deformation from the later prehistory of the Acacus Mts. (Southwestern Libya, Central Sahara). Int. J. Osteoarch. 18, 372–391.
Richards, M.B., Sykes, B.C., Hedges, R.E., 1995. Authenticating DNA extracted from ancient skeletal remains. J. Arch. Sci. 22, 291–299.
Richtsmeier, J.T., McGrath, J.W., 1986. Quantitative genetics of cranial nonmetric traits in random bred mice: heritability and etiology. Am. J. Phys. Anthropol. 69, 51–58.
Richtsmeier, J.T., Cheverud, J.M., Buikstra, J.E., 1984. The relationship between cranial metric and nonmetric traits in the rhesus macaques from Cayo Santiago. Am. J. Phys. Anthropol. 64, 213–222.
Ridley, R., 2002. Sex Estimation of Fetal and Infant Remains Based on Metric and Morphognostic Analyses. Unpublished Master of Arts Thesis.
Rightmire, G., 1976. Metric versus discrete traits in African skulls. In: Giles, E., Friedländer, J. (Eds.), The Measures of Man. Peabody Museum Press, Cambridge, pp. 209–220.
Rightmire, G.P., 1972. Cranial measurements and discrete traits compared in distance studies of African Negro skulls. Hum. Biol. 44, 263–276.
Rogers, A.R., Harpending, H.C., 1986. Migration and genetic drift in human populations. Evolution 40, 1312–1327.
Rogers, T.L., 1999. The Attribution of Ancestry for European and Indian (South Asian) Individuals Within a Forensic Context. Unpublished Doctoral Thesis.
Rogers, T.L., 2005. Determining the sex of human remains through cranial morphology. J. Forensic Sci. 50, 1–8.
Romanes, G.J., 1972. Cunningham's Textbook of Anatomy, 11th ed Oxford University Press, London.
Rose, J.C., 1977. Defective enamel histology of prehistoric teeth form Illinois. Am. J. Phys. Anthropol. 46, 439–446.
Rose, J.C., Goodman, A.H., Lallo, J.W., 1978. Histological enamel indicator of childhood stress in prehistoric skeletal samples. Am. J. Phys. Anthropol. 49, 511–516.

Rose, J.C., Condon, K.W., Goodman, A.H., 1985. Diet and dentition: developmental disturbances. In: Gilbert Jr., R.J., Mielke, J.H. (Eds.), The Analysis of Prehistoric Diets. Academic Press, New York, NY, pp. 281–338.

Roseman, C.C., Weaver, T.D., 2004. Multivariate apportionment of global human craniometric diversity. Am. J. Phys. Anthropol. 125, 257–263.

Rösing, F.W., 1982. Discreta des menschlichen Skeletts–ein kritischer Überblick. Homo 33, 100–130.

Rösing, F.W., 1984. Discreta of the Human Skeleton: a critical review. J. Hum. Evol. 13, 319–323.

Rsing, F.W., 1986. Kith or kin? on the feasability of kinship reconstructions in skeletons. In: David, R.A. (Ed.), Science in Egyptology. Manchester University Press, Manchester, pp. 223–237.

Rossmo, K., 2000. Geographic Profiling. CRC Press, Boca Raton, FL.

Rothhammer, F., Silva, C., 1990. Craniometrical variation among South American prehistoric populations: climatic, altitudinal, chronological and geographic contributions. Am. J. Phys. Anthropol. 82, 9–17.

Ruiz-Linares, A., Mich, E., Meyer, D., Cavalli-Sforza, L.L., 1995. Analysis of classical and DNA markers for reconstructing human population history. In: Brenner, S., Hanihara, K. (Eds.), The Origin and Past of Modern Humans as Viewed by DNA. World Scientific, Singapore, pp. 123–148.

Russell, F., 1900. Studies in cranial variation. Am. Nat. 34, 737–745.

Saiki, R.K., Gelfand, D.H., Stoffel, S., Scharf, S.J., Higuchi, R., Horn, G.T., et al., 1988. Primer-directed enzymatic amplification of DNA with a thermostable DNA polymerase. Science 239, 487–491.

Saller, K., 1957. KraniometrischeTechnik. In: Martin, R., Saller, K. (Eds.), Lehrbuch der Anthropologie, Vol 1. Fischer, Stuttgart, pp. 429–518.

Saller, K., 1959. Orbita. In: Martin, R., Saller, K. (Eds.), Lehrbuch der Anthropologie, Vol 2. Fischer, Stuttgart, pp. 1423–1436.

Sampson, H.W., Montgomery, J.L., Henryson, G.L., 1991. Atlas of the Human Skull. Texas A&M University Press, College Station, TX.

Sanghvi, L., Balakrishnan, V., 1972. Comparison of different measures of genetic distance between human populations. In: Weiner, J.S., Huizinga, J. (Eds.), The Assessment of Population Affinities in Man. Oxford University Press, London, pp. 25–36.

Sanghvi, L.D., 1953. Comparison of genetical and morphological methods for a study of biological differences. Am. J. Phys. Anthropol. 11, 385–404.

Santos, A.L., 1995. Death, sex, and nutrition: analysis of the cause of death in the Coimbra human skeletal collection. Antropol. Port. 13, 81–91.

Santos, A.L., 1999. TB files: new hospital data (1910–1936) on the Coimbra identified skeletal collection. In: Palfi, G., Dutour, O., Deak, J., Hutas, I. (Eds.), Tuberculosis: Past and Present. TB Foundation and Golden Book Publishers, Budapest–Szeged, pp. 127–134.

Santos, A.L., Roberts, C.A., 2001. A picture of Tuberculosis in young Portuguese people in the early 20$^{th}$ century: a multidisciplinary study of the skeletal and historical evidence. Am. J. Phys. Anthropol. 115, 38–49.

Sardi, M.L., Ramírez-Rozzi, F.V., 2005. A cross-sectional study of human craniofacial growth. Ann. Hum. Biol. 32, 390–396.

Sardi, M.L., Novellino, P.S., Pucciarelli, H.M., 2006. Craniofacial morphology in the Argentine Center-West: consequences of the transition to food production. Am. J. Phys. Anthropol. 130, 333--343.

Sarnat, B.G., 1970. The imprint method to determine orbital volume in the rabbit. Ophthalmologica 160, 142–151.

Sarnat, B.G., 1981. The orbit and eye: experiments on volume in young and adult rabbits. Acta Ophthalmol. 59, 12–16.

Saternus, K.S., Kernbach-Wighton, G., Koebke, J., 2008. The mobile condylus tertius occipitalis and fractures of the hypochordal clasp. Anthropol. Anz. 66, 155–165.

Sauer, N.J., 1992. Forensic anthropology and the concept of race: if races don't exist, why are forensic anthropologists so good at identifying them? Soc. Sci. Med. 34, 107–111.

Saunders, S.R., 1978. The Developmental and Distribution of Discontinuous Morphological Variation of the Human Infracranial Skeleton. National Museum of Canada, Archaeological Survey of Canada, Ottawa, ON, Paper No. 81.

Saunders, S.R., 1989. Nonmetric skeletal variation. In: Isçan, M.Y., Kennedy, K.A.R. (Eds.), Reconstruction of Life from the Skeleton. Wiley-Liss, New York, NY, pp. 95–108.

Saunders, S.R., 2000. Subadult skeletons and growth-related studies. In: Katzenberg, M.A., Saunders, S.R. (Eds.), Biological Anthropology of the Human Skeleton. Wiley-Liss, New York, NY, pp. 135–161.

Saunders, S.R., 2008. Juvenile skeletons and growth-related studies. In: Katzenberg, M.A., Saunders, S.R. (Eds.), Biological Anthropology of the Human Skeleton, 2nd ed Wiley-Liss, New York, NY, pp. 117–147.

Saunders, S.R., Barrans, L., 1999. What can be done about the infant category in skeletal samples? In: Hoppa, R.D., Fitzgerald, C.M. (Eds.), Human Growth in the Past: Studies from Bones and Teeth. Cambridge University Press, Cambridge, pp. 183–209.

Saunders, S.R., Rainey, D.L., 2008. In: Katzenberg, M.A., Saunders, S.R. (Eds.), Nonmetric Trait Variation in the Skeleton: Abnormalities, Anomalies, and Atavisms. John Wiley & Sons, Inc, Hoboken, NJ, pp. 533–559.

Sauvageau, A., Racette, S., 2008. Child and adolescent victims in forensic autopsy: a 5-year retrospective study. J. Forensic Sci. 53, 699–702.

Scarcini, C., Rossi, V., Messerini, P., 1980. Caratteri cranici discontinui in Sardi di Nuoro. Semin. Sci. Antropol. 2, 1–127.

Schejtman, R., Devoto, F.C.H., Arias, N.H., 1967. The origin and distribution of the elements of the human mandibular retromolar canal. Arch. Oral Biol. 12, 1261–1267.

Scheuer, L., Black, S., 2007. Osteology. In: Thompson, T., Black, S. (Eds.), Forensic Human Identification: An Introduction. CRC Press, New York, NY.

Schillaci, M.A., Irish, J.D., Wood, C.C., 2009. Further analysis of the population history of ancient Egyptians. Am. J. Phys. Anthropol. 139, 235–243.

Schiulli, P.W., Gramly, R.M., 1989. Analysis of the Ft. Laurens, Ohio, skeletal sample. Am. J. Phys. Anthropol. 80, 11–24.

Schultz, A.H., 1919a. Der Canalis cranio-pharyngeus persistensbeim Mensch und bei den Affen. Gegenbaurs Morphologisches Jahrbuch Leipzig 50, 417–426.

Schultz, A., 1919b. The development of the external nose in Whites and Negros. Contrib. Embryol. 34, 173–190.

Schultz, A.H., 1920. The development of the external nose in whites and negroes. Contrib. Embryol. 34, 175–190.

Schultz, A.H., 1940. The size of the orbit and of the eye in primates. Am. J. Phys. Anthropol. 26, 389–408.

Schwalbe, G., 1902. Der Schädel von Egisheim. Beiträge zur Anthropologie Elsaß-Lothringens 3. K. J. Trübner, Strassburg.

Schwartz, J.H., 1995. Skeleton Keys: An Introduction to Human Skeletal Morphology, Development and Analysis. Oxford Press, New York, NY.
Scott, G.R., Turner II, C.G., 1997. The Anthropology of Modern Human Teeth: Dental Morphology and Its Variation in Recent Human Populations. Cambridge University Press, Cambridge.
Scott, G.R., Halffman, C.M., Pedersen, P.O., 1991. Dental Conditions of Medieval Norsemen in the North Atlantic. Acta Archaeol. 62, 183–207.
Seldin, M.F., Morii, T., Collins-Schramm, H.E., Chima, B., Kittles, R., Criswell, L., et al., 2004. Putative ancestral origins of chromosomal segments in individual African Americans: implications for admixture mapping. Gen. Res. 14, 1076–1084.
Self, S.G., Leamy, L., 1978. Heritability of quasi-continuous skeletal traits in a randombred population of house mice. Genet 88, 109–120.
Selmer-Olsen, R., 1949. An odontological study of the Norwegian Lapps. Skrift Norske Vidensk-Akademi 3, 1–167.
Seltzer, C.C., 1937. A critique of the coefficient of racial likeness. Am. J. Phys. Anthropol. 23, 101–109.
Seselj, M., 2007. Geographic variatin in orbital shape in modern human populations. Am. J. Phys. Anthropol. 132, 215.
Shea, B.T., 1983. Allometry and heterochrony in the African apes. Am. J. Phys. Anthropol. 62, 275–289.
Shea, B.T., 1986. Ontogenetic approaches to sexual dimorphism in the anthropoids. Hum. Evol. 1, 97–100.
Shearer, M.H., 1989. Maternity patients' movement in the United States, 1820–1985. In: Chalmer, I., Enkin, M. (Eds.), Effective Care in Pregnancy and Childbirth. Oxford University Press, Oxford.
Sherwood, R.J., Meindl, R.S., Robinson, H.B., May, R.L., 2000. Fetal age: methods of estimation and effects of pathology. Am. J. Phys. Anthropol. 113, 305–315.
Shigematsu, M., Ishida, H., Goto, M., Hanihara, T., 2004. Morphological affinities between Jomon and Ainu: reassessment based on nonmetric traits. Anthropol. Sci. 112, 161–172.
Shinoda, K., Matzumura, H., Nishimoto, T., 1998. Genetical and morphological analysis on kinship of the Nakazuma Jomon people using mitochondrial DNA and tooth crown measurements. Zoo-archaeology 11, 1–21.
Shinohara, A.L., de Souza Melo, C.G., Silveira, E.M.V., Lauris, J.R.P., Andreo, J.C., de Castro Rodrigues, A., 2010. Incidence, morphology and morphometry of the foramen of Vesalius: complementary study for a safer planning and execution of the trigeminal rhizotomy technique. Surg. Radiol. Anat. 32, 159–164.
Silau, A.M., Nijo, B., Solow, B., Kjaer, I., 1994. Prenatal sagittal growth of the osseous components of the human palate. J. Cran. Genet. Dev. Biol. 14, 252–256.
Sillman, J.H., 1964. Dimensional changes of the dental arches: longitudinal study from birth to 25 years. Am. J. Orthodont. 39, 729–755.
Simms, D.L., Neely, J.G., 1989. Growth of the lateral surface of the temporal bone in children. Laryngoscope 99, 795–799.
Simms, T.M., Gracia, C., Mirabal, S., McCartney, Q., Herrera, R.J., 2008. The genetic legacy of the Transatlantic Slave Trade in the island of New Providence. Forensic Sci. Int.: Genet. 2, 310–317.
Simon, S., 2006. Statistical Evidence in Medical Trials: Mountain or Molehill, What Do the Data Really Tell Us? Oxford University Press, Oxford.
Sjøvold, T., 1973. The occurrence of minor non-metrical variants in the skeleton and their quantitative treatment for population comparisons. Homo 24, 204–233.
Sjøvold, T., 1977. Non-metrical divergence between skeletal populations: the theoretical foundation and biological importance of CAB Smith's mean measure of divergences. Ossa 4, 1–133.
Sjøvold, T., 1984. A report on the heritability of some cranial measurements and non-metric traits. In: Van Vark, G.N., Howells, W.W. (Eds.), Multivariate Statistical Methods in Physical Anthropology. D. Reidel Publishing Company, Boston, pp. 223–246.
Skrzat, J., Holiat, D., Walocha, J., 2003. A morphometrical study of the human palatine sutures. Folia Morphol. 62, 123–127.
Smith, C., 1972. Coefficients of biological distance. Ann. Hum. Genet. 36, 241–245.
Soafer, J.A., Smith, P., Kaye, E., 1986. Affinities between contemporary and skeletal Jewish and non-Jewish groups based on tooth morphology. Am. J. Phys. Anthropol. 70, 265–275.
Souza, P.D., Houghton, P., 1977. The mean measure of divergence and the use of non-metric data in the estimation of biological distances. J. Arch. Sci. 4, 163–169.
SPSS®. 2008. SPSS® Statistics Gradpack For Mac 17.0. Chicago, IL.
Stanton, W., 1960. The Leopard's Spots: Scientifie Attitudes Towards Race in American, 1815–59. University of Chicago Press, Chicago, IL.
Steegman, A.T., 1975. Human adaptations to cold. In: Damon, A. (Ed.), Physiological Anthropology. Oxford University Press, New York, NY, pp. 130–166.
Steele, D.G., Bramblett, C.A., 1988. The Anatomy and Biology of the Human Skeleton. Texas A&M University, College Station, Texas.
Steidel, S.E., 2006. An Issue Perspective. Missing and AbductedChildren: A Law- Enforcement Guide to Case Investigation and Program Management, third ed National Center for Missing and Exploited Children, Virginia.
Steinberg, M.E., Trueta, J., 1981. Effects of activity on bone growth and development of the rat. Clin. Orthop. Relat. Res. 156, 52–60.
Stewart, T.D., 1979. Essentials of Forensic Anthropology. Charles C Thomas, Springfield, IL.
Stewart, T.D., Kerley, E.R., 1979. Essentials of Forensic Anthropology: Especially as Developed in the United States. Charles C Thomas, Springfield, IL.
St. Hoyme, L.E., Iscan, M.Y., 1989. Determination of sex and race: accuracy and assumptions. In: Iscan, M.Y., Kennedy, K.A.R. (Eds.), Reconstruction of Life From the Skeleton. Alan R. Liss Inc, New York, NY, pp. 53–93.
Stojanowski, C., 2003. Matrix decomposition model for investigating prehistoric intracemetery biological variation. Am. J. Phys. Anthropol. 122, 216–231.
Stojanowski, C.M., Euber, J.K., 2011. Technical note: comparability of Hrdlička's catalog of crania data based on measurement landmark definitions. Am. J. Phys. Anthropol. 146, 143–149.
Stojanowski, C.M., Schillaci, M.A., 2006. Phenotypic approaches for understanding patterns of intracemetery biological variation. Yearb. Phys. Anthropol. 49, 49–88.
Stone, A.C., Stoneking, M., 1996. Genetic analyses of an 8000 yearold Native American skeleton. Ancient Biomol. 1, 83–87.

Stone, A.C., Stoneking, M., 1998. mtDNA analysis of a prehistoric Oneota population: implications for the peopling of the New World. Am. J. Hum. Genet. 62, 1153–1170.

Stone, A.C., Stoneking, M., 1999. Analysis of ancient DNA from a prehistoric Amerindian cemetery. Philos. T. R. Soc. B. 354, 153–159.

Stone, A.C., Wilbur, A.K., Buikstra, J.E., Roberts, C.A., 2009. Tuberculosis and leprosy in perspective. Yearb. Phys. Anthropol. 140, 66–94.

Stoneking, M., 1993. DNA and recent human evolution. Evol. Anthropol. 2, 60–73.

Stoneking, M., 1995. Ancient DNA: how do you know when you have it and what can you do with it? Am. J. Hum. Genet. 57, 1259–1262.

Strand Vidarsdottir, U.S., O'Higgins, P., 2003. Developmental variation in the facial skeleton of anatomically modern Homo sapiens. In: Thompson, J.L., Krovitz, G.E., Nelson, A.J. (Eds.), Patterns of Growth and Development in the Genus Homo. Cambridge University Press, Cambridge, pp. 114–143.

Strand Vidarsdottir, U.S., O'Higgins, P., Stringer, C., 2002. A geometric morphometric study of regional differences in the ontogeny of the modern human facial skeleton. J. Anat. 202, 211–229.

Stringer, C.B., Andrews, P., 1988. Genetic and fossil evidence for the origin of modern humans. Science 239, 1263–1268.

Stringer, C.B., Humphrey, L.T., Compton, T., 1997. Cladistic analysis of dental traits in recent humans using a fossil outgroup. J. Hum. Evol. 32, 389–402.

Stringer, C.B., Dean, M.C., Humphrey, L.T., 1999. Regional variation in human mandibular morphology. Am. J. Phys. Anthropol. 28 (Suppl), 260.

Stull, K.E., Kenyhercz, M.W., L'Abbé, E.N., 2014. Ancestry estimation in South Africa using craniometrics and geometric morphometrics. Forensic Sci. Int. 245, 206e1.

Suazo, G.I.C., Zavando, M.D.A., Smith, R.L., 2009. Is the conduct of Serres an anatomical variation in adults? Int. J. Morphol. 27, 43–47.

Sullivan, L.R., 1917. Growth of the nasal bridge in children. Am. Anthropol. 19, 406–409.

Sullivan, P.G., 1978. Skull, jaw and teeth growth patterns. In: Falkner, F., Tanner, J.M. (Eds.), Human Growth: Postnatal Growth. Plenum Press, New York, NY, pp. 381–412.

Sutter, R., Mertz, L., 2004. Nonmetric cranial trait variation and prehistoric biocultural change in the Azapa Valley, Chile. Am. J. Phys. Anthropol. 123, 130–145.

Sutter, R., Verano, J.W., 2007. Biodistance analysis of the Moche sacrificial victims from Huaca de la Luña Plaza 3C: matrix method test of their origins. Am. J. Phys. Anthropol. 132, 193–206.

Sutton, R.N., 1974. The practical significance of mandibular accessory foramina. Aust. Dent. J. 19, 167–173.

SYSTAT 9.0., 1998. SPSS, Inc. Standard Version.

Szathmary, E.J., Ossenberg, N.S., 1978. Are the biological differences between North American Indians and Eskimos truly profound? Curr. Anthropol. 19, 673–701.

Ta'ala, S.C., 2015. A brief history of the race concept in physical anthropology. In: Berg, G.E., Ta'ala, S.C. (Eds.), Biological Affinity in Forensic Identification of Human Skeletal Remains. CRC Press, Boca Raton, FL, pp. 1–16.

Tanner, J.M., 1988. Human Biology: An Introduction to Human Evolution, Variation, Growth and Adaptability, third ed Oxford University Press, Oxford.

Tenchini, L., 1904a. Sopra il canale infrasquamoso di Gruber nell'oumo. Archivio Italiano di Anatomia Embriologia 3, 1–36.

Tenchini, L., 1904b. Di un canale perforante arterioso (infraparietale) nella volta cranica dell'oumo adulto. Monitore Zoololgico Italiano 15, 101–110.

Terry, R.J., 1932. The clavicle of the American Negro. Am. J. Phys. Anthropol. 3, 351–379.

Thiele, K., 1993. The holy grail of the perfect character: the cladistic treatment of morphometric data. Cladistics 9, 275–304.

Thompson, A., 1903. Ethnographic Odontology: The Inca Peruvians.

Thompson, D.D., 1982. Forensic anthropology. In: Spencer, F. (Ed.), A History of American Physical Anthropology. Academic Press, New York, NY, pp. 357–359.

Tildesley, M.L., 1921. A first study of the burmese skull. Biometrika 13, 176–262.

Tillman, B., Lorenz, R., 1978. The stress at the human atlanto-occipital joint. Anat. Embryol. 153, 269–277.

Tobias, P.V., 1967. Olduvai Gorge: The Cranium of Australopithecus (Zinjanthropus) Boisei. Cambridge University Press, Cambridge.

Todd, T.W., 1921. Age changes in the pubic bone: II, the pubis of the male Negro-White hybrid; III, the pubis of the White female; IV, the pubis of the female Negro-White hybrid. Am. J. Phys. Anthropol. 4, 1–70.

Tomes, C.S., 1914. A Manual of Dental Anatomy: Human and Comparative. P. Blakiston's Son, Philadelphia, PA.

Tompkins, R.L., 1996. Human population variability in relative dental development. Am. J. Phys. Anthropol. 99, 79–102.

Torgersen, J., 1951a. Asymmetry and skeletal maturation. Acta Radiol. 36, 521–523.

Torgersen, J., 1951b. The developmental genetics and evolutionary meaning of the metopic suture. Am. J. Phys. Anthropol. 9, 193–210.

Torgersen, J., 1951c. Hereditary factors in the sutural pattern of the skull. Acta Radiol. 36, 374–382.

Torgersen, J., 1954. The occiput, the posterior cranial fossa and the cerebellum. In: Jansen, J., Brodal, A. (Eds.), Aspects of Cerebellar Anatomy. Johan Grundt Tanum, Oslo, pp. 396–418.

Torres, J.B., Stone, A.C., Kittles, R., 2013. An anthropological genetic perspective on Creolization in the Anglophone Caribbean. Am. J. Phys. Anthropol. 151, 135–143.

Torres-Rouff, C., Knudson, K.J., Hubbe, M., 2013. Issues of affinity: exploring population structure in the middle and regional developments periods of San Pedro de Atacama, Chile. Am. J. Phys. Anthropol. 152, 370–382.

Trinkaus, E., 1978. Bilateral asymmetry of human skeletal non-metric traits. Am. J. Phys. Anthropol. 49, 315–318.

Truslove, G.M., 1961. Genetical studies on the skeleton of the mouse. XXX. A search for correlations between some minor variants. Genet. Res. 2, 431–438.

Turner II, C.G., 1992. The dental bridge between Australia and Asia: following Macintosh into the East Asian hearth of humanity. Perspectives in Human Biology, 2. Archaeol. Oceania 27:143–152.

Turner II, C.G., Markowitz, M., 1990. Dental discontinuity between Late Pleistocene and recent Nubians. I. Peopling of the Eurafrican-South Asian triangle. Homo 41, 42–53.

Turner II, C.G., Nichol, C.R., Scott, G.R., 1991. Scoring procedures for key morphological traits of the permanent dentition: The Arizona State University Dental Anthropology System. In: Kelley, M.A., Larsen, C.S. (Eds.), Advances in Dental Anthropology. Wiley-Liss, New York, NY, pp. 13–31.

Tyrell, A.J., 2000. Skeletal non-metric traits and the assessment of inter- and intra-population diversity: past problems and future potential. In: Cox, M., Mays, S. (Eds.), Human Osteology in Archaeology and Forensic Science. Greenwich Medical Media, London, pp. 289–306.

Tyrell, A.J., Chamberlain, A.T., 1998. Non-metric trait evidence for modern human affinities and the distinctiveness of Neanderthals. J. Hum. Evol. 34, 549–554.

Ubelaker, D.H., 1978. Human Skeletal Remains: Excavation, Analysis and Interpretation. Smithsonian Institute Press, Washington, DC.

Ubelaker, D.H., 1989. Human Skeletal Remains: Excavation, Analysis, Interpretation, second ed Taraxacum, Washington, DC.

Vallois, M.H., Bennejeant, C.H., 1913. Le développement du canal dentaire inférieure et la vascularization des dents de la machoire inférieure aux differents ages. Bulletin et Memoires de la Societe d'Anthropologie de Paris 4, 568–584.

Van Vark, G.N., 1970. Some Statistical Procedures for the Investigation of Prehistoric Human Skeletal Material. V.R.B. Offsetdrukkerij, Groningen.

Verga, A., 1889. Poche parole sulla spina trocleare dell'orbita umana. Archivio per L'Antropologia e la Etnologia 19, 419–426.

Verneau, R., 1875. Le bassin dans les sexes et dans les races. J.B. Bailliere, Paris.

Vidic, B., 1967. Morphologic variations of the transverse palatine suture in Yugoslav skulls. J. Dent. Res. 46, 1473.

Vigilant, L., Stoneking, M., Harpending, H., Hawkes, K., Wilson, A.C., 1991. African populations and the evolution of human mitochondrial DNA. Science 253, 1503–1507.

Virchow, R., 1875. Über einige Merkmale niederer Menschenrassen am Schädel. der Berliner Akademie, Abhandi.

von Carabelli, G., 1842. Anatomie des Mundes. Braumuller und Seidel, Wien.

von Cramon-Taubadel, N., Lycett, S.J., 2008. Brief communication: human cranial variation fits iterative founder effect model with African origin. Am. J. Phys. Anthropol. 136, 108–113.

Waddington, C.H., 1942. Canalization of development and the inheritance of acquired characters. Nature 150, 563–565.

Waddington, C.H., 1956. Genetic assimilation of the bithorax phenotype. Evolution 10, 1–13.

Waldeyer, W., 1909. Der Processus retromastoideus. Abhandlungen Koniglich Preussischen Akademie der Wissenschaftliche 1–32.

Walker, P.L., Cook, D.C., Lambert, P., 1997. Skeletal evidence for child abuse: a physical anthropological perspective. J. Forensic Sci. 42, 196–207.

Washburn, S.L., 1951. The new physical anthropology. Trans. N.Y. Acad. Sci. 13, 258–304.

Watkins, J.E., 2004. Becoming American or becoming Indian? NAGPRA, Kennewick and cultural affiliation. J. Soc. Arcaeol. 4, 60–80.

Webb, W.S., Snow, C.E., 1945. The Adena people. University of Kentucky. Reports in Anthropology and Arch 6.

Weidenreich, F., 1941. The brain and its role in the phylogenetic transformation of the human skull. Trans. Am. Philos. Soc. 31, 321–442.

Weijs, W.A., Hillen, B., 1986. Correlations between the cross-sectional area of the jaw muscles and craniofacial size and shape. Am. J. Phys. Anthropol. 70, 423–431.

Weinker, C.W., 1987. Admixture in a biologically African caste of Black Americans. Am. J. Phys. Anthropol. 74, 265–273.

Wheeler, P.E., 1990. The significance of selective brain cooling in hominids. Am. J. Phys. Anthropol. 29, 405–423.

Whitnall, S.E., 1921. The Anatomy of the Human Orbit, second ed Oxford University Press, London.

Wiener, A.S., Belkin, R.B., Sonn, E.B., 1944. Distribution of the A1-A2-B-O, M-N, and Rh blood factors among Negroes of New York City. Am. J. Phys. Anthropol. 2, 187–194.

Wilbur, A.K., Bouwman, A.S., Stone, A.C., Roberts, C.A., Pfister, L.-A., Buikstra, J.E., et al., 2009. Deficiencies and challenges in the study of ancient tuberculosis DNA. J. Arch. Sci. 36, 1990–1997.

Wilkinson, L., Blank, G., Gruber, C., 1996. Desktop Data Analysis with SYSTAT. Prentice Hall, New Jersey.

Williams, B.A., Corruccini, R.S., 2007. The relationship between crown size and complexity in two collections. Dent. Anthropol. 20, 29–32.

Williams, B.A., Rogers, T.L., 2006. Evaluating the accuracy and precision of cranial morphological traits for sex determination. J. Forensic Sci. 51, 729–735.

Williams, S.E., Ross, A.H., 2009. Shifting morphological structure: comparing craniometric morphology in founding and descendant populations. Proc AAFS. American Academy of Forensic Sciences, Denver. Colorado Springs, CO.

Williams-Blangero, S., 1989. Phenotypic consequences of nonrandom migration in the Jirels of Nepal. Am. J. Phys. Anthropol. 80, 115–125.

Williams-Blangero, S., Blangero, J., 1989. Anthropometric variation and the genetic structure of the Jirels of Nepal. Hum. Biol. 61, 1–12.

Wolff, E., 1976. Anatomy of the Eye and Orbit. Lewis, London, pp. 18–19.

Wolpoff, M.H., 1968. Climatic influence on the skeletal nasal aperture. Am. J. Phys. Anthropol. 29, 405–424.

Wolpoff, M.H., Caspari, R., 1997. Race and Human Evolution. Simon and Schuster, New York, NY.

Wood-Jones, F., 1933. The non-metrical morphological characters of the skull as Criteria for racial diagnosis: Part IV. The non-metrical morphological characters of the Northern Chinese skull. J. Anat. 68, 96–108.

Workshop of European Anthropologists, 1980. Recommendations for age and sex diagnoses of skeletons. J. Hum. Evol. 9, 517–549.

Wright, S., 1951. The genetical structure of populations. Ann. Eugen. 15, 323–354.

Yamaguchi, B., 1967. A Comparative Osteological Study of the Ainu and the Australian Aborigines, Canberra, Australia Institute of Aboriginal Studies (Occasional Papers 10, Human Biology Series 2).

y'Edynak, G.J., Iscan, M.Y., 1993. Craniofacial evolution and growth. In: Iscan, M.Y., Helmer, R.P. (Eds.), Forensic Analysis of the Skull. Wiley Liss, New York, NY, pp. 11–27.

Yokley, T.R., 2009. Ecogeographic variation in human nasal passages. Am. J. Phys. Anthropol. 138, 11–22.

Zimmerman, L.J., Clinton, R.N., 1999. Case notes: Kennewick man and Native American graves protection and repatriation act woes. Int. J. Cult. Property 8, 212–228.

Zivanovic, S., 1980. Longitudinal grooves and canals of the human hard palate. Anat. Anz. 147, 161–167.

Zollikofer, C.P.E., Ponce De León, M.S., 2002. Visualizing Patterns of craniofacial shape variations in Homo sapiens. Proc. R. Soc. Biol. 269, 801.

# Appendix A

## CORRESPONDENCE ANALYSIS

```
#Correspondence Analysis of nonmetric data
#GetCA - Correspondence Analysis - modified from Portier's GetCa
library(MASS)
GetCa <- function(mydata)
{
xydata <- data.frame(mydata)
nf <- min(nrow(mydata),ncol(mydata))
ca <- corresp(xydata,nf)
minx <- min(ca$rscore[,1],ca$cscore[,1])
miny <- min(ca$rscore[,2],ca$cscore[,2])
maxx <- max(ca$rscore[,1],ca$cscore[,1])
maxy <- max(ca$rscore[,2],ca$cscore[,2])
plot(c(minx,maxx), c(miny,maxy),type="n",xlab="PCA1",ylab="PCA2")
text(ca$rscore[,1:2],type="p",rownames(ca$rscore),col="red",cex=1.5)
text(ca$cscore[,1:2],type="p",rownames(ca$cscore),col="blue",cex=1.5)
points(c(minx,maxx),c(0,0),type="l",lty=2)
points(c(0,0),c(miny,maxy),type="l",lty=2)
mysum <- sum(mydata)
Inertia <- round(ca$cor^2,4)
chisq <- Inertia*mysum
ti <- sum(Inertia)
tchisq <- sum(chisq)
perct <- (chisq/tchisq)*100
cperct <- cumsum(perct)
df <- (nrow(mydata)-1)*(ncol(mydata)-1)
list (sum=mysum,Singular_Value=ca$cor,Rscore=ca$rscore,Cscore=ca$cscore,Inertia=Inertia,ChiSq=chisq,
Total_Inertia=ti,Total_ChiSq=tchisq,Percent=perct,Cumulative=cperct,DF=df)
}
#Input data in matrix form
#INA provided as an example
INA <- matrix(c(1,9,64,11,6,13,59,66,41,48,33,159,76,3,18,46,60,2,6,1),nrow=5,ncol=4,byrow=TRUE)
INA
colnames(INA) <-c("White" , "Asian" , "African" , "Amerindian")
rownames(INA) <- c("Gut", "Inc Gut", "Str" , "Pa Sl" , "Sill")
INA <- data.frame(INA)
# Run the CA function
GetCa(INA)
```

# OPTIMIZED SUMMED SCORED ATTRIBUTES

## *Macromorphoscopics and OSSA Scoring Sheet*

**Anterior Nasal Spine (ANS)**

| Score | |
|---|---|
| 1 | Slight |
| 2 | Intermediate |
| 3 | Marked |

ANS Score = ☐

OSSA SCORE =

**Nasal Aperture Width (NAW)**

| Score | |
|---|---|
| 1 | Narrow |
| 2 | Medium |
| 3 | Broad |

NAW Score = ☐

OSSA SCORE =

**Inferior Nasal Aperture (INA)**

| Score | |
|---|---|
| 1 | Pronounced Slope |
| 2 | Moderate Slope |
| 3 | Straight |
| 4 | Partial Sill |
| 5 | Sill |

INA Score = ☐

OSSA SCORE =

**Nasal Bone Contour (NBC)**

| Score | |
|---|---|
| 0 | Low/Round |
| 1 | Oval |
| 2 | Steep/Marked Plateau |
| 3 | Steep/Narrow Plateau |
| 4 | Triangular |

NBS Score = ☐

OSSA SCORE =

**Interorbital Breadth (IOB)**

| Score | |
|---|---|
| 1 | Narrow |
| 2 | Intermediate |
| 3 | Wide |

IOB Score = ☐

OSSA SCORE =

**Post-Bregmatic Depression (PBD)**

| Score | |
|---|---|
| 0 | Absent |
| 1 | Present |

PBD Score = ☐

OSSA SCORE =

SUMMED SCORE =

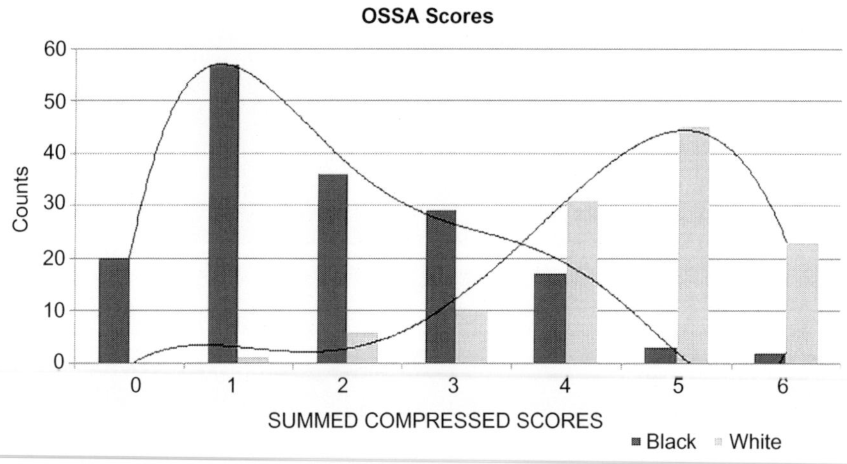

## NAÏVE BAYESIAN

```
###Naive Bayesian
###Script adapted from R code on CRAN website
bayes <- read.table("name.xxx", header = TRUE, sep = "\t", na.strings = "NA", dec = ".", strip.white = TRUE)
attach(bayes)
model <- naiveBayes(Class ~ ., data = bayes)
predict(model, bayes[1:20,-1])
predict(model, bayes[1:20,-1], type = "raw")
pred <- predict(model, bayes[,-1])
table(pred, bayes$Class)
```

## K-NEAREST NEIGHBOR

```
###k-nearest neighbor
###Script adapted from R code on CRAN website
knn (train, test, cl, k = 1, l = 0, prob = FALSE, use.all = TRUE)
{
train <- as.matrix(train)
if (is.null(dim(test)))
dim(test) <- c(1, length(test))
test <- as.matrix(test)
if (any(is.na(train)) || any(is.na(test)) || any(is.na(cl)))
stop("no missing values are allowed")
p <- ncol(train)
ntr <- nrow(train)
if (length(cl) != ntr)
stop("'train' and 'class' have different lengths")
if (ntr < k) {
warning(gettextf("k = %d exceeds number %d of patterns",
k, ntr), domain = NA)
k <- ntr
}
if (k < 1)
stop(gettextf("k = %d must be at least 1", k), domain = NA)
nte <- nrow(test)
if (ncol(test) != p)
stop("dims of 'test' and 'train differ")
clf <- as.factor(cl)
nc <- max(unclass(clf))
Z <- .C(VR_knn, as.integer(k), as.integer(l), as.integer(ntr),
as.integer(nte), as.integer(p), as.double(train), as.integer(unclass(clf)),
as.double(test), res = integer(nte), pr = double(nte),
integer(nc + 1), as.integer(nc), as.integer(FALSE), as.integer(use.all)) 107
res <- factor(Z$res, levels = seq_along(levels(clf)), labels = levels(clf))
if (prob)
attr(res, "prob") <- Z$pr
res
}
#now load training set and test set
train <- read.table("***.txt", header = TRUE, sep = "", na.strings = "NA", dec = ".", strip.white = TRUE)
test <- read.table("***.txt", header = TRUE, sep = "", na.strings = "NA", dec = ".", strip.white = TRUE)
test<-as.matrix(test)
train<-as.matrix(train)
#cl is a matrix of the factors for your training set
#replace GroupNo with name of factors and n with number of individuals
cl <- factor(c(rep("Group1",n), rep("Group 2",n)))
```

```
# select the number of neighbors to use for the classification (k), as well
#as various output options
knn(train, test, cl, k = 5, prob=T, use.all = T)
#this final line returns the class prediction for the test set
attributes(.Last.value)
```

## CANONICAL ANALYSIS OF THE PRINCIPAL COORDINATES

```
#The CAPdiscrim function
#By: Roeland Kindt (World Agroforestry Centre)
#In the BiodiversityR package for R
library(BiodiversityR)
library(vegan)
library(MASS)
data(dune)
data(dune.env)
#build the model
Ordination.model1 <- CAPdiscrim(dune~Management, data=dune.env,

        dist="bray", axes=2, m=0, add=FALSE)

Ordination.model1
plot1 <- ordiplot(Ordination.model1, type="none")
ordisymbol(plot1, dune.env, "Management", legend=TRUE)
# plot change in classification success against m
plot(seq(1:14), rep(-1000, 14), xlim=c(1, 14), ylim=c(0, 100), xlab="m",

        ylab="classification success (percent)", type="n")

for (mseq in 1:14) {

        CAPdiscrim.result <- CAPdiscrim(dune~Management, data=dune.env,
                dist="bray", axes=2, m=mseq)
        points(mseq, CAPdiscrim.result$percent)

}
#
```

# Index

*Note*: Page numbers followed by "*f*" and "*t*" refer to figures and tables, respectively.

## Z